ISNM

INTERNATIONAL SERIES OF NUMERICAL MATHEMATICS
INTERNATIONALE SCHRIFTENREIHE ZUR NUMERISCHEN MATHEMATIK
SÉRIE INTERNATIONALE D'ANALYSE NUMÉRIQUE

VOL. 47

General Inequalities 2

Proceedings of the Second International Conference
on General Inequalities
held in the Mathematical Research Institut at Oberwolfach, Black Forest
July 30–August 5, 1978

Edited by
E. F. Beckenbach

1980
Birkhäuser Verlag
Basel · Boston · Stuttgart

CIP-Kurztitelaufnahme der Deutschen Bibliothek

General Inequalities. – Basel, Boston, Stuttgart: Birkhäuser.
Bd. 1 mit d. Erscheinungsorten: Basel, Stuttgart. – Bd. 1 mit Parallelsacht.: Allgemeine Ungleichungen.
NE: PT
2. Proceedings of the Second International Conference on General Inequalities: held in the Math. Research Inst. at Oberwolfach, Black Forest, July 30 – August 5, 1978 / ed. by E. F. Beckenbach. – 1980.
(International series of numerical mathematics; Vol. 47)
ISBN 3–7643–1056–1

NE: Beckenbach, Edwin F. [Hrsg.]; Internationale Tagung über Allgemeine Ungleichungen ⟨02, 1978, Oberwolfach⟩; Mathematisches Forschungsinstitut ⟨Oberwolfach⟩

ISBN 3–7643–1056–1
Printed in Germany

Math Sci
Sep.

FOREWORD

The Second International Conference on General Inequalities was held from July 30 to August 5 at the Mathematische Forschungsinstitut in Oberwolfach (Black Forest, Germany). Unfortunately, Professors G. Aumann and M. Kuczma were unable to participate. Fortunately, Professors J. Aczél (Waterloo, Ont.) and W. Walter (Karlsrühe) were willing to join Professor E.F. Beckenbach (Los Angeles) as chairmen of the meeting. Professor R. Ger (Katowice) did an excellent job as secretary of the Organization Committee.

The meeting was opened by Professor E.F. Beckenbach and attended by 27 participants from Europe, America, Africa, Asia, and Australia.

Among the fields represented were functional and differential inequalities, convex functions, inequalities for sequences, and applications of inequalities to information theory, combinatorics, geometry, and functional analysis.

The Problems and Remarks sessions were steady sources of stimulation.

This meeting has shown again that the personal contact, made possible by such conferences, is particularly useful in the field of inequalities with its wide range of topics and rich possibilities for cross-fertilizations.

The meeting was closed by W. Walter who expressed the appreciation of the participants for the superb working conditions in the Institute and for the hospitality of its leaders and staff. The wish was expressed that the Third International Conference on General Inequalities be held in Oberwolfach in the spring of 1980.

Approved

J. Aczél

E. F. Beckenbach

E.F. Beckenbach

Wolfgang Walter

W. Walter

PARTICIPANTS

J. ACZÉL, University of Waterloo, Ontario, Canada
K. BARON, Silesian University, Katowice, Poland
E.F. BECKENBACH, University of California, Los Angeles, USA
J. BECKER, Technical University, West Berlin
D. BRYDAK, University of Port Harcourt, Nigeria
P.L. BUTZER, Rhein.-Westf. Technical University, Aachen, West Germany
F. FEHÉR, Rhein.-Westf. Technical University, Aachen, West Germany
D. GAŞPAR, University of Timoşoara, Romania
R. GER, Silesian University, Katowice, Poland
M. GOLDBERG, University of California, Los Angeles, USA
Ch. HENLEY, Harvard University, Cambridge, Massachusetts, USA
H.H. KAIRIES, Technical University, Clausthal-Zellerfeld, West Germany
P. KARDOS, University of Toronto, Toronto, Canada
H. KÖNIG, Institute of Mathematics, Saarbrücken, West Germany
M. KWAPISZ, University of Gdańsk, Poland
E. LUKACS, University of Erlangen, West Germany
D. MILMAN, University of Tel-Aviv, Israel
R. MOHAPATRA, American University of Beirut, Lebanon
A. OSTROWSKI, University of Basel, Switzerland
J. RÄTZ, University of Bern, Switzerland
D.K. ROSS, La Trobe University, Bundoora, Australia
D.C. RUSSELL, York University, Downsview, Toronto, Canada
D.R. SNOW, Brigham Young University, Provo, Utah, USA
J. SZARSKI, Jagiellonian University, Kraków, Poland
O. TAUSSKY-TODD, California Institute of Technology, Pasadena, USA
J. TODD, California Institute of Technology, Pasadena, USA
W. WALTER, University of Karlsrühe (TH), West Germany

SCIENTIFIC PROGRAM OF THE CONFERENCE

Monday, July 31

Opening of the conference, 9:45 E.F. BECKENBACH

Morning session Chairman: A. OSTROWSKI

H. KÖNIG: Some inequalities which occur in the theory of function algebras

J. TODD: Many values of mixed means

J. RÄTZ: On approximately additive mappings

Problems and remarks

Afternoon session Chairman: J. TODD

E.F. BECKENBACH: The formulas of Weierstrass and the topology of the fundamental theorem of algebra for minimal surfaces

H.H. KAIRIES: What is a "natural" generalization of the gamma function?

Problems and remarks

* * * * *

Tuesday, August 1

Early morning session Chairman: J. ACZÉL

M. KWAPISZ: General inequalities and fixed-point theorems

K. BARON: On a majorization of distances between the values of a family of functions and a fixed point

Late morning session Chairman: E.F. BECKENBACH

D. BRYDAK: Nonlinear functional inequalities

Problems and remarks

Afternoon session Chairman: J. RÄTZ

R. MOHAPATRA: Inequalities involving infinite matrices with nonnegative entries (joint work with P. JOHNSON)

R. GER: Homogeneity sets for Jensen-convex functions

D.R. SNOW: A functional inequality arising in combinatorics

Problems and remarks

* * * * *

Wednesday, August 2

Early morning session — Chairman: E. LUKACS

W. WALTER: Inequalities involving derivatives (joint work with R. REDHEFFER)

P.L. BUTZER: Jackson-type inequalities for a variety of processes in analysis

Late morning session — Chairman: D. MILMAN

O. TAUSSKY-TODD: Positive definite integral matrices

Problems and remarks

Afternoon excursion and discussion

* * * * *

Thursday, August 3

Early morning session — Chairman: J. SZARSKI

J. ACZÉL: On a new, unified theory of information

P. KARDOS: On the inequality $\sum_{i=1}^{n} p_i \frac{f_i(p_i)}{f_i(q_i)} \leq 1$

Late morning session — Chairman: W. WALTER

E. LUKACS: Inequalities for Fourier-Stieltjes transformations of functions of bounded variation

Problems and remarks

Afternoon session — Chairman: H. KÖNIG

J. SZARSKI: Comparison theorems for infinite systems of differential-functional equations with first-order partial derivatives

D.C. RUSSELL: L_p^m-extensions of a sequence (joint work with A. JAKIMOVSKI)

Problems and remarks

* * * * *

Friday, August 4

Early morning session Chairman: O. TAUSSKY-TODD

D. MILMAN: Eine geometrische Ungleichung und ihre Anwendung

M. GOLDBERG: Some combinatorial inequalities and C-numerical radii

Late morning session Chairman: D.C. RUSSELL

D.K. ROSS: N-th partial sums of special functions
(joint work with A. MAHAJAN)

Problems and remarks

Afternoon session Chairman: R. GER

D. GAŞPAR: Über die Interpolation von Operatoren vom schwachen Typ

F. FEHÉR: A generalized Schur-Hardy inequality on Köthe spaces

Problems and remarks

Closing of the conference, 17:45 W. WALTER

PREFACE

The Second International Conference on General Inequalities was held at the Mathematical Research Institute, Oberwolfach, Black Forest, in 1978.

Like the first volume of the General Inequalities series, the present Proceedings book consists mainly of papers presented at the related conference, and it also includes a few contributions by others who were invited to the conference but were unable to attend.

The mathematical papers in this volume have been grouped by the editor into ten roughly coherent sections, in addition to which there is a concluding section on Remarks and Problems.

Also, a new feature with this volume, there is an introductory historical essay concerning the founding and earliest days of the Institute, graciously provided by Irmgard Süss. This consists essentially of the first half of her previously published account. She has again kindly provided drawings for title pages of sections of the book, first a likeness of her late husband and then sketches showing scenes leading up to Lorenzenhof, the now-demolished hunting lodge where the Institute was originally housed. The sketch shown on page 15 was copied by her, especially for this volume, from an older oil painting of hers; the following ones are in-place drawings, dating from the 1940's. It is anticipated that the pattern of historical essays, and of drawings for the title pages, will be repeated in later volumes of the series.

As at the first General Inequalities Conference, family members and friends, this time including Susan Aczél, Elizabeth Lukacs, Margaret Ostrowski, Naomi Motzkin, June, Jennifer, Timothy, and Michelle Ross, Joy Russell, and Irmgard Süss, added greatly to the interest and content of stimulating conversations at meals, musicales, and other social events during the conference.

The editor is again deeply grateful to Elaine Barth of the U.C.L.A. Mathematics Department for expert editorial consultation and technical advice, and especially to Julie Honig, Phyllis Parris, and Debra Remetch of the Mathematics Department typing pool for the excellent and knowledgeable preparation of the typescript; and he sincerely thanks C. Einsele of Birkhäuser Verlag, Basel, and Alice and Klaus Peters of Birkhäuser Boston, Inc., for kind expressions of interest and encouragement.

E.F. Beckenbach, Editor
University of California, Los Angeles

CONTENTS

INEQUALITIES FOR SUMS, SERIES, AND INTEGRALS

FUNCTIONAL INEQUALITIES

INEQUALITIES OF APPROXIMATION THEORY

INEQUALITIES OF FUNCTIONAL ANALYSIS

INEQUALITIES OF OPERATOR THEORY

GEOMETRIC AND TOPOLOGICAL INEQUALITIES

INEQUALITIES OF PROBABILITY AND INFORMATION THEORY

REMARKS AND PROBLEMS

INDEXES

SKETCHES

by

Irmgard Süss

History

Wilhelm Süss (March 7, 1895 - May 21, 1958)
Professor of Mathematics at Freiburg University.
Founder of the Mathematical Research Institute,
Oberwolfach, Black Forest, 1944

ORIGIN OF THE MATHEMATICAL RESEARCH INSTITUTE OBERWOLFACH AT THE COUNTRYSEAT 'LORENZENHOF'

Irmgard Süss
Frankenweg 13
7800 Freiberg im Breisgau
WEST GERMANY

ANTECEDENTS CONCERNING LORENZENHOF

During the first decade of its existence, when its location in the Black Forest was not yet a definite decision and it seemed in no way essentially attached to geography, the mathematicians called their Institute simply by the name of the house, "Lorenzenhof." "Hof," meaning "court" in the simplest and in the highest sense of the word, appealed to their different tastes. The name originally belonged to the farm in the valley below, where there is a sawmill now. The big house that was built above on Lorenzenhof farm territory used to be called just "Little Castle" or the "Villa" by the village people. Other farms roundabout might not have offered a suitable name, diminutive forms of peasants' Christian names mostly being used to designate the farm. But "Lorenzenhof" just happened to sound dignified and vague enough for the name to be accepted as an inheritance from the valley farm.

Nobility. The present Lorenzenhof was the hunting lodge of one Baron Stoesser, Hessian Minister of State. The farm going bankrupt in 1905, he had been able to purchase the whole farm territory including its environing large areas of forest. American-dollar millions, won by marriage, are said to have contributed to the construction of this establishment, made especially expensive by the involved work of terracing and road building. It took three years, from 1905 to 1908, to complete it. The variety of architectural forms reminds one of that period of style in art, the "Jugendstil," and its imperial romanticism.

There was also a small house for the gardener and a nice little cozy-looking cottage for pigs, both stylishly in harmony with the main building, and two large heatable hothouses. All these gave way to the modern building in 1966. Another sizable building on the northern side, as well adapted in style, contained elegant horse stalls, a white-tiled stable for a cow, and room for coaches and a coachman. Cars are parking now in the space it occupied. A bit of the old splendor is still recalled by a trough of sandstone in front of the kitchen, meant for living trout.

The history of the change of proprietors is, on a small scale, a reflection of German history.

Foreign wealth. Baron Stoesser did not come back from the World War in 1918. Postwar inflation caused a general selling off, German values changing into the hands of those who owned foreign currency; and besides, the great times of nobility had become a thing of the past. A Belgian banker, a Mr. Hildesheim, bought the countryseat with its forests in 1928, leaving only the woods on the opposite side of the valley in possession of Baron Stoesser's heirs (v. Schubert).

Tradition reports Mr. Hildesheim to have been very popular with the village children owing to generous gifts of chocolate from his own factories, and with grownups by lavishly tipping them with five-mark pieces ever loose in his pockets. Moreover, he must have had a decided inclination to the pure, tranquil green of the meadows. So he cleared them -- much to the distress of his hungry mathematical successors -- of their original rich stock of fruit trees, and offered special rewards to the leaseholders, if they managed to do the lawn mowing in one day on account of the disturbance. The furniture of the ground floor and the bedrooms yet gave us evidence of his style of life, and so did an elegant pigeon-shooting pavillon by the row of maple trees uphill.

Black Forest timber trade. The Hitler period then broke out. In 1936, Göring's New National Law for Hunting was issued, depriving foreigners of shooting license within a frontier zone 50 km wide. Herewith the property, bought precisely for the sake of hunting, lost its value to the Belgian owner. So the existence of Lorenzenhof as an abode of luxury came to an end. Business took over.

A Black Forest dealer in timber, Mr. Rothfuss, could acquire possession. To him, the forests were of importance, not the château. For some time, anyhow, he lived in it with his wife and five children, but later moved into the gardener's cottage, turning the big house with a surrounding area of land into money, and keeping the wide forests for his lumber trade.

The National Socialist Party. The purchaser who entered the stage now, again corresponding to the course of history, was the State.

Some time before, the Baden Ministry of Education had got hold of the big hotels of Bad Rippoldsau. Rippoldsau Springs, a place nearby, once a flourishing health resort in the time of traveling Russian princes and horse carriages, had succumbed to the unfavorable general changes and ended in bankruptcy. The State had finally bought the buildings fully furnished, and established a teachers' training college there with board and lodging for the pupils.

In this connection, the Baden Ministry of Education contemplated the purchase of Lorenzenhof. The question arose, too, whether it might be useful as a dependency, possibly, to the Freiburg University. On the occasion of an educational meeting at Bad Peterstal in 1942, where Mr. Süss had to represent the University, he was taken along by several Ministry officials to have a look at it and give his opinion. He decidedly supported the plan to buy the place. In doing so, the Ministry invested a fund in its care, part of the "Pfälzischer Katholischer Schulfonds," which has been the actual owner to whom rents were payable, until, in 1967, the "Volkswagenwerk-Stiftung" took over. To the great disappointment of Mr. Süss in his position as university rector, however, he did not succeed in acquiring the place for Freiburg University. Other forces proved stronger, and the house was added to the teachers' training college of Rippoldsau as a branch establishment. Hence Lorenzenhof received its outfit as a boarding house for many persons, from the Rippoldsau hotel stock. The grand piano, also, and two imposing carpets came from there. A training camp for Alsatian teachers, first for men, later for young girls, to be imbued with the principles of National Socialism, that is what the house had come to be.

ANTECEDENTS CONCERNING THE MATHEMATICAL RESEARCH INSTITUTE

Change in the attitude of the Government toward scientific research. Once again a new era dawned. The final victory seemed to incline to the side of those powers that had not turned away from science with derision. The turning point was reached. With amazement, those concerned heard a quotation from a public speech Goebbels gave at Heidelberg: "We bow with deep respect before the men of science." The National Research Council (Reichsforschungs-rat) (NRC) was founded (1942-43) to organize science so as to win the war. "Their laboratory, their writing desk is the place where the gentlemen of the university belong," so Rust, Minister of Education in the Government in Berlin, told Süss in a private talk, having asked him to pay him company in his train compartment to Salzburg on his way from the university rectors' conference held in Vienna (in 1942). "When I, as assistant professor in Greifswald, saw you for the first time," Süss replied, "it sounded different. You said 'March, gentlemen, march!'" "I had to speak like that," said Rust, "at that time, in order to save you. None of you imagined the size of the imminent danger. There was such a storm of hatred against the intellectuals raging through Germany, universities would have been simply swept away if you had not got into line." A bitter resentment against Goebbels filled his soul. At a visit to Freiburg (June, 1943), in the privacy of the home of Mr. Süss, it moved him to the passionate exclamation: "We shall yet see which of the two will rule the world, the power of thought or the glibness of tongue" ("der Geist oder die Fresse").

So the political situation evidently was favorable to projects of scientific organization.

National Research Council. On September 8, 1942, Mentzel, Ministerial-director in the Ministry of Education in Berlin, in his capacity as President of the German Research Council, agreed to an allowance of RM 70 000 for editing mathematical literature, a sum Süss had demanded in his capacity as president of the German Mathematical Society (DMV).

On October 3, 1942, Mentzel already signed as President of the new National Research Council and delegated to Süss "the starting of an action to arrange teamwork for editing mathematical literature essential to military research."

On June 4, 1943, Staatsrat Prof. Dr. A. Esau wrote: "Within the NRC, newly created by the Reichsmarschall, it appears necessary to found a circle for mathematical research in the Department of Physics (Fachsparte Physik) delegated to me," and asked Süss "to accept the leading position in this field."

Dated November 3, 1944, the official request by Prof. Dr. Ing. W. Osenberg (Hannover and Nordheim), Head of the Planning Office (Assignment and Securing of Personnel) of the NRC, stated "...please start at once with an activity, by commission, which corresponds to that of Head of the Mathematics Section (Leiter der Fachsparte Mathematik)" ... "Months ago, I tendered propositions... Four weeks ago, I proposed to designate you as Head of the Section. For administrational reasons, your designation was not yet passed, as far as I know," so the same writing explains.

Finally, dated January 3, 1945, overdue, the designation came, signed by Göring, to wit, demanding that reports be given at intervals of six months. What could six months signify in a thousand years' empire!

From the point of view of the working committee, mathematics was classified as a subdivision of the Physics Section (Sparte Physik), which means that Süss as head of the Mathematics Circle did not belong to the Leading Staff (Führungsstab). Osenberg, it is assumed, attained independence for mathematics so very late, because the Party had reservations concerning the person of Süss. Only when the flood rose to their necks did they fully authorize him to a mandate he had executed for quite a time already. Anyway, grotesque though this belated request by Göring may seem, a report dispatched by Süss to the NRC on March 24, 1945, appears no less theatrical and strange, held against the background of the political events of the time. But there was a bitterly serious compulsion here: Important and unassailable research results had to be offered, against distrustful criticism, for the cause of the Institute was at perilous stake up to the very last moment of the regime.

What essentially mattered to Süss in this whole activity was, first, to be entitled to confer on mathematicians assignments describable as important for warfare. Süss was even successful in having fundamental research being declared of military importance; this enabled the mathematicians to pursue their own mathematical problems. Thus to keep science going was a task obviously natural for a president of the DMV, but also open to skepticism.

There was a second purpose, though, in Süss's activity, of a wider meaning and giving scope to his natural optimism. This was afforded by the so-called "Aktion Osenberg," in which Süss had his part. Its covert aim was to rescue and save for the dark German future scientific qualification and brain potential as a capital fund for starting anew after the catastrophe. In this sense the heads of their scientific departments worked with full conviction. Osenberg had obtained consent from the very highest official authorities to call back from their military duties scientists recommended for research of importance to the war. So Süss had the possibility of systematically fetching back from the front or any nonmathematical employment mathematicians of proven ability in research work. That meant the job of finding out their present address, of inducing their respective employers to release them, and (advised, of course, by his colleagues) of conferring upon them assignments corresponding to their own fields of interest. He managed that from his private study at Freiburg with the assistance of a lady secretary. The official letters Süss received generally gave an ultimate confirmation of agreements reached beforehand. The matters had usually been talked over personally, mostly confidentially, in advance. Instead of Prof. Esau, very soon Prof. W. Gerlach, Munich, was Head of the Physics Section, and he always united with Süss in most friendly cooperation.

<u>Offer of a Chair at Göttingen</u>. In the midst of this activity, in the spring of 1944, preliminaries opened, preceding an offer of a professorship in Göttingen. Two rivers joined their waters. The fact that Süss was in the exceptional position, created by the confidence of his mathematical colleagues on one side, his university colleagues on the other, of being President of the DMV as well as Rector of Freiburg University for more than the usual number of years, now gave him the lever to get his project of an institute into motion.

Already for quite a time, he had thought it desirable to bring into existence a central international institute for mathematics. His idea at that time was less a meeting place than a center provided with all literature and information, where any mathematician might obtain knowledge concerning the state reached in the treatment of any problem. Concurrent and double research, with resulting disappointment and waste of time and energy, might thus be turned into fruitful contacts. Mentzel in the Ministry proved amenable to the idea.

Now the flood rose so the ship could get into high waters.

To Süss, it went without saying that Göttingen must be upheld as the German stronghold of mathematics. So, to him, quite evidently Göttingen was the ideal place to establish the institute.

But "My remark that I had to consider a change of university has roused a real storm here as well as in the Baden Ministry of Education," he wrote to the dean in Göttingen, Prof. Kopfermann (a physicist), on June 22, 1944. And on July 8, 1944: "Min.Dir. Mentzel's point of view is that at present the question of war issues is of predominant importance, and that in this respect his urgent wish is to get done with a fundamental demand concerning mathematics in the NRC, which has been discussed for some time already, but only recently reaching actuality. One must not yet talk about it. But confidentially, I want to let you know that it means the foundation of a "National Mathematical Institute" of the NRC. Regarding this institute, I had always recommended especially Göttingen as the appropriate place. In spite of this, at this moment, no university town is taken into consideration, but rather a place not exposed to air raids.

"As it is, the Ministry of Education in Baden, wanting to keep me in Freiburg at least in the present difficult situation, has offered me a place of rare advantages in the Black Forest where I can hope to start with the most urgent work without delay and undisturbed. Therefore it was Mr. Mentzel's opinion that, for his part, the decision regarding the Göttingen problem might be delayed in my behalf (though he continues to support your intentions as promised), and that I ought to arrange for the foundation of the Institute in the Black Forest place."

Whereupon Prof. Kopfermann on August 1, 1944, wrote: "...a danger I want to emphasize. It is the following: If the Baden Government offers you a favorable place for the NMRI (National Mathematical Research Institute) in those parts now, there is a black outlook for this institute in as far as it will prove most difficult later on to transfer it from Baden to Göttingen. The next step will surely be that, once rid of the danger of bombs, its settling down in Freiburg will be aimed at. Then this institute, and probably you too, will be lost to Göttingen. Whereas you yourself, if I understood you, were convinced that its proper final place was Göttingen, an opinion which I absolutely support. To my view, the central question in the present situation seems to be: What guarantee might be given to ascertain later realization of this original plan concerning the NMRI?"

In answer to this, Süss, on August 26, 1944, replied: "The Baden Government, the University, and the town of Freiburg showed an interest in having me stay here which by far surmounts my expectation.

"In these uncertain times, to be obliged to tear such strong ties by definitely agreeing to go to Göttingen, either now or later, meant a brain-racking problem. Thus, Mr. Mentzel's resolution was a great relief to me, dispensing me of all momentary decision regarding the offered chair at Göttingen and deferring it to a time when conditions are less complicated. A formulation meanwhile touching the center of the question would be this: I unite the consciousness of the high honor and strong obligation of a call to Göttingen with the conviction that to conserve Göttingen as the internationally accepted stronghold has to be the aim of us mathematicians.

"The Baden Government felt they could not do without my experience as rector of the university in these difficult times and wanted to prolong my rectorate, which according to general official instructions ought to have ended now. As I insisted on the prevalent urgency of my duties concerning scientific organization, there followed the offer of a beautiful place for the temporary accomodation of the NMRI. The offer is explicitly made to me quite personally, not to the Mathematical Chair at Freiburg. There is not hidden behind this any ambition to obtain the Institute for Baden. On the contrary, it is only meant to enable me to pursue the interest of the Freiburg

University at the same time with that of the NMRI. It is to be welcomed with quite general objectivity, as it means the winning for science of a place favorable regarding air raids and quiet for work.

"Both Baden, and Mentzel just as myself, consider locating the NMRI there a solution for wartime only. It was stated unequivocally that the question of a definite establishment of the NMRI can be reasonably answered only after the end of the war, in unprejudiced consideration of the situation then in the universities. It does not seem possible to me to give exact guarantees for that special time. The ample spiritual and material basis that Göttingen presents, in my opinion, remains the decisive fact.

"Please don't believe me ungrateful or lacking collegial feeling, if I really avail myself of the governmental permission to put off my decision for the time being, in order to be able meanwhile to work in tranquility. The cordiality and intensity shown by you and the Göttingen colleagues obliges me to you most strongly..."

Founding of a National Institute of Mathematics. Dated August 3, 1944, the formal mandate by Mentzel ensued, and on August 29, 1944, details to this followed.

The position of Director of the NMRI was not meant to be just an honorary post, like the activity in the NRC had been. It was agreed that, in addition to official lodgings for himself and his family, he should be entitled to a continued salary of a university rector after the end of his rectorate. Owing to conditions at the end of the war, such agreements were not effectuated, and fighting for the existence of the Institute remained a matter of the heart as its creation had been. The connection with Göttingen was also destroyed in the universal ruin.

Selection of the place. The gentlemen of the Baden Ministry of Education who principally took pains in this matter were Ministerialdirector Gärtner, formerly school teacher (who later fell at Strassburg); Professor Fuhs, high school teacher, his assistant as Ministerial Counsel, who among Freiburg university people always went under the comradely name of Michel Fuhs; and Government Counsel Baumgratz, who after the war became chief of administration of the Freiburg University.

The kind of collaboration that was possible with Gärtner may be exemplified by an incident in another matter. Süss was expounding to him that it would not do to let a scholar like the biologist Oehlkers be continually tormented in regard to his Jewish wife since it would gradually render impossible any concentration in his work. It was not the first time that Süss discussed this point. Just then it concerned the Star of David. Gärtner ordered the respective documents to be brought, and under the eyes of Süss ran his pen through the indication 'Jewish' and scribbled 'non-Arian' in its place, thus warding off the danger. Without a word, he then passed on to other university matters.

Between Michel Fuhs and Süss, there was full confidence. Many a plan had they hatched together to step in helpfully against radicals, pedants, and denunciators, even outside the realms of the university. Their strategy helped to deliver, e.g., the high-school director Brühler from prison, who had been denunciated and arrested because of opinions uttered at a private evening party. Romantic nightly appointments in the black-darkened streets with a conniving public prosecutor played a part in this enterprise. On behalf of the Italian vice-consul Marco Doria, too, accused of espionage and imprisoned, they attempted various kinds of intervention, in this case in vain.

In all their pursuits they could count upon the assistance of the physicist Professor Steinke. Under the pressure of the sharp political wind of Königsberg, being near the Soviet frontier, he had become a Party member early enough to satisfy the conditions set for the office of 'Dozentenbundsführer' (Political leader of the Union of University teachers). He had taken upon himself this office with bitter reluctance, but out of friendship for Süss, because Süss had made his acceptance of the rectorate dependent on not having beside him a young political leader who would want to win for himself a 'little red coat' from the Party, but a colleague with his own devotion to science. This gave Süss considerable advantage in his dealings with the Party.

This general atmosphere of confidence helped greatly to effectuate Süss's plans regarding the Institute.

At the background of all this development there must have been, though not tangible and proven, the fact that Süss was on remarkably good terms with the top personality of educational administration, Rust.

Endeavors began immediately to make Süss stay in Baden by offering him a favorable place for the planned institute, comparatively safe from air raids. The "Jesuits' Castle" on a hillside close to Freiburg was one of the possibilities they suggested and inspected with Süss. It proved to demand too much renovation, unfeasible during the war. Then the gentlemen drove to the Lake of Constance, where old buildings of a convent were available below Birnau on the shore. But that, too, seemed unreasonable. Confidential talks were often held at the Süss's private dining table, that being a safe place where walls had no ears; and it was inconspicuous, also, for the officials from another town to go there, because it was so hard to get anything to eat elsewhere. So it was there that Michel Fuhs came out with the idea what Süss would think about Lorenzenhof if one could wrench it from political Party schooling. Since Süss already knew this house from the time of its purchase, this proposition quickly decided the future.

MATHEMATICS TAKING POSSESSION OF LORENZENHOF

Preliminary conditions. Science at this date had reached such high valuation by the government that mathematics was able to win the victory over the National-Socialist Party training at Lorenzenhof. The school of the young Alsatian girls had to clear out.

Nobody directly involved in this creation pursued any illusions or hopes that the catastrophe to Germany might be avoided. "Facing the future is like looking against a black wall," was the expression given by Michel Fuhs to the prevalent feeling at the above-mentioned dinner table. But the efforts were devoted to something that was meant to last beyond the war: A fortress of the intellect was being built that should stand firm in the storms expected, especially those of inner German insanity. So, in spite of everything, it was a promising enterprise for a politician of science.

Concerning the rectorate of the University, the Baden Ministry of Education suggested a compromise. Since the tasks of the Institute were of prime urgency according to highest orders and required the presence of its director, the prorector was to represent him at Freiburg, but Süss himself should remain available as rector for important affairs. The general situation had already reached such a state that the schools were obliged to release the upperclass pupils for war service after summer vacation. So Süss could assign his family as a whole to the new task.

Neighborly assistance. As a matter of course, the predecessor at Lorenzenhof was not too well pleased with having to quit the field and even later tried to spoil the fun by a denunciation. Whereas great satisfaction, one might say enthusiasm, was shown by the headmaster of Rippoldsau training college, Director Lutz. With all his power he helped to set the Institute going. Toward the end of August, he invited several professors of Freiburg University as lecturing guests to Rippoldsau. He met them at the station, walked with them from Wolfach to Rippoldsau, and hiking back two days later, he introduced Süss officially, so to speak, accompanied by his family and Professor Steinke, as new master of the Lorenzenhof, which had just been cleared.

He bade the serving personnel, four maids and a gardener's wife, to continue their work with undiminished zeal. Mathematics owed to Director Lutz that, apart from the necessary equipment, they could also keep the grand piano and those two decorative carpets from Rippoldsau, which he then was entitled to dispose of. Even a live pig was left by him to the Institute, and a little treasure of preserves from the garden, moreover a stock of wood for the chimney, of vital importance later. Furthermore, as necessity showed up, he continued helping with all sorts of things. The Süss family fetched these from Rippoldsau with bicycles and attached cart. They got his permission to cut the few stately towels on hand into pieces and to hem them on his sewing machine, so as to have one for each mathematician. They were well off in sewing thread, because Mr. Süss had brought some along from a mathematical trip to Romania.

For those who did not live here at that time, it may be worthwhile mentioning that one could not buy anything then besides one's scanty ration, except perhaps a painter's own paintings and Hitler portraits. The shop windows exhibited mainly big Hitler pictures wreathed with golden paper laurel, here and there surrounded by empty packages of something or other, or a few lonely pairs of cloggy wooden-soled shoes. If there was anything else, it was not for sale.

Asked for chests of drawers with washbasin sets, Mr. Lutz let the Institute profit of his good connections with the Rippoldsau mineral-water truck, which deposited them below Lorenzenhof in the 'Hirschen' archway. At that time, there was no other means of communication between Rippoldsau and Wolfach but the mineral-water truck and the truck transporting barium oxyde from the mine opposite Lorenzenhof, both privileged for military purposes. If somebody was lucky enough, he might be given a lift with his baggage by one of these trucks, but their schedule was very uncertain.

Ever and again, Mrs. Junghanns, the Hirschen hostess, lent the shelter of her archway for temporary storage of goods to be transported uphill, and always, Mr. Rothfuss was ready to help bring them up with his jeep.

Among the friendly neighbors who fundamentally helped the Institute to exist, there was Mr. Krauter also, owner of the sawdust factory in the valley below. He offered his reservoir as a swimming pool, and, with his own hands, he laid a connecting wire for electricity from his private water-power plant up to the Institute. Owing to this, the House subsisted on 'Krauter current' through all those difficult times when the public electricity plant at Hausach failed, which frequently occurred on account of air raids.

Furnishing the House. On September 1, 1944, the transformation of the maidens' boarding school into a place for mathematical work could be started.

There was a general order to the effect that the university mathematical library be removed to places not exposed to air raids, and Süss quickly started ordering and buying other available mathematical literature. A transportation firm was made to risk lending, under condition of immediate return, precious furniture-wrapping cloths, because of course there were no boxes or wrapping paper for books. The car center could be prevailed upon to grant a truck, and Mr. Süss's assistant, Dr. ter Hell, accompanied the transport and helped to unload it. Meanwhile, Mrs. Süss and Hilo Süss, occasionally assisted by one of the maids, had applied themselves to the task of clearing the political bookshelves. They carried the whole unwelcome inheritance of National-Socialist educational literature up to a small garret and stored it away in the strictest possible way of good order in heaps separated by labels, for the Party still swayed the scepter. Then the small crew dragged the shelves downstairs into the big room that had served as dining room to the young crowd, and Dr. ter Hell, in setting up the mathematical library, could lay the actual foundation stone for the future.

The duty of returning the furniture blankets without delay to Freiburg was shouldered by Mr. ter Hell and Mrs. Süss jointly, and they even learnt to praise their heavy load when they had to spend the night in the Offenburg station hall, on the stone floor densely covered with tired people waiting for irregular trains, where the old dirty furniture wraps afforded considerable comfort to their sleep.

Then they hurried back from Freiburg to continue preparations, while Mr. Süss was occupied with organization on a higher level in Freiburg or Berlin. One used to choose a train to Offenburg starting at three o'clock in the morning for fear of air raids, and hiked up from Hausach, maybe in lucky cases from Wolfach only, or otherwise cycled those 65 km over the mountains. Hiking the whole way, spending one night at Elzach, was no exception either.

Now it was most pleasant that Prof. Hellmuth Kneser appeared on the scene to have a look at the developing Institute. That meant help at the right moment, for it was rather hard for Mrs. Süss and Hilo alone to dismount the numerous beds in the dormitories and to distribute them into all the different rooms. But with three working together, it was fun. There were no washstands with running water as there are today in the rooms. The young teachers had used the laundry in the cellar as a common shower-bath room, for the lot of them. But Mr. Lutz sent the washbasin sets as mentioned above, and the study-bedrooms gradually got habitable.

It was a more difficult though easier task, being ticklish, to free all the rooms of the portraits representing diverse big Party-guns. That they were to be separated and preserved as property of the training camp, had to serve as an excuse in face of the household staff. The possibility of inspecting Party visitors made Mrs. Süss choose one large Hitler portrait from the lot, a reproduction of an oil painting which in subdued greenish and, that goes without saying, brownish hues, pursued a certain mimicry against the library wallpaper. This she hung up high above the bookshelves so nobody had to notice it if he did not absolutely wish to. The housekeeper was called in to help, and, in the act of fixing it, was influenced to the effect that she had to agree, this was the highest place of honor in the most important spot of the house, and how harmonious was the impression of its colors just there.

Thus, the House was prepared.

<u>Moving in</u>. Of course Mr. Kneser had not especially come to carry furniture, but only somewhat too early to a kind of foundation-council session

invited by Süss. About September 5, Mr. Sperner and Mr. Süss came hiking along with their rucksacks together, having met at Offenburg according to appointment on their way from Strassburg and Freiburg. So the first mathematical meeting could come to pass.

Mr. Sperner, having the choice between Scylla and Charybdis, parting with his university chair in Königsberg had accepted one offered in Strassburg, wishing at least to be in the West. But fortunately he was drawn into military service as a meteorologist, and being in the army was claimable, in the lines of the Osenberg Action, for scientific work at the Institute. He then took the responsibilities of a vice-director.

The order, issued from Berlin regarding removal of university libraries to air-raid-proof places, applied to Strassburg too. In a military retreat, Strassburg at all events was to be defended, and destruction by artillery and bombing was impending. Oberwolfach was designated as an appropriate place for safely stowing away the Strassburg mathematical library, and Mr. Sperner was ordered to survey the transportation of books with military trucks. Here they were arranged in separate shelves procured by special license from a Wolfach carpenter, and seemed much more reasonably placed than in any cellars whichsoever in the country.

In the beginning there was a general coming and going between Freiburg and Oberwolfach. There was university summer vacation, and the mathematicians from Freiburg partly stayed at Lorenzenhof and held colloquia there.

The first permanent residents were Mr. Threlfall and Mr. Seifert. These were colleagues whom Mr. Süss had early contacted about their willingness to let themselves be claimed. For already some time ago, Mr. Threlfall had required his services as an intermediary. Uttering hostile words against the government at table in his Frankfurt boarding house, he had contracted a denunciation and was menaced with the fearful institution called the "people's court of justice." It had been possible to arrange for his disappearance from his Frankfurt university chair to an employment with Mr. Seifert at the Military Institute for Aeronautical Investigation at Braunschweig. But obviously, under the prevailing circumstances, Lorenzenhof was the best imaginable place for his safety, and Mr. Süss was entitled now to demand the presence of both at the NRI.

There were several mathematicians, attached as guests to the Freiburg University Institute: Mr. Behnke, to whose activity at Münster bombs had put an end, further Mr. Bol, who had been ordered away from his chair at Greifswald University for military service with the spade, and Mr. Maak from Heidelberg, each of them secured against military claims by a commission from the NRC. Mr. Süss had made it possible also for the Alsatian colleague Pisot and the French colleague Roger, prisoner of war, to pursue their mathematical work at Freiburg University. Mr. Görtler had recently become Professor at Freiburg University, whereas the other official Freiburg colleague, Doetsch, was absent as an officer in Berlin and remained alien to the circle.

The destruction of the town and university of Freiburg, on November 27, 1944, deprived them, at one blow, of their working possibilities there. They all took refuge under the roof of Lorenzenhof, bringing their assistants and secretaries with them, rendering superfluous further plans about configuration of the Institute. On his own responsibility, Mr. Süss offered a home there as well to his French colleague Roger, who otherwise would have had to return to a prisoners' camp.

The other members of the mathematical staff in the beginning were: Miss Jägerschmidt as secretary for the NRC matters, the official assistants

Dr. ter Hell and Dr. Schubart, and the student assistants and candidates for a degree Miss Krawinkel and Miss Krepper, all from Freiburg; and Mr. Behnke and Mr. Seifert were joined by their assistants from Münster and Heidelberg, Miss Florack and Mr. Stakowski. Some further candidates from Freiburg took lodgings in the valley, Miss Bertling, Miss Natrop, and Miss Sander, to be able to study in the library, and moved into the house only later for protection during the actual passing of the war front.

Previous to the Freiburg air raid, measures of precaution had been started, at official bidding, in removing institutes of the university. Outposts, where work might be continued in case of danger to the town, were to be established. This action being officially supported, Mr. Süss had at last succeeded in his endeavors to have a car granted for transportation of the NRC records to Oberwolfach. It was always very difficult to get a car, but in this case the Security Service (SD) itself helped; it was Mr. Klein of the SD who made it possible.

So it came about, that exactly on the ominous day, November 27, 1944, at midday, a car held in front of Mr. Süss's private lodgings. Everybody present helped to stow the records and their chest of shelves away into the car, not heeding the howling sirens, whilst in the sky the airplanes circled reconnoitering for the evening raid. At 1 o'clock Mr. Süss started off to Lorenzenhof with his precious load, and at 8 o'clock in the evening Freiburg and his apartment were a heap of ruins. It was not unfavorable that Mr. Süss left his family, busy storing turnips for the winter, in the Freiburg home, when he drove up with those documents. For not a few people in leading positions were afterwards calumniated by rumors that they had previously been secretly warned of the imminent raid, the exact date of the attack being known beforehand to the German government, as menaced reprisals if Strassburg was defended. This ugly suspicion was promulgated even from the pulpit.

So, by an altogether lucky chance, the mathematical cause could be pursued without an interruption that might have been conclusive. For by a delay of only a few hours, the organizational center would have been paralyzed by the utter isolation of the ruined town, even if the papers had just been blown about and not burnt. So the NMRI now was the center of the Osenberg Action, that had been in Freiburg up to then.

Inequalities of Combinatorics and Number Theory

Lorenzenhof
A distant view from the southeast in the 1940's

A FUNCTIONAL INEQUALITY ARISING IN COMBINATORICS

Donald R. Snow
Department of Mathematics
Brigham Young University
Provo, Utah 84602
U.S.A.

ABSTRACT. In this paper, we discuss the functional inequality $p(n+m) \leq \binom{n+m}{n} p(n)\, p(m)$, which arises in tournament theory and other parts of combinatorics. A simple transformation removes the binomial coefficient, and then the solution set divides naturally into three classes of functions. One class consists of all the nonpositive functions since this inequality puts no restriction on such functions. The counting-function solutions, i.e., the nonnegative solutions, all lie in the other two classes and satisfy easily obtainable exponential growth bounds. This set of solutions also possesses a structure in the sense that various combinations of these solutions, e.g., sums and products, are again in the set. Various solution functions and properties of solutions are obtained by introducing a slack function to convert the functional inequality to a functional equation. The general solution to this functional equation is obtained by transforming it to another functional equation whose general solution is known. Solution functions found in this manner occur in pairs and are sometimes even from different solution classes. This slack-function concept has modifications, so it can be applied in other ways to the functional inequality and to other inequalities.

1. INTRODUCTION

The problem studied here is to find all functions $p(n)$ satisfying the inequality

$$p(n+m) \leq \binom{n+m}{m} p(n)p(m) \quad . \tag{1.1}$$

This inequality arises in tournament theory, where $p(n)$ is the maximum number of spanning paths in the tournament of n players [Moon (1968)]. It also arises in other combinatorics problems [Forcade (1971)]. Some information on solutions is given in [Moon (1968) and Szele (1943)].

Using the factorial representation of the binomial coefficients, we can write the inequality as

$$\frac{p(n+m)}{(n+m)!} \le \frac{p(n)p(m)}{n!\,m!} ,$$

so that, with $f(n) = \frac{p(n)}{n!}$, it reduces to

$$f(n+m) \le f(n)f(m) . \tag{1.2}$$

As the inequality has arisen, n is an integer ≥ 1. We shall assume here that n can be 0 as well. Note that the inequality is a generalization of one of the four fundamental Cauchy functional equations, and that all solutions to the equation also satisfy the inequality. By evaluating at $n = 0$, Cauchy's functional equation may be shown to have only $f(0) = 0$ or 1 as initial values. For the inequality, however, there are other possibilities, as will be shown. If f is assumed to be strictly positive, taking logarithms reduces the inequality to

$$\ln f(n+m) \le \ln f(n) + \ln f(m) ,$$

so $\ln f(n)$ is a subadditive function. Again we note that this is a generalization of another of Cauchy's four functional equations. The book by Moon and the paper by Szele attack the inequality from this point of view. If the possibility of $f(n) = 0$ for some n exists, then the logarithm approach is invalid. In this paper, the assumption $f(n) > 0$ will not be made, and hence the treatment will be more general.

If inequality (1.2) had a plus sign between $f(n)$ and $f(m)$ on the right-hand side, then it would be the subadditive inequality. If it had a multiplication sign on the left-hand side, it would describe submultiplicative functions. Thus by "interpolation of names," (1.2) can be referred to as the subaddiplicative inequality.

We note also that the inequality holds only for real-valued functions since it involves an inequality; that is, any complex generalizations of it must first involve taking some sort of "norm" to get corresponding real-valued functions.

2. SOLUTION CLASSES

The set of all functions satisfying (1.2) may be categorized into three classes, which we will call Classes N, P, and V (for negative, positive, and variable). These classes are defined by first evaluating at $n = 0$ to get

$$f(n + 0) \leq f(n)f(0) ,$$

or

(2.1) $$0 \leq f(n)[f(0) - 1] , \qquad \text{for all } n .$$

We see that the sign of $f(n)$ is determined by that of $f(0) - 1$. Evaluating this at $n = 0$, we get

(2.2) $$0 \leq f(0)[f(0) - 1] ;$$

this is a quadratic inequality for $f(0)$, implying

(2.3) $$f(0) \leq 0 \qquad \text{or} \qquad 1 \leq f(0) .$$

These are the corresponding generalizations of the Cauchy-equation initial conditions.

Class N $[f(0) - 1 < 0]$. In this case, inequality (2.1) implies that $f(n) \leq 0$ for all n. It may be observed, however, that any nonpositive function satisfies the inequality (1.2), so it is not restrictive in the class of nonpositive functions. Any function satisfying (1.2) and $f(0) - 1 < 0$ must also satisfy $f(0) \leq 0$ by (2.3). This class of solutions is the set of all nonpositive functions. The only other solution functions taking on any negative values must satisfy $f(0) - 1 = 0$, and hence be in class V, below.

Class P $[f(0) - 1 > 0]$. In this case, (2.1) implies $f(n) \geq 0$ for all n. Again, there are infinitely many solutions, e.g., e^{cn} and $an + b$, where $a \geq 0$, $b \geq 1$. But, unlike Class N, not all nonnegative functions are solutions; e.g., e^{n^2} is not a solution. Thus the inequality is restrictive in the set of nonnegative solutions.

Class V $[f(0) = 1]$. If, for a solution f, there are integers n_1, n_2 for which $f(n_1) < 0 < f(n_2)$, then (2.1) implies that $f(0) = 1$. Hence, into this class fall all solutions with variable sign, e.g., r^n, $r < 0$. This class also contains solutions of a single sign, e.g., r^n, $r > 0$. The only single-sign solutions in this class are nonnegative ones since $f(0) = 1 > 0$.

The chart in Figure 1 shows the signs of solutions in the three solution classes.

Class \ Sign	$f(n) \leq 0$	$f(n) \gtrless 0$	$f(n) \geq 0$
N $[f(0) < 1]$	x	∅	∅
V $[f(0) = 1]$	∅	x	x
P $[f(0) > 1]$	∅	∅	x

Figure 1. Chart of Signs of Solutions in Solution Classes.

The solutions of interest in combinatorics have nonnegative values, and hence are all in Classes V and P.

Figure 2 is a diagram illustrating the initial values of solutions in the three classes.

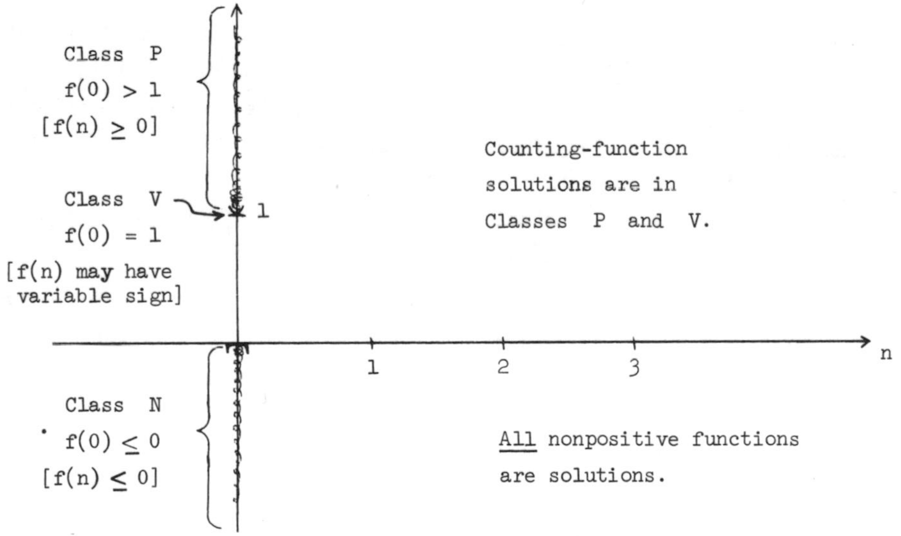

Figure 2. Initial Values and Solution Classes.

3. STRUCTURE OF THE COUNTING-FUNCTION SOLUTION SET

As indicated in Section 2, all solution functions of interest in combinatorics, i.e., $f(n) \geq 0$ for all n, lie in Classes P and V. Growth estimates for these nonnegative solutions are easily obtained as follows. Set $m = n$ and $m = 2n$ to get:

$$f(2n) \leq f(n)^2 \quad \text{and} \quad f(3n) \leq f(n)f(2n) \leq f(n)^3 ,$$

and, by induction, $f(kn) \leq f(n)^k$ for any positive integer k. Setting $n = 1$, we obtain

$$f(k) \leq f(1)^k \quad \text{for any positive integer } k . \tag{3.1}$$

Hence all nonnegative solutions are bounded by exponentials. If f takes on negative values, this inequality may still hold, but is not useful.

Szele [1943] and Moon [1968] obtain growth bounds by assuming $f(n) > 0$ for all n, taking logarithms, and using estimates for subadditive functions.

To illustrate the structure of the nonnegative solution set, suppose $f \geq 0$ and $g \geq 0$ are two solutions. Then

$$f(n + m)g(n + m) \leq f(n)f(m)g(n)g(m) = [f(n)g(n)][f(m)g(m)] ,$$

so we have:

Property (1). *If f and g are nonnegative solutions, then fg is also a nonnegative solution.*

We note that therefore the square of any nonnegative solution is another nonnegative solution.

We also have

$$f(n + m) + g(n + m) \leq f(n)f(m) + g(n)g(m) \leq [f(n) + g(n)][f(m) + g(m)] ,$$

so we have:

Property (2). *If f and g are nonnegative solutions, then $f + g$ is also a nonnegative solution.*

Property (3). *If f is a nonnegative solution, and $h \geq 1$ is any function, then hf is also a nonnegative solution.*

For any function $h \leq 0$, if f is a nonnegative solution then hf is also a solution, but is uninteresting.

Property (4). If $h \geq 0$ is a given function and hf is a solution for all solutions $f \geq 0$, then h is also a nonnegative solution.

To prove Property (4), let $f(n) = r^n$, $r > 0$. Then

$$h(n + m)r^{n+m} \leq h(n)r^n \, h(m)r^m ,$$

and so, canceling the powers of r, we see that $h(n)$ is also a solution. This property shows that there is almost a quotient-type relation in the nonnegative solution set.

The above properties give some ways of combining known nonnegative solutions to obtain new ones, and there are other ways still. It may be the case, however, that there is a "basis set" of nonnegative solutions, so that using Properties (1) - (3) yields all nonnegative solutions. This could be investigated further.

4. INTRODUCTION OF A SLACK FUNCTION

Functional inequality (1.2) can be converted to a functional equation by the introduction of a slack function, $F(n,m)$, as follows:

$$f(n + m) + F(n,m) = f(n)f(m) . \tag{4.1}$$

It is clear that any f satisfying (1.2) also satisfies (4.1), and that then the corresponding F satisfies

$$F(n,m) = f(n)f(m) - f(n + m) \tag{4.2}$$

and

$$F(n,m) \geq 0 . \tag{4.3}$$

On the other hand, if $F(n,m)$ and $f(n)$ are any functions satisfying (4.1) and (4.3), then f satisfies (1.2). Thus finding all solution pairs $[f,F]$ satisfying (4.1) and (4.3) is equivalent to finding all solutions f of (1.2). We shall show how some solutions to (4.1), and hence some to (1.2), can be found.

Note that solution pairs $[f,F]$ of (4.1) may also satisfy $F(n,m) \leq 0$

for all n,m, or F may be of variable sign. Hence (4.1) by itself has more solutions than inequality (1.2); but after a solution pair $[f,F]$ to (4.1) has been found, (4.3) can be checked, and if it is satisfied then f satisfies (1.2).

Any F satisfying (4.1) must have the form given in (4.2), i.e.,

$$F(n,m) = \varphi(n)\varphi(m) - \varphi(n+m)$$

for some $\varphi(n)$. Thus (4.1) may be written

$$f(n+m) - \varphi(n+m) = f(n)f(m) - \varphi(n)\varphi(m) , \tag{4.4}$$

where f and φ are not necessarily the same function. It is clear that given <u>any</u> φ, choosing $f \equiv \varphi$ yields a solution pair $[\varphi,\varphi]$ to (4.4), but this is not of much help. We shall show there are solution pairs to (4.4) in which the functions are different. We note here that if $[f,\varphi]$ is a solution pair to (4.4) and f satisfies inequality (1.2), then by (4.4), so does φ. Hence in a solution pair $[f,\varphi]$ to (4.4), either both f and φ are solutions to (1.2) or else neither is.

We first consider the relationship of possible initial conditions. Equation (4.4) yields

$$f(0) - \varphi(0) = f(0)^2 - \varphi(0)^2 ,$$

which is a quadratic equation for $f(0)$ in terms of $\varphi(0)$. It may be written as

$$[f(0) - \varphi(0)][f(0) + \varphi(0) - 1] = 0 , \tag{4.5}$$

so

$$f(0) = \varphi(0), \quad \text{i.e.,} \quad [\varphi(0),\varphi(0)] , \tag{4.6}$$

or

$$f(0) = 1 - \varphi(0), \quad \text{i.e.,} \quad [1 - \varphi(0) , \varphi(0)] , \tag{4.7}$$

or both are satisfied:

$$f(0) = \varphi(0) = 1 - \varphi(0)$$

which gives

$$f(0) = \varphi(0) = 1/2, \quad \text{i.e.,} \quad [1/2 , 1/2] . \tag{4.8}$$

Case (4.8) is not in the allowable range of initial conditions for inequality (1.2) (refer (2.3)), and hence is not of interest here. Clearly the case with $f \equiv \varphi$ satisfies (4.6), but there are also other possibilities.

Returning to (4.4), we transform it by

$$(4.9) \qquad \begin{cases} f(n) = c(n) + s(n) , \\ \varphi(n) = c(n) - s(n) , \end{cases}$$

or

$$(4.10) \qquad \begin{cases} c(n) = \frac{1}{2} [f(n) + \varphi(n)] , \\ s(n) = \frac{1}{2} [f(n) - \varphi(n)] , \end{cases}$$

to get:

$$(4.11) \qquad s(n + m) = s(n)c(m) + s(m)c(n) .$$

Since the transformation is invertible, the general solition to (4.11) transforms back to the general solution to (4.4). Note that $\sin n$ and $\cos n$ satisfy (4.11), suggesting the names for the transformation functions. Also,

$$s(n) \equiv 0 , \qquad c(n) = \text{arbitrary}$$

is the solution corresponding to $f \equiv \varphi$ as a solution pair to (4.4).

Aczél [1966, p. 205] obtained and listed all (complex) solutions to the continuous version of (4.11). These are

$$(4.12) \qquad \text{(i)} \quad c(x) \ \text{arbitrary} , \qquad s(x) \equiv 0 ,$$

$$(4.13) \qquad \text{(ii)} \quad c(x) = e_0(x) , \qquad s(x) = e_0(x)a(x) ,$$

$$(4.14) \qquad \text{(iii)} \quad c(x) = \frac{1}{2} [e_1(x) + e_2(x)] , \qquad s(x) = \frac{1}{2k} [e_1(x) - e_2(x)] ,$$

where $k \neq 0$ is an arbitrary complex constant, and where $a(x)$ and $e_j(x)$ satisfy

$$(4.15) \qquad a(x + y) = a(x) + a(y) ,$$

$$(4.16) \qquad e_j(x + y) = e_j(x)e_j(y) , \qquad j = 0,1,2 .$$

The nicely behaved (i.e., continuous, or bounded on an interval, etc.) solutions of the two Cauchy equations (4.15) and (4.16) are these:

(4.17) $$a(x) = \alpha x , \quad \alpha \text{ an arbitrary constant ,}$$

and

(4.18) $$e_j(x) = \alpha^x , \quad \alpha \text{ an arbitrary constant .}$$

Using (4.10) to transform back, we find that the "general" solution (there may still be additional discrete solutions) to equation (4.4) is

(4.19) (i) $f(n) \equiv \varphi(n) = \text{arbitrary}$,

(4.20) (ii) $f(n) = e_0(n)[1 + a(n)]$, $\varphi(n) = e_0(n)[1 - a(n)]$,

(4.21) $$\begin{cases} \text{(iii)} \quad f(n) = \frac{1}{2}\left[\left(1 + \frac{1}{k}\right)e_1(n) + \left(1 - \frac{1}{k}\right)e_2(n)\right] , \\ \qquad\qquad \varphi(n) = \frac{1}{2}\left[\left(1 - \frac{1}{k}\right)e_1(n) + \left(1 + \frac{1}{k}\right)e_2(n)\right] , \end{cases}$$

where $a(n)$ and $e_j(n)$ satisfy (4.15) and (4.16), respectively.

It should be remembered that the solutions given above include all complex solutions, and we are interested only in real solutions. There may be complex solutions to (4.15) and (4.16) which, when combined as in (4.20) and (4.21), yield real f and φ. We note that there is a symmetry between f and φ in the general solution, as we would expect, since they can be interchanged in (4.19) - (4.21) with the effect of only relabeling the solutions but still yielding all solutions.

The allowable initial conditions (4.6) and (4.7) put additional restrictions on the solutions:

Case (4.6): $f(0) = \varphi(0)$. Solutions (4.19) - (4.21) in this case require:

(i) All solutions of type (4.19) satisfy (4.6).

(ii) For solutions of type (4.20), we have

$$e_0(0)[1 + a(0)] = e_0(0)[1 - a(0)] ,$$

or

$$e_0(0)a(0) = 0 .$$

Since all solutions $a(n)$ of (4.17) satisfy $a(0) = 0$, (4.6) is not an additional restriction for solutions of this type.

(iii) For solutions of type (4.21) with $f(0) = \varphi(0)$, we have

$$\left(1 + \frac{1}{k}\right)e_1(0) + \left(1 - \frac{1}{k}\right)e_2(0) = \left(1 - \frac{1}{k}\right)e_1(0) + \left(1 + \frac{1}{k}\right)e_2(0) ,$$

which reduces to $e_1(0) = e_2(0)$. But initial conditions on (4.16) are $e_j(0) = 0$ or 1, and $e_j(0) = 0$ yields $e_j(n + 0) = e_j(n)e_j(0)$, so $e_j(n) \equiv 0$. Hence this restriction reduces to requiring that both f and φ must be identically 0 (which is already included in solution (4.19)) or else

$$e_1(0) = e_2(0) = 1 .$$

Case (4.7): $f(0) = 1 - \varphi(0)$. Solutions (4.19) - (4.21) for this case require:

(i) (4.19) requires that $f(0) = \varphi(0)$, so with $f(0) = 1 - \varphi(0)$, we have $f(0) = \varphi(0) = 1/2$, which is not an allowable initial condition for the inequality, so there are no solutions f of this type to inequality (1.2).

(ii) (4.20) in this case requires that

$$1 = e_0(0)[1 + a(0)] + e_0(0)[1 - a(0)] ,$$

so $e_0(0) = 1/2$. However, $e_0(0)$ satisfying (4.16) must have $e_0(0) = 0$ or 1. Hence there are no solutions of type (4.20) in this case.

(iii) (4.21) requires that

$$\frac{1}{2}\left[\left(1 + \frac{1}{k}\right)e_1(0) + \left(1 - \frac{1}{k}\right)e_2(0)\right] + \frac{1}{2}\left[\left(1 - \frac{1}{k}\right)e_1(0) + \left(1 + \frac{1}{k}\right)e_2(0)\right] = 1 ,$$

which reduces to

$$e_1(0) + e_2(0) = 1 .$$

Since $e_j(0) = 0$ or 1, this requires that one be 0 and the other 1. Thus if $e_2(0) = 0$ then $e_2(n) \equiv 0$ and $e_1(n) = \alpha^n$, so f and φ reduce to

$$f(n) = \frac{1}{2}\left(1 + \frac{1}{k}\right)\alpha^n , \qquad \varphi(n) = \frac{1}{2}\left(1 - \frac{1}{k}\right)\alpha^n .$$

If the initial conditions on the $e_j(n)$ are reversed, then f and φ are interchanged.

Summarizing, we have shown that all solutions to equation (4.4) which are of interest in our combinatorics inequality (1.2) are (remember that f and φ may be interchanged and that $a(n)$ and $e_j(n)$ satisfy (4.15) and (4.16), respectively) the following:

Solutions with $f(0) = \varphi(0)$:

(1) $f(n) \equiv \varphi(n) =$ arbitrary,

(2) $f(n) = e_0(n)[1 + a(n)]$, $\varphi(n) = e_0(n)[1 - a(n)]$,

(3) $f(n) = \frac{1}{2}\left[\left(1 + \frac{1}{k}\right)e_1(n) + \left(1 - \frac{1}{k}\right)e_2(n)\right]$,

$\varphi(n) = \frac{1}{2}\left[\left(1 - \frac{1}{k}\right)e_1(n) + \left(1 + \frac{1}{k}\right)e_2(n)\right]$,

where $e_1(0) = e_2(0) = 1$, and $k \neq 0$ is an arbitrary (real or complex) constant.

Solutions with $f(0) = 1 - \varphi(0)$:

(4) $f(n) = \frac{1}{2}\left(1 + \frac{1}{k}\right)\alpha^n$, $\varphi(n) = \frac{1}{2}\left(1 - \frac{1}{k}\right)\alpha^n$,

where $k \neq 0$ and α are arbitrary (real or complex) constants.

Cases (2) - (4) give us explicit solutions which can be checked to see if they satisfy the original inequality (1.2); but Case (1) incorporates many other types of solutions, and this approach does not give us any information concerning them. Note that the specific solutions mentioned in Section 2 are of types (2) - (4) or else are constructed from such solutions using the combinations mentioned in Section 3. It may be that all solutions to the inequality can be obtained in this way, in which case solutions (2) - (4) would form a sort of basis for the solution space. Note also that solutions f of the inequality (1.2) may correspond to other solutions φ of the inequality; and these may be in different classes, as defined in Section 3. There is a kind of "complementary function" idea here that could be pursued further.

5. CONCLUSIONS

We have discussed the inequality

$$p(n + m) \leq \binom{n+m}{m} p(n)\ p(m) ,$$

which arises in certain areas of combinatorics. By transforming to $f(n) = p(n)/n!$, the inequality reduces to $f(n + m) \leq f(n)f(m)$. We have seen how the solution set divides into three classes depending on the value of f at $n = 0$. We noted that solutions of interest in combinatorics, i.e., those which are ≥ 0, are contained in two of the classes, satisfy exponential growth bounds, and have a structure on them so that products, sums, and other combinations of such solutions are again solutions.

In Section 4 we converted the functional inequality into a functional equation in two unknown functions by introducing a slack function. We got the general solution to this equation by transforming it to a sine-cosine identity for which the general solution is known. The allowable initial conditions on the inequality impose additional restrictions on the solutions to the functional equation in order that they can also be solutions to the inequality. The solutions to the functional equation occur in pairs, each of which is a solution to the inequality, or else neither of which is. We have obtained solutions to the inequality in this way, and by forming combinations of these, can get others. It is conjectured that this approach may give all (nonnegative) solutions to the inequality, but this conjecture has not been investigated.

The idea of introducing a slack function can be modified in other ways for this inequality; e.g., it can be converted to the functional equation

$$f(n + m)G(n,m) = f(n)f(m) ,$$

in which $G(n,m) \geq 1$. This concept of converting a functional inequality into a functional equation appears to be applicable to other functional inequalities as well.

REFERENCES

1. Janos Aczél, Lectures on Functional Equations and Their Applications, Academic Press, New York, 1966.

2. Rodney W. Forcade, Hamiltonian Paths in Tournaments, Ph.D. Thesis, University of Washington, Seattle, 1971.

3. John W. Moon, Topics on Tournaments, Holt, Rinehart and Winston, New York, 1968.

4. Tibor Szele, Kombinatorikai vizsgálatok az irányított teljes gráffal kapcsolatban, Mat. és Fiz. Lapok 50 (1943), 223-256. For a German translation, see Kombinatorische Untersuchungen über gerichtete vollständige Graphen, Publ. Math. Debrecen 13 (1966), 145-168.

PAIRS OF SUMS OF THREE SQUARES OF INTEGERS WHOSE PRODUCT HAS THE SAME PROPERTY

Olga Taussky
Department of Mathematics
California Institute of Technology
Pasadena, California 91125
U.S.A.

ABSTRACT. In this article, pairs of sums of three squares of integers whose product has the same property will be divided into classes. It is possible, however, for a pair to belong to two different classes, in view of the different expressions that are sometimes possible for a given number as a sum of three squares.

Further, two applications of such pairs will be discussed, one to algebraic extensions with the quaternion group of order 8 as a Galois group, the other to a classical problem, going back to Gauss, of expressing a binary positive-definite integral quadratic form as the sum of three squares of integral linear forms.

1. INTRODUCTION

While 1, 2, 4, 8 are very popular in the theory of sums of squares, the number 3 is very "odd." In particular, it is well known that there is no identity

$$\sum_1^n x_i^2 \sum_1^n y_i^2 = \sum_1^n [\ell_i(x,y)]^2$$

for ℓ_i bilinear forms in the x_i, y_k, unless $n = 1, 2, 4, 8$, not even for ℓ_i replaced by $r_i(x,y)$, where the r_i are rational functions, unless n is a power of 2.

It was pointed out by van der Waerden that the exclusion of the cardinal 3 in the above identities was already observed indirectly by Legendre when he noticed that 3 and 21 are sums of three squares while their product 63 is not.

The reason for this lies in the fact that 7 is not a sum of three squares, for $3 \cdot 21$ being a sum of three squares would imply $3 \cdot 21/3^2 = 7 = \sum\square$, [1)] which in fact does not hold. (It is known that a sum of three

1) The symbol $\sum\square$ stands here and in what follows for "sum of 3 squares."

rational squares can also be expressed as a sum of three integral squares; see, e.g., Tate 1967, Serre 1970.)

However, if 7 is replaced by, e.g., 11, then we have $3 \cdot 11 = 33$ which is $\sum \square$, and $3 \cdot 33/3^2 = 11$ which is $\sum \square$, and $99 = 3^2 \cdot 11$ can be expressed as $\sum \square$, either by multiplying $11 = 3^2 + 1^2 + 1^2$ termwise by 9, or, alternatively, by $7^2 + 7^2 + 1^2$, which leads to a fractional representation of 11 as $\sum \square$.

2. THE LAGRANGE IDENTITY

The following identity will play a certain role in what follows:

$$\sum_1^3 x_i^2 \sum_1^3 y_i^2 = \left(\sum_1^3 x_i y_i\right)^2 + \sum_{i \neq j} (x_i y_j - x_j y_i)^2 .$$

It contains four terms on the right-hand side, and can be deduced from Euler's identity

$$\sum_1^4 x_i^2 \sum_1^4 y_i^2 = (x_1y_1 - x_2y_2 - x_3y_3 - x_4y_4)^2 + (x_1y_2 + x_2y_1 + x_3x_4 - x_4y_3)^2$$
$$+ (x_1y_3 - x_2y_4 + x_3y_1 + x_4y_2)^2 + (x_1y_4 + x_2y_3 - x_3y_2 + x_4y_1)^2$$

by replacing the indeterminates x_4, y_4 with 0 and by replacing y_2, y_3 with $-y_2$, $-y_3$. It is more useful in this work, however, to deduce it from the product of the norms of the two quaternions $x_1 + ix_2 + jx_3$, $y_1 - iy_2 - jy_3$.

3. COMPOSITION PAIRS

DEFINITIONS. A pair of integers a, b with the property that a, b, ab are all $\sum \square$ will be called a <u>composition pair</u>. A composition pair with the property that for some representation at least one term in the right-hand side of the Lagrange identity is zero will be called a <u>quaternion pair</u>. If the term $\sum x_i y_i$ is zero, it is called a <u>quaternion pair of class</u> D (D for dot product); if one of the $x_i y_j - x_j y_i = 0$, it will be called a <u>quaternion pair of class</u> V (V for vector product).

An example of a composition pair which is not a quaternion pair is $a = 163 = 9^2 + 9^2 + 1^2$, $b = 14 = 3^2 + 2^2 + 1^2$.

This leads to the following observation.

THEOREM 1. <u>There exist sums of three integral squares which allow a</u>

factorization into integers of the same kind, but which cannot be obtained as norms of quaternions with one component 0.

This is in contrast to facts about complex numbers or quaternions (see Hurwitz 1896, Lipschitz 1886). In particular, a quaternion with norm equal to $14 \cdot 163$ and one component 0 can be written as a product of quaternions of norms 14 and 163:

$$(2i - j - 3k)(12 + 3i + 3j + k) .$$

An example of a quaternion pair of class D which cannot be represented as a quaternion pair of class V is

$$a = 3 = 1^2 + 1^2 + 1^2 , \qquad b = 14 = 3^2 + 2^2 + 1^2 ,$$

with $3 \cdot 1 + 2 \cdot (-1) + 1 \cdot (-1) = 0$. It was pointed out by Catalan 1893 that it is not of class V. (Catalan studied the diophantine equation

$$\sum_1^3 x_i^2 \sum_1^3 y_i^2 = \sum_1^3 z_i^2 .)$$

An example of a quaternion pair of class V which cannot be represented as one of class D is

$$a = 3 = 1^2 + 1^2 + 1^2 , \qquad b = 9 = 2^2 + 2^2 + 1^2 = 3^2 ,$$

while the pair

$$a = 3 = 1^2 + 1^2 + 1^2 , \qquad b = 6 = 2^2 + 1^2 + 1^2$$

is both of class D and of class V.

The following theorem holds:

THEOREM 2. Let a, b be a quaternion pair of class D, such that $\sum x_i y_i = 0$ holds for a representation

$$a = \sum x_i^2 , \qquad b = \sum y_i^2 .$$

Then also

$$\sum x_i z_i = \sum y_i z_i = 0$$

for a suitable representation of $ab = \sum z_i^2$.

<u>Proof</u>. Under the assumption $\sum x_i y_i = 0$, we have the quaternion product

$$(x_1 + ix_2 + jx_3)(y_1 - iy_2 - jy_3) = i(x_2y_1 - x_1y_2) + j(x_3y_1 - x_1y_3) + k(x_3y_2 - x_2y_3) .$$

Hence z_1, z_2, z_3 may be taken as $\pm (x_2y_1 - x_1y_2)$, $\pm (x_3y_1 - x_1y_3)$, $\pm (x_3y_2 - x_2y_3)$ in any permutation desired. The result follows from the identity

$$x_3(x_2y_1 - x_1y_2) - x_2(x_3y_1 - x_1y_3) + x_1(x_3y_2 - x_2y_3) = 0 .$$

A similar computation shows that $\sum y_i z_i = 0$. □

THEOREM 3. <u>Let</u> a, b <u>be a quaternion pair of type</u> V <u>for a suitable representation</u>

$$a = \sum x_i^2 , \qquad b = \sum y_i^2$$

<u>such that</u>

$$x_i y_j - x_j y_i = 0$$

<u>for suitable values of</u> $i \neq j$. <u>Then also</u>

$$x_i z_j - x_j z_i = y_i z_j - y_j z_i = 0 .$$

<u>Proof</u>. Let, e.g., $x_1y_2 - x_2y_1 = 0$. Consider again the quaternion product used in the proof of Theorem 2, but replace the condition

$$\sum x_i y_i = 0 \qquad \text{with} \qquad x_1y_2 - x_2y_1 = 0 .$$

Hence the product turns out as a permutation of

$$\sum x_i y_i + j(x_3y_1 - x_1y_3) + k(x_3y_2 - x_2y_3) .$$

Thus we have to examine z_1, z_2, z_3 as a permutation of

$$\pm \sum x_i y_i , \ \pm (x_3y_1 - x_1y_3) , (x_3y_2 - x_2y_3) .$$

The expression

$$x_2(x_3y_1 - x_1y_3) - x_1(x_3y_2 - x_2y_3) = x_3(x_2y_1 - x_1y_2) = 0$$

proves the assertion. □

4. QUATERNION FIELDS

Here we study algebraic extensions of the field of rationals, Q, whose Galois group is the quaternion group of order 8. It is known (see Witt 1936, Reichardt 1936) that the quadratic subfields of such a field are generated by the square root of a sum of three squares. The whole field contains three quadratic subfields. Hence, if $Q(\sqrt{a})$, $Q(\sqrt{b})$, $a,b \in Q$, are subfields, the third one has to be $Q(\sqrt{ab})$, and hence a,b form a composition pair. However, not all composition pairs qualify, as is shown in the next theorem.

THEOREM 4. *A composition pair* a, b *with the property that* $Q(\sqrt{a})$, $Q(\sqrt{b})$ *are subfields of a quaternion field can be represented as a quaternion pair of class* D. *Conversely, every such pair leads to a subfield of a quaternion field.*

Proof. Let $Q(\sqrt{a})$, $Q(\sqrt{b})$ be subfields of a quaternion field. By a theorem of Witt 1936, it follows that the two quadratic forms

$$f_1 = ax_1^2 + bx_2^2 + \frac{1}{ab} x_3^2 , \qquad f_2 = y_1^2 + y_2^2 + y_3^2$$

are equivalent via a unimodular matrix with elements in Q. The condition is also sufficient. In Taussky (to appear) it is shown that this leads to the fact that the matrix

$$M = \begin{pmatrix} a & & \\ & b & \\ & & ab \end{pmatrix} \quad \text{satisfies} \quad M = YY' ,$$

with Y rational, and that this further implies that Y can even be chosen integral (for the last conclusion, see Hsia 1978, Verheiden, to appear). □

5. REMARKS. We present here some observations concerning composition pairs connected with integral positive-definite binary quadratic forms which can be expressed as sums of three squares of integral linear forms.

(i) The literature on such forms is fairly extensive, going back to Gauss; further, see Venkov 1931, whose work was studied by Rehm 1974, Mordell 1937, H. Braun 1937, Pall 1942. Expressing such a form as a sum of two or of four squares can be studied via Gaussian integers (see Mordell 1930 or Niven 1940) or by integral quaternions (Lipschitz quaternions, not Hurwitz) (see Mordell 1937, Pall and Taussky 1957).

(ii) The absence of a suitable algebra with three basis elements makes the case of three linear forms more complicated.

(iii) Let the form be given by

$$f = ax^2 + hxy + by^2 ,$$

with discriminant $\Delta + ab - h^2 > 0$ by assumption. Then the following results have been obtained previously:

Δ	0	one square	sum of 3 squares	arbitrary
f	one square	sum of 2 squares	sum of 4 squares	sum of 5 squares

Results in the case Δ = two or three squares, leading possibly to f equal to three squares, obtained, e.g., by Mordell, are too involved to describe in the table.

(iv) The following remark is now added to this investigation: If f is a sum of three squares, then the following matrix factorization holds:

$$\begin{pmatrix} a & h \\ h & b \end{pmatrix} = \begin{pmatrix} a_1 & a_2 & a_3 \\ b_1 & b_2 & b_3 \end{pmatrix} \begin{pmatrix} a_1 & b_1 \\ a_2 & b_2 \\ a_3 & b_3 \end{pmatrix} , \qquad a_i, b_i \in Z .$$

This leads to

$$a = \sum_1^3 a_i^2 , \qquad b = \sum_1^3 b_i^2 , \qquad h = \sum_1^3 a_i b_i .$$

Hence, if Δ = sum of two squares, then

$$ab = \Delta = h^2 + r^2 + s^2 , \qquad r, s \in Z ,$$

and therefore a,b form a composition pair.

Further, if $\Delta = \sum \square$ and f is a diagonal form, i.e., h = 0 and a,b are a quaternion pair of class D, then via the Lagrange identity it follows that f is a sum of three squares.

NOTE. It seems clear that in certain parts of these problems the study of rational representation is equivalent to that of integral representation.

This article is an extended version of a combination of a lecture at the Oberwolfach 1978 meeting on Inequalities and a lecture in a Special Session on Quadratic Forms at the Honolulu AMS meeting, March 1979. The author had help with the examples and exposition from D. Estes and R. Guralnick. From a reference supplied by E. Hlawka the author learned of Catalan's paper.

BIBLIOGRAPHY

1. H. Braun, Über die Zerlegung quadratischer Formen in Quadrate, J. Reine Angew. Math. 178 (1937), 38-62.

2. E. Catalan, Sur l'équation $(x^2+y^2+z^2)(x'^2+y'^2+z'^2) = u^2+v^2+w^2$, Mathesis (2) 3 (1893), 105-106.

3. E.N. Donkar, On sums of three integral squares in algebraic number fields, Amer. J. Math. 99 (1977), 1297-1328.

4. P. Erdös and C. Ko, On definite quadratic forms which are not the sum of two definite or semidefinite forms, Acta Arith. 3 (1939), 102-122.

5. Gauss, Disquisitiones Arith.

6. J. Hsia, Two theorems on integral matrices, Lin. and Multilin. Alg. 5 (1978), 257-264.

7. A. Hurwitz, Über die Zahlentheorie der Quaternionen, Nachr. Göttingen (1896), 303-330.

8. E. Landau, Elementare Zahlentheorie, 151-164, Chelsea Publ. Co., 1958.

9. R. Lipschitz, Recherches sur les transformations, par des substitutions réelles, d'une somme de deux ou de trois carrés en elle-même, Jour. de Math. (4) 2, (1886), 373-439.

10. L.J. Mordell, A new Waring's problem with squares of linear forms, Oxford Quart. J. 4 (1930), 276-288.

11. L.J. Mordell, An application of quaternions to the representation of a binary quadratic form as a sum of four linear squares, Oxford Quart. J. 8 (1937), 58-61.

12. L.J. Mordell, On the representation of a binary quadratic form as a sum of squares of linear forms, Math. Z. 35 (1932), 1-15.

13. I. Niven, Integers of quadratic fields as sums of squares, Trans. Amer. Math. Soc. 48 (1940), 405-417.

14. G. Pall, Quaternions and sums of three squares, Amer. J. Math. 64 (1942), 503-513.

15. G. Pall and O. Taussky, Application of quaternions to the representations of a binary quadratic form as a sum of four squares, Proc. Royal Irish Acad. 58 (1957), 23-28.

16. H.P. Rehm, On a theorem of Gausz concerning the integer solutions of the equation $x^2+y^2+z^2 = m$, Seminar Notes in Number Theory, California Institute of Technology, Ed. O. Taussky, 1974.

17. H. Reichardt, Über Normalkörper mit Quaternionen Gruppe, Math. Z. 41 (1936), 218-221.

18. J.-P. Serre, Cours d'arithmétique, Presses Universitaires de France, 1970.

19. J. Tate, Exercise 4.11, p. 359, in J.W.S. Cassels and A. Fröhlich, Algebraic Number Theory, Academic Press, 1967.

20. O. Taussky, Sums of Squares, Amer. Math. Monthly 77 (1977), 805-830.

21. O. Taussky, Results concerning composition of sums of three squares, to appear in Lin. and Multilin. Algebra.

22. W.A. Venkov, Über die Klassenanzahl positiver binärer quadratischer Formen, Math. Z. 33 (1931), 351-354.

23. B.L. van der Waerden, Hamiltons Entdeckung der Quaternionen, Veröffentlichung der Joachim Jungius Ges. der Wissenschaften, Göttingen, 1973, 1-14.

24. E. Verheiden, Thesis, California Institute of Technology, 1978.

25. A. Weil, Sur les sommes de trois et quatre carrés, L'Enseignement Math. 20 (1974), 215-222.

26. E. Witt, Konstruktion von galoisschen Körpern der Charakteristik p zu vorgegebener Gruppe der Ordnung p^f, J. Reine Angew. Math. 174 (1936), 237-245.

COMBINATORIAL INEQUALITIES, MATRIX NORMS, AND GENERALIZED NUMERICAL RADII

Moshe Goldberg
Department of Mathematics
University of California
Los Angeles, California 90024
U.S.A.

E. G. Straus
Department of Mathematics
University of California
Los Angeles, California 90024
U.S.A.

ABSTRACT. Two new combinatorial inequalities are presented. The main result states that if γ_j, $1 \leq j \leq n$, are fixed complex scalars with $\sigma \equiv |\sum \gamma_j| > 0$ and $\delta \equiv \max_{i,j} |\gamma_i - \gamma_j| > 0$, and if $\underset{\sim}{V}$ is a normed vector space over the complex field, then

$$\max_{\pi} |\Sigma_j \gamma_j a_{\pi(j)}| \geq [\sigma\delta/(2\sigma + \delta)] \max_j |a_j| ,$$

$$\forall a_1,\ldots,a_n \in \underset{\sim}{V} ,$$

π varying over permutations of n letters. Next, we consider an arbitrary generalized matrix norm N and discuss methods to obtain multiplicativity factors for N, i.e., constants $\nu > 0$ such that νN is submultiplicative. Using our combinatorial inequalities, we obtain multiplicativity factors for certain C-numerical radii which are generalizations of the classical numerical radius of an operator.

1. SOME NEW COMBINATORIAL INEQUALITIES

In a recent paper [5] we studied a somewhat less general version of the following problem: Given fixed complex scalars $\gamma_1,\ldots,\gamma_n$, and a normed vector space $\underset{\sim}{V}$ over the complex field $\mathbf{C}$, can we find a constant $K > 0$ such that the inequality

$$(1.1) \qquad \max_{\pi \in S_n} \left|\sum_{j=1}^{n} \gamma_j a_{\pi(j)}\right| \geq K \cdot \max|a_j| , \qquad \forall a_1,\ldots,a_n \in \underset{\sim}{V} ,$$

The research of the first author was sponsored in part by the Air Force Office of Scientific Research, Air Force System Command, USAF, under Grant AFOSR-76-3046. The work of the second author was supported in part by NSF Grant MPS 71-2884.

is satisfied? Here S_n is the symmetric group of n letters, and $|a_j|$ is the norm of the vector a_j.

We start with the following lemma.

LEMMA 1.1. *For any* $\gamma_1, \ldots, \gamma_n \in \mathbf{C}$ *and* $a_1, \ldots, a_n \in \underset{\sim}{V}$,

$$\max_{\pi} \left| \sum_j \gamma_j a_{\pi(j)} \right| \geq \frac{1}{2} \max_{i,j} |\gamma_i - \gamma_j| \cdot \max_{i,j} |a_i - a_j| .$$

Proof. We may rearrange the γ_j and the a_j so that

$$|\gamma_1 - \gamma_n| = \max_{i,j} |\gamma_i - \gamma_j| , \qquad |a_1 - a_n| = \max_{i,j} |a_i - a_j| .$$

Now consider the vectors

$$b_1 = \gamma_1 a_1 + \gamma_2 a_2 + \cdots + \gamma_{n-1} a_{n-1} + \gamma_n a_n ,$$

$$b_2 = \gamma_1 a_n + \gamma_2 a_2 + \cdots + \gamma_{n-1} a_{n-1} + \gamma_n a_1 .$$

We have

$$\max_{\pi} \left| \sum_j \gamma_j a_{\pi(j)} \right| \geq \max\{|b_1|, |b_2|\} \geq \frac{1}{2} |b_1 - b_2|$$

$$= \frac{1}{2} |\gamma_1 a_1 + \gamma_n a_n - \gamma_1 a_n - \gamma_n a_1|$$

$$= \frac{1}{2} |\gamma_1 - \gamma_n| \cdot |a_1 - a_n| ,$$

and the proof is complete. □

Denoting

$$(1.2) \qquad \sigma = \left| \sum_j \gamma_j \right| , \qquad \delta = \max_{i,j} |\gamma_i - \gamma_j| ,$$

we prove the following result.

THEOREM 1.2. *There exists a constant* $K > 0$ *that satisfies* (1.1) *if and only if* $\sigma\delta > 0$. *If* $\sigma\delta > 0$ *then* (1.1) *holds with* $K = \sigma\delta/(2\sigma + \delta)$.

Proof. Suppose $\sigma\delta = 0$. If $\sigma = 0$, take $a_j = a$, $1 \leq j \leq n$, for some $a \neq 0$; if $\delta = 0$, then the γ_j are equal, so choose a_j not all zero with $\sum a_j = 0$. In both cases,

$$\max_{\pi}\left|\sum_j \gamma_j\, a_{\pi(j)}\right| = 0 \quad \text{but} \quad \max_j |a_j| > 0 \;;$$

hence no $K > 0$ satisfies (1.1).

Conversely, suppose $\sigma\delta > 0$ and let us show that $K = \sigma\delta/(2\sigma + \delta)$ satisfies (1.1). The following proof, which is shorter than the original one in [5], is due to Redheffer and Smith [8].

Order the a_j so that

$$a_1 = \max_j |a_j| \;, \quad |a_1 - a_n| = \max_j |a_1 - a_j| \equiv \theta|a_1| \qquad (0 \le \theta \le 2) \;.$$

Thus, by Lemma 1.1,

$$\max_{\pi}\left|\sum_j \gamma_j\, a_{\pi(j)}\right| \ge \frac{\theta\delta}{2} \max_j |a_j| \;. \tag{1.3}$$

Next, consider the vectors

$$c_j = \gamma_j a_{1+j} + \gamma_2 a_{2+j} + \cdots + \gamma_n a_{n+j} \;, \qquad j = 1,\ldots,n \;,$$

where $k + j = (k + j) \bmod n$. We have

$$\begin{aligned} \max_{\pi}\left|\sum_j \gamma_j\, a_{\pi(j)}\right| &\ge \max_j |c_j| \ge \frac{1}{n}|c_1 + \cdots + c_n| \\ &= \frac{\sigma}{n}|a_1 + \cdots + a_n| \\ &= \frac{\sigma}{n}|na_1 - (a_1 - a_2) - (a_1 - a_3) - \cdots - (a_1 - a_{n-1})| \\ &\ge \frac{\sigma}{n}\{n|a_1| - (n-1)|a_1 - a_n|\} \\ &= \sigma(1 - \frac{n-1}{n}\theta) \max_j |a_j| \;. \end{aligned} \tag{1.4}$$

By (1.3) and (1.4), therefore,

$$\max_{\pi}\left|\sum_j \gamma_j\, a_{\pi(j)}\right| \ge \max\left\{\frac{\theta\delta}{2} \,,\, \sigma(1 - \frac{n-1}{n}\theta)\right\} \cdot \max_j |a_j| \;. \tag{1.5}$$

The expressions in the braces are functions of θ describing straight lines with opposite slopes and intersecting value $\sigma\delta/(2\sigma + \delta - 2\sigma/n.)$ Thus, for any θ,

$$\max\left\{\frac{\theta\delta}{2} \,,\, \sigma(1 - \frac{n-1}{n}\theta)\right\} \ge \frac{\sigma\delta}{2\sigma + \delta - 2\sigma/n} > \frac{\sigma\delta}{2\sigma + \delta} \;. \tag{1.6}$$

By (1.5) and (1.6), the theorem follows. □

What is the best (greatest) possible K which satisfies (1.1)? In answer to that question, Redheffer and Smith proved the following [8].

THEOREM 1.3. *If* $\sigma\delta > 0$, *then the best* K *for* (1.1) *satisfies*

$$(1.7)\qquad \frac{\sigma\delta}{2\sigma + \delta - 2\sigma/n} \leq K \leq \min\left\{\sigma\,,\ \frac{\sigma\delta}{2\sigma + \delta - 2\sigma/n - 2\delta/n}\right\}\,,$$

and the inequality on the right becomes an equality when the γ_j *and* a_j *are real numbers*.

We note that the left-hand inequality in (1.7) was established already in the proof of Theorem 1.2. For the complete proof of Theorem 1.3, see [2].

From Theorem 1.3, Redheffer and Smith immediately conclude that *while the Goldberg-Straus constant in Theorem* 1.2 *is not optimal for any* n, *it is the best that can be chosen independently of* n, *even if the* γ_j *and* a_j *are real*.

Under certain restrictions on the γ_j, we can improve the constant obtained in Theorem 1.2.

THEOREM 1.4. *If* $\gamma_1,\ldots,\gamma_n$ *are of the same argument, then* (1.1) *holds with* $K = \delta/2$.

Proof. We may assume that

$$\gamma_1 \geq \cdots \geq \gamma_n \,.$$

Arrange the a_j so that

$$|a_1| = \max_j |a_j|\,,$$

and let P be a projection of $\underset{\sim}{V}$ in the direction of a_1. We write

$$Pa_j = \lambda_j a_j\,, \qquad j = 1,\ldots,n\,,$$

and set

$$\rho_j = \operatorname{Re}\lambda_j\,, \qquad j = 1,\ldots,n\,.$$

Since

$$\lambda_1 = 1 \geq |\lambda_j| \ , \qquad j = 2,\ldots,n \ ,$$

it follows that

$$\rho_1 = 1 \geq |\rho_j| \ , \qquad j = 2,\ldots,n \ .$$

So we may order $a_2,\ldots,a_n$ to satisfy

$$1 = \rho_1 \geq \rho_2 \geq \cdots \geq \rho_n \ .$$

We have

$$(1.8) \qquad \max_{\pi} \left| \sum_j \gamma_j \, a_{\pi(j)} \right| \geq \max_{\pi} \left| P\left(\sum_j \gamma_j \, a_{\pi(j)}\right) \right|$$
$$= \max_{\pi} \left| \sum_j \gamma_j \lambda_j \right| \cdot |a_1| \geq \max_{\pi} \left| \mathrm{Re}\left(\sum_j \gamma_j \lambda_{\pi(j)}\right) \right| \cdot |a_1|$$
$$= \max_{\pi} \left| \sum_j \gamma_j \rho_{\pi(j)} \right| \cdot \max_j |a_j| \ .$$

Now, if $\rho_n \geq 0$, then

$$\max_{\pi} \left| \sum_j \gamma_j \rho_{\pi(j)} \right| = \sum \gamma_j \rho_j \geq \gamma_1 \rho_1 \geq \frac{1}{2}(\gamma_1 - \gamma_n) = \frac{\delta}{2} \ ;$$

and if $\rho_n < 0$, then, by Lemma 1.1,

$$\max_{\pi} \left| \sum_j \gamma_j \rho_{\pi(j)} \right| \geq \frac{\delta}{2} \max_{i,j} |\rho_i - \rho_j| = \frac{\delta}{2}(\rho_1 - \rho_n) \geq \frac{\delta}{2} \ .$$

This together with (1.8) completes the proof. □

Note that when the γ_j are of the same argument, then $\delta > 0$ implies $\sigma > 0$, in which case

$$\frac{\delta}{2} > \frac{\sigma\delta}{2\sigma + \delta} \ .$$

That is, the constant of Theorem 1.4 is indeed an improvement over the K of Theorem 1.2.

2. MATRIX NORMS AND GENERALIZED NUMERICAL RADII

In this section we review (mainly without proof) some of the results in [5] which lead to applications of our combinatorial inequalities.

We start with the following definitions [7]: let $\mathbf{C}_{n\times n}$ denote the algebra of $n \times n$ complex matrices. A mapping

$$N : \mathbf{C}_{n\times n} \to \mathbb{R}$$

is a <u>seminorm</u> if for all $A,B \in \mathbf{C}_{n\times n}$ and $\alpha \in \mathbf{C}$,

$$N(A) \geq 0 \ ,$$

$$N(\alpha A) = |\alpha| \ N(A) \ ,$$

$$N(A + B) \leq N(A) + N(B) \ .$$

If in addition

$$N(A) > 0 \ , \qquad \forall A \neq 0 \ ,$$

then N is a <u>generalized matrix norm</u>. Finally, if N is also (sub-) multiplicative, i.e.,

$$N(AB) \leq N(A)N(B) \ ,$$

we say that N is a <u>matrix norm</u>.

EXAMPLES. (i) If $|\cdot|$ is any norm on $\mathbf{C}^n$, then

$$\|A\| = \max\{|Ax| : |x| = 1\}$$

is a matrix norm on $\mathbf{C}_{n\times n}$. In particular, we recall the <u>spectral norm</u>

$$\|A\|_2 = \max\{(x^*A^*Ax)^{1/2} : x^*\mathbf{x} = 1\} \ .$$

(ii) The <u>numerical radius</u>,

$$r(A) = \max\{|x^*Ax| : x^*x = 1\} \ ,$$

is a nonmultiplicative generalized matrix norm (e.g., [6, §173,176], [3]).

In [5] we introduced the following generalization of the numerical radius: Given matrices $A,C \in \mathbf{C}_{n\times n}$, the C-numerical radius of A is the nonnegative quantity

$$r_C(A) = \max\{|\mathrm{tr}(CU^*AU)| : U \ \ n\times n \ \text{ unitary}\} \ .$$

It is not hard to see that

$$r(A) = r_C(A) \quad \text{with} \quad C = \mathrm{diag}(1,0,\ldots,0) \;;$$

thus $R(A)$ is a special case of $r_C(A)$.

It follows from the definition that for each C, r_C is a seminorm on $\mathbf{C}_{n\times n}$. We may then ask whether r_C is a generalized matrix norm. Since the situation is trivial for $n = 1$, we hereafter assume that $n \geq 2$.

THEOREM 2.1 ([5]). r_C _is a generalized matrix norm on_ $\mathbf{C}_{n\times n}$ _if and only if_ C _is a nonscalar matrix and_ $\mathrm{tr}\, C \neq 0$.

Next, we consider multiplicativity, which seems to be a complicated question.

For a given seminorm N and a constant $\nu > 0$, evidently

$$N_\nu \equiv \nu N$$

is a seminorm, too. Similarly, if N is a generalized matrix norm, then so is N_ν. In each case the new norm may or may not be multiplicative. If it is, we call ν a _multiplicativity factor_ for N.

It is an interesting fact that seminorms do not have multiplicativity factors, while generalized matrix norms always do. More precisely, we have the following result.

THEOREM 2.2 ([5]). (i) _A nontrivial seminorm has multiplicativity factors if and only if it is a generalized matrix norm_.

(ii) _If_ N _is a generalized matrix norm, then_ ν _is a multiplicativity factor if and only if_

$$\nu \geq \nu_N \equiv \max_{A,B\neq 0} \frac{N(AB)}{N(A)N(B)} .$$

Theorems 2.1 and 2.2 guarantee that r_C _has multiplicativity factors if and only if_ C _is nonscalar and_ $\mathrm{tr}\, C \neq 0$. In practice, however, Theorem 2.2 was of no help to us since we were unable to apply it to C-numerical radii.

An alternative way of obtaining multiplicativity factors is suggested by the following theorem of Gastinel [2] (originally in [1]).

THEOREM 2.3. Let N be a generalized matrix norm, M a matrix norm, and $\eta \geq \xi > 0$ constants such that

$$\xi M(A) \leq N(A) \leq \eta M(A), \qquad \forall A \in \mathbf{C}_{n\times n} .$$

Then any $\nu \geq \eta/\xi^2$ is a multiplicativity factor for N.

Proof. For $\nu \geq \eta/\xi^2$, we have

$$N_\nu(AB) \equiv \nu N(AB) \leq \nu\eta M(AB) \leq \nu\eta M(A)M(B) \leq \frac{\nu\eta}{\xi^2} N(A)N(B)$$
$$\leq \nu^2 N(A)N(B) = N_\nu(A)N_\nu(B) ,$$

and the proof is complete. □

Since any two generalized matrix norms on $\mathbf{C}_{n\times n}$ are equivalent, constants $\xi \geq \eta > 0$ as required in Theorem 2.3 always exist.

Having Gastinel's theorem and the inequalities of Section 1, we are now ready to obtain multiplicativity factors for C-numerical radii with Hermitian C.

Combining Lemmas 9 and 10 of [5], we state:

LEMMA 2.3. If C is Hermitian with eigenvalues γ_j, and if K satisfies (1.1), then

$$[\tfrac{K}{2}] \; \|A\|_2 \leq r_C(A) \leq \left[\sum_j |\gamma_j|\right] \|A_2\| , \qquad \forall A \in \mathbf{C}_{n\times n} .$$

Using the notation of (1.2), we prove:

THEOREM 2.4. Let C be Hermitian, nonscalar, with $\operatorname{tr} C \neq 0$ and eigenvalues γ_j. Then any ν with

$$\nu \geq 4 \sum |\gamma_j| \left(\frac{2\sigma + \delta}{\sigma\delta}\right)^2$$

is a multiplicativity factor for r_C; i.e., $\nu r_C \equiv r_{\nu C}$ is a matrix norm.

Proof. Since C is nonscalar, the γ_j are not all equal; and since $\operatorname{tr} C \neq 0$, $\sum \gamma_j \neq 0$. Thus $\sigma\delta > 0$, so inequality (1.1) is satisfied by the positive constant K of Theorem 1.2. By Lemma 2.3, therefore,

$$\frac{1}{2} \cdot \frac{\sigma\delta}{2\sigma + \delta} \|A\|_2 \le r_C(A) \le \sum |\gamma_j| \ \|A\|_2 , \qquad \forall A \in \mathbb{C}_{n\times n} ,$$

and Gastinel's theorem completes the proof. □

For Hermitian definite C, we improve Theorem 2.4 as follows.

THEOREM 2.5. *Let* C *be Hermitian nonnegative (nonpositive) definite. If* C *is nonscalar with eigenvalues* γ_j, *then any* ν *with* $\nu \ge 16\sigma/\delta^2$ *is a multiplicativity factor for* r_C.

Proof. Since C is Hermitian definite, the γ_j are of the same sign. So (1.1) holds with K of Theorem 1.4, and Lemma 2.3 implies that

$$\frac{\delta}{4} \|A\|_2 \le r_C(A) \le \sum |\gamma_j| \ \|A\|_2 = \sigma \|A\|_2 , \qquad \forall A .$$

Since C is nonscalar, the γ_j are not all equal; so $\delta > 0$, and Theorem 2.3 completes the proof. □

The optimal (least) multiplicativity factor for r, ν_r, is the subject of our last result.

THEOREM 2.6. νr *is a matrix norm if and only if* $\nu \ge 4$. *That is*, $\nu_r = 4$.

Proof. It is well known (e.g., [6, §173]) that

$$\frac{1}{2} \|A\|_2 \le r(A) \le \|A\|_2 , \qquad \forall A \in \mathbb{C}_{n\times n} .$$

Thus, by Gastinel's theorem, $\nu \ge 4$ is a multiplicativity factor for r, and by Theorem 2.2, $\nu_r \le 4$.

To show that $\nu_r \ge 4$, consider the $n \times n$ matrices

$$A = \begin{pmatrix} 0 & 1 \\ 0 & 0 \end{pmatrix} \oplus O_{n-2} , \qquad B = \begin{pmatrix} 0 & 0 \\ 1 & 0 \end{pmatrix} \oplus O_{n-2} .$$

A simple calculation shows that $r(A) = r(B) = 1/2$ and $r(AB) = 1$. Hence $r_\nu \equiv \nu r$ satisfies

$$r_\nu(AB) \le r_\nu(A) r_\nu(B)$$

if and only if $\nu \geq 4$, and the theorem follows. □

Note that the results of Theorems 2.4 - 2.6 depend neither on the dimension n nor on the space $\underset{\sim}{V}$.

REFERENCES

1. N. Gastinel, Matrices du Second Degré et Normes Générales en Analyse Numérique Linéaire. Thesis, Université de Grenoble, 1960.

2. N. Gastinel, Linear Numerical Analysis, Academic Press, New York, 1970.

3. M. Goldberg, On certain finite dimensional numerical ranges and numerical radii, Linear and Multilinear Algebra (1979), to appear.

4. M. Goldberg and E.G. Straus, Elementary inclusion relations for generalized numerical ranges, Linear Algebra Appl. 18 (1977), 1-24.

5. M. Goldberg and E.G. Straus, Norm properties of C-numerical radii, Linear Algebra Appl. 24 (1979), 113-131.

6. P.R. Halmos, A Hilbert Space Problem Book, Van Nostrand, New York, 1967.

7. A. Ostrowski, Über Normen von Matrizen, Math. Z., 63 (1955), 2-18.

8. R. Redheffer and C. Smith, On a surprising inequality of Goldberg and Straus, to appear.

THE CASE n = 2 OF THE GOLDBERG-STRAUS INEQUALITY

Raymond M. Redheffer
Department of Mathematics
University of California
Los Angeles, California 90024
U.S.A.

Carey Smith
Department of Mathematics
University of California
Los Angeles, California 90024
U.S.A.

ABSTRACT. It is shown by an example that the best (greatest possible) value of the constant K in the Goldberg-Straus combinatorial inequality for normed vectors over the complex field is less than the known best value of K for vectors over the real field. For $n = 2$, the exact best value of K is here determined in the complex case.

1. INTRODUCTION

For given real or complex values γ_j, a_j, $1 \leq j \leq n$, let

$$\sigma = \left| \sum_j \gamma_j \right| , \qquad \delta = \max_{i,j} |\gamma_i - \gamma_j| .$$

In the preceding article [1] in this book, it is shown that if $\sigma\delta > 0$ then there exists a constant $K > 0$ such that

$$\max_\pi \left| \sum_j \gamma_j a_{\pi(j)} \right| \geq K \max_j |a_j| . \tag{1}$$

Further, the best (greatest possible for all a_j, $1 \leq j \leq n$, with given σ, δ, and n) value of the constant K satisfies

$$\frac{\sigma\delta}{2\sigma + \delta - 2\sigma/n} \leq K \leq \min\left\{\sigma , \frac{\sigma\delta}{2\sigma + \delta - 2\sigma/n - 2\delta/n}\right\} , \tag{2}$$

and the inequality on the right becomes an equality when the γ_j and a_j are all real numbers.

We now observe that the best value of K is in fact less for complex γ_j, a_j than it is in the real case. For example, let $n = 3$ and

$$(\gamma_1,\gamma_2,\gamma_3) = (-3+i , 3+i , 3+i) , \qquad (a_1,a_2,a_3) = (1,0,0) .$$

Then, to two decimal places, the sums on the left in (1) have magnitude 3.16 for all permutations π; whereas, with K given by the expression on the right in (2), the expression on the right in (1) has value 3.32 to the same number of decimal places.

We shall here show that the exact best value of the constant K in (1), for $n = 2$ and the γ_j and a_j complex, is given by

$$K = \frac{\sigma\delta}{(\sigma^2 + \delta^2)^{1/2}} . \tag{3}$$

We note in passing that for $n = 2$ the expression on the right in inequality (2) reduces to $\min(\sigma,\delta)$, and that the value of K given in (3) satisfies

$$K = \frac{\sigma\delta}{(\sigma^2 + \delta^2)^{1/2}} < \min(\sigma,\delta), \qquad \sigma\delta > 0 .$$

2. THEOREM

The fact that the value (3) is optimum when $n = 2$ is equivalent to the following elementary result:

THEOREM. _Let_ a _and_ b _be nonzero complex numbers with_ $|a + b| = \sigma$, $|a - b| = \delta$, $\sigma\delta \neq 0$. _Let_ $z \in \mathbf{C}$ _be given_, $|z| \leq 1$. _Then_

$$\max(|az + b|, |a + bz|) \geq \frac{\sigma\delta}{(\sigma^2 + \delta^2)^{1/2}} .$$

Furthermore, for any specified (σ,δ), _there exist_ a, b, z _such that equality holds_.

In the course of the proof we shall characterize the (a,b,z) allowing equality.

Let $p = az + b$, $q = a + bz$. As z traverses $|z| \leq 1$, the point p traverses a disk with center b and radius $|a|$, while q traverses a disk with center a and radius $|b|$. We have to show that p and q cannot both be closer to the origin than the constant (3).

It should be observed that we never have $p = q = 0$, since this would entail $(a + b)(a - b) = 0$, which violates the hypothesis $\sigma\delta \neq 0$. Hence $\max(|p|,|q|)$ has a positive lower bound in $|z| \leq 1$, and we can suppose that z is chosen so that this value is attained.

3. LEMMA

We shall first establish the following preliminary result:

LEMMA. <u>At the value</u> z <u>which minimizes</u> $\max(|p|,|q|)$, <u>we have</u> $|p| = |q|$.

<u>Proof of Lemma</u>. Suppose, for example, that $|p| > |q|$ at the z in question. Then $|p|$ must be minimum subject to $|z| \leq 1$. Otherwise, we could make a slight change in z and reduce $|p|$ without getting into trouble from q. It is not possible that $p = 0$ at the minimum, since $|p| > |q|$, and hence, by the geometric interpretation mentioned above,

$$|a| < |b| \; , \qquad z = -\frac{b}{|b|}\frac{|a|}{a} \; , \qquad |p| = |b| - |a| \; .$$

From this it follows that

$$|a||b||q| = \left|a^2|b| - b^2|a|\right| \geq |a||b|(|b| - |a|) \; .$$

Hence, the supposed condition $|q| < |p|$ at the minimum of $|p|$ cannot hold, and the lemma follows. □

4. PROOF OF THEOREM

Turning now to the proof of the theorem, we consider how small $|p|$ can be when z is so chosen that $|p| = |q|$. Instead of assessing $|p|$, we can just as well assess

$$4|p|^2 = 2(|p|^2 + |q|^2) \; .$$

The latter expression gives

$$4|p|^2 = 2(|a|^2 + |b|^2)(1 + |z|^2) + 8(\mathrm{Re}\; z)(\mathrm{Re}\; a\bar{b}) \; .$$

The conditions $|a + b| = \sigma$ and $|a - b| = \delta$ are equivalent to the two equations

$$2(|a|^2 + |b|^2) = \sigma^2 + \delta^2, \qquad 4\;\mathrm{Re}\; a\bar{b} = \sigma^2 - \delta^2 \; .$$

Hence, we can write

$$4|p|^2 = (\sigma^2 + \delta^2)(1 + |z|^2) + 2(\mathrm{Re}\; z)(\sigma^2 - \delta^2) \; . \tag{4}$$

This is to be assessed from below when $|z| \leq 1$. To be sure, z is restricted by other relations when a and b are fixed. Nevertheless, if we assess $4|p|^2$ from below without any restriction on z, we shall certainly get a valid lower bound.

For given $|z|$, the expression (4) is least when the term involving Re z is as small as possible. This requires that z have the form

$$z = t\ \mathrm{sgn}(\delta^2 - \sigma^2), \qquad t \geq 0 \ \text{ real} .$$

Thus we are led to the problem

$$4|p|^2 = (\sigma^2 + \delta^2)(1 + t^2) - 2t|\sigma^2 - \delta^2| = \min, \qquad 0 \leq t \leq 1 .$$

It is readily checked that the solution is

$$t = \frac{|\sigma^2 - \delta^2|}{\sigma^2 + \delta^2}, \qquad \min = \frac{4\sigma^2\delta^2}{\sigma^2 + \delta^2} .$$

This gives the first part of the theorem and shows that the critical value of z is determined uniquely by

$$z = \frac{\delta^2 - \sigma^2}{\delta^2 + \sigma^2} .$$

Note that this z satisfies $|z| < 1$.

Given σ and δ, we must now construct a and b so that the minimum is attained. It is readily checked that $|p| = |q|$ holds for some real z, $|z| \neq 1$, if and only if $|a| = |b|$. Conversely, if $|a| = |b|$ then $|p| = |q|$ for all real z. When $|a| = |b|$, we get the correct σ and δ if and only if

$$4|a|^2 = \sigma^2 + \delta^2, \qquad 4 \ \mathrm{Re}\ a\bar{b} = \sigma^2 - \delta^2 .$$

It is necessary to show that these conditions are compatible. The first equation presents no difficulty; and, dividing the second by $4|a||b| = 4|a|^2$, we see that the second is equivalent to

$$\cos(\arg a - \arg b) = \frac{\sigma^2 - \delta^2}{\sigma^2 + \delta^2} .$$

Since the expression on the right has magnitude less than 1, this is possible too and the result follows. □

5. AN OPEN PROBLEM

Since the two bounds in the inequalities (2) differ only by a term

$O(1/n)$, there is not much point in getting any other approximate values for the best constant when γ_j and a_j are complex. It would be of interest, however, to get the exact value, especially if the exact value is comparable in simplicity to that found above for $n = 2$. Determination of the exact value for $n \geq 3$ is left as an open problem.

REFERENCES

1. Moshe Goldberg and E.G. Straus, Combinatorial Inequalities, Matrix Norms, and Generalized Numerical Radii, in E.F. Beckenbach (ed.), General Inequalities 2, Proceedings of the Second International Conference on General Inequalities, Mathematical Institute Oberwolfach, 1978, ISNM 47, Birkhäuser Verlag, Basel, Stuttgart, 1980, pp. 37-46. (Additional references are given here.)

2. Ray Redheffer and Carey Smith, On a surprising inequality of Goldberg and Straus, to appear in Amer. Math. Monthly.

Inequalities of Matrix Theory and Linear Algebra

INEQUALITIES INVOLVING INFINITE MATRICES WITH NONNEGATIVE ENTRIES

P.D. Johnson, Jr.
Department of Mathematics
American University of Beirut
Beirut
LEBANON

R.N. Mohapatra
Department of Mathematics
American University of Beirut
Beirut
LEBANON

ABSTRACT. For complete, normally quasinormed subspaces λ, μ of ω, the set of all sequences of scalars, and an infinite matrix A with nonnegative entries, we shall be interested in inequalities of the form

$$(*) \qquad \|A|x|\|_\lambda \leq K\|bx\|_\mu \qquad (x \in b^{-1}\mu) ,$$

where $b \in \omega$, and K is a positive constant. By introducing a method of comparing sequences, we shall obtain results on best possible inequalities of the form (*), best possible not by the smallness of K but by the smallness of the sequence b.

Our results have been applied to Hardy's inequality, and to some of its generalizations. In the process of our investigation, we have also obtained some best possible inequalities of the form (*).

1. INTRODUCTION

The space of all sequences of scalars will be denoted ω, and the subspace of only finitely nonzero sequences will be denoted φ. The k-th coordinate sequence will be denoted e_k, $k = 1,2,\ldots,$ and the sequence whose every entry is 1 will be denoted e. Operations on sequences will be coordinatewise. For instance, if

$$x = \{x_n\}, \qquad y = \{y_n\} ,$$

then

$$|x| = \{|x_n|\}, \qquad xy = \{x_n y_n\}, \qquad \text{and} \qquad x^p = \{x_n^p\} ;$$

this last requires some interpretation when x is not a sequence of positive numbers.

For $x,y \in \omega$, let $\langle x,y\rangle = \sum_n x_n y_n$, provided this series converges or diverges properly. Thus, $\langle \cdot, e_k\rangle$ can be taken to denote the k-th coordinate projection. The n-th finite section P_n is defined by

$$P_n = \sum_{k=1}^{n} \langle \cdot, e_k\rangle e_k ,$$

with $P_0 = 0$. The normal hull of $x \in \omega$ is denoted

$$N(x) = \{y \in \omega ; |y_n| \leq |x_n|, \quad n = 1,2,\cdots \} .$$

A set $S \subseteq \omega$ is normal if and only if $x \in S$ implies $N(x) \subseteq S$. A norm or quasinorm $\|\cdot\|$ on a normal subspace λ of ω will be called normal if and only if $y \in N(x) \subseteq \lambda$ implies $\|y\| \leq \|x\|$; equivalently, $\|\cdot\|$ is normal if and only if the closed unit ball in $(\lambda, \|\cdot\|)$ is normal. Note that the usual quasinorm $\|\cdot\|_p$ on ℓ_p, $0 < p \leq \infty$, is normal. Note that the coordinate projections are continuous on any normal, normally quasinormed subspace λ of ω (see [11]).

Throughout this paper, $A = (a_{mn})_{m,n \geq 1}$ will be an infinite matrix with nonnegative entries. The domain of A is given by

$$\text{dom } A = \{x \in \omega ; \sum_n a_{mn} x_n \text{ converges for each } m = 1,2,\cdots \} .$$

The linear transformation of dom A into ω determined by A will also be denoted by A. For $S \subseteq \omega$,

$$A^{-1}(S) = \{x \in \text{dom } A ; Ax \in S\} .$$

The object of this paper is to study inequalities of the form

$$\text{(1)} \qquad \|A|x|\|_\lambda \leq K\|bx\|_\mu \qquad (x \in b^{-1}\mu) ,$$

where $b \in \omega$, K is a positive constant, and λ, μ are complete, normal, normally quasinormed subspaces of ω. The root of this topic is Hardy's inequality [8], in which $\lambda = \mu = \ell_p$, $1 < p \leq \infty$, A is the Cesàro matrix, $b = e$, and the best possible K is $p(p-1)^{-1}$ (or 1, if $p = \infty$). Petersen [18], and subsequently Davies and Petersen [4], generalized Hardy's result to a class of inequalities of the form (1), in which $\lambda = \mu = \ell_p$, $1 \leq p < \infty$, and A is constrained to belong to a certain class of lower triangular matrices. The K is not completely lost track of in these results, but there is no way apparent of getting at the best possible K for all inequalities of the class.

We shall call inequalities of the form (1) HPD inequalities for Hardy-Petersen-Davies. We shall be interested in best possible HPD inequalities; not best possible by the smallness of K (indeed, the inequalities of interest may be throughout prefaced by the phrase "there exists K such that ..."), but by the smallness of the sequence b.

2. SMALL AND LARGE SEQUENCES

Preorder ω by defining $a < b$ if and only if $a = bc$ for some $c \in \ell_\infty$. Equivalently, $a < b$ if and only if $a.\ell_\infty \subseteq b.\ell_\infty$. Note that if $a < b$, then $a\lambda \subseteq b\lambda$ for any normal subspace λ of ω.

It is clear what it means for a sequence to be maximal, or to be maximum, in a set of sequences with respect to $<$. Namely, a sequence $a \in \lambda$ is maximal in λ if and only if $a < b \Rightarrow b < a$, $b \in \lambda$; and a sequence $a \in \lambda$ is maximum in λ if and only if $b < a$ for each $b \in \lambda$.

If $a < b$ and $b < a$, we call a and b equivalent. Note that x and $|x|$ are equivalent for any $x \in \omega$.

PROPOSITION 2.1. *Suppose* $\lambda \subseteq \omega$ *satisfies*

(a) $x \in \lambda \Rightarrow |x| \in \lambda$;

(b) *the sum of any two nonnegative sequences in* λ *is in* λ.

Then any a *that is maximal in* λ *is also maximum in* λ.

Proof. Assume a is maximal in λ, and $b \in \lambda$. Then $|a| + |b| \in \lambda$, and clearly $a < |a| + |b|$, so a and $|a| + |b|$ are equivalent, by the maximality of a. There exist $c_1, c_2, c_3 \in \ell_\infty$ such that $|a| + |b| = c_1 a$, $b = c_2|b|$, and $|a| = c_3 a$; then $b = c_2|b| = c_2(c_1 a - |a|) = c_2(c_1 - c_3)a$. Since $c_2(c_1 - c_3) \in \ell_\infty$, $b < a$; b was arbitrary, so a is maximum in λ. □

PROPOSITION 2.2. *If* λ *is a normal subspace of* ω, *then* b *is maximum in* λ *if and only if* $\lambda = b.\ell_\infty$.

The proof is straightforward. □

THEOREM 2.3. *Suppose* $(\lambda, \|\cdot\|)$ *is a complete normal, normally quasi-normed subspace of* ω. *Set* $S = \{n ; e_n \in \lambda\}$, *and define* b *by*

$$b_n = \|e_n\|^{-1}, \quad n \in S \; ; \quad b_n = 0, \quad n \notin S \; .$$

Then $\lambda \subseteq b.\ell_\infty$, and the following are equivalent:

(a) $\lambda = c.\ell_\infty$ for some $c \in \omega$;

(b) $\lambda = b.\ell_\infty$;

(c) $b \in \lambda$.

Proof. Since λ is a normal subspace of ω, $n \notin S$ implies $x_n = 0$ for all $x \in \lambda$.

Suppose $x \in \lambda$, and $n \in S$. Since $\|\cdot\|$ is normal,

$$|x_n| \, \|e_n\| = \|x_n e_n\| \leq \|x\| \; ,$$

so $|x_n| \leq \|x\| b_n$; clearly, the same holds for $n \notin S$. Thus $x \in N(\|x\| b) \subseteq b.\ell_\infty$.

Thus $\lambda \subseteq b.\ell_\infty$.

Clearly (b) implies (a). Suppose that (a) holds. Then $S = \{n; \, c_n \neq 0\}$. Note that $(\lambda, \|\cdot\|)$ is a Fichtenholz-Kantorovich (FK) space, since the coordinate projections are continuous on λ; but λ is also an FK space with the norm ρ defined by

$$\rho(x) = \sup_{n \in S} \; |c_n^{-1} x_n| \; .$$

Since a subspace of ω can be an FK space with at most one topology [6], ρ and $\|\cdot\|$ are equivalent, meaning there exist $m, M > 0$ such that $m\rho(x) \leq \|x\| \leq M\rho(x)$ for all $x \in \lambda$. For $n \in S$,

$$m\rho(e_n) = m|c_n^{-1}| \leq \|e_n\| = b_n^{-1} \leq M|c_n^{-1}| \; ,$$

and for $n \notin S$, $c_n = b_n = 0$. Consequently, b and c are equivalent, so $\lambda = b.\ell_\infty$, and in particular, $b = be \in \lambda$. Thus (c) holds.

If (c) holds, then, since λ is normal, $b.\ell_\infty \subseteq \lambda$, and the reverse inclusion has already been established. Thus (b) holds. □

REMARK. In Theorem 2.3, only the implications (a) implies (b) and (a) implies (c) require the completeness of $(\lambda, \|\cdot\|)$.

3. THE SUBSPACE $D(\mu,\lambda)$

For $\mu, \lambda \subseteq \omega$, set

$$D(\mu,\lambda) = \{x \in \omega \ ; \ x\omega \subseteq \lambda\} .$$

The following statements are easily verifiable:

(a) If λ is a subspace of ω, then so is $D(\mu,\lambda)$.

(b) If either μ or λ is normal, then $D(\mu,\lambda)$ is normal.

(c) If λ is a subspace of ω, then $D(\ell_\infty,\lambda)$ is the largest normal subset of λ, (and is a subspace of λ, by (a)).

(d) If μ is a normal sequence space and λ is a subspace of ω, then $D(\mu,\lambda) = D(\mu,D(\ell_\infty,\lambda))$; the inclusion $\supseteq$ follows from $D(\ell_\infty,\lambda) \subseteq \lambda$, and the inclusion $\subseteq$ from (c) and the normality of μ.

$D(\lambda,\ell_1)$ is called the Köthe-Toeplitz dual of λ, and is denoted by λ^x; λ^{xx} is $(\lambda^x)^x$. If $\lambda = \lambda^{xx}$, then λ is said to be perfect. Note that λ^x is perfect, for any $\lambda \subseteq \omega$.

PROPOSITION 3.1. <u>For any</u> $\mu,\lambda \subseteq \omega$, $D(\mu,\lambda) \subseteq D(\lambda^x,\mu^x)$, <u>with equality if</u> λ <u>is perfect</u>.

<u>Proof</u>. Suppose $b \in D(\mu,\lambda)$, $x \in \lambda^x$, and $y \in \mu$. Then $\langle |bx|,|y| \rangle = \langle |x|,|by| \rangle < \infty$, since $by \in \lambda$. Thus $bx \in \mu^x$, and therefore $D(\mu,\lambda) \subseteq D(\lambda^x,\mu^x)$. Now suppose λ is perfect. Then

$$D(\lambda^x,\mu^x) \subseteq D(\mu^{xx},\lambda^{xx}) = D(\mu^{xx},\lambda) \subseteq D(\mu,\lambda) ,$$

since $\mu \subseteq \mu^{xx}$. Thus $D(\lambda^x,\mu^x) = D(\mu,\lambda)$. □

For $x \in \omega$, let D_x denote the diagonal matrix with main diagonal sequence x.

If μ,λ are subspaces of ω, the association of $b \in D(\mu,\lambda)$ to the linear transformation $x \to bx$ from μ to λ is itself a linear transformation of $D(\mu,\lambda)$ into the space of all linear transformations from μ to λ. The association is an injection if μ satisfies the following:

For each n there exists $x \in \mu$ such that $x_n \neq 0$; in particular, this is so if $\varphi \subseteq \mu$. In this case, $D(\mu,\lambda)$ will be identified with its copy in the space of all linear transformations from μ to λ. If μ and λ are FK spaces, then $D(\mu,\lambda) \subseteq \mathcal{A}(\mu,\lambda)$, the space of continuous linear maps from μ to λ, for the action of $b \in D(\mu,\lambda)$ on λ is the same as that of the matrix D_b, and a matrix map between FK spaces is continuous [24, p. 204, Cor. 5].

PROPOSITION 3.2. <u>Suppose</u> $(\mu, \|\cdot\|_\mu)$, $(\lambda, \|\cdot\|_\lambda)$ <u>are quasinormed FK spaces, and for all</u> $n = 1,2,\ldots$, <u>there exists</u> $x \in \mu$ <u>such that</u> $x_n \neq 0$. <u>Then</u> $D(\mu,\lambda)$, <u>when equipped with the operator quasinorm</u> $\|\cdot\|$ <u>on</u> $\alpha(\mu,\lambda)$, <u>is an FK space. If both</u> λ <u>and</u> $\|\cdot\|_\lambda$ <u>are normal, or if both</u> μ <u>and</u> $\|\cdot\|_\mu$ <u>are normal, then</u> $\|\cdot\|$ <u>is normal on</u> $D(\mu,\lambda)$.

<u>Proof</u>. Let ρ denote the dual norm on λ', the space of continuous linear functionals on λ. Fix n, and let $x \in \mu$ be such that $x_n \neq 0$. Suppose $b \in D(\mu,\lambda)$. Then

$$|\langle b,e_n\rangle| = |x_n^{-1}\langle bx,e_n\rangle| \leq |x_n^{-1}|\ \rho(\langle\cdot,e_n\rangle)\ \|bx\|_\lambda$$

$$\leq |x_n|^{-1}\ \rho(\langle\cdot,e_n\rangle)\ \|x\|_\mu\ \|b\|\ .$$

Thus the coordinate projections are continuous on $(D(\mu,\lambda),\|\cdot\|)$.

Now suppose $\{b^{(n)}\}$ is a Cauchy sequence in $D(\mu,\lambda)$. Since $(\alpha(\mu,\lambda),\|\cdot\|)$ is complete, $\{b^{(n)}\}$ converges to some $T \in \alpha(\mu,\lambda)$. Because the coordinate projections are continuous on $D(\mu,\lambda)$, $b^{(n)}$ converges coordinatewise to some b. For each $x \in \mu$, $\{b^{(n)}x\}$ converges to Tx in λ; since the coordinate projections are continuous on λ, and $b^{(n)} \to b$ coordinatewise, it follows that $bx = Tx$. Thus $b \in D(\mu,\lambda)$, and the sequence $\{b^{(n)}\}$ converges to b in $(D(\mu,\lambda),\|\cdot\|)$. So $(D(\mu,\lambda),\|\cdot\|)$ is complete and is therefore an FK space.

Now suppose μ and $\|\cdot\|_\mu$ are normal, $b \in D(\mu,\lambda)$, and $c \in N(b)$. Then $c = bd$ for some $d \in \ell_\infty$ with $\|d\|_\infty \leq 1$. If $x \in \mu$ and $\|x\|_\mu \leq 1$, then $dx \in N(x) \subseteq \mu$ and $\|dx\|_\mu \leq \|x_\mu\| \leq 1$. Therefore,

$$\|c\| = \sup_{\|x\|_\mu \leq 1} \|bdx\| \leq \sup_{\|y\|_\mu \leq 1} \|by\|_\lambda = \|b\|\ ,$$

so $\|\cdot\|$ is normal on $D(\mu,\lambda)$.

Now suppose λ and $\|\cdot\|_\lambda$ are normal, $b \in D(\mu,\lambda)$, and $d \in \ell_\infty$, $\|d\|_\infty \leq 1$. For each $x \in \mu$, $bdx \in N(bx)$, whence $\|bdx\|_\lambda \leq \|bx\|_\lambda$. Clearly, then, $\|bd\| \leq \|b\|$, so $\|\cdot\|$ is normal. □

4. THE SUBSPACE nor-$A^{-1}(\lambda)$

We define

$$\text{nor-}A^{-1}(\lambda) = \{x \in \omega\ ;\ |x| \in A^{-1}(\lambda)\}\ .$$

The following are the essential facts about $\text{nor-}A^{-1}(\lambda)$, relevant to our purpose, from [11]. Assume from now on that λ is normal.

(a) $\text{nor-}A^{-1}(\lambda)$ is a normal subspace of ω, and is, in fact, the largest normal subset of $A^{-1}(\lambda)$ (i.e., $\text{nor-}A^{-1}(\lambda) = D(\ell_\infty, A^{-1}(\lambda))$.

(b) $\{n\ ;\ e_n \in \text{nor-}A^{-1}(\lambda)\} = \{n\ ;\ \text{for some } x \in \text{nor-}A^{-1}(\lambda),\ x_n \neq 0\} = \{n\ ;\ \text{the } n\text{-th column of } A \text{ is in } \lambda\}$.

(c) If λ is equipped with the normal quasinorm $\|\cdot\|$, and A has no zero columns, then $\||A|\cdot|\|$ is a normal quasinorm on $\text{nor-}A^{-1}(\lambda)$. Furthermore, if $\|\cdot\|$ is a norm, so is $\||A|\cdot|\|$.

(d) Suppose λ is equipped with a normal quasinorm $\|\cdot\|$, and $(\lambda,\|\cdot\|)$ is locally coordinatewise closed (LCC) (to be explained). Suppose A has no zero columns. Then if $(\lambda,\|\cdot\|)$ is complete, so is $(\text{nor-}A^{-1}(\lambda),\||A|\cdot|\|)$ (and thus $\text{nor-}A^{-1}(\lambda)$ is an FK space).

<u>Definition of</u> LCC. Let $\mathcal{P}$ denote the (product) topology of coordinatewise convergence on ω. Suppose $\mu \subseteq \omega$. By $(\mu,\mathcal{P})$ is meant μ considered with the relative topology induced by $\mathcal{P}$. If λ is a subspace of ω with a topological vector-space topology T, we call (λ,T) LCC if and only if there is a neighborhood base at the origin in (λ,T) comprised of sets which are closed in $(\lambda,\mathcal{P})$. We do not know of any non-LCC Hausdorff sequence space with a normal topology (see [11]), and there are easy general conditions sufficient for LCC; for instance, if T is the topology of uniform convergence on some class of normal subsets of λ^x, then (λ,T) is LCC. However, we do not know even that every normal, normally quasinormed, complete sequence space is LCC. In this connection, it is worth noting that such a space $(\lambda,\|\cdot\|)$ may be LCC even though its closed unit ball is not closed in $(\lambda,\mathcal{P})$. For instance, define $\|\cdot\|$ on ℓ_∞ by

$$\|x\| = \|x\|_\infty + \limsup |x_n| \ .$$

Then $\|\cdot\|$ is normal, and equivalent to $\|\cdot\|_\infty$ (so $(\ell_\infty,\|\cdot\|)$ is LCC); but

$$x^{(n)} = \sum_{k=1}^{n} e_k \ , \quad \text{satisfying } \|x^{(n)}\| = 1 \ ,$$

converges to e as $n \to \infty$, in $(\ell_\infty,\mathcal{P})$, and $\|e\| = 2$.

We are now in a position to apply the results of the preceding sections to the study of HPD inequalities and particularly to the question of best possible HPD inequalities. Henceforward, $(\lambda,\|\cdot\|_\lambda)$ and $(\mu,\|\cdot\|_\mu)$ will be normal, normally quasinormed, complete subspaces of ω, $(\lambda, \|\cdot\|_\lambda)$ will be LCC, $\varphi \subseteq \mu$, and A will have no zero columns.

To exploit the preceding results, we replace the inequality (1) by

$$\| A|b^{-1}x| \|_\lambda \leq K\|x\|_\mu \qquad (x \in \mu) . \tag{2}$$

It is clear that this inequality is the same as (1) when b has no zero entries, but we want to allow b to have zero entries. Let the n-th entry of b^{-1} be zero when $b_n = 0$, and let the b^{-1} mentioned in (1) be this b^{-1}, just defined. Then it is clear that (1) implies (2), by the normality of $\|\cdot\|_\mu$ (since $bb^{-1}x \in N(x)$). Clearly (2) implies (1), because, for $x \in b^{-1}\mu$, $bb^{-1}x = x$.

The point of switching from (1) to (2) is in this, that under our current hypotheses the existence of a K for which (2) holds is equivalent to $b^{-1} \in D(\mu,\text{nor-}A^{-1}(\lambda))$; and the question of the existence of a best possible HPD inequality becomes the question of the existence of a maximum, or maximal, sequence in $D(\mu,\text{nor-}A^{-1}(\lambda))$.

PROPOSITION 4.1. $D(\mu,\text{nor-}A^{-1}(\lambda))$ <u>is a normal FK space, with the normal quasinorm</u> $\|\cdot\|$ <u>defined by</u>

$$\|b\| = \sup_{\|x\|_\mu \leq 1} \| A|bx| \|_\lambda .$$

The proof is immediate from Proposition 3.2 and the remarks above about $\text{nor-}A^{-1}(\lambda)$. □

PROPOSITION 4.2. <u>The map</u> $b \to AD_b$ <u>is an isometric linear map of</u> $D(\mu,\text{nor-}A^{-1}(\lambda))$ <u>into</u> $\alpha(\mu,\lambda)$.

<u>Proof</u>. Let $\|\cdot\|$ denote both the quasinorm on $D(\mu,\text{nor-}A^{-1}(\lambda))$ defined in Proposition 4.1, and the operator quasinorm on $\alpha(\mu,\lambda)$. Note that if D is any diagonal matrix, then $A(D(x)) = (AD)(x)$ for any $x \in D^{-1}(\text{dom } A)$.

Clearly $b \to AD_b$ is a linear map of $D(\mu,\text{nor-}A^{-1}(\lambda))$ into some set of matrices. If $b \in D(\mu,\text{nor-}A^{-1}(\lambda))$, then

$$b\mu = D_b(\mu) \subseteq \text{nor-}A^{-1}(\lambda) \subseteq A^{-1}(\lambda) ,$$

so

$$A(D_b(\mu)) = (AD_b)\mu \subseteq \lambda \;;$$

thus $AD_b \in \mathcal{A}(\mu,\lambda)$, since a matrix map between FK spaces is continuous. Now

$$\|AD_b\| = \sup_{\|x\|_\mu \le 1} \|A(bx)\|_\lambda \le \sup_{\|x\|_\mu \le 1} \|A|bx|\,\|_\lambda = \|b\| \;;$$

the inequality holds because $\|\cdot\|_\lambda$ is normal and the entries of A are nonnegative. On the other hand, suppose $x \in \mu$, and $\|x\|_\mu \le 1$; let, for each n, y_n be such that

$$|y_n| = 1 \quad \text{and} \quad b_n y_n x_n = |b_n x_n| \;;$$

then $yx \in \mu$ and $\|yx\|_\mu = \|x\|_\mu \le 1$ by the normality of μ and $\|\cdot\|_\mu$. Therefore

$$\|AD_b\| \ge \|A(byx)\|_\lambda = \|A|bx|\,\|_\lambda \;;$$

this for any such x implies $\|AD_b\| \ge \|b\|$. □

THEOREM 4.3. <u>Suppose</u> $S = \{n\;;$ <u>the</u> n-<u>th column of</u> A <u>is in</u> $\lambda\}$ <u>and</u> $A^{(n)}$ <u>denotes the</u> n-<u>th column of</u> A. <u>Define</u> d <u>by</u>

$$d_n = \|e_n\|_\mu \, \|A^{(n)}\|_\lambda^{-1} \quad \underline{\text{if}} \quad n \in S, \quad d_n = 0 \quad \underline{\text{if}} \quad n \notin S\,.$$

<u>Then</u> $D(\mu,\text{nor-}A^{-1}(\lambda)) \subseteq d.\ell_\infty$ <u>and the following are equivalent</u>:

(a) $D(\mu,\text{nor-}A^{-1}(\lambda)) = c.\ell_\infty$ <u>for some</u> $c \in \omega$;

(b) $D(\mu,\text{nor-}A^{-1}(\lambda)) = d.\ell_\infty$;

(c) AD_b <u>maps</u> μ <u>into</u> λ.

The proof is straightforward from Theorem 2.3, with the λ there replaced by $\text{nor-}A^{-1}(\lambda)$ here. □

Clearly Theorem 4.3 gives in effect a strategy for deciding whether or not there is a best possible HPD inequality associated with A, μ, and λ. We shall make frequent use of it in what follows.

COROLLARY 4.4. <u>Suppose</u> $\|\cdot\|_\lambda$ <u>is a norm</u>, $\|e_n\|_\mu = 1$, $n = 1,2,\ldots,$ <u>and</u> S <u>is as in the theorem; set</u>

$$d_n = \|Ae_n\|_\lambda^{-1} \quad \underline{\text{for}} \quad n \in S, \quad d_n = 0 \quad \underline{\text{otherwise}}\,.$$

_If_ $\mu \subseteq \ell_1$, _then_ $D(\mu, \text{nor-}A^{-1}(\lambda)) = d.\ell_\infty$.

Proof. Observe that

$$\|AD_b(e_n)\|_\lambda = 1 \text{ if } n \in S, \quad \text{and} \quad \|AD_b(e_n)\|_\lambda = 0 \text{ if } n \notin S.$$

Since $(\lambda, \|\cdot\|_\lambda)$ is a complete normed space, and $\{AD_b(e_n) \; ; \; n = 1,2,\dots\}$ is bounded in λ, it follows that AD_b maps ℓ_1 into λ, and thus μ into λ. The conclusion now follows from the theorem. □

COROLLARY 4.5. _Suppose_ $\|\cdot\|_\lambda$ _is a norm, and_ d _is as in the previous corollary. Then for_ $0 < p \leq 1$,

$$D(\ell_p, \text{nor-}A^{-1}(\lambda)) = d.\ell_\infty .$$

COROLLARY 4.6. _Suppose_ A _has a matricial and transformational inverse_ A^{-1}, $1 \leq p \leq \infty$, b _is the sequence of_ $\ell_{p'}$ _norms of_ A^{-1} (_where_ $p^{-1} + p'^{-1} = 1$), _and_ $c = \{\|e_n\|_\mu\}_n$. _Then_

$$D(\mu, \text{nor-}A^{-1}(\ell_p)) \subseteq bc.\ell_\infty .$$

[Let $S = \{n \; ; \; b_n = \infty\}$, and e_s be the sequence with 1 at positions indexed by those $n \in S$, zero elsewhere. Let b' be obtained from b by placing zeroes at those positions indexed by $n \in S$. Then by $bc.\ell_\infty$ is meant $b'c.\ell_\infty + e_s\omega$.]

Proof. Let a be the sequence of ℓ_p norms of the columns of A. Let $A^{(n)}$ denote the n-th column of A, $R^{(n)}$ the n-th row of A^{-1}. Then, by Hölder's inequality,

$$1 = \langle R^{(n)}, A^{(n)} \rangle \leq \|R^{(n)}\|_{p'} \|A^{(n)}\|_p = b_n a_n ,$$

so $a^{-1} < b$. Consequently, $a^{-1}c.\ell_\infty \subseteq c.\ell_\infty \subseteq bc.\ell_\infty$. □

5. THE SUBSPACE $D(\mu, \text{nor-}A^{-1}(\ell_1))$

We have already seen a class of instances, in Corollaries 4.4 and 4.5, in which there is always a best possible HPD inequality, namely $\|A|dx|\|_\lambda \leq K\|x\|_\mu$, for some constant $K > 0$, with d as in Corollary 4.4. When $\lambda = \ell_1$, it turns out to be relatively easy to decide whether or not a best possible

HPD inequality exists, just because $\text{nor-}A^{-1}(\ell_1)$ is always a diagonal copy of ℓ_1 itself. We will get at this result through some more general propositions.

Note that if M is a matrix with nonnegative entries, and x and y are nonnegative sequences, then $\langle Mx,y\rangle = \langle x,M^t y\rangle$, with M^t denoting the transpose of M. Note also that for any $x,y \in \omega$,

$$\langle |x|,|M^t y|\rangle \leq \langle |x|,M^t|y|\rangle ,$$

because the entries of M are nonnegative.

PROPOSITION 5.1. <u>Suppose that</u> Λ <u>is a normal subspace of</u> ω, <u>and</u> B <u>is a matrix obtained from</u> A <u>by replacing each column of</u> A <u>not in</u> Λ^{xx} <u>by zero. Let</u>

$$S = \{n \text{ ; the } n\text{-th column of } A \text{ is in } \Lambda\} ,$$

<u>and let</u> e_S <u>denote the characteristic sequence of</u> S. <u>Then</u>

$$\text{nor-}A^{-1}(\Lambda) \subseteq e_S\cdot(B^t(\Lambda^x))^x ,$$

<u>with equality if</u> Λ <u>is perfect</u>.

<u>Proof</u>. Recall that if $n \notin S$, then $x_n = 0$ for all $x \in \text{nor-}A^{-1}(\Lambda)$. Consequently, $A|x| = B|x|$ and $x = e_S x$ for all $x \in \text{nor-}A^{-1}(\Lambda)$. Clearly $\Lambda^x \subseteq \text{dom } B^t$. Suppose that $y \in \Lambda^x$, and $x \in \text{nor-}A^{-1}(\Lambda)$. Then

$$\langle |x|,|B^t y|\rangle \leq \langle |x|,B^t|y|\rangle = \langle B|x|,|y|\rangle = \langle A|x|,|y|\rangle < \infty .$$

Thus $x \in (B^t(\Lambda^x))^x$, so $e_S x = x \in e_S\cdot(B^t(\Lambda^x))^x$.

Now suppose that Λ is perfect, and

$$x \in e_S\cdot(B^t(\Lambda^x))^x \subseteq (B^t(\Lambda^x))^x ;$$

then $B|x| = A|x|$, since $x_n = 0$ for $n \notin S$. Suppose $y \in \Lambda^x$. Then $|y| \in \Lambda^x$, so

$$\infty > \langle |x|,B^t|y|\rangle = \langle B|x|,|y|\rangle = \langle A|x|,|y|\rangle ,$$

and therefore $A|x| \in \Lambda^{xx} = \Lambda$. Thus $x \in \text{nor-}A^{-1}(\Lambda)$. □

COROLLARY 5.2. <u>If</u> Λ <u>is perfect, and all the columns of</u> A <u>are in</u> Λ, <u>then</u> $\text{nor-}A^{-1}(\Lambda)$ <u>is perfect</u>.

COROLLARY 5.3. <u>Suppose</u> λ <u>is perfect, and</u> $S = \{n\ ;$ <u>the</u> n-<u>th column of</u> A <u>is in</u> $\lambda\}$. <u>Let</u>

$$d_n = \|Ae_n\|_\lambda^{-1}, \quad \underline{\text{for}}\ n \in S\ , \qquad d_n = 0 \quad \underline{\text{for}}\ n \notin S\ .$$

<u>Then</u> $d\ell_1 \subseteq \text{nor-}A^{-1}(\lambda)$.

<u>Proof</u>. Recall that $(\lambda, \|\cdot\|_\lambda)$ is an FK space, by blanket hypothesis, and since λ is perfect, $\varphi \subseteq \lambda$. By the Banach-Steinhaus Theorem, then, the map $y \to \langle \cdot, y\rangle$ is an embedding of λ^x into λ', the continuous dual of λ. Let $\|\cdot\|'$ denote the dual norm on λ'. For $n \in S$, $y \in \lambda^x$,

$$|\langle Ae_n, y\rangle| \leq \|Ae_n\|_\lambda \cdot \|y\|' = d_n^{-1}\|y\|'\ .$$

Thus, if B is as in Proposition 5.1, then

$$B^t(\lambda^x) \subseteq d^{-1}.\ell_\infty\ ,$$

so

$$d.\ell_1 = e_S(d^{-1}.\ell_\infty)^x \subseteq e_S(B^t(\lambda^x))^x = \text{nor-}A^{-1}(\lambda). \quad \square$$

COROLLARY 5.4. <u>Suppose</u> λ <u>is perfect, and</u> d <u>is as in the preceding corollary. Then for any subset</u> Λ <u>of</u> ω,

$$d.\Lambda^x \subseteq D(\Lambda, \text{nor-}A^{-1}(\lambda))\ .$$

<u>Proof</u>. $d.\Lambda^x = dD(\Lambda, \ell_1) = D(\Lambda, d.\ell_1) \subseteq D(\Lambda, \text{nor-}A^{-1}(\zeta))$. $\square$

COROLLARY 5.5. <u>Suppose</u> λ <u>is perfect, and</u> d <u>is as in Corollary</u> 5.3. <u>Then for</u> $0 < p \leq 1$, $D(\ell_p, \text{nor-}A^{-1}(\lambda)) = d.\ell_\infty$.

<u>Proof</u>. By Corollary 5.4, $d(\ell_p)^x = d.\ell_\infty \subseteq D(\ell_p, \text{nor-}A^{-1}(\lambda))$. The reverse inclusion is part of Theorem 4.3 since $\|e_n\|_p = 1$. $\square$

REMARKS. (i) The difference between Corollary 4.5 and Corollary 5.5 is that in the former, $\|\cdot\|_\lambda$ must be a norm, while in the latter, λ must be perfect.

(ii) Clearly Corollary 5.5 holds with ℓ_p replaced by any μ such that $\|e_n\|_\mu = 1$ and $\mu^x = \ell_\infty$.

EXAMPLE 5.6. The common conclusion of Corollaries 4.5 and 5.5 need not hold if $\|\cdot\|_\lambda$ is not a norm and λ is not perfect. Fix $p \in (0,1]$, and suppose $q \in (0,p)$. Set $\lambda = \ell_q$, $\mu = \ell_p$; let A be any diagonal matrix with positive diagonal entries. Then d is the sequence of reciprocals of the diagonal entries of A. Then $\text{nor-}A^{-1}(\ell_q) = d.\ell_q$, so

$$D(\ell_p, \text{nor-}A^{-1}(\ell_q)) = D(\ell_p, d\ell_q) = dD(\ell_p,\ell_q) = d.\ell_r ,$$

where r is the positive number satisfying $p^{-1} + r^{-1} = q^{-1}$.

LEMMA 5.7. <u>Suppose</u> $M = (m_{kn})$ <u>is a matrix with nonnegative entries, and each row of</u> M <u>is in</u> ℓ_1. <u>Let</u> m <u>be the sequence of row sums of</u> M. <u>Then</u> $M(\ell_\infty))^x = m^{-1}.\ell_1$. [<u>In case</u> m <u>has zero entries, i.e.</u> M <u>has zero rows, by</u> $m^{-1}.\ell_1$ <u>we mean</u> $m^{-1}.\ell_1 + (e - e_S)\omega$, <u>where</u> $S = \{n \; ; \; m_n \neq 0\}$.]

<u>Proof</u>. Since $e \in \ell_\infty$,

$$M(\ell_\infty))^x \subseteq \{M(e)\}^x = m^{-1}.\ell_1 .$$

If $x \in \ell_1$, $y \in \ell_\infty$, then

$$\langle |My|, |m^{-1}x| \rangle \leq \langle M|y|, m^{-1}|x| \rangle = \sum_{k \in S} \left(\sum_{n=1}^{\infty} m_{kn}|y_n| \right) m_k^{-1}|x_k|$$

$$\leq \left(\sum_{k \in S} \left(\sum_{n=1}^{\infty} m_{kn} \right) m_k^{-1}|x_k| \right) = \|y\|_\infty \sum_{k \in S} |x_k| \leq \|y\|_\infty \|x\|_1 .$$

Thus $m^{-1}.\ell_1 \subseteq (M(\ell_\infty))^x$. [It is clear that $(e - e_S)\omega \subseteq (M(\ell_\infty))^x$.] □

PROPOSITION 5.8. <u>Let</u> $S = \{n \; ; \; Ae_n \in \ell_1\}$, <u>and define</u>

$$d_n = \|Ae_n\|_1^{-1} \text{ if } n \in S, \qquad d_n = 0 \text{ otherwise} .$$

<u>Then</u> $\text{nor-}A^{-1}(\ell_1) = d.\ell_1$.

The proof is straightforward from Lemma 5.7 and Proposition 5.1, with $\Lambda = \ell_1$. □

COROLLARY 5.9. <u>With</u> d <u>as in the Proposition,</u>

$$D(\Lambda, \text{nor-}A^{-1}(\ell_1)) = d.\Lambda^x, \quad \underline{\text{for any}} \quad \Lambda \subseteq \omega.$$

6. THE SUBSPACE $D(\ell_q, \text{nor-}A^{-1}(\ell_p))$

We shall only give the results which we can obtain on $D(\ell_q, \text{nor-}A^{-1}(\ell_p))$. The proofs will be given elsewhere.

PROPOSITION 6.1. *Suppose* $0 < p \leq \infty$, $S = \{n \; ; \; Ae_n \in \ell_p\}$,

$$d_n = \|Ae_n\|_p^{-1} \quad \underline{\text{for}} \quad n \in S \;, \qquad d_n = 0 \quad \underline{\text{otherwise}} \;.$$

If $D(\ell_p, \text{nor-}A^{-1}(\ell_p)) = b.\ell_\infty$ *for some* $b \in \omega$, *then* $D(\ell_q, \text{nor-}A^{-1}(\ell_p)) = d.\ell_\infty$ *for all* $q \in (0,p]$.

This leads to the following problem:

PROBLEM 6.2. Suppose $p > 0$, $p \neq 1, \infty$, and let d be defined as above, with respect to A and p. Does

$$D\left(\bigcup_{0<q<p} \ell_q, \text{nor-}A^{-1}(\ell_p)\right) = d.\ell_\infty$$

imply that $D(\ell_p, \text{nor-}A^{-1}(\ell_p)) = d.\ell_\infty$?

PROPOSITION 6.3. *Suppose* $1 < q \leq \infty$. *Then*

$$D(\ell_q, \text{nor-}A^{-1}(\ell_\infty)) = \left\{b \in \omega \; ; \left\{\sum_{k=1}^{\infty} (a_{nk}|b_k|)^{q'}\right\}_n \in \ell_\infty\right\}.$$

COROLLARY 6.4. *Suppose* $1 < q \leq \infty$, *and* $d_n = (\sup_n a_{nk})^{-1}$. *Then*

$$D(\ell_q, \text{nor-}A^{-1}(\ell_\infty)) = d.\ell_\infty$$

if and only if

$$\left\{\sum_{k=1}^{\infty} (a_{nk} \, d_k)^{q'}\right\}_n \in \ell_\infty \;.$$

EXAMPLE 6.5. Let $a_{nk} = (n - k + 1)^{-1}$, $n \geq k$, and $a_{nk} = 0$, $n < k$. Apply Corollaries 6.4 and 4.5 to see that $D(\ell_q, \text{nor-}A^{-1}(\ell_\infty)) = \ell_\infty$ for all $q \in (0,\infty)$. However, Corollary 6.4 and Theorem 4.3 guarantee that $D(\ell_\infty, \text{nor-}A^{-1}(\ell_\infty))$ is not ℓ_∞, nor any diagonal copy of ℓ_∞.

We shall next look at $D(\ell_q, \text{nor-}A^{-1}(\ell_p))$ with $1 \leq p < q \leq \infty$, and shall find that there is almost never a best possible HPD inequality of the form

$$\|Ad|x|\|_p \leq K\|x\|_q$$

in these cases (Cor. 6.9). We shall prefer to return to a more general setting. We also would use $\|\cdot\|$ for $\|\cdot\|_\lambda$ whenever the sequence space μ is not there. We define

$$K(\lambda) = \{x \in \lambda \; ; \; \|x - P_n(x)\| \to 0 \quad \text{as} \quad n \to \infty\} \; ;$$

λ is said to be AK (for abschnitt Konvergenz) if and only if $\lambda = K(\lambda)$. It is easy to see that $K(\lambda)$ is the closure of $\lambda \cap \varphi$ in $(\lambda, \|\cdot\|)$, and is normal.

The following lemma generalizes the usual characterization of compactness in ℓ_p, $0 < p < \infty$, and $c_0 = K(\ell_\infty)$.

LEMMA 6.6. <u>Suppose</u> λ <u>is AK, and</u> $F \subseteq \lambda$. <u>Then</u> F <u>is compact if and only if</u> F <u>is closed, bounded, and</u> $\lim_{n\to\infty} \sup_{x\in F} \|x - P_n(x)\| = 0$.

THEOREM 6.7. <u>The inclusion</u> $K(D(\mu, \text{nor-}A^{-1}(\lambda))) \subseteq \{b \in \omega \; ; \; AD_b$ <u>determines a compact map from</u> μ <u>to</u> $\lambda\}$, <u>holds, with equality if</u> λ <u>is AK</u>.

COROLLARY 6.8. <u>For</u> $1 \leq p < q < \infty$, $D(\ell_q, \text{nor-}A^{-1}(\ell_p))$ <u>is AK. Further</u>, $D(\ell_\infty, \text{nor-}A^{-1}(\ell_p))$ <u>is AK for every</u> $p \in (0, \infty)$.

COROLLARY 6.9. <u>Suppose that either</u> $1 \leq p < q < \infty$ <u>or</u> $0 < p < q = \infty$. <u>The following are equivalent</u>:

(a) $D(\ell_q, \text{nor-}A^{-1}(\ell_p)) = b.\ell_\infty$ <u>for some</u> $b \in \omega$;

(b) <u>only finitely many columns of</u> A <u>are in</u> ℓ_p;

(c) $D(\ell_q, \text{nor-}A^{-1}(\ell_p))$ <u>is finite dimensional</u>.

COROLLARY 6.10. <u>Suppose that either</u> $1 \leq p < q < \infty$ <u>or</u> $0 < p < q = \infty$. <u>If the sequence of</u> ℓ_p <u>norms of the columns of</u> A <u>is bounded away from zero, then</u> A <u>does not map</u> ℓ_q <u>into</u> ℓ_p.

In the last three sections of the paper, we shall be considering HPD inequalities with A restricted to certain classes of lower triangular matrices.

7. TOEPLITZ MATRICES

For $b \in \omega$, let T_b be the lower triangular matrix each of whose columns consists of the sequence b, starting from the main diagonal. That is, for $m \geq n$, the (m,n) entry of T_b is b_{m-n+1}.

Let $*$ denote the convolution on ω:

$$x * y = \left\{ \sum_{k=1}^{n} x_{n-k+1}\, y_k \right\}_n .$$

Then $b * y = T_b(y)$ for all $y \in \omega$.

Clearly T_b is invertible if and only if $b_1 = 0$.

Let σ denote the forward shift. Theorem 4.3 provides the following:

COROLLARY 7.1. *Suppose* $b \in \lambda$ *is a nonnegative sequence, not zero, and* λ *is invariant under* σ. *Let*

$$d_n = \|\sigma^{(n-1)}(b)\|_\lambda^{-1}\, \|e_n\|_\mu .$$

Then

$$D(\mu, \text{nor-}T_b^{-1}(\lambda)) \subseteq d.\ell_\infty ,$$

with equality if and only if T_b *maps* $d\mu$ *into* λ.

COROLLARY 7.2. *Suppose* $b \in \lambda$ *is nonnegative and not zero. Suppose* $\|e_n\|_\mu = 1$ *for all* n, *and* σ *is an isometry of* λ *into itself. Then*

$$D(\mu, \text{nor-}T_b^{-1}(\lambda)) \subseteq \ell_\infty ,$$

with equality if and only if $T_b(\mu) \subseteq \lambda$.

The next series of results is concerned with the inclusion $T_b(\lambda) \subseteq \lambda$; note that Corollary 7.2 shows that this inclusion gives rise to a best possible HPD inequality if b is nonnegative, $\varphi \subseteq \lambda$, and σ is an isometry of λ into itself. However, some of these results do not require the full force of the blanket hypothesis on λ. We shall state some results below whose proofs will be omitted.

PROPOSITION 7.3. *Suppose* b *is nonnegative and not zero,* Λ *is a normal subspace of* ω, *and* $\varphi \subseteq \Lambda$. *Then* $T_b(\Lambda) \subseteq \Lambda$ *if and only if* $\Lambda = \text{nor-}T_b^{-1}(\Lambda)$.

PROPOSITION 7.4. *Suppose* $b \in \ell_1$, *and* $(\Lambda,\|\cdot\|)$ *is a normed FK subspace of* ω *such that* $\sigma(\Lambda) \subseteq \Lambda$, *and the operator norm of* σ *is less than or equal to* 1. *Then* T_b *determines a continuous linear map of* Λ *into* Λ.

COROLLARY 7.5. *If* $b \in \ell_1$, b *is nonnegative and nonzero*, $(\Lambda,\|\cdot\|)$ *and* σ *satisfy the hypothesis of Proposition* 7.4, *and* Λ *is normal, then*

$$\text{nor-}T_b^{-1}(\Lambda) = \Lambda .$$

COROLLARY 7.6. *If*

$$g(z) = \sum_{n=1}^{\infty} b_n z^{n-1}$$

is analytic and nonzero in a disc of radius greater than 1 *centered at origin, and* $(\Lambda,\|\cdot\|)$ *satisfies the hypothesis of Proposition* 7.4, *then* T_b *determines an isomorphism of* Λ *onto* Λ.

COROLLARY 7.7. *Suppose* $b \in \ell_1$, *and* b *is nonnegative and nonzero. Then for* $1 \leq p \leq \infty$,

$$\|T_b|x|\|_p \leq C(p)\|x\|_p$$

for some constant $C(p)$ *depending only on* p, *and this HPD inequality is best possible in the sense that there is no sequence* a *with a subsequence tending to zero such that*

$$\|T_b|x|\|_p \leq K\|ax\|_p$$

for all x, *for some constant* K; *in the cases* $p = 1,\infty$, *the best possible constants are* $C(1) = C(\infty) = \|b\|_1$.

Proof. By Corollary 7.5,

$$\text{nor-}T_b^{-1}(\ell_p) = \ell_p ,$$

so

$$D(\ell_p,\text{nor-}T_b^{-1}(\ell_p)) = D(\ell_p,\ell_p) = \ell_\infty .$$

When $p = 1$, by changing the order of summation we find that the inequality is an equality with $C(1) = \|b\|_1$. That $C(\infty) = \|b\|_1$ is an easy consequence of the observation that the n-th row sum of T_b is

$$\sum_{k=1}^{n} b_k = \|b\|_1 ,$$

as $n \to \infty$. □

PROBLEM 7.8. Does Proposition 7.4 remain true if the assumption that the coordinate projections are continuous on Λ (implicit in the hypothesis that Λ be FK) is omitted?

From Corollary 7.7 we obtain the following best possible HPD inequalities:

COROLLARY 7.9. <u>Let</u> u <u>be a nonnegative sequence</u>, $1 \leq p < \infty$, $r \in (0,1)$, <u>and</u> $q > 1$. <u>Then</u>

$$\text{(i)} \quad \sum_{m=1}^{\infty} \left(\sum_{k=1}^{m} u_k (m-k)! \right)^p \leq C_1(p)^p \sum_m u_m^p ,$$

$$\text{(ii)} \quad \sum_{m=1}^{\infty} \left(\sum_{k=1}^{m} r^{-k} u_k \right)^p \leq C_2(p)^p \sum_m u_m^p ,$$

$$\text{(iii)} \quad \sum_{m=1}^{\infty} \left(\sum_{k=1}^{m} (m-k+1)^{-q} u_k \right)^p \leq C_3(p)^p \sum_m u_m^p .$$

To obtain (i), (ii), and (iii), put $b_n = (n-1)!^{-1}$, r^{n-1}, and n^{-q} in Corollary 7.7, respectively. □

We conclude this section by improving an HPD inequality due to Petersen [18], and by showing that there is no best possible improvement of the inequality. Petersen's inequality may be written as

$$\|Au\|_p \leq C\|a^{-1}u\|_p \quad \text{for } 1<p<\infty,\ u_n \geq 0,\ a = \{a_n\},\ a_n = n^{-1/2}, \text{ and } A = D_a T_a .$$

We shall improve this to $\|Au\|_p \leq C\|u\|_p$.

PROPOSITION 7.10. <u>For</u> $u_n \geq 0$ <u>and</u> $1 < p < \infty$,

$$\left(\sum_{m=1}^{\infty} \left(\sum_{n=1}^{m} u_n/(m(m-n+1))^{1/2} \right)^p \right)^{1/p} \leq 2p^2(p-1)^{-1} \left(\sum_{n=1}^{\infty} u_n^p \right)^{1/p} .$$

LEMMA 7.11. <u>For</u> $n \geq 1$, $1 < p < \infty$,

$$\sum_{m=n}^{\infty} [m^{p/2}(m-n+1)^{1/2}]^{-1} < (2p/(p-1))\, n^{(1-p)/2}$$

Proof. We have

$$\begin{aligned}\sum_{m=n}^{\infty} (m^{p/2}(m-n+1)^{1/2})^{-1} &= \left(\sum_{m=n}^{2n} + \sum_{m=2n+1}^{\infty}\right)(m^{p/2}(m-n+1)^{1/2})^{-1}\\ &< n^{-p/2}\sum_{m=n}^{2n}(m-n+1)^{-1/2} + \sum_{m=2n+1}^{\infty}(m^{p/2}(m-n+1)^{1/2})^{-1}\\ &= n^{-p/2}\sum_{m=n}^{n+1} m^{-1/2} + \sum_{m=n+1}^{\infty}[(m+n)^{p/2}(m+1)^{1/2}]^{-1}.\end{aligned}$$

It is easy to show by induction on n (starting with $n = 1$) that

$$\sum_{m=1}^{n+1} m^{-1/2} < 2n^{1/2} .$$

(In [17], p. 191, 3.1.12, it is shown that $\sum_{m=1}^{n+1} m^{-1/2} < 2(n+1)^{1/2} - 1$.)

Also, we have

$$\sum_{m=n+1}^{\infty}[(m+n)^{p/2}(m+1)^{1/2}]^{-1} \le \sum_{m=n+1}^{\infty}(m+1)^{-(p+1)/2} < \int_n^{\infty} x^{-(p+1)/2}dx = \left(\frac{2}{p-1}\right)n^{(1-p)/2}.$$

Thus

$$\sum_{m=n}^{\infty}(m^{p/2}(m-n+1)^{1/2})^{-1} < 2n^{-p/2}n^{1/2} + (2/(p-1))^{n(1-p)/2} = \frac{2p}{p-1}\, n^{(1-p)/2}. \quad \square$$

Proof of Proposition 7.10. Starting off by Lemma 1, [4], we have

$$\begin{aligned}&\sum_m\left(\sum_{n=1}^{m}(m(m-n+1)^{-1/2}u_n)\right)^p\\ &\le p\sum_m m^{-p/2}\sum_{n=1}^{m}(m-n+1)^{-1/2}u_n\left(\sum_{k=1}^{n}(m-k+1)^{-1/2}u_k\right)^{p-1}\\ &\le p\sum_m m^{-p/2}\sum_{n=1}^{m}(m-n+1)^{-1/2}u_n\left(\sum_{k=1}^{n}(n-k+1)^{-1/2}u_k\right)^{p-1}\\ &= p\sum_{n=1}^{\infty}\left(\sum_{k=1}^{n}(n-k+1)^{-1/2}u_k\right)^{p-1}u_n\sum_{m=n}^{\infty}(m^{p/2}(m-n+1)^{1/2})^{-1}\\ &\le p\,\frac{2p}{p-1}\sum_{n=1}^{\infty}\left(\sum_{k=1}^{n}(n-k+1)^{-1/2}u_k\right)^{p-1}u_n\, n^{(1-p)/2}\\ &= \frac{2p^2}{p-1}\sum_{m=1}^{\infty}\left(\sum_{n=1}^{m}(m(m-n+1))^{-1/2}u_n\right)^{p-1}u_m\end{aligned}$$

by Lemma 7.11.

Now by applying Hölder's inequality, and dividing both sides of the inequality by

$$\left(\sum_{n=1}^{m} ((m(m-n+1)^{-1/2} u_n)^p \right)^{1/p'} ,$$

we obtain the desired result. □

REMARK. In the above we have assumed that $u_n \neq 0$ for some n. The inequality is strict for $u \neq 0$.

Next we show that there is no best possible inequality of the form

$$\|Au\|_p \leq K\|du\|_p , \quad u_n \geq 0 ,$$

for each $p \in (1,\infty)$, where $A = D_a T_a$ with $a_n = n^{-1/2}$. Our result is the following.

PROPOSITION 7.12. <u>Suppose</u>

$$A = (a_{mn}) \ \underline{\text{with}} \ a_{mn} = (m(m-n+1)^{-1/2}, \quad m \geq n \ \underline{\text{and}} \ a_{mn} = 0, \quad m < n .$$

<u>Then for</u> $1 < p \leq \infty$, $D(\ell_p, \text{nor-}A^{-1}(\ell_p))$ <u>is not a diagonal copy of</u> ℓ_∞.

We shall need the following lemma for proving the proposition.

LEMMA 7.13. <u>Let</u>

$$d_n^p = \sum_{m=n}^{\infty} [m(m-n+1)]^{-1/2} .$$

<u>Then</u>

$$d_n^p \leq Cn^{1-p} \qquad (1 < p < 2) ,$$
$$d_n^2 \leq Cn^{-1} \log(n+1) ,$$
$$d_n^p \leq Cn^{-p/2} \qquad (2 < p < \infty) ,$$

C <u>being a constant depending only on</u> p.

<u>Proof</u>. Throughout, C will stand for a general constant and may take different values at each occurrence.

We have

$$d_n^p = \sum_{m=n}^{2n} [m(m - n + 1)]^{-p/2} + \sum_{m=2n+1}^{\infty} [m(m - n + 1)]^{-1/2}$$

$$= \sum_1 + \sum_2 , \quad \text{say} .$$

As in Lemma 7.11,

$$\sum_2 = \sum_{m=n+1}^{\infty} ((m + n)(m + 1))^{-p/2} \le \sum_{m=n+1}^{\infty} (m + 1)^{-p} \le Cn^{1-p} ,$$

for $1 < p < \infty$. For $1 < p < 2$,

$$\sum_1 \le n^{-p/2} \sum_{m=n}^{2n} (m - n + 1)^{-p/2} = n^{-p/2} \sum_{m=1}^{n+1} m^{-p/2} \le Cn^{1-p} .$$

For $p = 2$,

$$\sum_1 \le Cn^{-1} \log(n + 1) .$$

Thus $d_n^p \le Cn^{-1} \log(n + 1) + Cn^{-1}$, from which we see the required result in this case.

For $2 < p < \infty$,

$$\sum_1 = \sum_{m=n}^{2n} [m(m - n + 1)]^{-p/2} \le n^{-p/2} \sum_{m=n}^{2n} (m - n + 1)^{-p/2} \le Cn^{-p/2} .$$

Thus d_n^p has the requires estimates, as we see on adding the estimates of $\sum_1$ and $\sum_2$. □

LEMMA 7.14. _Suppose_ $M = (m_{kn})$ _is a matrix with nonnegative entries,_ V _is a normal subspace of_ dom M, _and_ $M(V) \subseteq S \subseteq \omega$. _Then_

$$M^t(S^x) \subseteq V^x ,$$

and for each $x \in V$, _and_ $y \in S^x$, $\langle Mx,y\rangle = \langle x,M^ty\rangle$.

Proof. Suppose $x \in V$ and $y \in S^x$. Then $|x| \in V$ and $|y| \in S^x$. By change of order of summation, we have

$$\infty > \langle M|x|,|y|\rangle = \langle |x|,M^t|y|\rangle \ge \langle |x|,|M^ty|\rangle .$$

Thus $M^ty \in V^x$. Also, the convergence of the absolute series implies $\langle Mx,y\rangle = \langle x,M^ty\rangle$. □

Proof of Proposition 7.12. Suppose first that $1 < p < \infty$, and set

$$d_n^{-1} = \left(\sum_{m=n}^{\infty} (m(m - n + 1))^{-p/2} \right)^{1/p} ,$$

the ℓ_p norm of the n-th column of A. By Theorem 4.3, it is sufficient to show that AD_b does not map ℓ_p into ℓ_p, or equivalently that $d \notin D(\ell_p, \text{nor-}A^{-1}(\ell_p))$. By Lemma 7.13, $d^{-1} < b^{-1}$, where

$$b_n = n^{1/p'},\ n^{1/2}(\log(n+1))^{-1/2}, \quad \text{or} \quad n^{1/2}$$

according as $1 < p < 2$, $p = 2$, or $p > 2$. Since $d^{-1} < b^{-1}$, we have $b < d$, so if suffices to show that $b \notin D(\ell_p, \text{nor-}A^{-1}(\ell_p))$, since the latter is a normal subspace of ω.

Now, $b \in D(\ell_p, \text{nor-}A^{-1}(\ell_p))$ if and only if $AD_b(\ell_p) \subseteq \ell_p$, if and only if $D_b A^t(\ell_{p'}) \subseteq \ell_{p'}$ (by Lemma 7.14). Thus it suffices to find $x \in \ell_{p'}$ such that

$$D_b A^t(x) \notin \ell_{p'} .$$

We take $x = \{n^{-\alpha}\}$, $\alpha = 2/p'$ in cases $1 < p < 2$ and $p = 2$, and $\alpha = 1/p' + 1/2$ when $p > 2$.

In any case,

$$D_b A^t(x) = \left\{ b_n \sum_{m=n}^{\infty} [m^{\alpha+1/2}(m - n + 1)^{1/2}]^{-1} \right\}_n .$$

Now,

$$b_n \sum_{m=n}^{\infty} [m^{\alpha+1/2}(m - n + 1)^{1/2}]^{-1} \geq b_n \sum_{m=n}^{\infty} m^{-\alpha-1} \geq \alpha^{-1} b_n n^{-\alpha} .$$

For different ranges of values of p, $b_n n^{-\alpha}$, and thus $D_b A^t(x)$ does not lie in $\ell_{p'}$.

Now suppose $p = \infty$, and set

$$d_n^{-1} = n^{-1/2} ,$$

the ℓ_∞ norm of the n-th column of A. The problem is to show that AD_d does not map ℓ_∞ to ℓ_∞; it suffices to show that the row sums of AD_d are unbounded. The 2m-th such sum is

$$(2m)^{-1/2} \sum_{n=1}^{2m} n^{1/2} (2m - n + 1)^{-1/2} \geq (2m)^{-1/2} \sum_{n=m+1}^{2m} n^{1/2}(2m - n + 1)^{-1/2} \geq cm^{1/2} ,$$

by integral comparison. □

This raises the following problem:

PROBLEM 7.15. Suppose the matrix A is as in Proposition 7.13, and d as in the proof.

(a) For $1<p\leq\infty$, for which $q\in(1,p)$ is $D(\ell_q, \text{nor-}A^{-1}(\ell_p)) = d.\ell_\infty$?

(b) Do there exist $p\in(1,\infty)$, $b\in c_0$, and K such that $\| A|x| \|_p \leq K\|bx\|_p$ for all x?

(c) Is e maximal with respect to < among the nondecreasing positive sequences in

$$D(\ell_p, \text{nor-}A^{-1}(\ell_p)) ,$$

for each $p\in(1,\infty)$?

8. THE MATRIX $A = D_aJ$

Let J stand for T_e, the lower triangular matrix with entry 1 on and below the main diagonal; a will be a positive sequence, and $A = D_aJ$, throughout this section. We shall only state our results concerning the matrix A, and will not prove them here.

PROPOSITION 8.1. *For* $1<p<\infty$,

$$a^{p-1}\,(J^t(a^p))^{-1} = \left\{a_n^{p-1}\left(\sum_{m=n}^{\infty} a_m^p\right)^{-1}\right\}_n \in D(\ell_p, \text{nor-}A^{-1}(\ell_p)) .$$

PROPOSITION 8.2. *If* $a^{-p}J^t(a^p)\in\ell_\infty$, $1<p<\infty$, *then*

$$D(\ell_p, \text{nor-}A^{-1}(\ell_p)) = a^{-1}.\ell_\infty .$$

COROLLARY 8.3. *If* $1<p<\infty$ and $a^{-p}J^t(a^p)\in\ell_\infty$ *then* $\{na_n\}\in\ell_p$.

Setting $a_n = (n-1)!^{-1}$ and observing that $a^{-p}J^t(a^p)$ is bounded, we have the following consequence of Proposition 8.2:

$$\sum_m (m-1)!^{-p}\left(\sum_{n=1}^{m} u_n\right)^p \leq C(p)^p \sum_n (u_n/(n-1)!)^p ,$$

for $u_n\geq 0$, $1<p<\infty$.

REMARK. Proposition 8.2 assures us that this inequality is best possible. A reprise of Petersen's proof in [18], for this particular case, shows that

$$C(p) \leq p \sum_{m=0}^{\infty} m!^{-p} .$$

9. THE SUBSPACE $ces_p^{(r)}$

Throughout this section, $A = D_a J$ with $a_n = n^{-r}$, and nor-$A^{-1}(\ell_p)$ will be denoted $ces_p^{(r)}$. The reason for this notation is that $ces_p^{(1)} = ces_p$, a name currently in use. (See [21].) Note that $ces_p^{(r)}$ is nontrivial if and only if $rp > 1$; in particular, $ces_\infty^{(r)}$ is nontrivial for every $r > 0$. The inclusion

$$\{n^{r-1}\}.\ell_p \subseteq ces_p^{(r)} ,$$

a consequence of Proposition 8.1 for $1 < p < \infty$, $rp > 1$, also holds for $p = \infty$, $r > 0$, because the row sums of $AD_{n^{r-1}}$ are bounded, implying that this matrix maps ℓ_∞ into ℓ_∞, which implies that $\{n^{r-1}\} \in D(\ell_\infty, ces_\infty^{(r)})$.

PROPOSITION 9.1. <u>Suppose</u> $0 < r < t$ <u>and</u> $0 < q < p \leq \infty$. <u>Then</u>

(a) $ces_p^{(r)} \subseteq ces_p^{(t)}$, <u>and the inclusion is proper if</u> $tp > 1$;

(b) $ces_q^{(r)} \subseteq ces_p^{(r)}$, <u>and the inclusion is proper if</u> $rp > 1$;

(c) <u>if</u> $r < 1$ <u>then</u> $\ell_p \not\subseteq ces_p^{(r)}$;

(d) <u>if</u> $rp > 1$, <u>then</u> $ces_p^{(r)} \not\subseteq \ell_\infty$;

(e) <u>if</u> $r \geq 1$, $1 \leq p \leq \infty$, <u>and</u> $rp > 1$, <u>then</u> $\ell_p \subseteq ces_p^{(r)}$.

PROBLEM 9.2. If $0 < p < 1$ and $rp > 1$, is $\ell_p \subseteq ces_p^{(r)}$?

REMARK. Hardy's inequality is the statement that $e = D(\ell_p, ces_p)$ for $1 < p < \infty$, so the fact that

$$\{n^{r-1}\} \in D(\ell_p, ces_p^{(r)}) , \quad 1 \leq p \leq \infty, \ rp > 1 ,$$

is a generalization of Hardy's inequality. Our next result is the statement that the HPD inequality derivable from this fact is not best possible, and even no best possible such inequality can be found for $p > 1$.

THEOREM 9.3. <u>Suppose</u> $1 < p \leq \infty$ <u>and</u> $rp > 1$. <u>Then</u> $D(\ell_q, ces_p^{(r)})$ <u>is not a diagonal copy of</u> ℓ_∞, <u>for</u> $1 < q \leq p$.

We omit the proofs since they will be given elsewhere. □

We are led to the following:

PROBLEM 9.4. Suppose $0 < p < 1$ and $rp > 1$. For which $q > 0$ is $D(\ell_q, ces_p^{(r)})$ a diagonal copy of ℓ_∞?

There are many other results concerning this sequence space $ces_p^{(r)}$ which will be proved elsewhere.

REFERENCES

1. T.A. Broadbent, A proof of Hardy's convergence theorem, J. London Math. Soc. 3 (1928), 242-243.

2. E.T. Copson, Note on series of positive terms, J. London Math. Soc. 2 (1927), 9-12.

3. E.T. Copson, Note on series of positive terms, J. London Math. Soc. 3 (1928), 49-51.

4. G.S. Davies and G.M. Petersen, On an inequality of Hardy's (II), Quart. J. Math. (Oxford) (2) 15 (1964), 35-40.

5. E.G. Elliot, A simple exposition of some recently proved facts as to convergency, J. London Math. Soc. 1 (1926), 93-96.

6. C. Goffman and G. Pedrick, First Course in Functional Analysis, Prentice-Hall, Englewood Cliffs, N.J. 1965.

7. K. Grandjot, On some identies relating to Hardy's convergence theorem, J. London Math. Soc. 3 (1928), 114-117.

8. G.H. Hardy, Note on a theorem of Hilbert, Math. Zeitschr. 6 (1920), 314-317.

9. G.H. Hardy, Remarks on three recent notes in the journal, J. London Math. Soc. 3 (1928), 166-169.

10. G.H. Hardy, J.E. Littlewood, and G. Pólya, Inequalities, Cambridge University Press, 1934.

11. P.D. Johnson and R.N. Mohapatra, Inverse images of normal sequence spaces under matrix transformations, and the spaces $ces(p_n)$, to appear.

12. Th. Kaluza and G. Szegö, Über Reihen mit lauter positiven Gliedern, J. London Math. Soc. 2 (1927), 266-272.

13. K. Knopp, Über Reihen mit positiven Gliedern, J. London Math. Soc. 3 (1928), 205-211.

14. E. Landau, A note on a theorem concerning series of positive terms, J. London Math. Soc. 1 (1926), 38-39.

15. I.J. Maddox, Continuous and Köthe-Toeplitz duals of certain sequence spaces, Proc. Camb. Phil. Soc. 65 (1969), 431-435.

16. I.J. Maddox, Elements of Functional Analysis, Cambridge University Press, 1970.

17. D.S. Mitrinovic, Analytic Inequalities, Springer Verlag, Berlin-Heidelberg-New York, 1970.

18. G.M. Petersen, An inequality of Hardy's, Quart. J. Math. (Oxford) (2) 13 (1962), 237-240.

19. H.P. Rosenthal, On quasi-complemented subspaces of Banach spaces with an appendix on compactness of operators from $L^p(\mu)$ to $L^r(\nu)$, J. Functional Analysis 4 (1969), 176-214.

20. H.H. Schaefer, Topological Vector Spaces, Macmillan, New York, 1966.

21. J.S. Shiue, On the Cesàro sequence spaces, Tamkang J. Math. 1 (1970), 19-25.

22. S. Simons, The sequence spaces (p_n) and $m(p_n)$, Proc. London Math. Soc. (3) 15 (1965), 422-436.

23. O. Szasz, On the product of two summability methods, Ann. Polon. Math. 25 (1952), 75-84.

24. A. Wilansky, Functional Analysis, Blaisdell, New York-Toronto-London, 1964.

ON PSEUDOCONVEX QUADRATIC FORMS

Siegfried Schaible
Industrieseminar
Universität Köln
5 Köln 41
WEST GERMANY

Richard W. Cottle
Department of Operations Research
Stanford University
Stanford, California 94305
U.S.A.

ABSTRACT. Cottle and Ferland characterized pseudoconvex quadratic forms on the semipositive orthant in terms of principal minors. Their proof is based on results by Martos, who related pseudoconvex quadratic forms to positive subdefinite matrices. We show that the criterion by Cottle and Ferland can be derived by specialization of a more recent characterization of pseudoconvex quadratic functions on arbitrary open convex sets without referring to positive subdefiniteness.

1. INTRODUCTION

In mathematical economics [1], [4], and in nonlinear optimization [6], [8], quasiconvexity and pseudoconvexity proved to be useful generalizations of convexity. Unfortunately, it is difficult to verify these properties for a given function since the definition of quasiconvexity and pseudoconvexity involves infinitely many inequalities not easily checked. Therefore, in recent years much emphasis has been put on deriving more practical characterizations of quasiconvex and pseudoconvex functions. In [9] such criteria were obtained for special classes of functions, such as composite functions, products and quotients, quadratic and cubic functions. More recently, pseudoconvex C^2-functions on open convex sets were characterized [2], [10]. In this connection also new criteria for pseudoconvex quadratic functions were obtained. In particular, a necessary and sufficient condition in terms of the principal minors of a bordered Hessian was derived.

In the present paper the foregoing criterion will be used to characterize (nonconvex) pseudoconvex quadratic forms on the positive orthant of R^n in terms of principal minors. The criterion obtained resembles one for convex quadratic forms. In a finite test, one has to check the sign of all principal minors.

This characterization was first proved in a recent paper by Cottle and Ferland [3] making use of results by Martos [7], who related pseudoconvex quadratic forms to positive subdefinite matrices. Our proof does not make use of positive subdefiniteness. Instead, the criterion is obtained by specialization of a more general result already given, characterizing pseudoconvex quadratic functions on arbitrary open convex sets in terms of determinants.

2. NOTATION AND DEFINITION

Let

$$Q(x) = \frac{1}{2} x^T A x \quad ,$$

where A is a real symmetric $n \times n$ matrix. Denote

$$R^n_{++} = \{x \in R^n \mid x_j > 0, \quad j = 1,\dots,n\} .$$

The quadratic form $Q(x)$ is said to be pseudoconvex [6] on R^n_{++} if the gradient inequality

$$(\bar{\bar{x}} - \bar{x})^T \nabla Q(\bar{x}) \geq 0$$

implies

$$Q(\bar{\bar{x}}) \geq Q(\bar{x}) \quad \text{for all} \quad \bar{x}, \bar{\bar{x}} \in R^n_{++} .$$

A convex function $Q(x)$ is necessarily pseudoconvex, but not conversely. We shall derive a finite criterion for nonconvex functions $Q(x)$ that are pseudoconvex on R^n_{++}. For this, we make use of a recent characterization in [2] involving the principal minors of the bordered Hessian [1]

$$D(x) = \begin{pmatrix} \nabla^2 Q(x) & \nabla Q(x) \\ \nabla Q(x)^T & 0 \end{pmatrix} = \begin{pmatrix} A & Ax \\ (Ax)^T & 0 \end{pmatrix} .$$

Let Γ_k be the set of monotone increasing sequences of k numbers from $\{1,2,\dots,n\}$; that is,

$$\Gamma_k = \{\gamma_k \mid \gamma_k = (i_1,\dots,i_k), \; 1 \leq i_1 < \cdots < i_k \leq n\} .$$

Let A_{γ_k} denote the principal submatrix of order k of A formed by the $(i_1,\dots,i_k)$-th row and column of A, where $\gamma_k = (i_1,\dots,i_k)$. The leading principal submatrix of order k of A is denoted by A_k.

We associate with $D(x)$ and A_{γ_k} the principal submatrix

$$D_{\gamma_k}(x) = \begin{pmatrix} \frac{\partial^2 Q(x)}{\partial x_{i_1}^2} & \cdots & \frac{\partial^2 Q(x)}{\partial x_{i_1}\partial x_{i_k}} & \frac{\partial Q(x)}{\partial x_{i_1}} \\ \vdots & & \vdots & \vdots \\ \frac{\partial^2 Q(x)}{\partial x_{i_k}\partial x_{i_1}} & \cdots & \frac{\partial^2 Q(x)}{\partial x_{i_k}^2} & \frac{\partial Q(x)}{\partial x_{i_k}} \\ \frac{\partial Q(x)}{\partial x_{i_1}} & \cdots & \frac{\partial Q(x)}{\partial x_{i_k}} & 0 \end{pmatrix}.$$

Similarly, $D_k(x)$ denotes the leading principal submatrix of order $k + 1$ of $D(x)$.

3. PRELIMINARY RESULTS

A criterion for pseudoconvex quadratic functions on arbitrary open convex subsets of R^n was derived in [2] (see Proposition 16). Based on a characterization in [9, Folgerung 4.6], it involves the principal minors of $D(x)$ and A. Specializing this result to quadratic forms on the positive orthant, we have:

LEMMA 1. *A quadratic form*

$$Q(x) = \frac{1}{2} x^T Ax$$

is pseudoconvex on R^n_{++} *if and only if for all* $x \in R^n_{++}$, $\gamma_k \in \Gamma_k$, *and* $k = 1,\dots,n$,

(i) $\det D_{\gamma_k}(x) \leq 0$ *and*

(ii) *if* $\det D_{\gamma_k}(x) = 0$ *then* $\det A_{\gamma_k} \geq 0$.

In addition to Lemma 1 we shall use the following result ([7], [9]):

LEMMA 2. *If*

$$Q(x) = \frac{1}{2} x^T Ax$$

is pseudoconvex on R^n_{++} *but not convex, then all entries of* A *are nonpositive; that is*, $A \leq 0$.

This essentially follows from the boundedness from above of nonconvex pseudoconvex quadratic functions [9]. Both Lemma 1 and Lemma 2 are derived from the same criterion on pseudoconvex quadratic functions ([9, Folgerung 4.6]). □

4. THEOREM

With the help of Lemma 1 and Lemma 2, we shall be able to prove the following criterion (for a different proof, see [3, Theorem 4.1, 4.2], in connection with [7, Theorem 5]).

THEOREM. Let $Q(x)$ be nonconvex on R^n. Then $Q(x)$ is pseudoconvex on R^n_{++} if and only if

$$A \leq 0 \tag{1}$$

and

$$\det A_{\gamma_k} \leq 0 \quad \text{for all} \quad \gamma_k \in \Gamma_k, \quad k = 1,\dots,n. \tag{2}$$

Proof. (a) Necessity. In view of Lemma 2, it remains to show that (2) holds. Suppose to the contrary that there exists a positive principal minor of A. For notational convenience, we may assume that this is a leading principal minor, that is, that

$$\det A_k > 0 \quad \text{for some} \quad k.$$

Let

$$x = \begin{pmatrix} x_k \\ 0 \end{pmatrix} \in R^n, \quad \text{where} \quad x_k \in R^k_{++}.$$

We have

$$\begin{aligned} \det D_k(x) &= \det \begin{pmatrix} A_k & A_k x_k \\ (A_k x_k)^T & 0 \end{pmatrix} = -\det \begin{pmatrix} A_k & 0 \\ (A_k x_k)^T & x_k^T A_k x_k \end{pmatrix} \\ &= -(x_k^T A_k x_k) \det A_k. \end{aligned} \tag{3}$$

Since $\det A_k > 0$, we see that $A_k \neq 0$. Hence $A_k \leq 0$ implies

$$x_k^T A_k x_k < 0$$

on R^k_{++}. Thus (3) yields $\det D_k(x) > 0$. Then there exists $\varepsilon \in R^{n-k}_{++}$ such that for

$$x_\varepsilon = \begin{pmatrix} x_k \\ \varepsilon \end{pmatrix} \in R^n_{++}$$

we have $\det D_k(x_\varepsilon) > 0$, contradicting (i) in Lemma 1.

(b) Sufficiency. We shall prove that (i) and (ii) in Lemma 1 hold. For notational convenience, we shall show this for leading principal minors

$$\det D_k(x) = \begin{pmatrix} A_k & (Ax)_k \\ (Ax)^T_k & 0 \end{pmatrix}.$$

Here $(Ax)_k$ denotes the vector formed by the first k components of Ax. Obviously,

$$\det D_1(x) = -(Ax)_1^2 \leq 0 \quad \text{on} \quad R^n_{++} ,$$

and if $\det D_1(x) = 0$ then $\det A_1 = a_{11} = 0$. It remains to verify (i) and (ii) in Lemma 1 for $k \geq 2$.

We partition A and $x \in R^n_{++}$ as follows:

$$A = \begin{pmatrix} A_k & B_k \\ B^T_k & C_k \end{pmatrix} \qquad x = \begin{pmatrix} x_k \\ y_k \end{pmatrix},$$

where $x_k \in R^k_{++}$, $y_k \in R^{n-k}_{++}$. Then we have

$$\det D_k(x) = \det \begin{pmatrix} A_k & A_k x_k + b_k y_k \\ (A_k x_k + B_k y_k)^T & 0 \end{pmatrix}$$

$$= \det \begin{pmatrix} A_k & A_k x_k + B_k y_k \\ (A_k x_k + B_k y_k)^T & x^T_k A_k x_k + 2x^T_k B_k y_k + y^T_k C_k y_k \end{pmatrix} - (x^T Ax) \det A_k$$

$$= \det \begin{pmatrix} A_k & B_k y_k \\ (B_k y_k)^T & y^T_k C_k y_k \end{pmatrix} - (x^T Ax) \det A_x .$$

Hence

$$(4) \qquad \det D_k(x) = \det N - (x^T Ax) \det A_k ,$$

where

(5) $$N = \begin{pmatrix} A_k & B_k y_k \\ (B_k y_k)^T & y_k^T C_k y_k \end{pmatrix} .$$

Because of (1), we have

$$x^T Ax \leq 0 \quad \text{on} \quad R^n_{++} .$$

Since $A \neq 0$ for the nonconvex function

$$Q(x) = \frac{1}{2} x^T Ax ,$$

we see that

(6) $$x^T Ax < 0 \quad \text{on} \quad R^n_{++} .$$

Hypothesis (2) then yields

(7) $$-(x^T Ax) \det A_k \leq 0 .$$

Hence, in view of (4), we have $\det D_k(x) \leq 0$ if

(8) $$\det N \leq 0 .$$

Thus (8) guarantees (i) in Lemma 1. Furthermore, the inequality in (8) is also sufficient for (ii) in Lemma 1 since $\det D_k(x) = 0$ implies $\det A_k = 0$, as seen from (6), (7), (8), and (4). Therefore, in order to finish the proof we have to verify (8).

If $A_k = 0$, then $\det N = 0$ since $k \geq 2$ is assumed. Suppose $A_k \neq 0$. Then there exists a nonzero principal minor in A_k. For notational convenience, we may assume that this is a leading principal minor denoted by $\det A_k^{11}$. We then partition A and N as follows:

(9) $$A = \begin{pmatrix} A_k^{11} & A_k^{12} & B_k^1 \\ (A_k^{12})^T & A_k^{22} & B_k^2 \\ (B_k^1)^T & (B_k^2)^T & C_k \end{pmatrix}, \qquad N = \begin{pmatrix} A_k^{11} & A_k^{12} & B_k^1 y_k \\ (A_k^{12})^T & A_k^{22} & B_k^2 y_k \\ (B_k^1 y_k)^T & (B_k^2 y_k)^T & y_k^T C_k y_k \end{pmatrix} .$$

The Schur complement S of A_k^{11} in A [5] is given by

(10) $$S = \begin{pmatrix} A_k^{22} & B_k^2 \\ (B_k^2)^T & C_k \end{pmatrix} - \begin{pmatrix} A_k^{12} \\ B_k^1 \end{pmatrix}^T (A_k^{11})^{-1}(A_k^{12}B_k^1) .$$

Schur's formula [5] yields

(11) $$\det S = \frac{\det A}{\det A_k^{11}} \geq 0 ,$$

because of (2).

In the same way, one can see that all principal minors of S are non-negative, considering the Schur complement of A_k^{11} in any principal submatrix of A that contains the rows and columns of A_k^{11}. Therefore S is positive semidefinite.

Then the Schur complement $\overline{S}$ of A_k^{11} in N is also positive semidefinite, since

$$\overline{S} = \begin{pmatrix} A_k^{22} & B_k^2 y_k \\ (B_k^2 y_k)^T & y_k^T C_k y_k \end{pmatrix} - \begin{pmatrix} A_k^{12} \\ B_k^1 y_k \end{pmatrix}^T (A_k^{11})^{-1}(A_k^{12}B_k^1 y_k)$$

$$= \begin{pmatrix} I & \underline{0} \\ 0 & y_k \end{pmatrix}^T S \begin{pmatrix} I & \underline{0} \\ 0 & y_k \end{pmatrix} .$$

Here I is the $\ell \times \ell$ identity matrix, 0 the $(n-k) \times \ell$ zero matrix, and $\underline{0}$ the zero column in R^ℓ, where ℓ denotes the dimension of A_k^{22}.

Positive semidefiniteness of $\overline{S}$ implies

$$\det \overline{S} \geq 0 .$$

Schur's formula then yields

$$\det N = \det A_k^{11} \cdot \det \overline{S} \leq 0 .$$

Hence (8) holds. □

5. DISCUSSION

The theorem shows that for (nonconvex) quadratic forms $Q(x)$ on the positive orthant, condition (ii) in Lemma 1 can be replaced by the stronger condition

$$\det D_{\gamma_k} = 0 \quad \text{implies} \quad \det A_{\gamma_k} = 0 .$$

According to the theorem, (nonconvex) pseudoconvex quadratic forms on R^n_{++} are characterized by nonpositive principal minors and a nonpositive matrix A. Apart from the latter condition, the criterion corresponds to the one for convex quadratic forms. These are characterized by nonnegative principal minors. We see that checking pseudoconvexity of a nonconvex quadratic form on R^n_{++} does not require more work than checking convexity.

An extension of the result in this paper to pseudoconvex quadratic functions and strictly pseudoconvex quadratic functions is in preparation [11].

The research for this paper was carried out at the Universities of Cologne and Bonn during the second author's visits there as recipient of the Senior U.S. Scientist Award from the Alexander von Humboldt-Stiftung (Bonn-Bad Godesberg, West Germany).

REFERENCES

1. K.J. Arrow and A.C. Enthoven, Quasi-concave programming, Econometrica 29 (1961), 779-800.

2. M. Avriel and S. Schaible, Second order characterizations of pseudoconvex functions, Mathematical Programming 14 (1978), 170-185.

3. R.W. Cottle and J.A. Ferland, Matrix-theoretic criteria for the quasi-convexity and pseudo-convexity of quadratic functions, Linear Algebra and its Applications 5 (1972), 123-136.

4. W. Eichhorn, Theorie der homogenen Produktionsfunktion, Springer Verlag, Berlin, Heidelberg, New York, 1970.

5. F.R. Gantmacher, The Theory of Matrices, Vol. I, Chelsea Publishing Company, New York, 1959.

6. O.L. Mangasarian, Pseudoconvex functions, J. SIAM Control. 3 (1965), 281-290.

7. B. Martos, Subdefinite matrices and quadratic forms, SIAM J. Appl. Math. 17 (1969), 1215-1223.

8. B. Martos, Nonlinear Programming, Theory and Methods, Amsterdam, 1975.

9. S. Schaible, Beiträge zur quasi-konvexen Programmierung, Dissertation, Köln, 1971.

10. S. Schaible, Second order characterizations of pseudoconvex quadratic functions, J. of Optimization Theory and Applications 21 (1977), 15-26.

11. S. Schaible, Quasiconvex, pseudoconvex, and strictly pseudoconvex quadratic functions, to appear.

SOME INEQUALITIES FOR POSITIVE DEFINITE MATRICES

Richard Bellman
Departments of Mathematics, Electrical Engineering, and Medicine
University of Southern California
Los Angeles, California 90007
U.S.A.

ABSTRACT. The purpose of this paper is to present some inequalities for positive definite matrices.

1. INTRODUCTION.

In Section 2 we give a matrix analogue of the Cauchy-Schwarz inequality, in Section 3 we present an inequality for traces, and in Section 4 we ask some open questions which are suggested by these results.

All the matrices that appear below are assumed to be positive definite. The elementary results that we use in deriving them will be found, for example, in [1].

2. AN ANALOGUE OF THE CAUCHY-SCHWARZ INEQUALITY

We start with the matrix identity

$$(A - B)^2 = A^2 + B^2 - AB - BA \ . \tag{1}$$

We now take the trace of both sides. We use the fact that the characteristic roots of the square of a positive definite matrix are the squares of the characteristic roots of the given matrix, together with the commutativity of the trace. In this way, we obtain the inequality

$$2 \ \mathrm{tr}(AB) \leq \mathrm{tr}(A^2) + \mathrm{tr}(B^2) \ . \tag{2}$$

Equality holds if and only if A and B are equal.

To obtain a multiplicative form, we replace A by $A/[\mathrm{tr}(A^2)]^{1/2}$ and B by the corresponding expression. Thus we obtain the desired analogue of the Cauchy-Schwarz inequality:

$$\mathrm{tr}(AB) \leq [\mathrm{tr}(A^2)]^{1/2} \ [\mathrm{tr}(B^2)]^{1/2} \ . \tag{3}$$

Equality holds if and only if B is a scalar multiple of A.

3. AN INEQUALITY FOR TRACES

We begin now with the identity

(1) $$(AB - BA)^2 = (AB)^2 + (BA)^2 - AB^2A - BA^2B .$$

We now observe that $AB - BA$ is a skew-symmetric matrix. This means that its characteristic roots are pure imaginary. Using this fact and the commutativity of the trace repeatedly, we obtain the result

(2) $$[\mathrm{tr}(AB)]^2 \leq \mathrm{tr}(A^2B^2) .$$

Equality holds if and only if A and B commute.

4. OPEN QUESTIONS

The inequalities above suggest several questions:

1. Is there a matrix analogue of the arithmetic mean-geometric mean inequality?

2. Does the result for traces hold for higher powers?

REFERENCE

1. R. Bellman, Introduction to Matrix Analysis, McGraw-Hill Book Company, New York, 1960; 2nd Edition, 1970.

INEQUALITIES CONNECTING EIGENVALUES AND NONPRINCIPAL SUBDETERMINANTS

Marvin Marcus
Institute for the Interdisciplinary Applications of Algebra and Combinatorics
University of California
Santa Barbara, California 93106
U.S.A.

Ivan Filippenko
Institute for the Interdisciplinary Applications of Algebra and Combinatorics
University of California
Santa Barbara, California 93106
U.S.A.

ABSTRACT. The nonprincipal subdeterminants of a normal matrix satisfy certain quadratic identities. In this paper, these identities are used to obtain upper bounds on such subdeterminants in terms of elementary symmetric functions of the moduli of the eigenvalues. The same analysis yields lower bounds on the spread of a normal matrix and on the Hilbert norm of an arbitrary matrix.

1. STATEMENT OF RESULTS

Let $\lambda_1,\ldots,\lambda_n$ be n complex numbers. The totality of n-square normal matrices with these numbers as eigenvalues is the set of all matrices A of the form

$$A = U^* DU , \tag{1}$$

where U is unitary and $D = \operatorname{diag}(\lambda_1,\ldots,\lambda_n)$. It is well known [1, p. 237] that for a fixed integer m, $1 \leq m \leq n$, the totality $W_m(\lambda)$ of m-square principal subdeterminants of all A defined by (1) is a region in the plane contained in the convex polygon

$$P_m(\lambda) = \mathcal{H}\{\lambda_{\omega(1)} \cdots \lambda_{\omega(m)}, \quad \omega \in Q_{m,n}\} . \tag{2}$$

The notation in (2) is this: $Q_{m,n}$ is the set of all $\binom{n}{m}$ integer sequences ω having domain $\{1,\ldots,m\}$ and range contained in $\{1,\ldots,n\}$, and satisfying $\omega(1) < \omega(2) < \cdots < \omega(m)$; $\mathcal{H}$ denotes the convex hull of the indicated products. Thus

The work of the first author was supported by the Air Force Office of Scientific Research under Grant AFOSR 4962078-C-0030.

$$W_m(\lambda) \subset P_m(\lambda) , \tag{3}$$

or in words, if A is a normal matrix with eigenvalues $\lambda_1,\ldots,\lambda_n$ then any m-square principal subdeterminant of A lies in the polygon $P_m(\lambda)$. It is also known that in contrast to the case $m = 1$ when $W_1(\lambda)$ is the numerical range of any A, it is not generally the case for $1 < m < n - 1$ that $W_m(\lambda)$ is a convex set [4].

The situation for m-square nonprincipal subdeterminants is remarkably different. To fix the notation, let k,m be fixed integers, $1 \leq k < m < n$, and let $W_{k,m}(\lambda)$ denote the totality of m-square subdeterminants of the matrices A in (1) which have precisely k main-diagonal elements in common with A. More precisely,

$$W_{k,m}(\lambda) = \{\det A[\alpha|\beta] : \alpha,\beta \in Q_{m,n}, \ |\operatorname{im}\alpha \cap \operatorname{im}\beta| = k, \ A \text{ defined by (1)}\} , \tag{4}$$

where $\operatorname{im}\alpha$ is the range of α and $A[\alpha|\beta]$ is the m-square submatrix of A lying in rows $\alpha(1),\ldots,\alpha(m)$ and columns $\beta(1),\ldots,\beta(m)$ of A. A slight modification of an argument found in [3, p. 220] shows that $W_{k,m}(\lambda)$ <u>is a closed circular disc centered at the origin</u>. Let $r_{k,m}(\lambda)$ denote the radius of this disc. Also let

$$E_m(|\lambda|) = E_m(|\lambda_1|,\ldots,|\lambda_n|)$$

denote the m-th elementary symmetric polynomial in $|\lambda_1|,\ldots,|\lambda_n|$, i.e.,

$$E_m(|\lambda|) = \sum_{\omega\in Q_{m,n}} \prod_{i=1}^{m} |\lambda_{\omega(i)}| .$$

The following is the main result of this paper.

THEOREM 1. *If* $n \geq 4$, $m \geq 2$, *and* $k \leq m - 2$, *then*

$$E_m(|\lambda|) \geq \begin{cases} 2(m - k + 1)r_{k,m}(\lambda) & \text{if } k < m - 2 , \\ 4r_{k,m}(\lambda) & \text{if } k = m - 2 . \end{cases} \tag{5}$$

In words, let A be a normal matrix with eigenvalues $\lambda_1,\ldots,\lambda_n$, $n \geq 4$. Let B be an m-square submatrix of A having precisely k main-diagonal entries lying on the main diagonal of A. If $k \leq m - 2$, then

$$(6) \qquad |\det B| \le \begin{cases} \dfrac{E_m(|\lambda|)}{2(m - k + 1)} & \text{if} \quad k < m - 2 , \\ \dfrac{E_m(|\lambda|)}{4} & \text{if} \quad k = m - 2 . \end{cases}$$

Recall that the <u>spread</u> of A [5, 6] is the number

$$s(A) = \max_{i,j} |\lambda_i - \lambda_j| .$$

We have the following result.

COROLLARY 1. *If* $2 < m < n$ *and the* m*-square submatrix* B *of* A *has no main-diagonal elements lying on the main diagonal of* A, *then*

$$(7) \qquad s(A) \ge \max \begin{cases} \sqrt{3}\left(2(m + 1)\binom{n}{m}^{-1}\right)^{1/m} |\det B|^{1/m} , \\ 2\sqrt{6}\,(n(n - 1))^{-1/2} |\det B|^{1/2} . \end{cases}$$

In the following corollary, A is an arbitrary n-square matrix $(n \ge 2)$. Let d_m be the greatest m-square subdeterminant of A (in absolute value), and let $\|A\|$ be the Hilbert norm of A, i.e., the greatest singular value of A.

COROLLARY 2. *If* $2 < m \le n$, *then*

$$\|A\| \ge \max \begin{cases} \left(2(m + 1)\binom{2n}{m}^{-1}\right)^{1/m} d_m^{1/m} , \\ 2(n(2n - 1))^{-1/2} d_2^{1/2} . \end{cases}$$

The remainder of the paper is divided into two sections. In Section 2, a combinatorial lemma about sets of sequences is established to be used later in analyzing some consequences of the quadratic Plücker relations for subdeterminants. In Section 3, the proofs of the above results are given.

2. A COMBINATORIAL LEMMA

Let $\Gamma_{m,n}$ denote the set of all n^m integer sequences with domain

$\{1,\ldots,m\}$ and range $\{1,\ldots,n\}$. Let $\alpha,\beta \in Q_{m,n}$ $(1 \le m \le n)$, and let $s,t \in \{1,\ldots,m\}$. Define $\alpha[s,t:\beta]$ to be the sequence in $\Gamma_{m,n}$ obtained from α by replacing $\alpha(s)$ with $\beta(t)$:

$$\alpha[s,t:\beta] = (\alpha(1),\ldots,\alpha(s-1),\beta(t),\alpha(s+1),\ldots,\alpha(m)) .$$

Similarly, $\beta[t,s:\alpha]$ denotes the sequence in $\Gamma_{m,n}$ obtained from β by replacing $\beta(t)$ with $\alpha(s)$:

$$\beta[t,s:\alpha] = (\beta(1),\ldots,\beta(t-1),\alpha(s),\beta(t+1),\ldots,\beta(m)) .$$

As s and t vary over the set $\{1,\ldots,m\}$, they give rise to the following two lists of sequences in $\Gamma_{m,n}$:

$$\begin{array}{lcc}
 & \underline{\alpha[s,t:\beta]\ \text{list}} & \underline{\beta[t,s:\alpha]\ \text{list}} \\
\text{Block } s=1 & \left\{\begin{array}{c}\alpha[1,1:\beta]\\ \vdots \\ \alpha[1,m:\beta]\end{array}\right. & \left.\begin{array}{c}\beta[1,1:\alpha]\\ \vdots \\ \beta[m,1:\alpha]\end{array}\right\} \\
 & \vdots & \vdots \\
\text{General Block } s & \left\{\begin{array}{c}\alpha[s,1:\beta]\\ \vdots \\ \alpha[s,m:\beta]\end{array}\right. & \left.\begin{array}{c}\beta[1,s:\alpha]\\ \vdots \\ \beta[m,s:\alpha]\end{array}\right\} \\
 & \vdots & \vdots \\
\text{Block } s=m & \left\{\begin{array}{c}\alpha[m,1:\beta]\\ \vdots \\ \alpha[m,m:\beta]\end{array}\right. & \left.\begin{array}{c}\beta[1,m:\alpha]\\ \vdots \\ \beta[m,m:\alpha]\end{array}\right\}
\end{array}$$

We shall refer to this array of sequences as "the twin lists." As indicated, the twin lists are arranged in m "blocks" (corresponding to $s = 1,\ldots,m$); each block has two columns (corresponding to α and β), each of which consists of m sequences (corresponding to $t = 1,\ldots,m$).

If $\gamma \in \Gamma_{m,n}$, we shall say that γ <u>appears in the twin lists</u> if the sequence $\gamma\sigma$ appears in the array for some permutation $\sigma \in S_m$.

LEMMA. *Suppose* $2 \le m < n$, *and consider the sequences*

$$\alpha = (1,2,\ldots,m) \in Q_{m,n}$$

and

$$\beta = (1,\ldots,k,m+1,\ldots,2m-k) \in Q_{m,n} ,$$

where $0 \le k \le m - 1$.

(i) *If* $k = m - 1$, *then* α *and* β *appear in every block in the twin lists for* α *and* β.

(ii) *If* $k \le m - 2$, *then*

(a) *in each of blocks* $s = 1,\ldots,k$ *in the twin lists, both* α *and* β *appear;*

(b) *in each of blocks* $s = k+1,\ldots,m$ *in the twin lists, neither* α *nor* β *appears in rows* $k+1,\ldots,m$;

(c) *in each of blocks* $s = k+1,\ldots,m$ *in the twin lists, each of the first* k *sequences on the left involves repeated integers;*

(d) *in the totality of rows* $k+1,\ldots,m$ *in blocks* $s = k+1,\ldots,m$ *in the twin lists, no sequence appears more than once if* $k < m - 2$, *and the sequences which appear do so exactly twice if* $k = m - 2$.

Proof. As an introduction, let us write out the general block in the twin lists for α and β:

$$\begin{array}{ccc}
 & \alpha[s,t:\beta] & \beta[t,s:\alpha] \\
 & (1,\ldots,s-1,1,s+1,\ldots,m) & (s,2,\ldots,k,m+1,\ldots,2m-k) \\
 & (1,\ldots,s-1,2,s+1,\ldots,m) & (1,s,\ldots,k,m+1,\ldots,2m-k) \\
 & \vdots & \vdots \\
\text{Block } s & (1,\ldots,s-1,k,s+1,\ldots,m) & (1,2,\ldots,s,m+1,\ldots,2m-k) \\
(1 \le s \le m) & (1,\ldots,s-1,m+1,s+1,\ldots,m) & (1,2,\ldots,k,s,\ldots,2m-k) \\
 & \vdots & \vdots \\
 & (1,\ldots,s-1,2m-k,s+1,\ldots,m) & (1,2,\ldots,k,m+1,\ldots,s)
\end{array}$$

(i) Suppose $k = m - 1$. Observe that if $s \le m - 1$, then block s in the twin lists for α and β has the form:

$$\begin{array}{ll}
(1,\ldots,s-1,1,s+1,\ldots,m) & (s,2,\ldots,m-1,m+1) \\
\vdots & \vdots \\
(1,\ldots,s-1,s,s+1,\ldots,m) & (1,2,\ldots,s,\ldots,m-1,m+1) \\
\vdots & \vdots \\
(1,\ldots,s-1,m-1,s+1,\ldots,m) & (1,2,\ldots,s,m+1) \\
(1,\ldots,s-1,m+1,s+1,\ldots,m) & (1,2,\ldots,m-1,s) \;.
\end{array}$$

(Notice that since $k = m - 1$, we have $\beta = (1,\ldots,m-1,m+1)$.) Thus α appears as the s-th sequence on the left, and β appears as the s-th sequence on the right. Now block $s = m$ in the twin lists for α and β has the form:

$$\begin{array}{ll}
(1,\ldots,m-1,1) & (m,2,\ldots,m-1,m+1) \\
(1,\ldots,m-1,2) & (1,m,\ldots,m-1,m+1) \\
\vdots & \vdots \\
(1,\ldots,m-1,m-1) & (1,2,\ldots,m,m+1) \\
(1,\ldots,m-1,m+1) & (1,2,\ldots,m-1,m) \;,
\end{array}$$

and we see that α appears as the m-th sequence on the right, while β appears as the m-th sequence on the left. This establishes (i).

(ii) Suppose $k \leq m - 2$.

(a) If $s \in \{1,\ldots,k\}$, an inspection of block s in the twin lists immediately shows that α appears as the s-th sequence on the left, and β appears as the s-th sequence on the right.

(b) Let $s \in \{k+1,\ldots,m\}$. Then block s in the twin lists for α and β has the form:

$$\begin{array}{lll}
 & \text{position } s & \\
 & \downarrow & \\
 & (1,\ldots,k,\ldots,1,\ldots,m) & (s,\ldots,k,m+1,\ldots,2m-k) \\
 & \vdots & \vdots \\
 & (1,\ldots,k,\ldots,k,\ldots,m) & (1,\ldots,s,m+1,\ldots,2m-k) \\
(8) & & \\
\text{rows} & \left\{\begin{array}{l}(1,\ldots,k,\ldots,m+1,\ldots,m) \\ (1,\ldots,k,\ldots,m+2,\ldots,m) \\ \vdots \\ (1,\ldots,k,\ldots,2m-k,\ldots,m)\end{array}\right. & \begin{array}{l}(1,\ldots,k,s,m+2,\ldots,2m-k) \\ (1,\ldots,k,m+1,s,\ldots,2m-k) \\ \vdots \\ (1,\ldots,k,m+1,\ldots,s) \;.\end{array} \\
k+1,\ldots,m & &
\end{array}$$

Observe that each sequence in rows $k+1,\dots,m$ in block s involves integers greater than m. Thus α does not appear in rows $k+1,\dots,m$ in block s. Next, the $(k+1)$-st sequence on the right in block s does not involve $m+1$,. the $(k+2)$-nd sequence does not involve $m+2$, and so on until finally the m-th sequence does not involve $2m-k$. Thus β does not appear on the right in rows $k+1,\dots,m$ in block s. Now if $s \le m-1$, then every sequence on the left in rows $k+1,\dots,m$ in block s involves m, and hence β does not appear on the left in these rows. If $s = m$, then rows $k+1,\dots,m$ in block s have left-hand side of the form

$$\begin{gathered}(1,\dots,k,k+1,\dots,m-1,m+1)\\(1,\dots,k,k+1,\dots,m-1,m+2)\\\vdots\\(1,\dots,k,k+1,\dots,m-1,2m-k)\ ,\end{gathered}$$

and each of these sequences involves $k+1$. But β does not involve $k+1$ since $k \le m-2$, so again β does not appear on the left in rows $k+1,\dots,m$ in block s. This completes the proof of (b).

(c) It is clear from the array (8) in the proof of (b) that if $s \in \{k+1,\dots,m\}$, then each of the first k sequences on the left in block s involves repeated integers.

(d) Let us examine the array (8) in the proof of (b) both for a fixed s and for different values of $s \in \{k+1,\dots,m\}$.

First, it is obvious that for a fixed $s \in \{k+1,\dots,m\}$, the sequences on the left in block s are all distinct, as are the sequences on the right.

Next, let $s,s' \in \{k+1,\dots,m\}$, $s \ne s'$, and observe that s does not occur in any sequence on the left in block s, whereas s does occur in every sequence on the left in block s'. Thus no sequence on the left in block s' appears on the left in block s. It follows from the preceding paragraph that in the totality of blocks $s = k+1,\dots,m$ in the twin lists, no sequence appears more than once on the left.

Again, let $s,s' \in \{k+1,\dots,m\}$, $s \ne s'$, and observe that s occurs in every sequence on the right in block s, whereas s does not occur in any sequence on the right in block s'. Thus no sequence on the right in block s' appears on the right in block s. As before, it follows that in the totality of blocks $s = k+1,\dots,m$ in the twin lists, no sequence appears more than once on the right.

If $s \in \{k+1,\ldots,m-1\}$, then each sequence on the left in block s involves m and hence does not appear on the right in block s' for any $s' \in \{k+1,\ldots,m-1\}$. Also, each sequence on the right in block $s = m$ involves m and hence does not appear on the left in block m.

Now suppose $k < m - 2$. We wish to show that in the totality of rows $k+1,\ldots,m$ in blocks $s = k+1,\ldots,m$ in the twin lists, no sequence appears more than once. By the above observations, we need verify only that no sequence on the left in rows $k+1,\ldots,m$ in blocks $s = k+1,\ldots,m-1$ appears on the right in rows $k+1,\ldots,m$ in block m, and that no sequence on the left in rows $k+1,\ldots,m$ in block m appears on the right in rows $k+1,\ldots,m$ in blocks $s = k+1,\ldots,m-1$. We reproduce the twin lists for α and β, omitting blocks $1,\ldots,k$ and rows $1,\ldots,k$ in each of the blocks $s = k+1,\ldots,m$:

$$\begin{array}{l} \text{Block } s, \\ k+1 \le s \le m-2; \\ t = k+1,\ldots,m \end{array} \quad \left\{ \begin{array}{ll} (1,\ldots,k,\ldots,m+1,\ldots,m-1,m) & (1,\ldots,k,s,m+2,\ldots,2m-k) \\ \vdots & \vdots \\ (1,\ldots,k,\ldots,2m-k,\ldots,m-1,m) & (1,\ldots,k,m+1,m+2,\ldots,s) \end{array} \right.$$

$$\begin{array}{l} \text{Block } s = m-1; \\ t = k+1,\ldots,m \end{array} \quad \left\{ \begin{array}{ll} (1,\ldots,k,\ldots,m-2,m+1,m) & (1,\ldots,k,m-1,m+2,\ldots,2m-k) \\ \vdots & \vdots \\ (1,\ldots,k,\ldots,m-2,2m-k,m) & (1,\ldots,k,m+1,m+2,\ldots,m-1) \end{array} \right.$$

$$\begin{array}{l} \text{Block } s = m; \\ t = k+1,\ldots,m \end{array} \quad \left\{ \begin{array}{ll} (1,\ldots,k,\ldots,m-2,m-1,m+1) & (1,\ldots,k,m,m+2,\ldots,2m-k) \\ \vdots & \vdots \\ (1,\ldots,k,\ldots,m-2,m-1,2m-k) & (1,\ldots,k,m+1,m+2,\ldots,m) . \end{array} \right.$$

Inspection of this array shows that each sequence on the left in rows $k+1,\ldots,m$ in blocks $s = k+1,\ldots,m-2$ involves $m - 1$ and hence does not appear on the right in block m; each sequence on the left in rows $k+1,\ldots,m$ in block $m - 1$ involves $m - 2$ and hence does not appear on the right in block m (since $k < m - 2$); each sequence on the left in rows $k+1,\ldots,m$ in block m involves $m - 1$ and hence does not appear on the right in rows $k+1,\ldots,m$ in blocks $s = k+1,\ldots,m-2$; each sequence on the left in rows $k+1,\ldots,m$ in block m involves $m - 2$ and hence does not appear on the right in rows $k+1,\ldots,m$ in block $m - 1$. This completes the required verification and establishes the assertion in (d) for the case $k < m - 2$.

Finally, suppose $k = m - 2$. Then if we consider the totality of rows $m-1\ (=k+1), m$ in blocks $s = m-1, m$ in the twin lists for α and β,

$$\begin{array}{lll} \text{Block } s = m-1; & \left\{\begin{array}{l}(1,\dots,m-2,m+1,m) \\ (1,\dots,m-2,m+2,m)\end{array}\right. & \begin{array}{l}(1,\dots,m-2,m-1,m+2) \\ (1,\dots,m-2,m+1,m-1)\end{array} \\ t = m-1,m & & \end{array}$$

$$\begin{array}{lll} \text{Block } s = m & \left\{\begin{array}{l}(1,\dots,m-2,m-1,m+1) \\ (1,\dots,m-2,m-1,m+2)\end{array}\right. & \begin{array}{l}(1,\dots,m-2,m,m+2) \\ (1,\dots,m-2,m+1,m)\ ,\end{array} \\ t = m-1,m & & \end{array}$$

we see immediately that every sequence which appears does so exactly twice. This establishes the assertion in (d) for the case $k = m - 2$. □

3. PROOFS

Proof of Theorem 1. We shall prove the equivalent statement that if $U \in U_n(\mathbb{C})$ is any unitary matrix, then

$$|\det(U^*AU)[\alpha|\beta]| \le \begin{cases} \dfrac{E_m(|\lambda_1|,\dots,|\lambda_n|)}{2(m-k+1)} & \text{if} \quad k < m-2\ , \\ \dfrac{1}{4} E_m(|\lambda_1|,\dots,|\lambda_n|) & \text{if} \quad k = m-2\ . \end{cases}$$

We begin by making the following two reductions. First, we may assume that A is diagonal,

$$A = \operatorname{diag}(\lambda_1,\dots,\lambda_n)\ .$$

Second, by effecting an appropriate permutation similarity transformation on the matrix U^*AU, we may assume

$$\alpha = (1,2,\dots,m) \quad \text{and} \quad \beta = (1,\dots,k,m+1,\dots,2m-k)\ .$$

Fix a matrix $U \in U_n(\mathbb{C})$, and let

$$\Delta = |\det(U^*AU)[\alpha|\beta]| = |C_m(U^*AU)_{\alpha,\beta}|\ ,$$

where $C_m(X)$ is the m-th compound matrix [1, p. 127]. For each $\nu \in Q_{m,n}$, let

$$p_\nu(\gamma)^\cdot = \det U[\nu|\gamma] \qquad \gamma \in \Gamma_{m,n} .$$

We have

$$\begin{aligned} C_m(U^*AU)_{\alpha,\beta} &= \sum_{\nu,\mu\in Q_{m,n}} C_m(U^*)_{\alpha,\nu}\, C_m(A)_{\nu,\mu}\, C_m(U)_{\mu,\beta} \\ &= \sum_{\nu\in Q_{m,n}} \overline{\det U[\nu|\alpha]}\,\det A[\nu|\nu]\,\det U[\nu|\beta] \\ &= \sum_{\nu\in Q_{m,n}} \overline{p_\nu(\alpha)}\,\lambda_\nu p_\nu(\beta) , \end{aligned}$$

where $\lambda_\nu = \lambda_{\nu(1)} \cdots \lambda_{\nu(m)}$. Therefore,

(9) $$\Delta \le \sum_{\nu\in Q_{m,n}} |\lambda_\nu||p_\nu(\alpha)||p_\nu(\beta)| .$$

Now the quadratic Plücker relations [2, p. 10] imply that for each $\nu \in Q_{m,n}$ and any $s \in \{1,\dots,m\}$,

(10) $$p_\nu(\alpha)p_\nu(\beta) = \sum_{t=1}^{m} p_\nu(\alpha[s,t:\beta])\; p_\nu(\beta[t,s:\alpha]) .$$

Taking absolute values in (10), applying the triangle inequality, and summing both sides on $s = k+1,\dots,m$, we obtain, for each $\nu \in Q_{m,n}$,

(11) $$|p_\nu(\alpha)||p_\nu(\beta)| \le \frac{1}{m-k} \sum_{s=k+1}^{m} \sum_{t=1}^{m} |p_\nu(\alpha[s,t:\beta])||p_\nu(\beta[t,s:\alpha])| .$$

Combining (9) and (11) yields

$$\Delta \le \frac{1}{m-k} \sum_{\nu\in Q_{m,n}} |\lambda_\nu| \left\{ \sum_{s=k+1}^{m} \sum_{t=1}^{m} |p_\nu(\alpha[s,t:\beta])||p_\nu(\beta[t,s:\alpha])| \right\},$$

and it follows from part (ii)(c) of the lemma in Section 2 and the arithmetic-geometric mean inequality that

(12) $$\begin{aligned} \Delta &\le \frac{1}{m-k} \sum_{\nu\in Q_{m,n}} |\lambda_\nu| \left\{ \sum_{s=k+1}^{m} \sum_{t=k+1}^{m} |p_\nu(\alpha[s,t:\beta])||p_\nu(\beta[t,s:\alpha])| \right\} \\ &\le \frac{1}{2(m-k)} \sum_{\nu\in Q_{m,n}} |\lambda_\nu| \left\{ \sum_{s=k+1}^{m} \sum_{t=k+1}^{m} |p_\nu(\alpha[s,t:\beta])|^2 + |p_\nu(\beta[t,s:\alpha])|^2 \right\}. \end{aligned}$$

Let us denote the double summation inside the brackets in the second inequality in (12) by $\{\Sigma_{s,t}\}$.

Since U is a unitary matrix, so is the m-th compound $C_m(U)$. Hence for each $\nu \in Q_{m,n}$, the sum of the squares of the moduli of the elements $p_\nu(\omega)$, $\omega \in Q_{m,n}$, in row ν of $C_m(U)$ is 1. It follows from parts (ii) (b), (d) of the lemma that

$$(13) \qquad \left\{\sum_{s,t}\right\} + |p_\nu(\alpha)|^2 + |p_\nu(\beta)|^2 \leq 1 \qquad \text{if} \quad k < m - 2 ,$$

$$(14) \qquad \frac{1}{2}\left\{\sum_{s,t}\right\} + |p_\nu(\alpha)|^2 + |p_\nu(\beta)|^2 \leq 1 \qquad \text{if} \quad k = m - 2 .$$

The remainder of the argument consists of a calculation performed in two cases.

Case **I**: $k < m - 2$. From (12) and (13) we conclude that

$$\begin{aligned}
\Delta &\leq \frac{1}{2(m-k)} \sum_{\nu\in Q_{m,n}} |\lambda_\nu|(1 - (|p_\nu(\alpha)|^2 + |p_\nu(\beta)|^2)) \\
&= \frac{1}{2(m-k)} \left[\sum_{\nu\in Q_{m,n}} |\lambda_\nu| - \sum_{\nu\in Q_{m,n}} |\lambda_\nu|(|p_\nu(\alpha)|^2 + |p_\nu(\beta)|^2)\right] \\
&\leq \frac{1}{2(m-k)} \left[\sum_{\nu\in Q_{m,n}} |\lambda_\nu| - 2 \sum_{\nu\in Q_{m,n}} |\lambda_\nu||p_\nu(\alpha)||p_\nu(\beta)|\right] \\
&\leq \frac{1}{2(m-k)} \sum_{\nu\in Q_{m,n}} |\lambda_\nu| - \frac{\Delta}{m-k} \qquad \text{(by (9))} .
\end{aligned}$$

Therefore

$$\Delta + \frac{\Delta}{m-k} \leq \frac{1}{2(m-k)} \sum_{\nu\in Q_{m,n}} |\lambda_\nu| ,$$

so that

$$\Delta \leq \frac{1}{2(m-k+1)} \sum_{\nu\in Q_{m,n}} |\lambda_\nu| = \frac{E_m(|\lambda_1|,\ldots,|\lambda_n|)}{2(m-k+1)} .$$

Case II: $k = m - 2$. From (12) (with $k = m - 2$) and (14) we conclude that

$$\begin{aligned}
\Delta &\leq \frac{1}{4} \sum_{\nu\in Q_{m,n}} |\lambda_\nu|\, 2(1 - (|p_\nu(\alpha)|^2 + |p_\nu(\beta)|^2)) \\
&= \frac{1}{2} \left[\sum_{\nu\in Q_{m,n}} |\lambda_\nu| - \sum_{\nu\in Q_{m,n}} |\lambda_\nu|(|p_\nu(\alpha)|^2 + |p_\nu(\beta)|^2)\right] \\
&\leq \frac{1}{2} \left[\sum_{\nu\in Q_{m,n}} |\lambda_\nu| - 2 \sum_{\nu\in Q_{m,n}} |\lambda_\nu||p_\nu(\alpha)||p_\nu(\beta)|\right]
\end{aligned}$$

$$\leq \frac{1}{2} \sum_{\nu \in Q_{m,n}} |\lambda_\nu| - \Delta \qquad \text{(by (9))} .$$

Therefore

$$2\Delta \leq \frac{1}{2} \sum_{\nu \in Q_{m,n}} |\lambda_\nu| ,$$

so that

$$\Delta \leq \frac{1}{4} \sum_{\nu \in Q_{m,n}} |\lambda_\nu| = \frac{1}{4} E_m(|\lambda_1|,\ldots,|\lambda_n|) .$$

Since $\Delta = |\det(U^*AU)[\alpha|\beta]|$, this completes the proof of the theorem. □

Proof of Corollary 1. Assume first that $2 < m < n$, and let $\alpha,\beta \in Q_{m,n}$ be sequences such that

$$\text{im } \alpha \cap \text{im } \beta = \emptyset, \qquad \text{so that} \qquad B = A[\alpha|\beta] .$$

For any $t \in \mathbf{C}$, $A - tI_n \in M_n(\mathbf{C})$ is a normal matrix with eigenvalues $\lambda_1 - t,\ldots,\lambda_n - t$, and since $\text{im } \alpha \cap \text{im } \beta = \emptyset$ we have

$$(A - tI_n)[\alpha|\beta] = A[\alpha|\beta] .$$

It follows by Theorem 1 that

$$|\det A[\alpha|\beta]| = |\det(A - tI_n)[\alpha|\beta]|$$
$$\leq \frac{E_m(|\lambda_1 - t|,\ldots,|\lambda_n - t|)}{2(m+1)} \leq \frac{\binom{n}{m}\left(\max_{1\leq i\leq n} |\lambda_i - t|\right)^m}{2(m+1)} .$$

Since this is true for each $t \in \mathbf{C}$, we have

$$(15) \qquad |\det A[\alpha|\beta]| \leq \frac{\binom{n}{m}\left(\min_{t\in\mathbf{C}} \max_{1\leq i\leq n} |\lambda_i - t|\right)^m}{2(m+1)} .$$

Now it is known [5] that any n points $\lambda_1,\ldots,\lambda_n$ in $\mathbf{C}$ are contained in a disc of radius

$$\frac{\max_{1\leq i,\, j\leq n} |\lambda_i - \lambda_j|}{\sqrt{3}} = \frac{s(A)}{\sqrt{3}} .$$

If t_0 is the center of this disk, then certainly

$$\max_{1\le i\le n} |\lambda_i - t_0| \le \frac{s(A)}{\sqrt{3}} ,$$

and hence

$$\min_{t\in \mathbf{C}} \max_{1\le i\le n} |\lambda_i - t| \le \frac{s(A)}{\sqrt{3}} . \tag{16}$$

The inequalities (15) and (16) together imply that

$$|\det A[\alpha|\beta]| \le \frac{\binom{n}{m}\left(\frac{s(A)}{\sqrt{3}}\right)^m}{2(m + 1)} ,$$

whence

$$s(A) \ge \sqrt{3}\left(\frac{2(m + 1)}{\binom{n}{m}}\right)^{1/m} |\det A[\alpha|\beta]|^{1/m} .$$

Since the sequences $\alpha,\beta \in Q_{m,n}$ were arbitrarily chosen subject to the condition $\operatorname{im}\alpha \cap \operatorname{im}\beta = \emptyset$, we conclude that

$$s(A) \ge \sqrt{3}\left[\frac{2(m + 1)}{\binom{n}{m}}\right]^{1/m} \max_{\substack{\alpha,\beta\in Q_{m,n}\\ \operatorname{im}\alpha\cap\operatorname{im}\beta=\emptyset}} |\det A[\alpha|\beta]|^{1/m}$$

whenever $2 < m < n$, and the inequality for the first expression on the right in (7) is established.

The proof of the inequality for the second expression on the right in (7) is virtually identical, the sole modification being that the application of Theorem 1 involves the case $m = 2$ rather than $m > 2$; this has the effect of replacing the constant $2(m + 1)$ by 4 throughout. □

Note that if A is hermitian (or skew hermitian), it is clear that

$$\min_{t\in \mathbf{C}} \max_{1\le i\le n} |\lambda_i - t| = \frac{s(A)}{2} . \tag{17}$$

Using (17) in place of (16) in the proofs of (7), we obtain the following specialization of Corollary 1.

_If_ A _is hermitian or skew hermitian and the_ m-_square submatrix_ B _of_ A _has no main-diagonal elements lying on the main diagonal of_ A, _then_

$$s(A) \ge 2\left(2(m + 1)\binom{n}{m}^{-1}\right)^{1/m} |\det B|^{1/m}, \quad 2 < m < n , \tag{18}$$

and

(19) $$s(A) \geq 4\sqrt{2}\,(n(n-1))^{-1/2}\,|\det B|^{1/2}.$$

Proof of Corollary 2. The matrix

$$\tilde{A} = \begin{bmatrix} 0 & A \\ A^* & 0 \end{bmatrix} \in M_{2n}(\mathbf{C})$$

is hermitian with eigenvalues $\pm\alpha_1, \ldots, \pm\alpha_n$, where

$$\alpha_1 = \|A\| \geq \alpha_2 \geq \cdots \geq \alpha_n \geq 0$$

are the singular values of A. Applying the inequality (18) to $\tilde{A}$, we see that if $2 < m \leq n$ then

$$s(\tilde{A}) \geq 2\left[\frac{2(m+1)}{\binom{2n}{m}}\right]^{1/m} \max_{\substack{\gamma,\omega \in Q_{m,2n} \\ \operatorname{im}\gamma \cap \operatorname{im}\omega = \emptyset}} |\det \tilde{A}[\gamma|\omega]|^{1/m}$$

$$\geq 2\left[\frac{2(m+1)}{\binom{2n}{m}}\right]^{1/m} \max_{\alpha,\beta \in Q_{m,n}} |\det A[\alpha|\beta]|^{1/m}.$$

Since $s(\tilde{A}) = 2\alpha_1$, the inequality for the first expression on the right in Corollary 2 follows. In the same way, application of (19) to $\tilde{A}$ yields the inequality for the second expression on the right in Corollary 2. □

REFERENCES

1. Marvin Marcus, Finite Dimensional Multilinear Algebra, Part I, Marcel Dekker, Inc., 1973.

2. Marvin Marcus, Finite Dimensional Multilinear Algebra, Part II, Marcel Dekker, Inc., 1975.

3. Marvin Marcus and Herbert Robinson, Bilinear functionals on the grassmannian manifold, Linear and Multilinear Algebra 3 (1975), 215-225.

4. Marvin Marcus, Derivations, Plücker relations, and the numerical range, Indiana University Mathematics J. 22 (1973), 1137-1149.

5. L. Mirsky, The spread of a matrix, Mathematika 3 (1956), 127-130.

6. L. Mirsky and R.A. Smith, The areal spread of matrices, Linear Algebra and Applications 2 (1969), 127-129.

7. L. Mirsky, Inequalities for normal and hermitian matrices, Duke Math. J. 14 (1957), 591-599.

Inequalities of Differential and Integral Operators

Lorenzenhof, 1946

Southeast side view, showing emergency topinambou field on the meadow slope at the right

MINIMUM PROPERTIES OF EIGENVALUES - ELEMENTARY PROOFS

Paul R. Beesack
Department of Mathematics
Carleton University
Ottawa, Ontario K1S 5B6
CANADA

ABSTRACT. The purpose of this paper is to use an elementary integral inequality and some simple linear algebra to give a completely elementary proof of the minimum properties of all eigenvalues of Sturm-Liouville problems. The results are a simplification of work published in [1], where singular cases were considered but general boundary conditions were not.

1. INTRODUCTION

We consider the Sturm-Liouville eigenvalue problem

$$(1') \qquad (ry')' + (\lambda p - q)y = 0 \ ,$$

$$(1'') \qquad \beta_a(a) - \alpha_a r(a)y'(a) = 0 \ , \qquad \beta_b y(b) + \alpha_b r(b)y'(b) = 0 \ ,$$

<u>where we assume that</u> $p,q,r \in C[a,b]$ <u>with</u> $r > 0$, $p \geq 0$ (<u>but</u> $p \not\equiv 0$ <u>on any subinterval of</u> $[a,b]$), <u>and</u> $\beta_a^2 + \alpha_a^2 > 0$, $\beta_b^2 + \alpha_b^2 > 0$. Under these hypotheses, it is known that there exists a real sequence $\{\lambda_n\}$ of eigenvalues of (1) such that for $\lambda = \lambda_n$ (and only for such values), (1) has nontrivial solutions $y = y_n$ $(n = 0,1,2,\ldots)$. Moreover, if $\lambda_0 < \lambda_1 < \cdots$, then $\lambda_n \to +\infty$, and y_n has exactly n zeros on (a,b). (See [7; 251], [4; 337], [2; 212], [6; 277].) We note that solutions of (1') are functions $y \in C^1[a,b]$ such that $(ry') \in C^1[a,b]$, which satisfy (1') on $[a,b]$.

LEMMA 1. <u>Under the above hypotheses, we have</u>

$$\int_a^b p y_i y_j \, dx = 0 \qquad \text{for} \quad i \neq j \ .$$

<u>Proof</u>. We have

$$y_j(ry_i')' + (\lambda_i p - q)y_i y_j = 0 \ ,$$

$$y_i(ry_j')' + (\lambda_j p - q)y_j y_i = 0 .$$

Now subtract and integrate over $[a,b]$ to obtain

$$(\lambda_i - \lambda_j)\int_a^b py_i y_j \, dx = \{y_i(ry_j') - y_j(ry_i')\}\Big|_a^b .$$

By the boundary conditions (1") on y_i, y_j, a consideration of the cases $\alpha_b = 0$, $\alpha_b \neq 0$, $\alpha_a = 0$, $\alpha_a \neq 0$ reduces the right-hand side of the last equation to zero, proving the result. (Note that if $\alpha_b = 0$, then $y(b) = 0$, and conversely, since not both $y(b) = 0$, $y'(b) = 0$ can hold.) □

If y is __any__ solution of (1'), then $y(ry')'$ is continuous on $[a,b]$, and

$$\int_a^b y(ry')' \, dx = y(ry')\Big|_a^b - \int_a^b ry'^2 \, dx .$$

In addition, we note that for any such y, on multiplying (1') by y and integrating over $[a,b]$, we obtain

$$\lambda\int_a^b py^2 \, dx = \int_a^b (ry'^2 + qy^2) \, dx + y(ry')\Big|_b^a . \tag{2}$$

If y is also a solution of (1"), this reduces to

$$\lambda\int_a^b py^2 \, dx = \int_a^b (ry'^2 + qy^2) \, dx + A(y) + B(y) , \tag{3}$$

where

$$A(y) = \begin{cases} 0 , & \underline{\text{if}} \quad \alpha_a = 0 \\ \dfrac{\beta_a}{\alpha_a} y^2(a), & \underline{\text{if}} \quad \alpha_a \neq 0 \end{cases} , \qquad B(y) = \begin{cases} 0 , & \underline{\text{if}} \quad \alpha_b = 0 \\ \dfrac{\beta_b}{\alpha_b} y^2(b), & \underline{\text{if}} \quad \alpha_b \neq 0 . \end{cases} \tag{4}$$

2. AN INTEGRAL INEQUALITY

We shall establish the following result.

THEOREM 1. __Under the preceding hypotheses on__ (1), __set__

$$\mathcal{D}_0 = \Big\{u \in AC[a,b] : u(a) = 0 \ \ \underline{\text{if}} \ \ \alpha_a = 0, \quad u(b) = 0 \ \ \underline{\text{if}} \ \ \alpha_b = 0 ;$$
$$\int_a^b ru'^2 \, dx < \infty , \quad \int_a^b pu^2 \, dx \neq 0\Big\} .$$

(__If__ $\alpha_a \neq 0$, $\mathcal{D}_0$ __includes no boundary condition at__ a, __and similarly for__ b;

only "essential" boundary conditions of (1") remain.) *For* $n \geq 1$, *set*

$$\mathcal{D}_n = \left\{ u \in \mathcal{D}_0 : \int_a^b p y_k u \, dx = 0 , \quad 0 \leq k \leq n-1 \right\} .$$

Then for all $n \geq 0$,

(5) $$\lambda_n = \min_{u \in \mathcal{D}_n} \left\{ \int_a^b (r u'^2 + q u^2) \, dx + A(u) + B(u) \right\} \Big/ \int_a^b p u^2 \, dx ,$$

where A, B *are defined by* (4). *The minimum in* (5) *is attained if and only if* $u = c y_n$ *for some constant* $c \neq 0$.

Proof for $n = 0$. Suppose first that $n = 0$, so that $y_0(x) \neq 0$ on (a,b). As can be seen by direct verification, for all $u \in AC[a,b]$ we have the identity (see also [5; 299])

$$r u'^2 + q u^2 - \lambda_0 p u^2 = \left(\frac{r y_0'}{y_0} u^2 \right)' + r \left(u' - \frac{y_0'}{y_0} u \right)^2 .$$

Hence integrating over $[a_1, b_1]$ for $a < a_1 < b_1 < b$, we obtain

(6) $$\int_{a_1}^{b_1} (r u'^2 + q u^2 - \lambda_0 \, p u^2) \, dx \geq \left(\frac{r y_0'}{y_0} u^2 \right) \Bigg|_{a_1}^{b_1} \equiv C(b_1) - C(a_1) ,$$

with equality precisely for $u = c y_0$ for some constant c. Here,

$$C(x) = \frac{r(x) y_0'(x)}{y_0(x)} u^2(x) .$$

Now if $\alpha_b \neq 0$ then $y_0(b) \neq 0$, as noted earlier. Hence in this case

$$C(b_1) \to -(\beta_b / \alpha_b) \, u^2(b) = -B(u) .$$

Similarly,

$$C(a_1) \to A(u) \qquad \text{if} \qquad \alpha_a \neq 0 .$$

On the other hand, if $\alpha_a = 0$, then $y_0(a) = 0$, and also $u(a) = 0$ from the definition of $\mathcal{D}_0$. But then

$$u(x) = \int_a^x u' \, dt = \int_a^x \frac{1}{\sqrt{r}} (\sqrt{r} \, u') \, dt , \qquad a \leq x \leq b ,$$

$$0 \leq u^2(x) \leq \left(\int_a^x \frac{dt}{r} \right) \left(\int_a^x r u'^2 \, dt \right) , \qquad a \leq x \leq b .$$

With no loss of generality, we may suppose $y_0(x) > 0$ on (a,b). Then

$$0 \leq \frac{u^2(x)}{y_0(x)} \leq \frac{\int_a^x \frac{dt}{r}}{y_0(x)} \int_a^x ru'^2\, dt\ , \qquad a < x < b\ ,$$

from which it follows that

$$u^2(x)/y_0(x) \to 0 \quad \text{as} \quad x \to a+\ .$$

Thus if $\alpha_a = 0$, then $C(a_1) \to 0 = A(u)$ as $a_1 \to a$. Similarly, if $\alpha_b = 0$, then $C(b_1) \to 0 = B(u)$ as $b_1 \to b-$. Now in (6) let $a_1 \to a$, $b_1 \to b$ to obtain

$$\int_a^b (ru'^2 + qu^2)\, dx + A(u) + B(u) \geq \lambda_0 \int_a^b pu^2\, dx \tag{7}$$

with equality precisely for $u = cy_0$. □

Now suppose $n \geq 1$. We shall first prove an intermediate result:

LEMMA 2. Let $n \geq 1$, so that the n-th eigenfunction y_n has consecutive zeros at $x_k \in (a,b)$, $1 \leq k \leq n$, where

$$x_0 = a < x_1 < x_2 < \cdots < x_n < b = x_{n+1}\ .$$

If $u \in \mathcal{D}_0$ satisfies the conditions $u(x_k) = 0$ $(1 \leq k \leq n)$, then

$$\lambda_n \int_a^b pu^2\, dx \leq \int_a^b (ru'^2 + qu^2)\, dx + A(u) + B(u)\ . \tag{8}$$

Moreover, equality holds in (8) if and only if $u(x) = c_k y_n(x)$ on $[x_{k-1}, x_k]$ $(1 \leq k \leq n + 1)$, for some constants c_k.

Proof of lemma. To prove Lemma 2, we essentially apply the case $n = 0$ just proved to the problem (1') on the successive subintervals $[x_{k-1}, x_k]$. For $k = 2,\ldots,n$ the boundary conditions (1") are replaced by $y(x_{k-1}) = y(x_k) = 0$, while for $[a, x_1]$ the boundary conditions consist of the first of (1") and $y(x_1) = 0$, and for $[x_n, b]$ they consist of the second of (1") and $y(x_n) = 0$. On each subinterval, the least eigenvalue is just λ_n, and y_n is a corresponding eigenfunction.

As at (7), for $1 \leq k \leq n + 1$, we obtain

$$\lambda_n \int_{x_{k-1}}^{x_k} pu^2\, dt \leq \int_{x_{k-1}}^{x_k} (ru'^2 + qu^2)\, dt + A_k(u) + B_k(u)\ ,$$

with equality precisely for $u = c_k y_n$. Here $A_k = B_k = 0$ for $2 \le k \le n$, while

$$B_1 = 0 , \quad A_{n+1} = 0 , \quad A_1 = A , \quad \text{and} \quad B_{n+1} = B ,$$

as defined by (4). Now sum over $k = 1,2,\dots,n+1$ to obtain (8), with equality as asserted there. □

Proof of Theorem 1 for $n \ge 1$. We now apply Lemma 2 to the case $n \ge 1$ of the theorem. To this end, take any $u \in \mathcal{D}_n$, again let $x_1,\dots,x_n$ denote the zeros of y_n in (a,b), and define the function

$$v(x) = \sum_{i=0}^{n-1} c_i y_i(x) - u(x) , \qquad a \le x \le b , \tag{9}$$

where $y_0,\dots,y_{n-1}$ are the first n eigenfunctions of (1), and the constants c_i are chosen to satisfy the system

$$\sum_{i=0}^{n-1} c_i y_i(x_k) = u(x_k) , \qquad 1 \le k \le n . \tag{10}$$

If all $u(x_k) = 0$, we can choose all $c_i = 0$ and then the inequality (8) holds for this $v = -u$. Hence we may, and do, assume that (10) is a nonhomogeneous system. We postpone for now the proof that it has a solution.

For v defined by (9) -- with arbitrary c_i -- note that if $\alpha_a = 0$ then $v(a) = 0$, and if $\alpha_b = 0$ then $v(b) = 0$, because u and also all y_i satisfy the boundary conditions in these cases. It follows that $v \in \mathcal{D}_0$, as well as $v(x_k) = 0$, $1 \le k \le n$. By (8) we have

$$\lambda_n \int_a^b pv^2 \, dx \le \int_a^b (rv'^2 + qv^2) \, dx + A(v) + B(v) . \tag{8'}$$

Now

$$\int_a^b pv^2 \, dx = \int_a^b pu^2 \, dx + \sum_0^{n-1} c_i^2 \int_a^b py_i^2 \, dx + 2 \sum_{i \ne j} c_i c_j \int_a^b py_i y_j \, dx - 2 \sum_0^{n-1} c_i \int_a^b puy_i \, dx$$

$$= \int_a^b pu^2 \, dx + \sum_0^{n-1} c_i^2 \int_a^b py_i^2 \, dx$$

by Lemma 1 and the orthogonality condition of $\mathcal{D}_n$. Also

$$\int_a^b qv^2 \, dx = \int_a^b qu^2 \, dx + \sum_0^{n=1} c_i^2 \int_a^b qy_i^2 \, dx + 2 \sum_{i \ne j} c_i c_j \int_a^b qy_i y_j \, dx - 2 \sum_0^{n-1} c_i \int_a^b quy_i \, dx ,$$

and

$$\int_a^b rv'^2\,dx = \int_a^b ru'^2\,dx + \sum_0^{n-1} c_i^2 \int_a^b ry_i'^2\,dx + 2\sum_{i\neq j} c_i c_j \int_a^b ry_i' y_j'\,dx - 2\sum_0^{n-1} c_i \int_a^b ru' y_i'\,dx \,.$$

However, by (1') with $y = y_i$ and Lemma 1,

$$\int_a^b ry_i' y_j'\,dx = ry_i' y_j\Big|_a^b + \int_a^b y_j(\lambda_i p - q)y_i\,dx = -\int_a^b qy_i y_j\,dx + ry_i' y_j\Big|_a^b \,.$$

Similarly, by the orthogonality conditions in $\mathfrak{D}_n$,

$$\int_a^b ry_i' u'\,dx = -\int_a^b quy_i\,dx + ry_i' u\Big|_a^b \,.$$

It follows that

$$\int_a^b (rv'^2 + qv^2)\,dx = \int_a^b (ru'^2 + qu^2)\,dx + \sum_0^{n-1} c_i^2 \int_a^b (ry_i'^2 + qy_i^2)\,dx$$

(11)

$$+ 2\sum_{i\neq j} c_i c_j (ry_i' y_j)\Big|_a^b - 2\sum_0^{n-1} c_i (ry_i' u)\Big|_a^b \,.$$

Suppose for now that $\alpha_a \alpha_b \neq 0$. As at (3), (4), the last two terms of (11) then reduce to

$$-2\frac{\beta_b}{\alpha_b}\sum_{i\neq j} c_i c_j y_i(b) y_j(b) + 2\frac{\beta_b}{\alpha_b}\sum_0^{n-1} c_i y_i(b) u(b)$$
$$-2\frac{\beta_a}{\alpha_a}\sum_{i\neq j} c_i c_j y_i(a) y_j(a) + 2\frac{\beta_a}{\alpha_a}\sum_0^{n-1} c_i y_i(a) u(a) \,.$$

Similarly, if $\alpha_a \alpha_b \neq 0$, we have

$$A(v) + B(v) = \frac{\beta_a}{\alpha_a} v^2(a) + \frac{\beta_b}{\alpha_b} v^2(b) = \sum_0^{n-1} c_i^2 \{A(y_i) + B(y_i)\} + A(u) + B(u)$$
$$+ 2\frac{\beta_b}{\alpha_a}\sum_{i\neq j} c_i c_j y_i(a) y_j(a) - 2\frac{\beta_a}{\alpha_a}\sum_0^{n-1} c_i y_i(a) u(a)$$
$$+ 2\frac{\beta_b}{\alpha_b}\sum_{i\neq j} c_i c_j y_i(b) y_j(b) - 2\frac{\beta_b}{\alpha_b}\sum_0^{n-1} c_i y_i(b) u(b) \,.$$

Hence, in this case we obtain

$$\int_a^b (rv'^2 + qv^2)\,dx + A(v) + B(v) = \int_a^b (ru'^2 + qu^2)\,dx + A(u) + B(u)$$
$$+ \sum_0^{n-1} c_i^2 \left\{\int_a^b (ry_i'^2 + qy_i^2)\,dx + A(y_i) + B(y_i)\right\}$$

$$= \int_a^b (ru'^2 + qu^2)\,dx + A(u) + B(u) + \sum_0^{n-1} c_i^2 \lambda_i \int_a^b py_i^2\,dx ,$$

on using (3) with $y = y_i$, $\lambda = \lambda_i$. The inequality (8') thus becomes

$$\lambda_n \left\{ \int_a^b pu^2\,dx + \sum_0^{n-1} c_i^2 \int_a^b py_i^2\,dx \right\} \leq \int_a^b (ru'^2 + qu^2)\,dx + A(u) + B(u) + \sum_0^{n-1} c_i^2 \lambda_i \int_a^b py_i^2\,dx ,$$

or

$$(12) \quad \lambda_n \int_a^b pu^2\,dx - \left\{ \int_a^b (ru'^2 + qu^2) + A(u) + B(u) \right\} \leq \sum_0^{n-1} (\lambda_i - \lambda_n) c_i^2 \int_a^b py_i^2\,dx .$$

Since all $\lambda_i < \lambda_n$, all

$$\int_a^b py_i^2\,dx > 0 ,$$

and at least one $c_i \neq 0$, it follows from (12) that

$$(13) \qquad \lambda_n < \left\{ \int_a^b (ru'^2 + qu^2)\,dx + A(u) + B(u) \right\} \Big/ \int_a^b pu^2\,dx .$$

In case $\alpha_a = 0$ or $\alpha_b = 0$, the corresponding boundary terms in (11) reduce to 0 at a or b since $y_i(a) = u(a) = 0$ or $y_i(b) = u(b) = 0$ in this case. The inequality (8') again leads to (12) and (13) in this case, as one readily verifies.

We note that (13) was obtained under the assumption that at least one $u(x_k) \neq 0$, so, in particular, $u \neq cy_n$ for any constant c. We now show that in this case the nonhomogeneous system (10) has a solution. Let $A = (a_{ij})$ with $a_{ij} = y_j(x_i)$ be the matrix of coefficients of this system. If A is singular, the corresponding homogeneous system of equations has a nontrivial solution $c_0, c_1, \ldots, c_{n-1}$. Now define

$$v = \sum_0^{n-1} c_i y_i .$$

As in the details following equation (10), we have $v \in \mathcal{D}_0$ and $v(x_k) = 0$ $(1 \leq k \leq n)$, so that (8') also holds for this v. Proceeding as before (but now with $u = 0$), we obtain in place of (12) the false inequality

$$0 \leq \sum_0^{n-1} c_i^2 (\lambda_i - \lambda_n) \int_a^b py_i^2\,dx .$$

Thus A must be nonsingular, and so (10) has a solution.

To complete the proof, it remains only to show that equality can hold in (8) <u>for</u> $u \in \mathcal{D}_n$ only if $u = cy_n$. So far, we have shown that equality can occur only when u satisfies the conditions $u(x_k) = 0$ $(1 \leq k \leq n)$ of Lemma 2. By that lemma, equality can then hold in (8) only if

$$(14) \qquad u(x) = c_k y_n(x) , \quad x_{k-1} \leq x \leq x_k , \quad 1 \leq k \leq n + 1 .$$

We now show that the only such u which also satisfy the orthogonality conditions of $\mathcal{D}_n$ have all c_k equal, thus completing the proof of the theorem. Suppose that u satisfies both (14) and

$$(15) \qquad \int_a^b py_i \, u \, dx = 0 , \quad 0 \leq i \leq n - 1 .$$

Then

$$\sum_{k=1}^{n+1} c_k \int_{x_{k-1}}^{x_k} py_i \, y_n \, dx = 0 \quad \text{for} \quad 0 \leq i \leq n - 1 .$$

However,

$$\int_a^b py_i \, y_n \, dx = \sum_{k=1}^{n+1} \int_{x_{k-1}}^{x_k} py_i \, y_n \, dx = 0 ,$$

by Lemma 1. Multiply the last equation by c_0 and subtract from each of the preceding equations to obtain

$$\sum_{k=2}^{n+1} (c_k - c_0) \int_{x_{k-1}}^{x_k} py_i \, y_n \, dx = 0 , \quad 0 \leq i \leq n - 1 .$$

This system of n equations in the $(c_k - c_0)$ has only the trivial solution $c_k \equiv c_0$ unless its coefficient matrix is singular. If, however, this were the case then there would be constants $a_0, \ldots, a_{n-1}$ not all zero such that

$$\sum_{i=0}^{n-1} a_i \int_{x_{k-1}}^{x_k} py_i \, y_n \, dx = 0 , \quad 2 \leq k \leq n + 1 .$$

Set

$$u = \sum_0^{n-1} a_i y_i \quad \text{so that} \quad \int_{x_{k-1}}^{x_k} py_n \, u \, dx = 0 \quad \text{for} \quad 2 \leq k \leq n + 1 ,$$

and hence in fact

$$\int_{x_1}^b py_n \, u \, dx = 0 .$$

Since $\int_a^b py_n \, u \, dx = 0$ by Lemma 1, it follows that $\int_a^{x_1} py_n \, u \, dx = 0$, and so

$$\int_a^{x_k} py_n\, u\, dx = 0 \qquad \text{for} \qquad 1 \leq k \leq n+1 .$$

As in the proof of Lemma 1, we also have

$$(\lambda_n - \lambda_i)\int_a^{x_k} py_n\, y_i\, dx = \{y_n(ry_i') - y_i(ry_n')\}\Big|_a^{x_k} ,$$

or since $y_n(x_k) = 0 \quad (1 \leq k \leq n)$,

$$\int_a^{x_k} py_n\, y_i\, dx = (\lambda_n - \lambda_i)^{-1}\{y_i(x_k)(ry_n')(x_k) + [y_i(ry_n') - y_n(ry_i')](a)\} .$$

Multiply this equation by a_i and sum over $0 \leq i \leq n-1$ to obtain, for $k = 1,2,\ldots,n$,

$$0 = \int_a^{x_k} py_n\, u\, dx = (ry_n')(x_k)\sum_{i=0}^{n-1} a_i \frac{y_i(x_k)}{\lambda_n - \lambda_i}$$
$$+ \sum_{i=0}^{n-1} a_i(\lambda_n - \lambda_i)^{-1}[y_i(ry_n') - y_n(ry_i')](a) .$$

By using the first of (1"), we see that the last term above has the value 0, so that since $(ry_n')(x_k) \neq 0$ for $1 \leq 1 \leq n$, we have

$$\sum_{i=0}^{n-1} \frac{a_i}{\lambda_n - \lambda_i} y_i(x_k) = 0 , \qquad 1 \leq k \leq n .$$

By hypothesis, not all $a_i/(\lambda_n - \lambda_i)$ are zero, so it follows that the matrix $(y_i(x_k))$ is singular. This contradicts our previous conclusion following (13). It follows that all $c_k \equiv c_0$ in (14), completing the proof of the theorem. □

REMARKS. We note that the above theorem remains valid, with only minor modifications to the proof, if it is supposed only that the n-th eigenfunction y_n has $k_n \leq n$ zeros on (a,b). Moreover, corresponding results hold for certain singular systems, that is, cases where a or b or both are infinite, or where one or more of the coefficients p, q, r are singular at the endpoints, or $r(x) = 0$ for $x = a$ or b. See [1] for a general theorem of this type.

3. MAXIMUM-MINIMUM CHARACTERIZATIONS OF EIGENVALUES

We can use Lemma 2 and Theorem 1 to obtain certain maximum-minimum characterizations of the eigenvalues of the Sturm-Liouville problem (1) under the hypotheses given there.

THEOREM 2. *For each* $n = 0,1,\ldots,$ *let*

$$\mathcal{H}_n = \{u : u(x_k) = 0 \text{ for at most } n \text{ distinct points } x_k \in (a,b)\} ,$$
$$\mathcal{H}_n(u) = \{v \in \mathcal{D}_0 : v = 0 \text{ if } u = 0\} , \qquad u \in \mathcal{H}_n ,$$
$$d_n(u) = \inf\{R(v) : v \in \mathcal{H}_n(u)\} ,$$

where R *is the Rayleigh quotient*

$$R(v) \equiv \left\{\int_a^b (rv'^2 + qv^2)\, dx + A(v) + B(v)\right\} \Big/ \int_a^b pv^2\, dx . \tag{16}$$

Then

$$\lambda_n = \sup\{d_n(u) : u \in \mathcal{H}_n\} . \tag{17}$$

Proof. Since y_n has n zeros on (a,b), it follows from Lemma 2 that

$$\lambda_n = d_n(y_n) \le \sup\{d_n(u) : u \in \mathcal{H}_n\} .$$

To prove the opposite inequality, take any $u \in \mathcal{H}_n$ and suppose the zeros of u on (a,b) are $x_1,\ldots,x_k$, where $k \le n$. We now construct a function $v \in \mathcal{H}_n(u)$ such that $R(v) \le \lambda_n$. This will prove $d_n(u) \le \lambda_n$ for all $u \in \mathcal{H}_n$, whence (17) will follow. In fact, it suffices to take

$$v = \sum_0^n c_i y_i .$$

We have $v \in \mathcal{H}_n(u)$ if the c_i (not all 0) can be chosen so that

$$\sum_{i=0}^n c_i y_i(x_j) = 0 , \qquad 1 \le j \le k \ (\le n) .$$

Such a nontrivial solution always exists for this homogeneous system. But then precisely as in the case of the function v in the proof of Theorem 1, but with $u \equiv 0$ and $(n - 1)$ replaced by n, it follows that

$$\int_a^b (rv'^2 + qv^2)\, dx + A(v) + B(v) = \sum_0^n c_i^2 \lambda_i \int_a^b py_i^2\, dx ,$$
$$\lambda_n \int_a^b pv^2\, dx = \lambda_n \sum_0^n c_i^2 \int_a^b py_i^2\, dx .$$

Thus,

$$\lambda_n \int_a^b pv^2\,dx \geq \int_a^b (rv'^2 + qv^2)\,dx + A(v) + B(v)$$

is clear, so that $R(v) \leq \lambda_n$ holds, completing the proof of (17). □

The above result is given in Courant-Hilbert [3; 463] and attributed there to K. Hohenemser. A second maximum-minimum characterization of λ_n is due to R. Courant [3; 406] and can be formulated as follows.

THEOREM 3. *Let* $\mathcal{C}_n$ *be the class of all* n-*tuples* $(v_0,\ldots,v_{n-1})$ *of functions such that*

$$0 < \int_a^b pv_i^2\,dx < \infty \quad \textit{for} \quad 0 \leq i \leq n-1 ,$$

and set

$$C_n(v_0,\ldots,v_{n-1}) = \left\{u \in \mathcal{D}_0 : \int_a^b puv_i\,dx = 0 , \quad 0 \leq i \leq n-1\right\} ,$$

$$d_n(v_0,\ldots,v_{n-1}) = \inf \{R(u) : u \in C_n(v_0,\ldots,v_{n-1})\} .$$

Then

(18) $$\lambda_n = \sup \{d_n(v_0,\ldots,v_{n-1}) : (v_0,\ldots,v_{n-1}) \in \mathcal{C}_n\} .$$

Proof. By Theorem 1 we have $d_n(y_0,\ldots,y_{n-1}) = \lambda_n$, so that

$$\lambda_n \leq \sup \{d_n(v_0,\ldots,v_{n-1}) : (v_0,\ldots,v_{n-1}) \in \mathcal{C}_n\} .$$

Now, for any $(v_0,\ldots,v_{n-1}) \in \mathcal{C}_n$, define the function

$$u(x) = \sum_0^n c_i y_i(x) ,$$

where the c_i are any nontrivial solution of the n homogeneous equations (in $n + 1$ unknowns)

$$\int_a^b puv_j\,dx = \sum_0^n c_i \int_a^b pv_j\, y_i\,dx = 0 \qquad (0 \leq j \leq n-1) .$$

Then $u \in C_n(v_0,\ldots,v_{n-1})$ and, as in the proof of Theorem 2, $\lambda_n \geq R(u) \geq d_n(v_0,\ldots,v_{n-1})$, completing the proof of (18). □

REFERENCES

1. P.R. Beesack, Elementary proofs of the extremal properties of the eigenvalues of the Sturm-Liouville equation, Can. Math. Bull. 3 (1960), 59-77.

2. E. Coddington and N. Levinson, Theory of Ordinary Differential Equations, McGraw-Hill Book Company, Inc., New York, 1955.

3. R. Courant and D. Hilbert, Methods of Mathematical Physics, V. 1, Interscience Publishers, Inc., New York, 1953.

4. P. Hartman, Ordinary Differential Equations, S.M. Hartman, Baltimore, 1973.

5. J. Hersch, Propriétés de convexité du type de Weyl pour des problèmes de vibration ou d'équilibre, Jour. math. et de phys. appl. (ZAMP) 12 (1961), 298-322.

6. E. Kamke, Differentialgleichungen reeller Funktionen, Akademische Verlagsgesellschaft, Berlin, 1930, reprinted by Chelsea Publishing Company, N.Y., 1947.

7. W.T. Reid, Ordinary Differential Equations, John Wiley and Sons, Inc., New York, 1971.

INFINITE SYSTEMS OF FIRST-ORDER PARTIAL-DIFFERENTIAL FUNCTIONAL INEQUALITIES

J. Szarski
Mathematical Institute
Jagiellonian University
Reymonta 4
30-059 Kraków
POLAND

ABSTRACT. This paper deals with an infinite system of differential-functional inequalities of the form

$$u_x^i(x,y) \leq f^i(x,y,u(x,y),u,u_y^i(x,y)) \quad (i=1,2,\dots)$$

in

$$P = \{(x,y)\ ;\ x_0 \leq x < x_0 + b,\ \ |y_k| \leq b_k - C(x - x_0)\}\ .$$

Here

$$y = (y_1,\dots,y_n)\ ,\quad u = (u^1,u^2,\dots)\ :$$

$$P \ni (x,y) \to u(x,y) = (u^1(x,y),u^2(x,y),\dots) \in \ell^\infty$$

is the unknown function,

$$u_y^i(x,y) = \mathrm{grad}_y\ u^i(x,y)\ ,$$

and f^i is a functional of the map u.

1. DEFINITIONS AND NOTATIONS

Put

$$(1.1)\quad P = \{(x,y)\ :\ x_0 \leq x < x_0 + b,\ \ |y_k| \leq b_k - C(x - x_0),\ \ k = 1,\dots,n\}\ ,$$

where

$$0 \leq C < \infty, \qquad 0 < b_k < \infty, \qquad 0 < b, \qquad 0 \leq \min_k(b_k) - Cb\ .$$

Denote

$$P_0 = V_0 \cup P\ ,$$

where

$$V_0 = V \cup (P \cap \{(x_0,y)\}) ,$$

and V is a fixed set (possibly empty) contained in $\{(x,y) : x < x_0\}$.

Let X stand for the space of mappings

$$w = (w^1,w^2,\dots) : P_0 \ni (x,y) \to w(x,y) = (w^1(x,y),w^2(x,y),\cdots) \in \ell^\infty ,$$

where w^j are continuous in P. We recall that ℓ^∞ is the Banach space of real bounded sequences $s = (s^1,s^2,\dots)$ with the norm

$$\|s\|_{\ell^\infty} = \sup\{|s^j| : j = 1,2,\dots \} .$$

If in particular

$$w^j(x,y) = c \qquad (j = 1,2,\dots) ,$$

where c is a constant, then we denote the corresponding mapping by c. We denote by $C^1_\infty(P)$ the subspace of X composed of mappings $w = (w^1,w^2,\dots)$ such that $w^j \in C^1(P)$ $(j = 1,2,\dots)$.

If $w \in X$ and

$$[w] := \sup\{w^j(x,y) : (x,y) \in P_0, \quad j = 1,2,\dots\} < \infty ,$$

then for every $x \geq x_0$ we put

$$[w]_x := \sup\{w^j(\tilde{x},\tilde{y}) : (\tilde{x},\tilde{y}) \in P_0, \quad \tilde{x} \leq x, \quad j = 1,2,\dots\} .$$

It is clear that

$$[w]_x = [w] \quad \text{for} \quad x \geq x_0 + b .$$

We denotc

$$[w]_x^0 := \max\{0,[w]_x\} . \tag{1.2}$$

For $w,\tilde{w} \in X$, we introduce the partial order

$$w \leq \tilde{x} \iff w^j(x,y) \leq \tilde{w}^j(x,y), \qquad (x,y) \in P_0, \quad j = 1,2,\dots .$$

Let the real functions

$$f^i(x,y,s,w,q) \qquad (i = 1,2,\ldots)$$

be defined for

$$(x,y) \in P, \quad s \in \ell^\infty, \quad w \in E, \quad q = (q_1,\ldots,q_n) \in R^n ,$$

where E is a subset (not necessarily a linear subspace) of X.

We say that the functions f^i $(i = 1,2,\ldots)$ satisfy the monotonicity condition W_+ if the function f^i is increasing (weakly) with respect to each variable

$$s^1,\ldots,s^{i-1},s^{i+1},\ldots,w \in E$$

separately.

2. THEOREM ON INFINITE SYSTEMS OF DIFFERENTIAL-FUNCTIONAL INEQUALITIES

THEOREM. Suppose the real functions

$$f^i(x,y,s,w,q) \qquad (i = 1,2,\ldots)$$

are defined for

$$(x,y) \in P, \quad s \in \ell^\infty, \quad w \in E, \quad q = (q_1,\ldots,q_n) \in R^n ,$$

where E is a subset of the space X, and let E have the following property: for any constant $c \geq 0$,

$$w \in E \Rightarrow w - c \in E .$$

Let the functions f^i $(i = 1,2,\ldots)$ satisfy the monotonicity condition W_+. Assume that whenever

$$w \geq \tilde{w} \quad \text{and} \quad [w - \tilde{w}] < \infty ,$$

the Lipschitz condition

$$(2.1) \qquad |f^i(x,y,s,w,q) - f^i(x,y,\tilde{s},\tilde{w},\tilde{q})| \leq B(\|s - \tilde{s}\|_{\ell^\infty} + [w - \tilde{w}]_X) + C\sum_{k=1}^{n} |q_k - \tilde{q}_k| \qquad (i = 1,2,\ldots)$$

is satisfied with some constant $B > 0$. Here C is the constant appearing in the definition (1.1) of P.

Let

$$u, v \in E \cap C^1_\infty(P)$$

be solutions of the inequalities

$$u^i_x(x,y) \leq f^i(x,y,u(x,y),u,u^i_y(x,y)), \quad (x,y) \in P, \tag{2.2}$$

where

$$u^i_y(x,y) = \operatorname{grad}_y u^i(x,y),$$

$$v^i_x(x,y) \geq f^i(x,y,v(x,y),v,v^i_y(x,y)), \quad (x,y) \in P, \tag{2.3}$$

$$u^i(x,y) \leq v^i(x,y), \quad (x,y) \in V_0 \quad (i = 1,2,\ldots). \tag{2.4}$$

Suppose finally that

$$[u - v] < \infty. \tag{2.5}$$

Under these assumptions, we have

$$u \leq v. \tag{2.6}$$

Proof. It is obvious that (2.6) is equivalent to

$$[u - v] \leq 0. \tag{2.7}$$

In order to obtain (2.7), we shall prove first that

$$[u - v]_{x_0+h} \leq 0, \tag{2.8}$$

with h given by the formula

$$h := \min\{b, B^{-1} \ln(5/4)\}. \tag{2.9}$$

Put

$$z := u - v$$

and notice that by (2.1), (2.2), (2.3), the monotonicity condition W_+, and the definition (1.2), we have in

$$P^h := P \cap \{(x,y) : x < x_0 + h\}$$

the following inequality:

$$\begin{aligned} z^i_x(x,y) &\le f^i(x,y,u(x,y),u,u^i_y(x,y)) - f^i(x,y,v(x,y),v,v^i_y(x,y)) \\ &\le f^i(x,y,u(x,y),u,u^i_y(x,y)) - f^i(x,y,u^1(x,y)-[z]^0_x,\dots, \\ &\qquad u^{i-1}(x,y)-[z]^0_x,v^i(x,y),u^{i+1}(x,y)-[z]^0_x,u-[z]^0_x,v^i_y(x,y)) \\ &\le 2B[z]^0_{x_0+h} + B|z^i(x,y)| + C\sum_{k=1}^{n} |z^i_{y_k}(x,y)| \ . \end{aligned}$$

Hence, it follows that for every $i = 1,2,\dots$ we have

$$z^i_x(x,y) \le 2B[z]^0_{x_0+h} + B|z^i(x,y)| + C\sum_{k=1}^{n} |z^i_{y_k}(x,y)| \tag{2.10}$$

in P^h. Inequalities (2.4) imply that

$$z^i(x_0,y) \le 0 \ . \tag{2.11}$$

By the differential and initial inequalities (2.10) and (2.11), using a well-known theorem on differential inequalities [1], we conclude that for every $i = 1,2,\dots$ we have

$$z^i(x,y) \le 2[z]^0_{x_0+h}\,[\exp B(x - x_0) - 1] \quad \text{in} \quad P^h ,$$

and consequently, since by (2.9) we have

$$x - x_0 \le B^{-1}\ln(5/4) \quad \text{in} \quad P^h ,$$

we obtain

$$z^i(x,y) \le \frac{1}{2}\,[z]^0_{x_0+h} \quad \text{in} \quad P^h .$$

Remembering that by (2.4) we have $z^i(x,y) \le 0$ for $(x,y) \in V_0$, we get from the last inequality

$$[z]^0_{x_0+h} \le \frac{1}{2}\,[z]^0_{x_0+h} \ .$$

Hence, it follows that

$$[z]^0_{x_0+h} \leq 0 ,$$

which is equivalent to (2.8).

Now, substitute

$$x_0 + h \text{ for } x_0 , \quad \tilde{P} = P \setminus P^h \text{ for } P , \quad \tilde{V}_0 = V \cup \overline{P^h} \text{ for } V_0 ,$$

and check that by (2.8) we have

$$u^i(x,y) - v^i(x,y) \leq 0 \quad \text{for} \quad (x,y) \in \tilde{V}_0 .$$

Hence, we see that the previous argument holds in $\tilde{P}$, and thus we get

$$[u - v]_{x_0+2h} \leq 0 .$$

Proceeding in this way a finite number of times (say p times), we obtain

(2.12) $$[u - v]_{x_0+ph} \leq 0$$

and

(2.13) $$ph \geq b .$$

By (2.13), inequality (2.12) is equivalent to (2.7), and this completes the proof. □

REFERENCE

1. J. Szarski, Differential Inequalities, Polish Scientific Publishers, Warszawa, 1965.

INEQUALITIES FOR FOURIER-STIELTJES TRANSFORMATIONS OF FUNCTIONS OF BOUNDED VARIATION

Eugene Lukacs
3727 Van Ness Street N.W.
Washington, D.C. 20016
U.S.A.

ABSTRACT. In this paper we consider analytic Fourier transforms of functions of bounded variation and derive estimates for these functions.

1. INTRODUCTION

Let $F(x)$ be a function of bounded variation. Then the transform

$$f(t) = \int_{-\infty}^{\infty} e^{itx}\, dF(x) \tag{1}$$

exists. It is known that a function of bounded variation can be represented as the difference of two bounded, nondecreasing functions:

$$F(x) = G_2(x) - G_1(x) , \tag{1a}$$

so that

$$f(t) = \int_{-\infty}^{\infty} e^{itx}\, dG_2(x) - \int_{-\infty}^{\infty} e^{itx}\, dG_1(x) = g_2(t) - g_1(t) . \tag{2}$$

Without loss of generality, we can assume that

$$G_1(-\infty) = G_2(-\infty) = 0 ;$$

this does not affect $f(t)$. Let

$$C_j = \int_{-\infty}^{\infty} dG_j(x)$$

be the total variation of $G_j(x)$; then the total variation of $F(x)$ is $C_1 + C_2$.

The transform (1) of a function of bounded variation is said to be <u>analytic</u> if there exist two functions $A_1(z)$ and $A_2(z)$ of the complex variable $z = t + iy$ which are regular (holomorphic) in some circle $|z| < \rho$ and if, for some $\Delta > 0$,

$$A_j(t) = g_j(t) \quad \text{for} \quad |t| < \Delta \quad (j = 1,2) .$$

Since the $G_j(x)$ are distribution functions, if properly normed, we can use the properties of analytic characteristic functions to see that there exist two strips

$$-\alpha_j < \text{Im } z < \beta_j \ , \quad \alpha_j > 0 \ , \quad \beta_j > 0 \qquad (j = 1,2)$$

in which the functions $g_j(t)$ can be continued to be regular and admit the representation

$$g_j(z) = \int_{-\infty}^{\infty} e^{izx} \, dG_j(x) \qquad (j = 1,2) .$$

Let $\alpha = \min(\alpha_1,\alpha_2)$, $\beta = \min(\beta_1,\beta_2)$. Then we have

$$(3) \qquad f(z) = \int_{-\infty}^{\infty} e^{izx} \, dF(x) = \int_{-\infty}^{\infty} e^{izx} \, dG_2(x) - \int_{-\infty}^{\infty} e^{izx} \, dG_1(x)$$

for $-\alpha < \text{Im } z < \beta$.

2. AN ESTIMATE

For $-\alpha < \text{Im } z_j < \beta$ $(j = 1,2)$, we have

$$|f(z_1) - f(z_2)| = \left| \int_{-\infty}^{\infty} (e^{iz_1x} - e^{iz_2x}) \, dF(x) \right| .$$

Writing $z_j = t_j + iy_j$, we see, by (1a), that

$$(4) \quad |f(z_1)-f(z_2)| = \left| \int_{-\infty}^{\infty} e^{it_1x-y_1x} [1 - \exp(i(t_2-t_1)x-(y_2-y_1)x] \, d[G_2(x)-G_1(x)] \right| .$$

We note that

$$(5) \quad |1 - \exp[i(t_2-t_1)x-(y_2-y_1)x]|^2 = 1 - 2e^{-(y_2-y_1)x} \cos(t_2-t_1)x + e^{-2(y_2-y_1)x} .$$

We shall apply Schwarz's inequality to (4) and also use the validity of the integral representation in the strip $-\alpha < \text{Im } z < \beta$. We assume therefore that

$$(6) \qquad -\alpha < 2y_1 < \beta \ , \qquad -\alpha < 2(y_2 - y_1) < \beta \ , \qquad -\alpha < y_2 < \beta .$$

In this way, we get

$$(7) \quad \left| \int_{-\infty}^{\infty} e^{it_1x-y_1x} \{1 - \exp[i(t_2 - t_1)x - (y_2 - y_1)x]\} \, dG_j(x) \right|^2$$
$$\leq g_j(2iy_1) \int_{-\infty}^{\infty} [1 + 2e^{-(y_2-y_1)x} + e^{-2(y_2-y_1)x}] \, dG_j(x)$$

$$= g_j(2iy_1)[C_j + 2g_j(iy_2 - iy_1) + g_j(2iy_2 - 2iy_1)]$$

for $j = 1,2$. Hence it follows from (4) that

$$(8) \quad |f(z_1) - f(z_2)|^2 \leq \sum_{j=1}^{2} g_j(2iy_1)[C_j + 2g_j(iy_2 - iy_1) + g_j(2iy_2 - 2iy_1)]$$

provided (6) holds.

3. AN ALTERNATIVE ESTIMATE

We next derive a different estimate for $|f(z_1) - f(z_2)|$. We have

$$\left|\int_{-\infty}^{\infty} e^{it_1x}[e^{-y_1x} - e^{-y_2x}e^{i(t_2-t_1)x}]dG_j(x)\right| \leq \int_{-\infty}^{\infty} |e^{-y_1x} - e^{-y_2x}e^{i(t_2-t_1)x}|dG_j(x) .$$

We use this inequality and the relation

$$(9) \quad \left|e^{-y_1x} - e^{-y_2x}e^{i(t_2-t_1)x}\right|^2 = e^{-2y_1x} - 2e^{-(y_1+y_2)x}\cos(t_2-t_1)x + e^{-2y_2x} ,$$

and apply Schwarz' inequality, to see that

$$\left|\int_{-\infty}^{\infty} e^{itx}[e^{-y_1x} - e^{-y_2x}e^{i(t_2-t_1)x}]\, dG_j(x)\right|^2$$

$$\leq C_j \int_{-\infty}^{\infty} [e^{-2y_1x} + 2e^{-(y_1+y_2)x} + e^{-2y_2x}]\, dG_j(x)$$

$$= C_j[g_j(2iy_1) + 2g_j(iy_1 + iy_2) + g_j(2iy_2)] .$$

Therefore,

$$(10) \qquad |f(z_1) - f(z_2)|^2 \leq \sum_{j=1}^{2} C_j[g_j(2iy_1) + 2g_j(iy_1 + iy_2) + g_j(2iy_2)$$

provided $-\alpha < 2y_1 < \beta$, $-\alpha < 2y_2 < \beta$.

4. COMPARISON OF ESTIMATES

Inequalities (8) and (10) both give estimates for $|f(z_1) - f(z_2)|^2$. In some cases (8) is preferable, in other cases (10).

EXAMPLE. Consider the function

$$F(x) = e^{-|x|} .$$

This is a function of bounded variation with

$$G_1(x) = 0 \quad \text{for} \quad x \leq 0 , \qquad G_1(x) = 1 - e^{-x} \quad \text{for} \quad x \geq 0$$

and

$$G_2(x) = e^{x} \quad \text{for} \quad x \leq 0 , \qquad G_2(x) = 1 \quad \text{for} \quad x \geq 0 .$$

Here

$$C_1 = C_2 = 1 .$$

Then for $y_1 = -1/4$, $y_2 = -1/8$, (8) yields a better estimate, while for $y_1 = 1/4$, $y_2 = -1/8$ the estimate of (10) is better.

We write

$$\text{(11a)} \qquad T_1(y_1,y_2) = \sum_{j=1}^{2} g_j(2iy_1)[C_j + 2g_j(iy_2 - iy_1) + g_j(2iy_2 - 2iy_1)] ,$$

$$\text{(11b)} \qquad T_2(y_1,y_2) = \sum_{j=1}^{2} C_j[g_j(2iy_1) + 2g_j(iy_1 + iy_2) + g_j(2iy_2)] .$$

Then we have the estimate

$$\text{(12)} \qquad |f(z_1) - f(z_2)|^2 \leq \min[T_1(y_1,y_2), T_2(y_1,y_2)] ,$$

provided that $-\alpha < 2y_1 < \beta$, $-\alpha < 2y_2 < \beta$, $-\alpha < 2(y_2 - y_1) < \beta$.

5. PARTICULAR CASES

We discuss next particular cases where better estimates can be obtained.

Suppose $t_1 = t_2 = t$, while

$$-\alpha < 2y_1 < \beta , \qquad -\alpha < y_2 < \beta , \qquad -\alpha < 2(y_2 - y_1) < \beta .$$

Then by the method which yielded (8) we obtain the estimate

$$\text{(8a)} \quad |f(t+iy_1) - f(t+iy_2)|^2 \leq \sum_{j=1}^{2} g_j(2iy_1)[C_j - 2g_j(iy_2-iy_1) + g_j(2iy_2-2iy_1)] .$$

In a similar way, we obtain an inequality analogous to (10):

$$\text{(10a)} \quad |f(t+iy_1) - f(t+iy_2)|^2 \leq \sum_{j=1}^{2} C_j[g_j(2iy_1) - 2g_j(iy_1+iy_2) + g_j(2iy_2)]$$

provided that $-\alpha < 2y_1 < \beta$, $-\alpha < 2y_2 < \beta$.

We next put $z_2 = 0$, that is, $t_2 = y_2 = 0$. Then $f(0) = C_2 - C_1$ and we write $z_1 = z = t + iy$ to obtain from (8) the inequality

(8b) $$|f(t + iy) - (C_2 - C_1)|^2 \leq \sum_{j=1}^{2} g_j(2iy)[C_j + 2g_j(-iy) + g_j(-2iy)] .$$

In the same way, from (10) we obtain the relation

(10b) $$|f(t + iy) - (C_2 - C_1)|^2 \leq \sum_{j=1}^{2} C_j[g_j(2iy + 2g_j(iy) + C_j]$$

provided $-\alpha < 2y < \beta$.

We consider next the case where $F(x)$ is a distribution function. Then

$$G_2(x) = F(x) , \quad G_1(x) \equiv 0 , \quad C_2 = 1 , \quad C_1 = 0 ,$$

and also

$$g_1(z) \equiv 0 , \quad f(z) = g_2(z) .$$

The transform $f(z)$ is then an analytic characteristic function, and we obtain from (8b) and (10b) the inequalities

(13a) $$|f(t + iy) - 1|^2 \leq f(2iy)[1 + 2f(-iy) + f(-iy)]$$

and

(13b) $$|f(t + iy) - 1|^2 \leq f(2iy) + 2f(iy) + 1$$

provided $-\alpha < 2y < \beta$.

If in (5) we put

(14) $$y_1 = y_2 = y ,$$

we see that

(5a) $$|1 - \exp[i(t_2 - t_1)x]|^2 = 2[1 - \cos(t_2 - t_1)x] .$$

Considering (14) and using Schwarz' inequality, we get

$$\left\{\int_{-\infty}^{\infty} e^{it_1x-yx}\{1 - \exp[i(t_2 - t_1)x]\}\, dG_j(x)\right\}^2$$

$$\leq 2\int_{-\infty}^{\infty} e^{-2yx}\, dG_j(x) \int_{-\infty}^{\infty}[1 - \cos(t_2-t_1)x]\, dG_j(x)$$

$$= 2g_j(2iy)[C_j - \operatorname{Re} g_j(t_2 - t_1)] .$$

Using (4) and (14), we see that

(15) $$|f(t_1 + iy) - f(t_2 + iy)|^2 \leq 2 \sum_{j=1}^{2} g_j(2i_y)[C_j - \operatorname{Re} g_j(t_2 - t_1)]$$

provided that $-\alpha < 2y < \beta$.

6. A MODIFICATION

Select a real v so that $-\alpha < v < \beta$. Then

$$f(z + iv) = g_2(z + iv) - g_1(z + iv)$$

is the Fourier-Stieltjes transform of a function of bounded variation which is analytic in the strip

$$-(\alpha + v) < \operatorname{Im} z < \beta - v .$$

We consider the function

$$k(z) = f(z + iv)$$

and write

$$h_j(z) = g_j(z + iv) \qquad (j = 1,2) .$$

Then

$$k(z) = h_2(z) - h_1(z) .$$

We write

$$C'_j = h_j(0) = g_j(iv) \qquad (j = 1,2) .$$

We now apply (15) to $k(z)$ and write

$$C'_j = h_j(0) = g_j(iv) .$$

We then see that

$$|k(t_1 + iy) - k(t_2 + iy)|^2 \leq 2 \sum_{j=1}^{2} h_j(2iy)[C'_j - \operatorname{Re} h_j(t_2 - t_1)] .$$

This relation is valid if

$$2 \operatorname{Im} z = 2y \in (-\alpha - v, \beta - v) .$$

Since

$$h_j(iy) = g_j(iy + iv) ,$$

we get

$$|f(t_1+iy+iv) - f(t_2+iy+iv)|^2 \leq 2 \sum_{j=1}^{2} g_j(2iy+iv)[C_j' - \text{Re } h_j(t_2 - t_1)]$$

$$= 2 \sum g_j(2iy+iv)[g_j(iv) - \text{Re } g_j(t_2-t_1+iv)] \;.$$

Putting $t_2 = t + \theta$, $t_1 = \theta$, we see that

$$|f(\theta+iy+iv) - f(t+\theta+iy+iv)|^2 \leq 2 \sum_{j=1}^{2} g_j(2iy+iv)[g_j(iv) + \text{Re } g_j(t+iv)] \;.$$

Now we set $y = 0$, so that

$$(16) \qquad |f(\theta+iv) - f(t+\theta+iv)|^2 \leq 2 \sum_{j=1}^{2} g_j(iv)[g_j(iv) - \text{Re } g_j(t+iv)] \;.$$

This relation is valid for all t and all θ, and for all v such that $-\alpha < v < \beta$.

Finally, we put $\theta = 0$ in (16) to obtain the inequality

$$(17) \qquad |f(iv) - f(t + iv)|^2 \leq 2 \sum_{j=1}^{2} g_j(iv)[g_j(iv) - \text{Re } g_j(t + iv)] \;,$$

valid for $-\alpha < v < \beta$.

REMARK. Inequality (15) is valid only in the strip $-\alpha/2 < y < \beta/2$. We used it to derive a modification, namely (17), which is valid in the whole strip $-\alpha < v < \beta$.

Inequalities for Sums, Series, and Integrals

ℓ_1-BOUNDS FOR INNER PRODUCTS

Vencil Skarda
Department of Mathematics
Brigham Young University
Provo, Utah 84602
U.S.A.

ABSTRACT. Let $a = \{a_n\}$ and $b = \{b_n\}$ be absolutely convergent real sequences. In terms of the ℓ_1-norm, their inner product $a \cdot b = \sum a_n b_n$ can be bounded as follows:

$$a \cdot b \le \frac{1}{4}(\|a+b\| + \|a\| - \|b\|)(\|a+b\| - \|a\| + \|b\|) ,$$

$$a \cdot b \ge -\frac{1}{2}(\|a\| + \|b\| - \|a+b\|) \max(\|a\|,\|b\|) ,$$

$$a \cdot b \ge -\frac{1}{4}(\|a-b\| + \|a\| - \|b\|)(\|a-b\| - \|a\| + \|b\|) ,$$

$$a \cdot b \le \frac{1}{2}(\|a\| + \|b\| - \|a-b\|) \max(\|a\|,\|b\|) .$$

Each of these inequalities gives the sharpest bound possible in terms of the norms which it involves. Necessary and sufficient conditions for equality are also discussed in each case.

1. INTRODUCTION

The inner product $a \cdot b = \sum a_n b_n$ of two sequences or finite-dimensional vectors is often estimated in terms of ℓ_p-norms $\|a\|_p \equiv (\sum |a_n|^p)^{1/p}$, which appear in the Hölder, Cauchy, and related inequalities as described in [1], [2], and [3]. Except for restrictive cases like the Chebyshev inequality or indirect cases like the Abel inequality, we see very few inner-product bounds -- if any -- done exclusively in terms of the ℓ_1-norm.

This paper presents sharp upper and lower bounds for $a \cdot b$ in terms of the values of $\|a\|_1$ and $\|b\|_1$, along with either $\|a+b\|_1$ or $\|a-b\|_1$.

2. UPPER AND LOWER BOUNDS

In the following, $a = (a_1,\ldots,a_n,\ldots)$ will represent a typical sequence, e_k will represent the k-th unit sequence $(\ldots,0,1,0,\ldots)$, and an unindexed $\sum$ will represent summation over the positive integers.

We start with the first inequality.

THEOREM 1. _For any absolutely convergent real sequences_ a _and_ b, _we have_

$$\sum a_n b_n \le \frac{1}{4}\left(\sum |a_n + b_n| + \sum |a_n| - \sum |b_n|\right)\left(\sum |a_n + b_n| - \sum |a_n| + \sum |b_n|\right) .$$

Equality occurs here if and only if either

(i) a _is the zero sequence_ (0,...,0,....).

(ii) b _is the zero sequence, or_

(iii) a _equals_ ce_k _and_ b _equals_ de_k, _with_ c _and_ d _both positive or both negative_.

Proof. For any n, the signs of both a_n and b_n can be reversed with no effect on the truth of this inequality. Without loss of generality, we shall assume that $a_n + b_n \ge 0$ for all n.

We shall first consider the case where each of the summations is restricted to the set S of positive integers n for which $a_n b_n \ge 0$, and for which a_n and b_n are both nonnegative. Here we have

$$\sum_{n\in S} a_n b_n = \sum_{j\in S} a_j \sum_{k\in S} b_k - \sum_{j\in S} \sum_{\substack{k\in S \\ j\neq k}} a_j b_k$$

$$\le \sum_{n\in S} a_n \sum_{n\in S} b_n \tag{1}$$

$$= \sum_{n\in S} \frac{1}{2}((a_n + b_n) + a_n - b_n) \sum_{n\in S} \frac{1}{2}((a_n + b_n) - a_n + b_n)$$

$$= \frac{1}{4} \sum_{n\in S} (|a_n + b_n| + |a_n| - |b_n|) \sum_{n\in S} (|a_n + b_n| - |a_n| + |b_n|) .$$

These summations may now be extended over the remaining n's -- if any -- where $a_n b_n < 0$. In this case, the sum on the left side would decrease and make the inequality proper, if it weren't proper already. Because of the triangle inequality for absolute values, each of the sums on the right-hand side either would increase or would not change at all.

If equality holds in this theorem, no terms such as those described in the preceding paragraph can be involved. Moreover, inequality (1) must collapse to equality. This requires that each of the terms $a_j b_k$ $(j \neq k)$ in the double summation subtracted there needs to equal zero. Unless condition (ii) holds in the theorem, b is not the zero sequence, and one of its elements --

say b_k -- is nonzero. Then all of the a_j, $j \neq k$, are equal to zero. Unless condition (i) holds, the element a_k is nonzero, and all b_j, $j \neq k$, are equal to zero. This is the situation described in condition (iii), with $c = a_k$ and $d = b_k$. □

The corresponding lower bound assumes a surprisingly different form.

THEOREM 2. For any absolutely convergent real sequences a and b we have

$$\frac{1}{2}\max\left(\sum |a_n|, \sum |b_n|\right)\left(\sum |a_n+b_n| - \sum |a_n| - \sum |b_n|\right) \le \sum a_n b_n .$$

Equality can happen when either of these sequences, say a, is arbitrary, but only when the other sequence satisfies either

(i) that $a_n b_n = 0$ for all n, or

(ii) that sequence b equals ce_k, where $|c| \ge \|a\|_1$ and where c and a_k have opposite signs.

Proof. We may assume, again without loss of generality, that $a_n + b_n \ge 0$ for each n. Define

$$A = \sum_{n\in S} a_n, \qquad C = -\sum_{n\in T} a_n, \qquad E = \sum_{n\in U} a_n,$$

$$B = -\sum_{n\in S} b_n, \qquad D = \sum_{n\in T} b_n, \qquad \text{and} \qquad F = \sum_{n\in U} b_n, \qquad \text{where}$$

$S = \{n : a_n > 0,\ b_n < 0\}$, $T = \{n : a_n < 0,\ b_n > 0\}$, $U = \{n : a_n \ge 0,\ b_n \ge 0\}$. These sums are all nonnegative. Now the claimed inequality can be written

$$\frac{1}{2}\max(A+C+E, B+D+F)((A-B-C+D+E+F) - (A+C+E) - (B+D+F)) \le \sum a_n b_n ,$$

which is equivalent to

$$(2) \qquad (B+C)\max(A+C+E, B+D+F) \ge -\sum_{n\in S} a_n b_n - \sum_{n\in T} a_n b_n - \sum_{n\in U} a_n b_n .$$

We shall prove this by combining

$$(3) \qquad (B+C)\max(A+C+E, B+D+F) \ge AB + CD ,$$

which we shall prove in different cases below, with the following:

(4) $$AB = -\sum_{j\in S} a_j \sum_{k\in S} b_k = -\sum_{n\in S} a_n b_n - \sum_{j\in S}\sum_{\substack{k\in S\\ j\neq k}} a_j b_k \geq -\sum_{n\in S} a_n b_n ,$$

(5) $$CD = -\sum_{j\in T} a_j \sum_{k\in T} b_k = -\sum_{n\in T} a_n b_n - \sum_{j\in T}\sum_{\substack{k\in T\\ j\neq k}} a_j b_k \geq -\sum_{n\in T} a_n b_n , \quad \text{and}$$

(6) $$0 \geq -\sum_{n\in U} a_n b_n .$$

Equality occurs in inequality (2) if, and only if, it occurs simultaneously in inequalities (3),(4),(5), and (6). Equality can occur in inequality (4) only when the double summation vanishes there, i.e., when the set S is empty or when it contains only one element. Similarly, inequality (5) collapses only if the set T is empty or contains only one element. Inequality (6) is an equality only if $a_n b_n$ equals zero for all n's in the set U.

If the sets S and T are both empty, then we have $A = B = C = D = 0$, and (3) holds as an equality. Equality in (6) gives condition (i) of the theorem.

If the set S is empty and if the set T is nonempty, then we have $A = B = 0$, $C > 0$, and $D > 0$. Inequality (3) is then equivalent to $D \leq \max(C+E, D+F)$, which is true because of the nonnegativity of F. Equality holds here if, and only if, we have $C + E \leq D$ and $F = 0$, which gives condition (ii) of the theorem. The only member of the set T, in this case, is k.

If the set S is nonempty while T is empty, a similar situation holds.

If the sets S and T are both nonempty, then the sums A, B, C, and D are all positive, and inequality (3) follows -- as a proper inequality -- from the following contradiction: denial or equality would require both

$$(B+C)(A+C) \leq AB + CD \quad \text{and} \quad (B+C)(B+D) \leq AB + CD ,$$

which yield respectively $D - A$ and $A - D$ each being at least as great as $B + C$, which is positive. But $D - A$ and $A - D$ cannot both be positive. □

The corresponding inequalities in terms of the ℓ_1-norms of the sequences a, b, and $a - b$ follow from both of the above results when each b is replaced by $-b$ and when each inequality is multiplied throughout by -1.

THEOREM 3. *For any absolutely convergent real sequences* a *and* b *we have*

$$\sum a_n b_n \geq -\frac{1}{4}\left(\sum |a_n - b_n| + \sum |a_n| - \sum |b_n|\right)\left(\sum |a_n - b_n| - \sum |a_n| + \sum |b_n|\right) .$$

Equality occurs only when

(i) *either* a *or* b *is the zero sequence, or when*

(ii) a *equals* ce_k *and* b *equals* de_k, *for some* k, *and where* c *and* d *have opposite signs*.

THEOREM 4. *For any absolutely convergent real sequences* a *and* b *we have*

$$\sum a_n b_n \leq \frac{1}{2} \max\left(\sum |a_n| , \sum |b_n|\right)\left(\sum |a_n| + \sum |b_n| - \sum |a_n - b_n|\right) .$$

Equality can happen only when either of the sequences, say a, *is arbitrary and when the other satisfies either*

(i) *that* $a_n b_n$ *equals zero for all* n, *or*

(ii) *that* b *equals* ce_k, *where* $|c| \leq \|a\|$ *and where* c *and* a_k *are both positive or both negative*.

3. EXAMPLE

Let a be the vector (3,4) and let b be the vector (4,-3), so that we have $\|a\|_1 = \|b\|_1 = 7$ and $\|a + b\|_1 = \|a - b\|_1 = 8$. If it were not known that the inner product $a \cdot b$ is equal to zero, it could be bounded above by 16 in Theorem 1 and by 21 in Theorem 4. Also, it would be bounded below by -16 in Theorem 3 and by -21 in Theorem 2.

The Cauchy inequality, with the Euclidean norm, would yield only $-25 \leq a \cdot b \leq 25$.

Theorems 1 and 4 seem to be stronger when the inner product $a \cdot b$ is negative. Theorems 2 and 3 seem to be stronger when it is positive. This may happen because the Cauchy inequality involves neither $\|a + b\|$ nor $\|a - b\|$.

It is admitted, however, that there are many other cases where the Cauchy inequality is more powerful than the inequalities presented in this paper.

4. REMARKS

The inequalities proved above have some interesting relationships with other inequalities.

Whenever sequences a and b coincide, all four of these inequalities reduce to

$$\sum a_n^2 \leq \left(\sum |a_n|\right)^2 ,$$

or $\|a\|_2 \leq \|a\|_1$, a special case of the Pringsheim-Lüroth-Jensen inequality: that $\|a\|_p$ is a decreasing function of p, for $p > 1$, unless the sequence a is a multiple of some e_k [1, p. 18], [2, p. 28]. An interesting property common to these inequalities is that none of them is "homogeneous in $\sum$," as defined in [2, p. 4]. Consequently, none of them should be expected to have any mean-value or integral analogues.

If the ℓ_1-norms were replaced by ℓ_2-norms in Theorems 1 and 3, the resulting bounds would read:

$$\frac{1}{4}(\|a\|_2 - \|b\|_2)^2 - \frac{1}{4}\|a-b\|_2^2 \leq a \cdot b \leq \frac{1}{4}\|a+b\|_2^2 - \frac{1}{4}(\|a\|_2 - \|b\|_2)^2 ,$$

which is "homogeneous in $\sum$," in addition to being true. Indeed, after being simplified, it reduces to the Cauchy inequality.

REFERENCES

1. E.F. Beckenbach and R. Bellman, Inequalities, Springer-Verlag, Berlin and New York, 2nd Edition, 1965.

2. G.H. Hardy, J.E. Littlewood, and G. Pólya, Inequalities, Cambridge University Press, London and New York, 2nd Edition, 1952.

3. D.S. Mitrinović, Analytic Inequalities, Springer-Verlag, Berlin and New York, 1970.

ON THE LOCATION OF THE INTERMEDIATE POINT IN TAYLOR'S THEOREM

S. Haber
Applied Mathematics Division
National Bureau of Standards
Washington, D.C. 20234
U.S.A.

O. Shisha
Department of Mathematics
University of Rhode Island
Kingston, R.I. 02881
U.S.A.

ABSTRACT. It is here shown that, under suitable conditions, the intermediate point in Taylor's theorem must lie in the left half of the interval considered.

1. THEOREM

We shall establish the following result.

THEOREM. *Let* a,b *satisfy* $-\infty < a < b < \infty$, *let* n *be an integer* ≥ 1, *and let* f *be a real function with* $f^{(n-1)}$ *continuous in* $[a,b]$ *and* $f^{(n)}$ *convex in* (a,b). *If* $n > 1$, *suppose also that*

$$f^{(n)}(x) \geq f^{(n)}\left(\frac{a+b}{2}\right)$$

throughout $(a, \frac{a+b}{2})$. *Then*

$$f(b) - \sum_{k=0}^{n-1} \frac{f^{(k)}(a)}{k!}(b-a)^k \geq \frac{f^{(n)}((a+b)/2)}{n!}(b-a)^n . \tag{1}$$

COROLLARY. *Let the left-hand side of* (1) *equal*

$$\frac{f^{(n)}(c)}{n!}(b-a)^n, \qquad a < c < b .$$

If

$$f^{(n)}(x) < f^{(n)}\left(\frac{a+b}{2}\right) \quad \text{throughout} \quad \left(\frac{a+b}{2}, b\right),$$

then $c \leq (a+b)/2$. *If* $n = 1$, *and*

$$f'(x) < f'\left(\frac{a+b}{2}\right) \quad \text{throughout} \quad \left(a, \frac{a+b}{2}\right),$$

then $c \geq (a+b)/2$.

2. PROOF

We shall use in the proof of the theorem the fact (cf. [2], p. 15) that if F is a real function, convex in (a,b), and if $a \leq x-h < x+h \leq b$, then

$$(2) \qquad \int_{x-h}^{x+h} F(t)\,dt \geq 2hF(x) \ ,$$

where the integral is a proper or improper Riemann integral, possibly diverging to $+\infty$.

If $n = 1$, then by (2),

$$f(b) - f(a) = \int_a^b f'(t)\,dt \geq f'\left(\frac{a+b}{2}\right)(b - a) \ ,$$

namely, (1).

Assume now that $n > 1$. Then (with an obvious interpretation if $n = 2$),

$$\begin{aligned} f(b) - \sum_{k=0}^{n-1} \frac{f^{(k)}(a)}{k!}(b-a)^k &= \int_a^b \int_a^{t_n} \cdots \int_a^{t_2} f^{(n)}(t_1)\,dt_1 dt_2 \cdots dt_n \\ &\geq \int_a^b \int_a^{t_n} \cdots \int_a^{t_3} (t_2 - a) f^{(n)}\left(\frac{a+b}{2}\right) dt_2 \cdots dt_n \\ &= f^{(n)}\left(\frac{a+b}{2}\right) \frac{(b-a)^n}{n!} \ . \qquad \square \end{aligned}$$

3. EXAMPLE

As an example, with $n = 1$, take $f(x) \equiv x^p$, where $p \geq 2$ or $0 \leq p \leq 1$, and where $a \geq 0$. We obtain

$$(b^p - a^p)/(b - a) \geq p\left(\frac{a+b}{2}\right)^{p-1} \ ,$$

an inequality proved, with greater effort, in [1].

REFERENCES

1. S. Haber, An elementary inequality, Internat. J. Math. and Math. Sci. 2 (1979), 531-535.

2. A.W. Roberts and D.E. Varberg, Convex Functions, Academic Press, New York, 1973.

ON HÖLDER'S INEQUALITY

J. Aczél
Faculty of Mathematics
University of Waterloo
Waterloo, Ontario N2L 3G1
CANADA

E.F. Beckenbach
Department of Mathematics
University of California
Los Angeles, California 90024
U.S.A.

ABSTRACT. It is pointed out that the normalization $1/p + 1/q = 1$ in Hölder's inequality can be replaced by relations of the form $1/p + 1/q \leq 1/r$ or $1/p + 1/q \geq 1/r$ if the inequality is suitably adjusted. A single symmetric form, including all cases, is given. It is further noted that apparent adhesion to the normalization has perhaps unnecessarily restricted investigations of inequalities only indirectly related to Hölder's inequality.

1. REMARKS

It is well known (see [2, p. 24, Th. 12]), but perhaps not always remembered, that in the standard Hölder inequality,

$$(1) \qquad \sum f_i g_i \leq \left(\sum f_i^p\right)^{1/p} \left(\sum g_i^q\right)^{1/q}, \qquad p > 1, \quad \frac{1}{p} + \frac{1}{q} = 1,$$

the condition $\frac{1}{p} + \frac{1}{q} = 1$ is a normalization that can be dropped if the inequality is suitably adjusted.

Thus if $p > 0$, $q > 0$, and

$$(2) \qquad \frac{1}{p} + \frac{1}{q} = \frac{1}{r},$$

then

$$\frac{p}{r} > 1, \qquad \frac{1}{p/r} + \frac{1}{q/r} = 1,$$

and accordingly (1) can be applied to the values f_i^r and g_i^r to yield

$$\sum f_i^r g_i^r \leq \left[\sum (f_i^r)^{p/r}\right]^{r/p} \left[\sum (g_i^r)^{q/r}\right]^{r/q},$$

whence, on taking r-th roots, we obtain

$$(3) \quad \left(\sum f_i^r g_i^r\right)^{1/r} \leq \left(\sum f_i^p\right)^{1/p} \left(\sum g_i^q\right)^{1/q}, \qquad p > 0, \quad q > 0, \quad \frac{1}{p} + \frac{1}{q} = \frac{1}{r}.$$

Similarly, if $p > 0$, $q < 0$, and (2) holds with $r > 0$, then

$$\frac{r}{p} > 1 , \qquad \frac{1}{r/p} + \frac{1}{-q/p} = 1 ,$$

and (1) applied to the values of $f_i^p g_i^p$ and g_i^{-p} yields

$$\Sigma (f_i^p g_i^p) g_i^{-p} \le \left[\Sigma (f_i^p g_i^p)^{r/p}\right] \left[\Sigma (g_i^{-p})^{-q/p}\right]^{-p/q} ,$$

which reduces to

(4) $$(\Sigma f_i^r g_i^r)^{1/r} \ge (\Sigma f_i^p)^{1/p} (\Sigma g_i^q)^{1/q} , \qquad p>0,\ q<0,\ r>0,\ \frac{1}{p} + \frac{1}{q} = \frac{1}{r} .$$

In the same way, for the two remaining arrangements of positive and negative values of p, q, r satisfying (2), applications of (1) to suitable powers of the f_i, g_i, and $f_i g_i$ yield

(5) $$(\Sigma f_i^r g_i^r)^{1/r} \le (\Sigma f_i^p)^{1/p} (\Sigma g_i^q)^{1/q} , \qquad p>0,\ q<0,\ r<0,\ \frac{1}{p} + \frac{1}{q} = \frac{1}{r} ,$$

and

(6) $$(\Sigma f_i^r g_i^r)^{1/r} \ge (\Sigma f_i^p)^{1/p} (\Sigma g_i^q)^{1/q} , \qquad p<0,\ q<0,\ \frac{1}{p} + \frac{1}{q} = \frac{1}{r} .$$

The second standard, or normalized, Hölder inequality,

(7) $$\Sigma f_i g_i \ge (\Sigma f_i^p)^{1/p} (\Sigma g_i^q)^{1/q} , \qquad 0 < p < 1 , \quad \frac{1}{p} + \frac{1}{q} = 1 ,$$

is a special case of (4).

2. SYMMETRIC FORM

The standard Hölder inequalities (1) and (7) emphasize a single given real value p and its related conjugate value q. The forms (3)-(6) emphasize two given real values, p and q, and their related value r. The following formulation, using slightly altered notation, emphasizes all three values, p, q, and r, equally:

If the sets of positive values (f), (g), (h) *satisfy* $f_i g_i h_i = 1$ *for all* i, *and the nonzero real numbers* p, q, r *satisfy*

(8) $$\frac{1}{p} + \frac{1}{q} + \frac{1}{r} = 0 ,$$

then

$$(9)\quad (\Sigma f_i^p)^{1/p}(\Sigma g_i^q)^{1/q}(\Sigma h_i^r)^{1/r} \begin{Bmatrix} \geq 1 \\ \leq 1 \end{Bmatrix} \text{ \underline{if all but one of} } p,q,r \text{ \underline{are} } \begin{Bmatrix} \text{\underline{positive}} \\ \text{\underline{negative}} \end{Bmatrix}.$$

This result, and all the foregoing results, can be extended in an obvious way to the general case of k sets of positive values, and k corresponding nonzero real numbers all but one of which are of the same sign.

3. SUMS, INTEGRALS, AND MEANS

We have tacitly assumed that the foregoing inequalities involve simple, finite sums. As in the standard Hölder inequalities (1) and (7), however, the sums in the inequalities (3)-(6) and (9) might be interpreted as being multiple or infinite.

Also like the standard Hölder inequalities, these inequalities are "homogeneous in Σ," and accordingly they admit finite and infinite mean-value formulations, single and multiple integral analogues of all sorts, and integral-mean analogues.

As they stand, the foregoing inequalities involve sums of order p, q, r. Now the <u>sum or order</u> r,

$$(\Sigma f_i^r)^{1/r},$$

decreases monotonically from $\min_i f_i$ to 0 as r increases from $-\infty$ to 0^-, and it decreases from $+\infty$ to $\max_i f_i$ as r increases from 0^+ to $+\infty$ [2, p. 28, Th. 19]; that is, the sum of order r increases from 0 to $\min_i f_i$ as $1/r$ increases from $-\infty$ to 0^-, and it increases from $\max_i f_i$ to $+\infty$ as $1/r$ increases from 0^+ to $+\infty$.

Accordingly, with suitable conventions, the domains of p, q, r might be extended appropriately in the inequalities to include the values $\pm\infty$, 0^+, and 0^-.

Also, because of the monotonic character of the sums of order p, q, r, the restrictions on p, q, r might be relaxed in each of (3)-(6) from the equation (2), and in (9) from the equation (8), to an appropriate inequality. Thus with p and q fixed, the condition (2) might be replaced in (3)-(6), respectively, with

(3') $+\infty \geq \frac{1}{p} + \frac{1}{q} \geq \frac{1}{r} \geq -\infty$, (5') $+\infty \geq \frac{1}{p} + \frac{1}{q} \geq \frac{1}{r} \geq -\infty$,

(4') $-\infty \leq \frac{1}{p} + \frac{1}{q} \leq \frac{1}{r} \leq +\infty$, (6') $-\infty \leq \frac{1}{p} + \frac{1}{q} \leq \frac{1}{r} \leq +\infty$.

For the top line and the bottom line of (9), the condition (8) might be replaced by

(8a) $+\infty \geq \frac{1}{p} + \frac{1}{q} + \frac{1}{r} \geq 0$, (8b) $-\infty \leq \frac{1}{p} + \frac{1}{q} + \frac{1}{r} \leq 0$,

respectively.

For values of r other than the ones here given, the right-hand and left-hand members of the inequalities for sums of order p, q, r are not comparable.

The mean of order r,

$$\left(\frac{1}{n} \sum_{i=1}^{n} f_i^r\right)^{1/r} \quad \text{or} \quad \left(\frac{1}{b-a} \int_a^b f^r\right)^{1/r} ,$$

increases monotonically, from $\min f$ to $\max f$ (or from $\operatorname{ess\,inf} f$ to $\operatorname{ess\,sup} f$, depending on the context), as r increases from $-\infty$ to $+\infty$ [2, p. 26, Th. 16]. Accordingly, for mean-value versions of the inequalities, the conditions (3'), (4'), and (8a) must be interchanged with (5'), (6'), and (8b), respectively.

Again, for values of r other than these, the right-hand and left-hand members of the inequalities for mean values of order p, q, r are not comparable.

For integral (not integral-mean) versions, the members of the inequalities are comparable only for the single values of r originally given.

Incidentally and trivially, for all versions of (9), whether sum, integral, or mean-value, the condition $fgh = 1$ might be replaced by $fgh \geq 1$ for the top line of (9), and by $fgh \leq 1$ for the bottom line.

4. PROBLEMS

Since the inequalities (3)-(6) follow quite directly from (1), any property of (1) can be expected to yield an analogous property of (3)-(6).

For example, knowing the conditions under which the sign of equality holds in (1), we can trace these conditions through the derivation of (3)-(6) to obtain the conditions under which the sign of equality holds in (3)-(6).

Again, from the inverse of (1),

$$\sum f_i g_i \geq c \left(\sum f_i^p\right)^{1/p} \left(\sum g_i^q\right)^{1/q} ,$$

where the best value of C is a known function of

$$\max_i f_i\ , \quad \min_i f_i\ , \quad \max_i g_i\ , \quad \min_i g_i\ ,$$

we can in the same way derive inverses of (3)-(6), together with the best values of the constants for these inverse inequalities. This program has been carried through by Chung-Lie Wang, who first in an earlier version of [3] dealt with the integral analogue of (3) and its inverse, and then in the published revision, following a suggestion by one of the present authors, kindly included the integral analogues of (4)-(6) and their inverses.

Finally, other results related to (1), but less directly so, invite the formulation of analogous statements involving (3)-(6), and the investigation of their possible validity.

For example, consider the known inequalities ([2, p. 193, Th. 261])

$$\int_{-\infty}^{\infty} |f'|^2 \le \left(\int_{-\infty}^{\infty} |f|^2\right)^{1/2}\left(\int_{-\infty}^{\infty} |f''|^2\right)^{1/2}$$

and ([2, p. 187, Th. 259])

$$\int_0^{\infty} |f'|^2 \le 2\left(\int_0^{\infty} |f|^2\right)^{1/2}\left(\int_0^{\infty} |f''|^2\right)^{1/2} .$$

These inequalities have been generalized, seemingly with (1) in mind, respectively to ([2, p. 195, Th. 269])

$$\int_{-\infty}^{\infty} |f'|^2 \le \left(\int_{-\infty}^{\infty} |f|^p\right)^{1/p}\left(\int_{-\infty}^{\infty} |f''|^q\right)^{1/q} , \qquad p > 1, \ \ \frac{1}{p} + \frac{1}{q} = 1 ,$$

and ([1])

$$\int_0^{\infty} |f'|^2 \le K(p)\left(\int_0^{\infty} |f|^p\right)^{1/p}\left(\int_0^{\infty} |f''|^q\right)^{1/q} , \qquad p > 1, \ \ \frac{1}{p} + \frac{1}{q} = 1 ,$$

where $K(p)$ is a positive constant, the only known best value of which is $K(2) = 2$.

With (3) in mind, one might now investigate whether or not the further generalizations

$$\left(\int_{-\infty}^{\infty} |f'|^{2r}\right)^{1/r} \le \left(\int_{-\infty}^{\infty} |f|^p\right)^{1/p}\left(\int_{-\infty}^{\infty} |f''|^q\right)^{1/q} , \qquad p>0, \ q>0, \ \ \frac{1}{p} + \frac{1}{q} = \frac{1}{r} ,$$

and

$$\left(\int_0^{\infty} |f'|^{2r}\right)^{1/2r} \le K(p,q)\left(\int_0^{\infty} |f|^p\right)^{1/p}\left(\int_0^{\infty} |f''|^q\right)^{1/q} , \qquad p>0, \ q>0, \ \ \frac{1}{p} + \frac{1}{q} = \frac{1}{r} ,$$

are valid, with $K(p,q) > 0$, and, if so, what the best value of $K(p,q)$ might be, other than $K(2,2) = 2$.

REFERENCES

1. W.N. Everitt and M. Giertz, On the integro-differential inequality $\|f'\|_2^2 \le K\|f\|_p\|f\|_q$, Jour. Math. Anal. Appl. 45, 639-653, 1974.

2. G.H. Hardy, J.E. Littlewood, and G. Pólya, Inequalities, Cambridge Univ. Press, London and New York, 1934; 2nd Edition, 1952.

3. Chung-Lie Wang, Variants of the Hölder inequality and its inverses, Canad. Math. Bull. 20 (1977), 377-384.

ON SOME INTEGRAL INEQUALITIES OF E.T. COPSON

Paul R. Beesack
Department of Mathematics
Carleson University
Ottawa, Ontario K1S 5B6
CANADA

ABSTRACT. Six recently established inequalities of E.T. Copson, which are generalizations of Hardy's inequality, are here extended to additional cases of the exponents involved, and in some cases are proved under a more natural convergence bypothesis.

1. INTRODUCTION

In a recent paper [1], E.T. Copson proved six integral inequalities which are generalizations of Hardy's inequality (cf. [3, Theorem 347]). We state these results briefly as follows, where in all cases the functions φ and f are nonnegative and measurable on $\mathbb{R}^+$, and

$$\Phi(x) = \int_0^x \varphi \, dt , \qquad F_1(x) = \int_0^x f\varphi \, dt , \qquad F_2(x) = \int_x^\infty f\varphi \, dt$$

all exist for $x > 0$, while $M = (p/|c-1|)^p$.

(1) $\displaystyle\int_0^b F_1^p \Phi^{-c} \varphi \, dx \le M \int_0^b f^p \Phi^{p-c} \varphi \, dx$ if $p \ge 1$, $c > 1$, $0 < b \le \infty$;

(2) $\displaystyle\int_a^\infty F_1^p \Phi^{-c} \varphi \, dx \ge M \int_a^\infty f^p \Phi^{p-c} \varphi \, dx$ if $0 < p \le 1$, $c > 1$, $0 < a < \infty$, and $\Phi(x) \to \infty$ as $x \to \infty$;

(3) $\displaystyle\int_a^\infty F_2^p \Phi^{-c} \varphi \, dx \le M \int_a^\infty f^p \Phi^{p-c} \varphi \, dx$ if $p \ge 1$, $c < 1$, $0 < a < \infty$;

(4) $\displaystyle\int_0^b F_2^p \Phi^{-c} \varphi \, dx \ge M \int_0^b f^p \Phi^{p-c} \varphi \, dx$ if $0 < p \le 1$, $c < 1$, $0 < b \le \infty$;

(5) $\displaystyle\int_0^b F_1^p \Phi^{-1} \varphi \, dx \le p^p \int_0^b f^p \Phi^{p-1} \left\{\log \frac{\Phi(b)}{\Phi(x)}\right\}^p \varphi \, dx$ if $p \ge 1$, $0<b<\infty$;

(6) $\displaystyle\int_a^\infty F_2^p \Phi^{-1} \varphi \, dx \ge p^p \int_a^\infty f^p \Phi^{p-1} \left\{\log \frac{\Phi(x)}{\Phi(a)}\right\}^p \varphi \, dx$ if $0<p\le 1$, $0<a<\infty$.

In all cases, it is assumed also that the integral $\int F_i^p \Phi^{-c} \varphi \, dx$ on the left-hand side of (1) - (6) is convergent. In cases (1), (3), (5), this assumption is rather unnatural, the natural hypothesis in these cases being that the greater integral on the right-hand side converge. The question arises as to whether or not (1), (3), (5) are valid under such a hypothesis. A second question which suggests itself is: Are there analogous results for $p < 0$? The answer to both questions is "Yes," and all that is required to show this is a rearrangement of Copson's proofs and an application of the elementary inequalities

$$(7) \qquad \begin{aligned} (u+v)^p &\geq u^p + pu^{p-1} v \qquad && (p < 0 \text{ of } p > 1) , \\ (u+v)^p &\leq u^p + pu^{p-1} v && (0 < p < 1) . \end{aligned}$$

The inequalities (7) are valid for all $u \geq 0$, $u + v \geq 0$ (if $p > 0$), or $u > 0$, $u + v > 0$ (if $p < 0$), and equality holds only if $v = 0$. Here we adopt the usual convention $0 \cdot \infty = 0$. These inequalities are proved in [3; Theorem 41]; see also [2; p. 45].

We arrange our analysis so as to deal with all cases of p and $c \neq 1$, as well as F_1, F_2, simultaneously to obtain inequalities involving boundary terms. We then obtain conditions under which the boundary terms have finite limits, and indicate the resulting inequalities. We actually obtain at least twelve inequalities (for $c \neq 1$) by this approach.

2. ANALYSIS

As in [1], set

$$u(x) = F_i^p(x) \, \Phi^{1-c}(x) , \qquad 0 < a \leq x \leq b < \infty , \quad i = 1,2 .$$

Then

$$u' = (-1)^{i-1} p F_i^{p-1} f \varphi \, \Phi^{1-c} + (1-c) F_i^p \Phi^{-c} \varphi \qquad \text{a.e.} ;$$

hence

$$(8) \qquad \int_a^b F_i^p \Phi^{-c} \varphi \, dx = (-1)^i [p/(1-c)] \int_a^b F_i^{p-1} \Phi^{1-c} f \varphi \, dx + (1-c)^{-1} F_i^p \Phi^{1-c} \Big|_a^b ,$$

or

$$(8') \qquad I(a,b) = |p/(1-c)| \; K(a,b) + (1-c)^{-1} F_i^p \Phi^{1-c} \Big|_a^b ,$$

where

$$(9) \qquad I(a,b) \equiv \int_a^b F_i^p \Phi^{-c} \varphi \, dx , \qquad K(a,b) \equiv \int_a^b F_i^{p-1} \Phi^{1-c} f \varphi \, dx .$$

For later use, we also define J(a,b):

$$J(a,b) \equiv \int_a^b f^p \Phi^{p-c} \varphi \, dx . \tag{10}$$

In (8'), we suppose i, p, c are chosen so that $(-1)^i[p/(1-c)] > 0$. Also when $p < 0$ we assume f, φ are <u>strictly</u> positive on $\mathbb{R}^+$.

Now

$$K(a,b) = \int_a^b \left\{ f \Phi^{(p-c)/p} \varphi^{1/p} \right\} \left\{ F_i^{p-1} \Phi^{-c(p-1)/p} \varphi^{(p-1)/p} \right\} dx ,$$

so by Hölder's inequality we obtain

$$K(a,b) \leq J^{1/p}(a,b) I^{(p-1)/p}(a,b) \quad \text{if} \quad p > 1 ,$$

with the opposite inequality holding if $p < 0$ or $0 < p < 1$. By (8'), this gives

$$|p/(1-c)| \, J^{1/p} I^{(p-1)/p} \geq I - (1-c)^{-1} F_i^p \Phi^{1-c} \Big|_a^b \geq 0 \quad \text{if} \quad p > 1 , \tag{11}$$

with the opposite inequality holding if $p < 0$ or $0 < p < 1$. If we now raise both sides of (11) to the power p and apply (7) with

$$u = I , \qquad v = -(1-c)^{-1} F_i^p \Phi^{1-c} \Big|_a^b ,$$

after simplification we obtain

$$|p/(1-c)|^p \, J + p(1-c)^{-1} F_i^p \Phi^{1-c}(b) \geq I + p(1-c)^{-1} F_i^p \Phi^{1-c}(a) \tag{12a}$$

in case $p < 0$ or $p > 1$, and

$$|p/(1-c)|^p \, J + p(1-c)^{-1} F_i^p \Phi^{1-c}(b) \leq I + p(1-c)^{-1} F_i^p \Phi^{1-c}(a) \tag{12b}$$

if $0 < p < 1$. We note that if $p = 1$ then $K = J$ and both of (12) hold, with equality, since they reduce to (8').

The inequalities (12) are the basic inequalities; they determine the <u>direction</u> of the final inequalities. To analyze the boundary terms, we deal separately with the cases $i = 1,2$.

3. THE CASE $i = 1$

When $i = 1$, p and c must satisfy $p/(1-c) < 0$ by the remark following (10), and we assume this in the following analysis. First, if

$I(a,b)$ is convergent for $a = 0$ or $b = \infty$ we note that for $0 < \alpha < \beta < \infty$,

$$I(\alpha,\beta) = \int_\alpha^\beta F_1^p \Phi^{-c} \varphi \, dx \geq F_1^p(\alpha)(1-c)^{-1}[\Phi^{1-c}(\beta) - \Phi^{1-c}(\alpha)] \quad \text{if} \quad p > 0 ,$$

while

$$I(\alpha,\beta) \leq F_1^p(\beta)(1-c)^{-1}[\Phi^{1-c}(\beta) - \Phi^{1-c}(\alpha)] \quad \text{if} \quad p < 0 .$$

When $p > 0$, $c > 1$ must hold, so

$$(13) \qquad (c-1)^{-1} F_1^p(\alpha)\Phi^{1-c}(\alpha) \leq I(\alpha,\beta) + (c-1)^{-1} F_1^p(\alpha)\Phi^{1-c}(\beta) .$$

From (13) we at once obtain, for all $\beta > 0$ (or $\alpha > 0$),

$$(13') \qquad 0 \leq \overline{\lim_{\alpha\to 0}} \, (c-1)^{-1} F_1^p(\alpha)\Phi^{1-c}(\alpha) \leq I(0,\beta) \quad \text{if} \quad p > 0 ;$$

$$(13'') \qquad 0 \leq (c-1)^{-1} F_1^p(\alpha)\Phi^{1-c}(\alpha) \leq I(\alpha,\infty) \quad \text{if} \quad p > 0 \quad \text{and} \quad \Phi(\infty) = \infty .$$

When $p < 0$, we obtain no results of this kind since the inequality involving $F_1^p(\beta)\Phi^{1-c}(\beta)$ runs in the wrong direction.

Next we see what limit results can be obtained if $J(a,b)$ is convergent for $a = 0$ or $b = \infty$. For $0 < \alpha < \beta < \infty$, we have

$$F_1(\beta) = F_1(\alpha) + \int_\alpha^\beta f\varphi \, dt = F_1(\alpha) + \int_\alpha^\beta \left\{f\Phi^{(p-c)/p}\varphi^{1/p}\right\}\left\{\Phi^{(c-p)/p}\varphi^{(p-1)/p}\right\} dt$$

$$\leq F_1(\alpha) + J(\alpha,\beta)^{1/p}\left\{\left(\frac{p-1}{c-1}\right)\left[\Phi^{(c-1)/(p-1)}(\beta) - \Phi^{(c-1)/(p-1)}(\alpha)\right]\right\}^{(p-1)/p}$$

if $p > 1$, with the opposite inequality in case $p < 0$ or $0 < p < 1$. Hence if $p > 1$, we have

$$(14) \qquad \begin{aligned} F_1(\beta)\Phi^{(1-c)/p}(\beta) &\leq F_1(\alpha)\,\Phi^{(1-c)/p}(\beta) \\ &\quad + J^{1/p}(\alpha,\beta)\left\{\left(\frac{p-1}{c-1}\right)\left[1 - (\Phi(\alpha)/\Phi(\beta))^{(c-1)/(p-1)}\right]\right\}^{(p-1)/p}, \end{aligned}$$

with $\geq$ holding in case $p < 0$ or $0 < p < 1$. Omitting details, we can use (14) and its reverse to obtain the following results: For $p < 0$, $c < 1$,

$$(14') \qquad 0 \leq \overline{\lim_{\beta\to\infty}} \, F_1^p(\beta)\Phi^{1-c}(\beta) \leq [(1-p)/(1-c)]^{p-1} J(\alpha,\infty) \quad \text{if} \quad \Phi(\infty) = \infty ;$$

$$(14'') \qquad 0 \leq F_1^p(\beta)\Phi^{1-c}(\beta) \leq [(p-1)/(c-1)]^{p-1} J(0,\beta) \quad \text{if} \quad p > 1, \; c > 1,$$

or if $p < 0$, $c < 1$,

$$(14''') \quad 0 \le \overline{\lim_{\beta \to \infty}} \; F_1^p(\beta)\Phi^{1-c}(\beta) \le [(p-1)/(c-1)]^{p-1} \, J(\alpha,\infty) \quad \text{if} \quad p > 1, \quad c > 1, \quad \Phi(\infty) = \infty .$$

Before proceeding to the case $i = 2$ or $p/(1-c) > 0$, we apply the results (13) and (14) to (12a) and (12b) which, in our case, can be written in the form

$$(12a') \quad I + |p/(1-c)| \, F_1^p(b)\,\Phi^{1-c}(b) \le |p/(1-c)|^p \, J + |p/(1-c)| \, F_1^p(a)\,\Phi^{1-c}(a) ,$$

if $p < 0$ or $p > 1$, while for $0 < p < 1$, we have

$$(12b') \quad I + |p/(1-c)| \, F_1^p(b)\,\Phi^{1-c}(b) \ge |p/(1-c)|^p \, J + |p/(1-c)| \, F_1^p(a)\,\Phi^{1-c}(a) .$$

If $p > 1$, $c > 1$, or if $p < 0$, $c < 1$, we use (12a') and (14") to obtain, for $0 < b < \infty$,

$$(15') \qquad I(0,b) + |p/(1-c)| \, F_1^p(b)\,\Phi^{1-c}(b) \le |p/(1-c)|^p \, J(0,b) ,$$

which is an improvement of (1) for finite b, and is valid whenever $J(0,b)$ converges.

Similarly, if $p > 1$, $c > 1$, or if $p < 0$, $c < 1$, it follows that for $0 < a < \infty$,

$$(15'') \qquad \begin{aligned} & I(a,\infty) + \lim_{b \to \infty} |p/(1-c)| \, F_1^p(b)\,\Phi^{1-c}(b) \\ & \le |p/(1-c)|^p \, J(a,\infty) + |p/(1-c)| \, F_1^p(a)\,\Phi^{1-c}(a) , \end{aligned}$$

and this is a <u>new</u> inequality. From (15') we also obtain

$$(16) \qquad I(0,\infty) + \lim_{b \to \infty} |p/(1-c)| \, F_1^p(b)\,\Phi^{1-c}(b) \le |p/(1-c)|^p \, J(0,\infty) ,$$

which is, in general, an improvement of (1) for $b = \infty$ $(p > 1, \; c > 1)$. By (14''') or (14'), we see that the limit in (15") and (16) is 0 if $\Phi(\infty) = \infty$, so (16) reduces to (1) for $p > 1$, $c > 1$ in this case. Note that if $\Phi(\infty) = \gamma > 0$ is finite, then (15') shows that the monotone limit $\lim_{b\to\infty} F_1^p(b)$ must also be finite. This case can actually occur; for example, take

$$f(x) = \varphi(x) = 1 \quad \text{for} \quad 0 \le x \le 1 \qquad \text{and} \qquad f(x) = \varphi(x) = 0 \quad \text{for} \quad x > 1 .$$

If $p < 0$, $c < 1$, the limit in (15") is also 0 if $\Phi(\infty)$ is finite provided $F_1(\infty) = \infty$, because

$$F_1^p(b)\,\Phi^{1-c}(b) \to 0 \cdot \gamma^{1-c} = 0$$

in this case.

Now suppose $0 < p < 1$, so that (12b') applies, and we assume the convergence of $I(a,b)$ for $a = 0$ or $b = \infty$. By (12b') and (13"), we see that if $0 < p < 1$ and $c > 1$, then for $0 < a < \infty$ we have

$$(17') \qquad I(a,\infty) \geq |p/(1-c)|^p\, J(a,\infty) + |p/(1-c)|\, F_1^p(a)\,\Phi^{1-c}(a) \quad \text{if} \quad \Phi(\infty) = \infty ,$$

which is an improvement of (2). Similarly using (12b') and (13'), we obtain for $0 < b < \infty$, the new inequality

$$(17'') \qquad I(0,b) + |p/(1-c)|\, F_1^p(b)\,\Phi^{1-c}(b) \geq |p/(1-c)|^p\, J(0,b) .$$

Letting either $a \to 0$ in (17') or $b \to \infty$ in (17"), and using (13') or (13"), we obtain

$$(18) \qquad I(0,\infty) \geq |p/(1-c)|^p\, J(0,\infty) \quad \text{if} \quad \Phi(\infty) = \infty, \quad 0 < p < 1 ,$$

which is (2) for $a = 0$.

4. THE CASE $i = 2$

We now turn to the case $i = 2$, where p, c must satisfy the condition $p/(1-c) > 0$, which is assumed in what follows. In those cases where we assume the convergence of $I(a,b)$ for $a = 0$ or $b = \infty$ in (12b), we use the fact that, for $0 < \alpha < \beta < \infty$,

$$I(\alpha,\beta) = \int_\alpha^\beta F_2^p\, \Phi^{-c}\, \varphi\, dx \geq F_2^p(\beta)(1-c)^{-1}[\Phi^{1-c}(\beta) - \Phi^{1-c}(\alpha)] \qquad (p > 0) .$$

Hence we have

$$(19) \qquad (1-c)^{-1} F_2^p(\beta)\,\Phi^{1-c}(\beta) \leq I(\alpha,\beta) + (1-c)^{-1} F_2^p(\beta)\,\Phi^{1-c}(\alpha) \qquad (p > 0) ;$$

for $p < 0$, no useful result is obtained. By (19), we have

$$(19') \qquad 0 \leq (1-c)^{-1} F_2^p(\beta)\,\Phi^{1-c}(\beta) \leq I(0,\beta) , \qquad p > 0, \quad c < 1, \quad \beta > 0 ,$$

$$(19'') \quad 0 \leq \overline{\lim_{\beta\to\infty}}\, (1-c)^{-1} F_2^p(\beta)\,\Phi^{1-c}(\beta) \leq I(\alpha,\infty) , \qquad p > 0, \quad c < 1, \quad \alpha > 0 .$$

For $0 < \alpha < \beta < \infty$, we also have

$$F_2(\alpha) = F_2(\beta) + \int_\alpha^\beta f\,\varphi\,dt$$

and so, proceding as in (14), we obtain

$$(20)\quad F_2(\alpha)\Phi^{(1-c)/p}(\alpha) \le F_2(\beta)\Phi^{(1-c)/p}(\alpha) + J^{1/p}(\alpha,\beta)\left\{\left(\frac{1-p}{c-1}\right)\left[1-(\Phi(\alpha)/\Phi(\beta))^{(c-1)/(p-1)}\right]\right\}^{(p-1)/p}$$

if $p > 1$, with the opposite inequality for $p < 0$ or $0 < p < 1$. From (20), it follows that

$$(20')\quad 0 \le \overline{\lim_{\alpha\to 0}}\, F_2^p(\alpha)\,\Phi^{1-c}(\alpha) \le [(1-p)/(c-1)]^{p-1}\, J(0,\beta) \quad \text{if} \quad p < 0,\ c > 1\ ;$$

$$(20'')\quad 0 \le F_2^p(\alpha)\Phi^{1-c}(\alpha) \le [(1-p)/(c-1)]^{p-1}\, J(\alpha,\infty) \quad \text{if} \quad p < 0,\ c > 1 \quad \text{or} \quad p > 1,\ c < 1 \ \text{and}\ \Phi(\infty) = \infty\ ;$$

$$(20''')\quad 0 \le \overline{\lim_{\alpha\to 0}}\, F_2^p(\alpha)\,\Phi^{1-c}(\alpha) \le [(p-1)/(1-c)]^{p-1}\, J(0,\beta) \quad \text{if} \quad p > 1,\ c < 1\ .$$

Now for the case $i = 2$, the boundary terms in (12a), (12b) are positive since $p/(1-c) > 0$. Again we deal with (12a) first and so assume $J(a,b)$ converges for $a = 0$ or $b = \infty$.

For $p > 1$, $c < 1$ or $p < 0$, $c > 1$, (20") implies that, for $0<a<\infty$,

$$(21')\quad |p/(1-c)|^p\, J(a,\infty) \ge I(a,\infty) + |p/(1-c)|\, F_2^p(a)\,\Phi^{1-c}(a) \quad \text{if} \quad \Phi(\infty) = \infty\ .$$

In the case $p > 1$, $c < 1$, (21') holds even if $\Phi(\infty) = \gamma > 0$ is finite since then

$$F_2^p(b)\,\Phi^{1-c}(b) \to 0\cdot\gamma^{1-c} = 0 \quad \text{as} \quad b \to \infty$$

is clear. Hence in this case (21') is an improvement of (3). Moreover, by (20') or (20''') it follows from (12a) that for $p > 1$, $c < 1$, or $p < 0$, $c > 1$, and $0 < b < \infty$, we have

$$(21'')\quad |p/(1-c)|^p\, J(0,b) + |p/(1-c)|\, F_2^p(b)\,\Phi^{1-c}(b) \ge I(0,b)\ ,$$

and this is a <u>new</u> inequality. From (21") and (20"), we obtain

$$(22)\quad |p/(1-c)|^p J(0,\infty) \ge I(0,\infty) \quad \text{for}\quad p>1,\ c<1;\ \text{or}\ p<0,\ c>1,\ \Phi(\infty)=\infty.$$

We turn to the case $0 < p < 1$, so (12b) applies, and we assume the convergence of $I(a,b)$ for $a = 0$ or $b = \infty$. By (12b) and (19'), for $0<b<\infty$ we have

$$(23')\quad |p/(1-c)|^p J(0,b) + |p/(1-c)| F_2^p(b)\Phi^{1-c}(b) \le I(0,b) \quad \text{if} \quad 0<p<1, \quad c<1 ,$$

and this is an improvement of (4) for finite b. Similarly, (12b) and (19") imply that for $0 < a < \infty$ we have

$$(23'')\quad |p/(1-c)|^p J(a,\infty) \le I(a,\infty) + |p/(1-c)| F_2^p(a)\Phi^{1-c}(a) \quad \text{if} \quad 0<p<1, \quad c<1 ,$$

and this inequality is <u>new</u>. Using either (23') and (19"), or (23") and (19'), we obtain

$$(24)\qquad |p/(1-c)|^p J(0,\infty) \le I(0,\infty) \quad \text{if} \quad 0 < p < 1, \quad c < 1 ,$$

which is (4) for $b = \infty$.

For the inequalities (5) and (6) corresponding to $c = 1$, we shall merely indicate the beginning of the analysis, and the final inequalities one may obtain, leaving all details as a problem for the reader. The methods are analogous to those used above for $c \neq 1$ and, as in [1], we begin by setting

$$v_1(x) = \Phi(x)/\Phi(a) , \qquad v_2(x) = \Phi(b)/\Phi(x) , \qquad 0 < a \le x \le b ,$$

and

$$u(x) = F_i^p(x) \log v_j(x) \qquad (i,j = 1,2) .$$

Then

$$u' = (-1)^{i-1} p F_i^{p-1} f \varphi \log v_j + (-1)^{j-1} F_i^p \Phi^{-1} \varphi \qquad \text{a.e.} ,$$

so integrating over $[a,b]$ we obtain

$$(25)\qquad I(a,b) = |p| K(a,b) + (-1)^{j-1} F_i^p \log v_j \Big|_a^b ,$$

where i, j, p are chosen so that $(-1)^{i+j-1} p > 0$, and now

$$(26)\quad I(a,b) = \int_a^b F_i^p \Phi^{-1} \varphi \, dx , \qquad K(a,b) = \int_a^b F_i^{p-1} \log v_j \, f \, \varphi \, dx ,$$

$$(27)\qquad J(a,b) = \int_a^b f^p \Phi^{p-1} (\log v_j)^p \varphi \, dx .$$

The final inequalities obtained are these:

$$(28)\quad \int_0^b F_1^p \Phi^{-1}\varphi\,dx \le p^p \int_0^b f^p \Phi^{p-1}(\log[\Phi(b)/\Phi(x)])^p \varphi\,dx \quad (p>1,\ \ 0<b<\infty)\ ;$$

$$(29)\quad \int_a^\infty F_2^p \Phi^{-1}\varphi\,dx \le p^p \int_a^\infty f^p \Phi^{p-1}(\log[\Phi(x)/\Phi(a)])^p \varphi\,dx \quad (p>1,\ \ 0<a<\infty)\ ;$$

$$(30)\quad \int_a^\infty F_1^p \Phi^{-1}\varphi\,dx \le |p|^p \int_a^\infty f^p \Phi^{p-1}(\log[\Phi(x)/\Phi(a)])^p \varphi\,dx \quad (p<0,\ \ 0<a<\infty)$$

provided $\Phi(\infty) = \infty$, or even if $\Phi(\infty) < \infty$ but $F_1(\infty) = \infty$;

$$(31)\quad \int_0^b F_2^p \Phi^{-1}\varphi\,dx \le |p|^p \int_0^b f^p \Phi^{p-1}(\log[\Phi(b)/\Phi(x)])^p \varphi\,dx \quad (p<0,\ \ 0<b<\infty)\ ;$$

$$(32)\quad \int_0^b F_1^p \Phi^{-1}\varphi\,dx \ge p^p \int_0^b f^p \Phi^{p-1}(\log[\Phi(b)/\Phi(x)])^p \varphi\,dx \quad (0<p<1,\ \ 0<b<\infty);$$

$$(33)\quad \int_a^\infty F_2^p \Phi^{-1}\varphi\,dx \ge p^p \int_a^\infty f^p \Phi^{p-1}(\log[\Phi(x)/\Phi(a)])^p \varphi\,dx \quad (0<p<1,\ \ 0<a<\infty).$$

The inequality (30) actually holds in <u>all</u> cases and, in general, may be improved to

$$\int_a^\infty F_1^p\, \Phi^{-1}\, \varphi\, dx + \lim_{b\to\infty}\ |p|\ F_1^p(b)\, \log[\Phi(b)/\Phi(a)] \le |p|^p \int_a^\infty f^p\, \Phi^{p-1}(\log[\Phi(x)/\Phi(a)])^p\, \varphi\, dx\ ,$$

where the limit term is 0 in the cases indicated at (30).

REFERENCES

1. E.T. Copson, Some integral inequalities, <u>Proc. Roy. Soc. Edinburgh 75A</u> 13 (1975/76), 157-164.

2. G. Chrystal, <u>Algebra, an Elementary Textbook</u>, <u>v. 2</u>, <u>7th ed.</u>, Chelsea reprint, New York, 1964.

3. G.H. Hardy, J.E. Littlewood, and G. Pólya, <u>Inequalities</u>, <u>2nd ed.</u>, Cambridge, 1952.

ON ENVELOPING SERIES FOR SOME OF THE SPECIAL FUNCTIONS, AND ON INTEGRAL INEQUALITIES INVOLVING THEM

Dieter K. Ross
Department of Mathematics
La Trobe University
Victoria 3083
AUSTRALIA

Arvind Mahajan
Department of Mathematics
La Trobe University
Victoria 3083
AUSTRALIA

ABSTRACT. The work of the present paper deals with enveloping series for certain of the special functions of mathematical physics. In many (but not all) cases, the Maclaurin-series expansion of the function concerned envelops the function itself and can be regarded as an asymptotic expansion of the function about the origin.

An important case refers to the hypergeometric function ${}_2F_1(a,b;c;x)$, which has simple upper and/or lower bounds whenever its Maclaurin-series expansion has coefficients with nonconstant sign. A similar result is found for certain other higher-order hypergeometric functions, including the confluent hypergeometric function ${}_1F_1(a;b;x)$. The methods described here have applications to other classes of functions, including those referred to in Truesdell's "Essay toward a unified theory of special functions." It is Truesdell's essay which has prompted the present approach to the subject.

1. INTRODUCTION

Many of the special functions of mathematical physics, particularly those which can be derived from a Sturm-Liouville type of differential equation, are enveloped (see Pólya and Szegö [10]) by their Maclaurin-series expansion. The simplest and best-known of these are the trigonometric cosine and sine functions, for these satisfy the inequalities

$$(1)\quad (-1)^{n+1}\left[\cos x - \sum_{\nu=0}^{n} \frac{(-1)^{\nu} x^{2\nu}}{(2\nu)!}\right] \geq 0 \quad \text{for each } n \in \mathbb{N} \text{ and } x \in \mathbb{R} ,$$

and

(2) $$(-1)^{n+1}\left[\sin x - \sum_{\nu=0}^{n} \frac{(-1)^\nu x^{2\nu+1}}{(2\nu+1)!}\right] \geq 0 \quad \text{for each } n \in \mathbb{N} \text{ and } x \geq 0 .$$

Here $\mathbb{N}$ is used to denote the positive integers, and $\mathbb{R}$ to denote the set of all real numbers. These are old results; they appear, for example, in Durell and Robson [3], who obtained them by starting with the simple inequality $\cos x \leq 1$, for all $x \in \mathbb{R}$, and integrating with respect to x, $(2n+1)$ times.

The inequalities given above can be used to prove similar results for many other special functions, but only a few of these will be given here. Unless otherwise stated, all of the formulas quoted can be found in Abramowitz and Stegun [1]. In all cases, they have been cross-checked with other books or original research papers, which are too numerous to mention here.

2. THE BESSEL FUNCTIONS OF THE FIRST KIND $J_\alpha(x)$, with $\alpha > -1$, $x \geq 0$

It is known that

(3) $$J_\alpha(x) = \frac{2(x/2)^\alpha}{\Gamma(1/2)\Gamma(\alpha+(1/2))} \int_0^1 (1-t^2)^{\alpha-(1/2)} \cos(tx)\, dt ,$$

where $\Gamma(\beta)$ denotes the Euler gamma function, provided that $\alpha > -1/2$, $x \geq 0$. (The case $-1/2 \geq \alpha > -1$ will be treated anon.) It follows from (1) that

$$(-1)^{n+1}\left[(1-t^2)^{\alpha-(1/2)} \cos(tx) - \sum_{\nu=0}^{n} \frac{(-1)^\nu x^{2\nu}}{(2\nu)!} (1-t^2)^{\alpha-(1/2)}\, t^{2\nu}\right] \geq 0$$

for each $n \in \mathbb{N}$, $x \in \mathbb{R}$, and $0 \leq t \leq 1$. On multiplying the above by the factor $2(x/2)^\alpha/\Gamma(1/2)\Gamma(\alpha+(1/2))$, and integrating with respect to t, this inequality becomes

$$(-1)^{n+1}\left[J_\alpha(x) - \sum_{\nu=0}^{n} \frac{(-1)^\nu x^{2\nu+\alpha}}{(2\nu)!\, A_\alpha} \int_0^1 (1-t^2)^{\alpha-(1/2)}\, t^{2\nu}\, dt\right] \geq 0 ,$$

where $A_\alpha = 2^{\alpha-1}\,\Gamma(1/2)\Gamma(\alpha+(1/2))$.

Since the integral appearing in the previous line is related to the beta function, this can be transformed, by the duplication formula for the gamma function, to give

(4) $$(-1)^{n+1}\left[J_\alpha(x) - \sum_{\nu=0}^{n} \frac{(-1)^\nu (x/2)^{2\nu+\alpha}}{\nu!\,\Gamma(\nu+\alpha+1)}\right] \geq 0 \qquad \text{for each } n \in \mathbb{N} .$$

In other words, $J_\alpha(x)$ is enveloped by the n-th partial sums of its Maclaurin-series expansion under the conditions $\alpha > -1/2$, $x \geq 0$.

The above inequality (4) can be extended to $\alpha > -1$, $x \geq 0$, and $n \in \mathbb{N}$, but $n \neq 0$. The proof depends on the existence of the identity

$$\int_0^x t^{-\alpha+1} J_\alpha(t)\, dt = 2^{1-\alpha}/\Gamma(\alpha) - x^{1-\alpha} J_{\alpha-1}(x) , \qquad \alpha > 0 ,$$

which is applied to the inequality (4).

This is not a new result; it first appeared as a problem proposed by Askey [2], who published a partial but different proof two years later, in 1976.

3. THE STURVE FUNCTIONS $H_\alpha(x)$, WITH $\alpha > -1$, $x \geq 0$

The Sturve functions are very much like the Bessel function described previously, except that the cosine in the integral representation (3) is replaced by the sine function. Thus

$$H_\alpha(x) = \frac{2(x/2)^\alpha}{\Gamma(1/2)\Gamma(\alpha+(1/2))} \int_0^1 (1 - t^2)^{\alpha-(1/2)} \sin(tx)\, dt ,$$

provided $\alpha > -1/2$, $x \geq 0$. In this case, the analysis follows precisely the same line as for the Bessel functions, but here the starting point is inequality (2), and the conclusion is

$$(5) \qquad (-1)^{n+1}\left[H_\alpha(x) - \sum_{\nu=0}^{n} \frac{(-1)^\nu (x/2)^{2\nu+\alpha+1}}{\Gamma(\nu+(3/2))\Gamma(\nu+\alpha+(3/2))}\right] \geq 0 \qquad \text{for each} \quad n \in \mathbb{N} .$$

Once again, this inequality can be shown to be valid for $\alpha > -1$, $x \geq 0$, and for each $n \in \mathbb{N}$, except $n = 0$, by using the identity

$$\int_0^x t^{1-\alpha} H_\alpha(t)\, dt = 2^{-\alpha} x/\Gamma(3/2)\Gamma(\alpha+(3/2)) - x^{1-\alpha} H_{\alpha-1}(x) , \qquad \alpha > 0 .$$

The result for Struve functions appears to be new, for the authors have not found this inequality in the literature.

4. THE LAGUERRE POLYNOMIAL $L_n^{(\alpha)}(x)$, WITH $\alpha > -1$, $x \geq 0$, $n \in \mathbb{N}$

It is interesting to note that the earlier-mentioned inequalities for the Bessel functions $J_\alpha(x)$ can be used to derive other enveloping series for $e^{-x} L_n^{(\alpha)}(x)$. The method is quite simple; it makes use of the identity

$$e^{-x} L_n^{(\alpha)}(x) = \frac{x^{-\alpha/2}}{n!} \int_0^\infty e^{-t}\, t^{n+(\alpha/2)}\, J_\alpha(2\sqrt{tx})\, dt .$$

The proof is based on the extension of (4) to $\alpha > -1$, by replacing x by $2\sqrt{tx}$, for then, on multiplying by the obvious factors and integrating with respect to t, it appears that

$$(6) \qquad (-1)^{m+1}\left[e^{-x} L_n^{(\alpha)}(x) - \sum_{\nu=0}^{m} \binom{n+\nu+\alpha}{n} \frac{(-x)^\nu}{\nu!}\right] \geq 0 \qquad \text{for all} \quad m \in \mathbb{N} .$$

Here the notation $\binom{n+\beta}{n}$ needs some explanation for noninteger values of β. It is taken to mean

$$\Gamma(n+\beta+1)/\Gamma(n+1)\Gamma(\beta+1) = (\beta)_n/n! ,$$

where $(\beta)_n$ is the Pochhammer symbol. In (6), the case $n = 0$ requires separate treatment; but because $L_0^{(\alpha)}(x) = 1$, in this case the inequality amounts to

$$(7) \qquad (-1)^{m+1}\left[e^{-x} - \sum_{\nu=0}^{m} \frac{(-x)^\nu}{\nu!}\right] \geq 0 \qquad \text{for} \quad m \in \mathbb{N} ,$$

and this can be proved more easily by noting that

$$e^{-x} \leq 1 \qquad \text{for all} \quad x \geq 0$$

and integrating this inequality m times. The inequality (7), which is important in its own right, will be required later.

5. THE HERMITE POLYNOMIALS $H_n(x)$, WITH $x \geq 0$ AND $n \in \mathbb{N}$

In order to clarify what is meant by a Hermite polynomial, it suffices to say that Hermite polynomials are orthogonal polynomials associated with the interval $(-\infty,\infty)$ and with weight function $\exp(-x^2)$. In this case, it is known that

$$e^{-x^2} H_n(x) = 2^{n+1} \pi^{-1/2} \int_0^\infty e^{-t^2} t^n \cos(2tx - (n\pi/2))\, dt ,$$

and this may be used in the same way as before to prove that

$$(8a) \qquad (-1)^{m+1}\left[(-1)^n e^{-x^2} H_{2n}(x) - 2^{2n} n! \sum_{\nu=0}^{m} (-1)^\nu \binom{n+\nu-(1/2)}{n} \frac{x^{2\nu}}{\nu!}\right] \geq 0$$

and

$$(8b) \qquad (-1)^{m+1}\left[(-1)^n e^{-x^2} H_{2n+1}(x) - 2^{2n+1} n! \sum_{\nu=0}^{m} (-1)^\nu \binom{n+\nu+(1/2)}{n} \frac{x^{2\nu+1}}{\nu!}\right] \geq 0$$

for all $m \in \mathbb{N}$, with $x \in \mathbb{R}$ in the former case, and $x \geq 0$ in the latter case. The same results can be deduced from the known relationships between the Laguerre and Hermite polynomials, together with the inequality (6).

6. OTHER RESULTS BASED ON THE COSINE, SINE, AND EXPONENTIAL INEQUALITIES, WHEN $x \geq 0$, $n \in \mathbb{N}$

It is clear from the method developed so far that the following inequalities apply to the cosine, sine, and Fresnel integrals:

$$(-1)^{n+1}\left[\int_0^x \frac{1-\cos t}{t}\,dt - \sum_{\nu=1}^{n+1} \frac{(-1)^{\nu+1}\, x^{2\nu}}{2\nu\,(2\nu)!}\right] \geq 0\ , \quad \text{but for all } x \in \mathbb{R}\ ,$$

$$(-1)^{n+1}\left[\int_0^x \frac{\sin t}{t}\,dt - \sum_{\nu=0}^{n} \frac{(-1)^{\nu}\, x^{2\nu+1}}{(2\nu+1)(2\nu+1)!}\right] \geq 0\ ,$$

$$(-1)^{n+1}\left[\int_0^x \cos t^2\,dt - \sum_{\nu=0}^{n} \frac{(-1)^{\nu}\, x^{4\nu+1}}{(4\nu+1)(2\nu)!}\right] \geq 0\ ,$$

and

$$(-1)^{n+1}\left[\int_0^x \sin t^2\,dt - \sum_{\nu=0}^{n} \frac{(-1)^{\nu}\, x^{4\nu+3}}{(4\nu+3)(2\nu+1)!}\right] \geq 0\ .$$

On the other hand, the exponential inequality referred to in (7) leads to enveloping series for the error function, the complementary exponential integral, and the incomplete gamma function. Thus,

$$(-1)^{n+1}\left[\int_0^x e^{-t^2}\,dt - \sum_{\nu=0}^{n} \frac{(-1)^{\nu}\, x^{2\nu+1}}{(2\nu+1)\,\nu!}\right] \geq 0\ ,$$

$$(-1)^{n+1}\left[\int_0^x \frac{1-e^{t}}{t}\,dt - \sum_{\nu=1}^{n+1} \frac{(-1)^{\nu+1}\, x^{\nu}}{\nu\,\nu!}\right] \geq 0\ ,$$

and

$$(-1)^{n+1}\left[\int_0^x e^{-t}\, t^{\alpha-1}\,dt - \sum_{\nu=0}^{n} \frac{(-1)^{\nu}\, x^{\nu+\alpha}}{(\nu+\alpha)\,\nu!}\right] \geq 0 \qquad \text{for} \quad \alpha > 0\ .$$

Obviously many other such results can be found by equally simple manipulations. One of the more interesting examples is an inequality, involving the confluent hypergeometric function ${}_1F_1(a;b;x)$, which can be deduced from (7). Thus

$$(-1)^{n+1}\left[e^{-x} - \sum_{\nu=0}^{n} \frac{(-1)^{\nu} x^{\nu}}{\nu!}\right] \geq 0 \qquad \text{for} \quad x \geq 0,\quad n \in \mathbb{N}\ ,$$

implies that

$$(-1)^{n+1}\left[\int_0^1 e^{-tx}\, t^{b-a-1}(1-t)^{a-1}\,dt - \sum_{\nu=0}^{n} \frac{(-1)^{\nu}\, x^{\nu}\, \Gamma(\nu+b-a)\,\Gamma(a)}{\nu!\,\Gamma(\nu+b)}\right] \geq 0$$

provided $b > a > 0$. However, the integral in the above line is equal to

$$\frac{\Gamma(a)\,\Gamma(b-a)}{\Gamma(b)}\, e^{-x}\ {}_1F_1(a;b;x) ,$$

and so

$$(-1)^{n+1}\left[e^{-x}\ {}_1F_1(a;b;x) - \sum_{\nu=0}^{n} \frac{(-1)^{\nu}\, x^{\nu}(b-a)_{\nu}}{\nu!\,(b)_{\nu}}\right] \geq 0 ,$$

provided that $x \geq 0$, $n \in \mathbb{N}$, and $b > a > 0$. The restrictions on a, b, and x may be removed by making use of the Kummer identity

$$e^{-x}\ {}_1F_1(a;b;x) = {}_1F_1(b-a;b;-x) ,$$

in which case the above inequality may be replaced by the more attractive form

(9) $$\frac{(a)_{n+1}}{(b)_{n+1}}\, x^{n+1}\left[{}_1F_1(a;b;x) - \sum_{\nu=0}^{n} \frac{(a)_{\nu}\, x^{\nu}}{(b)_{\nu}\,\nu!}\right] \geq 0, \qquad -b \notin \mathbb{N} .$$

See Section 8, where the method is described in more detail.

7. THE BINOMIAL THEOREM FOR $(1+x)^{\alpha}$, WITH $x > -1$, $\alpha \in \mathbb{R}$

All the functions considered thus far except for the one in (9) have had series expansions with coefficients of alternating sign when $x > 0$. Thus, it is natural to ask if there exist similar inequalities for other elementary functions which do not have coefficients of strictly alternating sign in their expansions. The answer is "Yes," and perhaps the simplest of these is the function $(1+x)^{\alpha}$. In this case, there exist values of x and α within the specified ranges $x > -1$, $\alpha \in \mathbb{R}$, for which the coefficients in the Maclaurin-series expansion are not of alternating sign, even when x is replaced by $-x$. Nevertheless, inequalities involving the n-th partial sum do exist, for Gerber [8] proved that

(10) $$\binom{\alpha}{n+1} x^{n+1}\left[(1+x)^{\alpha} - \sum_{\nu=0}^{n} \binom{\alpha}{\nu} x^{\nu}\right] \geq 0 \qquad \text{for each} \quad n \in \mathbb{N} ,$$

with the term in square brackets equal to zero if, and only if, α is one of the integers $0,1,2,\ldots,n$, provided that $x > -1$, $x \neq 0$. Gerber's method is rather complicated, for he uses a method of induction involving both n and α; but a simplified proof of the same result appears in Ross [11].

8. THE HYPERGEOMETRIC FUNCTION ${}_2F_1(a,b;c;x)$

One of the most important applications of the inequality (10) refers to the hypergeometric function which can be defined by the series

(11) $${}_2F_1(a,b;c;x) = 1 + \sum_{\nu=1}^{\infty} \frac{(a)_\nu\,(b)_\nu\,x^\nu}{(c)_\nu\,\nu!}\,.$$

This is convergent for $|x| < 1$, as proved by the ratio test. Notice that, in fact, the series terminates whenever a or b is a nonpositive integer, and is without meaning if c is a nonpositive integer, unless a and/or b is a negative integer and

$$c = -(m+1), -(m+2), -(m+3), \ldots ,$$

where m is the greater of the integer $-a$ and/or $-b$. In the above case, the series (11) is convergent for all $x \in \mathbb{R}$. Notice that the series is unchanged if a and b are interchanged. For a fuller discussion of these points, see Szegö [13].

Now it is known that the hypergeometric function under discussion has the integral representation

(12) $${}_2F_1(a,b;c;x) = \frac{\Gamma(c)}{\Gamma(c-b)\,\Gamma(b)} \int_0^1 t^{b-1}\,(1-t)^{c-b-1}\,(1-tx)^{-a}\,dt$$

when $c > b > 0$, provided a and x are such that the integral exists. This point need not be labored here, for the conditions are quite obvious.

An inequality involving the n-th partial sum of the series in (11) can now be found by using the result for the binomial theorem given in (10). On replacing x by $-tx$, multiplying by the appropriate factors, and integrating with respect to t, it appears that

(13) $$(a)_{n+1}\,x^{n+1}\left[{}_2F_1(a,b;c;x) - \sum_{\nu=0}^{n} \frac{(a)_\nu\,(b)_\nu\,x^\nu}{(c)_\nu\,\nu!}\right] \geq 0\,,$$

where the first term in the series is taken to be 1 when $\nu = 0$, provided $c > b > 0$ with a and x so chosen that the integral (12) exists.

In the other cases, where $c > 0 > b$ or $0 > c > b$, the inequality in (13) must be modified. Then

(14) $$\frac{(a)_{n+1}\,(b)_{n+1}}{(c)_{n+1}}\,x^{n+1}\left[{}_2F_1(a,b;c;x) - \sum_{\nu=0}^{n} \frac{(a)_\nu\,(b)_\nu\,x^\nu}{(c)_\nu\,\nu!}\right] \geq 0\,,$$

whenever the series is meaningful (i.e., $-c \notin \mathbb{N}$) and $c > b$. This result follows by applying the fact that

$$\frac{ab}{c}\int_0^x {}_2F_1(a+1,b+1;c+1;t)\,dt = {}_2F_1(a,b;c;x) - 1$$

to (14) as often as required.

The same inequality (14) is valid when $c < b$. This can easily be proved for $b > 0$ by using the identity

$$ {}_2F_1(a,b;c;x) = (1-x)^{c-a-b}\ {}_2F_1(c-a,c-b;c;x) , $$

together with the uniqueness theorem for the Maclaurin-series expansions. The extension to $b < 0$ is equally simple and can be deduced from the identity

$$ c\ {}_2F_1(a,b-1;c;x) + (a-b)x\ {}_2F_1(a,b;c+1;x) = c\ {}_2F_1(a-1,b;c;x) . $$

The fact that the inequality (14) applies whenever the series is meaningful is a very strong result. In fact, only a few inequalities for the general hypergeometric functions are known (see Flett [6] and Erber [4]). Of course, there is an obvious extension to the higher-order hypergeometric function ${}_pF_q$, in case $p = q$ or $p = q + 1$, which is based on the identity

$$ {}_pF_q(a_1,a_2,\dots,a_p;b_1,b_2,\dots,b_q;x) $$
$$ = \frac{\Gamma(b_1)}{\Gamma(a_1)\Gamma(b_1-a_1)} \int_0^1 t^{a_1-1}(1-t)^{b_1-a_1-1}\ {}_{p-1}F_{q-1}(a_2,\dots,a_p;b_2,\dots,b_q;xt)\, dt . $$

The inequality (14) can be applied to the Jacobi polynomials, which may be defined by the relation

$$ P_n^{(\alpha,\beta)}(x) = \binom{n+\alpha}{n} {}_2F_1(-n,n+\alpha+\beta+1;\alpha+1;(1/2)-(1/2)x) . $$

Hence, it is an easy matter to show that

$$ (-1)^{m+1}\left[P_n^{(\alpha,\beta)}(x) - \binom{n+\alpha}{n} \sum_{\nu=0}^{m} \frac{(-n)_\nu (n+\alpha+\beta+1)_\nu\ (1-x)^\nu}{2^\nu (\alpha+1)_\nu\ \nu!}\right] \geq 0 $$

for $\alpha > -1$, $\alpha+\beta > -1$, $|x| \leq 1$, and $m = 0,1,\dots,n$, provided the term under the summation sign is replaced by 1 when $m = 0$. A particular case of this was proved by Askey [2], who restricted his argument to the case $-1 \leq x \leq 1$ with $\alpha \geq \beta > -1$. In fact, these two results overlap.

Obviously many other inequalities of this kind can be obtained by using special values for a, b, and c in the hypergeometric function. The simplest of these are the enveloping series for $\sinh^{-1}(x)$, $\tan^{-1}(x)$, and $\log(1 + x)$, which are referred to by Pólya and Szegö [10], and which could be proved by much more elementary methods.

The work to date is obviously related to the study of the sign of the remainder in the Maclaurin-series expansions of certain special functions. Thus, the techniques mentioned so far lead in a natural way to the study of integral inequalities involving these functions.

9. INTEGRAL INEQUALITIES

It is well known (see Titchmarsh [14]) that a function f which is analytic within the circle $|z| < R$ in the complex z-plane may be written in the form

$$f(z) = S_n(z) + R_n(z) \qquad \text{for each } n \in \mathbb{N} ,$$

where

$$S_n(z) = \sum_{\nu=0}^{n} a_\nu z^\nu$$

is the sum of the first $(n+1)$ terms and will be called its n-th partial sum, and where the remainder is

$$R_n(z) = \frac{1}{n!} \int_0^z (z - t)^n D^{n+1} \{f(t)\} \, dt . \tag{15}$$

Here the symbol D^i is used to denote the i-th derivative. Notice that the counting starts with the zero-th term a_0, which corresponds to the value of $f(0)$.

For each of the special functions mentioned thus far, the remainder has a predetermined sign and in many cases is an upper bound (lower bound) for the function when n is odd (even). This means that the sign of many integrals can be found without actually evaluating the integral. There exists an extensive literature dealing with the positivity of certain integrals (see, for example, Gasper [7], which contains a fairly recent bibliography). Two very simple examples will now be given, in order to illustrate the method:

(a) $$S_n \equiv \int_0^x (x - t)^n \sin t \, dt \geq 0 \qquad \text{when} \quad x \geq 0 \quad \text{and} \quad n \in \mathbb{N} ,$$

(b) $$C_n \equiv \int_0^x (x - t)^{n+1} \cos t \, dt \geq 0 \qquad \text{when} \quad x \geq 0 \quad \text{and} \quad n \in \mathbb{N} .$$

These results depend on the formula for the remainder term, given in (15), in the power-series expansions of the cosine and sine functions, plus the inequalities (1) and (2). In fact, it is a simple matter to strengthen the above results to include noninteger values of n. This can be achieved by integrating them by parts so as to obtain

$$S_{n+1} = x^{n+1} - (n+1)\,C_{n-1} \qquad \text{and} \qquad nS_{n-1} = C_{n-1}$$

whenever $n > 1$. But, since $\cos t \leq 1$, it appears that $x^{n+1} \geq (n+1)C_{n-1}$, which implies that $S_{n+1} \geq 0$. Hence

$$(16) \qquad S_\alpha \equiv \int_0^x (x-t)^\alpha \sin t\,dt \geq 0 \qquad \text{when} \quad x \geq 0 \quad \text{and} \quad \alpha \geq 0\ ,$$

and

$$(17) \qquad C_\alpha \equiv \int_0^x (x-t)^{\alpha+1} \cos t\,dt \geq 0 \qquad \text{when} \quad x \geq 0 \quad \text{and} \quad \alpha \geq 0\ .$$

(Here, it is important to note that $S_0 = 1 - \cos x \geq 0$.) As well as knowing when S_α and C_α are positive, it is useful to find enveloping series for these functions. In fact, a further generalization can be obtained by replacing the x in inequalities (1) and (2) by tx, multiplying by the positive factor $(1-t)^{\alpha-1}t^{\beta-1}$, and integrating with respect to t. Thus

$$(-1)^{n+1}\left[\int_0^1 (1-t)^{\alpha-1}\,t^{\beta-1}\cos(tx)\,dt - \sum_{\nu=0}^{n} \frac{(-1)^\nu x^{2\nu}\Gamma(\alpha)}{(2\nu)!\,(2\nu+\beta)_\alpha}\right] \geq 0 \quad \text{for} \quad x \in \mathbb{R}\ ,$$

and

$$(-1)^{n+1}\left[\int_0^1 (1-t)^{\alpha-1}\,t^{\beta-1}\sin(tx)\,dt - \sum_{\nu=0}^{n} \frac{(-1)^\nu\,x^{2\nu+1}\,\Gamma(\alpha)}{(2\nu+1)!\,(2\nu+\beta+1)_\alpha}\right] \geq 0 \quad \text{for} \quad x \geq 0\ ,$$

where $n \in \mathbb{N}$ and $\alpha, \beta > 0$.

Now it is a straightforward matter to show that the two integrals

$$\int_0^1 (1-t)^{\alpha-1}\,t^{\beta-1}\begin{Bmatrix}\cos(tx)\\ \sin(tx)\end{Bmatrix} dt$$

cannot be positive for all $\alpha, \beta > 0$ and all $x \geq 0$, for, by a simple change of variable, it becomes clear that the former integral equals

$$\cos x \int_0^1 t^{\alpha-1}(1-t)^{\beta-1}\cos(tx)\,dt + \sin x \int_0^1 t^{\alpha-1}(1-t)^{\beta-1}\sin(tx)\,dt\ ,$$

and the above positivity hypothesis would lead to a contradiction for x in the third quadrant, where $\sin x$ and $\cos x$ are both negative. What is important here is that these integrals may be written as hypergeometric functions ${}_2F_3$'s, which are also enveloped by their n-th partial sums just like those in (14).

Now Truesdell [15] in his "Essay on a unified theory of functions" has shown that many of the special functions satisfy an equation of the form

$$\frac{\partial F(x,\alpha)}{\partial x} = F(x,\alpha+1) .$$

This is precisely the kind of result which can be used to generate integral inequalities via the remainder theorem (15) and the method of the first few sections of this paper. To begin with, results for Bessel functions will now be obtained.

10. INTEGRALS INVOLVING THE BESSEL FUNCTION $J_\alpha(x)$, WITH $x \geq 0$, $\alpha > -1$

Now it is well known that

$$J_{-m}(t) = (-1)^m J_m(t) \quad \text{for all} \quad m \in \mathbb{N} .$$

Thus, on applying a result of Truesdell [15], it appears that

$$D^{n+1}\left[t^{-m/2} J_m(2\sqrt{t})\right] = (-1)^{n+1} t^{-(m+n+1)/2} J_{m+n+1}(2\sqrt{t})$$

for all $n \in \mathbb{N}$. However, the inequality in (4) implies that the remainder after n terms in the power-series expansion for

$$t^{-m/2} J_m(2\sqrt{t})$$

has the same sign as $(-1)^{n+1}$. In other words,

$$\int_0^x (x-t)^n t^{-(m+n+1)/2} J_{m+n+1}(2\sqrt{t})\, dt \geq 0 \quad \text{for all} \quad x \geq 0 .$$

In fact, this inequality is valid for other values of m and n. This can be proved in the same manner as the inequalities in (16) and (17). The final result obtained is that

$$(18) \quad \int_0^x (x-t)^\beta t^{-\alpha/2} J_\alpha(2\sqrt{t})\, dt \geq 0 \quad \text{for all} \quad x \geq 0, \quad \alpha,\beta > -1 .$$

A similar but less general result was obtained by Steinig [12], who employed an oscillation theorem of Makai [9]. This inequality is also given by Gasper [7], who made an elementary change of variable.

11. INTEGRALS INVOLVING THE STRUVE FUNCTION $H_\alpha(x)$ WITH $x \geq 0$, $\alpha > -1$

It is possible to find an integral inequality of the type (18) for the Struve function, in spite of the fact that this function does not satisfy the "F-equation" referred to by Truesdell [15]. In order to find this inequality, it is advantageous to begin with the function

$$f(t,\alpha) \equiv t^{-\alpha/2} H_\alpha(2\sqrt{t}) \qquad \text{for} \quad t \geq 0 \quad \text{and} \quad \alpha > -1 .$$

From the enveloping series given in (5), it is seen that

$$f(0,\alpha) = 0 \qquad \text{and} \qquad f(t,\alpha) \leq t^{1/2}/\Gamma(3/2)\Gamma(\alpha+(3/2))$$

under the conditions stated above. Hence, the integral

$$R(\alpha,\beta) \equiv \int_0^x (x - t)^\beta f(t,\alpha)\, dt , \qquad \text{with} \qquad \beta > -1 ,$$

is such that

$$(19) \qquad (\beta + 1)|R(\alpha,\beta)| \leq x^{\beta+(3/2)} \Gamma(\beta + 2)/\Gamma(\alpha+(3/2))\Gamma(\beta+(5/2)) .$$

On the other hand, it is easy to verify that

$$\frac{\partial}{\partial t} f(t,\alpha) = \frac{t^{-1/2}}{\Gamma(1/2)\Gamma(\alpha+(3/2))} - f(t,\alpha+1) .$$

Then, on multiplying the above identity by $(x - t)^{\beta+1}$ and integrating the left-hand side by parts, it appears that

$$(\beta + 1)R(\alpha,\beta) = x^{\beta+(3/2)} \frac{\Gamma(\beta + 2)}{\Gamma(\alpha+(3/2))\Gamma(\beta+(5/2))} - R(\alpha+1,\beta+1) .$$

Hence, from (19), it follows that

$$(20) \qquad R(\alpha,\beta) = \int_0^x (x - t)^\beta t^{-\alpha/2} H_\alpha(2\sqrt{t})\, dt \geq 0$$

for all $x \geq 0$ and $\alpha,\beta > -1$. The extension to the range $-1 < \beta \leq 0$ follows by integrating the inequality (20), which is valid for $\alpha > -1$, $\beta \geq 0$, by parts. Thus

$$R(\alpha,\beta) = \beta R(\alpha,\beta-1) - \beta x^{\beta+(1/2)}\Gamma(\beta)/\Gamma(\alpha+(3/2))\Gamma(\beta+(3/2)) \geq 0 ,$$

and the result follows.

It is clear from the differential properties of the hypergeometric function that many of the integral inequalities can be obtained just as easily. To name one more, it is clear that

$$\int_0^x (x - t)^m e^{-t} L_m^{(\alpha+m)}(t)\, dt \geq 0 \qquad \text{for} \quad x \geq 0, \quad m \in \mathbb{N} , \quad \alpha > -1 ,$$

because the Laguerre polynomials satisfy

$$\frac{\partial}{\partial t}\left\{e^{-t}\, L_m^{(\alpha)}(t)\right\} = -e^{-t}\, L_m^{(\alpha+1)}(t)\ ,$$

and because the remainder R_n for the function $e^{-t}\, L_m^{(\alpha)}(t)$ depends only on the parity of n. The same result can also be obtained by using Rodrigues' formula for the Laguerre polynomials. Finally, it is a simple matter to use these methods to verify that Lommel's function $s_{u,\nu}(x)$ satisfies the inequality

$$\text{(21)} \qquad \Gamma(\tfrac{1}{2}(u-\nu+1))\, s_{u,\nu}(x) > 0 \quad \text{for} \quad x > 0, \quad \text{provided} \quad u+\nu > -1\ .$$

This is a simple consequence of the integral representation

$$s_{u,\nu}(x) = 2^{\frac{(u-\nu+1)}{2}}\, \Gamma(\tfrac{1}{2}(u-\nu+1))\, x^{\frac{(u+\nu+1)}{2}} \int_0^1 (1-t^2)^{\frac{(u+\nu-1)}{2}}\, t^{\frac{(\nu-u+1)}{2}}\, J_{\frac{(u-\nu+1)}{2}}(tx)\, dt$$

(see Erdélyi, et al. [5]), together with the inequality in (18). The inequality (21) is like a result proved by Gasper [7] and Steinig [12], who used more restrictive conditions on u and ν. Obviously our result is meaningful only if $u-\nu$ is not an odd, negative integer.

12. REMARKS

It is clear that the methods described so far can be extended in many different directions by quite elementary methods. For example, no mention has been made of the fact that the sign of the remainder is unchanged if the function is subjected to a Mellin or Laplace transform which has a positive kernel, or of the well-established theory of monotone functions. Thus, Williamson [16] has proved that a completely monotone function is enveloped by its Taylor-series expansion, and that the product of two such functions is itself completely monotone. It follows that if $f(x)$ and $g(x)$ are enveloped by their Taylor-series expansions about every point $x_0 \in \mathbb{R}$, then so is the function defined by $h(x) = f(x)g(x)$. This is a very deep theorem; it leads to innumerable integral inequalities, some of which already appear in the literature. They are referred to by Gasper [7]. However, the proof that a function is completely, or even k-times, monotone is usually difficult, so that the present techniques are preferred by the present authors.

ACKNOWLEDGEMENTS. This work was completed whilst one of the authors (D.K. Ross) was on study leave in the Department of Chemistry at the University of Southampton. He wishes to take this opportunity to thank Dr. R.E.W. Jansson for his hospitality, and Professor T.D. Howroyd for making available a travel grant to the Department of Mathematics at the University of New Brunswick. It was during the latter visit that the paper was completed.

REFERENCES

1. M. Abramowitz and I.A. Stegun (eds.), Handbook of Mathematical Functions, Dover Publications, Inc., New York, 1965.

2. R. Askey, One-sided approximation to special functions, Siam Rev. 16 (1974), 545-546; 18 (1976), 121-122.

3. C.V. Durell and A. Robson, Advanced Trigonometry, G. Bell and Sons, Ltd., 1949.

4. T. Erber, Inequalities for hypergeometric functions, Arch. Rational Mech. and Anal. 4 (1959-1960), 341-351.

5. A. Erdélyi, W. Magnus, F. Oberhettinger, and F.G. Tricomi, Higher Transcendental Functions, Vol. II, McGraw-Hill, New York, 1953.

6. T.M. Flett, Some inequalities for a hypergeometric integral, Edin. Math. Soc. Proc. 18 (1972), 31-34.

7. G. Gasper, Positive integrals of Bessel functions, Siam J. Math. Anal. 6 (1975), 868-881.

8. L. Gerber, An extension of Bernoulli's inequality, Amer. Math. Monthly 75 (1968), 875-876.

9. E. Makai, On a monotonic property of certain Sturm-Liouville functions, Acta. Math. Acad. Sci. Hungar. 3 (1952), 165-172.

10. G. Pólya and G. Szegö, Problems and Theorems in Analysis, Vol. I, Springer-Verlag, New York, 1972.

11. D.K. Ross, A note on a generalisation of Bernoulli's inequality for the binomial theorem, to appear.

12. J. Steinig, The sign of Lommel's function, Trans. Amer. Math. Soc. 163 (1972), 123-129.

13. G. Szegö, Orthogonal Polynomials, Amer. Math. Soc. Colloq. Publ. 23, Providence, R.I., 1967.

14. E.C. Titchmarsh, The Theory of Functions, Oxford University Press, 1950.

15. C. Truesdell, An Essay Toward a Unified Theory of Special Functions, Princeton University Press, 1948.

16. R.E. Williamson, Multiply monotone functions and their Laplace transforms, Duke Math. J. 23 (1956), 189-207.

Functional Inequalities

Lorenzenhof, 1946
West side view, from the road

A GENERALIZATION OF THEOREMS CONCERNING A NONLINEAR FUNCTIONAL INEQUALITY IN A SINGLE VARIABLE

Dobiesław Brydak
Institute of Mathematics
Pedagogical University
30-011 Kraków
POLAND

ABSTRACT. A generalization of a comparison theorem for the functional inequality

$$\psi[f(x)] \le g[x,\psi(x)] ,$$

where ψ is an unknown function, is here presented. An application of this theorem to the theory of nonlinear functional equations is also given.

1. INTRODUCTION

In this paper we shall deal with the functional inequality

$$\psi[f(x)] \le g[x,\psi(x)] , \tag{1}$$

and with the functional equation

$$\varphi[f(x)] = g[x,\varphi(x)] \tag{2}$$

related to inequality (1), where f and g are given functions and ψ and φ are unknown functions. Some comparison theorems for inequality (1) have been given in [1] and [2]. The theorems given in [1] have been proved under the assumption of a Lipschitz condition on g. Here we shall give a generalization of those theorems, replacing the Lipschitz condition with a nonlinear inequality. Applying this theorem to the equation (2), we obtain a generalization of the uniqueness theorem proved in [3]. The theorems given in the present paper are analogous to theorems in the theory of differential inequalities (see, for example, [5]).

2. HYPOTHESES AND DEFINITION

In the sequel we shall assume the following hypotheses:

Hypothesis H_1: The function f is defined, continuous, and strictly increasing in the interval $I = [\xi,b)$, and

$$\xi < f(x) < x \quad \text{for} \quad x \in (\xi,b) .$$

Hypothesis H_2: The function g is defined and continuous in a set $\Omega \subset R^2$ containing the point (ξ,η), where η is a solution of the equation

$$\eta = g(\xi,\eta) . \tag{3}$$

Moreover, for every $x \in I$, the set $\Omega_x = \{y : x,y \in \Omega\}$ is an open interval,

$$g(x,\Omega_x) \subset \Omega_{f(x)} ,$$

and g is strictly increasing with respect to the second variable in Ω_x when $x \in I$.

Let us consider the functional equation

$$\varphi[f(x)] = G[x,\varphi(x)] , \tag{4}$$

where G is a given function. Equation (4) will be called a <u>comparison equation</u> in U_1 if the following conditions are fulfilled:

(i) The function G is defined in a neighborhood

$$U = U_1 \times U_2 = [\xi,c) \times (-d,d) , \qquad c,d > 0 ,$$

of the point $(\xi,0)$, and the function G fulfills the hypothesis H_2 in U.

(ii) If a function ψ is a continuous solution of the inequality

$$\psi[f(x)] \geq G[x,\psi(x)] \tag{5}$$

in U_1, and φ is a continuous solution of equation (4) in U_1, then the inequality

$$\psi(\xi) \leq 0 \tag{6}$$

implies the inequality

$$\psi(x) \leq 0 . \tag{7}$$

(iii) $\varphi(x) = 0$ is the only continuous solution of equation (4) in U_1, satisfying the condition $\varphi(0) = 0$.

3. LEMMAS

First we are going to quote here the following result:

LEMMA 1. Let the hypotheses H_1 and H_2 be fulfilled, and let $x_0 \in (\xi, b)$. If ψ and φ are continuous solutions of (1) and (2), respectively, in I, and $\psi(x_0) < \varphi(x_0)$, then $\psi[f^n(x_0)] < \varphi[f^n(x_0)]$ for $n = 0,1,\ldots,$ where f^n denotes the n-th iterate of the function f.

This lemma has been proved in [1]. Its very important consequence is the following:

LEMMA 2. Let the hypotheses H_1 and H_2 be fulfilled, and let ψ and φ be continuous solutions of (1) and (2), respectively, in I. If

$$\psi(x) \geq \varphi(x) \quad \text{for} \quad x \in [\xi, a) \subset I, \tag{8}$$

then

$$\psi(x) \geq \varphi(x) \quad \text{for} \quad x \in I. \tag{9}$$

Proof. Let us assume that inequality (8) holds, and that there exists a point $x_0 \in I$, $a_0 < x_0$, such that $\psi(x_0) < \varphi(x_0)$. It follows from the hypothesis H_1 that there exists a positive integer n such that

$$f^n(x_0) \in [\xi, a_0), \quad \text{because} \quad f^n(x_0) \to \xi$$

(see [4]). It also follows from Lemma 1 that

$$\psi[f^n(x_0)] < \varphi[f^n(x_0)],$$

which contradicts inequality (8). Therefore the lemma has been proved. □

4. THEOREMS

Now we are able to prove the following:

THEOREM 1. Let the hypotheses H_1 and H_2 be fulfilled, and let equation (4) be a comparison equation in U_1. Moreover, let

(10) $|g(x,y_1) - g(x,y_2)| \geq G(x,|y_1-y_2|)$ *for* $(x,y_1),(x,y_2) \in V$,

where

$$V = V_1 \times V_2 , \quad V_1 = [\xi,a) \subset U_1 , \quad V_2 = (\eta - d', \eta + d') , \quad 0 < d' < \frac{d}{2} .$$

If ψ *and* φ *are continuous solutions of* (1) *and* (2), *respectively, in* I, *and*

(11) $$\psi(\xi) \geq \varphi(\xi) = \eta ,$$

then inequality (9) *holds*.

Proof. First let us assume that

(12) $$\psi(\xi) = \eta .$$

Put

(13) $$\bar{\psi}(x) = \min[\psi(x),\varphi(x)] \quad \text{for} \quad x \in V_1 ,$$

(14) $$\psi_0(x) = \varphi(x) - \bar{\psi}(x) \quad \text{for} \quad x \in V_1 .$$

Since both ψ and φ satisfy (1) in V_1, the function $\bar{\psi}(x)$ also satisfies (1) in V_1 (see [1]). Moreover, from (14) and (13) we obtain

(15) $$\psi_0(x) \geq 0 \quad \text{for} \quad x \in V_1 ,$$

and thus

(16) $$\varphi(x) \geq \bar{\psi}(x) \quad \text{for} \quad x \in V_1 .$$

Since the functions ψ and φ are continuous in I, there exists an $a_0 \in (\xi,a_0)$ such that $\psi(x),\varphi(x) \in V_2$ for $x \in V_0 = [\xi,a_0)$, because of (11) and (12). Therefore $\bar{\psi}(x),\psi_0(x) \in V_2$, in view of (13) and (14). It follows from (14), (1), (16), (15), hypothesis H_2, and (10) that

$$\psi_0[f(x)] = \varphi[f(x)] - \bar{\psi}[f(x)] \geq g[x,\varphi(x)] - g[x,\bar{\psi}(x)]$$

$$\geq G[x,\varphi(x) - \bar{\psi}(x)] = G[x,\psi_0(x)]$$

for $x \in V_0$. Thus the function ψ_0 satisfies inequality (5) in V_0. Since (4) is a comparison equation in $U_1 \supset V_1 \supset V_0$, it follows that $\psi_0(x) \leq 0$

for $x \in V_0$, because $\psi_0(\xi) = 0$, by virtue of (12), (13), and (14). Therefore $\psi_0(x) = 0$ for $x \in V_0$, in view of (15). Since $V_0 \subset V_1$, the last equality, together with (14) and (13), implies that $\psi(x) \geq \varphi(x)$ for $x \in V_0$. Hence inequality (9) follows because of Lemma 2.

In the case where $\psi(\xi) > \varphi(\xi)$, inequality (9) holds in a neighborhood of the point ξ, because ψ is continuous at ξ, and thus (9) also holds in the whole interval I, because we can apply Lemma 2 again. This completes the proof. □

As an application of Theorem 1, we can obtain a theorem concerning the uniqueness of continuous solution of equation (2). Namely, we are going to prove the following result:

THEOREM 2. *If the hypotheses* H_1 *and* H_2 *are fulfilled, then equation* (2) *has at most one continuous solution* φ *in* I *satisfying the condition*

$$\varphi(\xi) = \eta \,, \tag{17}$$

where η *is a solution of* (3).

Proof. Let φ_1 and φ_2 be continuous solutions of equation (2) in I, satisfying condition (17). Thus the function

$$\psi(x) = \varphi_1(x) - \varphi_2(x) \qquad \text{for} \quad x \in I \tag{18}$$

satisfies inequality (5) in I because, in view of (10),

$$\begin{aligned}\psi[f(x)] &= \varphi_1[f(x)] - \varphi_2[f(x)] \\ &= |g[x,\varphi_1(x)] - g[x,\varphi_2(x)]| \geq G[x,\psi(x)] \qquad \text{for} \quad x \in V_0 \,,\end{aligned}$$

where V_0 is such a neighborhood of ξ that $V_0 \subset V_1$ and $\psi(x) \in V_2$ for $x \in V_0$. Since equation (4) is a comparison one, it follows that

$$\psi(x) = 0 \qquad \text{for} \quad x \in V_0 \,, \tag{19}$$

by virtue of (18) and (17). We are going to prove that (19) holds in the whole interval I. Indeed, let us assume that there exists a point $x_0 \in I \setminus V_0$ such that

$$\varphi_1(x_0) \neq \varphi_2(x_0) .$$

We may assume that

$$\varphi_1(x_0) < \varphi_2(x_0) .$$

The hypothesis H_1 implies (see [4]) that there exists a positive integer n such that

$$f^n(x_0) \in V_0 , \qquad \text{whence} \qquad \varphi_1[f^n(x_0)] < \varphi_2[f^n(x_0)] ,$$

by virtue of Lemma 1 (when we put φ_1 in place of ψ, and φ_2 in place of φ). This contradicts equality (19), already proved. Therefore

$$\varphi_1(x) = \varphi_2(x) \qquad \text{for} \qquad x \in I ,$$

and this ends the proof. □

REFERENCES

1. D. Brydak, On functional inequalities in a single variable, Dissertationes Math. (to appear).

2. D. Brydak, Nonlinear functional inequalities in a single variable, pp. 181-189 in E.F. Beckenbach (ed.), General Inequalities 1 (Proc. Oberwolfach Conference, May 10-15, 1976), ISNM 41, Birkhäuser Verlag, Basel and Stuttgart, 1978.

3. D. Czaja-Pośpiech and M. Kuczma, Continuous solutions of some functional equations in the indeterminate case, Ann. Polon. Math. 24 (1970), 9-20.

4. M. Kuczma, Functional Equations in a Single Variable, Monografie Mat. 46, Warszawa, 1968.

5. I. Szarski, Differential Inequalities, Monografie Mat. 43, Warszawa, 1965.

GENERALIZED SUBADDITIVITY AND CONVEXITY

Bogdan Choczewski
Institute of Mathematics
University of Mining and Metallurgy
30-059 Kraków
POLAND

Zbigniew Powązka
Institute of Mathematics
Pedagogical University
30-011 Kraków
POLAND

ABSTRACT. Functional inequalities in two variables, generalizing the inequalities of subadditive and/or Jensen-convex functions, are considered. Theorems both on the form and on some properties of their continuous solutions are given.

1. INTRODUCTION

In the present paper, we deal with the functional inequality

$$g(ax + by + c) \leq A(g(x),g(y)) \,, \tag{A}$$

where a, b, c are given real numbers. In particular, we consider two special cases of A:

$$g(x + y) \leq B(g(x),g(y)) \,, \tag{B}$$

generalizing the inequality of subadditive functions, for which $B(u,v) = u + v$; and

$$g((x + y)/2) \leq C(g(x),g(y)) \,, \tag{C}$$

more general than the inequality of Jensen-convex functions, for which $C(u,v) = (u + v)/2$.

In the sequel, the symbols J and X will have the following meaning:

$J \subset R$ is an open, proper or improper interval .

X is a linear topological space over R, endowed with such a topology that vector addition in X, and multiplication of vectors by reals, are continuous operations. Moreover, the functions $A,B,C : J \times J \to J$ are assumed to be continuous in J^2.

For inequalities (A) - (C), we consider solutions $g : X \to J$ which are continuous in X. The results obtained are of two kinds: on the form of solutions of (A) and (B) (Sections 2 and 3), and on some properties of solutions of (C) (Sections 4 and 5).

We shall make use of a fundamental result, quoted below, concerning the continuous solutions $f : R \to J$ of the functional equation

$$f(ax + by + c) = A(f(x), f(y)) , \tag{I}$$

which is due to J. Aczél; cf. [1], p. 77.

LEMMA 1. *If there exists a function* $f : R \to J$, *strictly monotonic and continuous in* R, $f(R) = J$, *such that*

$$A(u,v) = f(af^{-1}(u) + bf^{-1}(v) + c), \qquad u,v \in J , \tag{1}$$

then the function f *satisfies equation* (I) *in* R. *Conversely, if equation* (I) *has in* R *a solution* f *from* R *onto* J *which is continuous and strictly monotonic in* R, *then the function* A *has the form* (1).

2. FORM OF SOLUTIONS OF (A)

THEOREM 1. *Let* $A : J^2 \to J$ *be continuous in* J^2. *If equation* (I) *has a continuous, strictly increasing solution* $f : R \to J$, $f(R) = J$, *then every continuous solution* $g : X \to J$ *of* (A) *can be represented as the composition*

$$g = f \circ h \tag{2}$$

of that f *and a continuous solution* $h : X \to R$ *of the functional inequality*

$$h(ax + by + c) \leq ah(x) + bh(y) + c , \qquad x,y \in X . \tag{3}$$

Proof. According to Lemma 1, the function A has the form (1), with the function f taken from the assumption. If $g : X \to J$ is a continuous solution of (A), then by (1) we have

$$g(ax + by + c) \leq f(af^{-1}(g(x)) + bf^{-1}(g(y)) + c) .$$

for every $x,y \in X$. Since the inverse function $f^{-1} : J \to R$ exists and is strictly increasing, we get

$$f^{-1}(g(ax + by + c)) \leq af^{-1}(g(x)) + bf^{-1}(g(y)) + c .$$

Putting

$$h := f^{-1} \circ g ,$$

we see that it satisfies inequality (3) and is continuous in X. The formula for h yields (2) for our g. On the other hand, every function given by (2) with functions f and h fulfilling the assumptions of the theorem obviously is a continuous solution of (A). □

3. INEQUALITY (B)

As a direct consequence of Theorem 1, we get the following characterization of continuous solutions $g : X \to J$ of inequality (B).

THEOREM 2. Let $B : J^2 \to J$ be continuous in J^2. If, moreover, the interval J with the operation B performed on its elements forms a group, then every continuous solution $g : X \to J$ of (B) is given by formula (2), where now $f : R \to J$ is a strictly increasing, continuous solution of the equation

$$\text{(II)} \qquad f(x + y) = B(f(x),f(y)) , \qquad x,y \in X ,$$

and $h : X \to R$ is a subadditive functional, i.e.,

$$h(x + y) \leq h(x) + h(y) .$$

Proof. The assumptions on B (in particular that it is a group operation in J) imply the existence of a function $f : R \to J$ satisfying all the conditions named in the theorem. This is a result due to J. Aczél [1], p. 57. Thus to complete the proof it is enough to apply Theorem 1 with $a = b = 1$, $c = 0$. □

REMARK 1. The same result as in Theorem 2 has been obtained in the case $X \neq R$ by D. Brydak [5].

REMARK 2. Theorem 1, when applied to equation (II), shows the form of all its continuous solutions in the topological space X. They are given by formula (2), where h is an arbitrary continuous linear functional on X.

This results from the fact that an arbitrary continuous additive functional is also homogeneous.

4. PROPERTIES OF SOLUTIONS OF (C)

Together with inequality (C), we consider the equation

$$\text{(III)} \qquad f((x + y)/2) = C(f(x),f(y)) , \qquad x,y \in X .$$

We accept the following hypotheses:

(H) The function $C : J^2 \to J$ is continuous in J^2, and there exists a continuous, strictly increasing solution f, from R onto J, of equation (III).

If hypotheses (H) are fulfilled, then, according to Theorem 1, continuous solutions $G : X \to J$ of (C) are given by formulas (2) and (3) with $a = b = 1/2$, $c = 0$; i.e., we have

$$\text{(4)} \qquad G(x) = f(k(x)) , \qquad x \in X ,$$

where $k : X \to R$ is any Jensen-convex, continuous functional:

$$\text{(5)} \qquad k((x + y)/2) \leq (k(x) + k(y))/2 .$$

A similar formula to (4) holds for continuous solutions of equation (III) in X. We obtain it by repeating the argument used in [1], p. 43, in the case $X = R$, to find the continuous solutions in X of Jensen's functional equation

$$\text{(6)} \qquad \varphi((x + y)/2) = (\varphi(x) + \varphi(y))/2 .$$

THEOREM 3. *Assume* (H) *to hold. Every continuous solution* $F : X \to J$ *of* (III) *has the form*

$$\text{(7)} \qquad F(x) = f(h(x) + d) , \qquad x \in X ,$$

where $h : X \in R$ *is a continuous linear functional and* $d := f^{-1}(F(0))$. *The formula*

$$\varphi(x) = h(x) + d , \qquad x \in X ,$$

presents the general continuous solution of equation (6).

After these preparations, we shall prove a comparison theorem for inequality (C), to the effect that its solutions enjoy a property similar to the maximum principle for harmonic functions.

Note first the following property of Jensen-convex functionals $k : X \to R$, which can be proved in the same way as in the case $X = R$; cf. [6], pp. 155-157.

LEMMA 2. Let $W \subset X$ be a convex set. If $k : W \to R$ is a continuous convex functional (i.e., (5) holds in W), then for every $x_i \in W$ and non-negative numbers p_i,

$$\sum p_i = 1 , \qquad i = 1,\dots,n ; \quad n \in N ,$$

we have the inequality

$$k(\sum p_i x_i) \leq \sum p_i k(x_i) . \tag{8}$$

THEOREM 4. Assume (H) to hold, and let $W \subset X$ be a convex, closed set. Denote by ∂W the boundary of W. If $G : X \to J$ is a continuous solution of (C) in X; $F : X \to J$ is a continuous solution of (III) in X; and

$$G(x) = F(x) \quad \text{for} \quad x \in \partial W , \tag{9}$$

then

$$G(x) \leq F(x) \quad \text{for} \quad x \in W . \tag{10}$$

Proof. If ∂W is not empty, then W is the minimal convex set containing ∂W, i.e., its convex hull: $W = \operatorname{conv} \partial W$. Thus every point of W is a convex linear combination of points from ∂W (cf. [2], p. 81). Take an $x \in W$. Then there are

$$x_i \in \partial W \quad \text{and} \quad p_i \geq 0 , \quad \sum p_i = 1 , \quad i = 1,\dots,n ,$$

such that

$$x = \sum p_i x_i . \tag{11}$$

The function G can be written in form (4); thus, by (11),

$$G(x) = f(k(\sum p_i x_i)) ,$$

where f is strictly increasing and k satisfies (8). Hence

$$G(x) \leq f(\sum p_i k(x_i)) . \tag{12}$$

Since $x_i \in \partial W$, by (9) we have $G(x_i) = F(x_i)$. Both functions can be written in the form involving the function f, viz. (4) and (7), respectively. Consequently,

$$G(x_i) = f(k(x_i)) = f(h(x_i) + d) = F(x_i) ,$$

which implies

$$k(x_i) = h(x_i) + d ,$$

where h is a continuous linear functional. This, when used in (12), yields

$$G(x) \leq f(\sum p_i(h(x_i) + d)) = f(\sum p_i h(x_i) + d \sum p_i)$$

$$= f(h(\sum p_i x_i) + d) = f(h(x) + d) = F(x) ,$$

i.e., (10), and the proof is complete. □

REMARK 3. As is seen from the proof of Theorem 4, if we take

$$W = \operatorname{conv}\{a_1, \dots, a_n\} ,$$

where the a_i are given vectors from X, then to get the statement of Theorem 4 we need to assume (9) only for $x = a_i$.

Similarly, as in the proof of Theorem 4, using formula (7), we can obtain a kind of uniqueness theorem for equation (III).

THEOREM 5. <u>Let hypotheses</u> (H) <u>be fulfilled, and let</u> W <u>and</u> ∂W <u>be as in Theorem</u> 4. <u>If</u> $F_i : X \to J$, $i = 1,2$, <u>are continuous solutions of equation</u> (III), <u>and</u> $F_1(x) = F_2(x)$ <u>on</u> ∂W, <u>then the equality is valid also on</u> W.

5. BECKENBACH'S CONVEXITY

In this section, we take $X = R$ (endowed with the natural topology) and accept hypotheses (H).

A geometric property of convex functions can be interpreted as follows:

The graph of any continuous solution of (5), connecting two points of the plane, lies under the graph of the continuous solution of (6) which is determined by these points (over a suitable interval). We are going to show that a similar relation holds for solutions of (C) and (III). To this end, we introduce after E.F. Beckenbach [3] a family of functions and the notion of convexity with respect to this family (in the form proposed in [4]).

DEFINITION. (a) We denote by $\Phi(J;p,q)$ the two-parameter family of functions $\varphi : J \to R$ having the properties:

(i) φ is continuous in J.

(ii) For given points (x_i,y_i), $x_i \in J$, $i = 1,2$, $x_1 \neq x_2$, there is a unique function of the family, the graph of which connects the two points.

(b) A function $\psi : R \to R$ is said to be convex with respect to the family $\Phi(R;p,q)$ (shortly: Φ-convex) if for any real $x_1,x_2 \in J$ it fulfills the inequality

$$\psi(\tfrac{1}{2}(x_1 + x_2)) \leq \varphi_1^2(\tfrac{1}{2}(x_1 + x_2)) , \tag{13}$$

where φ_1^2 is the member of $\Phi(R;p,q)$ determined by the conditions

$$\varphi_1^2(x_i) = \psi(x_i) , \qquad i = 1,2 . \tag{14}$$

REMARK 4. E.F. Beckenbach proved in [3] that if ψ is a continuous Φ-convex function then it satisfies the inequality

$$\psi(x) \leq \varphi_1^2(x)$$

in the interval, the endpoints of which are x_1 and x_2.

LEMMA 3. Let hypotheses (H) be fulfilled. The family $\mathfrak{F}(R;p,q)$ of continuous solutions $F : R \to J$ of (III) is given by the formula

$$F(x) = f(px + q) , \qquad x \in R , \tag{15}$$

and it satisfies the conditions (a) of the Definition.

The proof of Lemma 3 is straightforward. Note only, that formula (15) is the same as (7) for $X = R$; cf. [1], p. 78. □

Now we can formulate:

THEOREM 6. Let hypotheses (H) be fulfilled. A continuous function $g : R \to J$ satisfies inequality (C) in R if and only if it is convex with respect to the family $\mathfrak{F}(R;p,q)$ of continuous solutions of equation (III) in R.

Proof. By Lemma 3, $\mathfrak{F}$-convexity makes sense. Given a function g, continuous and $\mathfrak{F}$-convex, denote by f_1^2 the element of the family $\mathfrak{F}$ (i.e., a solution of (III)) determined by conditions (14) with $\psi = g$. Taking into account (13), (III), and (14), we get

$$g(\tfrac{1}{2}(x_1 + x_2)) \leq f_1^2(\tfrac{1}{2}(x_1 + x_2)) = C(f_1^2(x_1),f_1^2(x_2)) = C(g(x_1),g(x_2)) \;;$$

i.e., the function g satisfies inequality (C) in R, as the x_i were arbitrary reals.

Similarly, if g is a continuous solution of (C), and f_1^2 has the same meaning as above, then by (C), (14), and (III), we obtain

$$g(\tfrac{1}{2}(x_1 + x_2)) \leq C(g(x_1),g(x_2)) = C(f_1^2(x_1),f_1^2(x_2)) = f_1^2(\tfrac{1}{2}(x_1 + x_2)) \;,$$

i.e. relation(13), which means that g is $\mathfrak{F}$-convex. □

REMARK 5. The relation among continuous solutions of inequality (C) and equation (III), announced at the beginning of this section, results from Theorem 7 on account of Remark 4.

REFERENCES

1. J. Aczél, Lectures on Functional Equations and Their Applications, Academic Press, New York, 1966.

2. A. Alexiewicz, Analiza Funkcjonalna, Polskie Wydawnictwo Nautowe, Warszawa, 1969.

3. E.F. Beckenbach, Generalized convex functions, Bull. Amer. Math. Soc. 43 (1937), 363-371.

4. E.F. Beckenbach and R.H. Bing, On generalized convex functions, Trans. Amer. Math. Soc. 58 (1945), 220-230.

5. D. Brydak, On a functional inequality, Aequationes Math., to appear.

6. O. Haupt and G. Aumann, Differential- und Integralrechnung, Berlin, 1948.

HOMOGENEITY SETS FOR JENSEN-CONVEX FUNCTIONS

Roman Ger
Department of Mathematics
Silesian University
40-007 Katowice
POLAND

ABSTRACT. For a convex subset Δ of a real vector space X and a function $f : \Delta \to \mathbb{R}$, the homogeneity set H_f is defined by

$$H_f := \{\lambda \in [0,1] : f(\lambda x + (1-\lambda)y) \leq \lambda f(x) + (1-\lambda)f(y) \text{ for all } x,y \in \Delta\} .$$

In this paper, homogeneity sets of Jensen-convex functions are discussed.

1. INTRODUCTION

In this paper, the letters $\mathbb{R}$ and $\mathbb{Q}$ will stand for the fields of all real and all real rational numbers, respectively. Given a convex subset Δ of a real vector space X, and a function $f : \Delta \to \mathbb{R}$, we put

$$H_f := \{\lambda \in [0,1] : f(\lambda x + (1-\lambda)y) \leq \lambda f(x) + (1-\lambda)f(y) \quad \text{for all} \quad x,y \in \Delta\}.$$

In the sequel, H_f will be called the <u>homogeneity set</u> for f.

The following lemma is obvious.

LEMMA 1. *The homogeneity set H_f of any given function $f : \Delta \to \mathbb{R}$ is nonvoid (contains 0 and 1) and has the property: $H_f = 1 - H_f$ (symmetry with respect to 1/2).*

A function $f : \Delta \to \mathbb{R}$ is called <u>Jensen-convex</u> if and only if $1/2$ is a member of its homogeneity set, that is, if and only if the inequality

$$f\left(\frac{x+y}{2}\right) \leq \frac{f(x) + f(y)}{2}$$

is satisfied for all $x,y \in \Delta$.

The usual convexity corresponds to the case in which $H_f = [0,1]$.

2. SUBFIELDS AND HOMOGENEITY SETS

It is well known (see, for instance, [1], [2], or [3]) that $\mathbb{Q} \cap [0,1] \subset H_f$ for each Jensen-convex function $f : \Delta \to \mathbb{R}$. Consequently, for each Jensen-convex function we have

$$\mathbb{Q} \cap [0,1] \subset H_f \subset \mathbb{R} \cap [0,1] \ . \tag{1}$$

In view of (1), the following question seems now to be very natural: Assume that a subfield K of $\mathbb{R}$ and a convex subset Δ of a real vector space X are given; does there exist a (Jensen-convex) function $f : \Delta \to \mathbb{R}$ such that $H_f = K \cap [0,1]$? We shall prove that the answer is positive; this result is inspired by a work of J. Rätz [4] who proved, among other things, that any subfield K of $\mathbb{R}$ is of the form

$$\{\alpha \in \mathbb{R} : f(\alpha x) = \alpha f(x) \quad \text{for all} \quad x \in X\}$$

for a certain additive functional on X.

THEOREM 1. <u>Let a real vector space</u> X, <u>a convex subset</u> Δ <u>of</u> X, <u>with card</u> $\Delta \geq 2$, <u>and a subfield</u> K <u>of</u> $\mathbb{R}$ <u>be given. Then there exists a function</u> $f : \Delta \to \mathbb{R}$ <u>such that its homogeneity set</u> H_f <u>coincides with</u> $K \cap [0,1]$.*

<u>Proof</u>. Assume first that

$$\{-h_0, 0, h_0\} \subset \Delta \quad \text{for some} \quad h_0 \in X \setminus \{0\} \ . \tag{2}$$

Take a subfield K of $\mathbb{R}$ and any algebraical (Hamel) basis H_K of X over K, such that $h_0 \in H_K$. Consider a functional $f_0 : X \to K$ being an additive extension of the function $g_0 : H_K \to K$ given by the formula

$$g_0(h) = \begin{cases} -1 & \text{for} \quad h = h_0 \ , \\ 0 & \text{otherwise} \ , \end{cases}$$

and put

$$f := f_0|_\Delta \ .$$

---

* Such a function is certainly Jensen-convex. The assumption card $\Delta \geq 2$ is essential since, otherwise, we have always $H_f = [0,1]$ (for any function).

Evidently, $K \cap [0,1] \subset H_f$. We have to show that every $\lambda \in [0,1] \setminus K$ lies outside of H_f. To this end, for a given $\lambda \in [0,1] \setminus K$, it suffices to find an $x \in \Delta$ such that

$$f(\lambda x + (1-\lambda)0) = f(\lambda x) > \lambda f(x) = \lambda f(x) + (1-\lambda)f(0) .$$

Consider the following two cases:

Case 1: h_0 does not appear in the Hamel expansion of λh_0. Then, taking $x := h_0$, we have $f(\lambda x) = f(\lambda h_0) = 0 > -\lambda = \lambda f(h_0) = \lambda f(x)$.

Case 2: $\lambda h_0 = \alpha h_0 + \alpha_1 h_1 + \cdots + \alpha_n h_n$, $\alpha_i \in K$, $h_i \in H_K$ for $i \in \{1,\ldots,n\}$ and $\alpha \in K \setminus \{0\}$. Evidently, $K \not\ni \lambda \neq \alpha \in K$, and so we have only two possibilities:

(i) $\lambda > \alpha$; then, taking $x := h_0$, we have $f(\lambda x) = f(\lambda h_0) = -\alpha > -\lambda = \lambda f(h_0) = \lambda f(x)$.

(ii) $\lambda < \alpha$; then, taking $x := -h_0$, we have $f(\lambda x) = f(-\lambda h_0) = -f(\lambda h_0) = \alpha > \lambda = \lambda f(-h_0) = \lambda f(x)$.

We can now remove assumption (2). For, observe that jointly with points $a,b \in \Delta$, $a \neq b$ (card $\Delta \geq 2$), Δ contains the whole segment $\overline{a;b}$. Put

$$z := \tfrac{1}{2}(a + b) , \qquad \Delta_0 := \Delta - z , \qquad \text{and} \qquad h_0 := \tfrac{1}{2}(a - z) .$$

Now, Δ_0 is convex and $\{-h_0,0,h_0\} \subset \Delta_0$, whence, by means of the first part of our proof, there exists a function

$$f : \Delta_0 \to K \qquad \text{such that} \qquad H_f = K \cap [0,1] .$$

Let $g(x) := f(x - z)$ for $x \in \Delta$; now, an easy calculation shows that $H_f = H_g$. This completes our proof. □

REMARK 1. The function f "constructed" in the above proof takes its values in the field K only. Evidently, uniqueness cannot be expected; observe, for instance, that if f realizes the assertion of Theorem 1, then so does $\alpha f + a|_\Delta$, where α is a positive real constant and a is an additive functional on X whose homogeneity field contains a given field $K \subset \mathbb{R}$.

3. A CONVERSE QUESTION

Has any homogeneity set for a Jensen-convex function $f : \Delta \to \mathbb{R}$ to be the intersection of a subfield of $\mathbb{R}$ with the interval $[0,1]$? Up to now, we do not know the full answer to this question. However, we have the following, in which, for sets A and B contained in $\mathbb{R}$, we define $\frac{A}{B}$ by

$$\frac{A}{B} := \left\{\frac{\alpha}{\beta} \in \mathbb{R} : \alpha \in A, \quad \beta \in B \setminus \{0\}\right\} .$$

THEOREM 2. Assume that Δ is a convex subset of a real vector space and $f : \Delta \to \mathbb{R}$ is a Jensen-convex function with a homogeneity set H_f. If

$$2H_f \subset H_f \cup \frac{1}{H_f} , \tag{3}$$

then there exists a field $K \subset \mathbb{R}$ such that $H_f = K \cap [0,1]$; K is simply the field $\langle H_f \rangle$ generated by H_f.

Before presenting the proof, we shall give two lemmas. Note that neither of them has (3) as an assumption.

LEMMA 2. Assume that Δ is a convex subset of a real vector space and $f : \Delta \to \mathbb{R}$ is a Jensen-convex function with a homogeneity set H_f. Then, for every $\lambda \in H_f$, we have

$$\lambda H_f + (1-\lambda)H_f = H_f . \tag{4}$$

In particular, $H_f \cdot H_f = H_f$ and $2H_f = H_f + H_f$ (midpoint convexity).

Proof. Take any $x,y \in \Delta$ and $\lambda,\mu_1,\mu_2 \in H_f$. It is not hard to check that

$$L := [\lambda\mu_1 + (1-\lambda)\mu_2]x + [1-(\lambda\mu_1 + (1-\lambda)\mu_2)]y$$

$$= \lambda[\mu_1 x + (1-\mu_1)y] + (1-\lambda)[\mu_2 x + (1-\mu_2)y] .$$

Hence

$$f(L) \le \lambda f(\mu_1 x + (1-\mu_1)y) + (1-\lambda)f(\mu_2 x + (1-\mu_2)y)$$

$$\le \lambda[\mu_1 f(x) + (1-\mu_1)f(y)] + (1-\lambda)[\mu_2 f(x) + (1-\mu_2)f(y)]$$

$$= [\lambda\mu_1 + (1-\lambda)\mu_2]f(x) + [1 - (\lambda\mu_1 + (1-\lambda)\mu_2)]f(y) ;$$

that is,

$$\lambda\mu_1 + (1-\lambda)\mu_2 \in H_f .$$

Thus, (4) has been proved. In particular,

$$H_f = 1 \cdot H_f \subset H_f \cdot H_f = \bigcup \{\lambda H_f : \lambda \in H_f\}$$

$$= \bigcup \{\lambda H_f + (1-\lambda) \cdot 0 : \lambda \in H_f\} \subset \bigcup \{\lambda H_f + (1-\lambda) H_f : \lambda \in H_f\} = H_f ,$$

whereas the equality $2H_f = H_f + H_f$ results from (4) by setting $\lambda = \frac{1}{2} \in H_f$, and the proof is finished. □

LEMMA 3. <u>Under the assumptions of the previous lemma, the field</u> $\langle H_f \rangle$ <u>generated by</u> H_f <u>coincides with</u> $\frac{H}{H}$, <u>where</u> $H := H_f - \frac{1}{2}$.

<u>Proof</u>. First, we shall prove that $\frac{H}{H}$ is a field. For, note that, on account of Lemma 2,

$$H \cdot H = \left(H_f - \frac{1}{2}\right) \cdot \left(H_f - \frac{1}{2}\right) \subset H_f \cdot H_f - \frac{1}{2}(H_f + H_f) + \frac{1}{4}$$

$$= H_f - H_f + \frac{1}{4} = H - H + \frac{1}{4} = H + H + \frac{1}{4} = 2H + \frac{1}{4} ,$$

since H is symmetric with respect to zero (cf. Lemma 1) as well as midpoint convex. Now, take any

$$x \in \frac{H}{H} \quad \text{and} \quad y \in \frac{H}{H} \setminus \{0\} ;$$

then

$$\frac{x}{y} \in \frac{H}{H} \cdot \frac{H}{H} \subset \frac{2H + \frac{1}{4}}{2H + \frac{1}{4}} = \frac{H + \frac{1}{8}}{H + \frac{1}{8}} \subset \frac{H + H}{H + H} = \frac{2H}{2H} = \frac{H}{H} ,$$

because

$$\frac{1}{8} = \frac{5}{8} - \frac{1}{2} \in H_f - \frac{1}{2} , \quad \text{as} \quad \mathbb{Q} \cap [0,1] \subset H_f .$$

Similarly, for $x,y \in \frac{H}{H}$, we have

$$x - y \in \frac{H \cdot H - H \cdot H}{HH} \subset \frac{2H - 2H}{2H + \frac{1}{4}} = \frac{H - H}{H + \frac{1}{8}} \subset \frac{H + H}{H + H} = \frac{H}{H} .$$

Consequently, $\langle H \rangle = \frac{H}{H}$. On the other hand,

$$\langle H \rangle = \langle H + \tfrac{1}{2} \rangle = \langle H_f \rangle ,$$

since $\frac{1}{2} \in H$. This ends the proof. □

Proof of Theorem 2. Put, as previously, $H = H_f - \frac{1}{2}$. We have $\frac{H}{H} \cap [0,\infty] = \frac{H_f}{H_f}$. Indeed,

$$[0,\infty] \supset \frac{H_f}{H_f} = \frac{H + \frac{1}{2}}{H + \frac{1}{2}} \subset \frac{H + H}{H + H} = \frac{H}{H} ;$$

on the other hand, by assumption,

$$2H_f - 1 \subset (H_f - 1) \cup \left(\frac{1}{H_f} - 1\right) ,$$

whence

$$(2H_f - 1) \cap [0,1] \subset \{0\} \cup \left(\frac{1}{H_f} - 1\right) \subset \frac{1 - H_f}{H_f} = \frac{H_f}{H_f} ,$$

and, consequently, since H is symmetric with respect to zero,

$$\frac{H}{H} \cap [0,\infty) = \frac{H \cap [0,\frac{1}{2}]}{H \cap [0,\frac{1}{2}]} = \frac{\left(H_f - \frac{1}{2}\right) \cap [0,\frac{1}{2}]}{\left(H_f - \frac{1}{2}\right) \cap [0,\frac{1}{2}]}$$

$$= \frac{(2H_f - 1) \cap [0,1]}{(2H_f - 1) \cap [0,1]} \subset \frac{H_f}{H_f} \cdot \frac{H_f}{H_f} = \frac{H_f}{H_f} .$$

Now, by means of Lemma 3,

$$\langle H_f \rangle \cap [0,1] = \frac{H}{H} \cap [0,1] = \frac{H_f}{H_f} \cap [0,1] .$$

Note that hypothesis (3) may also be expressed as follows: For

$$\lambda \in H_f \cap [0,\tfrac{1}{2}] ,$$

we have 2λ in H_f, whereas 2λ belongs to $\frac{1}{H_f}$ provided

$$\lambda \in H_f \cap (\tfrac{1}{2},1] .$$

We shall use this to prove that $\langle H_f \rangle \cap [0,1] = H_f$.

Evidently: $H_f \subset \langle H_f \rangle \cap [0,1]$. Let

$$\lambda = \frac{\alpha}{\beta} , \qquad \alpha,\beta \in H_f , \qquad 0 \le \alpha \le \beta > 0 ;$$

we may suppose $\frac{1}{2} < \beta \le 1$, since otherwise we can represent λ in the form $(2^p\alpha)/(2^p\beta)$, where p is a positive integer so chosen that $1/2 < 2^p\beta \le 1$

(by assumption, we still have $2^p\alpha$ and $2^p\beta$ in H_f). Thus $2\beta > 1$, and the representation $2\beta = 1/\varepsilon$, $\varepsilon \in H_f$, follows by assumption, again; therefore,

$$\lambda = \frac{2\alpha}{2\beta} = 2(\alpha\varepsilon) \leq 1$$

and, since $H_f \ni \alpha\varepsilon \leq 1/2$ (cf. Lemma 2), we get $\lambda = 2(\alpha\varepsilon) \in H_f$ by applying the assumption once more. This completes the proof. □

REMARK 2. Using (3), one may prove that

$$\langle H_f\rangle = \frac{H_f}{H_f} \cup \left(-\frac{H_f}{H_f}\right) \quad \text{and get the equality} \quad \langle H_f\rangle \cap [0,1] = \frac{H_f}{H_f} \cap [0,1]$$

in a shorter way. However, it seems worthwhile for us to derive the representation

$$\langle H_f\rangle = \frac{H}{H}$$

without the use of (3), as has been done in Lemma 3.

REMARK 3. In the case where $H_f = K \cap [0,1]$, with K being a subfield of $\mathbb{R}$, condition (3) is certainly satisfied. Thus (3) is a necessary and sufficient condition for H_f to be of the above form.

4. ALTERNATIVE CONDITIONS

In what follows, we are going to give alternative conditions in place of (3).

LEMMA 4. Under the assumptions of Lemma 2, the following implications hold true:

$$(5) \qquad \lambda \in H_f \quad \text{and} \quad \frac{\lambda}{1-\lambda} \in H_f \quad \text{imply} \quad 2\lambda \in H_f\ ;$$

$$(6) \qquad \lambda \in H_f \quad \text{and} \quad \frac{1-\lambda}{\lambda} \in H_f \quad \text{imply} \quad 2\lambda \in \frac{1}{H_f}\ .$$

Proof. Take $x,y \in \Delta$ and suppose that the hypothesis of (5) is fulfilled. Then, obviously, $\lambda \in [0,1/2]$ and

$$f(2\lambda x + (1-2\lambda)y) = f\left(\lambda x + (1-\lambda)\left[\frac{\lambda}{1-\lambda}x + \frac{1-2\lambda}{1-\lambda}y\right]\right)$$
$$\leq \lambda f(x) + (1-\lambda)f\left(\frac{\lambda}{1-\lambda}x + \left(1-\frac{\lambda}{1-\lambda}\right)y\right) \leq 2\lambda f(x) + (1-2\lambda)f(y)\ .$$

As regards (6), if

$\frac{1-\lambda}{\lambda} \in H_f$ then $\frac{1}{\lambda} \in 2 - \omega$ with $\omega \in H_f$, i.e., $\frac{1}{2\lambda} = 1 - \frac{1}{2}\omega$;

certainly, $\omega/2$ belongs to H_f since so do $1/2$ and ω and Lemma 2 holds. Consequently:

$$f\left(\frac{1}{2\lambda} x + \left(1 - \frac{1}{2\lambda}\right)y\right) = f\left(\left(1 - \frac{1}{2}\omega\right)x + \frac{1}{2}\omega y\right) \leq \left(1 - \frac{1}{2}\omega\right)f(x) + \frac{1}{2}\omega f(y)$$
$$= \frac{1}{2\lambda} f(x) + \left(1 - \frac{1}{2\lambda}\right)f(y) ,$$

which was to be proved. □

THEOREM 3. Under the assumptions of Lemma 2, H_f is of the form $K \cap [0,1]$, where K is a subfield of $\mathbb{R}$, if and only if one of the following two conditions is satisfied:

$$\left(\frac{1}{H_f} - 1\right) \cap [0,1] \subset H_f ; \tag{7}$$

$$\frac{H_f}{H_f} \cap [0,1] \subset H_f . \tag{8}$$

Proof. The necessity is obvious in each case. To prove the sufficiency of (7), according to Lemma 4 and Theorem 2 it is enough to show that for any $\lambda \in H_f$ we have

$$\frac{\lambda}{1-\lambda} \in H_f \quad \text{or} \quad \frac{1-\lambda}{\lambda} \in H_f .$$

Take a $\lambda \in H_f$; then one of the numbers

$$\frac{\lambda}{1-\lambda} \quad \text{and} \quad \frac{1-\lambda}{\lambda}$$

belongs to $[0,1]$. If

$$\frac{\lambda}{1-\lambda} =: \alpha \in [0,1] ,$$

then

$$\frac{1}{1+\alpha} = 1 - \lambda \in H_f ,$$

whence, by (7),

$$\frac{\lambda}{1-\lambda} = \alpha \in H_f ;$$

if

$$\frac{1-\lambda}{\lambda} = \frac{1}{\lambda} - 1 \in [0,1] ,$$

then, again by (7), it also belongs to H_f.

The sufficiency of (8) results from the fact that (8) immediately implies (7). This ends our proof. □

The question as to whether or not any homogeneity set for a Jensen-convex function has to be the intersection of a subfield (a subring?) of $\mathbb{R}$ with the unit interval still remains open.

REFERENCES

1. J.L.W.V. Jensen, Sur les fonctions convexes et les inequalities entre les valeurs moyennes, Acta Math. 30 (1906), 175-193.

2. M. Kuczma, Convex functions, Centro Internazionale Matematico Estivo, Functional Equations and Inequalities, La Mendola, 20-28 agosto 1970, Proceedings, Roma-Cremonese 1971, 195-213.

3. D.S. Mitrinović, Analytic Inequalities, Springer-Verlag, Berlin-Heidelberg-New York, 1970.

4. J. Rätz, On the homogeneity of additive mappings, Aequationes Mathematicae 14 (1976), 67-71.

Inequalities of Operator Theory

ON AN INTERPOLATION PROBLEM AND SPLINE FUNCTIONS

A. Jakimovski
Department of Mathematics
Tel-Aviv University
Tel-Aviv
ISRAEL

D.C. Russell
Department of Mathematics
York University
Downsview, Ontario M3J 1P3
CANADA

ABSTRACT. A unified method is presented for determining conditions under which functions of a specified degree of smoothness can be found, from different classes of function spaces, which take prescribed values at all points of a given bi-infinite sequence. Further, the existence of optimal solutions is examined, namely those for which some higher derivative has minimum norm, and some inequalities are given which estimate these minima.

1. INTRODUCTION AND DEFINITIONS

Let ω denote the space of all doubly-infinite complex-valued sequences, and $\omega\uparrow$ the space of all doubly-infinite real-valued monotone strictly increasing sequences. Suppose that $x = (x_i)_{i\in\mathbb{Z}} \in \omega\uparrow$, where x is a fixed sequence, and denote

$$a := \inf x_i \geq -\infty , \quad b := \sup x_i \leq +\infty .$$

For a prescribed sequence $y = (y_i)_{i\in\mathbb{Z}} \in \omega$, the problem of finding a function $F : (a,b) \to \mathbf{C}$ belonging to a preassigned linear space $\mathcal{S}$ of functions, and such that

$$F(x_i) = y_i \quad \text{for every} \quad i \in \mathbb{Z} , \tag{1.1}$$

is called the <u>interpolation problem</u> $IP(y; \mathcal{S},x)$. The symbol $IP(y; \mathcal{S},x)$ (sometimes abbreviated to $IP(y; \mathcal{S})$ for a given fixed x) will also denote the set of all its solutions (which may be empty). A solution of $IP(y; \mathcal{S},x)$ is also called an <u>$\mathcal{S}$-extension of</u> y. It is the object of this paper to consider the existence and nature of the solutions of $IP(y; \mathcal{S},x)$ for certain

The authors acknowledge support from the Deutscher Akademischer Austauschdienst, the Israel Commission for Basic Research, and the Natural Sciences and Engineering Research Council of Canada, during preparation of this paper.

choices of the space $\mathbb{S}$. When $x_i = i$ $(\forall i \in \mathbb{Z})$, we obtain the <u>cardinal interpolation problem</u> CIP(y; $\mathbb{S}$), which has been extensively considered by other authors, particularly by Schoenberg (e.g., see [12], [14], [15], [16]). For simplicity of exposition, we shall assume throughout that $a = -\infty$, $b = +\infty$; however, all our results remain valid with the real line $\mathbb{R}$ replaced appropriately by the interval (a,b).

We therefore suppose throughout that $x \in \omega\uparrow$, unbounded at both ends, and we denote $X_k = (x_k, x_{k+1}]$, $k \in \mathbb{Z}$, with length $|X_k| = x_{k+1} - x_k$. As usual, $L_p(E)$ denotes the space of measurable functions, either p-th power Lebesgue integrable $(1 \le p < +\infty)$ or essentially bounded $(p = +\infty)$, over the measurable set $E \subseteq \mathbb{R}$, with

$$\|f\|_{p,E} = \left(\int_E |f|^p\right)^{1/p} \quad (1 \le p < +\infty), \qquad \|f\|_{\infty,E} = \operatorname*{ess\,sup}_E |f| .$$

We write $L_p = L_p(\mathbb{R})$ and $\|f\|_p = \|f\|_{p,\mathbb{R}}$; and unless otherwise stated, $\sup_k$ and $\sum_k$ range over all $k \in \mathbb{Z}$. Apart from the L_p spaces, we consider also, for $1 \le p \le +\infty$, the spaces

$$C^0_{p,x} := \{f : \lim_{|k|\to\infty} |X_k|^{-1/p}\|f\|_{p,X_k} = 0\}, \quad \|f\|_{C^0_{p,x}} := \sup_k (|X_k|^{-1/p}\|f\|_{p,X_k}) ;$$

(1.2) $$L_{(p),x} := \{f : \|f\|_{L_{(p),x}} := \sum_k |X_k|^{1-1/p} \|f\|_{p,X_k} < +\infty\} .$$

It is easy to verify by Hölder's inequality that

(1.3) $$C^0_{p,x} \subseteq C^0_{r,x} \quad \text{and} \quad L_{(p),x} \subseteq L_{(r),x}, \qquad 1 \le r < p \le +\infty ;$$

also $L_{(1),x} = L_1$, and in the cardinal case (where $x_i = i$, $\forall i \in \mathbb{Z}$) we have $L_{(\infty),x} = L_{[1]}$ in the notation of Schoenberg [14]. The spaces $C^0_{p,x}$ and $L_{(p),x}$ are in fact "direct sums of Banach spaces" of the form $(\sum_k \oplus \Lambda_k)_\lambda$ as used, for example, in Lindenstrauss and Tzafriri [9], (Λ_k) being a sequence of Banach spaces and λ a sequence space.

The spaces $\mathbb{S}$ to be treated here in connection with the interpolation problem IP(y; $\mathbb{S}$,x) will be one of the following (in all cases $m \in \mathbb{Z}^+$):

(1.4) $$L^m_p := \{F : F^{(m-1)} \in AC(\mathbb{R}), \ F^{(m)} \in L_p(\mathbb{R}) \} ,$$

(1.5) $$L^m_{(p),x} := \{F : F^{(m-1)} \in AC(\mathbb{R}), \ F^{(m)} \in L_{(p),x}\} ,$$

(1.6) $$V^m := \{G : G^{(m-2)} \in AC(\mathbb{R}),\ G^{(m-1)} \in BV(\mathbb{R})\} ;$$

if $m = 1$, the condition on $G^{(m-2)}$ is to be omitted, and $G^{(m-1)} \in BV(\mathbb{R})$ is interpreted to mean that $G^{(m-1)}$ is a normalized function of bounded variation on $\mathbb{R}$, equal almost everywhere to the $(m-1)$-th derivative of G. The respective seminorms $\|\cdot\|_{\mathcal{S}}$ are

$$\|F\|_{L_p^m} := \|F^{(m)}\|_p , \quad \|F\|_{L^m_{(p),x}} := \|F^{(m)}\|_{L_{(p),x}} , \quad \|G\|_{V^m} := \int_{\mathbb{R}} |dG^{(m-1)}| .$$

The notation in (1.4) follows that of Schoenberg [14]; L_p^m is also denoted by $\mathcal{H}^{m,p}$, $\mathcal{H}_p^m$, $H^{m,p}$ (e.g., [6], [8], [2]). Characterizations of L_p^m are given by Schoenberg [12; for $p = 2$] and by Jerome and Schumaker [8; for $1 < p < +\infty$]. The spaces V^m are used by Subbotin [18, Section 3].

To identify the sequences y in $IP(y; \mathcal{S}, x)$, we must consider the sequences spaces

(1.7)
$$\ell_{m,p,x} := \{u \in \omega : \|u\|_{m,p,x} := (m^{-1} \sum_k (x_{k+m} - x_k)|u_k|^p)^{1/p} < \infty\} ;$$
$$\ell_p := \{u \in \omega : \|u\|_p := (\sum_k |u_k|^p)^{1/p} < \infty\} \qquad (1 \le p < +\infty) ;$$
$$\ell_{m,\infty,x} := \ell_\infty := \{u \in \omega : \|u\|_{m,\infty,x} := \|u\|_\infty := \sup_k |u_k| < \infty\} ;$$
$$c^0 := \{u \in \omega : \lim_{|k|\to\infty} u_k = 0\} \quad \text{with the norm of } \ell_\infty .$$

For a fixed sequence $x \in \omega\uparrow$ and a complex-valued function f defined at x_i $(\forall i \in \mathbb{Z})$, the divided differences $f[x_k,\dots,x_{k+r}] = [x_k,\dots,x_{k+r}]f$ $(k \in \mathbb{Z},\ r \ge 0)$ are defined inductively by $f[x_k] = f(x_k)$ and $f[x_k,\dots,x_{k+r+1}] = (f[x_k,\dots,x_{k+r}] - f[x_{k+1},\dots,x_{k+r+1}])/(x_k - x_{k+r+1})$ $(r = 0,1,2,\dots)$. For $u \in \omega$, $u[x_k,\dots,x_{k+r}]$ denotes $f[x_k,\dots,x_{k+r}]$, where $u_i = f(x_i)$. It is well known that

$$u[x_k,\dots,x_{k+r}] = \sum_{i=k}^{k+r} u_i/w'_{kr}(x_i) , \qquad w_{kr}(t) = (t-x_k) \cdots (t-x_{k+r}) ;$$

and that, for $x_i = i$,

$$m!u[k,\dots,k+r] = (-1)^r \Delta^r u_k ,$$

where

$$\Delta^0 u_k = u_k, \quad \Delta u_k = u_k - u_{k+1}, \quad \Delta^r u_k = \Delta(\Delta^{r-1} u_k) \qquad (r = 2,3,\ldots) .$$

In Theorem 8 below, we give existence theorems for $IP(y; \mathcal{S},x)$ by showing that, for $m \in \mathbb{Z}^+$,

$$(1.8) \qquad IP(y; L_p^m,x) \neq \emptyset \iff \{y[x_k,\ldots,x_{k+m}]\}_{k\in\mathbb{Z}} \in \ell_{m,p,x} \qquad (1 \leq p \leq +\infty),$$

$$(1.9) \qquad IP(y; L_{(p),x}^m,x) \neq \emptyset \iff \{y[x_k,\ldots,x_{k+m}]\}_{k\in\mathbb{Z}} \in \ell_{m,1,x} \qquad (1 < p \leq +\infty),$$

$$(1.10) \qquad IP(y; V^m,x) \neq \emptyset \iff \{y[x_k,\ldots,x_{k+m}]\}_{k\in\mathbb{Z}} \in \ell_{m,1,x} .$$

In the cardinal case, (1.8) reduces to

$$(1.11) \qquad CIP(y; L_p^m) \neq \emptyset \iff \{\Delta^m y_k\}_{k\in\mathbb{Z}} \in \ell_p \qquad (1 \leq p \leq +\infty) ,$$

which is due to Subbotin ([17] for $p = +\infty$; [18] for $1 \leq p < +\infty$). Schoenberg [14, Theorem 1] proves (1.11) independently for $1 \leq p \leq +\infty$, and also writes the right-hand side of (1.11) as $y \in \ell_p^m$, so we may similarly denote the right-hand side of (1.8) as $y \in \ell_{p,x}^m$; that is,

$$(1.12) \qquad \begin{aligned} \ell_{p,x}^m &:= \{y \in \omega : \{y[x_k,\ldots,x_{k+m}]\}_{k\in\mathbb{Z}} \in \ell_{m,p,x}\} , \\ \|y\|_{\ell_{p,x}^m} &:= \|\{y[x_k,\ldots,x_{k+m}]\}_{k\in\mathbb{Z}}\|_{m,p,x} , \end{aligned}$$

where $\|\cdot\|_{m,p,x}$ is defined as in (1.7). The cardinal case of (1.10) is also obtained by Subbotin [18, Section 3], who uses it to get the case $p = 1$ of (1.11); while Schoenberg [14, Theorem 1] obtains the cardinal case of (1.9) with $p = +\infty$, and uses that to get the case $p = 1$ of (1.11).

In these previous papers, as well as in the present paper, spaces of spline functions are used. For $m \in \mathbb{Z}^+$, denote by π_{m-1} the set of all polynomials (in a real variable, with complex coefficients) of degree not exceeding $m - 1$. The linear space $\mathcal{S}_{m,x}$ of spline functions of degree $m - 1$ or order m, with knots at $x = (x_i)$, is defined by

$$(1.13) \qquad \mathcal{S}_{m,x} := \{S(\cdot) : S \in C^{m-2}(\mathbb{R}) \text{ and } S|_{(x_i,x_{i+1}]} \in \pi_{m-1} \quad (\forall\, i \in \mathbb{Z})\} ;$$

if $m = 1$, the condition $S \in C^{m-2}(\mathbb{R})$ is omitted. In the proofs of [14], extensive use was made of the invariance of a space of cardinal splines with respect to the group of translations by integers. This property no longer holds for a space $\mathcal{S}_{m,x}$ of spline functions with arbitrary knots $x = (x_i)$, so a different approach is needed. In Section 2 below, we first document some properties of spline functions, of which the main important new result is given in Lemma 5. By using these properties, we show in Section 3 that $\mathcal{S}_{m,x} \cap L_p$ $(1 \leq p \leq +\infty)$ is a Banach space isomorphic to the sequence space $\ell_{m,p,x}$; and, knowing Schauder bases for the two spaces (when $1 \leq p < +\infty$), we can characterize the continuous linear functionals on $\mathcal{S}_{m,x} \cap L_p$. We then relate the $IP(y; L_p^m,x)$ to the existence of continuous linear functionals on $\mathcal{S}_{m,x} \cap L_p$ possessing special properties. In the case $p = 2$, the results can be made sharper, since $\mathcal{S}_{m,x} \cap L_2$ is a Hilbert space. The equivalence (1.8) was first obtained by de Boor [2, Section 4; 3, p. 125] (and, with some restrictions on the sequence x, by Golomb [6]); de Boor's method (for $1 \leq p \leq +\infty$) is by direct construction of a solution, while our method departs from this by recognizing the isomorphism between the function space and the sequence space, and using this to develop a procedure which can be used in a wide variety of interpolation problems -- for instance, it gives (1.9) and (1.10), which are new. Following Schoenberg's method for the cardinal case, we deduce the case $p = 1$ of (1.8) from (1.9).

For a general interpolation problem $IP(y; \mathcal{S},x)$, we say that F_* is an <u>optimal solution</u> (or <u>extremal solution</u>) when $F_* \in IP(y; \mathcal{S},x)$ and

(1.14) $$\|F_*\|_{\mathcal{S}} \leq \|F\|_{\mathcal{S}} \quad \text{for all} \quad F \in IP(y; \mathcal{S},x) .$$

By using the Riesz Representation Theorem for L_p, or analogues of this for other spaces, our general method can also specify the existence of optimal solutions, and we do this in the cases where $\mathcal{S} = L_p^m, L_{(p),x}^m, V^m$. For $IP(y; L_p^m,x)$ $(1 < p < +\infty)$, a condition for the existence of a unique optimal solution was given by Golomb [6, Theorem 2.2]. Schoenberg [14, Theorem 9] was able to identify the unique optimal solution of $CIP(y; L_2^m)$, $y \in \ell_2^m$, as a spline function of degree $2m - 1$ with simple knots at the integers (see also [12, Theorem 7]); we shall show (Theorem 9) that this result generalizes directly to $IP(y; L_2^m,x)$.

2. SPLINE FUNCTIONS AND PRELIMINARY RESULTS

We suppose throughout that $x \in \omega\uparrow$, $m \in \mathbb{Z}^+$, and recall the definitions of divided differences and spline functions in the Introduction. Define

$$t_+^0 = 1 \quad (t > 0), \qquad t_+^0 = 0 \quad (t \leq 0), \qquad \text{and} \qquad t_+^{m-1} = t^{m-1} \cdot t_+^0 \qquad (m = 2,3,\ldots) .$$

The so-called B-splines (basic splines) $M_k(t)$ are, for each t, divided differences of the function $f(u) = m(u - t)_+^{m-1}$; more precisely, we write

$$(2.1) \qquad M_k(t) = M_{k,m}(t) = M_{k,m}(t;x) = m[x_k,\ldots,x_{k+m}]_{(\cdot - t)_+^{m-1}} \qquad (k \in \mathbb{Z},\ t \in \mathbb{R}) .$$

We shall also use the normalized basic splines

$$(2.2) \qquad N_k(t) = N_{k,m}(t) = N_{k,m}(t;x) = \frac{1}{m}(x_{k+m} - x_k)M_{k,m}(t;x) \qquad (k \in \mathbb{Z},\ t \in \mathbb{R}) .$$

We remark that for $x_i = i$, $M_k(t)$ and $N_k(t)$ have the same value. The properties of these splines have been well documented; see Schoenberg [11], [13] (and the supplement to this paper by T.N.E. Greville), Curry and Schoenberg [5], and Marsden [10], and for an excellent survey see de Boor [4]. Thus $M_k(\cdot) \in \mathcal{S}_{m,x}$, $N_k(\cdot) \in \mathcal{S}_{m,x}$, and we have the following lemmas.

LEMMA 1. *For any* $k \in \mathbb{Z}$:

$$(2.3) \qquad \begin{gathered} N_{k,m}(t;x) > 0 \ \ \textit{if} \ \ t \in (x_k, x_{k+m}) \quad (m > 1) \quad \textit{or if} \quad t \in (x_k, x_{k+m}] \quad (m = 1), \\ N_{k,m}(t;x) = 0 \ \ \textit{otherwise} ; \end{gathered}$$

for any $r \in \mathbb{Z}$ *and* $x_r < t \leq x_{r+1}$,

$$(2.4) \qquad \sum_{k=r-m+1}^{r} N_{k,m}(t;x) = 1 ;$$

$$(2.5) \qquad \int_{\mathbb{R}} N_{k,m}(t;x)\, dt = \int_{x_k}^{x_{k+m}} N_{k,m}(t;x)\, dt = \frac{1}{m}(x_{k+m} - x_k) .$$

Proof. See, for example, Curry and Schoenberg [5, Section 1] and Marsden [10, (2.10)]; (2.4) is obtainable from (2.6) below by differentiating $m-1$ times with respect to z, and (2.5) by taking $F(t) = t^m$ in (2.21). □

LEMMA 2. *Let* $r,s \in \mathbb{Z}$, $r \leq s$, $x_r < t \leq x_{s+1}$, *and* $z \in \mathbf{C}$; *then*

$$(2.6) \qquad (t - z)^{m-1} = \sum_{k=r-m+1}^{s} (x_{k+1} - z) \cdots (x_{k+m-1} - z)\, N_{k,m}(t;x) .$$

In particular,

(2.7) $$(t - x_r)_+^{m-1} = \sum_{k=r}^{\infty} (x_{k+1} - x_r) \cdots (x_{k+m-1} - x_r)\, N_{k,m}(t;x) \ .$$

Proof. For (2.6), see Marsden [10, Theorem 1] (the proof being attributed to T.N.E. Greville). To obtain (2.7), take $z = x_r$ (r fixed) and $s \to +\infty$ in (2.6), and note that if $k \geq r$ and $t \leq x_r$ then $N_k(t) = 0$; while if $r - m + 1 \leq k \leq r - 1$ then $(x_{k+1} - x_r) \cdots (x_{k+m-1} - x_r) = 0$. The series in (2.7) is of course finite, by (2.3), the number of terms depending on t. □

LEMMA 3. The map $T_{m,x} : \omega \to \mathcal{S}_{m,x}$ defined by

(2.8) $$S(t) = \sum_{k \in \mathbb{Z}} \alpha_k N_{k,m}(t;x) \qquad (\forall\, t \in \mathbb{R})$$

is bijective. That is, for each $\alpha \in \omega$, (2.8) defines a spline function $S = T_{m,x}(\alpha) \in \mathcal{S}_{m,x}$; and to each $S \in \mathcal{S}_{m,x}$ there corresponds a unique $\alpha = T_{m,x}^{-1}(S) \in \omega$. Further, $S(t)$ vanishes for $t < x_n$ if and only if $\alpha_k = 0$ for $k < n$.

Proof. See Schoenberg [13, Theorem 2 (p. 259)] or Curry and Schoenberg [5, Theorem 4]. The series in (2.8) is actually finite, by (2.3). □

LEMMA 4. Let $S \in \mathcal{S}_{m,x}$, $n \in \mathbb{Z}$, and $S(t) = 0$ for $t < x_n$, so that (by Lemma 3) there is a unique $\alpha \in \omega$, with $\alpha_k = 0$ for $k < n$, such that

(2.9) $$S(t) = \sum_{k=n}^{\infty} \alpha_k N_{k,m}(t;x) \qquad (\forall\, t \in \mathbb{R}) \ .$$

Define the sequence $\beta = (\beta_r)_{r \geq n}$ by

(2.10) $$\alpha_k = \sum_{r=n}^{k} (x_{k+1} - x_r) \cdots (x_{k+m-1} - x_r)\, \beta_r \qquad (k = n, n+1, n+2, \ldots) \ ;$$

then

(2.11) $$S(t) = \sum_{r=n}^{\infty} \beta_r (t - x_r)_+^{m-1} \qquad (\forall\, t \in \mathbb{R}) \ .$$

Proof. We note that $(\beta_r)_{r \geq n}$ is defined uniquely in terms of $(\alpha_k)_{k \geq n}$, since (2.10) is of the form $\alpha = A\beta$, where A is a lower-triangular matrix with nonzero diagonal elements; in fact, it is easy to obtain the inverse matrix A^{-1} to show that

$$(2.12)\qquad \beta_r = \sum_{k=\max(n,r-m)}^{r} \frac{(-1)^m(x_{k+m}-x_k)\,\alpha_k}{w'_{km}(x_r)}, \qquad w_{km}(u) = (u-x_k)\cdots(u-x_{k+m}).$$

However, (2.9), (2.10), and Lemma 2 (2.7) show at once that

$$S(t) = \sum_{k=n}^{\infty}\left(\sum_{r=n}^{k}(x_{k+1}-x_r)\cdots(x_{k+m-1}-x_r)\,\beta_r\right)N_k(t)$$

$$= \sum_{r=n}^{\infty}\beta_r\sum_{k=r}^{\infty}(x_{k+1}-x_r)\cdots(x_{k+m-1}-x_r)\,N_k(t) = \sum_{r=n}^{\infty}\beta_r(t-x_r)_+^{m-1},$$

where the series are all finite, the number of terms depending on the value of t. □

LEMMA 5. *Let* $S \in \mathcal{S}_{m,x}$, *with corresponding sequence* $\alpha = T_{m,x}^{-1}(S)$ (*as in Lemma* 3). *For each* $k \in \mathbb{Z}$, *define an integer* $\nu = \nu(k,m)$ *satisfying*

$$(2.13)\qquad k \le \nu \le k+m-1 \quad \text{and} \quad x_{\nu+1}-x_\nu = \max_{k\le i\le k+m-1}(x_{i+1}-x_i),$$

and partition the interval $[x_\nu, x_{\nu+1}]$ *by the points*

$$(2.14)\qquad u_{ki} = x_\nu + \frac{i}{2m}(x_{\nu+1}-x_\nu) \qquad (i = 0,1,\ldots,2m);$$

let θ_{kj} *be any numbers satisfying*

$$(2.15)\qquad \theta_{kj} \in [u_{k,2j+1}, u_{k,2j+2}] \qquad (j = 0,1,\ldots,m-1).$$

Then there are numbers a_{kj} $(j = 0,1,\ldots,m-1)$ *such that*

$$(2.16)\qquad |a_{kj}| \le m!(2m^2)^{(1/2)m(m-1)} \qquad (0 \le j \le m-1,\ k \in \mathbb{Z})$$

and such that

$$(2.17)\qquad \alpha_k = \sum_{j=0}^{m-1} a_{kj}\,S(\theta_{kj}) \quad \textit{for each} \quad k \in \mathbb{Z}.$$

Proof. If $m = 1$, then a function $S \in \mathcal{S}_{1,x}$ is a constant in each interval $(x_k, x_{k+1}]$, so that $S(\theta_{k0}) = \alpha_k$ and (2.17) holds with $a_{k0} = 1$.

Assume now that $m > 1$ and $k \in \mathbb{Z}$. Write

$$s_i = (x_{k+i}-x_k)/(x_{k+m}-x_k) \quad (1\le i\le m-1), \qquad t_j = (\theta_{kj}-x_k)/(x_{k+m}-x_k) \quad (0\le j\le m-1);$$

then the identity

$$\prod_{i=1}^{m-1} (z + s_i) = \sum_{j=0}^{m-1} a_{kj}(z + t_j)^{m-1} \qquad (z \in \mathbb{C}) \tag{2.18}$$

is equivalent to the system of linear equations

$$\sum_{j=0}^{m-1} a_{kj} t_j^i = b_i \qquad (i = 0,1,\dots,m-1) , \tag{2.19}$$

where

$$b_0 = 1, \quad b_i = \binom{m-1}{i}^{-1} \sum_{1 \le n_1 < \cdots < n_i \le m-1} s_{n_1} s_{n_2} \cdots s_{n_i} \qquad (1 \le i \le m-1) .$$

The determinant of the system (2.19) is the Vandermonde determinant

$$D = \prod_{0 \le i < j \le m-1} (t_i - t_j) = \prod_{0 \le i < j \le m-1} \{(\theta_{ki} - \theta_{kj})/(x_{k+m} - x_k)\} ,$$

and the hypotheses on $\{u_{ki}\}$ and $\{\theta_{kj}\}$ give

$$|D| \ge (2m^2)^{-(1/2)m(m-1)}$$

By Cramer's rule, we have $a_{kj} = D_j/D$, where D_j is the determinant of the $m \times m$ matrix (b_{in}) for which $b_{ij} = b_i$ and $b_{in} = t_n^i$ for $n \ne j$. The definitions of s_i and t_j show that $0 \le s_i \le 1$ $(0 \le i \le m-1)$ and $0 \le t_j \le 1$ $(1 \le j \le m-1)$ and hence $|b_{in}| \le 1$ $(i,n = 0,1,\dots,m-1)$, whence $|D_j| \le m!$ and so

$$|a_{kj}| = |D_j/D| \le m!(2m^2)^{(1/2)m(m-1)} \qquad (0 \le j \le m-1) .$$

Now if we put $z = (x_k - x_r)/(x_{k+m} - x_k)$ in (2.18), we get

$$\prod_{i=1}^{m-1} (x_{k+i} - x_r) = \sum_{j=0}^{m-1} a_{kj} (\theta_{kj} - x_r)^{m-1} \qquad \text{for any } r \in \mathbb{Z} . \tag{2.20}$$

Given $S \in \mathcal{S}_{m,x}$ $(m > 1)$ with corresponding sequence α as in (2.8), take an arbitrary $k \in \mathbb{Z}$, choose $n < k - m$, and define

$$S_1(t) = \sum_{j=n}^{\infty} \alpha_j N_j(t) \qquad (\forall\, t \in \mathbb{R}) ;$$

thus $S_1 \in \mathcal{S}_{m,x}$, $S_1(t) = 0$ for $t < x_n$, and $S_1(t) = S(t)$ for $t \ge x_k$. Then, by (2.10) and (2.20),

$$\alpha_k = \sum_{r=n}^{k} (x_{k+1}-x_r)\cdots(x_{k+m-1}-x_r)\beta_r = \sum_{r=n}^{\nu} (x_{k+1}-x_r)\cdots(x_{k+m-1}-x_r)\,\beta_r$$

$$= \sum_{r=n}^{\nu} \beta_r \sum_{j=0}^{m-1} a_{kj}(\theta_{kj}-x_r)^{m-1} = \sum_{j=0}^{m-1} a_{kj} \sum_{r=n}^{\nu} \beta_r(\theta_{kj}-x_r)^{m-1}$$

$$= \sum_{j=0}^{m-1} a_{kj}\, S_1(\theta_{kj})$$

by Lemma 4 (2.11), since $x_\nu < \theta_{kj} \le x_{\nu+1}$ $(j = 0,1,\ldots,m-1)$. Now, in the last sum, $S_1(\theta_{kj}) = S(\theta_{kj})$ (because $\theta_{kj} > x_k$), and this proves the lemma. □

For cardinal splines, there is an expansion which bears a resemblance to (2.17) in Schoenberg [15, Theorem 5]; however, in the latter the expansion is in terms of the derivatives of S at the knots (i.e., the integers). In (2.17) we have an expression in terms of values of S alone, with coefficients a_{kj} which are uniformly bounded, with a bound, and a fixed number of terms, depending on m only; this makes (2.17) useful for numerical work.

LEMMA 6. <u>Let</u> $x \in \omega\uparrow$, $m \in \mathbb{Z}^+$. <u>If, for a sequence</u> $y \in \omega$,

$$y[x_k,\ldots,x_{k+m}] = 0 \quad \underline{\text{for every}} \quad k \in \mathbb{Z}\,,$$

<u>then</u> $\exists\, P \in \pi_{m-1}$ <u>such that</u> $y_k = P(x_k)$ $(\forall\, k \in \mathbb{Z})$.

<u>Proof</u>. A proof can be found in Jakimovski and Russell [7, Lemma 2]. □

LEMMA 7. <u>Let</u> $x \in \omega\uparrow$, $m \in \mathbb{Z}^+$. <u>If</u> $F^{(m-1)} \in AC[x_k,x_{k+m}]$, <u>then</u>

$$F[x_k,\ldots,x_{k+m}] = \frac{1}{m!}\int_{x_k}^{x_{k+m}} M_{k,m}(t;x)\, F^{(m)}(t)\, dt\,. \tag{2.21}$$

<u>If</u> $G \in V^m[x_k,x_{k+m}]$ (<u>definition</u> (1.6) <u>restricted to</u> $[x_k,x_{k+m}]$), <u>then</u>

$$G[x_k,\ldots,x_{k+m}] = \frac{1}{m!}\int_{x_k}^{x_{k+m}} M_{k,m}(t;x)\, dG^{(m-1)}(t)\,. \tag{2.22}$$

<u>Proof</u>. The results are based on a theorem of Peano; e.g., see [5, Section 1]. □

3. THE INTERPOLATION PROBLEMS $IP(y;\, L_p^m, x)$, $IP(y;\, L_{(p),x}^m, x)$

THEOREM 1. <u>Let</u> $x \in \omega\uparrow$, $m \in \mathbb{Z}^+$, $1 \le p \le +\infty$. <u>Then in each of the</u>

following cases:

(a) $\Lambda = L_p$, (b) $\Lambda = C^0_{p,x}$, (d) $\Lambda = L_{(p),x}$,

Λ is a Banach space, and $\mathcal{S}_{m,x} \cap \Lambda$ is a closed linear subspace of Λ.

(e) For $1 \leq p < +\infty$, $p^{-1} + q^{-1} = 1$, we have $(C^0_{p,x})^* \cong L_{(q),x}$. More precisely:

(i) If $f \in L_{(q),x}$ then $H(h) := \int_{\mathbb{R}} hf \quad (\forall h \in C^0_{p,x})$ defines

$$H \in (C^0_{p,x})^* \quad \text{and} \quad |H(h)| \leq \|h\|_{C^0_{p,x}} \|f\|_{L_{(q),x}} .$$

(ii) To each $H \in (C^0_{p,x})^*$ there corresponds a unique $f \in L_{(q),x}$ such that

$$H(h) = \int_{\mathbb{R}} hf \quad (\forall h \in C^0_{p,x}) \quad \text{and} \quad \|H\| = \|f\|_{L_{(q),x}} .$$

[Note: Theorem 1 (c) is given later. The symbol Λ^* denotes the continuous dual of a space Λ, namely the space of all continuous linear functionals on Λ. The elements of the space $\mathcal{S}_{m,x} \cap L_p$ are sometimes called $H^{m,p}$-splines (e.g., [6]).]

Proof. The proofs that the given spaces Λ are Banach spaces are either known or straightforward.

(a) We prove that $\mathcal{S}_{m,x} \cap L_p$ is closed in L_p, the proofs in the other cases being similar. Let $(P_k)_{k\in\mathbb{Z}^+}$, $P_k \in \pi_{m-1}$, be a sequence of polynomials convergent a.e. in some interval (a,b) to a function f; then $\exists\, q \in \pi_{m-1}$ such that $f(t) = q(t)$ a.e. in (a,b) and, for each i, $0 \leq i \leq m-1$, $P^{(i)}_k(t) \to q^{(i)}(t)$ $(k \to \infty)$ uniformly on $[a,b]$.

Suppose $1 \leq p \leq +\infty$. Let $S_n \in \mathcal{S}_{m,x}$ $(n \in \mathbb{Z}^+)$, $g \in L_p$, and $S_n \to g$ in the L_p-norm. Then $\exists\, (S_{n_k})_{k\in\mathbb{Z}^+}$ convergent a.e. in $\mathbb{R}$ to g. By the first part of the proof applied to each interval $(x_\nu, x_{\nu+1})$, $\exists\, q_\nu \in \pi_{m-1}$ such that $g(t) = q_\nu(t)$ a.e. in $(x_\nu, x_{\nu+1})$ and, for $0 \leq i \leq m-2$, $S^{(i)}_{n_k}(t) \to q^{(i)}_\nu(t)$ $(k \to \infty)$ uniformly on $[x_\nu, x_{\nu+1}]$, while $S^{(m-1)}_{n_k}(t) \to q^{(m-1)}_\nu(t)$ on $(x_\nu, x_{\nu+1}]$. With the definition $S(t) := q_\nu(t)$ for $t \in (x_\nu, x_{\nu+1}]$, it follows that $S \in \mathcal{S}_{m,x} \cap L_p$ and that $g(\cdot) = S(\cdot)$ a.e. on $\mathbb{R}$. Hence $\mathcal{S}_{m,x} \cap L_p$ is closed in $L_p(\mathbb{R})$.

(e) (i) If $f \in L_{(q),x}$ we see directly from Hölder's inequality that

$$|H(h)| \leq \int_{\mathbb{R}} |hf| = \sum_k \int_{X_k} |hf| \leq \sum_k \|h\|_{p,X_k} \|f\|_{q,X_k}$$

$$= \sum_k (|X_k|^{-1/p}\|h\|_{p,X_k})(|X_k|^{1/p}\|f\|_{q,X_k}) \leq \|h\|_{C^0_{p,x}} \|f\|_{L_{(q),x}} .$$

Thus $H \in (C^0_{p,x})^*$ and $\|H\| \leq \|f\|_{L_{(q),x}}$.

(ii) The proof of (ii) utilizes the well-known Riesz Representation Theorem for the general continuous linear functional on L_p $(1 \leq p < +\infty,$ $p^{-1} + q^{-1} = 1)$. For a given $H \in (C^0_{p,x})^*$, we apply this theorem on each interval X_k to obtain functions $f_k \in L_q(X_k)$ with the required representation, and then define $f \in L_{(q),x}$ by $f(t) := f_k(t)$ on X_k $(\forall k \in \mathbb{Z})$. Then for each $h \in C^0_{p,x}$ we define a sequence of functions in $C^0_{p,x}$, with compact support and converging in norm to h, and application of the functional H to this sequence gives the required representation for $H(h)$. By suitable choice of h, we can also ensure that $\|H\| \geq \|f\|_{L_{(q),x}}$. This, together with the result in (i), gives us the final result. □

THEOREM 2. <u>For a given sequence</u> α, <u>let</u> $S(t)$ <u>be defined by</u> (2.8). <u>Then</u>

(3.1)
$$\text{(a)} \quad \alpha \in \ell_{m,p,x} \Rightarrow S \in \mathcal{S}_{m,x} \cap L_p \qquad (1 \leq p \leq +\infty),$$
$$\|S\|_p \leq \|\alpha\|_{m,p,x} ;$$

(3.2)
$$\text{(b)} \quad \alpha \in c^0 \Rightarrow S \in \mathcal{S}_{m,x} \cap C^0_{p,x} \qquad (1 \leq p \leq +\infty),$$
$$\|S\|_{C^0_{p,x}} \leq m^{1/p} \|\alpha\|_\infty .$$

<u>Proof</u>. (a) This part of the theorem is due to de Boor [1, Section 3; 4, Theorem 5.2]; for completeness we sketch the proof. The case $p = +\infty$ of (3.1) is immediate, by (2.8) and (2.4). If $1 \leq p < +\infty$, we write (2.8) in the form

$$S = \sum_k \alpha_k N_k^{1/p} N_k^{1/q} \qquad (p^{-1} + q^{-1} = 1)$$

and apply Hölder's inequality to get, by (2.3) and (2.4),

$$|S(t)|^p \leq \sum_k |\alpha_k|^p N_k(t) \qquad (\forall t \in \mathbb{R}) . \tag{3.3}$$

Taking the integral over $\mathbb{R}$ and using (2.5) and definition (1.7), we get (3.1).

(b) Suppose $\alpha \in \ell_\infty$. If, for any given $r \in \mathbb{Z}$, $t \in X_r$, then the summations in (a) range over $r-m+1 \leq k \leq r$. Thus for $p = +\infty$ we get

$$\|S\|_{\infty,X_r} \leq \|\alpha\|_\infty ,$$

while for $1 \leq p < +\infty$ we see, from (3.3), (2.3), (2.4), that

$$|S(t)|^p \leq \sum_{k=r-m+1}^{r} |\alpha_k|^p \qquad (t \in X_r) ,$$

and integration over X_r then gives

$$\|S\|_{p,X_r} \leq (m|X_r|)^{1/p} \|\alpha\|_\infty ; \tag{3.4}$$

by definition (1.2), (3.2) now follows. If $\alpha \in c^0$, we must verify in addition that $S \in \mathcal{S}_{m,x} \cap C^0_{p,x}$. Clearly $S \in \mathcal{S}_{m,x}$; and $S \in C^0_{p,x}$ because, given $\varepsilon > 0$, we can replace the $\|\alpha\|_\infty$ in (3.4) by ε, for sufficiently large $|r|$. □

THEOREM 3. <u>For a given</u> $S \in \mathcal{S}_{m,x}$, <u>let</u> α <u>be defined by</u> (2.8) (<u>according to Lemma</u> 3). <u>Then</u>

(a) $\quad S \in \mathcal{S}_{m,x} \cap L_p \Rightarrow \alpha \in \ell_{m,p,x} \qquad (1 \leq p \leq +\infty)$,

$$\|\alpha\|_{m,p,x} \leq A_m \|S\|_p , \qquad A_m = m!(2m^2)^{(1/2)m(m-1)+1} ; \tag{3.5}$$

(b) $\quad S \in \mathcal{S}_{m,x} \cap C^0_{p,x} \Rightarrow \alpha \in c^0 \qquad (1 \leq p \leq +\infty)$,

$$\|\alpha\|_\infty \leq m^{-1} A_m \|S\|_{C^0_{p,x}} \tag{3.6}$$

<u>Proof</u>. If $S \in \mathcal{S}_{m,x}$ then, for any $k \in \mathbb{Z}$, S is continuous on $(x_k, x_{k+m}]$ and hence on every interval

$$I_{kj} := [u_{k,2j+1}, u_{k,2j+2}] \qquad (j = 0,1,\ldots,m-1) ,$$

where u_{ki} is defined as in (2.13) and (2.14). Let $1 \leq p < +\infty$. Then, by the mean-value theorem for integrals, $\exists\, \theta_{kj} \in I_{kj}$ $(j = 0,1,\ldots,m-1)$ such that

$$\frac{1}{2m}(x_{\nu+1} - x_\nu)\, |S(\theta_{kj})|^p = \int_{I_{kj}} |S(t)|^p \, dt . \tag{3.7}$$

Now by Lemma 5, applying Hölder's inequality to (2.17) and using (2.16), we obtain

$$|\alpha_k|^p \leq A \sum_{j=0}^{m-1} |S(\theta_{kj})|^p , \qquad A = m^{p-1}[m!(2m^2)^{(1/2)m(m-1)}]^p ,$$

so that, from (3.7) and (2.13),

$$\frac{1}{m}(x_{k+m} - x_k)|\alpha_k|^p \leq (x_{\nu+1} - x_\nu)|\alpha_k|^p \leq 2m\,A \sum_{j=0}^{m-1} \int_{I_{kj}} |S|^p \leq 2m\,A \int_{X_\nu} |S|^p . \tag{3.8}$$

Hence

$$|\alpha_k| \leq m^{-1} A_m |X_\nu|^{-1/p} \|S\|_{p,X_\nu} , \tag{3.9}$$

with A_m as in (3.5); and (3.9) holds also for $p = +\infty$, since we may then choose any $\theta_{kj} \in I_{kj}$ $(j = 0,1,\ldots,m-1)$ and get, from Lemma 5,

$$|\alpha_k| \leq \sum_{j=0}^{m-1} |a_{kj}| \max_{0 \leq j \leq m-1} |S(\theta_{kj})| \leq m \cdot m!(2m^2)^{(1/2)m(m-1)} \|S\|_{\infty,X_\nu} . \tag{3.10}$$

(a) Suppose $S \in \mathcal{S}_{m,x} \cap L_p$. If $p = +\infty$, we get (3.5) from (3.10). If $1 \leq p < +\infty$, then from (3.8), since $X_\nu \subseteq (x_k, x_{k+m}]$, we obtain

$$\frac{1}{m} \sum_{k=-M}^{N} (x_{k+m} - x_k)|\alpha_k|^p \leq 2mA \cdot m \int_{x_{-M}}^{x_{N+m}} |S|^p \leq 2m^2 A \|S\|_p^p \leq A_m^p \|S\|_p^p ;$$

and letting $M,N \to \infty$ we get (3.5).

(b) Suppose $S \in \mathcal{S}_{m,x} \cap C^0_{p,x}$. Then the right-hand side of (3.9) tends to zero as $|k| \to \infty$ $(\text{since } k \leq \nu \leq k+m-1)$, so $\alpha \in c^0$; and taking suprema on both sides of (3.9) gives (3.6). □

Part (a) of Theorem 3 has been obtained by a different method (with a constant less than A_m) by de Boor [1, Section 3; 4, Theorem 5.2].

THEOREM 4. Let the map $S = T_{m,x}(\alpha)$ be defined by (2.8) in each of the following cases:

(a) $$T_{m,x} : \ell_{m,p,x} \to \mathcal{S}_{m,x} \cap L_p \qquad (1 \leq p \leq +\infty) ,$$

(b) $$T_{m,x} : c^0 \to \mathcal{S}_{m,x} \cap C^0_{p,x} \qquad (1 \leq p \leq +\infty) .$$

In each case, the map is bijective; and the two spaces are isomorphic Banach spaces under this map.

Proof. The results follow, respectively, from parts (a), (b) of Theorems 1, 2, 3. □

THEOREM 5. In each of the cases: (a) $\Lambda = L_p$ $(1 \le p < +\infty)$, (b) $\Lambda = C^0_{p,x}$ $(1 \le p \le +\infty)$, $\{N_{k,m}(\cdot;x)\}_{k\in\mathbb{Z}}$ is a Schauder basis in $\mathcal{S}_{m,x} \cap \Lambda$, with the representation

$$S(\cdot) = \lim_{M,N\to\infty} \sum_{k=-M}^{N} \alpha_k N_{k,m}(\cdot;x) \quad \text{for each} \quad S \in \mathcal{S}_{m,x} \cap \Lambda, \quad \alpha = T^{-1}_{m,x}(S) ,$$

where the limit is in the Λ-norm. Since $M_{k,m}(\cdot;x) = mN_k(\cdot;x)/(x_{k+m} - x_k)$, $\{M_{k,m}(\cdot;x)\}_{k\in\mathbb{Z}}$ is likewise a Schauder basis in $\mathcal{S}_{m,x} \cap \Lambda$.

Proof. Given $S \in \mathcal{S}_{m,x}$, choose $\alpha = T^{-1}_{m,x}(S)$ by Lemma 3, and denote

$$S_{M,N}(t) = \sum_{k=-M}^{N} \alpha_k N_{k,m}(t;x) .$$

(a) If $S \in \mathcal{S}_{m,x} \cap L_p$ $(1 \le p < +\infty)$ then, by Theorem 3 (a), $\alpha \in \ell_{m,p,x}$; and applying Theorem 2 (3.1) (and the last sentence of Lemma 3) to the function $S(\cdot) - S_{M,N}(\cdot)$, we get

$$(3.11) \qquad \|S(\cdot) - S_{M,N}(\cdot)\|_p^p \le \left(\sum_{k=-\infty}^{-M-1} + \sum_{k=N+1}^{\infty} \right) (x_{k+m} - x_k)|\alpha_k|^p \to 0 \quad \text{as} \quad M,N \to \infty .$$

(b) If $S \in \mathcal{S}_{m,x} \cap C^0_{p,x}$ $(1 \le p \le +\infty)$ then $\alpha \in c^0$, and (using (3.2) instead of (3.1)) (3.11) is replaced by

$$(3.12) \qquad \|S(\cdot) - S_{M,N}(\cdot)\|_{C^0_{p,x}} \le m^{1/p} \sup_{k<-M,\, k>N} |\alpha_k| \to 0 \quad \text{as} \quad M,N \to \infty .$$

To show that the representations are unique, suppose that $S(\cdot) = \sum_k \alpha^*_k N_{k,m}(\cdot;x)$, with convergence in the appropriate norm. Then there is convergence a.e. to $S(t)$, and hence, by the uniqueness of the representation in Lemma 3, we have $\alpha^*_k = \alpha_k$ $(\forall k \in \mathbb{Z})$. □

Part (a) of Theorem 5 has been given by de Boor [1, p. 273; 4, p. 17].

THEOREM 6. In each of the cases:

(a) $\Lambda = L_q$, $\Lambda^\dagger = L_p$, $\lambda = \ell_{m,p,x}$ $(1 < p \le +\infty,\ p^{-1} + q^{-1} = 1)$,

(b) $\Lambda = C^0_{q,x}$, $\Lambda^\dagger = L_{(p),x}$, $\lambda = \ell_{m,1,x}$ $(1 < p \le +\infty,\ p^{-1} + q^{-1} = 1)$,

we have the following results:

(i) $z \in \lambda \iff \exists\, H \in (\mathcal{S}_{m,x} \cap \Lambda)^*, \quad z_k = H(M_k(\cdot)) \qquad (\forall\, k \in \mathbb{Z})$.

(ii) <u>If</u> $f \in \Lambda^\dagger$ <u>and</u>

$$H(S) = \int_{\mathbb{R}} Sf \qquad (\forall\, S \in \mathcal{S}_{m,x} \cap \Lambda) , \tag{3.13}$$

<u>then</u> $H \in (\mathcal{S}_{m,x} \cap \Lambda)^*$.

(iii) <u>If</u> $H \in (\mathcal{S}_{m,x} \cap \Lambda)^*$, <u>then</u> $\exists\, f_* \in \Lambda^\dagger$, <u>satisfying</u> (3.13) <u>and such that</u>

$$\|H\| = \|f_*\|_{\Lambda^\dagger} = \min\{\|f\|_{\Lambda^\dagger} : f \in \Lambda^\dagger \text{ and } f \text{ satisfies } (3.13)\} . \tag{3.14}$$

<u>Proof</u>. (i) Consider first the case (a) $\Lambda = L_q$, $\Lambda^\dagger = L_p$, $\lambda = \ell_{m,p,x}$ $(1 < p \le +\infty)$, and write $\mu = \ell_{m,q,x}$, $\mu^\dagger = \{u \in \omega : \|u\| := (m^{p-1} \sum_k (x_{k+m} - x_k)^{1-p} |u_k|^p)^{1/p} < \infty\}$ (for $p = +\infty$, $\|u\|_{\mu^\dagger} := \sup_k m(x_{k+m} - x_k)^{-1}|u_k|$). Then μ has Schauder basis $\{e^k\}_{k\in\mathbb{Z}}$, where $e^k = (\cdots,0,0,1,0,0,\cdots)$ with 1 in the k-th position, and it is easy to see that $\mu^* \cong \mu^\dagger$. Then, by Theorem 4, $\mathcal{S}_{m,x} \cap \Lambda \cong \mu$, and by Theorem 5 we have the correspondence between the basis elements:

$$e^k \longleftrightarrow N_k(\cdot) = \frac{1}{m}(x_{k+m} - x_k)\, M_k(\cdot) .$$

Thus, given $H \in (\mathcal{S}_{m,x} \cap \Lambda)^*$ with $z_k = H(M_k(\cdot))$, we can define $H_1(\cdot)$ uniquely by

$$H_1(e^k) = H(N_k(\cdot)) = \frac{1}{m}(x_{k+m} - x_k)\, H(M_k(\cdot)) = \frac{1}{m}(x_{k+m} - x_k)\, z_k .$$

Thus $H_1 \in \mu^* \cong \mu^\dagger$; hence $\{\frac{1}{m}(x_{k+m} - x_k)\, z_k\}_{k\in\mathbb{Z}} \in \mu^\dagger$, and computation of the norm shows that this is equivalent to $z \in \lambda$. A reversal of the argument gives the converse.

Case (b) follows exactly the same pattern, with $\mu = c^0$, $\mu^\dagger = \ell_1$.

(ii) These follow from Theorem 1(e)(i), the corresponding result for L_q^*, and the fact that $\mathcal{S}_{m,x} \cap \Lambda$ is a linear subspace of Λ in each case.

(iii) If $H \in (\mathcal{S}_{m,x} \cap \Lambda)^*$ then, by the Hahn-Banach Theorem, $H(\cdot)$ can be extended to a continuous linear functional on Λ with the same norm as $H(\cdot)$. By the Riesz Representation Theorem for L_q^* in case (a), and by Theorem 1(e)(ii) in case (b), there then exists a function $f_* \in \Lambda^\dagger$ satisfying (3.13) and $\|H\| = \|f_*\|_{\Lambda^\dagger}$. Now take any $f \in \Lambda^\dagger$ for which (3.13) holds.

Then $H(S) \leq \|S\|_\Lambda \|f\|_{\Lambda^\dagger}$, whence $\|H\| \leq \|f\|_{\Lambda^\dagger}$, so that $\|f_*\|_{\Lambda^\dagger} \leq \|f\|_{\Lambda^\dagger}$. □

In the case $p = q = 2$, Theorem 6(a)(iii) can be improved as follows.

THEOREM 6'. Write $\mathcal{S}_2 := \mathcal{S}_{m,x} \cap L_2$. If $H \in \mathcal{S}_2^*$, then there exists a unique $S_0 \in \mathcal{S}_2$ such that

$$H(S) = \int_{\mathbb{R}} S\,\overline{S}_0 \qquad (\forall S \in \mathcal{S}_2) \tag{3.15}$$

and such that

$$\|H\| = \|S_0\|_2 \,. \tag{3.16}$$

Moreover, for each $f \in L_2(\mathbb{R})$ for which

$$H(S) = \int_{\mathbb{R}} S\,f \qquad (\forall S \in \mathcal{S}_2)\,,$$

we have

$$\|S_0\|_2 < \|f\|_2 \quad \text{unless} \quad f(\cdot) = \overline{S}_0(\cdot) \quad \text{a.e. in } \mathbb{R}\,. \tag{3.17}$$

Proof. Since L_2 is a Hilbert space and (by Theorem 1(a)) $\mathcal{S}_2 := \mathcal{S}_{m,x} \cap L_2$ is closed in L_2, $\mathcal{S}_2$ is therefore a Hilbert space, with the inner product $\langle S_1, S_2\rangle = \int_{\mathbb{R}} S_1 \overline{S}_2$. Thus, by the Riesz Representation Theorem for Hilbert spaces, there is a unique $S_0 \in \mathcal{S}_2$ satisfying (3.15) and (3.16). Now take any $f \in L_2$ for which $H(S) = \int_{\mathbb{R}} S\,f$ $(\forall S \in \mathcal{S}_2)$; in particular, taking $S = S_0$ here and in (3.15), we get $\int_{\mathbb{R}} S_0(f - \overline{S}_0) = 0$, whence, by orthogonality,

$$\|f\|_2^2 - \|S_0\|_2^2 = \|f - \overline{S}_0\|_2^2 > 0$$

unless $f(\cdot) = \overline{S}_0(\cdot)$ a.e. in $\mathbb{R}$. □

THEOREM 7. If $\Lambda = L_p$ or if $\Lambda = L_{(p),x}$ $(1 \leq p \leq +\infty)$, write

$$\mathfrak{F}(y;\Lambda) := \{f \in \Lambda : y[x_k,\ldots,x_{k+m}] = \int_{\mathbb{R}} M_k\, f \qquad (\forall k \in \mathbb{Z})\}\,. \tag{3.18}$$

Then

(i) $F \in IP(y;\Lambda^m) \Rightarrow f := \frac{1}{m!} F^{(m)} \in \mathfrak{F}(y;\Lambda)$.

(ii) $f \in \mathfrak{F}(y;\Lambda) \Rightarrow \exists\, F \in IP(y;\, \Lambda^m)$ with $f = \frac{1}{m!} F^{(m)}$ a.e.

Proof. (i) Lemma 7 gives the result, the support of $M_{k,m}(t;x)$ being $[x_k, x_{k+m}]$.

(ii) Let $f \in \mathfrak{F}(y;\Lambda)$ and let $F_1(\cdot)$ be an m-th indefinite integral of $m!f$. Denote $z_k = F_1(x_k)$ $(\forall\, k \in \mathbb{Z})$. Then, by hypothesis and Lemma 7 (2.21), $(z - y)[x_k,\ldots,x_{k+m}] = 0$ and hence, by Lemma 6, $\exists\, P \in \pi_{m-1}$ with $y_k = z_k + P(x_k)$, whence $F := F_1 + P \in IP(y;\Lambda^m)$; moreover, $F^{(m)} = F_1^{(m)} = m!f$ a.e.. □

THEOREM 8 (a). Let $x \in \omega\uparrow$, $m \in \mathbb{Z}^+$.

(i) If $1 \le p \le +\infty$, then $y \in \ell^m_{p,x} \Longleftrightarrow IP(y;\, L^m_p) \ne \emptyset$.

(ii) If $1 < p \le +\infty$ and $y \in \ell^m_{p,x}$, then $IP(y;\, L^m_p)$ has an optimal solution F_*, and

$$(3.19)\qquad \|F_*^{(m)}\|_p \le K\|y\|_{\ell^m_{p,x}}, \quad K = K_m = (m!)^2(2m^2)^{(1/2)m(m-1)+1}.$$

(iii) If $1 < p < +\infty$ and $y \in \ell^m_{p,x}$, then $IP(y;\, L^m_p)$ has exactly one optimal solution.

THEOREM 8 (b). Let $x \in \omega\uparrow$, $m \in \mathbb{Z}^+$, $1 < p \le +\infty$.

(i) $y \in \ell^m_{1,x} \Longleftrightarrow IP(y;\, L^m_{(p),x}) \ne \emptyset$.

(ii) If $y \in \ell^m_{1,x}$, then $IP(y;\, L^m_{(p),x})$ has an optimal solution F_*, and

$$(3.20)\qquad \|F_*^{(m)}\|_{L_{(p),x}} \le K'\|y\|_{\ell^m_{1,x}}, \qquad K' = K'_m = m^{-1} K_m.$$

Proof. (a)(i) Let $1 < p \le +\infty$ (we shall add the case $p = 1$ after proving part (b)). By using the definition of $\mathfrak{F}$ in (3.18), substitution of $z_k = y[x_k,\ldots,x_{k+m}]$ in Theorem 6 (a) (without using (3.14)) gives

$$y \in \ell^m_{p,x} \Longleftrightarrow \exists\, f \in \mathfrak{F}(y;\, L_p),$$

and, coupled with Theorem 7 (with $\Lambda = L_p$), this gives the first result.

(ii) If $1 < p \le +\infty$ and $y \in \ell^m_{p,x}$, then by Theorem 6 (a) (using (3.14)) $\exists\, f_* \in \mathfrak{F}$ such that

(3.21) $$\|f_*\|_p = \min\{\|f\|_p : f \in \mathfrak{F}\} .$$

Then, by Theorem 7 (ii), $\exists\, F_* \in IP$, with $f_* = \frac{1}{m!} F^{(m)}$ a.e., so that

$$\|f_*\|_p = \frac{1}{m!} \|F_*^{(m)}\|_p .$$

Now take $F \in IP$; then by Theorem 7 (i),

$$f := \frac{1}{m!} F^{(m)} \in \mathfrak{F}$$

and, by (3.21), $\|F_*^{(m)}\|_p \leq \|F^{(m)}\|_p$ for any $F \in IP$. Hence F_* is an optimal solution of $IP(y;\, L_p^m)$. It follows, moreover, from Theorem 6 (a), that $\exists\, H \in (\mathcal{S}_{m,x} \cap L_q)^*$ such that

$$\|H\| = \frac{1}{m!} \|F_*^{(m)}\|_p \quad \text{and} \quad z_k := y[x_k, \ldots, x_{k+m}] = H(M_{k,m}(\cdot\,;x)) \qquad (\forall\, k \in \mathbb{Z}) .$$

Then for each $S \in \mathcal{S}_{m,x} \cap L_q$ and $\alpha = T_{m,x}^{-1}(S)$, from Theorem 5 (a) we have

$$H(S) = \frac{1}{m} \sum_k (x_{k+m} - x_k)\, \alpha_k\, H(M_{k,m}(\cdot\,;x)) = \frac{1}{m} \sum_k (x_{k+m} - x_k)\, \alpha_k\, z_k .$$

Applying Hölder's inequality and using Theorem 3 (a), we get

$$|H(S)| \leq \|\alpha\|_{m,q,x}\, \|z\|_{m,p,x} \leq A_m\, \|S\|_q\, \|z\|_{m,p,x} .$$

Hence $\|F_*^{(m)}\|_p = m!\|H\| \leq m!\, A_m \|z\|_{m,p,x} = K\|z\|_{m,p,x}$.

(iii) If $1 < p < +\infty$ then L_p is strictly convex, and the simple argument given by Golomb [6; see the first paragraph of the proof of Theorem 2.2] shows that $IP(y;\, L_p^m)$ cannot then have more than one optimal solution.

(b) The pattern of proof for this case is identical with that of part (a) ((i) and (ii)) above, employing in the proof the (b) parts of the appropriate theorems.

It remains to deal with the case $p = 1$ of (a)(i). As de Boor [2, p. 114] remarks, the $\Leftarrow$ implication is elementary: for, from Theorem 7 (i),

$$F \in IP(y;L_p^m) \Rightarrow y[x_k, \ldots, x_{k+m}] = \frac{1}{m!} \int_{\mathbb{R}} M_k F^{(m)} = \frac{m}{m!} (x_{k+m} - x_k)^{-1} \int_{x_k}^{x_{k+m}} N_k F^{(m)} ,$$

and an application of Hölder's inequality (and of Lemma 1) gives

$$m^{-1} \sum_k (x_{k+m} - x_k)\, |y[x_k, \ldots, x_{k+m}]|^p \leq (m!)^{-p} \sum_k \int_{x_k}^{x_{k+m}} |F^{(m)}|^p .$$

Augmenting this with the simple case $p = +\infty$, we get

$$(3.22)\qquad F \in IP(y;L_p^m) \Rightarrow y \in \ell_{p,x}^m, \text{ and } \|y\|_{\ell_{p,x}^m} \leq \frac{m^{1/p}}{m!}\|F^{(m)}\|_p \qquad (1 \leq p \leq +\infty) .$$

For the reverse implication in the case $p = 1$, the inclusion $L_{(p),x}^m \subseteq L_1^m$ and an appeal to (b)(i) of this theorem gives

$$(3.23)\qquad y \in \ell_{1,x}^m \Rightarrow IP(y;\, L_{(p),x}^m) \neq \emptyset \Rightarrow IP(y;\, L_1^m) \neq \emptyset \qquad (1 < p \leq +\infty) ,$$

and the proof of Theorem 8, (a) and (b), is therefore complete. □

As remarked in Section 1 above, Theorem 8 (a)(i) is due to de Boor [1, Section 4], and Theorem 8 (a)(iii) essentially to Golomb [6, Theorem 2.2] (he showed that, for $1 < p < +\infty$, if $IP(y;L_p^m)$ has a solution, then it has a unique optimal solution). For comments on (3.19) and (3.20), see Remark (vi) in Section 5 below.

THEOREM 9. Let $x \in \omega\uparrow$, $m \in \mathbb{Z}^+$. If $y \in \ell_{2,x}^m$, then the unique optimal solution of $IP(y;\, L_2^m)$ is a spline function $S_* \in \mathcal{S}_{2m,x}$. Moreover, S_* is the only solution of $IP(y;\, L_2^m)$ in $\mathcal{S}_{2m,x}$.

Proof. The existence of a unique optimal solution is guaranteed by Theorem 8 (a). However, if in the second part of the proof of Theorem 8 (a)(ii), we make use of Theorem 6' as a supplement to Theorem 6 (a), we see that $IP(y;\, L_2^m)$ has optimal solution S_*, where

$$\frac{1}{m!}\, S_*^{(m)} = S_0 \in \mathcal{S}_{m,x} \cap L_2 ;$$

i.e., S_* is an m-th indefinite integral of a function in $\mathcal{S}_{m,x}$, and hence S_* is in $\mathcal{S}_{2m,x}$.

Now suppose that $S_1, S_2 \in \mathcal{S}_{2m,x} \cap IP(y;\, L_2^m)$. Then, by Theorem 6 (a)(ii), the functions

$$H_j(S) = \frac{1}{m!}\int_{\mathbb{R}} S\, S_j^{(m)} \qquad (\forall\, S \in \mathcal{S}_{m,x} \cap L_2) \qquad (j = 1,2)$$

satisfy $H_j \in (\mathcal{S}_{m,x} \cap L_2)^*$ and then, by Theorem 7 (i),

$$y[x_k,\ldots,x_{k+m}] = H_1(M_k(\cdot)) = H_2(M_k(\cdot)) \qquad (\forall\, k \in \mathbb{Z}) .$$

Since H_1 and H_2 agree at the basis elements, we have $H_1 = H_2$ and therefore $S_1^{(m)} = S_2^{(m)}$ a.e.; hence $\sigma := S_1 - S_2 \in \pi_{m-1}$, and since $\sigma(x_k) = 0$ $(\forall\, k \in \mathbb{Z})$ it follows that $\sigma = 0$, i.e., $S_1 = S_2$. □

As a corollary of Theorem 9, we obtain the cardinal case $(x_i = i, \forall\, i \in \mathbb{Z})$, which has been proved by Schoenberg [14, Theorem 9].

4. THE INTERPOLATION PROBLEM $IP(y;\, V^m, x)$

Recalling the definition of V^m in (1.6), we remark first that if we wish merely to establish an existence theorem for $IP(y;\, V^m)$ (corresponding to Theorem 8 (i)), then in one direction a treatment similar to the case $p = 1$ of (3.22) (using Lemma 7 (2.22) instead of (2.21)) easily gives

(4.1) $$G \in IP(y; V^m) \Rightarrow y \in \ell^m_{1,x} \quad \text{and} \quad \|y\|_{\ell^m_{1,x}} \leq \frac{m}{m!} \|G\|_{V^m} .$$

The inclusion $L_1^m \subseteq V^m$ and an appeal to the case $p = 1$ of Theorem 8 (a) gives the reverse implication:

(4.2) $$y \in \ell^m_{1,x} \Rightarrow IP(y;\, L_1^m) \neq \emptyset \Rightarrow IP(y;\, V^m) \neq \emptyset .$$

However, if we want to establish the existence of an optimal solution and an inequality corresponding to (3.19) or (3.20), or an independent proof of the sufficiency of $y \in \ell^m_{1,x}$, we need to follow through a sequence of theorems using the space $C^0 := C^0(\mathbb{R})$ of functions continuous on $\mathbb{R}$ and tending to zero at $\pm\infty$, with the norm of L_∞.

Since spline functions of degree 0 are step functions and not necessarily continuous, it is best to dispose of the case $m = 1$ separately. Noting that $\ell^1_{1,x} = v$, the space of sequences of bounded variation, with $\|y\|_v := \sum_k |y_k - y_{k+1}|$, we have:

(i) $G \in IP(y;V^1) \Rightarrow \sum_k |y_k - y_{k+1}| = \sum_k |G(x_k) - G(x_{k+1})| \leq \int_{\mathbb{R}} |dG| < \infty$.

(ii) If $y \in v$, choose $G_*(t) = y_{k+1}$ on $(x_k, x_{k+1}]$ $(\forall\, k \in \mathbb{Z})$; then $y_k = G_x(x_k)$ $(\forall\, k \in \mathbb{Z})$ and

$$\int_{\mathbb{R}} |dG_*| = \sum_k |G_*(x_k) - G_*(x_{k+1})| = \sum_k |y_k - y_{k+1}| < \infty .$$

(iii) Let $y \in v$ and take $G \in IP(y;V^1)$; then from (i) and (ii) we have $\|G_*\|_{V^1} = \|y\|_v \leq \|G\|_{V^1}$, so G_* is optimal.

THEOREM 1 (c). <u>Let</u> $m > 1$. <u>Then</u> $\mathcal{S}_{m,x} \cap C^0$ <u>is closed in</u> L_∞.

Proof. The space C^0 is closed in L_∞ and, by Theorem 1 (a), $\mathcal{S}_{m,x} \cap L_\infty$ is closed in L_∞. □

THEOREM 4 (c). Let $m > 1$. The map $T_{m,x} : c^0 \to \mathcal{S}_{m,x} \cap C^0$, with $S = T_{m,x}(\alpha)$ defined by (2.8), is bijective, and it provides an isomorphism between c^0 and $\mathcal{S}_{m,x} \cap C^0$.

Proof. For $m > 1$, $\mathcal{S}_{m,x} \cap C^0 = \mathcal{S}_{m,x} \cap C^0_{\infty,x}$, with the same L_∞-norm. So Theorems 2 (b) and 3 (b) (with $p = +\infty$) give the bijectivity; the addition of Theorem 1 (c), together with (3.2) and (3.6) $(p = +\infty)$, gives the isomorphism. □

THEOREM 5 (c). Let $m > 1$. Then Theorem 5 holds with $\Lambda = C^0$.

Proof. Take the case $p = +\infty$ of Theorem 5 (b). □

THEOREM 6 (c). Let $m > 1$.

(i) $z \in \ell_{m,1,x} \Rightarrow \exists\, H \in (\mathcal{S}_{m,x} \cap C^0)^*,\quad z_k = H(M_k(\cdot)) \qquad (\forall\, k \in \mathbb{Z})$.

(ii) If $g \in V := BV(\mathbb{R})$ and

$$H(S) = \int_{\mathbb{R}} S\, dg \qquad (\forall\, S \in \mathcal{S}_{m,x} \cap C^0) , \tag{4.3}$$

then $H \in (\mathcal{S}_{m,x} \cap C^0)^*$.

(iii) If $H \in (\mathcal{S}_{m,x} \cap C^0)^*$, then $\exists\, g_*$ satisfying (4.3) and such that

$$\|H\| = \|g_*\|_V = \min\{\|g\|_V : g \in V \text{ and } g \text{ satisfies } (4.3)\} . \tag{4.4}$$

Proof. Follow the proof of Theorem 6 with $\Lambda = C^0$, $\Lambda^\dagger = V$, $\lambda = \ell_{m,1,x}$, $\mu = c^0$, $\mu^\dagger = \ell_1$, and use the Riesz Representation Theorem for $(C^0)^*$. □

THEOREM 7 (c). Let $m \geq 1$ and denote

$$\mathcal{G}(y;V^m) := \{g \in V : y[x_k,\dots,x_{k+m}] = \int_{\mathbb{R}} M_k\, dg \qquad (\forall\, k \in \mathbb{Z})\} . \tag{4.5}$$

Then

(i) $G \in IP(y;V^m) \Rightarrow g := \frac{1}{m!} G^{(m-1)} \in \mathcal{G}(y;V^m)$;

(ii) $g \in \mathcal{G}(y;V^m) \Rightarrow \exists\, G \in IP(y;V^m)$ with $g = \frac{1}{m!} G^{(m-1)}$ a.e.

Proof. Analogous to Theorem 7, using Lemma 7 (2.22) instead of (2.21). □

THEOREM 8 (c). Let $x \in \omega\uparrow$, $m \in \mathbb{Z}^+$.

(i) $$y \in \ell^m_{1,x} \iff IP(y;V^m) \neq \emptyset .$$

(ii) If $y \in \ell^m_{1,x}$, then $IP(y;V^m)$ has an optimal solution G_*, and

$$(4.6) \qquad \|G_*^{(m-1)}\|_V \leq K' \|y\|_{\ell^m_{1,x}} , \qquad K' = K'_m = m^{-1} (m!)^2 (2m^2)^{(1/2)m(m-1)+1} .$$

Proof. For $m > 1$, the proof is analogous to that of Theorem 8 (a), but it uses the (c) parts of the appropriate theorems. The case $m = 1$ was already dealt with. □

5. CONCLUDING REMARKS

(i) There is a strict inclusion in (1.3), between the spaces $L_{(p),x}$, and between the spaces $C^0_{p,x}$. This is easy to show by examples: for take any fixed p in $1 < p \leq +\infty$, suppose $x_k \to +\infty$ $(k \to +\infty)$, choose k_0 so that $x_{k_0} \leq 1 < x_{k_0+1}$, and let

$$\varepsilon_k = (x_{k+1} - x_k)/x^p_{k+1} \qquad \text{for} \quad k \geq k_0 .$$

Define $f(t) = g(t) = 0$ for $t \leq x_{k_0}$; and for $t \in (x_k, x_{k+1}]$ $(k \geq k_0)$ define

$$f(t) = g(t) = 0 \qquad \text{for} \quad x_k < t < x_{k+1} - \varepsilon_k ,$$

$$f(t) = 1, \quad g(t) = x_{k+1} \qquad \text{for} \quad x_{k+1} - \varepsilon_k \leq t \leq x_{k+1} .$$

Then

$$f \in L_{(r),x} \setminus L_{(p),x} \quad \text{and} \quad g \in C^0_{r,x} \setminus C^0_{p,x}, \qquad \text{for} \quad 1 \leq r < p .$$

Two further observations arise from this:

(ii) Although $L^m_{(\infty),x} \subset L^m_{(p),x} \subset L^m_{(1),x} = L^m_1 \subset V^m$ $(1 < p < +\infty$, $m \in \mathbb{Z}^+)$, nevertheless (Theorem 8 (i)) the necessary and sufficient condition on y in order that it can be interpolated at x by some function from one of these spaces is the same condition, $y \in \ell^m_{1,x}$, whichever space we take. The question therefore arises as to whether, given $y \in \ell^m_{1,x}$, there exists a solution of the interpolation problem which is in one of the spaces but not in a smaller space.

(iii) Although $C^0_{\infty,x} \subset C^0_{p,x} \subset C^0_{1,x}$ $(1 < p < +\infty)$, it follows from Theorem 4 (b) that, for fixed m and x, the sets $\mathcal{S}_{m,x} \cap C^0_{p,x}$ $(1 \leq p \leq +\infty)$ are identical, and as normed spaces they are isomorphic. In particular, taking the case $p = +\infty$ in (3.2) and $1 \leq p < +\infty$ in (3.6), we get the interesting <u>inequality</u>

$$(5.1) \quad \sup_k \left(\frac{1}{x_{k+1} - x_k} \int_{x_k}^{x_{k+1}} |S(t)|^p \, dt \right)^{1/p} \geq m A_m^{-1} \sup_{\mathbb{R}} |S(t)| \qquad (1 \leq p < +\infty),$$

with $A_m = m!(2m^2)^{(1/2)m(m-1)+1}$, valid for any spline function $S(\cdot)$ of order m (degree $m - 1$) with knots at x. It would be interesting to obtain a better value for A_m than the one given here.

(iv) The definitions of the spaces $C^0_{p,x}$ and $L_{(p),x}$ in (1.2) depend only on p being constant in each interval X_k. Consequently it is possible to <u>replace</u> p <u>in these definitions by a sequence</u> $p = (p_k)$, $1 \leq p_k \leq +\infty$. All the theorems concerning these spaces then go through in the more general setting (with restrictions $p_k \neq 1$ or $p_k \neq +\infty$ as appropriate and, for example, with the replacement of $m^{1/p}$ on the right side of (3.2) by $\sup_k m^{1/p_k} \leq m$). Note that part (i) of Theorem 8 (b) is also valid for $p = 1$, since $L_{(1),x} = L_1$; hence we may have $1 \leq p_k \leq +\infty$ in Theorem 8 (b)(i), and $1 < p_k \leq +\infty$ in 8 (b)(ii). Also we may replace p by p_k, with $1 \leq p_k \leq +\infty$, in the inequality (5.1) above.

(v) It is interesting to note that our Lemma 5 gives almost immediately the following result used frequently by de Boor (e.g., see [2, Lemma; 3, p. 123]):

<u>Given</u> $m \in \mathbb{Z}^+$, $\exists\, D_m$ <u>such that</u> $\forall\, x \in \omega\uparrow$, $\forall\, k \in \mathbb{Z}$, $\exists\, h_k(\cdot) \in L_\infty$ <u>with</u>

$$(5.2) \qquad \operatorname{supp} h_k \subseteq [x_k, x_{k+m}], \qquad \int_{\mathbb{R}} h_k N_j = \delta_{kj} \quad \underline{\text{for all}} \quad j,$$

<u>and</u>

$$(5.3) \qquad \|h_k\|_p \leq D_m (x_{k+m} - x_k)^{-1/q} \qquad (1 \leq p \leq +\infty, \quad p^{-1} + q^{-1} = 1).$$

<u>Proof</u>. For any $S \in \mathcal{S}_{m,x}$ and $\alpha_k = \alpha_k(S)$ defined by $S(t) = \sum_i \alpha_i N_i(t)$, we have by (3.8) (with $p = 1$), for any largest subinterval $X_\nu \subseteq (x_k, x_{k+m}]$,

$$|\alpha_k(S)| \leq A_m (x_{k+m} - x_k)^{-1} \|S\|_{\infty, X_\nu}, \qquad A_m = m!\,(2m^2)^{(1/2)m(m-1)+1}.$$

Thus $\alpha_k(\cdot)$ is a continuous linear functional on $\{S|_{X_\nu} : S \in \mathcal{S}_{m,x}\}$ with the $L_1(X_\nu)$-norm, and so, by the Riesz Representation Theorem, there is a unique $h_k(\cdot) \in L_\infty(X_\nu)$ such that

$$(5.4) \qquad \alpha_k(S) = \int_{X_\nu} h_k S \quad (\forall S \in \mathcal{S}_{m,x}) \quad \text{and} \quad \|h_k\|_\infty \le A_m(x_{k+m} - x_k)^{-1} .$$

Extend the definition of $h_k(\cdot)$ to the whole of $\mathbb{R}$ by defining it to be zero outside X_ν (hence $\operatorname{supp} h_k \subseteq [x_k, x_{k+m}]$). Now (5.3) follows from

$$\|h_k\|_p^p = \int_{X_\nu} |h_k|^p \le |X_\nu| \; \|h_k\|_\infty^p \le (x_{k+m} - x_k) \, A_m^p \, (x_{k+m} - x_k)^{-p} .$$

Finally, choosing the spline $S(t) = N_j(t)$, with corresponding sequence $\alpha_k(N_j) = \delta_{kj}$ (since $N_j(t) = \sum_i \delta_{ij} N_i(t)$), we see from (5.4) that $\delta_{kj} = \int_{\mathbb{R}} h_k N_j$. □

(vi) Given $y \in \ell^m_{p,x}$, define the functional

$$(5.5) \qquad \mathcal{L}^m_{p,x}(y) := \inf\{\|F^{(m)}\|_p : F \in IP(y; L^m_p, x)\} \qquad (1 \le p \le +\infty) .$$

Then Theorem 8 (a)(ii) shows that $\exists F_* \in IP(y; L^m_p, x)$ with $\|F_*^{(m)}\|_p = \mathcal{L}^m_{p,x}(y)$, if $1 < p \le +\infty$, and that

$$(5.6) \qquad \|\mathcal{L}^m_{p,x}\| := \sup\{\mathcal{L}^m_{p,x}(y) : \|y\|_{\ell^m_{p,x}} \le 1\} \le K_m .$$

Thus $\|\mathcal{L}^m_{p,x}\|$ is the <u>best possible (least) value of</u> K in (3.19). Its values have been determined in the <u>cardinal case</u> by Subbotin ([17] for $p = +\infty$; [18] for $1 \le p < +\infty$) and by Schoenberg ([14, Theorem 5] for $p = 2$). For example,

$$(5.7) \qquad \phi_m := \|\mathcal{L}^m_{\infty,\mathbb{Z}}\| = \frac{1}{2}\left(\frac{\pi}{2}\right)^{m+1} \left[\sum_{i=1}^{\infty} (-1)^{(m+1)(i-1)}/(2i - 1)^{m+1}\right]^{-1} ,$$

giving the sequence of values $(\phi_m) = (1, 2, 3, \frac{24}{5}, \frac{15}{2}, \frac{720}{61}, \frac{315}{17}, \ldots)$. In the general (noncardinal) case, de Boor [3, Theorem 4.1] has obtained the bound K in (3.19) of $m!D_m$, where

$$\frac{1}{2}\left(\frac{\pi}{2}\right)^m \le D_m \le 2m \cdot 9^{m-1} ,$$

and he conjectures from numerical evidence that the best possible bound in Theorem 8 (a) which will serve independently of p and x is of the order of $m!2^m$. We have a slightly different bound in Theorem 8 (b) and (c) (for $L^m_{(p),x}$ and V^m) from the one we obtain in 8 (a) (for L^m_p), so similar questions arise for these other spaces also. For example, Schoenberg [14, Theorem 3] shows that the best constant K' in the case $p = +\infty$, $\{x_i\} = \mathbb{Z}$, of (3.20) (i.e., for his interpolation problem $CIP(y; L_{[1]})$) is the ϕ_m in (5.7).

REFERENCES

1. C. de Boor, The quasi-interpolant as a tool in elementary polynomial spline theory, Approximation Theory (Symposium, Texas, 1973, ed. G.G. Lorentz), pp. 269-276, Academic Press, New York/London, 1973.

2. C. de Boor, How small can one make the derivatives of an interpolating function?, J. Approx. Theory 13 (1975), 105-116.

3. C. de Boor, On local linear functionals which vanish at all B-splines but one, Theory of Approximation (Conference Proc., Calgary, 1975, ed. A.G. Law and B.N. Sahney), pp. 120-145, Academic Press, New York/London, 1976.

4. C. de Boor, Splines as linear combinations of B-splines: a survey, Approximation Theory II (Symposium Proc., Texas, 1976, ed. G.G. Lorentz, C.K. Chui, L.L. Schumaker), pp. 1-47, Academic Press, New York/London, 1976.

5. H.B. Curry and I.J. Schoenberg, On Pólya frequency functions IV: the fundamental spline functions and their limits, J. d'Analyse Math. 17 (1966), 71-107.

6. M. Golomb, $H^{m,p}$-extensions by $H^{m,p}$-splines, J. Approx. Theory 5 (1972), 238-275.

7. A. Jakimovski and D.C. Russell, On the Hausdorff moment problem, General Inequalities 1 (Conference Proc., Oberwolfach, 1976, ed. E.F. Beckenbach), pp. 63-81, Birkhäuser-Berlag, Basel/Stuttgart, 1978.

8. J.W. Jerome and L.L. Schumaker, Characterizations of functions with higher order derivatives in $\mathcal{L}_p$, Trans. Amer. Math. Soc. 143 (1969), 363-371.

9. J. Lindenstrauss and L. Tzafriri, Classical Banach Spaces I, Springer-Verlag, Berlin/Heidelberg/New York, 1977.

10. M.J. Marsden, An identity for spline functions with applications to variation-diminishing spline approximations, J. Approx. Theory 3 (1970), 7-49.

11. I.J. Schoenberg, On variation-diminishing approximation methods. On Numerical Approximation (M.R.C. Symposium, ed. R.E. Langer), pp. 249-274, Univ. of Wisconsin Press, Madison, 1959.

12. I.J. Schoenberg, Spline interpolation and the higher derivatives, Proc. Nat. Acad. Sci. U.S.A. 51 (1964), 24-28.

13. I.J. Schoenberg, On spline functions, Inequalities (Symposium Proc., 1965, ed. O. Shisha), pp. 255-291, Academic Press, New York/London, 1967.

14. I.J. Schoenberg, Cardinal interpolation and spline functions, J. Approx. Theory 2 (1969), 167-206.

15. I.J. Schoenberg, Cardinal interpolation and spline functions: II. Interpolation of data of power growth, J. Approx. Theory 6 (1972), 404-420.

16. I.J. Schoenberg, Cardinal Spline Interpolation, Soc. Indust. Appl. Math., Philadelphia, 1973.

17. Ju.N. Subbotin, On the relations between finite differences and the corresponding derivatives, Proc. Steklov Inst. Math. 78 (1965), 24-42 (in Russian); Amer. Math. Soc. Translations (1967), 23-42.

18. Ju.N. Subbotin, Interpolation by functions with n-th derivative of minimum norm, Proc. Steklov Inst. Math. 88 (1967), 30-60 (in Russian); Amer. Math. Soc. Translations (1969), 31-63.

ON APPROXIMATELY ADDITIVE MAPPINGS

Jürg Rätz
Mathematisches Institut
Universität Bern
CH-3012 Bern
SWITZERLAND

Dedicated to Professor Walter Nef on his sixtieth birthday

ABSTRACT. The stability question for additive mappings under various conditions on their domains and ranges is studied. The main aspects are existence, uniqueness, and continuity of an approximating additive mapping (Sections 4 and 5). Suitable examples demonstrate the limits of the scope of our theorems (Section 6). The monogenic subsets of the domain and the behavior of the mappings on these turn out to be of central importance.

1. INTRODUCTION

The question (originally posed by S. Ulam) as to when an approximately additive, multiplicative, convex, subharmonic, or isometric mapping can be approximated by an additive, multiplicative, convex, subharmonic, or isometric mapping, respectively, has been investigated by many authors (cf., e.g., [11], [12]; [19], [3]; [15], [8]; [9]; [13], [14], [6]). This is a question of stability, and for a survey of this notion cf., e.g., [20], pp. 63-69; I thank Dr. D. Brydak for this reference. My deep gratitude goes to Dr. J.D. Aczél for having supported this work by inviting me to the University of Waterloo, and to Dr. John A. Baker for having drawn my attention to this kind of problem.

In connection with additive mappings, D.H. Hyers [11] proved that if δ is a positive real number and f a mapping from a Q-vector space X into a Banach space Y satisfying the functional inequality

$$\|f(x_1) + f(x_2) - f(x_1 + x_2)\| \leq \delta \quad \text{for all} \quad x_1, x_2 \in X$$

of approximate additivity, then there exists a unique additive mapping $\ell : X \to Y$ with the property $\|f(x) - \ell(x)\| \leq \delta$ for every $x \in X$. By modifications of the procedure in [11], it is possible to find other situations in which a similar conclusion holds. The presentation of some of these is the purpose of the present paper.

2. GENERAL HYPOTHESES

For creating a situation more general than the one investigated in [11], a choice is necessary. That situation certainly is covered by the framework of the following general hypotheses:

(H1) $(X,*)$ is a groupoid; i.e., X is a nonempty set and $* : X \times X \to X$ a binary operation.

(H2) $(Y,+)$ is a Q-vector space.

(H3) $\emptyset \neq V \subset Y$.

(H4) $f : X \to Y$, $f(x_1) + f(x_2) - f(x_1 * x_2) \in V$ for all $x_1, x_2 \in X$.

For further hypotheses (H1'), (H2'), cf. Section 5 and Remark 2.

3. PRELIMINARIES AND NOTATION

N, Z, Q, R, R_+^*, C denote the sets of positive integers, integers, rational, real, positive real, and complex numbers, respectively. For intervals of R, we use the symbols $[a,b]$, $[a,b[$, etc. $\mathfrak{R}$ stands for the usual topology on R, cl for closure, and $\mathfrak{U}(a)$ for the filter of neighborhoods of the point a. The powers of an element x of a groupoid are defined by

$$x^1 := x \; ; \qquad x^{m+1} := x * x^m \qquad (m \in N) \; . \tag{1}$$

They are merely left powers, and some care is necessary in the absence of power associativity (cf. Definition 1). For a characterization of those abelian groups $(Y,+)$ which are Q-vector spaces, cf., e.g., [21], p. 258, Exercises 26.12, 26.13. By 0 we denote the zero vector and the scalar zero (it will always be clear from the context what is meant), and by $\underline{0}$ the constant mapping with value 0. By Hom(X,Y), under the hypotheses (H1) and (H2), we always mean the set

$$\{\ell : X \to Y \; ; \; \ell(x_1 * x_2) = \ell(x_1) + \ell(x_2) \quad (\forall\, x_1, x_2 \in X)\} \; .$$

We shall make extensive use of the familiar arithmetic of sets in vector spaces (cf., e.g., [22], p. 22 ff.), from which we mention here only

(2) $s(tA) = (st)A$ for all scalars s,t ;

(3) $sA + tA = (s + t)A$ for all nonnegative scalars s,t $\Longleftrightarrow$ A is convex with respect to the respective scalar field .

4. EXISTENCE AND UNIQUENESS

The following abbreviations will be used:

$(\exists\ \ell,f,V)$ There exists $\ell \in \mathrm{Hom}(X,Y)$ such that $f(x) - \ell(x) \in V$ for every $x \in X$.

$(\exists\,!\ell,f,V)$ Condition $(\exists\ \ell,f,V)$ holds, and moreover ℓ is unique.

The first two theorems are very simple; they describe purely algebraic situations.

THEOREM 1. <u>If</u> (H1), (H2), (H3), (H4) <u>hold, and if moreover for every</u> $x \in X$ <u>there exists</u> $x' \in X$ <u>with the property</u> $x * x' = x'$, <u>then</u> $(\exists\,!\ell,f,V)$, <u>namely</u> $\ell = \underline{0}$.

<u>Proof</u>. Let $x \in X$ be arbitrary. By (H4),

$$f(x) = f(x) + f(x') - f(x') = f(x) + f(x') - f(x * x') \in V ,$$

i.e., $\ell = \underline{0}$ has the required property. Assume that $\ell \in \mathrm{Hom}(X,Y)$ and $x \in X$. Then

$$\ell(x) + \ell(x') = \ell(x * x') = \ell(x') ;$$

hence $\ell(x) = 0$, i.e., $\ell = \underline{0}$, so ℓ is unique. □

REMARK 1. The special hypothesis in Theorem 1 (saying that every x of X is absorbed from the right by some element $\mathbf{x}'$ of X) is trivially satisfied if X has a right zero element or if every element of X is idempotent. An inspection of the proof also shows that (H2) could be replaced here by the weaker condition that $(Y,+)$ is a (not necessarily abelian) group.

For later purposes, we establish the following technical lemma.

LEMMA 1. *Let* (H1), (H2), (H3), (H4) *hold, with* V $\mathbb{Q}$-*convex. If* $p,q \in \mathbb{N}$, $p < q$, *and* $x \in X$, *then*

$$(q - p)f(x) + f(x^p) - f(x^q) \in (q - p)V .$$

Proof. From (H4) and (1), we obtain $f(x) + f(x^p) - f(x^{p+1}) \in V$, $f(x) + f(x^{p+1}) - f(x^{p+2}) \in V$, ... , $f(x) + f(x^{q-1}) - f(x^q) \in V$, and by adding and using $\mathbb{Q}$-convexity of V via (3), we furthermore have

$$(q - p)f(x) + f(x^p) - f(x^q) \in V + \dots + V = (q - p)V ,$$

i.e., the assertion. □

THEOREM 2. *Let* (H1), (H2), (H3), (H4) *hold, with* V $\mathbb{Q}$-*convex*.

(a) *If for every* $x \in X$ *the set* $\{f(x^q) ; q \in \mathbb{N}\}$ *is finite, then* $(\exists \ell,f,V)$, *for instance with* $\ell = \underline{0}$.

(b) *If for every* $x \in X$ *the set* $\{x^q ; q \in \mathbb{N}\}$ *is finite, i.e., if* $(X,*)$ *is a so-called periodic groupoid, then* $(\exists ! \ell,f,V)$, *namely* $\ell = \underline{0}$.

Proof. (a) Let $x \in X$ be arbitrary. Then there exist $p,q \in \mathbb{N}$ such that $p < q$ and $f(x^p) = f(x^q)$. Lemma 1 now ensures

$$(q - p)f(x) \in (q - p)V ;$$

hence, by (2), $f(x) \in V$. So $(\exists \ell,f,V)$ holds with $\ell = \underline{0}$.

(b) $\mathrm{Hom}(X,Y) = \{\underline{0}\}$ follows from the fact that 0 is the only element of Y of finite order, and now the assertion is a consequence of part (a). □

The next theorem needs some more preparations.

LEMMA 2. *If* (H1), (H2), (H3), (H4) *hold, with* V $\mathbb{Q}$-*convex and* $0 \in V$, *then we have*:

(a) $t \in [0,1] \cap \mathbb{Q}$ *implies* $tV \subset V$; *i.e.,* V *is* $\mathbb{Q}$-*starlike with respect to* 0.

(b) $f(x) - \frac{1}{q} f(x^q) \in V$ *for every* $q \in \mathbb{N}$ *and every* $x \in X$.

Proof. For $v \in V$ and $t \in [0,1] \cap \mathbb{Q}$, we get

$$tv = (1 - t)0 + tv \in V ,$$

which ensures part (a).

For $q = 1$, assertion (b) becomes $0 \in V$, which is true. Now let q satisfy $q \geq 2$. Lemma 1, applied for $p = 1$, yields

$$(q - 1)f(x) + f(x) - f(x^q) \in (q - 1)V ,$$

i.e.,

$$qf(x) - f(x^q) \in (q - 1)V , \quad \text{i.e.,} \quad f(x) - \frac{1}{q} f(x^q) \in \frac{q - 1}{q} V \subset V ,$$

the last step being guaranteed by part (a). Therefore assertion (b) holds. □

REMARK 2. Q-vector spaces offer themselves as quite natural tools for our purposes. As we wish to use boundedness and convergence in Y from now on, we furnish Y with a vector topology $\mathfrak{T}$, where the scalar field Q is supposed to be topologized by its usual absolute value $|\cdot|$. We then briefly say that

(H2') $(Y,+,\mathfrak{T})$ is a topological $(Q,|\cdot|)$-vector space .

If K is a topological field containing $(Q,|\cdot|)$ as a subfield, if Y is a topological K-vector space, and if we restrict multiplication $\cdot : K \times Y \to Y$ to $Q \times Y$, then Y becomes a topological $(Q,|\cdot|)$-vector space. It must be emphasized that the additive group of Y and the topology $\mathfrak{T}$ remain unchanged, and so does the uniformity of the additive group. Since $(Q,|\cdot|)$ is a topological subfield of R and of C, with their respective usual absolute values, we are sure to include in our considerations the most important examples of topological vector spaces.

REMARK 3. $\mathfrak{T}$-bounded sets in a topological vector space $(Y,+,\mathfrak{T})$ are introduced in most texts for $K = R$ or $K = C$. It is an easy exercise to see that, for $(Q,|\cdot|)$-vector spaces $(Y,+,\mathfrak{T})$, the definition "$S \subset Y$ $\mathfrak{T}$-bounded if and only if for every $U \in \mathfrak{U}(0)$ there exists $t \in Q$, $t > 0$, such that $tS \subset U$" has the following consequences (cf., e.g., [22], p. 178):

(B1) $S \subset Y$ $\mathfrak{T}$-bounded if and only if for any sequences (y_n) in S, (t_n) in Q with $t_n \to 0$ $(n \to \infty)$, we have $t_n y_n \to 0$ $(n \to \infty)$.

(B_2) $S \subset T \subset Y$, T $\mathfrak{T}$-bounded $\Rightarrow$ S $\mathfrak{T}$-bounded.

(B3) $S, T \subset Y$ $\mathfrak{T}$-bounded, $t \in Q \Rightarrow S + T$, tS, $\mathrm{cl}\, S$ $\mathfrak{T}$-bounded.

THEOREM 3. Let (H1), (H2'), (H3), (H4) hold, with V Q-convex and $0 \in V$. If for every $x \in X$ there exists a sequence $(q(n,x))$ $(n \in N)$ of positive integers such that $q(n,x) \to +\infty$ $(n \to \infty)$, and such that the set

$$\{f(x^{q(n,x)})\ ;\ n \in N\}$$

is $\mathfrak{T}$-bounded, then $f(x) \in \mathrm{seqcl}\, V$ for all $x \in X$; i.e., $(\exists\, \ell, f, \mathrm{seqcl}\, V)$ holds, e.g., with $\ell = \underline{0}$.

Here $\mathrm{seqcl}\, V$ denotes the sequential closure of the set V.

Proof. Let $x \in X$ be arbitrary. By (B1), $\mathfrak{T}$-boundedness of

$$\{f(x^{q(n,x)})\ ;\ n \in N\} \qquad \text{and} \qquad \frac{1}{q(n,x)} \to 0 \qquad (n \to \infty)$$

imply

$$y_n := \frac{1}{q(n,x)} \cdot f(x^{q(n,x)}) \to 0 \ ,$$

i.e.

$$f(x) - y_n \to f(x) \qquad (n \to \infty) \ .$$

By Lemma 2(b), $f(x) - y_n \in V$ for all $n \in N$, so $f(x) \in \mathrm{seqcl}\, V$. □

COROLLARY 1. If (H1), (H2'), (H3), (H4) hold, with V Q-convex and $0 \in V$, and if $f(X)$ is $\mathfrak{T}$-bounded, then $f(X) \subset \mathrm{seqcl}\, V$.

REMARK 4. Theorem 3 contains a so-called resonance theorem. If we define

$$f_n : X \to Y \qquad \text{by} \qquad f_n(x) := f(x^{q(n,x)}) \qquad (x \in X, \quad n \in N) \ ,$$

the hypothesis says that the family (f_n) is pointwise $\mathfrak{T}$-bounded on X. Now if V is $\mathfrak{T}$-bounded, so is $f(X)$, by (B3), (B2), and

$$f(X) \subset \mathrm{seqcl}\, V \subset \mathrm{cl}\, V \ .$$

Since $f_n(X) \subset f(X)$ for every $n \in N$, (f_n) turns out to be uniformly $\mathfrak{T}$-bounded. This argument of course leans very heavily on (H4); in the absence of (H4) it collapses, as suitable examples show.

We are going to consider one more situation in which we obtain a conclusion of the $(\exists\, \ell, f, V)$ type. Here, too, we need some specific preparations.

DEFINITION 1. A groupoid $(X,*)$ is called <u>power-associative</u> if the left powers (cf. (1)) satisfy

$$x^{m+n} = x^m * x^n \quad \text{for all} \quad m,n \in N \quad \text{and every} \quad x \in X\,. \tag{4}$$

This means that for every $x \in X$ the set $\{x^n\,;\, n \in N\}$ forms a commutative subsemigroup of $(X,*)$. By induction we easily get, from (1) and (4),

$$(x^p)^q = x^{pq} \quad \text{for all} \quad p,q \in N \quad \text{and every} \quad x \in X\,. \tag{5}$$

Power-associativity is a weak substitute for associativity. For a construction of power-associative nonassociative operations, cf., e.g., [2], p. 555.

LEMMA 3. <u>Let</u> (H1), (H2'), (H3), (H4) <u>hold, with</u> $(X,*)$ <u>power-associative</u>, V <u>Q-convex and</u> $\mathfrak{T}$<u>-bounded, and</u> $0 \in V$. <u>If</u> $k \in N$, $k \geq 2$, <u>then the sequence</u>

$$(k^{-n}\, f(x^{k^n}))_{n\in N}$$

<u>satisfies the "uniform Cauchy condition": For every</u> $U \in \mathfrak{U}(0)$ <u>there exists</u> $n_0 \in N$ <u>such that</u> $x \in X$ <u>and</u> $m,n \in N$, $m,n \geq n_0$ <u>imply</u>

$$k^{-m}\, f(x^{k^m}) - k^{-n}\, f(x^{k^n}) \in U\,.$$

<u>Proof</u>. Let $U \in \mathfrak{U}(0)$ be arbitrary. Since V is $\mathfrak{T}$-bounded, there exists $t \in Q$, $t > 0$, such that $tV \subset U$. Choose $n_0 \in N$ such that

$$k^{-n_0} < t\,.$$

Let $x \in X$ be arbitrary and $m,n \in N$ such that $n \geq m \geq n_0$. For $m = n$, we have

$$k^{-m}\, f(x^{k^m}) - k^{-n}\, f(x^{k^n}) = 0 \in U\,.$$

In the following, let $n > m$. From (5), we get

$$x^{k^n} = x^{k^m \cdot k^{n-m}} = (x^{k^m})^{k^{n-m}}\,,$$

and Lemma 2(b) with x^{k^m} instead of x yields

$$k^{-m} f(x^{k^m}) - k^{-n} f(x^{k^n}) = k^{-m}[f(x^{k^m}) - k^{-n+m} f((x^{k^m})^{k^{n-m}})] \in k^{-m} V ,$$

and Lemma 2(a) ensures

$$k^{-m} V \subset k^{-n_0} V \subset tV \subset U ,$$

which completes the proof. □

THEOREM 4. Let (H1), (H2'), (H3), (H4) hold, with $(X,*)$ power-associative and V Q-convex and $\mathfrak{T}$-bounded, $0 \in V$. Let $(Y,+,\mathfrak{T})$ be sequentially complete, and assume that there is $k \in N$, $k \geq 2$, such that

$$(6) \qquad f((x_1 * x_2)^{k^n}) = f(x_1^{k^n} * x_2^{k^n}) \quad \text{for all} \quad x_1,x_2 \in X; \quad n \in N .$$

Then $(\exists\, \ell, f, \text{seqcl } V)$.

Proof. (a) By Lemma 3,

$$(k^{-n} f(x^{k^n}))_{n\in\mathbf{N}}$$

is a Cauchy sequence for each $x \in X$. Sequential completeness of $(Y,+,\mathfrak{T})$ ensures the existence of at least one limit of each such sequence. For every $x \in X$, choose one and call it $\ell'(x)$.

(b) For arbitrary $x_1,x_2 \in X$, $n \in N$, from (6) and (H4) we get

$$f(x_1^{k^n}) + f(x_2^{k^n}) - f((x_1 * x_2)^{k^n}) \in V .$$

Since V is $\mathfrak{T}$-bounded and $k^{-n} \to 0$ $(n \to \infty)$, by virtue of (B1) we obtain

$$(7) \qquad k^{-n} f(x_1^{k^n}) + k^{-n} f(x_2^{k^n}) - k^{-n} f((x_1 * x_2)^{k^n}) \to 0 \qquad (n \to \infty) ,$$

and on the other hand from part (a) of this proof we have

$$(8) \quad k^{-n}f(x_1^{k^n}) + k^{-n}f(x_2^{k^n}) - k^{-n}f((x_1 * x_2)^{k^n}) \to \ell'(x_1) + \ell'(x_2) - \ell'(x_1 * x_2)$$
$$(n \to \infty) .$$

Since $(Y,\mathfrak{T})$ is a regular topological space (cf., e.g., [5], p. 9, Proposition 4),

$$y,y',y_n \in Y , \quad y_n \to y, \quad y_n \to y' \quad (n \to \infty)$$

implies $y' \in \mathrm{cl}\{y\}$. [This is true even in so-called R_1-spaces (cf. [7], p. 889-890), but false in general in T_1-spaces.] So from (7) and (8) we get

$$(9) \qquad \ell'(x_1) + \ell'(x_2) - \ell'(x_1 * x_2) \in \mathrm{cl}\{0\} \quad \text{for all} \quad x_1,x_2 \in X .$$

(c) The next step is to replace $\ell' : X \to Y$ by an additive mapping ℓ, i.e., to correct the possibly unrelated choice of the values of ℓ'. Since $\mathrm{cl}\{0\}$ is a linear subspace of Y, there is an algebraically complementary linear subspace Y_1 of $\mathrm{cl}\{0\}$ in Y (cf., e.g., [22], p. 32-33). By definition,

$$Y_1 \cap \mathrm{cl}\{0\} = \{0\}, \qquad Y_1 + \mathrm{cl}\{0\} = Y .$$

So every $y \in Y$ has a unique representation

$$y = y_1 + w \quad \text{with} \quad y_1 \in Y_1, \quad w \in \mathrm{cl}\{0\} .$$

Now $g : Y \to Y_1$, $h : Y \to \mathrm{cl}\{0\}$ are well-defined by

$$(10) \qquad y = g(y) + h(y) \qquad (y \in Y) ,$$

and they turn out to be Q-linear. If $j : Y_1 \to Y$ denotes the natural injection, we put

$$\ell : X \to Y , \qquad \ell := j \circ g \circ \ell' .$$

Let $x_1,x_2 \in X$ be arbitrary. Then

$$\ell(x_1) + \ell(x_2) - \ell(x_1 * x_2) = g[\ell'(x_1)] + g[\ell'(x_2)] - g[\ell'(x_1 * x_2)]$$

$$= g[\ell'(x_1) + \ell'(x_2) - \ell'(x_1 * x_2)] \in g[\mathrm{cl}\{0\}] ,$$

by (9). But by (10), $g[\mathrm{cl}\{0\}] = \{0\}$; i.e.,

$$\ell(x_1) + \ell(x_2) - \ell(x_1 * x_2) = 0 ;$$

i.e., $\ell \in \mathrm{Hom}(X,Y)$.

(d) Finally, we have to show that ℓ approximates f in the required sense. Let $x \in X$ be arbitrary. Then by (10),

$$\ell(x) - \ell'(x) = g[\ell'(x)] - \ell'(x) = - h[\ell'(x)] \in \mathrm{cl}\{0\} ;$$

i.e., since translations in Y are homeomorphisms,

$$\ell(x) \in \ell'(x) + \mathrm{cl}\{0\} = \mathrm{cl}[\ell'(x) + \{0\}] = \mathrm{cl}\{\ell'(x)\} .$$

By construction of ℓ',

$$k^{-n} f(x^{k^n}) \to \ell'(x) ,$$

and $\ell(x) \in \mathrm{cl}\{\ell'(x)\}$ now ensures

$$k^{-n} f(x^{k^n}) \to \ell(x) \qquad (n \to \infty) .$$

From Lemma 2 (b), we conclude

$$f(x) - k^{-n} f(x^{k^n}) \in V \qquad \text{for every} \quad n \in N ,$$

so $f(x) - \ell(x) \in \mathrm{seqcl}\ V$. Therefore, $(\exists\ \ell, f, \mathrm{seqcl}\ V)$. □

We may look at Theorem 4 from a different point of view:

COROLLARY 2. Under the hypotheses of Theorem 4, $\mathrm{Hom}(X,Y) = \{0\}$ implies $f(X) \subset \mathrm{seqcl}\ V$.

REMARK 5. The condition

(11) $$(x_1 * x_2)^k = x_1^k * x_2^k \qquad \text{for all} \quad x_1, x_2 \in X ,$$

for a fixed $k \in N$, $k \geq 2$, is a weak substitute for commutativity of $*$. By use of power-associativity via (5), and by induction, we derive

$$(x_1 * x_2)^{k^n} = x_1^{k^n} * x_2^{k^n} \qquad (n \in N;\ x_1, x_2 \in X)$$

from (11). Therefore (11) implies (6), but the converse is not true: Let

$$(X,*) := (GL(2,R),\cdot) , \qquad (Y,+) := (R,+) ,$$

$$\psi : Y \to Y, \qquad f := \psi \circ \det : X \to Y, \qquad x_1 := \begin{pmatrix} 1 & 1 \\ 0 & 1 \end{pmatrix}, \qquad x_2 := \begin{pmatrix} 1 & 0 \\ 1 & 1 \end{pmatrix} .$$

Then (11) is violated for every $k \in N$, $k \geq 2$, but (6) holds. For this reason, we prefer assuming (6) in Theorem 4. There are many contributions in the literature about the role of (11) in group or ring theory. E.g., (11) for $k = 2$ is sufficient for a not necessarily associative ring with identity to be commutative (cf. [16]). For arbitrary monoids, however, so *a fortiori* for power-associative groupoids, "(11) for every $k \in N$" does not imply commutativity: For $A = \{a,b\}$, $a \neq b$, the transformation semigroup consisting of the identical mapping and the two constant mappings on A is an idempotent noncommutative monoid.

In Theorems 1 and 2, the question of uniqueness of ℓ could be settled. For Theorems 3 and 4, this is done by Theorem 5. Theorems 4 and 5 extend Theorem 1 in [11].

LEMMA 4. *If* (H1), (H2') *hold, if*

$$f : X \to Y \quad \textit{and} \quad \ell_1, \ell_2 \in \mathrm{Hom}(X,Y) \ ,$$

and if

$$W_1 := \{f(x) - \ell_1(x) \ ; \ x \in X\}$$

is $\mathfrak{T}$*-bounded, then the following statements are equivalent*:

(i) $W_2 := \{f(x) - \ell_2(x) \ ; \ x \in X\}$ *is* $\mathfrak{T}$*-bounded*.

(ii) $\ell_1(x) - \ell_2(x) \in \mathrm{cl}\{0\}$ *for every* $x \in X$.

Proof. Suppose (i) holds, and let $x \in X$, $n \in N$ be arbitrary. Then $x^n \in X$; i.e.,

$$n(\ell_1(x) - \ell_2(x)) = n\ell_1(x) - n\ell_2(x) = \ell_1(x^n) - \ell_2(x^n)$$
$$= \ell_1(x^n) - f(x^n) + f(x^n) - \ell_2(x^n) \in (-W_1) + W_2 \ .$$

Since W_1, W_2 are $\mathfrak{T}$-bounded, so is $(-W_1) + W_2$, by (B3), and by (B1) the constant sequence with value

$$\ell_1(x) - \ell_2(x)$$

converges to 0 as $n \to \infty$. Therefore

$$0 \in \mathrm{cl}\{\ell_1(x) - \ell_2(x)\} \ ;$$

and since $(Y,\mathfrak{T})$ is regular (as a matter of fact, the weaker property R_0 would be sufficient; cf. [7], p. 888), we get

$$\ell_1(x) - \ell_2(x) \in \mathrm{cl}\{0\} \ ;$$

i.e., (ii) holds.

Now let (ii) hold. For every $x \in X$, we have

$$f(x) - \ell_2(x) = f(x) - \ell_1(x) + \ell_1(x) - \ell_2(x) \in W_1 + \mathrm{cl}\{0\} ,$$

so $W_2 \subset W_1 + \mathrm{cl}\{0\}$. Regularity of $(Y,\mathfrak{T})$ guarantees that $\mathrm{cl}\{0\}$ is contained in any neighborhood U of 0, and hence that $\mathrm{cl}\{0\}$ is $\mathfrak{T}$-bounded. By (B3) and (B2), so is W_2; i.e. (i) holds. □

THEOREM 5. _If_ V _is_ $\mathfrak{T}$_-bounded and_ $(Y,+,\mathfrak{T})$ _is a Hausdorff space, then the mapping_ $\ell \in \mathrm{Hom}(X,Y)$ _in Theorems_ 3 _and_ 4 _is uniquely determined_.

Proof. Since V is $\mathfrak{T}$-bounded, so is seqcl V (cf. Remark 4). If $\ell_1,\ell_2 \in \mathrm{Hom}(X,Y)$ such that

$$f(x) - \ell_i(x) \in \mathrm{seqcl}\, V \qquad (x \in X,\ i \in \{1,2\}) ,$$

then by Lemma 4, $\ell_1(x) - \ell_2(x) \in \mathrm{cl}\{0\} = \{0\}$ $(x \in X)$; i.e., $\ell_1 = \ell_2$. □

5. CONTINUITY

Here (H1) is replaced by

(H1') $(X,*,\gamma)$ is a topological groupoid, i.e., $* : X \times X \to X$ is continuous .

In Theorems 1, 2, 3, with (H1') instead of (H1), we always have available a continuous approximating $\ell \in \mathrm{Hom}(X,Y)$, namely $\ell = \underline{0}$, no matter whether or not f is continuous. So it is natural to study the situation of Theorem 4, and besides this a different one including that of Theorem 2 in [11].

THEOREM 6. _Let the hypotheses of Theorem_ 4 _hold with_ (H1') _instead of_ (H1), _and let_ $\ell \in \mathrm{Hom}(X,Y)$ _be such that_

$$f(x) - \ell(x) \in \mathrm{seqcl}\, V \qquad (\forall\, x \in X) .$$

Then we have:

(a) _For each_ $x_0 \in X$, _continuity of_ f _at every point_ $x_0^{k^n}$ $(n \in N)$ _implies continuity of_ ℓ _at_ x_0.

(b) _If_ f _is continuous on_ X, _so is_ ℓ.

Proof. (a) For every $m \in N$, the mapping

$$\mu_m : X \to X \quad \text{defined by} \quad \mu_m(x) = x^m \quad (\forall x \in X)$$

is continuous on X. For $m = 1$, this is trivial, and since

$$\mu_{m+1}(x) = x * x^m = *(\mu_1(x), \mu_m(x)) ,$$

continuity of μ_m implies that of μ_{m+1}. We define

$$f_n : X \to Y \quad \text{by} \quad f_n(x) := k^{-n} f(x^{k^n}) \quad (\forall x \in X, \ \forall n \in N) .$$

It turns out that every f_n is continuous at x_0. From the final part of the proof of Theorem 4, we know that

$$f_n(x) \to \ell(x) \quad (n \to \infty)$$

for every $x \in X$. Regularity of $(Y,\mathfrak{T})$ and Lemma 3 imply that $f_n \to \ell$ $(n \to \infty)$ uniformly on X, and by a standard procedure we obtain continuity of ℓ at x_0.

(b) As an immediate consequence of (a), statement (b) is true. □

COROLLARY 3. _In Theorem_ 6(a) _we obtain continuity of_ ℓ _on the entire space_ X _if_ $(X,*,\gamma)$ _is a topological group_.

Proof. By Theorem 6(a), ℓ is continuous at x_0; so by a well-known fact (cf., e.g., [4], p. 29, Proposition 23), ℓ is continuous on X. □

After the foregoing complements to Theorem 4, we come to an independent continuity theorem.

DEFINITION 2. Let K denote a subfield of C, with the usual absolute value $|\cdot|$. A subset B of a K-vector space Y is called _autophorbic_ (i.e., eating itself) if for any family $(\rho_1,\ldots,\rho_n)$ of elements of $R_+^* \cap K$ there exists $s \in N$ such that

$$\rho_1 B + \cdots + \rho_n B \subset sB .$$

A topological K-vector space Y is called _locally autophorbic_ if Y has a neighborhood base at 0 consisting of autophorbic sets.

REMARK 6. (a) Every locally convex K-vector space Y is locally autophorbic. In fact, Y has a neighborhood base at 0 consisting of convex and circled sets U (cf., e.g., [17], pp. 177, 206). All these sets are autophorbic:

$$\rho_1 U + \cdots + \rho_n U = (\rho_1 + \cdots + \rho_n)U$$

since U is convex, and

$$(\rho_1 + \cdots + \rho_n)U \subset ([\rho_1 + \cdots + \rho_n] + 1)U$$

since U is circled.

(b) Every locally bounded K-vector space is locally autophorbic. (Locally bounded spaces are those which have a $\mathfrak{T}$-bounded neighborhood of 0; they were introduced by D.H. Hyers [10].) In fact, Y has a neighborhood base at 0 consisting of $\mathfrak{T}$-bounded and circled sets U (cf., e.g., [22], p. 168, Fact (x), and (B2)). All these sets are autophorbic: Since $\rho_1 U + \cdots + \rho_n U$ is bounded by (B3), there exists

$$\sigma \in R_+^* \cap K \quad \text{such that} \quad \rho_1 U + \cdots + \rho_n U \subset \sigma U ,$$

and circledness implies $\sigma U \subset ([\sigma] + 1)U$.

THEOREM 7. _Hypotheses_: (a) $(X,*,\gamma)$ _is a topological group_.

(b) $(Y,+,\mathfrak{T})$ _is a locally autophorbic topological_ K-_vector space_.

(c) $f : X \to Y$ _and_ $\ell \in \mathrm{Hom}(X,Y)$.

(d) W _is a_ $\mathfrak{T}$-_bounded subset of_ Y _such that_

$$f(x) - \ell(x) \in W$$

for all $x \in X$.

Assertion: _If_ f _is continuous at a single point_ x_0 _of_ X, _then_ ℓ _is continuous on the whole of_ X.

Proof. Let e be the identity element of X, and assume that ℓ is not continuous at e. Then there is a net $(x_\delta)_{\delta \in D}$ of elements of X such that $x_\delta \to e$ but

$$\ell(x_\delta) \not\to \ell(e) = 0 .$$

Hence there exists $U_0 \in \mathfrak{U}(0)$ such that

$$D' = \{\delta \in D\ ;\quad \ell(x_\delta) \notin U_0\}$$

is a cofinal subset of D. By hypothesis (b), U_0 contains an autophorbic set $U_1 \in \mathfrak{U}(0)$. <u>A fortiori</u>,

(12) $$\ell(x_\delta) \notin U_1 \quad \text{for all} \quad \delta \in D' .$$

Now $\mathfrak{T}$-boundedness of W implies that of $-W$, and for suitable

$$\rho_1, \rho_2 \in R_+^* \cap K$$

we have

(13) $$(-W) \subset \rho_1 U_1 , \quad W \subset \rho_2 U_1 .$$

Since U_1 is autophorbic, there exists $m \in N$ with the property

$$\rho_1 U_1 + U_1 + \rho_2 U_1 \subset m U_1 .$$

This and (12) yield

(14) $$m \cdot \ell(x_\delta) \notin \rho_1 U_1 + U_1 + \rho_2 U_1 \quad \text{for all} \quad \delta \in D' .$$

From $x_\delta \to e$, we get

$$x_\delta^m * x_0 \to x_0 ,$$

and since f is continuous at x_0, there is $\delta_0 \in D$ such that

$$\delta \in D, \quad \delta \geq \delta_0 \quad \text{implies}$$
$$f(x_\delta^m * x_0) - f(x_0) \in U_1 ,$$

and now for a suitable $\delta_1 \in D'$,

(15) $$f(x_{\delta_1} * x_0) - f(x_0) \in U_1 .$$

On the other hand, from (15) and (13) we obtain

$$m \cdot \ell(x_{\delta_1}) = \ell(x_{\delta_1}^m) = \ell(x_{\delta_1}^m * x_0) - \ell(x_0) = \ell(x_{\delta_1}^m * x_0) - f(x_{\delta_1}^m * x_0) + f(x_{\delta_1}^m * x_0) - f(x_0)$$
$$+ f(x_0) - \ell(x_0) \quad \in \quad (-W) + U_1 + W \subset \rho_1 U_1 + U_1 + \rho_2 U_1 ,$$

a contradiction of (14). So ℓ is continuous at e, i.e., continuous on X (cf. the proof of Corollary 3). □

6. EXAMPLES AND COMMENTS

REMARK 7. Some smallness condition on V is needed to make our statements $(\exists\ \ell,f,V)$, $(\exists!\ell,f,V)$ nontrivial. We chose $\mathfrak{T}$-boundedness as the main condition in this direction. Notice that in the case of pseudometric vector spaces, metric boundedness would be too weak since Y itself may be metrically bounded and $V = Y$ would become possible.

EXAMPLE 1. Let $(X,*) = (Z_2,+)$, $Y = R$, $V = \{0,2\}$, $f(0) = 0$, $f(1) = 1$, $\mathfrak{T} = \mathfrak{R}$. Then all the hypotheses of Theorems 2, 3, 4 except Q-convexity of V are satisfied, and furthermore

$$\text{seqcl } V = V \quad \text{and} \quad \text{Hom}(X,Y) = \{\underline{0}\} .$$

But $f(1) - \ell(1) = 1 - 0 = 1 \notin V$, so $(\exists\ \ell,f,V)$ does not hold. This example shows that Q-convexity of V in Theorems 2, 3, 4 as well as the special hypothesis in Theorem 1 are essential.

EXAMPLE 2. Let $(X,*) = (R,+)$, $Y = Q$, $V = [0,1] \cap Q$, $f(x) = -[x]$ $(\forall\, x \in X)$, and let $\mathfrak{T}$ be the topology on Q given by $|\cdot|$. Then (H1), (H2'), (H3), (H4) are satisfied ((H4) even with $\{0,1\}$ instead of V). Furthermore, V is Q-convex, $\mathfrak{T}$-bounded, $0 \in V$, and $\text{seqcl } V = V$. Finally, (4) and (6) hold. But $(\exists\ \ell,f,V)$ is not true, for if it were we would have

$$0 \leq f(x) - \ell(x), \quad \ell(x) \leq f(x) = -[x] = 0 \qquad (\forall\, x \in [0,1[) .$$

Now if $j : Q \to R$ is the inclusion mapping, then $j \circ \ell \in \text{Hom}(R,R)$, and it follows from a theorem of G. Darboux (cf., e.g., [1], pp. 32-33) that

$$\ell(x) = j(\ell(x)) = cx \qquad (\forall\, x \in R) ,$$

and $\ell(R) \subset Q$ requires $c = 0$, so $\ell = \underline{0}$. But $f(1) - \ell(1) = -1 \in V$, so ℓ cannot exist. This example simultaneously shows that the finiteness condition in Theorem 2(a),(b), pointwise boundedness in Theorem 3 (as explained in Remark 4), and sequential completeness in Theorem 4 are essential there. By the way, the inequality

$$k^{-n} - x > -[k^n x] \cdot k^{-n} \geq -x \qquad (\forall n \in N)$$

directly shows that $(-[k^n x] \cdot k^{-n})_{n \in N}$ is a Cauchy sequence (as it must be by Lemma 3) but that it is not convergent in Q whenever $x \in R \setminus Q$.

REMARK 8. The proof of Theorem 3 shows that forming the sequences

$$\left(\frac{1}{q(n,x)} \cdot f(x^{q(n,x)})\right)_{n \in N}$$

means annihilating functions with $\mathfrak{T}$-bounded ranges. For instance, if

$$f : R \to R, \quad f(x) = -[x] \quad (x \in R), \qquad \text{we may write} \quad f(x) = (-x) + (x - [x]) ,$$

and the procedure is to destroy the bounded nonadditive part $x - [x]$ and to keep the additive part $(-x)$ for approximation. Notice that this additive decomposition of f fails in Example 2 because the range Q is too narrow.

REMARK 9. If we insist on $0 \in V$ and Q-convexity of V, the goodness of approximation in the statement

$$f(x) - \ell(x) \in V \qquad (\forall x \in X)$$

cannot be sharpened in general, as pointed out in [11], pp. 222-223. But in special cases an improvement is possible: Let

$$f : R \to R, \quad f(x) = |x|/(1 + |x|) \quad (x \in R) .$$

Then

$$f(X) = f(R) = [0,1[$$

is $\mathfrak{R}$-bounded, and Theorems 3 and 5 imply $\ell = \underline{0}$. On the other hand,

$$V \supset \{f(x_1) + f(x_2) - f(x_1 + x_2) \; ; \; x_1, x_2 \in R\} = [0,2[\; .$$

REMARK 10. R_+^*, with multiplication in the role of addition and exponentiation

$$(c,x) \to x^c \qquad (c \in R, \; x \in R_+^*)$$

as multiplication of vectors by scalars, is an R-vector space, so it may also be considered as a Q-vector space. It is known that the topology $\mathfrak{R}|R_+^*$

induced by $\mathfrak{R}$ on R_+^* can be derived from the norm

$$\|\cdot\| := |\cdot| \circ \ln \quad \text{on} \quad R_+^*$$

(cf., e.g., [18], p. 103, Beispiel 1), so it is a vector topology. Clearly ln is a bijective isometry from the normed space onto the Banach space $(R,|\cdot|)$, with topology $\mathfrak{R}$. Therefore $(R_+^*,\|\cdot\|)$ also is complete. Now a unified treatment of the question of approximation of f by ℓ in the four following cases can be based on the theorems in [11] or on our Theorems 4, 5, and 7:

$$f : R \to R \qquad |f(x_1)+f(x_2)-f(x_1+x_2)| \leq \delta \ , \qquad \ell \in \mathrm{Hom}(R,R) \ ;$$

$$f : R \to R_+^* \qquad \|f(x_1)\cdot f(x_2)\cdot f(x_1+x_2))^{-1}\| \leq \delta \ , \qquad \ell \in \mathrm{Hom}(R,R_+^*) \ ;$$

$$f : R_+^* \to R \qquad |f(x_1)+f(x_2) - f(x_1\cdot x_2)| \leq \delta \ , \qquad \ell \in \mathrm{Hom}(R_+^*,R) \ ;$$

$$f : R_+^* \to R_+^* \ , \qquad \|f(x_1)\cdot f(x_2)\cdot (f(x_1\cdot x_2))^{-1}\| \leq \delta \ , \qquad \ell \in \mathrm{Hom}(R_+^*,R_+^*) \ .$$

In this way, we get four analogous stability theorems for the four Cauchy functional equations. But a different point of view is possible in this connection: In a recent paper [3] the case $f : X \to R$, X a Q-vector space, $|f(x_1)\cdot f(x_2) - f(x_1+x_2)| \leq \delta$ was investigated with a result completely different from the ones just mentioned.

REFERENCES

1. J. Aczél, Lectures on Functional Equations and Their Applications, Academic Press, New York, San Francisco, London, 1966.

2. A.A. Albert, Power-associative rings, Trans. Amer. Math. Soc. 64 (1948), 552-593.

3. John A. Baker, J. Lawrence, F. Zorzitto, The Stability of the equation $f(x + y) = f(x)f(y)$, to appear.

4. N. Bourbaki, Topologie générale, chap. 3 et 4, 3e édition, Hermann, Paris, 1960.

5. N. Bourbaki, Espaces vectoriels topologiques, chap. 1 et 2, 2e édition, Hermann, Paris, 1966.

6. D.G. Bourgin, Approximate isometries, Bull. Amer. Math. Soc. 52 (1946), 704-714.

7. A.S. Davis, Indexed systems of neighborhoods for general topological spaces, Amer. Math. Monthly 68 (1961), 886-893.

8. J.W. Green, Approximately convex functions, Duke Math. J. 19 (1952), 499-504.

9. J.W. Green, Approximately subharmonic functions, Proc. Amer. Math. Soc. 3 (1952), 829-833.

10. D.H. Hyers, A note on linear topological spaces, Bull. Amer. Math. Soc. 44 (1938), 76-80.

11. D.H. Hyers, On the stability of the linear functional equation, Proc. Nat. Acad. Sci. USA 27 (1941), 222-224.

12. D.H. Hyers, Transformations with bounded n-th differences, Pacific J. Math. 11 (1961), 591-602.

13. D.H. Hyers and S.M. Ulam, On approximate isometries, Bull. Amer. Math. Soc. 51 (1945), 288-292.

14. D.H. Hyers and S.M. Ulam, Approximate isometries of the space of continuous functions, Ann. Math. 48 (1947), 285-289.

15. D.H. Hyers and S.M. Ulam, Approximately convex functions, Proc. Amer. Math. Soc. 3 (1952), 821-828.

16. E.C. Johnson, D.L. Outcalt, and A. Yaqub, An elementary commutativity theorem for rings, Amer. Math. Monthly 75 (1968), 288-289.

17. G. Köthe, Topologische lineare Räume I, Springer, Berlin, Göttingen, Heidelberg, 1960.

18. H. Schubert, Topologie, Teubner, Stuttgart, 1964.

19. H.N. Shapiro, Note on a problem in number theory, Bull. Amer. Math. Soc. 54 (1948), 890-893.

20. S.M. Ulam, Problems in Modern Mathematics, Wiley, New York, 1964.

21. S. Warner, Modern Algebra, Vol. I, Prentice-Hall, Englewood Cliffs, N.J., 1965.

22. A. Wilansky, Functional Analysis, Blaisdell, New York, Toronto, London, 1964.

Inequalities of Functional Analysis

Hörsaal Lorenzenhof.

Northern side, main entrance

NEW VERSIONS OF THE HAHN-BANACH THEOREM

Benno Fuchssteiner
Fachbereich Mathematik
Gesamthochschule Paderborn
D479 Paderborn
WEST GERMANY

Heinz König
Fachbereich Mathematik
der Universität des Saarlandes
D 6600 Saarbrücken
WEST GERMANY

ABSTRACT. The Hahn-Banach theorem is perhaps the most fundamental individual theorem in abstract analysis. It is in the literature in countless forms. Yet there is still demand for versions which at the same time have simple shape and admit fast and widespread application. The present note claims to present some versions of this sort. The Main Version 1.1 is due to König and has been announced in [5] without its complicated initial proof. The present simple proof via the Fundamental Lemma 1.2 is due to Fuchssteiner. We also present the extended versions of the minimax theorem which follow from the above Hahn-Banach results.

The Hahn-Banach theorem has meanwhile been lifted to a new level of abstraction in a paper of Rodé [7]. His Theorem contains our Main Version 1.1, but to obtain the latter one in this manner would be much more involved, so that our presentation seems to retain independent interest.

1. MAIN VERSION AND FUNDAMENTAL LEMMA

Let E be a real vector space, and let E^* consist of the real-linear real-valued functionals on E.

1.1 MAIN VERSION. <u>Let</u> $\theta : E \to \mathbb{R}$ <u>be sublinear, and consider on the nonvoid subset</u> $T \subset E$ <u>the function</u> $\tau : T \to \mathbb{R}$ <u>with</u> $\tau \leq \theta | T$. <u>Assume that there is a pair of numbers</u> $\alpha, \beta > 0$ <u>such that</u>

$$\operatorname*{Inf}_{w \in T} (\theta(w - \alpha u - \beta v) - \tau(w) + \alpha\tau(u) + \beta\tau(v)) \leq 0 \qquad \forall\, u,v \in T .$$

<u>Then there exists</u> $\varphi \in E^*$ <u>such that</u> $\varphi \leq \theta$ <u>and</u> $\tau \leq \varphi | T$.

The proof is after the usual scheme: One applies to an appropriate modified sublinear functional the primitive Hahn-Banach version that below each sublinear functional there exists a linear one. We define $Q : E \to \mathbb{R}$ to be

$$Q(x) = \operatorname*{Inf}_{\substack{u \in T \\ t > 0}} (\theta(x + tu) - t\tau(u)) \qquad \forall x \in E ,$$

which is finite valued since the Inf is to be taken over a set of numbers $\geq -\theta(-x) > -\infty$. One verifies that

$$Q(x) \leq \theta(x) \qquad \forall x \in E \qquad \text{and} \qquad \tau(x) \leq -Q(-x) \qquad \forall x \in T .$$

From this one deduces for $\varphi \in E^*$ the equivalence: $\varphi \leq Q \iff \varphi \leq \theta$ and $\tau \leq \varphi|T$. Thus after the primitive Hahn-Banach theorem it remains to prove that the functional Q is sublinear. This will be done via the following Fundamental Lemma.

The Fundamental Lemma can be established on a fixed nonvoid cone $F \subset E$ (defined to be closed under addition and under multiplication with positive numbers) rather than on all of E, at the expense that we have to consider functions with values in $\mathbb{R} \cup \{-\infty\} =: \mathbb{R}^-$. In case that $0 \in F$, a sublinear $\theta : F \to \mathbb{R}^-$ is seen to fulfill $\theta(0) = 0$, except for the constant $\theta = -\infty$.

1.2 FUNDAMENTAL LEMMA. Let $P : F \to \mathbb{R}^-$ be such that for each $x \in F$ the function $t \mapsto P(tx)$ is upper semicontinuous (=: USC) on $]0,\infty[$. Assume that there is a pair of numbers $\alpha,\beta > 0$ such that

$$(*) \qquad P(\alpha x + \beta y) \leq \alpha P(x) + \beta P(y) \qquad \forall x,y \in F .$$

Define $Q : F \to \mathbb{R}^-$ to be

$$Q(x) = \operatorname*{Inf}_{t>0} \frac{1}{t} P(tx) \qquad \forall x \in F .$$

Then Q is sublinear. Furthermore, in case $\alpha + \beta \neq 1$, we have

$$Q(x) = \lim_{n \to \infty} \frac{P((\alpha + \beta)^n x)}{(\alpha + \beta)^n} \qquad \forall x \in F ,$$

where the limit exists since $P((\alpha + \beta)x) \leq (\alpha + \beta) P(x) \quad \forall x \in F$ in view of $(*)$.

The Fundamental Lemma will be proved in Section 2. To deduce the Main Version from the Fundamental Lemma, we assume the situation of 1.1. Define

$P : E \to \mathbb{R}$ to be

$$P(x) = \operatorname*{Inf}_{u \in T} (\theta(x + u) - \tau(u)) \qquad \forall\, x \in E \;,$$

which is seen to be finite valued, as above. Then the functional $Q : E \to \mathbb{R}$ defined earlier turns out to be

$$Q(x) = \operatorname*{Inf}_{t>0} \frac{1}{t} P(tx) \qquad \forall\, x \in E \;,$$

so that P and Q are connected as in 1.2. Thus it remains to show that the functional P satisfies the assumptions of 1.2 with $F = E$.

(i) For $x,u \in E$, we have

$$|\theta(tx + u) - \theta(sx + u)| \leq \Theta((t - s)x) = |t - s|\, \Theta(x) \qquad \forall\, s,t \in \mathbb{R} \;,$$

where

$$\Theta : \theta(x) = \operatorname{Max}(\theta(x),\theta(-x)) \qquad \forall\, x \in E$$

is the associated seminorm. It follows that for $x,u \in E$ the function $t \mapsto \theta(tx + u) - \tau(u)$ is continuous on $\mathbb{R}$, and hence that for $x \in E$ the function $t \mapsto P(tx)$, as the Inf of a family of continuous functions, is USC on $\mathbb{R}$.

(ii) For $x,y \in E$ and $u,v \in T$, we have

$$\begin{aligned} P(\alpha x + \beta y) &= \operatorname*{Inf}_{w \in T} (\theta(\alpha x + \beta y + w) - \tau(w)) \\ &= \operatorname*{Inf}_{w \in T} (\theta(\alpha(x + u) + \beta(y + v) + (w - \alpha u - \beta v)) - \tau(w)) \\ &\leq \alpha\theta(x + u) + \beta\theta(y + v) + \operatorname*{Inf}_{w \in T} (\theta(w - \alpha u - \beta v) - \tau(w)) \\ &\leq \alpha(\theta(x + u) - \tau(u)) + \beta(\theta(y + v) - \tau(v)) \;, \end{aligned}$$

so that we obtain

$$P(\alpha x + \beta y) \leq \alpha P(x) + \beta P(y) \qquad \forall\, x,y \in E \;.$$

This completes the proof of 1.2 $\Rightarrow$ 1.1. □

2. PROOF OF THE FUNDAMENTAL LEMMA

(i) We define $H : F \to \mathbb{R}^-$ to be

$$H(x) = \operatorname*{Inf}_{n \in \mathbb{Z}} \frac{P((\alpha+\beta)^n x)}{(\alpha+\beta)^n} = \lim_{n\to\infty} \frac{P((\alpha+\beta)^n x)}{(\alpha+\beta)^n} \qquad \forall\, x \in F\ .$$

It follows that

$$H(\alpha x + \beta y) \leq \alpha H(x) + \beta H(y) \qquad \forall\, x,y \in F\ ,$$
$$H((\alpha+\beta)x) = (\alpha+\beta)\, H(x) \qquad \forall\, x \in F\ ,$$

and that for each $x \in F$ the function $t \mapsto H(tx)$ is USC on $]0,\infty[$.

(ii) We claim that H is convex on F. Let M consist of the numbers $t \in [0,1]$ such that

$$H((1-t)x + ty) \leq (1-t)\, H(x) + tH(y) \qquad \forall\, x,y \in F$$

(with the usual convention $0(-\infty) := 0$). Then

(1) $0,1 \in M$,

(2) $s,t \in M \Rightarrow \lambda := \dfrac{\alpha s + \beta t}{\alpha + \beta} \in M$.

In fact, $\forall\, x,y \in F$ we have

$$\begin{aligned} H((1-\lambda)x + \lambda y) &= H\left(\frac{\alpha(1-s) + \beta(1-t)}{\alpha+\beta}\, x + \frac{\alpha s + \beta t}{\alpha+\beta}\, y\right) \\ &= \frac{1}{\alpha+\beta}\, H(\alpha((1-s)x + sy) + \beta((1-t)x + ty)) \\ &\leq \frac{\alpha}{\alpha+\beta}\, H((1-s)x + sy) + \frac{\beta}{\alpha+\beta}\, H((1-t)x + ty) \\ &\leq \frac{\alpha}{\alpha+\beta}\, ((1-s)H(x) + sH(y)) + \frac{\beta}{\alpha+\beta}\, ((1-t)H(x) + tH(y)) \\ &= (1-\lambda)\, H(x) + \lambda H(y)\ . \end{aligned}$$

From (1) and (2) it follows that

(3) $\overline{M} = [0,1]$,

(4) M is closed ,

and hence $M = [0,1]$, which is the assertion. In fact, $[0,1] \setminus M$ consists of the $t \in\,]0,1[$ such that

$$\exists\, x,y \in F \quad \text{with} \quad H((1-t)x + ty)) > (1-t)H(x) + tH(y)\ ,$$

or

$$\exists\ x,y \in F \quad \text{with} \quad H(x + y) > (1 - t)\, H\left(\frac{x}{1 - t}\right) + tH\left(\frac{y}{t}\right),$$

and hence is open after the USC behavior of H as described in (i).

(iii) For $x \in F$, we have

$$\operatorname*{Inf}_{t>0} \frac{1}{t} H(tx) = \operatorname*{Inf}_{t>0} \operatorname*{Inf}_{n \in \mathbb{Z}} \frac{P((\alpha + \beta)^n\, tx)}{(\alpha + \beta)^n\, t} = \operatorname*{Inf}_{t>0} \frac{1}{t} P(tx) = Q(x)\ .$$

(iv) We claim that Q is subadditive and hence sublinear on F. In fact, for $x,y \in F$ we have $\forall\, s,t > 0$, after (ii), (iii),

$$Q(x + y) \leq (s + t)\, H\left(\frac{1}{s + t}\,(x + y)\right) = (s + t)\, H\left(\frac{s}{s + t}\left(\frac{x}{s}\right) + \frac{t}{x + t}\left(\frac{y}{t}\right)\right)$$

$$\leq sH\left(\frac{x}{s}\right) + tH\left(\frac{y}{t}\right) \quad \text{and hence} \quad \leq Q(x) + Q(y)\ .$$

(v) Assume now that $\alpha + \beta \neq 1$. We claim that $H(tx) = tH(x) \quad \forall\, x \in F$ and $t > 0$, so that (iii) implies that $H = Q$, which remains to be proved. In fact, for $p \in \mathbb{Z}$ with $0 < t < (\alpha + \beta)^p$ and $n \in \mathbb{Z}$, we have

$$H\left([((\alpha+\beta)^p - t)(\alpha+\beta)^n + t]x\right) = (\alpha+\beta)^p\, H\left(\left(1 - \frac{t}{(\alpha+\beta)^p}\right)(\alpha+\beta)^n x + \frac{t}{(\alpha+\beta)^p}\, x\right)$$

$$\leq (\alpha+\beta)^p\left(\left(1 - \frac{t}{(\alpha+\beta)^p}\right)(\alpha+\beta)^n H(x) + \frac{t}{(\alpha+\beta)^p}\, H(x)\right)$$

$$= ((\alpha+\beta)^p - t)(\alpha+\beta)^n\, H(x) + tH(x)\ .$$

Now the function $s \mapsto H(sx)$ is convex on $]0,\infty[$ and therefore is either always $= -\infty$ or always finite valued and hence continuous. We can assume the latter case. Let $n \to \pm\infty$ such that $(\alpha + \beta)^n \to 0$. Then $H(tx) \leq tH(x)$. This holds true $\forall\, x \in F$ and $t > 0$, so that in fact we have $=$. The proof of 1.2 is complete. □

3. SPECIALIZATIONS OF THE MAIN VERSION

We start with a version of the familiar Hahn-Banach extension theorem. Here we have to take $\alpha = \beta = 1$. We want to emphasize, however, that the extension version is much less powerful and flexible than the subsequent ones.

3.1 EXTENSION VERSION. Let $\theta : E \to \mathbb{R}$ be sublinear, and on an additive subgroup $T \subset E$ let $\tau : T \to \mathbb{R}$ be additive with $\tau \leq \theta|T$. Then there exists $\varphi \in E^*$ such that $\varphi \leq \theta$ and $\tau = \varphi|T$.

Let us turn to more efficient specializations. First we mention the version $\tau = \text{const}$. Here it is natural to restrict $\alpha,\beta > 0$ to $\alpha + \beta = 1$. For $\alpha = \beta = 1/2$ this has been the basic theorem in [2], [3]. Next we quote the version $\tau = 0$. It requires no restriction on $\alpha,\beta > 0$. For $\alpha = \beta = 1$, this has already been obtained in [3]. The version $\tau = 0$ will be the source for all that follows.

3.2 HOMOGENEOUS VERSION. <u>Let</u> $\theta : E \to \mathbb{R}$ <u>be sublinear. Assume that the nonvoid subset</u> $T \subset E$ <u>is such that there is a pair of numbers</u> $\alpha,\beta > 0$ <u>with</u>

$$\operatorname*{Inf}_{w \in T} \theta(w - \alpha u - \beta v) \leq 0 \qquad \forall\, u,v \in T .$$

<u>If</u> $\theta|T \geq 0$, <u>then there exists</u> $\varphi \in E^*$ <u>such that</u> $\varphi \leq \theta$ <u>and</u> $\varphi|T \geq 0$.

An important special case is $E = C(X,\mathbb{R})$, with X a compact Hausdorff space $\neq \emptyset$, and

$$\theta = \text{Max}: \theta(f) = \text{Max } f \qquad \forall\, f \in C(X,\mathbb{R}) .$$

As in [2], [3], we extend the result to the cone $USC(X)$ of the USC functions $X \to \mathbb{R}^-$.

3.3 USC VERSION. <u>Let the nonvoid subset</u> $T \subset USC(X)$ <u>and the numbers</u> $\alpha,\beta > 0$ <u>be such that for all</u> $f,g \in T$ <u>and</u> $\varepsilon > 0$ <u>there exists</u> $h \in T$ <u>with</u> $h \leq \alpha f + \beta g + \varepsilon$. <u>If</u> $\text{Max } f \geq 0 \;\; \forall\, f \in T$, <u>then there exists</u> $\varphi \in \text{Prob}(X)$ <u>such that</u> $\varphi(f) \geq 0 \;\; \forall\, f \in T$.

We turn to a close relative. On a nonvoid set X, consider $E = B(X,\mathbb{R})$, the space of bounded functions $X \to \mathbb{R}$, and

$$\theta = \text{Sup}: \theta(f) = \text{Sup } f \qquad \forall\, f \in B(X,\mathbb{R}) .$$

Define $\text{AProb}(X)$ to consist of the $\varphi \in B(X,\mathbb{R})^*$ with $\varphi \leq \text{Sup}$. The functionals $\varphi \in \text{AProb}(X)$ have various simple characterizations; see, for example, [1] Appendix 1. As before, we extend the result to the cone $USB(X)$ of the upper semibounded functions $X \to \mathbb{R}^-$. For $\varphi \in \text{AProb}(X)$, it is natural to define

$$\varphi(f) := \text{Inf}\{\varphi(F) : f \leq F \in B(X,\mathbb{R})\} \qquad \forall\, f \in USB(X) .$$

One verifies that in particular the extended functional $\varphi : USB(X) \to \mathbb{R}^-$ remains additive, a fact which here is much more obvious than in the measure-theoretic USC situation.

3.4 USB VERSION. Let the nonvoid subset $T \subset USB(X)$ and the numbers $\alpha,\beta > 0$ be such that for all $f,g \in T$ and $\varepsilon > 0$ there exists $h \in T$ with $h \leq \alpha f + \beta g + \varepsilon$. If $\operatorname{Sup} f \geq 0 \quad \forall f \in T$, then there exists $\varphi \in AProb(X)$ such that $\varphi(f) \geq 0 \quad \forall f \in T$.

3.5 CONSEQUENCE. Let X be a compact Hausdorff space $\neq \emptyset$. For each $\varphi \in Prob(X)$, there exists $\Phi \in AProb(X)$ such that not only $\Phi|C(X,\mathbb{R}) = \varphi$ but also $\Phi(f) = \varphi(f) \quad \forall f \in USC(X)$.

In fact, this results from 3.4 applied to

$$T := \{f \in B(X,\mathbb{R}) : f \geq \text{some } F \in USC(X) \text{ with } \varphi(F) \geq 0\} .$$

Note that for $\varphi \in Prob(X)$ and $\Phi \in AProb(X)$ with $\Phi|C(X,\mathbb{R}) = \varphi$, one always has

$$\Phi(f) \leq \varphi(f) \qquad \forall f \in USC(X) ,$$

but $<$ is possible. A simple example can be formed with the Dirac functional $\varphi = \delta_a \in Prob(X)$ and $f = \chi_a \in USC(X)$, where $a \in X$ is not an isolated point of X.

An important common specialization of 3.3 and 3.4 is the case that X is finite. Let us restrict our attention to finite-valued functions.

3.6 FINITE VERSION. Let the nonvoid subset $T \subset \mathbb{R}^r$ and the numbers $\alpha,\beta > 0$ be such that for all $u,v \in T$ and $\varepsilon > 0$ there exists $x \in T$ with $x \leq \alpha u + \beta v + \varepsilon$. If

$$\operatorname{Max}(x_1,\ldots,x_r) \geq 0 \qquad \forall x \in T ,$$

then there exist $\sigma_1,\ldots,\sigma_r \geq 0$ with $\sigma_1 + \cdots + \sigma_r = 1$ such that

$$\sigma_1 x_1 + \cdots + \sigma_r x_r \geq 0 \qquad \forall x \in T .$$

The above Hahn-Banach versions are powerful work horses. They often allow us to cut down lengthy proofs to a few lines and, what is more important, can lead to more adequate forms of results. Decisive for their easy application is the weak form of the assumption "There is a pair of numbers $\alpha,\beta > 0$ such that ..." instead of, for example, "For all pairs $\alpha,\beta > 0$ with $\alpha + \beta = 1$ ... ." There are numerous examples in [1], [2], [3], [4].

4. THE BARYCENTER LEMMA

It can be expected that the minimax theorem as obtained in [2],[6] admits extended versions which correspond to the above results. We start to extend the barycenter lemma [2],[6].

4.1 FINITE VERSION REFORMULATED. Consider $f_1,\ldots,f_r : X \to \mathbb{R}$ on the nonvoid set X. Assume that there is a pair of numbers $\alpha,\beta > 0$ such that for all $x,y \in X$ and $\varepsilon > 0$ there exists $z \in X$ with

$$\alpha f_\ell(x) + \beta f_\ell(y) \leq f_\ell(z) + \varepsilon \qquad \forall \ell = 1,\ldots,r .$$

If $\mathrm{Min}(f_1,\ldots,f_r) \leq 0$ on X, then there exists a convex combination $f \in \mathrm{Conv}(f_1,\ldots,f_r)$ such that $f \leq 0$ on X.

This follows upon application of 3.3 or 3.4 or 3.6 to the set

$$T := \{\hat{x} := -(f_1(x),\ldots,f_r(x)) : x \in X\} \subset \mathbb{R}^r = C(\{1,\ldots,r\},\mathbb{R}) = B(\{1,\ldots,r\},\mathbb{R}) .$$

We see that the functions $f_1,\ldots,f_r$ could have been allowed to take values in $\mathbb{R} \cup \{\infty\}$ as well. In what follows, however, the opposite case of functions with values in $\mathbb{R} \cup \{-\infty\} = \mathbb{R}^-$ will be needed. This is a nontrivial extension, the first simple treatment of which appears to be due to Neumann [6]. For the sake of completeness, we include the explicit transfer of his idea.

4.2 EXTENDED FINITE VERSION. Consider $f_1,\ldots,f_r \in \mathrm{USB}(X)$ on the nonvoid set X. Assume that there is a pair of numbers $\alpha,\beta > 0$ such that for all $x,y \in X$ and $\varepsilon > 0$ there exists $z \in X$ with

$$\alpha f_\ell(x) + \beta f_\ell(y) \leq f_\ell(z) + \varepsilon \qquad \forall \ell = 1,\ldots,r .$$

If $\mathrm{Min}(f_1,\ldots,f_r) \leq 0$ on X, then to each $\varepsilon > 0$ there exists a convex combination $f \in \mathrm{Conv}(f_1,\ldots,f_r)$ (with the convention $0(-\infty) := 0$) such that $f \leq \varepsilon$ on X.

There are trivial examples which show that the conclusion cannot be maintained as in 4.1: Take $X = \{0,1\}$ and define $f_1, f_2 \in USB(X)$ to be $f_1(0) = 1$, $f_1(1) = -\infty$ and $f_2(0) = 0$, $f_2(1) = 1$.

Proof of 4.2. Let

$$D := \{x \in X : f_1(x), \ldots, f_r(x) > -\infty\} .$$

If $D = \emptyset$, then

$$f := \frac{1}{r}(f_r + \cdots + f_r)$$

will do. If $D \neq \emptyset$, then after 4.1 applied to $f_1|D, \ldots, f_r|D$ there are real $\sigma_1, \ldots, \sigma_r \geq 0$ with $\sigma_1 + \cdots + \sigma_r = 1$ such that

$$\sigma_1 f_1 + \cdots \sigma_r f_r \leq 0$$

on D. Let now $M > 0$ with $f_1, \ldots, f_r \leq M$ and put

$$\tau_\ell := \left(1 - \frac{\varepsilon}{M}\right)\sigma_\ell + \frac{\varepsilon}{rM} \qquad \forall \ell = 1, \ldots, r .$$

Then it is obvious that $\tau_1 f_1 + \cdots + \tau_r f_r \leq \varepsilon$ on X. □

4.3 USB BARYCENTER LEMMA. Let the nonvoid subset $T \subset USB(X)$ on the set X and the numbers $\alpha, \beta > 0$ be such that for all $x, y \in X$ and $\varepsilon > 0$ there exists $z \in X$ with

$$\alpha f(x) + \beta f(y) \leq f(z) + \varepsilon \qquad \forall f \in T .$$

If for some $\varphi \in AProb(X)$ we have

$$\varphi(f) \geq 0 \qquad \forall f \in T ,$$

then

$$\operatorname{Sup} f \geq 0 \qquad \forall f \in Min(T) ,$$

where $Min(T)$ is defined to consist of the functions $f = Min(f_1, \ldots, f_r)$ with $f_1, \ldots, f_r \in T$.

Proof. (i) The case $\alpha + \beta > 1$ requires separate treatment. First we show that in this case $f \leq 0$ $\forall f \in T$. In fact, assume that $F(a) > 0$ for some $F \in T$ and $a \in X$. Then after the assumption applied to

$$x = y = a \quad \text{and} \quad \varepsilon = \frac{1}{2}(\alpha + \beta - 1)F(a) > 0 ,$$

there exists $b \in X$ with

$$(\alpha + \beta)F(a) \leq F(b) + \frac{1}{2}(\alpha + \beta - 1)F(a) ,$$

or

$$F(b) \geq \frac{1}{2}(1 + \alpha + \beta)F(a) .$$

Via induction, we obtain $a_n \in X$ with

$$F(a_n) \geq \left(\frac{1}{2}(\alpha + \beta + 1)\right)^n F(a) \qquad \forall\, n \in \mathbb{N} .$$

It follows that $F(a_n) \to \infty$ for $n \to \infty$, which is impossible.

(ii) Let $\alpha+\beta > 1$ and fix $f = \mathrm{Min}(f_1,\dots,f_r)$ with $f_1,\dots,f_r \in T$. We have to show that $\mathrm{Sup}\, f \geq 0$. Assume that $\mathrm{Sup}\, f < 0$ and hence $\mathrm{Sup}\, f < -\delta$ for some $\delta > 0$. Then we have a decomposition $X = X(1) \cup \cdots \cup X(r)$ into pairwise disjoint $X(\ell) \subset X$ such that $f_\ell \leq -\delta$ on $X(\ell)$ $\forall\, \ell = 1,\dots,r$. In view of (i), it follows that

$$f_\ell + \delta\chi_{X(\ell)} \leq 0$$

and hence

$$\delta\varphi(\chi_{X(\ell)}) \leq \varphi(f_\ell) + \delta\varphi(\chi_{X(\ell)}) = \varphi(f_\ell + \delta\chi_{X(\ell)}) \leq 0 ,$$

so that $\varphi(\chi_{X(\ell)}) = 0$ $\forall\, \ell = 1,\dots,r$. Thus $\varphi(1) = 0$, which is a contradiction.

(iii) Let now $\alpha+\beta \leq 1$. Fix $f = \mathrm{Min}(f_1,\dots,f_r)$ with $f_1,\dots,f_r \subset T$ and assume that $\mathrm{Sup}\, f < 0$ and hence

$$\mathrm{Sup}\, f \leq -\delta , \quad \text{or} \quad f + \delta = \mathrm{Min}(f_1+\delta, \dots, f_r+\delta) \leq 0 ,$$

on X for some $\delta > 0$. In view of $\alpha + \beta \leq 1$, the version 4.2 can be applied to the functions $f_1+\delta, \dots, f_r+\delta$. For $\varepsilon := \delta/2$ we thus obtain real numbers $\sigma_1,\dots,\sigma_r \geq 0$ with $\sigma_1 + \cdots + \sigma_r = 1$ such that

$$\sum_{\ell=1}^{r} \sigma_\ell(f_\ell + \delta) \leq \frac{\delta}{2} \quad \text{or} \quad \sum_{\ell=1}^{r} \sigma_\ell f_\ell \leq -\frac{\delta}{2} \quad \text{on } X .$$

It follows that

$$0 \leq \sum_{\ell=1}^{r} \sigma_\ell \varphi(f_\ell) = \sum_{\ell=1}^{r} \varphi(\sigma_\ell f_\ell) = \varphi\left(\sum_{\ell=1}^{r} \sigma_\ell f_\ell\right) \leq \mathrm{Sup}\left(\sum_{\ell=1}^{r} \sigma_\ell f_\ell\right) \leq -\frac{\delta}{2} .$$

We thus arrive at a contradiction, which proves the assertion. □

In order to obtain the USC barycenter lemma, we combine the above result with 3.5 and with the usual Dini theorem [2], which can be stated as follows.

4.4 DINI THEOREM. <u>Let</u> X <u>be a compact Hausdorff space. For each nonvoid</u> $T \subset USC(X)$ <u>with</u> $F := \mathrm{Inf}_{f \in T} f \in USC(X)$, <u>we have</u> $\mathrm{Inf}_{f \in \mathrm{Min}(T)} \mathrm{Max}\, f = \mathrm{Max}\, F$.

4.5 USC BARYCENTER LEMMA. <u>Let the nonvoid subset</u> $T \subset USC(X)$ <u>on the compact Hausdorff space</u> X <u>and the numbers</u> $\alpha, \beta > 0$ <u>be such that for all</u> $x, y \in X$ <u>and</u> $\varepsilon > 0$ <u>there exists</u> $z \in X$ <u>with</u>

$$\alpha f(x) + \beta f(y) \leq f(z) + \varepsilon \qquad \forall f \in T .$$

<u>If for some</u> $\varphi \in \mathrm{Prob}(X)$ <u>we have</u>

$$\varphi(f) \geq 0 \qquad \forall f \in T ,$$

<u>then</u>

$$F := \underset{f \in T}{\mathrm{Inf}}\ f \in USC(X)$$

<u>has</u> $\mathrm{Max}\, F \geq 0$; <u>that is, there exists</u> $a \in X$ <u>such that</u> $f(a) \geq 0 \quad \forall f \in T$.

5. EXTENDED VERSIONS OF THE MINIMAX THEOREMS

Now as in [2] we combine 3.4 with 4.3, and 3.3 with 4.5, to obtain the following extended minimax theorems.

5.1 USB MINIMAX THEOREM. <u>Assume that the nonvoid subset</u> $T \subset USB(X)$ <u>on the set</u> X <u>satisfies</u>:

(i) <u>There is a pair of numbers</u> $\alpha, \beta > 0$ <u>such that for all</u> $f, g \in T$ <u>and</u> $\varepsilon > 0$ <u>there exists</u> $h \in T$ <u>with</u> $h \leq \alpha f + \beta g + \varepsilon$.

(ii) <u>There is a pair of numbers</u> $\sigma, \tau > 0$ <u>such that for all</u> $x, y \in X$ <u>and</u> $\varepsilon > 0$ <u>there exists</u> $z \in X$ <u>with</u> $\sigma f(x) + \tau f(y) \leq f(z) + \varepsilon \quad \forall f \in T$.

<u>If</u> $\mathrm{Sup}\, f \geq 0 \quad \forall f \in T$, <u>then</u> $\mathrm{Sup}\, f \geq 0 \quad \forall f \in \mathrm{Min}(T)$.

5.2 USC MINIMAX THEOREM. <u>Assume that the nonvoid subset</u> $T \subset USC(X)$ <u>on the compact Hausdorff space</u> X <u>satisfies:</u>

(i) <u>There is a pair of numbers</u> $\alpha, \beta > 0$ <u>such that for all</u> $f, g \in T$

and $\varepsilon > 0$ there exists $h \in T$ with $h \leq \alpha f + \beta g + \varepsilon$.

(ii) There is a pair of numbers $\sigma,\tau > 0$ such that for all $x,y \in X$ and $\varepsilon > 0$ there exists $z \in X$ with $\sigma f(x) + \tau f(y) \leq f(z) + \varepsilon \quad \forall f \in T$.

If $\operatorname{Max} f \geq 0 \quad \forall f \in T$, then

$$F := \operatorname*{Inf}_{f \in T} f \in USC(X)$$

has $\operatorname{Max} F \geq 0$; that is, there exists $a \in X$ such that $f(a) \geq 0 \quad \forall f \in T$.

There are trivial examples which show that the conclusion in 5.1 cannot be the same as in 5.2: Let $X = [0,\infty[$ and $T \subset USB(X)$ consist of the monotone increasing functions $f : X \to \mathbb{R}$ with $f(x) \to 0$ for $x \to \infty$. The same remark applies to 4.3 and 4.5.

We conclude with the remark that both from 5.1 and from 5.2 we obtain a more familiar minimax theorem when we restrict assumptions (i) and (ii) to pairs of numbers $\alpha,\beta > 0$ with $\alpha + \beta = 1$ and $\sigma,\tau > 0$ with $\sigma + \tau = 1$: Then the assumptions and hence the conclusions carry over from T to $T - c := \{f - c : f \in T\}$ for fixed $c \in \mathbb{R}$, and thus the assertions can be formulated in the form of familiar equalities.

REFERENCES

1. Klaus Barbey and Heinz König, Abstract Analytic Function Theory and Hardy Algebras, Lect. Notes Math. 493, Springer-Verlag, Berlin-Heidelberg-New York, 1977.

2. Heinz König, Über das von Neumannsche Minimax-Theorem, Arch. Math. 19 (1968), 482-487.

3. Heinz König, On Certain Applications of the Hahn-Banach and Minimax Theorems, Arch. Math. 21 (1970), 583-591.

4. Heinz König, Sublineare Funktionale, Arch. Math. 23 (1972), 500-508.

5. Heinz König, Neue Methoden und Resultate aus Funktionalanalysis und konvexer Analysis, Oper. Res. Verf. 28 (1978), 6-16.

6. Michael Neumann, Bemerkungen zum von Neumannschen Minimax-theorem, Arch. Math. 29 (1977), 96-105.

7. Gerd Rodé, Eine abstrakte Version des Satzes von Hahn-Banach, Arch. Math. 31 (1978), 474-481.

ON INTERPOLATION OF WEAK-TYPE OPERATORS

Dumitru Gaşpar
Department of Mathematics
University of Timişoara
1900 Timişoara
S.R. ROMANIA

ABSTRACT. It is the aim of this paper to describe all optimal interpolation pairs for the Banach couples of Lorentz spaces that occur in the theorem of Marcinkiewicz.

1. INTRODUCTION

We begin with some definitions and notations. Let $(X,\mathcal{A},\mu)$ be a positive σ-finite measure space and $L^p(\mu)$, $L^{p,q}(\mu)$ the corresponding Lebesgue and Lorentz spaces, respectively. Recall that the L_p-norm can be expressed with the aid of the nonincreasing rearrangement function f^* of f as follows:

$$\|f\|_p = \left(\int_0^\infty (f^*(t))^p\, dt\right)^{1/p}, \qquad p \in [1,\infty),$$

$$\|f\|_p = \text{ess sup } f^*(t), \qquad p = \infty,$$

while the $L^{p,q}$-norm is given by

$$\|f\|_{p,q} = \left(\int_0^\infty (t^{1/p} f^{**}(t))^q \frac{dt}{t}\right)^{1/q} \cong \left(\int_0^\infty (t^{1/p} f^*(t))^q \frac{dt}{t}\right)^{1/q},$$

$$p \in (1,\infty), \quad q \in [1,\infty),$$

$$\|f\|_{p,q} = \text{ess sup } t^{1/p} f^{**}(t), \qquad p \in (1,\infty), \quad q = \infty,$$

where

$$f^{**}(t) = \frac{1}{t}\int_0^t f^*(s)\, ds, \qquad t \in (0,\infty).$$

It is well known that

$$L^p(\mu) = L^{p,p}(\mu)$$

with equivalent norms, and that the continuous embeddings

$$(*)\qquad L^{p,1}(\mu) \subset L^{p,q}(\mu) \subset L^{p,\infty}(\mu)$$

hold true.

We also recall that a <u>Banach couple</u> consists of two Banach spaces which are continuously embedded in a linear topological space. For a pair of Banach spaces A, B, we shall denote by $\mathfrak{B}(A,B)$ the space of all bounded linear operators from A into B. For a pair of Banach couples A_1, A_2 and B_1, B_2, we shall denote by $\mathfrak{B}(A_1,A_2;B_1,B_2)$ the space of all linear operators from $A_1 + A_2$ into $B_1 + B_2$ such that they map continuously A_j into B_j $(j = 1,2)$. A pair of Banach spaces A, B is an <u>interpolation pair</u> with respect to the "interpolation segment" $[A_1,B_1;A_2,B_2]$ if each operator $T \in \mathfrak{B}(A_1,A_2;B_1,B_2)$ maps continuously A into B. It will be said to be <u>optimal</u> if for each other interpolation pair $\overline{A}$, $\overline{B}$, with $\overline{A} \supset A$ and $\overline{B} \subset B$, we have necessarily $\overline{A} = A$ and $\overline{B} = B$.

We now consider two positive σ-finite measure spaces $(X,\mathfrak{a},\mu)$, $(Y,\mathfrak{B},\nu)$ and let

$$\sigma = [\alpha_1,\beta_1;\alpha_2,\beta_2]$$

be a closed line segment in the open (unit) square $(0,1) \times (0,1)$ with end-points $(\alpha_1,\beta_1),(\alpha_2,\beta_2)$. A pair $\mathfrak{X}$, $\mathfrak{Y}$ of Banach function spaces of μ-measurable functions, ν-measurable functions, respectively, will be called:

(a) <u>a strong σ-interpolation pair</u> if it is an interpolation one with respect to

$$\left[L^{1/\alpha_1}(\mu),\ L^{1/\beta_1}(\nu);\ L^{1/\alpha_2}(\mu),\ L^{1/\beta_2}(\nu)\right] ;$$

(b) <u>a restricted strong σ-interpolation pair</u> if it is an interpolation one with respect to

$$\left[L^{1/\alpha_1,1}(\mu),\ L^{1/\beta_1}(\nu);\ L^{1/\alpha_2,1}(\mu),\ L^{1/\beta_2}(\nu)\right] ;$$

(c) <u>a weak σ-interpolation pair</u> if it is interpolation one with respect to

$$\left[L^{1/\alpha_1}(\mu),\ L^{1/\beta_1,\infty}(\nu);\ L^{1/\alpha_2}(\mu),\ L^{1/\beta_2,\infty}(\nu)\right] ;$$

(d) <u>a restricted weak σ-interpolation pair</u> if it is an interpolation one with respect to

$$\left[L^{1/\alpha_1,1}(\mu),\ L^{1/\beta_1,\infty}(\nu);\ L^{1/\alpha_2,1}(\mu),\ L^{1/\beta_2,\infty}(\nu)\right].$$

The purpose of the convexity theorems is to determine the Lebesgue or Lorentz pairs, corresponding to an inner point (α,β) of σ, which are σ-interpolation pairs in the sense of (a), (b), (c), or (d); that is, to prove a $(1/\alpha,1/\beta)$-strong type inequality under the hypothesis of strong or weak-type inequalities at the endpoints of σ.

We can now give a brief historical view of the most important convexity theorems:

$L^{1/\alpha}(\mu)$, $L^{1/\beta}(\nu)$ <u>is, for each</u> $(\alpha,\beta) \in \mathring{\sigma}$,

- <u>a strong</u> σ-<u>interpolation pair</u> (M. Riesz, 1926; O. Thorin, 1939);
- <u>a restricted strong</u> σ-<u>interpolation pair</u> (Stein - G. Weiss, 1959);
- <u>a weak</u> σ-<u>interpolation pair</u> (Marcinkiewicz, 1939);
- <u>a restricted weak</u> σ-<u>interpolation pair</u> (Calderón, Hunt, Stein, Weiss, Krein, Semenov, 1959-1964).

2. THE CLASSICAL RESULTS

We shall discuss the foregoing results more closely, and also the stronger one including the pairs of Lorentz spaces as interpolation pairs. In what follows, we refer to the following two statements of Riesz-Thorin and Marcinkiewicz theorems, respectively.

THEOREM A (Riesz-Thorin) (A.1). <u>For each</u> $(\alpha,\beta) \in \sigma$, <u>the spaces</u> $L^{1/\alpha}(\mu)$, $L^{1/\beta}(\nu)$ <u>form a strong</u> σ-<u>interpolation pair</u>.

(A.2). <u>For each</u> $(\alpha,\beta) \in \mathring{\sigma}$ <u>and every</u> $\gamma \in [0,1]$, <u>the spaces</u> $L^{1/\alpha,1/\gamma}(\mu)$, $L^{1/\beta,1/\gamma}(\nu)$ <u>form a strong</u> σ-<u>interpolation pair</u>.

From now on we shall deal only with restricted weak σ-interpolation pairs, and therefore we shall call these simply weak σ-interpolation pairs.

THEOREM B (Marcinkiewicz) (B.1). <u>For each</u> $(\alpha,\beta) \in \mathring{\sigma}$, <u>the spaces</u> $L^{1/\alpha}(\mu)$, $L^{1/\beta}(\nu)$ <u>form a weak</u> σ-<u>interpolation pair</u>.

(B.2). <u>For each</u> $(\alpha,\beta) \in \mathring{\sigma}$ <u>and every</u> $\gamma \in [0,1]$, <u>the spaces</u> $L^{1/\alpha,1/\gamma}(\mu)$, $L^{1/\beta,1/\gamma}(\nu)$ <u>form a weak</u> σ-<u>interpolation pair</u>.

Regarding closely these two statements, we naturally ask the following two questions.

QUESTION 1. What is the reason that, in the two theorems above, there appear the same families of σ-interpolation pairs, although the imposed conclusion in Theorem A is stronger than that in Theorem B?

In the proofs of these theorems (see, for example, [3]), the $(\theta,q;K)$-interpolation method of J. Peetre is essentially used. For this reason, it is meaningful to ask what might be the relation between the spaces

$$(L^{p_1,1},L^{p_2,1})_{\theta,q;K};\ (L^{p_1,\infty},L^{p_2,\infty})_{\theta,q;K};\ (L^{p_1},L^{p_2})_{\theta,q;K}.$$

So if we have in view only the pairs of Lorentz spaces as interpolation pairs, we then can reply in the following manner. After application of the stability theorem for the $(\theta,q;K)$-interpolation method (see [3, Theorem 3.2.20]), the three spaces above are equal, and this is the reason that in (A.2), (B.2) the right-hand terms as well as the left-hand terms of the interpolation pairs are Lorentz spaces. In particular, we can also obtain the interpolation pairs from (A.1), (B.1).

QUESTION 2. In the statements (A.2) and (B.2) appear the greater families of interpolation pairs. Because of this, we ask the question: Is the family of Lorentz spaces the greatest one for which the theorems remain valid?

An answer to this question is partially contained in the work of D.W. Boyd [2], where the particular case

$$\sigma \subset \Delta = \{(\alpha,\alpha),\ \ \alpha \in (0,1)\},\ \mu = \nu$$

is considered. Namely, D.W. Boyd describes all weak σ-interpolation spaces for such a segment. Before we state this result, some definitions from the fields of rearrangement invariant Banach spaces are needed.

A <u>norm-function</u> on the measure space $(X,\mathcal{A},\mu)$ is a functional

$$\rho : \mathfrak{M}^+(X,\mathcal{A},\mu) \to [0,\infty]$$

such that for all

$$f,g,f_n \in \mathfrak{M}(X,\mathcal{A},\mu),\qquad E \in \mathcal{A},\ \ \mu(E) < \infty,\ \text{and}\ \ a \geq 0$$

the following conditions are fulfilled:

(i) $\rho(f) = 0 \Rightarrow f = 0$ a.e., $\rho(af) = a\rho(f)$, $\rho(f + g) \leq \rho(f) + \rho(g)$;

(ii) $f \leq g \Rightarrow \rho(f) \leq \rho(g)$;

(iii) $\rho(\chi_E) < \infty$ and $\int_E f \, d\mu \leq C_E \rho(f)$, in which C_E does not depend on f;

(iv) $f_n \uparrow f$ a.e. $\Rightarrow \rho(f_n) \uparrow \rho(f)$.

If ρ is a norm-function on $(X,\mathfrak{A},\mu)$, then

$$L^\rho(\mu) := \{f \in \mathfrak{M}(X,\mathfrak{A},\mu) : \rho(|f|) < \infty\}$$

is a Banach space under the norm

$$\|f\|_\rho = \rho(|f|) .$$

The space $L^\rho(\mu)$ is called a Banach function space. If ρ verifies

(v) $f^* = g^* \Rightarrow \rho(f) = \rho(g)$,

then ρ is called a rearrangement invariant norm, or briefly an r. i. norm, and $L^\rho(\mu)$ is an r. i. space.

In the case that the measure space $(X,\mathfrak{A},\mu)$ does not contain atoms or is purely atomic, as was proved by Luxemburg [7], for an r. i. norm on $(X,\mathfrak{A},\mu)$ there exists an r. i. norm ρ^* on $(0,\infty)$ endowed with the usual Lebesgue measure in such a way that

$$\rho(f) = \rho^*(f^*) \quad \text{for all} \quad f \in \mathfrak{M}^+(X,\mathfrak{A},\mu) .$$

We then define the indicator function (see [2])

$$h_\rho(s) := \sup\{\rho^*(f^*(st) : \rho^*(f^*(t)) \leq 1\}$$

and the lower and upper indices

$$\beta_\rho := \lim_{s \to \infty} \frac{-\ln h_\rho(s)}{\ln s} , \qquad \alpha_\rho := \lim_{s \to 0} \frac{-\ln h_\rho(s)}{\ln s} .$$

Now the above-mentioned result of Boyd has the following statement:

THEOREM C. Let $\sigma = [\alpha_1,\alpha_1;\alpha_2,\alpha_2]$ be a closed line segment contained in the diagonal Δ of the unit square, and let $L^\rho(\mu)$ be a Banach function space.

(a) If $L^\rho(\mu)$, $L^\rho(\mu)$ is a weak σ-interpolation pair, then $L^\rho(\mu)$ is necessarily a rearrangement invariant space.

(b) <u>If</u> ρ <u>is an r. i. norm, then</u> $L^{\rho}(\mu)$, $L^{\rho}(\mu)$ <u>is a weak</u> σ-<u>interpolation pair if and only if</u>

$$\alpha_1 < \beta_\rho \leq \alpha_\rho < \alpha_2 \ .$$

As is well known, by studying this problem with the aid of his abstract real ρ-interpolation method C. Bennett [1] has proved the following:

(b') <u>If</u> ρ <u>is an r. i. norm, then</u> $\alpha_1 < \beta_\rho \leq \alpha_\rho < \alpha_2$ <u>if and only if</u>

$$L^{\rho}(\mu) = (L^{1/\alpha_1}(\mu), L^{1/\alpha_2}(\mu))_{\tau,k} ,$$

<u>where</u> τ <u>is a certain r. i. norm on</u> $(0,\infty)$ <u>such that</u> $0 < \beta_\tau \leq \alpha_\tau < 1$.

3. THE GENERAL RESULT

It is our aim now to generalize this theorem in the case of interpolation with change of measure and with σ not necessarily contained in Δ. In what follows, we may assume that $(X,\mathfrak{A},\mu)$ and $(Y,\mathfrak{B},\nu)$ have infinite measures and satisfy the condition (P) of [4, p. 294].

THEOREM 1. <u>If</u> ρ',ρ'' <u>are two function-norms on</u> $(X,\mathfrak{A},\mu)$ <u>and</u> $(Y,\mathfrak{B},\nu)$, <u>respectively, so that</u> $L^{\rho'}(\mu)$, $L^{\rho''}(\nu)$ <u>is an optimal weak</u> σ-<u>interpolation pair, then</u> ρ' <u>and</u> ρ'' <u>are necessarily r. i. norms</u>.

The <u>proof</u> results if we combine an argument of Aronszajn with another argument of D.W. Boyd from [2]. □

It is then natural to seek weak σ-interpolation pairs, consisting of r. i. spaces.

For, let τ be an r. i. norm on $(0,\infty)$ such that

$$0 < \beta_\tau \leq \alpha_\tau < 1 \ .$$

THEOREM 2. <u>If</u> $1 < p_1,p_2 < \infty$, <u>then</u>

$$(L^{p_1,1}(\mu),L^{p_2,1}(\mu))_{\tau,k} = (L^{p_1}(\mu),L^{p_2}(\mu))_{\tau,k}$$

$$= (L^{p_1,\infty}(\mu),L^{p_2,\infty}(\mu))_{\tau,k} \ .$$

Proof. It is easy to check that $L^{p,q}(\mu)$ is a space which belongs to the class

$$\mathcal{H}(1 - 1/p, L^1(\mu), L^\infty(\mu))$$

for all $q \in [1,\infty]$ (see [3]). Now we can apply Theorem 2 (see also Theorem 3) of [5] for $q = 1$ and $q = \infty$, and the theorem results. □

COROLLARY 1. *The spaces* $(L^{1/\alpha_1}(\mu), L^{1/\alpha_2}(\mu))_{\tau,k}$; $(L^{1/\beta_1}(\nu), L^{1/\beta_2}(\nu))_{\tau,k}$ *form an optimal weak* σ-*interpolation pair*.

COROLLARY 2. *The spaces* $(L^{1/\beta_1}(\nu), L^{1/\beta_2}(\nu))_{\tau,k}$; $(L^{1/\alpha_1}(\mu), L^{1/\alpha_2}(\mu))_{\tau,k}$ *form an optimal weak* σ'-*interpolation pair, where* σ' *is the segment symmetric to* σ, *with respect to the diagonal* Δ, *and is equal to* $[\beta_1,\alpha_1; \beta_2,\alpha_2]$. (For optimalities, see Theorem 11 of [4].)

Thus we have also an answer to Question 2, because these are evidently also strong σ-interpolation pairs and σ'-interpolation pairs, respectively.

THEOREM 3. *Let*

$$L^{\rho'}(\mu),\ L^{\rho''}(\nu)$$

be an optimal weak σ-*interpolation pair; then there exists an r. i. norm* τ *on* $(0,\infty)$ *such that*

$$L^{\rho'}(\mu) = (L^{1/\alpha_1}(\mu), L^{1/\alpha_2}(\mu))_{\tau,k},$$
$$L^{\rho''}(\nu) = (L^{1/\beta_1}(\nu), L^{1/\beta_2}(\nu))_{\tau,k}.$$

Proof. It is a well-known fact that if an interpolation pair A, B with respect to two Banach couples A_1, A_2 and B_1, B_2 is optimal, then B, A is an interpolation pair with respect to the Banach couples B_1, B_2 and A_1, A_2 (see, for example, Theorem 4.6, p. 46 of [6]). It results for our situation that

$$L^{\rho''}(\nu), L^{\rho'}(\mu)$$

is an interpolation pair with respect to the Banach couples

$$L^{1/\beta_1,\infty}(\nu), L^{1/\beta_2,\infty}(\nu) \quad \text{and} \quad L^{1/\alpha_1,1}(\mu), L^{1/\alpha_2,1}(\mu) .$$

By the embeddings (*), we find that

$$L^{\rho''}(\nu), L^{\rho'}(\mu)$$

is a weak σ'-interpolation pair. Now applying Theorem 4 of [5] and Theorem 8 of [4] completes the proof. □

REMARK. It is not difficult to see that, if $\sigma \subset \Delta$, $\mu = \nu$, and $L^{\rho}(\mu), L^{\rho}(\mu)$ is a weak σ-interpolation pair, then it is an optimal one.

Indeed, because of the embeddings (*), it is clear that the identity operator I belongs to

$$\mathcal{B}(L^{1/\alpha_1,1}(\mu), L^{1/\alpha_2,1}(\mu); L^{1/\alpha_1,\infty}(\mu), L^{1/\alpha_2,\infty}(\mu)) ,$$

and consequently if $\mathfrak{X}, \mathfrak{Y}$ is a weak σ-interpolation pair then $\mathfrak{X} \subset \mathfrak{Y}$. This means that if $\mathfrak{X}_0$ is such that $\mathfrak{X}_0, \mathfrak{X}_0$ is a weak σ-interpolation pair, then it is an optimal one.

Thus our Corollaries 1 and 2 and Theorem 3 generalize exactly Theorem C, as well as Theorem B.

REFERENCES

1. C. Bennett, Banach function spaces and interpolation methods. I. The abstract theory, Journ. of Functional Analysis 17 (1974), 409-440; II. Interpolation of weak type operators, Linear Operators and Approximation, Proc. Conf. Oberwolfach 1974, pp. 129-139, Birkhäuser Verlag (ISNM 25), Stuttgart-Basel, 1975.

2. D.W. Boyd, Indices of function spaces and their relationship to interpolation, Canad. J. Math. 21 (1969), 1245-1254.

3. P.L. Butzer and H. Berens, Semi-Groups of Operators and Approximation, Grundlehren 145, Springer Verlag, Berlin-Heidelberg-New York, 1967.

4. A.P. Calderón, Spaces between L^1 and L^∞ and the theorem of Marcinkiewicz, Studia Math. 26 (1966), 273-299.

5. D. Gaşpar and Şt. Bisz, On an abstract interpolation method, Analele Univ. Timişoara, Ser. Şt. Mat., XVI, 2 (1978), 119-139.

6. S.G. Krein, Ju. I. Petunin, E.M. Semenov, Interpolijatzja lineinih operatorov, Moskwa, Nauka, 1978.

7. W.A.J. Luxemburg, Rearrangement-invariant Banach function spaces, _Queen's Paper in Pure and Applied Mathematics_ 10 (1967), 83-144.

A GENERALIZED SCHUR-HARDY INEQUALITY ON NORMED KÖTHE SPACES

F. Fehér
Lehrstuhl A für Mathematik
Rheinisch-Westfälische Technische Hochschule
Aachen

ABSTRACT. The Schur-Hardy inequality for Köthe norms being already established in a previous paper, its connections with the Hilbert-inequality on double integrals are now considered. Moreover, several applications of both inequalities are given, e.g. to the Weyl integral operator, and to particular Köthe norms. As a tool, rearrangement invariant spaces of "fundamental type" are introduced.

1. THE INEQUALITY

The normed Köthe space L^ρ is the space of all Lebesgue measurable, real valued functions f with $\|f\|_\rho := \rho(|f|) < \infty$, functions which coincide a.e. being identified. Here ρ denotes a function norm on the set $P((0,\infty))$ of all nonnegative, measurable functions on $(0,\infty)$, i.e. a mapping $\rho: P((0,\infty)) \to [0,\infty]$ such that for all $f,g \in P$

(i) $\rho(f) = 0 \Leftrightarrow f = 0$ a.e.;

$\rho(\lambda f) = \lambda\rho(f) \quad (\lambda > 0); \quad \rho(f+g) \leq \rho(f) + \rho(g);$

(ii) $f \leq g$ a.e. $\Rightarrow \rho(f) \leq \rho(g)$.

The dilation operator E_s on L^ρ is defined by $(E_s f)(t) := f(st)$, $s,t > 0$, and its operator norm on L^ρ, regarded as a function of $s > 0$, is called the indicator function $h(s,L^\rho)$, or briefly $h(s)$. The associate norm on P, namely

$$\rho'(g) := \sup \{\int_0^\infty f(t)g(t);\ f \in P,\ \rho(f) \leq 1\} \qquad (g \in P)$$

is again a function norm, and defines the associate Köthe space $L^{\rho'}$. Basic is the Hölder inequality (see e.g. A.C. Zaanen [15])

$$\int_0^\infty f(t)g(t)dt \leq \rho(f)\rho'(g). \tag{1.1}$$

The Schur-Hardy inequality in question is concerned with kernel operators in the sense of A.C. Zaanen [16], A.R. Schep [10], i.e.,

$$(Kf)(t) := \int_0^\infty K(t,s)f(s)ds, \tag{1.2}$$

$K(t,s)$ being a nonnegative kernel which is homogeneous of degree $\gamma \in \mathbb{R}$. Generalizing a method of proof of E.R. Love [8] we give a direct proof of

THEOREM 1.1 (Schur-Hardy inequality). *Let* $\gamma \in \mathbb{R}$, *and* $K(t,s)$ *be a nonnegative, Lebesgue measurable function of* $t,s \geq 0$ *which is homogeneous of degree* γ, *and assume* L^ρ *to be a complete normed Köthe space such that*

$$A_\rho := \int_0^\infty K(1,s)s^{-(1+\gamma)}h(s,L^\rho)ds < \infty.$$

Then for any f *with* $(\cdot)^{1+\gamma}f \in L^\rho$

$$\|Kf\|_\rho \leq A_\rho \|(\cdot)^{1+\gamma}f\|_\rho . \tag{1.3}$$

Proof. For any $t > 0$ one has with the substitution $s = tu$

$$\begin{aligned} |(Kf)(t)| &\leq \int_0^\infty K(t,tu)|f(tu)|t\,du \\ &= \int_0^\infty K(1,u)t^{1+\gamma}|(E_u f)(t)|du \\ &= \int_0^\infty K(1,u)u^{-(1+\gamma)}|(E_u((\cdot)^{1+\gamma}f))(t)|du. \end{aligned}$$

Passing to the norms on both sides yields (1.3). □

The particular case $\gamma = -1$ and $\|\cdot\|_\rho = \|\cdot\|_p$ $(1 \leq p < \infty)$ of (1.3) is the classical Schur-Hardy inequality, since $h(s,L^p) = s^{-1/p}$. For $p = 2$ it is due to I. Schur. For $1 < p < \infty$ it is e.g. to be found in [6] but with an indirect proof given via Hilbert's inequality concerning double integrals. This in its turn is proved by means of three other theorems, and does not include the case $p=1$, nor arbitrary $\gamma \in \mathbb{R}$ and arbitrary Köthe norms. Moreover, it can even be shown that, conversely, the Hilbert inequality can easily be deduced from Theorem 1.1. As a matter of fact one has

COROLLARY 1.2 (Hilbert inequality). <u>Let</u> L^ρ, γ, <u>and</u> $K(t,s)$ <u>be given as in Thm.</u> 1.1. <u>Then</u>

a) $$\int_0^\infty K(1,u)h(u,L^{\rho'})du = \int_0^\infty K(u,1)u^{-(1+\gamma)}h(u,L^\rho)du =: B_\rho .$$

<u>For any</u> f <u>with</u> $(\cdot)^{1+\gamma} f \in L^\rho$ <u>and any</u> $g \in L^{\rho'}$ <u>one has</u>

b) $$\left|\int_0^\infty\int_0^\infty K(t,s)f(t)g(s)dt\,ds\right| \leq B_\rho \|(\cdot)^{1+\gamma}f\|_\rho \|g\|_{\rho'} .$$

For the proof of a), observe that $sh(s,L^{\rho'}) = h(1/s,L^\rho)$. Hence

$$\begin{aligned}\int_0^\infty K(1,u)h(u,L^{\rho'})du &= \int_0^\infty K(1,u)h(1/u,L^\rho)u^{-1}du \\ &= \int_0^\infty K(1,1/v)h(v,L^\rho)v^{-1}dv \\ &= \int_0^\infty v^{-(1+\gamma)}K(v,1)h(v,L^\rho)dv = B_\rho .\end{aligned}$$

Concerning the proof of b), let $\tilde{K}(t,s) := t^{-(1+\gamma)}K(t,s)$; then

$$(\tilde{K}f)(t) := \int_0^\infty \tilde{K}(t,s)f(s)ds$$

is again a kernel operator, and, by Hölder's inequality (1.1),

$$\begin{aligned}\left|\int_0^\infty\int_0^\infty K(t,s)f(t)g(s)dt\,ds\right| &= \left|\int_0^\infty t^{1+\gamma}f(t)(\tilde{K}g)(t)dt\right| \\ &\leq g(|(\cdot)^{1+\gamma}f|)\rho'(|\tilde{K}g|).\end{aligned}$$

Since the kernel of $\tilde{K}$ is homogeneous of degree -1, the Schur-Hardy inequality (1.3) applies to $\rho'(|\tilde{K}g|) \equiv \|\tilde{K}g\|_{\rho'}$ with $\gamma = -1$ and ρ' instead of ρ, yielding the Hilbert inequality of b) since $\tilde{K}(1,s) = K(1,s)$. □

Let us remark that a modified version of (1.3), which makes use of the nonincreasing rearrangement f* of a function f, namely

(1.4) $$\|Kf\|_\rho \leqslant \left(\int_0^\infty K^*(1,s)s^{-(1+\gamma)}h(s,L^\rho)ds\right)\|(\cdot)^{1+\gamma}f^*\|_\rho$$

can be proved similarly, see [3]. (1.4) yields the modified Hilbert's inequality

(1.5) $$\left|\int_0^\infty\int_0^\infty K(t,s)f(t)g(s)dt\,ds\right| \leqslant \left(\int_0^\infty K^*(s,1)s^{-(1+\gamma)}h(s,L^\rho)ds\right)\|(\cdot)^{1+\gamma}f^*\|_\rho\|g\|_{\rho'},$$

since the left-hand side of (1.5) is, with $(\overline{K}f)(s) := \int_0^\infty K(t,s)f(t)dt$, equal to $|\int_0^\infty (\overline{K}f)(s)g(s)ds|$, which again can be estimated by Hölder's inequality (1.1).

2. KÖTHE NORMS OF FUNDAMENTAL TYPE

Let L^ρ be a Köthe space containing the characteristic functions $\chi_{(0,t)}$ of the intervals $(0,t)$, $t > 0$. Then the fundamental function τ_ρ of L^ρ is defined by $\tau_\rho(t) := \|\chi_{(0,t)}\|_\rho$, see e.g. [17]. Since there is already quite a number of results on Köthe spaces in terms of the fundamental function, it may be of interest to reformulate the inequalities of Schur-Hardy and Hilbert in terms of τ_ρ instead of the indicator function. For this purpose we define

DEFINITION 2.1. <u>A Köthe norm</u> ρ <u>is said to be of "fundamental type", iff the indicator function of</u> L^ρ <u>is given by</u>

(2.1) $$h(s,L^\rho) := \sup_{t>0}\frac{\tau_\rho(t)}{\tau_\rho(st)}.$$

Since $\tau_\rho(t) = \|E_s\chi_{(0,st)}\|_\rho$ and $\tau_\rho(st) = \|\chi_{(0,st)}\|_\rho$, (2.1) can be rewritten as

(2.2) $$h(s,L^\rho) = \sup_{t>0}\frac{\|E_s\chi_{(0,st)}\|_\rho}{\|\chi_{(0,st)}\|_\rho};$$

i.e., if ρ is of fundamental type, then the norm $h(s,L^\rho)$ of the dilation operator E_s is already determined by its impact upon a very simple subclass of functions of L^ρ.

In connection with a problem on the Hardy-property, raised by R. O'Neil,

T. Shimogahi [12] constructed a Köthe space which has the same fundamental function as L^2 but a different indicator function; hence this space is not of fundamental type. On the other hand, Definition 2.1 is not empty, as the following lemma shows:

LEMMA 2.2. <u>The Lebesgue spaces</u> L^p $(1 \leq p \leq \infty)$, <u>the Lorentz spaces</u> L^{pq} $(1 \leq p,q < \infty)$, <u>the generalized Lorentz spaces</u> $\Lambda(\phi,p)$ $(p \geq 1)$, <u>and the Orlicz spaces</u> $L_{M\Psi}$ <u>(with strictly increasing Young function</u> Ψ) <u>are of fundamental type.</u>

<u>Proof</u>. In case of Lebesgue or Lorentz spaces $(h(s,L^p) = h(s,L^{pq}) = s^{-1/p})$, (2.1) obviously holds since $\tau_\rho(t) = t^{1/p}$. For the generalized Lorentz spaces $\Lambda(\phi,p)$ D.W. Boyd [1] proved that $h(s,\Lambda(\phi,p)) = N(s)^{1/p}$ with

$$N(s) := \sup_{t>0} \frac{\Phi(t)}{\Phi(st)} \qquad (s > 0)$$

and $\Phi(t) := \int_0^t \phi(u)du$. Hence (2.1) follows by observing that

$$\tau_{\Lambda(\phi,p)}(t) = \Phi(t)^{1/p} .$$

In case of Orlicz spaces we first compute the norm of $\chi_{(0,t)}$:

$$\tau_{L_{M\Psi}}(t) = \|\chi_{(0,t)}\|_{L_{M\Psi}} = \inf \{c > 0\colon M_\Psi(\tfrac{1}{c}\chi_{(0,t)}) \leq 1\},$$

where $\Psi(t) = \int_0^t \psi(u)du$, and

$$M_\Psi(\tfrac{1}{c}\chi_{(0,t)}) := \int_0^\infty \Psi(\tfrac{1}{c}\chi_{(0,t)}(u))du = \int_0^\infty \int_0^{\frac{1}{c}\chi_{(0,t)}(u)} \psi(s)ds\, du$$

$$= \int_0^t \int_0^{1/c} \psi(s)ds\, du = \int_0^t \Psi(1/c)du = t\Psi(1/c) .$$

This gives that (compare [9])

$$\tau_{L_{M\Psi}}(t) = \inf \{c > 0\colon t\Psi(1/c) \leq 1\} = 1/\Psi^{-1}(1/t)$$

if Ψ is strictly increasing. On the other hand (see D.W. Boyd [1]), $h(s,L_{M\Psi}) = 1/G(s)$ with $G(s) = \inf_{t>0} \{\Psi^{-1}(st)/\Psi^{-1}(t)\}$. Hence

$$h(s,L_{M\Psi}) = \frac{1}{\inf\limits_{t>0}\{\Psi^{-1}(t)/\Psi^{-1}(t/s)\}} = \frac{1}{\inf\limits_{t>0}\{\Psi^{-1}(1/t)/\Psi^{-1}(1/st)\}}$$

$$= \sup_{t>0}\frac{\Psi^{-1}(1/st)}{\Psi^{-1}(1/t)} = \sup_{t>0}\frac{\tau_{L_{M\Psi}}(t)}{\tau_{L_{M\Psi}}(st)},$$

yielding (2.1) for the Orlicz space $L_{M\Psi}$. □

REMARK. The example of Shimogaki actually shows that there is no general connection between the concept of indicator function and that of fundamental function. Nevertheless, by Lemma 2.2, those spaces which are among the most important ones with respect to applications are of fundamental type; these give a positive answer to O'Neil's problem.

In terms of the fundamental function the inequalities of Schur-Hardy and of Hilbert, respectively, read:

$$\text{(2.3)}\qquad \|Kf\|_\rho \leq \left(\int_0^\infty K(1,s)s^{-(1+\gamma)} \sup_{t>0}[\tau_\rho(t)/\tau_\rho(st)]ds\right)\|(\cdot)^{1+\gamma}f\|_\rho$$

$$\text{(2.4)}\qquad \left|\int_0^\infty\int_0^\infty K(t,s)f(t)g(s)dt\, ds\right| \leq$$

$$\leq \left(\int_0^\infty K(u,1)u^{-(1+\gamma)} \sup_{t>0}[\tau_\rho(t)/\tau_\rho(ut)]du\right)\|(\cdot)^{1+\gamma}f\|_\rho\|g\|_{\rho'},$$

if the Köthe norm ρ is of fundamental type, e.g. in particular for Lebesgue, Lorentz and Orlicz norms.

3. APPLICATION TO PARTICULAR KERNEL OPERATORS

As a first example we consider the averaging operator P_θ, $\theta > 0$, defined by

$$(P_\theta f)(t) := t^{-\theta}\int_0^t s^{\theta-1}f(s)ds \qquad (t > 0),$$

and its dual operator

$$(P_\theta' f)(t) := t^{-\theta}\int_t^\infty s^{\theta-1}f(s)ds.$$

Both operators are kernel operators, their kernels $t^{-\theta}s^{\theta-1}\chi_{(0,t)}(s)$ and

$t^{-\theta}s^{\theta-1}\chi_{(t,\infty)}(s)$ being homogeneous of degree $\gamma=-1$. So Theorem 1.1 and Corollary 1.2 apply to these operators. Actually, Theorem 1.1 reduces in this case to a generalized Hardy inequality

$$(3.1) \qquad \| t^{-\theta} \int_0^t s^{\theta-1} f(s)ds \|_\rho \leq \left(\int_0^1 s^{\theta-1} h(s,L^\rho)ds\right) \| f\|_\rho$$

and its dual

$$(3.1') \qquad \| t^{-\theta} \int_t^\infty s^{\theta-1} f(s)ds \|_\rho \leq \left(\int_1^\infty s^{\theta-1} h(s,L^\rho)ds\right) \| f\|_\rho \ ,$$

valid for any complete Köthe norm ρ, in particular for the norms of Section 2. The case $\theta=1$, $\|\cdot\|_\rho=\|\cdot\|_p$ is that of the classical Hardy inequality and its dual, see [6, pp. 240,244].

Corollary 1.2, applied to the averaging operator P_θ, reads

$$(3.2) \qquad \left|\int_0^\infty f(t)\left(t^{-\theta}\int_0^t s^{\theta-1} g(s)ds\right)dt\right| \leq \left(\int_1^\infty u^{-\theta} h(u,L^\rho)du\right)\| f\|_\rho \| g\|_{\rho'} \ .$$

In particular, for L^{pq} norms one has with $1/p+1/p'=1$, $1/q+1/q'=1$

$$(3.3) \qquad \left|\int_0^\infty f(t)\left(t^{-\theta}\int_0^t s^{\theta-1} g(s)ds\right)dt\right| \leq \frac{p}{p(\theta-1)+1} \| f\|_{pq} \| g\|_{p'q'}$$

provided $1/p > 1-\theta$.

Our second example is that of fractional integration of order $\lambda>0$ in the sense of Riemann-Liouville, namely

$$(I_\lambda f)(t) = \frac{1}{\Gamma(\lambda)} \int_0^t (t-s)^{\lambda-1} f(s)ds \ ,$$

and its dual, the Weyl integral

$$(W_\lambda f)(t) = \frac{1}{\Gamma(\lambda)} \int_t^\infty (s-t)^{\lambda-1} f(s)ds \ .$$

The kernels of these integrals are homogeneous of degree $\gamma=\lambda-1$. In particular, for L^p norms one has by Theorem 1.1 (see also [3])

$$(3.4) \qquad \| I_\lambda f\|_p \leq \frac{\Gamma(1-\lambda-1/p)}{\Gamma(1-1/p)} \| (\cdot)^\lambda f\|_p$$

if $0<\lambda<1-1/p$, and (compare [6, p. 245])

$$\|W_\lambda f\|_p \leqslant \frac{\Gamma(1/p)}{\Gamma(1/p+\lambda)} \|(\cdot)^\lambda f\|_p \qquad (\lambda>0, p\geqslant 1). \tag{3.4'}$$

A modified version of I_λ leads to Flett's inequality for Köthe norms, see T.M. Flett [4], E.R. Love [8], and [3].

Similarly, the kernel of the operator

$$(T_r f)(t) := t^{-r} \int_0^t f(s)ds ,$$

which was brought into discussion by R. Mohapatra (Beirut) during the conference, is homogeneous of degree $\gamma=-r$, and Theorem 1.1 yields that

$$\|T_r f\|_\rho \leqslant \left(\int_0^1 s^{r-1} h(s,L^\rho)ds\right) \|(\cdot)^{1-r} f\|_\rho . \tag{3.5}$$

In particular, for L^{pq} norms with $pr>1$,

$$\|T_r f\|_{pq} \leqslant \frac{p}{pr-1} \|(\cdot)^{1-r} f\|_{pq} . \tag{3.6}$$

Finally we consider the kernel $(0<\alpha\leqslant 1)$

$$K_\alpha(t,s) = (t+s)^{-\alpha} .$$

In case of Lebesgue norms and $\alpha=1$, Corollary 1.2 applied to this kernel gives exactly the classical Hilbert inequality (see e.g. [6, p. 226]):

$$\int_0^\infty \int_0^\infty \frac{|f(s)g(t)|}{s+t} ds\, dt \leqslant \frac{\pi}{\sin \pi/p} \|f\|_p \|g\|_{p'}, \qquad \left(\frac{1}{p}+\frac{1}{p'}=1\right), \tag{3.7}$$

noting that

$$B_p = \int_0^\infty \frac{s^{-1/p'}}{1+s} ds = \int_1^\infty (u-1)^{-1/p'} u^{-1} du = \int_0^1 v^{1/p'-1} (1-v)^{-1/p'} dv$$

$$= \Gamma(1/p')\Gamma(1-1/p') = \frac{\pi}{\sin \pi/p} .$$

Observe that the constant B_p of Corollary 1.2 cannot be improved, since it is known that the constant $\pi/\sin(\pi/p)$ in (3.7) is best possible.

In the general case $0<\alpha\leq 1$, we apply the modified Hilbert inequality (1.5) to the Lebesgue norm $\|\cdot\|_q$ to deduce, with $\gamma=-\alpha$ and $1/q+1/q'=1$

$$\int_0^\infty\int_0^\infty \frac{f(t)g(s)}{(t+s)^\alpha}\,dt\,ds \leq \frac{\Gamma(\alpha-1/q)\Gamma(1/q)}{\Gamma(\alpha)}\,\|(\cdot)^{1-\alpha}f^*\|_q\|g\|_{q'}\,.$$

Now, recalling the definition of Lorentz norms, one has with $1/p=1-\alpha+1/q$

$$\|(\cdot)^{1-\alpha}f^*\|_q = (p/q)^{1/q}\|\cdot\|_{pq} \leq (p/q)^{1/q}\|f\|_{pp} = (p/q)^{1/q}\|f\|_p\,,$$

and hence

$$\int_0^\infty\int_0^\infty \frac{f(t)g(s)}{(t+s)^\alpha}\,dt\,ds \leq \frac{\Gamma(\alpha-1/q)\Gamma(1/q)}{\Gamma(\alpha)}\,\left(\frac{p}{q}\right)^{1/q}\|f\|_p\|g\|_{q'}\,. \tag{3.8}$$

The condition $1/p+1/q'=2-\alpha\geq 1$ needed here is exactly the condition of E.K. Godunova [5], V.I. Levin - S.B. Stečkin [7], and also agrees with the condition in the corresponding inequality for sums instead of integrals (see [6, Thm. 339]).

REFERENCES

1. D.W. Boyd, The Hilbert transform on rearrangement-invariant spaces. Canad. J. Math. 19 (1967), 599-616.
2. P.L. Butzer - F. Fehér, Generalized Hardy and Hardy-Littlewood inequalities in rearrangement-invariant spaces. Comment. Math. Prace Mat. Tomus Specialis in Honorem Ladislai Orlicz I (1978), 41-64.
3. F. Fehér, A note on a paper of E.R. Love. Bull. Austral. Math. Soc. (in print).
4. T.M. Flett, A note on some inequalities. Proc. Glasgow Math. Assoc. 4 (1958), 7-15.
5. E.K. Godunova, Generalization of two-parameter Hilbert's inequality (Russian). Izv. Vysš. Učebn. Zav. Mat. No. 1, (56) (1967), 35-39.
6. G.H. Hardy - J.E. Littlewood - G. Pólya, Inequalities. Cambridge University Press, Cambridge 1959.
7. V.I. Levin - S.B. Stečkin, Inequalities. Amer. Math. Soc. Transl. (2) 14 (1960), 1-29.
8. E.R. Love, Some inequalities for fractional integrals. In: Linear Spaces and Approximation. (Proc. Oberwolfach Conference, August 20-27, 1977; P.L. Butzer - B. Sz.-Nagy, eds.) ISNM Vol. 40, Birkhäuser, Basel, 1978, pp. 177-184.

9. M. Milman, Some new function spaces and their tensor products. Notas de Matematica, Universidad de Los Andes, 1978.

10. A.R. Schep, Kernel Operators. Thesis, Leiden 1977.

11. R. Sharpley, Interpolation of n pairs and counterexamples employing indices. J. Approximation Theory 13 (1975), 117-127.

12. T. Shimogaki, Hardy-Littlewood majorants in function spaces. J. Math. Soc. Japan 17 (1965), 365-373.

13. T. Shimogaki, A note on norms of compression operators on function spaces. Proc. Japan Acad. 46 (1970), 239-242.

14. I. Schur, Bemerkungen zur Theorie der beschränkten Bilinearformen mit unendlich vielen Veränderlichen. J. Reine Angew. Math. 140 (1911), 1-28.

15. A.C. Zaanen, Integration. North-Holland Publishing Company. Amsterdam 1967.

16. A.C. Zaanen, Kernel operators. In: Linear Spaces and Approximation. (Proc. Oberwolfach Conference, August 20-27, 1977; P.L. Butzer - B. Sz.-Nagy, eds.), ISNM Vol. 40, Birkhäuser, Basel, 1978, pp. 23-31.

17. M. Zippin, Interpolation of operators of weak type between rearrangement invariant function spaces. J. Functional Analysis 7 (1971), 267-284.

MEAN VALUES AND FUNCTION SPACES

H.-H. Kairies
Mathematisches Institut der Technischen Universität
3392 Clausthal-Zellerfeld
WEST GERMANY

ABSTRACT. For a weight function $u : \mathbb{N} \to \mathbb{R}_+$ necessary conditions and sufficient conditions are established to get nontrivial solutions $f : [0,1] \to \mathbb{R}$ of the infinite system of interpolation equations

$$f(x) = u(p) \sum_{k=0}^{p-1} f\left(\frac{x+k}{p}\right), \quad 1 \leqq p < \infty ,$$

in certain function spaces.

1. INTRODUCTION

Let be $T \subset \mathbb{R}$, $f : T \to \mathbb{R}$ and $u : \mathbb{N} \to \mathbb{R}_+$ (the set of positive real numbers). Assume that

$$(1) \qquad \exists\, p \in \mathbb{N},\ p \geqq 2 \quad \forall x \in T : \ f(x) = u(p) \sum_{k=0}^{p-1} f\left(\frac{x+k}{p}\right)$$

holds. This functional equation is of interpolation type and can be interpreted in the following way : f at the point x is a homogeneously weighted mean value of f at the p equidistant points $(x+k)/p$, $0 \leqq k \leqq p-1$. The weight $u(p)$ may depend on the number p of interpolation points.

Functions f , which satisfy (1) simultaneously for all $p \in \mathbb{N}$, are called replicative (see [6], [8]).

Here are some elementary examples :

$f : \mathbb{R} \setminus \mathbb{Z} \to \mathbb{R}$, $f(x) = \cot \pi x$ with $u(p) = 1/p$,

$f : \mathbb{R} \setminus \mathbb{Z} \to \mathbb{R}$, $f(x) = \log(2 \sin \pi x)$ with $u(p) = 1$,

$f : \mathbb{R} \to \mathbb{R}$, $f(x) = B_m(x)$ with $u(p) = p^{m-1}$,

B_m ($m \in \{0, 1, 2, 3, \ldots\}$) being the m-th Bernoulli polynomial.

Power functions and constant functions occur frequently in our considerations. They shall be denoted by special symbols :
$\tau_\alpha(x) := x^\alpha$ and $\sigma_\alpha(x) := \alpha$.
In this paper we are mainly concerned with functions $f: [0,1] \to \mathbb{R}$, satisfying (1) for $p \in M \subset \mathbb{N}$ and we shall write shortly $(2)_M$ instead of

$$(2) \qquad \forall x \in [0,1] \quad \forall p \in M : \quad f(x) = u(p) \sum_{k=0}^{p-1} f\left(\frac{x+k}{p}\right) .$$

In Section 2 we collect some preliminary results about $(2)_M$.
In Section 3 we derive necessary conditions for the weight function u , implied by the existence of a solution f of $(2)_{\mathbb{N}}$ in a certain function space. In Section 4 we give sufficient conditions for the weight function u to ensure the existence of a solution f of $(2)_{\mathbb{N}}$ in a certain function space.

Both the properties of the function spaces involved and the corresponding properties of the weight functions u are expressed in terms of characteristic inequalities. Clearly the zero function σ_0 satisfies (1) and $(2)_M$ for any weight function $u: \mathbb{N} \to \mathbb{R}_+$ and thus has to be excluded as a trivial exceptional case from most of our further considerations.

2. PRELIMINARY RESULTS

The Remarks 1 and 2 refer to the special importance of the interval $[0,1]$ occuring in (2).

REMARK 1. Let $f: [0,1] \to \mathbb{R}$ satisfy (1) for $T = [0,1]$. Define $g: \mathbb{R} \to \mathbb{R}$ by $g(x) := f(x)$ for $0 \leqq x < 1$ and by $g(x+1) = g(x)$ for $x \in \mathbb{R}$. Then g satisfies (1) for $T = \mathbb{R}$. The proof may be found in [3] or [8].

REMARK 2. Assume again that $f: [0,1] \to \mathbb{R}$ satisfies (1) for $T = [0,1]$. Then $f(1) - f(0) = u(p)\,[f(1) - f(0)]$, hence necessarily $f(0) = f(1)$ in case $u(p) \neq 1$. If $u(p) = 1$, equation (1) does not impose any restriction on the values $f(0)$ and $f(1)$. So we may, if necessary, redefine $f(1)$ to be $f(0)$ and (1) remains still valid. Thus we may assume that every solution $f: [0,1] \to \mathbb{R}$ of (1) satisfies $f(0) = f(1)$ and (Remark 1) can be extended by 1-periodicity to a function satisfying (1) for all $x \in \mathbb{R}$. In the sequel we make use of this fact and denote the 1-periodic extension of f again by f.

The following remarks indicate, that multiplicative weight functions u are especially important in connection with $(2)_{\mathbb{N}}$.

REMARK 3. Assume $(2)_{\{p\}}$ and $(2)_{\{q\}}$ to be true. Then

$$f(x) = u(p) \sum_{k=0}^{p-1} \left[u(q) \sum_{m=0}^{q-1} f\left(\frac{(x+k)/p + m}{q} \right) \right] = u(p)u(q) \sum_{k=0}^{pq-1} f\left(\frac{x+k}{pq}\right) .$$

Thus if $f \neq \sigma_0$ satisfies $(2)_{\mathbb{N}}$, necessarily

(3) $\qquad \forall p, q \in \mathbb{N} : \quad u(p)\, u(q) = u(pq) \quad .$

Hence in this case $u: \mathbb{N} \to \mathbb{R}_+$ is a completely multiplicative arithmetic function.

REMARK 4. Let $f \neq \sigma_0$ satisfy $(2)_{\mathbb{N}}$ and assume furthermore

(4) $\qquad \exists \beta \in \mathbb{R}_+ \quad \forall p \in \mathbb{N} : \quad u(p+1)/u(p) \leqq \beta \quad .$

Then $v := \log \circ u$ satisfies $v(pq) = v(p) + v(q)$ (Remark 3), and $v(p+1) - v(p) \leqq \log \beta$ for all $p, q \in \mathbb{N}$. By a theorem of Wirsing [7] necessarily $v(p) = \alpha \log p$ with some $\alpha \in \mathbb{R}$. Hence under the above assumptions the weight function u must be a power function: $u(p) = p^{\alpha}$.

In the last remark of this section we show, that a surprisingly simple property of f is sufficient to imply: $(2)_{\{p\}}$ has exactly one pair (f, u) of solutions.

REMARK 5. Let $f \neq \sigma_0$ satisfy $(2)_{\{p\}}$ for some $p \geq 2$ and assume the existence of $\gamma := \int_0^1 f(t)\,dt \neq 0$ (in the Riemann sense). By Remark 3 we have $f(x) = [u(p)]^m \sum_{k=0}^{p^m-1} f(\frac{x+k}{p^m})$ for every $x \in [0,1]$ and every $m \in \mathbb{N}$. Passing to the limit $m \to \infty$ we obtain

$$(5) \qquad \forall x \in [0,1] : \; f(x) = \gamma \cdot \lim_{m \to \infty} [p \cdot u(p)]^m \, .$$

Since (5) can be valid only for a constant function f, necessarily $f = \sigma_\gamma$ and consequently $u(p) = \frac{1}{p}$. On the other hand, $(2)_{\mathbb{N}}$ is satisfied for $f = \sigma_\gamma$ and $u = \tau_{-1}$ for any $\gamma \neq 0$.

3. NECESSARY CONDITIONS FOR THE WEIGHT FUNCTION

In the following sections we shall always assume that $f \in L^1[0,1]$. Hence the Fourier coefficients $a_k = 2 \int_0^1 f(t) \cos 2\pi kt \, dt$ and $b_k = 2 \int_0^1 f(t) \sin 2\pi kt \, dt$ exist, and the formal Fourier series of f will be denoted by F:

$$F(x) = a_0/2 + \sum_{k=1}^{\infty} (a_k \cos 2\pi kx + b_k \sin 2\pi kx) \, .$$

Moreover we define $N := \{g \in L^1[0,1] \mid g(x) = 0 \text{ a.e. in } [0,1]\}$.

THEOREM 1. <u>Let</u> $f \in L^1[0,1]$ <u>satisfy</u> $(2)_{\mathbb{N}}$. <u>Then</u>

(a) $u = \tau_{-1} \;\Rightarrow\; F(x) = a_0/2$,

(b) $u \neq \tau_{-1} \;\Rightarrow\; F(x) = \sum_{k=1}^{\infty} \left(\frac{a_1}{k\,u(k)} \cos 2\pi kx + \frac{b_1}{k\,u(k)} \sin 2\pi kx \right)$.

<u>Proof.</u> Let be $p \in \mathbb{N}$ and $k \in \{0,1,2,3,\ldots\}$. Then

$$a_k = 2 \int_0^1 f(t) \cos 2\pi kt \, dt = 2 \int_0^1 u(p) \sum_{n=0}^{p-1} f(\frac{t+n}{p}) \cos 2\pi kt \, dt = p\,u(p)\,a_{kp}$$

(see [3]). For $k = 0$ and $u \neq \tau_{-1}$ (recall: $\tau_\alpha(x) = x^\alpha$) we obtain $a_0 = 0$. For $k = 1$ we get $a_p = a_1 / p\,u(p)$ and $k \geq 2$ yields no other information from $a_k = p\,u(p)\,a_{kp}$, since u is multiplicative as a consequence of $(2)_{\mathbb{N}}$.

Similarly we obtain $b_p = b_1 / p\,u(p)$ and therefore

$$F(x) = \frac{a_0}{2} + \sum_{k=1}^{\infty} \left(\frac{a_1}{k\,u(k)} \cos 2\pi kx + \frac{b_1}{k\,u(k)} \sin 2\pi kx \right) .$$

Hence (b) is proved. Observe that in case (a) $k\,u(k) = 1$, thus $a_k = a_1$ and $b_k = b_1$ for all $k \in \mathbb{N}$. By the Riemann-Lebesgue lemma $a_1 = b_1 = 0$ and (a) is proved. □

REMARK 6. Let $f \in L^1[0,1]$ satisfy $(2)_{\mathbb{N}}$ with $u = \tau_{-1}$. This implies by Theorem 1 : $F(x) = a_0/2$, hence $f(x) = a_0/2$ a.e. in $[0,1]$. But f is not necessary a (pointwise) constant function. Example : Define $\varphi : [0,1] \to \mathbb{R}$ by $\varphi(x) := 1$ for $x \in \mathbb{Q} \cap [0,1]$ and $\varphi(x) := 0$ otherwise. Then $\varphi \in L^r[0,1]$ for every $r > 0$ and φ satisfies $(2)_{\mathbb{N}}$ with $u = \tau_{-1}$.

In the sequel we denote by

$BV\,[0,1]$ the space of functions of bounded variation over $[0,1]$ and by

$Lip_\alpha\,[0,1]$ the space of functions g of period 1, which satisfy a Lipschitz condition $|g(t+\delta) - g(t)| \leqq \gamma |\delta|^\alpha$.

THEOREM 2. <u>Let</u> $f : [0,1] \to \mathbb{R}$, $f \notin N$, <u>satisfy</u> $(2)_{\mathbb{N}}$ <u>with</u> $u \neq \tau_{-1}$. <u>Then</u>

(a) $f \in L^1\,[0,1] \;\Rightarrow\; \lim_{k\to\infty} 1/(k\,u(k)) = 0$,

(b) $f \in L^r\,[0,1]\,,\; 1 < r \leqq 2 \;\Rightarrow\; \sum_{k=1}^{\infty} \left(\frac{1}{k\,u(k)}\right)^{\frac{r}{r-1}} < \infty$,

(c) $f \in BV\,[0,1] \;\Rightarrow\; \exists\, b \in \mathbb{R}\;\; \forall k \in \mathbb{N} : \; u(k) \geqq b > 0$,

(d) $f \in Lip_\alpha[0,1]\,,\; \alpha > \frac{1}{\rho} - \frac{1}{2} \;\Rightarrow\; \left[\sum_{k=n}^{\infty} \left(\frac{1}{k\,u(k)}\right)^\rho\right]^{\frac{1}{\rho}} \leqq c\, n^{\frac{1}{\rho} - \frac{1}{2} - \alpha}$.

<u>Proof.</u> By Theorem 1 the Fourier series F of f has the form

$$F(x) = \sum_{k=1}^{\infty} \left(a_1 \frac{\cos 2\pi kx}{k\,u(k)} + b_1 \frac{\sin 2\pi kx}{k\,u(k)} \right) .$$

Because of $f \notin N$ and the completeness of the trigonometric system in $L^1[0,1]$ we have $\max\{ |a_1|, |b_1| \} > 0$.

(a) : The Riemann–Lebesgue lemma implies $\lim 1/(k\,u(k)) = 0$.

(b) : The Hausdorff–Young theorem states : If $f \in L^r[0,1]$, $1 < r \leqq 2$, then necessarily

$$\left(\sum_{n=-\infty}^{\infty} |c_n|^s \right)^{\frac{1}{s}} \leqq \|f\|_r \quad ,$$

where $\frac{1}{r} + \frac{1}{s} = 1$ and $c_n = \int_0^1 f(t)\, e^{-2\pi i n t}\, dt$, $n \in \mathbb{Z}$.

Consequently $\sum_{k=1}^{\infty} |a_k|^{\frac{r}{r-1}}$ and $\sum_{k=1}^{\infty} |b_k|^{\frac{r}{r-1}}$ are both convergent, hence $\sum_{k=1}^{\infty} \left(\frac{1}{k\,u(k)}\right)^{\frac{r}{r-1}}$ is convergent.

(c) : By means of a simple substitution we get

$$a_k = 2 \int_0^1 f(t) \cos 2\pi k t \; dt = (-1)^n \, 2 \int_0^1 f\left(x + \frac{n}{2k}\right) \cos 2\pi k x \; dx$$

for $n \in \{0, 1, 2, 3, \dots\}$. Here we make use of Remark 2 . Hence

$$k a_k = \int_0^1 \sum_{n=0}^{k-1} \left[f\left(x + \frac{n}{k}\right) - f\left(x + \frac{2n+1}{2k}\right) \right] \cos 2\pi k x \; dx \quad .$$

Therefore $k\,|a_k| \leqq \int_0^1 V\, dx = V$, V being the total variation of f over any interval of length 1 . Similarly $k\,|b_k| \leqq V$ and $u(k) \geqq \frac{1}{V} \max\{|a_1|, |b_1|\} > 0$. Note that our hypotheses imply: $V > 0$.

(d) : We use again Remark 2 and a theorem of Lorentz [5] : $f \in \mathrm{Lip}_\alpha[0,1]$ and $\alpha > \frac{1}{\rho} - \frac{1}{2}$, $0 < \rho \leqq 2$, imply :

$$\left[\sum_{k=n}^{\infty} \left(|a_k|^\rho + |b_k|^\rho \right) \right]^{\frac{1}{\rho}} \leqq c^* n^{\frac{1}{\rho} - \frac{1}{2} - \alpha} \quad ,$$

c^* depending only of the Lipschitz constant. Since $a_k = a_1 / (k\,u(k))$ and $b_k = b_1 / (k\,u(k))$ our assertion follows with a modified constant c . □

REMARK 7. A consequence of the special case $\rho = 1$ of (d) is

$$(d^*) \quad f \in \mathrm{Lip}_\alpha[0,1] ,\ \alpha > \frac{1}{2} \quad \Rightarrow \quad \sum_{k=1}^{\infty} \frac{1}{k\,u(k)} < \infty \quad .$$

Roughly, Theorem 2 states: The "nicer" the solution space the "greater" are the average values of the weight function u . The implications on u are from step to step more restrictive, beginning in (a) with $\lim 1/(k\,u(k)) = 0$ and ending up in (d^*) with $\sum 1/(k\,u(k)) < \infty$.

4. SUFFICIENT CONDITIONS FOR THE WEIGHT FUNCTION

We define functions $s, c : \mathbb{R} \to \mathbb{R}$ by

$$(7) \qquad s(x) := \sum_{k=1}^{\infty} \frac{\sin 2\pi kx}{k\,u(k)} \quad \text{and} \quad c(x) := \sum_{k=1}^{\infty} \frac{\cos 2\pi kx}{k\,u(k)} ,$$

where $u : \mathbb{N} \to \mathbb{R}_+$ has values which guarantee the convergence of the series. In the following remark we state an important property of the functions s and c .

REMARK 8. Suppose $u : \mathbb{N} \to \mathbb{R}_+$ is multiplicative and $s, c : \mathbb{R} \to \mathbb{R}$. Then

$$(8) \qquad \forall x \in \mathbb{R} \quad \forall p \in \mathbb{N} : s(x) = u(p) \sum_{k=0}^{p-1} s\left(\frac{x+k}{p}\right), \; c(x) = u(p) \sum_{k=0}^{p-1} c\left(\frac{x+k}{p}\right) .$$

The proof is by straightforward computation, using elementary facts about roots of unity (see [3] or [8]). (8) remains true, if any linear method of summation is applied to the defining series (7).

The statements of the following theorem are formulated in analogy to the "reverse" statements of Theorem 2. We prove in fact a bit more: In (a) and (b) we compute all nontrivial solutions f in the given function space.

THEOREM 3. <u>Let</u> $u : \mathbb{N} \to \mathbb{R}_+$ <u>be multiplicative. Then</u>

(a) $\displaystyle\sum_{k=1}^{\infty} \frac{1}{k\,u(k)} < \infty \quad \Rightarrow \quad \exists f \in C[0,1],\; f \neq \sigma_0 : (2)_{\mathbb{N}}$,

(b) $\displaystyle\sum_{k=n}^{\infty} \frac{1}{k\,u(k)} = O(n^{-\alpha}),\; 0 < \alpha < 1 \quad \Rightarrow \quad \exists f \in \mathrm{Lip}_\alpha[0,1],\; f \neq \sigma_0 : (2)_{\mathbb{N}}$,

(c) $\displaystyle\sum_{k=1}^{\infty} \left(\frac{1}{k\,u(k)}\right)^r < \infty ,\; 1 < r \leq 2 \quad \Rightarrow \quad \exists f \in L^s[0,1],\; f \notin N : (2)_{\mathbb{N}}$.

Proof. (a) : Assume the existence of a solution $f \in C[0,1]$ of $(2)_{\mathbb{N}}$, $f \neq \sigma_0$. Because of $\sum 1/(ku(k)) < \infty$ necessarily $u \neq \tau_{-1}$. In view of Theorem 1 the Fourier series F of f has the form

$$F(x) = \sum_{k=1}^{\infty} (a_1 \cos 2\pi kx + b_1 \sin 2\pi kx)/(ku(k)) .$$

Now $\sum 1/(ku(k)) < \infty$ implies the absolute convergence of $F(x)$, hence we have $F(x) = a_1 c(x) + b_1 s(x)$, s and c as defined in (7). Thus necessarily by Fejér's theorem:

$f(x) = a_1 c(x) + b_1 s(x)$.

On the other hand by Remark 8, the function f^*, given by $f^*(x) = ac(x) + bs(x)$ is a solution of $(2)_{\mathbb{N}}$ and clearly $f^* \in C[0,1]$ for any $a, b \in \mathbb{R}$.

(b) : Assume there is a solution $f \in Lip_\alpha[0,1]$ of $(2)_{\mathbb{N}}$, $f \neq \sigma_0$.

Since $\sum_{k=n}^{\infty} 1/(ku(k)) = O(n^{-\alpha})$, the Fourier series of f is given by $F(x) = a_1 c(x) + b_1 s(x)$ and again by Fejér's theorem necessarily $f(x) = a_1 c(x) + b_1 s(x)$.

On the other hand f^*, given by $f^*(x) = a\,c(x) + b\,s(x)$ is a solution of $(2)_{\mathbb{N}}$. f^* coincides with its Fourier series and the Fourier coefficients satisfy the condition $\sum_{k=n}^{\infty} (|a_k| + |b_k|) = O(n^{-\alpha})$. This implies $f^* \in Lip_\alpha[0,1]$ by a theorem of Lorentz [5] .

Note that both the statements of Lorentz we used in the proofs of Theorems 2 and 3 cannot be improved in a sense described in [5].

(c) : Define $c_n := \frac{1-i}{2nu(n)}$, $c_{-n} := \frac{1+i}{2nu(n)}$ for $n \in \mathbb{N}$ and $c_0 := 0$.

Then $\sum_{n=-\infty}^{\infty} |c_n|^r < \infty$ because of our hypotheses $\sum_{k=1}^{\infty} (\frac{1}{ku(k)})^r < \infty$, and by the Hausdorff-Young theorem there exists a function $f \in L^s[0,1]$ (recall $\frac{1}{r} + \frac{1}{s} = 1$), whose Fourier coefficients are just the c_n, $n \in \mathbb{Z}$, given above. Now if $f \in L^s[0,1]$, the functions $x \mapsto \frac{1}{2}(f(x) + f(-x))$ and $x \mapsto \frac{1}{2}(f(x) - f(-x))$ belong as well to $L^s[0,1]$ and their Fourier series are $c(x)$ resp. $s(x)$.

By the Carleson-Hunt theorem [2] $c(x)$ is convergent a.e. in $[0,1]$. Denote the exeptional set by E and define

$$E^* := \{x \in [0,1] \mid x = \frac{y+p}{k} \; ; \; y \in E \; , \; p \in \mathbb{N} \; , \; 0 \leqq k \leqq p-1\} \; .$$

E^* is of measure 0. Now

$$c^*(x) := \begin{cases} 0 & \text{for } x \in E^* \\ c(x) & x \in [0,1] \setminus E^* \end{cases}$$

is pointwise convergent and we have $c^* \in L^s[0,1]$, $c^* \notin N$ and c^* satisfies (pointwise) $(2)_{\mathbb{N}}$. A similar reasoning applies to $s(x)$. □

REMARK 9. Note that in the important case $r = 2$ the condition $\sum_{k=1}^{\infty} (\frac{1}{k u(k)})^2 < \infty$ is both necessary and sufficient to ensure the existence of a nontrivial solution f of $(2)_{\mathbb{N}}$. This fact was already stated in [4].

REFERENCES

1. N.K. Bary, A Treatise on Trigonometric Series, Pergamon Press, Oxford, 1964.
2. R.A. Hunt, On the convergence of Fourier series, Proc. Conf. Southern Illinois Univ.: Orthogonal Expansions and their Continuous Analogues, Southern Illinois Univ. Press (1968), 235-255.
3. H.-H. Kairies, Multiplikationstheoreme (Habilitationsschrift), Braunschweig, 1971.
4. H.-H. Kairies, On homogeneously weighted mean values, Aequationes Math. 12 (1975), 265-266.
5. G.G. Lorentz, Fourier-Koeffizienten und Funktionenklassen, Math. Z. 51 (1948), 135-149.
6. P. Schroth, On $(1, b_p)$-replicative functions with isolated discontinuities, Aequationes Math., to appear.
7. E. Wirsing, A characterization of $\log n$ as an additive arithmetic function, Symposia Math. IV (1970), 45-57.
8. M.F. Yoder, Continuous replicative functions, Aequationes Math. 13 (1975), 251-261.

Inequalities of Approximation Theory

THE BANACH-STEINHAUS THEOREM WITH RATES, AND APPLICATIONS TO VARIOUS BRANCHES OF ANALYSIS

P.L. Butzer
Lehrstuhl A für Mathematik
Rheinisch-Westfälische Technische Hochschule
51 Aachen
FEDERAL REPUBLIC OF GERMANY

ABSTRACT. The purpose of this survey paper is to examine the applicabilities of the Banach-Steinhaus theorem in a version equipped with rates in the light of results obtained at Aachen during the past two years. These lie in a variety of fields, namely in (a) Fourier analysis, (b) quadrature formulae, (c) mean ergodic theory, (d) algebraic approximation, (e) probability theory, (f) numerical analysis, and (g) signal theory. In each case direct theorems involving rates of convergence are presented. The hypotheses of the general theorem applied basically consist of two inequalities: one involves the rate of increase of the operator norm, the other a Jackson-type inequality.

1. INTRODUCTION

One of the half-dozen basic theorems of functional analysis is the uniform-boundedness principle. It is the principle underlying the Banach-Steinhaus theorem, the latter essentially stating that a family of bounded linear operators is convergent to some limit operator on a Banach space if and only if the operators are uniformly bounded as well as convergent on a dense subspace. As the name already signifies, this theorem is concerned with operators the norms of which are uniformly bounded.

Several years ago (see [16]) this theorem was equipped with rates in the sense that necessary and sufficient conditions were given such that the family of operators tends to the limit operator with a specific rate of convergence; these are a condition upon the operator norms (they may be unbounded) together with a Jackson-type inequality for the operators. Just as the Banach-

Steinhaus theorem can be applied to study the *convergence* behaviour of a variety of operators, the purpose of this survey paper will be to show that the general theorem with rates can be utilized to describe the *rate* of the convergence of these operators. These applications occur in various fields and deal with (i) estimates of 2π-periodic continuous functions by the partial sums of their Fourier series in terms of the modulus of continuity, (ii) estimates of 2π-periodic functions by the de La Vallée Poussin singular integral, (iii) derivative-free error estimates of integrals by quadrature formulae, (iv) rate of convergence in the mean ergodic theorem for Cesàro averages in the discrete case, (v) direct pointwise approximation estimates for Bernstein polynomials, (vi) pointwise approximation estimates for the Szász-Mirakjan operators, (vii) central limit theorem of probability theory with rates, (viii) weak law of large numbers with rates, (ix) Lax equivalence theorem of numerical analysis with rates, (x) rate of convergence for the Shannon sampling series in case of duration limited functions.

The applications (i) and (v), first considered in Dickmeis-Nessel [26], recover the classical results known to be best possible; those of (iii) and (iv) are to be found in [16]. In (vi) a recent estimate by Becker [3] is reconsidered. The material of (vii) and (viii) is based on new results of Butzer and Hahn [12] and [9]; this time the proofs follow as applications of the general theorem with rates. Results of the type dealt with in (ix) have received much attention in Aachen in the past years, see e.g. [20], [10], [27], [11]. Here it will be shown that the Lax theorem with rates can also be deduced as a corollary of our general theorem with rates. The Shannon sampling theorem of (x), or called the cardinal interpolation series, has been studied by only a few mathematicians in the past fourty years (contrary to the situation in communication engineering circles). In this respect recent results of Splettstößer, Stens and the author are considered in (x) from the point of view of the general theorem.

In order to handle these heterogeneous applications from our general point of view, particularly those of (v), (vi) and (ix), it will turn out that the original theorem with rates, that of [16], is not general enough. For this purpose an extended version involving the rate of closeness of two families of operators, due to Dickmeis and Nessel [26], is employed.

Under the general framework the structure of the proofs of the different applications is reduced to their basic essentials, namely to the verification of two inequalities: one involves the order of the operator norms and may also be termed a stability condition, the other is a Jackson - type inequality. In [14] Butzer and Junggeburth gave a brief survey of results known on Jackson inequalities for best approximation as well as for certain linear processes, emphasizing the interconnections with Voronovskaja - type relations and saturation. In this work Jackson - type inequalities are presented in connection with the Banach - Steinhaus theorem equipped with rates on the basis of eight further applications. It must also be emphasized that all estimates presented are best possible of their kind, at least in those cases where known results are reproduced, although this is not explicitly mentioned each time.

Prof. R.J. Nessel kindly read the entire manuscript with meticulous care and gave valuable suggestions. Dr. W. Dickmeis checked the material of Secs. 2, 5, and aided with the proofs in Sec. 11. Dr. L. Hahn gave useful suggestions in connection with the proofs of the theorems in Secs. 9 and 10. Dr. M. Becker read over Secs. 7 and 8. Drs. W. Splettstößer and R.L. Stens gave helpful advice concerning Sec. 12. To all the author would like to express his sincere thanks.

Parts of the material of this paper were presented by the author while he held a R. and H. Britton lectureship at McMaster University, Hamilton, Ont. in Sept. of 1978, and in colloquium talks given at the University of Pittsburgh on Sept. 18, 1978, at Pennsylvania State University, University Park, on Sept. 19, 1978, and at the University of Virginia, Charlottesville, on Sept. 21, 1978.

2. BANACH - STEINHAUS THEOREM WITH RATES

2.1 The Classical Theorem and Theorem with Rates

Before stating the theorem with rates of convergence let us recall the Banach - Steinhaus theorem in its classical form.

Below, let $\mathbb{Z}$, $\mathbb{P}$, $\mathbb{N}$ be the set of all, of all non - negative, of all positive integers, respectively. For normed linear spaces X, Y, let [X,Y] be the space of all bounded linear operators mapping X into Y. Let $U \subset X$ be a linear manifold with seminorm $|\cdot|_U$, and $\overline{U}$ its closure with respect to the norm of X.

THEOREM A. <u>A sequence</u> $\{T_n\}_{n\in\mathbb{P}}$ <u>of bounded linear operators mapping a Banach space</u> X <u>into a normed linear space</u> Y <u>is convergent to a bounded linear operator</u> $T: X\to Y$, i.e.,

$$\text{(a)}' \qquad \lim_{n\to\infty} \|T_n f - Tf\|_Y = 0 \qquad (f\in X)$$

<u>if and only if</u>

$$\text{(b)}' \quad \text{(i)} \qquad \|T_n\|_{[X,Y]} \leqslant M < \infty \qquad (n\in\mathbb{P})$$

$$\text{(ii)} \qquad \lim_{n\to\infty} \|T_n f - Tf\|_Y = 0 \qquad (f\in U),$$

<u>where</u> U <u>is a dense linear manifold of</u> X.

Note that is is possible to replace (b)' (ii) by the (weaker) condition

(c)' (ii) $\{T_n f\}_{n\in\mathbb{P}}$ <u>is a Cauchy sequence in</u> Y <u>for each</u> $f\in U$ <u>with</u> $\overline{U}=X$, Y <u>now being a Banach space</u>.

The basic concept needed in order to equip the assertion (a)' with rates is the modified K-functional of $f\in X$, defined for all $t\geqslant 0$ by

$$(2.1) \qquad K(t,f) \equiv K(t,f;X,U) := \inf_{g\in U} \{\|f-g\|_X + t|g|_U\}.$$

It is known that K(t,f) is a continuous, monotone, concave function of t for each $f\in X$ with

$$(2.2) \qquad \lim_{t\to 0+} K(t,f) = 0 \qquad (f\in\overline{U})$$

having the further properties

$$(2.3) \qquad K(t,f) \leqslant \begin{cases} \|f\|_X & (f\in X) \\ t|f|_U & (f\in U). \end{cases}$$

It may be used to describe smoothness properties of $f \in X$, serving as a substitute of the modulus of continuity to which it is equivalent in concrete instances (see Sec. 2.3).

The simplest version of the Banach - Steinhaus theorem with rates is the following one. It suffices in order to deduce error estimates for quite a number of applications. This is a normed linear space version of a form first given for locally convex Hausdorff spaces in [16]. A more sophisticated version (for Banach spaces) covering a wider range of applications is presented in Sec. 2.2.

THEOREM I. _Let_ X, Y _be normed linear spaces_, T_n, $T \in [X,Y]$, _and_ $\{\varphi(n)\}_{n\in\mathbb{P}}$, $\{\psi(n)\}_{n\in\mathbb{P}}$ _two sequences of non-negative real numbers with_ $0<\psi(n)<c_\psi$, $n\in\mathbb{P}$. _The following assertions are equivalent_ $(n\in\mathbb{P})$:

(a) $$\|T_n f - Tf\|_Y \leq \frac{c_1}{\psi(n)} K(\varphi(n)\psi(n),f;X,U) \qquad (f\in X);$$

(b)

(i) $$\|T_n\|_{[X,Y]} \leq c_2/\psi(n)$$

(ii) $$\|T_n f - Tf\|_Y \leq c_3\varphi(n)|f|_U \qquad (f\in U).$$

The c_i _are constants independent of_ f _and_ n.

Proof. The fact that (a) ⇒ (b) (ii) together with

(2.4) $$\|T_n f - Tf\|_Y \leq (c_1/\psi(n))\|f\|_X \qquad (f\in X; n\in\mathbb{P})$$

follows directly by (2.3). So $\|T_n - T\|_{[X,Y]} \leq c_1/\psi(n)$, and therefore

$$\|T_n\|_{[X,Y]} \leq \|T_n - T\|_{[X,Y]} + \|T\|_{[X,Y]}$$

$$\leq c_1/\psi(n) + c_\psi\|T\|_{[X,Y]}/\psi(n) =: c_2/\psi(n).$$

Concerning (b) ⇒ (a), one has by (b) (i)

$$\|T_n f - Tf\|_Y \leq \|T_n f\|_Y + \|Tf\|_Y \leq [(c_2 + c_\psi\|T\|_{[X,Y]})/\psi(n)]\|f\|_X =:$$

$$=: [c_2'/\psi(n)]\|f\|_X \qquad (f \in X; n \in \mathbb{P}).$$

One therefore has for any $f \in X$, $g \in U$, $n \in \mathbb{P}$

$$\|T_n f - Tf\|_Y \leq \|(T_n - T)(f-g)\|_Y + \|(T_n - T)g\|_Y$$

$$\leq (c_2'/\psi(n))\|f-g\|_X + c_3\varphi(n)|g|_U$$

$$\leq \max\{c_2', c_3\}(1/\psi(n))[\|f-g\|_X + \varphi(n)\psi(n)|g|_U],$$

noting (b) (ii). Taking the infimum over all $g \in U$ now yields (a) with $c_1 = \max\{c_2', c_3\}$. □

Note that the inequality of part (a), which is valid for all $f \in X$, "interpolates" between two end-points, given by the inequality $\|T_n - T\|_{[X,Y]} \leq c_1'/\psi(n)$ which is equivalent to (b) (i), and the inequality of (b) (ii), the so-called Jackson-type inequality of order $\varphi(n)$ on X for the sequence $\{T_n\}_{n \in \mathbb{P}}$, valid for all $f \in U$. Note that condition (b) (ii) even allows the norms of T_n to be unbounded.

One can interpret Thm. I as a Banach-Steinhaus theorem with rates as follows: Set $\psi(n) \equiv 1$, $n \in \mathbb{P}$, let $\varphi(n) \to 0$ as $n \to \infty$, and let $\overline{U} = X$, X now being a Banach space. Then statements (a) and (b) take on the forms

(a) $\|T_n f - Tf\|_Y \leq c_1 K(\varphi(n), f; X, U) \qquad (f \in \overline{U} = X)$

(b) (i) $\|T_n\|_{[X,Y]} \leq c_2$,

(ii) $\|T_n f - Tf\|_Y \leq c_3 \varphi(n)|f|_U \qquad (f \in U)$.

Since the right-hand sides of (a) and (b) (ii) tend to zero for $n \to \infty$ in view of (2.2), statements (a) and (b) "contain" those of (a)' and (b)'.

Observe that in comparison with the hypotheses of Thm. A the spaces X and Y of Thm. I need not be Banach spaces, just normed linear spaces. The proof of Thm. I is simpler than that of Thm. A in the sense that it gets along without the uniform boundedness principle; this is so since the estimate by the K-functional, being stronger than (a)', practically takes over the role of this principle.

Finally note that assertion (b) (ii) can also be replaced by a Cauchy-sequence type condition. This follows from

COROLLARY I. Let X be a normed linear space, Y a Banach space, let $\overline{U} = X$, and $\lim_{n\to\infty} \varphi(n) = 0$. The following assertions are equivalent for the sequence $\{T_n\}_{n\in\mathbb{P}} \subset [X,Y]$ (for $n,m \in \mathbb{P}$):

(a) There exists $T \in [X,Y]$ such that

$$\|T_n f - Tf\|_Y \leq c_1 K(\varphi(n), f; X, U) \qquad (f \in X),$$

(b)

(i) $\|T_n\|_{[X,Y]} \leq c_2$

(ii) $\|T_n f - T_m f\|_Y \leq c_3[\varphi(n) + \varphi(m)]\,|f|_U \qquad (f \in U).$

The fact that (a) ⇒ (b) follows similarly as in the proof of Thm. I. Concerning (b) ⇒ (a), condition (b) (ii) states that $\{T_n f\}_{n\in\mathbb{P}}$ is a Cauchy sequence in Y for every $f \in U$ with $\overline{U} = X$, since $\lim_{n\to\infty} \varphi(n) = 0$. Condition (c)' (ii) in conjunction with (b)' (i) delivers the existence of an operator $T \in [X,Y]$ such that (a)' holds. Taking the limit for $m \to \infty$ in (b) (ii) then yields (b) (ii) of Thm. I. The implication (b) ⇒ (a) now follows by Thm. I.

2.2 A More Refined Theorem with Rates

The first extension of the Banach-Steinhaus theorem to one with rates, namely Thm. I, is not powerful enough to cover all of the standard examples, one being the pointwise approximation by Bernstein polynomials. For this purpose let us present the following generalization due to Dickmeis-Nessel [26].

Let J be an arbitrary index set, and $A(J)$ the set of all non-negative, real-valued functions defined on J. The elements of $A(J)$ will serve as a measure of the rate of convergence.

THEOREM II. Let X be a Banach space, Y a normed linear space, and let $\{T_j\}_{j\in J}$, $\{F_j\}_{j\in J}$ be two families of operators belonging to $[X,Y]$ with

$$\|F_j\|_{[X,Y]} \leqslant c_F/\psi(j) \qquad (j\in J), \tag{2.5}$$

where $\psi\in A(J)$ with $0<\psi(j)<c_\psi$ for $j\in J$, c_F, c_ψ being certain constants. Moreover, let $\varphi\in A(J)$. The following assertions are equivalent:

(a) $$\|T_jf - F_jf\|_Y \leqslant \frac{c_1}{\psi(j)} K(\varphi(j)\psi(j),f;X,U) \qquad (f\in X),$$

(b) (i) $\|T_j\|_{[X,Y]} \leqslant c_2/\psi(j)$,

(ii) $\|T_jf - F_jf\|_Y \leqslant c_3\varphi(j)|f|_U \qquad (f\in U)$

(c) (i), (ii) $$\|T_jf - F_jf\|_Y \leqslant \begin{cases} M_f/\psi(j) & (f\in X) \\ c_3\varphi(j)|f|_U & (f\in U), \end{cases}$$

the constants c_1, c_2, c_3 being independent of $j\in J$ and f, and M_f depends only on f.

Proof. The fact that (a)$\Rightarrow$(b) (ii) follows as in the proof of Thm. I with $c_2=c_1+c_F$, and $c_3=c_1$. Concerning (b) (i)$\Rightarrow$(c) (i),

$$\|T_jf - F_jf\|_Y \leqslant \|T_jf\|_Y + \|F_jf\|_Y \leqslant \frac{c_2}{\psi(j)}\|f\|_X + \frac{c_F}{\psi(j)}\|f\|_X$$

for all $f\in X$, $j\in J$, noting (2.5). This gives (c) (i) with $M_f=(c_2+c_F)\|f\|_X$.

Concerning (c)$\Rightarrow$(a), (c) (i) implies by the uniform boundedness principle that there is a constant $M'>0$ with $\psi(j)\|T_j - F_j\|_{[X,Y]} \leqslant M'$, $j\in J$. Also using (c) (ii) one therefore has for any $f\in X$, $g\in U$, $j\in J$,

$$\begin{aligned}\|T_jf - F_jf\|_Y &\leqslant \|(T_j-F_j)(f-g)\|_Y + \|(T_j-F_j)g\|_Y \\ &\leqslant \frac{M'}{\psi(j)}\|f-g\|_X + c_2\varphi(j)|g|_U \\ &\leqslant \max\{M',c_2\}(1/\psi(j))[\|f-g\|_X + \varphi(j)\psi(j)|g|_U] .\end{aligned}$$

Taking the infimum over all $g \in U$ now yields (a) with $c_1 = \max\{M', c_2\}$. □

Note that just as in Thm. I one could prove the implications (a)$\Leftrightarrow$(b) of Thm. II without proceeding via part (c). In that case X need not be complete since the uniform boundedness principle was only used to prove that (c)$\Rightarrow$(a).

2.3 K-Functional and Moduli of Continuity

The applications in this paper deal with X being one of the spaces $C_{2\pi}$, $C_B(\mathbb{R})$ or $C[a,b]$; these are spaces of continuous functions defined on $\mathbb{R}$ (:= real numbers) or $[a,b]$, respectively, which are 2π-periodic in case of $C_{2\pi}$ and uniformly continuous and bounded on $\mathbb{R}$ in case of $C_B(\mathbb{R})$, endowed with the norms

$$\|f\|_{C_{2\pi}} = \|f\|_{C_B} := \sup_{x\in\mathbb{R}} |f(x)|, \quad \|f\|_{C[a,b]} := \sup_{x\in[a,b]} |f(x)|.$$

A further space is $L^p_{2\pi}$, $1 \leq p < \infty$, of 2π-periodic, measurable functions on $\mathbb{R}$ with the norm $\|f\|_p := \{(1/2\pi)\int_{-\pi}^{\pi} |f(x)|^p dx\}^{1/p}$, as well as C_k (see Sec. 8 for definition). The subspaces $U \subset X$ in question are spaces of r-fold differentiable functions, namely ($r \in \mathbb{N}$)

$$U = X^r := \{f \in X; f^{(j)} \in X, 1 \leq j \leq r\}$$

with seminorm $|f|_U := \|f^{(r)}\|_X$.

In these instances the K-functional (2.1) is equivalent to the classical rth modulus of continuity of $f \in X$, defined by

$$\omega_r(t,f;X) := \sup_{0\leq h\leq t} \Big\| \sum_{k=0}^{r} (-1)^{r-k}\binom{r}{k} f(x+kh)\Big\|_X \qquad (t \geq 0)$$

(the sup being restricted to those arguments belonging to the domain of definition) in the form (see [8, p. 192; 258], [25, p. 122], the literature cited there, as well as La. 6 of Sec. 12)

$$(2.6) \qquad c_{1,r}\,\omega_r(t,f;X) \leq K(t^r,f;X,X^r) \leq c_{2,r}\,\omega_r(t,f;X),$$

the (positive) constants $c_{1,r}$, $c_{2,r}$ being independent of $f \in X$ and $t \geq 0$.

The estimates will also be expressed in terms of the Lipschitz class of order α, $0<\alpha\leq r$, defined by

$$\mathrm{Lip}_r(\alpha;X) := \{f\in X;\omega_r(t,f;X) = \mathcal{O}(t^\alpha)\}.$$

Since $\omega_r(t,f;X)\leq t^{r-1}\omega_1(t,f^{(r-1)};X)$, one has that $f^{(r-1)}\in \mathrm{Lip}_1(\alpha;X)$, $0<\alpha\leq 1$, implies $f\in \mathrm{Lip}_r(r-1+\alpha;X)$.

3. PARTIAL SUMS OF FOURIER SERIES

Consider the nth partial sum of the trigonometric Fourier series of $f\in C_{2\pi}$, namely $(n\in\mathbb{P},k\in\mathbb{Z})$

$$(3.1)\qquad (S_nf)(x) := \sum_{k=-n}^{n} f^\wedge(k)e^{ikx},\quad f^\wedge(k) := \frac{1}{2\pi}\int_{-\pi}^{\pi} f(u)e^{-iku}\,du\,.$$

LEMMA 1. <u>The operators</u> $S_n\in[C_{2\pi},C_{2\pi}]\equiv[C_{2\pi}]$ <u>satisfy</u>

$$(3.2)\qquad \|S_n\|_{[C_{2\pi}]}\leq c_2\log n$$

$$(3.3)\qquad \|S_nf-f\|_{C_{2\pi}}\leq c_3\frac{\log n}{n^r}\|f^{(r)}\|_{C_{2\pi}}\qquad (f\in C_{2\pi}^r).$$

The second follows by the well-known inequality (cf. [15, p. 105])

$$\|S_nf-f\|_{C_{2\pi}}\leq (1+\|S_n\|_{[C_{2\pi}]})E_n(f;C_{2\pi}),$$

$E_n(f;C_{2\pi})$ being the best approximation of $f\in C_{2\pi}$ by trigonometric polynomials of degree n, together with the classical Jackson inequality (cf. [15, p. 97], [14, p. 88])

$$E_n(f;C_{2\pi})\leq \frac{c_4}{n^r}\|f^{(r)}\|_{C_{2\pi}}\qquad (f\in C_{2\pi}^r).$$

To apply Thm. I., following [26], choose $X=Y=C_{2\pi}$ with $T_n=S_n$, $T=I$ (= identity), $\psi(n)=1/\log n$, $\varphi(n)=\log n/n^r$, and $U=C_{2\pi}^r$, $|f|_U=\|f^{(r)}\|_{C_{2\pi}}$. This regives by (2.6) the estimate

THEOREM 1. <u>The partial sums</u> $S_n f$ <u>of the Fourier series of</u> $f \in C_{2\pi}$ <u>satisfy the inequality</u>

$$\| S_n f - f \|_{C_{2\pi}} \leq c_5 \log n \, \omega_r(\tfrac{1}{n}, f; C_{2\pi}),$$

<u>the constant</u> c_5 <u>being independent of</u> f <u>and</u> $n \in \mathbb{N}$. <u>In particular, if</u> $f^{(r-1)} \in \mathrm{Lip}_1(\alpha, C_{2\pi})$, $0<\alpha\leq 1$, <u>then</u>

$$\| S_n f - f \|_{C_{2\pi}} = \mathcal{O}(\log n / n^{r-1+\alpha}).$$

4. SINGULAR INTEGRAL OF DE LA VALLÉE POUSSIN

This integral, often used to establish the famous Weierstraß approximation theorem for periodic functions (cf. [34, p.13]), is defined for $f \in X_{2\pi} = C_{2\pi}$ or $L^p_{2\pi}$, $1 \leq p < \infty$, $n \in \mathbb{N}$, by

$$(4.1) \qquad (V_n f)(x) := \frac{1}{2\pi} \int_{-\pi}^{\pi} f(x-u) v_n(u) du, \quad v_n(x) := \frac{(n!)^2}{(2n)!} (2 \cos \frac{x}{2})^{2n} .$$

It is seen to define a polynomial summation process of the Fourier series of $f \in X_{2\pi}$ when rewritten as

$$(V_n f)(x) = \sum_{k=-n}^{n} \frac{(n!)^2}{(n-k)!(n+k)!} f^\wedge(k) e^{ikx} .$$

LEMMA 2. <u>The operators</u> $V_n \in [X_{2\pi}, X_{2\pi}]$ <u>satisfy</u>

$$(4.2) \qquad \| V_n \|_{[X_{2\pi}]} \leq 1$$

$$(4.3) \qquad \| V_n f - f \|_{X_{2\pi}} \leq \frac{\pi^2}{4} \frac{1}{n+1} \| f'' \|_{X_{2\pi}} \qquad (f \in X^2_{2\pi}).$$

This result, particularly the Jackson-type inequality (4.3) (see e.g. [14] for a proof), reveals that in Thm. I one may choose $X = Y = X_{2\pi}$ with $T_n = V_n$, $T = I$, $\psi(n) = 1$, $\varphi(n) = 1/(n+1)$, and $U = X^2_{2\pi}$, $|f|_U = \| f'' \|_{X_{2\pi}}$. Again using (2.6) this gives the well-known (cf. [15, p. 113])

THEOREM 2. <u>The de La Vallée Poussin integral</u> $V_n f$ <u>of</u> $f \in X_{2\pi}$ <u>satisfies</u>

$$\|V_n f - f\|_{X_{2\pi}} \leqslant c_6 \omega_2\left(\frac{1}{\sqrt{n+1}}, f; X_{2\pi}\right).$$

<u>If</u> $f \in \mathrm{Lip}_2(\alpha; X_{2\pi})$, $0<\alpha\leqslant 2$, <u>then</u> $\|V_n f - f\|_{X_{2\pi}} = \mathcal{O}(n^{-\alpha/2})$.

5. NUMERICAL INTEGRATION

When the integral $Qf := \int_a^b f(x)dx$ is not readily available, one often approximates it by a quadrature formula

$$(5.1) \qquad Q_n f := \sum_{k=1}^{n} A_{k,n} f(x_{k,n}) \qquad (n \in \mathbb{N}),$$

where $A_{k,n}$ are certain weights and $x_{k,n}$ certain nodes with $a \leqslant x_{1,n} < x_{2,n} < \ldots < x_{n,n} \leqslant b$. If $f \in C[a,b]$, Q_n and Q are bounded, linear functionals on $C[a,b,]$. The well-known result of Pólya (1933) (which is indeed a simple application of Thm. A) then states that

$$\lim_{n\to\infty} |Q_n f - Qf| = 0 \qquad (f \in C[a,b])$$

if and only if

$$\text{(i)} \qquad \sum_{k=1}^{n} |A_{k,n}| \leqslant M < +\infty \qquad (n \in \mathbb{N})$$

$$\text{(ii)} \qquad \lim_{n\to\infty} |Q_n p_j - Qp_j| = 0$$

for all $p_j(x) := \sum_{k=0}^{j} a_k x^k$, all $j \in \mathbb{N}$. Now to apply Thm. I, first note that $\|Q_n\|_{[C[a,b],\mathbb{R}^1]} = \sum_{k=1}^{n} |A_{k,n}|$. If the quadrature formula is assumed to be exact for polynomials $p_m(x)$ of fixed degree m, i.e., $Q_n p_m = Qp_m$, then the Peano kernel theorem yields that

$$Q_n f - Qf = \int_a^b f^{(m+1)}(u) \frac{1}{m!} (Q_n - Q)_x (x-u)_+^m du \qquad (f \in C^{m+1}[a,b]),$$

the index x meaning that the functional $Q_n - Q$ is applied to $(x-u)_+^m$ considered as a function of x, where

$$(x-u)_+^m = \begin{cases} (x-u)^m, & x \geq u \\ 0, & x < u. \end{cases}$$

For $f \in C^{m+1}[a,b]$ this gives the Jackson-type inequality

$$(5.3) \qquad |Q_n f - Qf| \leq \frac{1}{m!} \int_a^b |(Q_n - Q)_x (x-u)_+^m| du \, \|f^{(m+1)}\|_{C[a,b]} ;$$

moreover,

$$(5.4) \qquad \|Q_n - Q\|_{[C^{m+1}[a,b], \mathbb{R}^1]} = \frac{1}{m!} \int_a^b |(Q_n - Q)_x (x-u)_+^m| du .$$

So in Thm. I we may take $X = C[a,b]$, $Y = \mathbb{R}^1$, $U = C^{m+1}[a,b]$, $m \geq 0$, $T_n = Q_n$, $T = Q$, $\psi(n) = 1$, and $\varphi(n) = n^{-(m+1)}$ if the integral in (5.4) is of order $n^{-(m+1)}$, to deduce

THEOREM 3. <u>If</u> $Q_n p_m = Qp_m$ <u>for</u> m <u>fixed, then for all</u> $n \geq m$

$$(5.5) \qquad |Q_n f - Qf| \leq c_1 \omega_{m+1}(\tfrac{1}{n}, f; C[a,b]) \qquad (f \in C[a,b])$$

<u>if and only if</u>

$$(5.6) \quad (i) \quad \sum_{k=1}^{n} |A_{k,n}| \leq M, \qquad (ii) \quad \frac{1}{m!} \int_a^b |(Q_n - Q)_x (x-u)_+^m| du \leq \frac{c_2}{n^{m+1}} .$$

<u>If</u> $f^{(m)} \in \mathrm{Lip}(\alpha; C[a,b])$, $0 < \alpha \leq 1$, <u>and</u> (5.6) <u>holds, then</u>

$$|Q_n f - Qf| = \mathcal{O}\left(\frac{1}{n^{m+\alpha}}\right).$$

Note that (5.5) is a so-called derivative-free error estimate for the quadrature formula $Q_n f \approx Qf$; see e.g. G. Hämmerlin [31], H. Brass [6] and Davis-Rabinowitz [24, p. 232] in this respect.

Observe that conditions (5.6) (i) and (ii) are readily verified for the composite Newton-Cotes formulae which include the trapezoidal and Simpson's rule. Thus for the particular case of the trapezoidal formula one has for $f \in C^2[a,b]$

$$\left|\int_a^b f(x)dx - \left(\frac{b-a}{n}\right)\left[\frac{f(x_{0,n})+f(x_{n,n})}{2} + \sum_{k=1}^{n-1} f(x_{k,n})\right]\right|$$

$$\leqslant \frac{(b-a)^3}{12\,n^2}\ \|f''\|_{C[a,b]}\ ,$$

$$\int_a^b |(Q_n-Q)_x|\,(x-u)_+^1\,du \leqslant \frac{(b-a)^3}{12\,n^2}\ .$$

6. MEAN ERGODIC THEOREM

Let T be a bounded linear operator mapping the Banach space X into itself such that $\|T^n\|_{[X]} \leqslant M$, $n \in \mathbb{P}$. If, for simplicity, X is reflexive, the mean ergodic theorem asserts that

$$\lim_{n\to\infty} \left\|\frac{1}{n+1}\sum_{k=0}^{n} T^k f - Pf\right\|_X = 0 \qquad (f \in X),$$

where P is the bounded linear projection of X on the null space N(I-T) parallel to $\overline{R(I-T)}$, the closure of the range of I-T. Here $X = N(I-T) \oplus \overline{R(I-T)}$.

The question to be considered is the rate of convergence of $\sigma_n(T)f := (n+1)^{-1}\sum_{k=0}^{n} T^k f$ to Pf on a linear manifold of X, a problem first considered by Butzer - Westphal [21,22]. For this purpose one needs two basic inequalities, the second being of Jackson - type (see [22] for a proof),

$$\|\sigma_n(T)\|_{[X]} \leqslant M \qquad (n \in \mathbb{P})$$

$$\|\sigma_n(T)f - Pf\|_X \leqslant \frac{M+1}{n+1}\,\|Bf\|_X \qquad (f \in D(B); n \in \mathbb{N}),$$

B being the linear operator with domain $D(B) = N(I-T) \oplus R(I-T)$ and range in X defined by $Bf = g$, where $g \in X$ is uniquely determined by $(I-P)f = (I-T)g$ and $Pg = \theta$. Note that $\overline{D(B)} = X$.

Therefore one may apply Thm. I to the case $X = Y$, $T_n = \sigma_n(T)$, $T = P$ with $\varphi(n) = (n+1)^{-1}$, $\psi(n) = 1$, $|f|_U = \|Bf\|_X$, $U = D(B)$. This gives

THEOREM 4. <u>One has</u>

$$\left\| \frac{1}{n+1} \sum_{k=0}^{n} T^k f - Pf \right\|_X \leq c\, K\left(\frac{1}{n+1}, f; X, D(B)\right) \qquad (f \in X).$$

Results of the above type do not only hold for the $(C,1)$ but also for the (C,α) - means for $\alpha \geq 1$ (see [32]) as well as for the Abel means of the iterates $\{T^n\}_{n \in \mathbb{P}}$, namely

$$A_r(T) := (1-r) \sum_{k=0}^{\infty} r^k T^k \qquad (0 < r < 1).$$

In the latter case, if f belongs to the space

$$\mathrm{Lip}_1(\alpha;X) := \{f \in X; K(t,f;X,D(B)) = \mathcal{O}(t^\alpha)\},$$

$0<\alpha \leq 1$, then (see [22])

$$\| A_r(T)f - Pf \|_X = \mathcal{O}((1-r)^\alpha) \qquad (r \to 1-).$$

It may be interesting to add that in connection with Thm. 4 the following is known (see [21]): if for $f \in X$ one has $\| \sigma_n(T)f - Pf \|_X = o(n^{-1})$, then $f \in N(I-T)$. If X is reflexive, then $\| \sigma_n(T)f - Pf \| = \mathcal{O}(n^{-1})$ iff $f \in D(B)$.

7. BERNSTEIN POLYNOMIALS

These are defined for $f \in C[0,1]$, $x \in [0,1]$ by

(7.1) $$(B_n f)(x) := \sum_{k=0}^{n} f\left(\frac{k}{n}\right) \binom{n}{k} x^k (1-x)^{n+k} \qquad (n \in \mathbb{P})$$

and have the properties that

(7.2) $$|(B_n f)(x)| \leq \|f\|_{C[0,1]} \qquad (f \in C[0,1])$$

(7.3) $$|(B_n f)(x) - f(x)| \leq \frac{x(1-x)}{2n} \|f''\|_{C[0,1]} \qquad (f \in C^2[0,1])$$

for all $x \in [0,1]$, $n \in \mathbb{N}$ (cf. [33], [23, p. 117]). In particular, $B_n \in [C[0,1]]$. Introducing the evaluation functional $f_x^*(f) := f(x)$ for $f \in C[0,1]$, $x \in [0,1]$ (cf. [28]), one has $f_x^* \in [C[0,1], \mathbb{R}] := C^*$ and $f_x^* B_n \in C^*$ for any $x \in [0,1]$, $n \in \mathbb{P}$.

Following [26], let us set $J = \{j = (x,n); x \in [0,1], n \in \mathbb{P}\}$,

$T_j = f *_x B_n$, $F_j = f *_x$. The basic inequalities (7.2), (7.3) then turn out to be

$$|T_j f| \leqslant \|f\|_{C[0,1]} \qquad (f \in C[0,1])$$

$$|T_j f - F_j f| \leqslant \frac{x(1-x)}{2n} \|f''\|_{C[0,1]} \qquad (f \in C^2[0,1])$$

for all $x \in [0,1]$. In particular, $\|T_j\|_{C*} \leqslant 1$. Moreover, $\|F_j\|_{C*} = 1$ (cf. (2.5)). So we can apply Thm. II with $X = C[0,1]$, $Y = \mathbb{R}$, $\psi(j) = 1$, $\varphi(j) = x(1-x)/2n$, and $U = C^2[0,1]$, to give

THEOREM 5. <u>For the Bernstein polynomials one has</u>

$$|(B_n f)(x) - f(x)| \leqslant c\omega_2(\sqrt{x(1-x)/2n}, f; C[0,1]),$$

<u>the constant</u> c <u>being independent of</u> $f \in C[0,1]$, $x \in [0,1]$ <u>and</u> $n \in \mathbb{N}$. <u>In particular, if</u> $f \in \mathrm{Lip}_2(\alpha; C[0,1])$, $0<\alpha\leqslant 2$, <u>then</u>

$$|(B_n f)(x) - f(x)| = O([\frac{x(1-x)}{n}]^{\alpha/2}).$$

This shows that it is also possible to deduce pointwise approximation estimates from our general theorems.

8. SZÁSZ - MIRAKJAN OPERATORS

These are defined for $f \in C[0,\infty)$ ($\equiv$ the set of continuous functions on $[0,\infty)$) by

$$(8.1) \qquad (G_n f)(x) := e^{-nx} \sum_{k=0}^{\infty} f(\frac{k}{n}) \frac{(nx)^k}{k!} \qquad (x \in [0,\infty); n \in \mathbb{P}).$$

Corresponding to the unbounded interval, the function f may be unbounded with polynomial growth at infinity. More precisely, following M. Becker [3], for $k \in \mathbb{P}$ let

$$C_k := \{f \in C[0,\infty);\ w_k f \text{ uniformly continuous and bounded on } [0,\infty)\}$$

$$\|f\|_k := \sup_{x \in [0,\infty)} w_k(x)|f(x)|, \quad w_k(x) := (1+x^k)^{-1}, \quad w_o(x) = 1 .$$

LEMMA 3. *Let* $k \in \mathbb{P}$. *The operators* G_n *have the following properties for each* $x \in [0,\infty)$:

a) *For all* $f \in C_k$ *there is a constant* M_k *such that*

$$w_k(x)|(G_n f)(x)| \leq M_k \|f\|_k , \tag{8.3}$$

b) *For all* $f \in C_k^2 := \{g \in C_k; g''(x) \in C_k\}$ *there exists a constant* M_k' *such that*

$$w_k(x)|(G_n f)(x) - f(x)| \leq \frac{x}{2n} M_k' \|f''\|_k \qquad (n \in \mathbb{N}). \tag{8.4}$$

In particular, $G_n \in [C_k]$ for each $k \in \mathbb{P}$. Introducing the functional $f_x^*(f) = w_k(x)f(x)$, $f \in C_k$, $x \in [0,\infty)$, then $f_x^* \in [C_k,\mathbb{R}] := C_k^*$ and $f_x^* G_n \in C_k^*$ for any $x \in [0,\infty)$, $n \in \mathbb{P}$. Setting $J = \{j = (x,n); x \in [0,\infty), n \in \mathbb{N}\}$, $T_j = f_x^* G_n$, $F_j = f_x^*$, then (8.3), (8.4) take on the form

$$|T_j f| \leq M_k \|f\|_k \qquad (f \in C_k)$$

$$|T_j f - F_j f| \leq \frac{x}{2n} M_k' \|f''\|_k \qquad (f \in C_k^2)$$

for all $x \in [0,\infty)$, $n \in \mathbb{N}$. In particular, $\|T_j\|_{C_k^*} \leq M_k$. Moreover, $\|F_j\|_{C_k^*} \leq 1$. So we may apply Thm. II with $X = C_k$, $Y = \mathbb{R}$, $U = C_k^2$, and $\varphi(j) = x/2n$, $\psi(j) = 1$, to regain

THEOREM 6. *For the Szász - Mirakjan operators one has*

$$|(G_n f)(x) - f(x)| \leq c\omega_{2,k}(\sqrt{x/2n}, f; C_k),$$

the constant c *being independent of* $f \in C_k$, $n \in \mathbb{N}$, *and* $x \in [0,\infty)$.

Here one utilizes the fact that the K - functional $K(x/2n, f; C_k, C_k^2)$ is equivalent to the modulus

$$\omega_{2,k}(\delta, f; C_k) := \sup_{0 \leq h \leq \delta} \|f(\cdot+2h) - 2f(\cdot+h) + f(\cdot)\|_k ,$$

a result implicitly proven e.g. in [3].

It is possible to extend the foregoing results to functions which are allowed to have exponential growth at infinity (see [3]), this time using the original locally convex version of Thm. I (see [16]).

It would also be feasible to apply Thm. II to establish the counterparts of Thm. 6 for the Baskakov and Favard operators. This would regive parts of the results of [3] and [4], respectively.

9. CENTRAL LIMIT THEOREM WITH RATES

Let $\{Z_i\}_{i\in\mathbb{P}}$ be a sequence of real, independent (not necessarily identically distributed (i.d.)) random variables (r.vs.) defined on an arbitrary probability space (Ω,A,P). Let F_{Z_i} be the distribution function (d.f.) of $Z_i:\Omega\to\mathbb{R}$, i.e., $F_{Z_i}(z)=P(\{\omega\in\Omega : Z_i(\omega)\leqslant z\})$ for each $z\in\mathbb{R}$. Assume without loss of generality that the expectation $E(Z_i)(:=\int_{\mathbb{R}} z\,dF_{Z_i}(z))=0$, $i\in\mathbb{P}$ (otherwise apply results to $Y_i := Z_i - E(Z_i)$). Abbreviate the variance as $V(Z_i)(:=E([Z_i-E(Z_i)]^2))=\sigma_i^2$. Let Z^* be a normally distributed r.v. with $E(Z^*)=0$ and $V(Z^*)=1$, thus $F_{Z^*}(z)=(1/\sqrt{2\pi})\int_{-\infty}^{z}\exp(-u^2/2)du$. Set $S_n := \sum_{i=0}^{n} Z_i$, and $s_n^2 := \sum_{i=0}^{n}\sigma_i^2$.

The sequence $\{Z_i\}_{i\in\mathbb{P}}$ with $0<V(Z_i)<\infty$ is said to satisfy the central limit theorem if

$$\sup_{u\in\mathbb{R}} |F_{S_n/s_n}(u) - F_{X^*}(u)| = o(1) \qquad (n\to\infty) \tag{9.1}$$

or, equivalently, if

$$\sup_{y\in\mathbb{R}} \left|\int_{\mathbb{R}} f(z+y)dF_{S_n/s_n}(z) - \int_{\mathbb{R}} f(z+y)dF_{Z^*}(z)\right| = o_f(1) \qquad (n\to\infty) \tag{9.2}$$

for all $f\in C_B^r(\mathbb{R})$, where $r\in\mathbb{P}$ is arbitrary fixed. When comparing (9.1) with (9.2) first note that (9.2) is equivalent to that condition which arises when the sup in (9.2) is replaced by its value at $y=0$, and that (9.1) can be written in a similar form with $f(z)=\chi_{(-\infty,u]}(z) := 1$ for $z\in(-\infty,u]$, $=0$ otherwise, since

$$F_{S_n/s_n}(u) = \int_{\mathbb{R}} \chi_{(-\infty,u]}(z)F_{S_n/s_n}(z) .$$

Concerning the rate of convergence in (9.1), H. Cramér, A.C. Berry, and G.C. Esseen (1937/45) showed that

$$\sup_{u\in\mathbb{R}} |F_{S_n/s_n}(u) - F_{Z*}(u)| \leq \frac{c}{s_n^3} \sum_{i=0}^{n} \beta_{3,i} \tag{9.3}$$

where $\beta_{3,i} := E(|Z_i|^3)$. Note that this estimate is of order $\mathcal{O}(n^{-1/2})$ provided the Z_i are i.d., i.e., $F_{Z_i} = F_Z$, $i \in \mathbb{P}$. Concerning the error estimate in (9.2) we have

THEOREM 7. <u>For</u> $f \in C_B(\mathbb{R})$ <u>one has for</u> $n \in \mathbb{P}$

$$\Delta_n := \sup_{y\in\mathbb{R}} \left|\int_{\mathbb{R}} f(z+y)dF_{S_n/s_n}(z) - \int_{\mathbb{R}} f(z+y)dF_{Z*}(z)\right|$$

$$\leq c'\omega_3\left(\left[\frac{1}{2s_n^3} \sum_{i=0}^{n} \beta_{3,i}\right]^{1/3}, f; C_B(\mathbb{R})\right). \tag{9.4}$$

<u>In particular</u>, $f'' \in \mathrm{Lip}_1(\alpha; C_B(\mathbb{R}))$, $0<\alpha\leq 1$, <u>implies</u>

$$\Delta_n = \mathcal{O}\left(\left[\frac{1}{2s_n^3} \sum_{i=0}^{n} \beta_{3,i}\right]^{(2+\alpha)/3}\right) \qquad (n \in \mathbb{P}). \tag{9.5}$$

<u>Proof</u>. To apply Thm. I set

$$(T_n f)(y) = \int_{\mathbb{R}} f(z+y)dF_{S_n/s_n}(z), \quad (Tf)(y) = \int_{\mathbb{R}} f(z+y)dF_{Z*}(z).$$

Then T_n, $T \in [C_B(\mathbb{R})]$ with $\|T_n\|_{[C_B]} = \|T\|_{[C_B]} = 1$. So choose $X = Y = C_B(\mathbb{R})$, and $\psi(n) = 1$, $n \in \mathbb{P}$. Concerning the Jackson-type inequality, let us show that

$$\Delta_n \equiv \|T_n f - Tf\|_{C_B} \leq \frac{1}{2s_n^3} \sum_{i=0}^{n} \beta_{3,i} \|f^{(3)}\|_{C_B} \tag{9.6}$$

for all $f \in C^3(\mathbb{R})$, $n \in \mathbb{P}$. Since the operators $A_i \in [C_B(\mathbb{R})]$, defined by $(A_i f)(y) := \int_{\mathbb{R}} f(z+y)dF_{Z_i}(z)$, $i \in \mathbb{P}$, are linear, contractive and moreover commutative (the r.vs. Z_i being independent), one has indeed

$$\|T_n f - Tf\|_{C_B} \leq \sum_{i=0}^{n} \left\|\int_{\mathbb{R}} f\left(\frac{z}{s_n} + \cdot\right)d\left[F_{Z_i}(z) - F_{\sigma_i Z*}(z)\right]\right\|_{C_B}.$$

By the Taylor series expansion the integral I_i within the norm is equal to

$$I_i = f(y) \int_{\mathbb{R}} d\left[F_{Z_i}(z) - F_{\sigma_i Z^*}(z)\right] + \frac{f'(y)}{s_n} \int_{\mathbb{R}} z\,d\left[F_{Z_i}(z) - F_{\sigma_i Z^*}(z)\right]$$

$$+ \frac{f''(y)}{2s_n^2} \int_{\mathbb{R}} z^2 d\left[F_{Z_i}(z) - F_{\sigma_i Z^*}(z)\right] + \frac{1}{6s_n^3} \int_{\mathbb{R}} z^3 f^{(3)}(\eta) d\left[F_{Z_i}(z) - F_{\sigma_i Z^*}(z)\right]$$

where $|\eta - y| \leq |z|/s_n$. It follows readily that the first three terms of I_i vanish for each $y \in \mathbb{R}$, so that

$$\| I_i \|_{C_B} \leq \frac{1}{6s_n^3} \left[\beta_{3,i} + 4 \frac{\sigma_i^3}{\sqrt{2\pi}} \right] \| f^{(3)} \|_{C_B} \leq \frac{\beta_{3,i}}{2s_n^3} \| f^{(3)} \|_{C_B}$$

(since $\sigma_i = (\sigma_i^2)^{1/2} \leq (\beta_{3,i})^{1/3}$, and $4/\sqrt{2\pi} < 2$). This yields (9.6).

In view of (9.6) we may finally take $\varphi(n) := (1/2s_n^3) \sum_{i=0}^n \beta_{3,i}$, and $U = C_B^3(\mathbb{R})$ with $|f|_{C_B^3} = \| f^{(3)} \|_{C_B}$. The theorem now follows by (2.6). □

Note that Thm. 7 could readily be extended to the modulus of continuity of order $r \in \mathbb{P}$ provided $\beta_{r,i} := E(|Z_i|^r) < \infty$, $i \in \mathbb{P}$, and

$$E(Z_i^j) := \int_{\mathbb{R}} z^j dF_{Z_i}(z) = \sigma_i^j E(Z^{*j})$$

for $3 \leq j \leq r-1$, $i \in \mathbb{P}$. If $f^{(r-1)} \in \mathrm{Lip}_1(\alpha; C_B(\mathbb{R}))$, $0 < \alpha \leq 1$, this would yield

$$(9.7) \qquad \Delta_n = \mathcal{O}\left(\left[\frac{1}{s_n^r} \sum_{i=0}^n \beta_{r,i} \right]^{(r+\alpha-1)/r} \right).$$

This estimate is of order $\mathcal{O}(n^{-(r-2)/2})$ provided the Z_i are i.d. and $f \in C_B^r(\mathbb{R})$.

On the other hand, it would also be possible to sharpen the estimate in (9.3) to essentially the same order as that given by (9.7) provided the same conditions upon the moments are satisfied. Instead of a smoothness condition upon f such as $f \in C_B^r(\mathbb{R})$ ($\subset \mathrm{Lip}_r(\alpha; C_B(\mathbb{R})$, $0 < \alpha \leq r$), one then needs in the i.d. case the Cramér condition

$$\limsup_{|v|\to\infty} \left|\int_{\mathbb{R}} e^{ivz} dF_Z(z)\right| < 1$$

which is actually a smoothness condition upon the d.f. However, the proof of this result is very long and has to make use of heavy Fourier analytic machinery (see e.g. V.V. Petrov [36, pp. 134 ff]).

10. WEAK LAW OF LARGE NUMBERS

A further application of Thm. I in probability theory is the weak law of large numbers (WLLN) with rates. Again let $\{Z_i\}_{i\in\mathbb{N}}$ be a sequence of real, independent (not necessarily i.d.) r.vs. defined on (Ω,A,P) with $E(Z_i)=0$, $i\in\mathbb{N}$.

The sequence $\{Z_i\}_{i\in\mathbb{N}}$ is said to satisfy the WLLN if, for each $\varepsilon>0$,

(10.1) $$\lim_{n\to\infty} P(\{\omega\in\Omega; |S_n(\omega)/n|\geqslant\varepsilon\}) = 0$$

or, equivalently, if (see e.g. [1 , p. 220])

(10.2) $$\lim_{n\to\infty} \sup_{y\in\mathbb{R}} \left|\int_{\mathbb{R}} f(z+y)\,d\, F_{S_n/n}(z) - F_{Z^o}(z)\right| = 0$$

for each $f\in C_B^r(\mathbb{R})$, $r\in\mathbb{P}$ arbitrary fixed. Here Z^o is the r.v. with d.f. $F_{Z^o}(z)=0$ for $z<0$, $=1$ for $z\geqslant 0$. In this respect one has

LEMMA 4. <u>The sequence $\{Z_i\}_{i\in\mathbb{N}}$ satisfies the WLLN provided</u>

(10.3) $$\sigma_i^2 := E(X_i^2) < +\infty \quad (i\in\mathbb{N}), \quad \sum_{i=1}^n \sigma_i^2 = o(n^2) \qquad (n\to\infty).$$

Concerning rates in (10.1), L.E. Baum and M. Katz [2] showed in particular in the case of i.d. r.vs. that $E(Z^r)<\infty$ for $r\in\mathbb{N}$ implies

(10.4) $$P(\{\omega\in\Omega; |S_n(\omega)/n|\geqslant\varepsilon\}) = o_\varepsilon(n^{-r+1}) \qquad (n\to\infty)$$

for each $\varepsilon>0$. Although this means that the rate in (10.4) is arbitrarily good provided the moments of sufficiently high order are finite, the disadvantage is that the little-o term in (10.4) depends decisively on ε (e.g. if $\varepsilon_n = n^{-1/2}$, then not even (10.1) holds in view of the CLT).

Concerning the error estimate in (10.2) we have

THEOREM 8. <u>For</u> $f \in C_B(\mathbb{R})$ <u>one has with</u> $n \in \mathbb{N}$

$$\Delta_n' := \sup_{y \in \mathbb{R}} \left| \int_{\mathbb{R}} f(z+y)\,d\left[F_{S_n/n}(z) - F_{Z^o}(z)\right]\right| \tag{10.5}$$

$$\leqslant c\,\omega_2\left(\left[\frac{1}{2n^2}\sum_{i=1}^{n}\sigma_i^2\right]^{1/2}, f; C_B(\mathbb{R})\right).$$

<u>In particular</u>, <u>if</u> $f' \in \mathrm{Lip}_1(\alpha; C_B(\mathbb{R}))$, $0<\alpha\leqslant 1$, <u>then</u>

$$\Delta_n' = O\left(\left[\frac{1}{2n^2}\sum_{i=1}^{n}\sigma_i^2\right]^{(1+\alpha)/2}\right). \tag{10.6}$$

<u>Proof</u>. To apply Thm. I take $(T_n f)(y) := \int_{\mathbb{R}} f(z+y)dF_{S_n/n}(z)$, and $(Tf)(y) := \int_{\mathbb{R}} f(z+y)dF_{Z^o}(z)(= f(y))$. Then T_n, $T \in [C_B(\mathbb{R})]$ with $\|T_n\|_{[C_B]} = \|T\|_{[C_B]} = 1$. Hence $X = Y = C_B(\mathbb{R})$, and $\psi(n) \equiv 1$, $n \in \mathbb{N}$. Concerning the Jackson-type inequality there holds $(n \in \mathbb{N})$

$$\Delta_n' \equiv \|T_n f - Tf\|_{C_B} \leqslant \left(\frac{1}{2n^2}\sum_{i=1}^{n}\sigma_i^2\right)\|f''\|_{C_B} \qquad (f \in C_B^2(\mathbb{R})). \tag{10.7}$$

Indeed, by the Taylor series expansion $\Delta_n' \leqslant \sum_{i=1}^{n} \|I_i'\|_{C_B}$, where

$$I_i'(y) := \int_{\mathbb{R}} f(z/n + y)\,d\left[F_{Z_i}(z) - F_{Z^o}(z)\right]$$

$$\leqslant f(y)\int_{\mathbb{R}} d\left[F_{Z_i}(z) - F_{Z^o}(z)\right] + \frac{f'(y)}{n}\int_{\mathbb{R}} z\,d\left[F_{Z_i}(z) - F_{Z^o}(z)\right]$$

$$+ \frac{1}{2n^2}\int_{\mathbb{R}} z^2 f''(\eta_z)\,d\left[F_{Z_i}(z) - F_{Z^o}(z)\right]$$

with $|\eta_z - y| \leqslant z/n$. Since the first two integrals on the right vanish for each

$y \in \mathbb{R}$, one has $\| I_i' \|_{C_B} \leqslant (\sigma_i^2/2n^2) \| f'' \|_{C_B}$. This gives (10.7). Therefore $\varphi(n) := (1/2n^2) \sum_{i=1}^n \sigma_i^2$, and $U = C_B^2(\mathbb{R})$ with $|f|_{C_B^2} = \| f'' \|_{C_B}$. The estimate (10.5) now follows by (2.6). □

Note that Thm. 8 contains La. 4. Indeed, $f \in C_B^2(\mathbb{R})$ implies $f \in \mathrm{Lip}_2(2, C_B(\mathbb{R}))$, which gives

$$\Delta_n' \leqslant (1/2n^2) \sum_{i=1}^n \sigma_i^2 = o(1) \qquad (n \to \infty)$$

in view of (10.3). The result now follows on account of the equivalence of (10.1) with (10.2). On the other hand, La. 4 also follows immediately from inequality (10.7).

If the r. vs. are i.d. and $f' \in \mathrm{Lip}_1(1; C_B(\mathbb{R}))$, then Δ_n' is of order $O(n^{-1})$. Moreover, this order cannot be improved (unless $F_{Z_i} = F_{Z^0}$, $i \in \mathbb{N}$; see [29]). However, in the case of r. vs. that are not necessarily i.d., the estimates (10.5), (10.6) give rates that are as good as $O(n^{-2})$.

The above matter is to be found in a much more general form but with another approach to the proofs in [12] (see also [13]).

Let us now show that it is also possible to deduce Thm. 5 on Bernstein polynomials from Th. 8 by specializing the r. vs. Z_i. Indeed, let Z_i be independent i.d. Bernoulli r. vs. with parameter $x \in [0,1]$, i.e., $P(\{\omega \in \Omega; Z_i(\omega) = 1\}) = x$, $P(\{Z_i = 0\}) = 1 - x$. Then apply Thm. 8 to the centered r. vs. $Z_i' := Z_i - x$ for which $E(Z_i') = 0, E(Z_i'^2) = \sigma_i^2 \equiv V(Z_i) = x(1-x)$. It follows with $S_n' := (1/n) \sum_{i=1}^n Z_i'$ that

$$\int_{\mathbb{R}} f(z+y) dF_{S_n'/n}(z) = \sum_{k=0}^n \binom{n}{k} x^k (1-x)^{n-k} f(\tfrac{k}{n} - x + y).$$

So Thm. 5 follows from Th. 8 by setting $y = x$, noting that the class $C_B^2(\mathbb{R})$ can here be replaced by $C^2[0,1]$.

Thm. 6 on the Szász - Mirakjan operators can also be deduced from Thm. 8. Indeed, let Z_i be independent, i.d. Poisson r. vs. with parameter $x \in [0,\infty)$, i.e., $P(\{\omega \in \Omega; Z_i(\omega) = k\}) = e^{-t} t^k/k!$, each $k \in \mathbb{N}$. Then apply Thm. 8 to the r. vs.

$Z_i' = Z_i - x$ for which $E(Z_i') = 0$ and $E(Z_i'^2) = V(Z_i) = x$. One then has

$$\int_{\mathbb{R}} f(z+y)\,dF_{S'/n}(z) = e^{-nx} \sum_{k=0}^{\infty} \frac{(nx)^k}{k!} f(\tfrac{k}{n} - x + y).$$

The result follows by setting $y = x$, noting that $C_B^2(\mathbb{R})$ is now the class $C_B^2[0,\infty)$.

In this matter see also L. Hahn [30].

11. LAX EQUIVALENCE THEOREM WITH RATES

Consider the initial-value problem

$$\frac{d}{dt} w(t) = Aw(t) \quad (t \geq 0), \quad w(0) = f \quad (f \in X), \tag{11.1}$$

where A is a closed linear operator with domain D(A) dense in the Banach space X and range in X, and f is a given element in X describing the initial state. This problem is said to be *properly* (or correctly) *posed* if there exists a one-parameter semigroup $\{E(t);t \geq 0\}$ of (evolution) operators of class (C_o) (i.e. $E(0) = I$, $E(s)E(t) = E(s+t)$ for all $s,t \geq 0$, $\lim_{t\to 0+} \|E(t)f-f\|_X = 0$, all $f \in X$; see e.g. [8]) such that the solution of the problem is of the form $w(t) = E(t)f$ for each $f \in X$, $t \geq 0$, it being unique. In this case A may be regarded as the infinitesimal generator of the semigroup. This semigroup may, without loss of generality, be assumed to be uniformly bounded, i.e.,

$$\|E(t)\|_{[X]} \leq M \qquad (t \geq 0). \tag{11.2}$$

In numerical analysis one is interested in approximating the family of "exact" operators $\{E(t);t \geq 0\}$ by powers of some family of operators $\{E_\tau;\tau \geq 0\} \subset [X]$, usually interpreted as a certain finite difference scheme. For this purpose the following definitions are basic.

Let $\varphi(\tau)$ be a non-negative function on $[0,\infty)$, and $\psi(n,\tau)$ a function on $\mathbb{P}\times[0,\infty)$, monotonely decreasing with n such that

$$0 < \psi(n,\tau) < c_\psi \qquad (n \in \mathbb{N}, \tau \in [0,\infty)), \tag{11.3}$$

with $\psi(0,\tau) = c_1'$ (without loss of generality). The family $\{E_\tau;\tau \geq 0\} \subset [X]$ is said to be ordinarily *stable* [or *stable of order* $O(1/\psi(n,\tau))$] if there exists a constant $c_s > 0$ such that

$$\|E_\tau^n\|_{[X]} \leq c_s \quad [\text{or} \leq c_s/\psi(n,\tau)] \qquad (\tau \geq 0, n \in \mathbb{P}). \tag{11.4}$$

The family $\{E_\tau;\tau \geq 0\}$ is said to be ordinarily *consistent* [or *consistent of order* $O(\varphi(\tau))$] on a linear manifold $U \subset X$ with respect to the family of operators $\{E(\tau);\tau \geq 0\} \subset [X]$, if [or if there exists $c_c > 0$ such that]

$$\|[E_\tau - E(\tau)]E(t)f\| = o(\tau) \quad [\text{or} \leq c_c \tau\varphi(\tau)|f|_U] \tag{11.5}$$

for all $f \in U$ with $\overline{U} = X$, all $\tau \geq 0$, uniformly in $t \geq 0$. Here $|f|_U$ is a suitable seminorm on U.

In this terminology the Lax theorem in its standard form reads (see e.g. [37])

THEOREM OF LAX (1954/56): <u>Given a properly posed initial - value problem</u> (11.1) <u>in</u> X <u>and a finite difference scheme</u> $\{E_\tau;\tau \geq 0\} \subset [X]$ <u>satisfying the ordinary consistency condition. Then ordinary stability is necessary and sufficient for ordinary convergence, i.e.,</u>

$$\lim_{j\to\infty} \|E_{\tau_j}^{n_j} f - E(t)f\|_X = 0 \tag{11.6}$$

<u>for each sequence</u> $\{(n_j,\tau_j)\}_{j \in \mathbb{N}}$ <u>with</u> $\tau_j \to 0$; $n_j\tau_j \to t$ <u>as</u> $j \to \infty$.

Our aim now is to equip the convergence assertion (11.6) of the Lax theorem with rates. For this purpose let us first observe that

$$\|E_{\tau_j}^{n_j} f - E(t)f\|_X \leq \|E_{\tau_j}^{n_j} f - E(n_j\tau_j)f\|_X + \|E(n_j\tau_j)f - E(t)f\|_X. \tag{11.7}$$

If stability and consistency are considered with orders in the sense of (11.4), (11.5), then *convergence with orders* will be defined via the growth of the error $\|E_\tau^n f - E(n\tau)f\|_X$ in terms of n and τ for suitable, smooth f, due to the fact that in contrast with the first term, the second term on the right in (11.7) only depends upon the exact solution, namely E(t).

The Lax theorem with rates, first established in the setting of arbitrary Banach spaces in [20], following up work in Besov spaces in the sufficiency direction begun by Peetre - Thomée [35], now takes on the following form.

THEOREM 9. <u>Given a properly posed initial - value problem</u> (11.1) <u>in</u> X, <u>and a finite difference approximation</u> $\{E_\tau;\tau\geqslant 0\}$ <u>that is consistent of order</u> $\mathcal{O}(\varphi(\tau))$ <u>on</u> $U\subset X$ <u>with respect to the semigroup</u> $\{E(t);t\geqslant 0\}$ <u>satisfying</u> (11.2). <u>The following assertions are equivalent for all</u> $n\in\mathbb{N}$, $\tau>0$:

(a) $$\|E_\tau^n f - E(n\tau)f\|_X \leqslant \frac{c_1}{\psi(n,\tau)}\, K(n\tau\varphi(\tau),f;X,U) \qquad (f\in X),$$

(b) $$\|E_\tau^n\|_{[X]} \leqslant c_s/\psi(n,\tau),$$

(c) $$\|E_\tau^n f - E(n\tau)f\|_X \leqslant \frac{c_2}{\psi(n,\tau)} \begin{cases} M_f & (f\in X) \quad \text{(i)}\\ n\tau\varphi(\tau)|f|_U & (f\in U). \quad \text{(ii)}\end{cases}$$

<u>Proof</u>. To apply Thm. II take $J=\{j=(n,\tau);n\in\mathbb{N},\tau\geqslant 0\}$, $X=Y$, $T_j = E_\tau^n$, $F_j = E(n\tau)$. Then T_j, $F_j\in[X]$, $j\in J$, and

(11.8) $$\|F_j\|_{[X]} = \|E(n\tau)\|_{[X]} \leqslant (Mc_\psi)/\psi(n,\tau)$$

in view of (11.2) and (11.3). So condition (2.5) is satisfied with $\psi(j) := \psi(n,\tau)$. The Jackson - type inequality given by (c) (ii) of Thm. II here takes on the form (c) (ii), so that $\varphi(j) := n\tau\varphi(\tau)/\psi(n,\tau)$.

The fact that (a) $\Rightarrow$ (b) now follows by Thm. II (a) $\Rightarrow$ (b) (i). Concerning (b) $\Rightarrow$ (c) (ii), one makes use of the consistency condition of the hypothesis. Indeed,

$$\|E_\tau^n f - E(n\tau)f\|_X \leqslant \sum_{k=1}^{n} \|E_\tau^{n-k}\|_{[X]}\|[E_\tau - E(\tau)]E((n-k-1)\tau)f\|_X$$

$$\leqslant \sum_{k=1}^{n} \frac{c_s}{\psi(n-k,\tau)}\, c_c\tau\varphi(\tau)|f|_U \leqslant \frac{c_s c_c n\tau}{\psi(n-1,\tau)}\,\varphi(\tau)|f|_U$$

for all $f \in U$, $n \in \mathbb{N}$, $\tau \geq 0$, noting that $\psi(n,\tau)$ is decreasing with respect to n. This gives (c) (ii) since $\psi(n-1,\tau) \geq \psi(n,\tau)$.

The assertions (b) ⇒ (c) (i) and (c) ⇒ (a) follow directly from the corresponding parts of Th. II. This completes the proof. □

There is an alternative version of the Lax equivalence theorem on the convergence of the solution of the discrete problem to that of the given properly posed initial - value problem. This states that consistency plus stability is equivalent to convergence. This theorem can also be equipped with rates in the sense that all three concepts are considered with rates, as was shown in [10], [27]. Let us now show that this version may also be deduced as an easy application of Thm. II.

THEOREM 10. Given a properly posed initial - value problem (11.1) for which the associated family of (uniformly bounded) semigroup operators $\{E(t); t \geq 0\} \subset [X]$ satisfies the additional hypothesis

$$|E(t)f|_U \leq c' |f|_U \qquad (f \in U, t \geq 0) \tag{11.9}$$

with $\psi(1,\tau) = c_2'$ (instead of $\psi(0,\tau) = c_1'$ as in (11.3)). The following assertions are equivalent for the family of difference operators $\{E_\tau; \tau \geq 0\}$ $(\tau \geq 0, n \in \mathbb{N})$:

(a) $$\| E_\tau^n f - E(n\tau)f \|_X \leq \frac{c_1}{\psi(n,\tau)} K(n\tau\varphi(n), f; X, U) \qquad (f \in X),$$

(b) The scheme $\{E_\tau\}$ is stable of order $\mathcal{O}(1/\psi(n,\tau))$ and consistent of order $\mathcal{O}(\varphi(\tau))$ on U with respect to $\{E(t)\}$,

(c) $$\| E_\tau^n f - E(n\tau)f \|_X \leq \frac{c_3}{\psi(n,\tau)} \begin{cases} M_f & (f \in X) \quad \text{(i)} \\ n\tau\varphi(\tau)|f|_U & (f \in U) \quad \text{(ii)} \end{cases}.$$

Proof. The implications (a) ⇒ (b) (i) (= stability), (c) ⇒ (a) follow directly from Thm. II. Concerning (a) ⇒ (b) (ii) (= consistency), (a) implies by (2.3) when replacing f by $E(t)f$ and setting $n = 1$,

$$\|E^1_\tau(E(t)f) - E(\tau)(E(t)f)\|_X \leqslant c''\tau\varphi(\tau)|f|_U \qquad (f \in U)$$

with $c'' := c_1c'/\psi(1,\tau)$, noting (11.9). The fact that (b)$\Rightarrow$(c) follows as in the proof of Thm. 9. □

12. SHANNON SAMPLING THEOREM

One of the basic theorems of signal theory is the Whittaker - Kotel'nikov - Shannon sampling theorem according to which any band - limited signal function $f(t)$ can be exactly reconstructed from its sampled values. If the signal $f(t)$ is not band - limited but time - limited, an alternative model, studied by J.L. Brown [7] and Butzer - Splettstößer [17,18,19], (see also the extensive literature cited there) states that it can be approximately reconstructed from its samples. More precisely, if $f \in C_1(\mathbb{R}) := \{f \in C_B(\mathbb{R});\ f(t) = 0,\ \text{all } |t| > 1\}$ (one may take $|t|>1$ without loss of generality), and $f^\wedge(v) := \int_{\mathbb{R}} f(t)\exp(-ivt)dt \in L^1(\mathbb{R})$, then

$$\lim_{n\to\infty} \Big\| \sum_{k=-n}^{n} f(\tfrac{k}{n}) \frac{\sin \pi(nt-k)}{\pi(nt-k)} - f(t)\Big\|_{C_B} = 0. \tag{12.1}$$

This series interpolates f at the nodes $t = k/n$, each fixed n, since

$$\frac{\sin \pi(nt-k)}{\pi(nt-k)} = \begin{cases} 1, & t = k/n \\ 0, & t = m/n,\ m \neq k,\ m \in \mathbb{Z}. \end{cases}$$

To apply Thm. I set

$$(W_nf)(t) := \sum_{k=-n}^{n} f(\tfrac{k}{n})\mathrm{si}\{\pi(nt-k)\},$$

where $\mathrm{si}\{t\} := \sin t/t$. The operators $W_n \in [C_1(\mathbb{R}), C_B(\mathbb{R})]$ satisfy two basic inequalities; see R.L. Stens [38] for a proof.

LEMMA 5. <u>For the operators W_n one has</u>

(a) $$\|W_n\|_{[C_1,C_B]} = \sup_{t\in\mathbb{R}} \sum_{k=-n+1}^{n-1} |\mathrm{si}\{\pi(nt-k)\}| \leqslant 2 + \frac{2}{\pi}\log(n+1) \quad (n \in \mathbb{N}).$$

b) <u>To each</u> $r \in \mathbb{P}$ <u>there exists a constant</u> $c = c(r)$ <u>such that</u>

$$\|W_n f - f\|_{C_B} \le c \frac{\log(n+1)}{n^r} \|f^{(r)}\|_{C_B} \qquad (f \in C_1^r(\mathbb{R}); n \in \mathbb{N}).$$

So one can choose $X = C_1(\mathbb{R})$, $Y = C_B(\mathbb{R})$, $T_n = W_n$, $T = I$, $\psi(n) = 1/\log(n+1)$, $\varphi(n) = \log(n+1)/n^r$, and $U = C_1^r(\mathbb{R})$ with $|f|_U = \|f^{(r)}\|_{C_B}$ to give

THEOREM 11. <u>For the</u> W_n <u>one has</u>

$$\|W_n f - f\|_{C_B} \le c' \log(n+1) \omega_r\left(\frac{1}{n^r}, f; C_1(\mathbb{R})\right). \tag{12.2}$$

<u>In particular, if</u> $f^{(r-1)} \in \mathrm{Lip}_1(\alpha; C_1(\mathbb{R}))$, $0<\alpha\le 1$, <u>then</u>

$$\|W_n f - f\|_{C_B} = \mathcal{O}\left(\frac{\log(n+1)}{n^{r-1+\alpha}}\right).$$

For the proof one also needs the fact that the present K-functional is equivalent to the modulus in (12.2). This is given by the following lemma. Since the result does not seem to be shown anywhere, let us add a proof due to R.L. Stens.

LEMMA 6. <u>One has for</u> $f \in C_1(\mathbb{R})$, $r \in \mathbb{N}$,

$$K(t, f; C_1(\mathbb{R}), C_1^r(\mathbb{R})) \le c_r \omega_r(t, f; C_1(\mathbb{R})) \qquad (0 < t \le 1/2 r^2), \tag{12.3}$$

c_r <u>being a constant independent of</u> f <u>and</u> t.

<u>Proof</u>. First assume that $f(x) = 0$ for $|x| \ge 1 - r^2 t$. Following along the lines of the classical proof (e.g. [8, p. 192], Butzer - Scherer, J. Approximation Theory <u>5</u> (1972), p. 317) set

$$g(x) \equiv g(x; f) := - \sum_{k=1}^{r} (-1)^r \binom{r}{k} F_r(x, kt/r),$$

where

$$F_r(x,y) := \int_0^1 \dots \int_0^1 f(x + y(u_1 + \dots + u_r)) du_1 \dots du_r \qquad (x \in \mathbb{R}; y>0).$$

The function g belongs to $C_1^r(\mathbb{R})$, and one has

$$\|f-g\|_{C_B} \leq \omega_r(t,f;C_1(\mathbb{R})),$$

$$t^r\|g^{(r)}\|_{C_B} \leq r^r(2^r-1)\omega_r(t,f;C_1(\mathbb{R})).$$

This would imply the assertion since

$$K(t^r,f) \leq \|f-g\|_{C_B} + t^r\|g^{(r)}\|_{C_B} .$$

To verify (12.3) for arbitrary $f\in C_1(\mathbb{R})$ set

$$f_t(x) := -\sum_{k=1}^{r} (-1)^k\binom{r}{k}f\left(x+k\,\frac{xr^2t}{1-r^2t}\right) \qquad (x\in\mathbb{R};0<t\leq 1/2\,r^2).$$

Then $f_t(x)=0$ for $|x|\geq 1-r^2t$, and by the first step

$$K(t^r,f) \leq \|f-g(f_t)\|_{C_B} + t^r\|g^{(r)}(f_t)\|_{C_B}$$

$$\leq \|f-f_t\|_{C_B} + \{r^r(2^r-1)+1\}\omega_r(t,f_t;C_1(\mathbb{R})).$$

Now one has that

$$\|f-f_t\|_{C_B} = \sup_{x\in[-1,1]} \left|\sum_{k=0}^{r} (-1)^k\binom{r}{k}f\left(x+k\,\frac{xr^2t}{1-r^2t}\right)\right|$$

$$\leq \omega_r(2r^2t,f;C_1(\mathbb{R})) \leq (2r^2)^r\omega_r(t,f;C_1(\mathbb{R})),$$

$$\omega_r(t,f_t;C_1(\mathbb{R}))\leq \omega_r(t,f_t-f;C_1(\mathbb{R})) + \omega_r(t,f;C_1(\mathbb{R}))$$

$$\leq 2^r\|f_t-f\|_{C_B} + \omega_r(t,f;C_1(\mathbb{R})).$$

This completes the proof of the second step. □

It may be of interest to compare the above theorem with Tm. 1 concerning the corresponding estimate for the partial sums of the Fourier series.

REFERENCES

1. H. Bauer, Wahrscheinlichkeitstheorie und Grundzüge der Maßtheorie (2nd. ed.) De Gruyter, Berlin 1974.

2. L.E. Baum and M. Katz, Convergence rates in the law of large numbers. Trans. Amer. Math. Soc. 120 (1965), 108 - 123.

3. M. Becker, Global approximation theorems for Szász-Mirakjan and Baskakov operators in polynomial weight spaces. Indiana Univ. Math. J. 27 (1978), 127 - 142.

4. M. Becker, P.L. Butzer and R.J. Nessel, Saturation for Favard operators in weighted function spaces. Studia Math. 59 (1976), 139 - 153.

5. M. Becker, D. Kucharski and R.J. Nessel, Global approximation theorems for the Szász - Mirakjan operators in exponential weight spaces. In: Linear Spaces and Approximation (Proc. Conf. Oberwolfach 1977, P.L. Butzer, B. Sz.-Nagy, Eds.), ISNM 40, Birkhäuser Verlag, Basel 1978, pp. 319 - 333.

6. H. Brass, Quadraturverfahren. Studia Mathematica, Skript 3, Vandenhoeck + Ruprecht, Göttingen 1977.

7. J.L. Brown, Jr., On the error in reconstructing a non - bandlimited function by means of the bandpass sampling theorem. J. Math. Anal. Appl. 18 (1967), 75 - 84.

8. P.L. Butzer and H. Berens, Semi-Groups of Operators and Approximation, Springer Verlag, Berlin-Heidelberg-New York 1967.

9. P.L. Butzer, W. Dickmeis, L. Hahn and R.J. Nessel, Lax-type theorems and a unified approach to some limit theorems in probability theory with rates. Resultate der Mathematik (in print).

10. P.L. Butzer, W. Dickmeis, Hu. Jansen and R.J. Nessel, Alternative forms with orders of the Lax equivalence theorem in Banach spaces. Computing (Arch. Elektron. Rechnen) 17 (1977), 335 - 342.

11. P.L. Butzer, W. Dickmeis and R.J. Nessel, Lax-type theorems with orders in connection with inhomogeneous evolution equations in Banach spaces. In: Linear Spaces and Approximation (Proc. Conf. Oberwolfach 1977, P.L. Butzer, B. Sz.-Nagy, Eds.), ISNM 40, Birkhäuser Verlag, Basel 1978, pp. 531 - 546.

12. P.L. Butzer and L. Hahn, General theorems on rates of convergence in distribution of random variables, I: General limit theorems; II. Applications to the stable limit laws and weak law of large numbers. J. Multivariate Anal. 8 (1978), 181 - 201; 202 - 221.

13. P.L. Butzer, L. Hahn and U. Westphal, On the rate of approximation in the central limit theorem. J. Approximation Theory 13 (1975), 327 - 340.

14. P.L. Butzer and J. Junggeburth, On Jackson - type inequalities in approximation theory. In: General Inequalities 1. (Proc. Conf. Oberwolfach 1976, E.F. Beckenbach, Ed.) ISNM 41, Birkhäuser Verlag, Basel 1978, pp. 85 - 114.

15. P.L. Butzer and R.J. Nessel, Fourier Analysis and Approximation, Academic Press, New York, and Birkhäuser Verlag, Basel 1971.

16. P.L. Butzer, K. Scherer and U. Westphal, On the Banach - Steinhaus theorem and approximation in locally convex spaces. Acta Sci. Math. (Szeged) 34 (1973), 25 - 34.

17. P.L. Butzer and W. Splettstößer, A sampling theorem for duration - limited functions with error estimates. Information and Control 34 (1977), 55 - 65.

18. P.L. Butzer and W. Splettstößer, Approximation und Interpolation durch verallgemeinerte Abtastsummen. Forschungsberichte des Landes Nordrhein-Westfalen Nr. 2708, Westdeutscher Verlag, Opladen 1978.

19. P.L. Butzer and W. Splettstößer, On quantization, truncation and jitter errors in the sampling theorem and its generalizations (to appear).

20. P.L. Butzer and R. Weis, On the Lax equivalence theorem equipped with orders. J. Approximation Theory 19 (1977), 239 - 252.

21. P.L. Butzer and U. Westphal, The mean ergodic theorem and saturation. Indiana Univ. Math. J. 20 (1971), 1163-1174.

22. P.L. Butzer and U. Westphal, Ein Operatorenkalkül für das approximationstheoretische Verhalten des Ergodensatzes im Mittel. In: Linear Operators and Approximation I (Proc. Conf. Oberwolfach 1971; P.L. Butzer, J.P. Kahane and B. Sz.-Nagy, Eds.) ISNM 20, Birkhäuser Verlag, Basel 1972, pp. 102 - 113.

23. P.J. Davis, Interpolation and Approximation, Blaisdell, New York - London 1963.

24. P.J. Davis and P. Rabinowitz, Methods of Numerical Integration. Academic Press, New York - San Francisco - London 1975.

25. R. DeVore, Degree of approximation. In: Approximation Theory II (Proc. Conf. Austin, Texas 1976; G.G. Lorentz, C.K. Chui, L.L. Schumaker, Eds.), Academic Press, New York - San Francisco - London 1976, pp. 117 - 161.

26. W. Dickmeis and R.J. Nessel, On Banach - Steinhaus theorems with orders. Comment. Math. Prace Mat. Tomus Specialis in Honorem Ladislai Orlicz I (1978), 95 - 107.

27. W. Dickmeis and R.J. Nessel, Classical approximation processes in connection with Lax equivalence theorems with orders, Acta Sci. Math. (Szeged) 40 (1978), 33 - 48.

28. H. Esser, On pointwise convergence estimates for positive linear operators on $C[a,b]$. Nederl. Akad. Wetensch. Indag. Math. 38 (1976), 189 - 194.

29. L. Hahn, Inverse theorems on the rate of approximation for certain limit theorems in probability theory. In: Linear Spaces and Approximation (Proc. Conf. Oberwolfach 1977, P.L. Butzer, B. Sz.-Nagy, Eds.) ISNM 40, Birkhäuser Verlag, Basel 1978, pp. 583 - 601.

30. L. Hahn, Stochastic methods in connection with theorems for positive linear operators (to appear).

31. G. Hämmerlin, Über ableitungsfreie Schranken für Quadraturfehler. I; II. Ergänzungen und Möglichkeiten zur Verbesserung. Num. Math. 5 (1963), 225 - 233; 7 (1965), 232 - 237.

32. D. Leviatan and U. Westphal, On the mean ergodic theorem and approximation. Mathematica (Cluj) 15 (38) (1973), 83 - 88.

33. G.G. Lorentz, Bernstein Polynomials, University of Toronto Press, Toronto 1953.

34. I.P. Natanson, Constructive Function Theory. Vol. I: Uniform Approximation. Frederick Ungar, New York 1964 (Orig. Russ. ed. Moscow 1949).

35. J. Peetre and V. Thomée, On the rate of convergence for discrete initial-value problems. Math. Scand. 21 (1967), 159 - 176.

36. V.V. Petrov, Sums of Independent Random Variables. Springer Verlag, Berlin - Heidelberg - New York 1975.

37. R.D. Richtmyer and K.W. Morton, Difference Methods for Initial - Value Problems. Interscience, New York - London - Sydney 1967.

38. R.L. Stens, Approximation of duration - limited functions by sampling sums (to appear).

HARNACK'S INEQUALITIES FOR OPERATORS*

Ky Fan
Department of Mathematics
University of California
Santa Barbara, California 93106
U.S.A.

ABSTRACT. In this paper, alternative versions of Harnack's inequalities are established for operators.

1. INTRODUCTION

Let $\mathcal{H}$ be a complex Hilbert space. By an operator we shall always mean a bounded linear transformation on $\mathcal{H}$. The real and imaginary parts of an operator A will be denoted by $\operatorname{Re} A$ and $\operatorname{Im} A$, respectively, i.e.,

$$\operatorname{Re} A = \frac{A + A^*}{2}, \qquad \operatorname{Im} A = \frac{A - A^*}{2i}.$$

For two Hermitian operators A, B on $\mathcal{H}$, we write $A \leq B$ to indicate that $B - A$ is a positive operator, i.e., $((B - A)x,x) \geq 0$ for all $x \in \mathcal{H}$. The notation $A < B$ will mean that $B - A$ is positive and invertible.

For a complex function f analytic on the open disk $|z| < \rho$ and for an operator A on $\mathcal{H}$ with $\|A\| < \rho$, $f(A)$ will denote the operator defined by the usual Riesz-Dunford integral ([1], p. 568)

$$f(A) = \frac{1}{2\pi i}\int_{C} f(z)(zI - A)^{-1}\, dz ,$$

where I stands for the identity operator on $\mathcal{H}$, and C is a positively oriented simple closed rectifiable contour lying in the disk $|z| < \rho$ and encircling the spectrum of A. The limit used in defining the integral is taken in the norm topology (i.e., uniform topology) for operators.

In our recent paper [2], the classical Harnack's inequalities were extended to the following result for operators.

PROPOSITION 1. *Let* A *be an operator on* $\mathcal{H}$ *with* $\|A\| < 1$. *Let* n *be a positive integer. Let* g *be analytic on the open unit disk* $\Delta = \{z : |z| < 1\}$ *such that* $\operatorname{Re} g(z) > 0$ *for all* $z \in \Delta$, $g(0) = 1$, *and* $g'(0) =$

*The work on this paper was supported in part by a grant from the National Science Foundation.

$g''(0) = \cdots = g^{(n-1)}(0) = 0$ <u>in case</u> $n \geq 2$. <u>Then</u>

$$[I - g(A)^*][I - g(A)] \leq [I + g(A)^*]\, A^{n*}A^n[I + g(A)] \,, \tag{1}$$

$$\frac{1 - \|A^n\|}{1 + \|A^n\|} \leq \|g(A)\| \leq \frac{1 + \|A^n\|}{1 - \|A^n\|} \,. \tag{2}$$

<u>There is strict inequality in</u> (1) <u>if and only if</u> $A^{n*}A^n > 0$ <u>and</u> g <u>is not of the form</u>

$$g(z) = (1 + \eta z^n)(1 - \eta z^n)^{-1}$$

<u>for some constant</u> η <u>with</u> $|\eta| = 1$.

In the present note, we shall prove two other versions of Harnack's inequalities for operators.

2. THE FIRST ALTERNATIVE VERSION

The following lemma will be needed in our proof of Proposition 2.

LEMMA 1. <u>Let</u> A <u>be an operator on</u> $\mathcal{H}$ <u>with</u> $\|A\| < 1$, <u>and let</u> $0 < \rho < 1$. <u>Then the inequality</u>

$$\left\| (I + A)(I - A)^{-1} - \frac{1 + \rho^2}{1 - \rho^2} I \right\| \leq \frac{2\rho}{1 - \rho^2} \tag{3}$$

<u>holds if and only if</u> $\|A\| \leq \rho$.

<u>Proof</u>. Inequality (3) is equivalent to

$$\left[(I - A^*)^{-1}(I + A^*) - \frac{1 + \rho^2}{1 - \rho^2} I\right] \left[(I + A)(I - A)^{-1} - \frac{1 + \rho^2}{1 - \rho^2} I\right] \leq \frac{4\rho^2}{(1 - \rho^2)^2} I \,,$$

which may be written

$$(I + A^*)(I + A) + \left(\frac{1 + \rho^2}{1 - \rho^2}\right)^2 (I - A^*)(I - A) - \frac{1 + \rho^2}{1 - \rho^2} \{(I - A^*)(I + A) + (I + A^*)(I - A)\}$$

$$\leq \frac{4\rho^2}{(1 - \rho^2)^2} (I - A^*)(I - A) \,,$$

or

$$(1 - \rho^2)^2(I + A^*)(I + A) + (1 + \rho^2)^2(I - A^*)(I - A) - 2(1 + \rho^2)(1 - \rho^2)(I - A^*A)$$

$$\leq 4\rho^2(I - A^*)(I - A) \,.$$

The last inequality may be written

$$(1 - \rho^2)\{(I + A^*)(I + A) + (I - A^*)(I - A)\} \leq 2(1 + \rho^2)(I - A^*A) ,$$

or

$$(1 - \rho^2)(I + A^*A) \leq (1 + \rho^2)(I - A^*A) ,$$

which is the same as $A^*A \leq \rho^2 I$, i.e., $\|A\| \leq \rho$. Hence (3) is equivalent to $\|A\| \leq \rho$. □

PROPOSITION 2. <u>Let</u> A <u>be an operator on</u> $\mathcal{H}$ <u>with</u> $\|A\| < 1$, <u>and let</u> n <u>be a positive integer. Let</u> g <u>be analytic on the open unit disk</u> Δ <u>such that</u> $\mathrm{Re}\, g(z) > 0$ <u>on</u> Δ, $g(0) = 1$, <u>and</u> $g'(0) = g''(0) = \cdots = g^{(n-1)}(0) = 0$ <u>in case</u> $n \geq 2$. <u>Then</u>

$$\left\| g(A) - \frac{1 + \|A^n\|^2}{1 - \|A^n\|^2} I \right\| \leq \frac{2\|A^n\|}{1 - \|A^n\|^2} , \tag{4}$$

$$\frac{1 - \|A^n\|}{1 + \|A^n\|} I \leq \mathrm{Re}\, g(A) \leq \frac{1 + \|A^n\|}{1 - \|A^n\|} I , \tag{5}$$

$$- \frac{2\|A^n\|}{1 - \|A^n\|^2} I \leq \mathrm{Im}\, g(A) \leq \frac{2\|A^n\|}{1 - \|A^n\|^2} I . \tag{6}$$

<u>Proof</u>. Define f by

$$f(z) = \frac{g(z) - 1}{g(z) + 1} .$$

Then f is analytic on Δ, $f(\Delta) \subset \Delta$, and $f(0) = f'(0) = \cdots = f^{(n-1)}(0) = 0$. By an operator analogue of Schwarz's lemma ([2], Cor. 2), we have

$$\|f(A)\| \leq \|A^n\| .$$

By an application of Lemma 1, the last inequality implies

$$\left\| (I + f(A))(I - f(A))^{-1} - \frac{1 + \|A^n\|^2}{1 - \|A^n\|^2} I \right\| \leq \frac{2\|A^n\|}{1 - \|A^n\|^2} ,$$

which is precisely (4), since

$$g(z) = \frac{1 + f(z)}{1 - f(z)} \qquad \text{and} \qquad g(A) = (I + f(A))(I - f(A))^{-1} .$$

From (4) we derive

$$\pm \operatorname{Re}\left[g(A) - \frac{1 + \|A^n\|^2}{1 - \|A^n\|^2} I\right] \leq \left\|g(A) - \frac{1 + \|A^n\|^2}{1 - \|A^n\|^2} I\right\| \cdot I \leq \frac{2\|A^n\|}{1 - \|A^n\|^2} \cdot I ,$$

and therefore (5). Similarly, (6) is seen from

$$\pm \operatorname{Im} g(A) = \pm \operatorname{Im}\left[g(A) - \frac{1 + \|A^n\|^2}{1 - \|A^n\|^2} I\right] \leq \left\|g(A) - \frac{1 + \|A^n\|^2}{1 - \|A^n\|^2} I\right\| \cdot I \leq \frac{2\|A^n\|}{1 - \|A^n\|^2} I .$$

□

3. THE SECOND ALTERNATIVE VERSION

LEMMA 2. *Let* A *be an operator on* $\mathcal{H}$. *If* $\|A\| \leq \rho < 1$, *then*

$$\operatorname{Re} A(I - A)^{-1} \geq -\frac{\rho}{1 + \rho} I . \tag{7}$$

Equality occurs if and only if $A = -\rho I$.

Proof. As

$$\operatorname{Re} A(I - A)^{-1} = \frac{1}{2}(I - A^*)^{-1}\{(I - A^*)A + A^*(I - A)\}(I - A)^{-1}$$
$$= (I - A^*)^{-1}(\operatorname{Re} A - A^*A)(I - A)^{-1} ,$$

(7) is equivalent to

$$\operatorname{Re} A - A^*A \geq -\frac{\rho}{1 + \rho}(I - A^*)(I - A) ,$$

or

$$\rho I - A^*A + (1 - \rho) \operatorname{Re} A \geq 0 .$$

This last inequality may be written

$$(\rho^2 I - A^*A) + (1 - \rho)(\rho I + \operatorname{Re} A) \geq 0 . \tag{8}$$

Since $\|A\| \leq \rho < 1$, we have

$$\rho^2 I - A^*A \geq 0 , \qquad -\operatorname{Re} A \leq \|A\| I \leq \rho I ,$$

and therefore (8), which is equivalent to the desired inequality (7). Also, equality in (8) holds if and only if

$$\rho^2 I - A^*A = 0 \qquad \text{and} \qquad \rho I + \operatorname{Re} A = 0 .$$

In other words, equality in (7) occurs if and only if $A = -\rho I$. □

Part of the following result duplicates with (5).

PROPOSITION 3. *Let* f *be analytic on* $|z| < \rho$, *and let* β *be a real number such that*

$$\operatorname{Re} f(z) < \beta \quad \text{for} \quad |z| < \rho . \tag{9}$$

Then for every operator A *on* $\mathcal{H}$ *with* $\|A\| < \rho$, we have

$$\operatorname{Re} f(A) \leq \left\{\frac{\rho - \|A\|}{\rho + \|A\|} \operatorname{Re} f(0) + \frac{2\|A\|}{\rho + \|A\|} \beta\right\} \cdot I . \tag{10}$$

Equality in (10) *occurs if and only if either* $A = 0$; *or* A *and* f *are of the forms*

$$A = -\bar{\eta}\alpha I , \tag{11}$$

$$f(z) = \frac{\rho w_0 + (\bar{w}_0 - 2\beta)\eta z}{\rho - \eta z} , \tag{12}$$

with $|\eta| = 1$, $0 < \alpha < \rho$, *and* $\operatorname{Re} w_0 < \beta$.

Proof. Define φ on the open unit disk Δ by

$$\varphi(z) = f(0) + 2[\operatorname{Re} f(0) - \beta] \frac{z}{1 - z} .$$

Then φ is analytic and univalent on Δ. Using the fact that

$$|z| < 1 \iff 1 + 2 \operatorname{Re} \frac{z}{1 - z} > 0$$

and $\operatorname{Re} f(0) < \beta$, we infer that

$$|z| < 1 \iff \operatorname{Re} \varphi(z) < \beta .$$

Define g on Δ by

$$g(z) = \varphi^{-1} \circ f(\rho z) .$$

Then g is analytic on Δ, $g(\Delta) \subset \Delta$, and $g(0) = 0$. By the operator analogue of Schwarz's lemma ([2], Cor. 2), we have $\|g(B)\| \leq \|B\|$ for every operator B with $\|B\| < 1$, so

$$\|\varphi^{-1} \circ f(\rho B)\| \leq \|B\| \quad \text{for} \quad \|B\| < 1 ,$$

or

$$\|\varphi^{-1} \circ f(A)\| \leq \frac{\|A\|}{\rho} \quad \text{for} \quad \|A\| < \rho. \tag{13}$$

According to Lemma 2, we have

$$\operatorname{Re} C(I - C)^{-1} \geq - \frac{\|C\|}{1 + \|C\|} I \quad \text{for} \quad \|C\| < 1 .$$

Therefore,

$$\begin{aligned} \operatorname{Re} \varphi(C) &= [\operatorname{Re} f(0)] \cdot I + 2[\operatorname{Re} f(0) - \beta] \cdot \operatorname{Re} C(I - C)^{-1} \\ &\leq [\operatorname{Re} f(0)] \cdot I - 2[\operatorname{Re} f(0) - \beta] \frac{\|C\|}{1 + \|C\|} \cdot I \end{aligned} \tag{14}$$

holds for every operator C with $\|C\| < 1$.

Take $C = \varphi^{-1} \circ f(A)$ with $\|A\| < \rho$. Then

$$\|C\| \leq \frac{\|A\|}{\rho}$$

by (13), and therefore

$$\frac{\|C\|}{1 + \|C\|} \leq \frac{\|A\|}{\rho + \|A\|} . \tag{15}$$

As $\varphi(C) = f(A)$, the desired inequality (10) follows immediately from (14) and (15).

It remains to examine the case where equality occurs in (10). Clearly there is equality when $A = 0$. Suppose that equality in (10) holds for some operator $A \neq 0$ with $\|A\| < \rho$. Then we must have equality in (15), so $\|C\| = \|A\|/\rho$, i.e.,

$$\left\|g\left(\frac{A}{\rho}\right)\right\| = \left\|\varphi^{-1} \circ f(A)\right\| = \frac{\|A\|}{\rho} .$$

Since $A \neq 0$, this can happen only when g is of the form $g(z) = \eta z$ with some constant η of absolute value 1 ([2], Cor. 2). Then $f(\rho z) = \varphi \circ g(z) = \varphi(\eta z)$, or

$$f(z) = \varphi\left(\frac{\eta}{\rho} z\right) = f(0) + 2[\operatorname{Re} f(0) - \beta] \frac{\eta z}{\rho - \eta z} , \tag{16}$$

which is precisely (12) with $w_0 = f(0)$. From (16) we derive

$$\operatorname{Re} f(A) = [\operatorname{Re} f(0)] \cdot I + 2[\operatorname{Re} f(0) - \beta] \cdot \operatorname{Re} \eta A(\rho I - \eta A)^{-1} .$$

Comparing this with equality in (10), which can be written

$$\operatorname{Re} f(A) = [\operatorname{Re} f(0)] \cdot I - 2[\operatorname{Re} f(0) - \beta] \frac{\|A\|}{\rho + \|A\|} I ,$$

we obtain

$$\operatorname{Re} \eta A(\rho I - \eta A)^{-1} = - \frac{\|A\|}{\rho + \|A\|} I . \tag{17}$$

Since $\|A\| < \rho$, (17) implies $\eta A = -\|A\| \cdot I$ (by Lemma 2), so A must be of the form (11) with $0 < \alpha < \rho$. Thus, if equality in (10) holds for some $A \neq 0$ with $\|A\| < \rho$, then A and f must be of the forms (11), (12) with $|\eta| = 1$, $0 < \alpha < \rho$, and $\operatorname{Re} w_0 < \beta$. Conversely, the fact that equality in (10) holds for such A and f can also be easily verified. □

REFERENCES

1. N. Dunford and J.T. Schwartz, Linear Operators, Part I: General Theory, Interscience, New York (1958).

2. K. Fan, Analytic functions of a proper contraction, Math. Z. 160 (1978), 275-290.

GENERAL INEQUALITIES AND FIXED-POINT PROBLEMS

Marian Kwapisz
Institute of Mathematics
University of Gdansk
80-952 Gdansk
POLAND

ABSTRACT. The aim of the present paper is to give some general results on fixed-point problems in the setting of an abstract set equipped only with a rather simple mathematical structure.

1. INTRODUCTION

Many practical problems lead us to solving the fixed-point problem $x = f(x)$, where the set X and the mapping $f : X \to X$ are given. The fixed-point problem is a purely set-theoretic problem. Unfortunately, the tools of set theory are often not satisfactory to solve these problems effectively. In view of this, we accordingly need to introduce into X some mathematical structure which makes us able to solve the problem efficiently. We note that sometimes the structure mentioned does not have to be particularly rich.

The general idea of this paper is close to the ideas which in particular cases can be found in [4], [9], [11], [12] (see also [1]-[3], [5]-[8]). We note that there exists a rather extensive bibliography of the problem under consideration, but it is not the purpose of the present paper to give a review of the literature of this problem.

I. INEQUALITIES AND FIXED POINTS IN PARTIALLY ORDERED SETS

2. SETS WITH CONVERGENT DECREASING SEQUENCES

Let us first introduce an assumption.

ASSUMPTION (A_1). Assume that:

(i) $(P, \leq)$ is a partially ordered set.

(ii) For some decreasing sequences $\{u_n\}$, $u_n \in P$, $u_{n+1} \leq u_n$, $n \in N = \{0,1,\dots\}$, there exist uniquely defined elements called their limits; we write this

$$u = \lim_{n \to \infty} u_n \quad \text{or} \quad u_n \searrow u .$$

(iii) The limit has the properties:

(a) $\lim_{n\to\infty} u_{n+k} = \lim_{n\to\infty} u_n$, $k \in N$;

(b) if $u_n = u$, $u_n, u \in P$, $n \in N$ then $u_n \searrow u$;

(c) if $u_n \leq v_n$, $u_n, v_n \in P$, $n \in N$ and $u_n \searrow u$, $v_n \searrow v$, then $u \leq v$.

Let the mapping $\phi : P \to P$ be given. We say it is <u>isotone</u> if and only if

$$u \leq v \Rightarrow \phi(u) \geq \phi(v) ,$$

and we say it is <u>continuous</u> if and only if always

$$u_n \searrow u \Rightarrow \phi(u_n) \searrow \phi(u) .$$

By ϕ^n we denote the n-th iterate of ϕ, that is,

$$\phi^0(u) = u, \quad \phi^{n+1}(u) = \phi(\phi^n(u)) .$$

Now we can formulate a first result.

THEOREM 1. *If*

(i) *Assumption* (A_1) *holds*,

(ii) *the continuous mapping* ϕ *is isotone*,

(iii) *there exists* $u_0 \in P$ *such that* $\phi(u_0) \leq u_0$,

(iv) $\{\phi^n(u_0)\}$ *converges*,

then there exists at least one fixed point of ϕ, *say* u^*,

$$\phi^n(u_0) \searrow u^* ,$$

and u^* *is maximal in the set*

$$\{u \mid u \leq u_0, \ u \leq \phi(u), \ u \in P\} .$$

Proof. By assumptions, there exists u^* such that

$$\phi^n(u_0) \searrow u^* .$$

By the continuity of ϕ and by the relation

$$\phi^{n+1}(u_0) = \phi(\phi^n(u_0)) ,$$

we infer that u^* is a fixed point of ϕ. To prove the last part of the assertion, take

$$p \in P , \quad p \leq u_0 , \quad \text{and} \quad p \leq \phi(p) .$$

By induction, we find

$$p \leq \phi^n(u_0), \quad n \in N .$$

Now letting $n \to \infty$, we get $p \leq u^*$. To finish the proof, it is sufficient to observe that obviously

$$u^* \in \{u \leq u_0, \ u \leq \phi(u), \ u \in P\} . \quad \square$$

REMARK 1. Good models for P satisfying (A_1) are (with usual partial order and convergence):

R^m -- m-dimensional euclidean space,

$C(\Omega,R^m)$ -- the space of all R^m-valued continuous functions defined on a compact set Ω,

$L(\Omega,R^m)$ -- the space of all R^m-valued Lebesgue integrable functions,

$C_0(\Omega,R^m)$ -- the space of all R^m-valued upper semicontinuous functions (with pointwise convergence).

REMARK 2. Sometimes it may happen that all decreasing sequences in P are convergent. This occurs, for instance, if we take for P some subsets of the spaces mentioned in Remark 1. Thus it takes place for R^m_+ ($u \in R^m_+$ if and only if $u \geq 0$), $L(\Omega,R^m_+)$, and $C_0(\Omega,R^m_+)$ (with pointwise convergence) but not for $C(\Omega,R^m_+)$ (with uniform convergence).

REMARK 3. The convergence of $\{\phi^n(u_0)\}$ assumed in Theorem 1 obviously takes place if all decreasing sequences in P converge.

REMARK 4. In Theorem 1, instead of assumption (iv) we can use the stronger one: The mapping ϕ transforms any decreasing sequence into a convergent one.

3. SETS WITH CONVERGENT INCREASING SEQUENCES

Let us now consider the case when in the set P the convergence of increasing sequences is assumed.

ASSUMPTION (A_2). We assume that (A_1) holds with the change of the word "decreasing" to "increasing" and the symbol "$\searrow$" to "$\nearrow$".

We have now the following result.

THEOREM 2. *If*

(i) *Assumption* (A_2) *holds*,

(ii) *the continuous mapping* Φ *is isotone*,

(iii) *there exists* $v_0 \in P$ *such that* $\Phi(v_0) \geq v_0$,

(iv) *the sequence* $\{\Phi^n(v_0)\}$ *converges*,

then there exists at least one fixed point of Φ, *say* v^*,

$$\Phi^n(v_0) \nearrow v^* ,$$

and v^* *is minimal in the set*

$$\{v \mid v \geq v_0, \quad v \geq \Phi(v), \quad v \in P\} .$$

The proof of this theorem is quite similar to that of Theorem 1. □

As a simple consequence of Theorems 1 and 2 we get:

THEOREM 3. *If*

(i) *both assumptions* (A_1) *and* (A_2) *are satisfied*,

(ii) *the continuous (with respect to both convergences) mapping* Φ *is isotone*,

(iii) *there exist elements* $u_0, v_0 \in P$ *such that* $v_0 \leq u_0$ *and*

$$\Phi(u_0) \leq u_0 , \qquad v_0 \leq \Phi(v_0) ,$$

(iv) *the sequences* $\{\Phi^n(u_0)\}$, $\{\Phi^n(v_0)\}$ *converge*,

then there exist, in the interval $[v_0, u_0]$, *minimal and maximal fixed points* v^* *and* u^* *of the mapping* Φ, *respectively*

$$\Phi^n(v_0) \nearrow v^0 , \qquad \Phi^n(u_0) \searrow u^* ,$$

and

$$v_0 \leq \phi^n(v_0) \leq \phi^{n+1}(v_0) \leq v^* \leq u^* \leq \phi^{n+1}(u_0) \leq \phi^n(u_0) \leq u_0 , \qquad n \in N .$$

<u>Moreover if</u> $p, s \in [v_0, u_0]$ <u>and</u>

$$p \leq \phi(p) , \qquad s \geq \phi(s) ,$$

<u>then</u>

$$v_0 \leq p \leq u^* , \qquad v^* \leq s \leq u_0 .$$

<u>Finally if in addition</u> $u^* = v^* = \tilde{u}$, <u>then</u>

$$v_0 \leq p \leq \tilde{u} \leq s \leq u_0 .$$

REMARK 5. By Theorems 1, 2, and 3, we find a way of solving the inequalities $p \leq \phi(p)$ and $s \geq \phi(s)$.

REMARK 6. In applications of the results mentioned above, the difficulty is to find elements u_0 and v_0 having the properties needed. This difficulty can be avoided if in P there exist minimal and the maximal elements, say 0 and 1, respectively. In this case we can take $u_0 = 1$ and $v_0 = 0$.

4. DEPENDENCE OF MAXIMAL FIXED POINT ON ϕ AND u_0.

Let us now consider the dependence of the maximal fixed point of ϕ (defined in Theorem 1) on ϕ and u_0. We denote this point by $u^*(\phi, u_0)$.

THEOREM 4. <u>If</u>

(i) <u>assumption</u> (A_1) <u>holds</u>,

(ii) <u>the mappings</u> $\phi, \psi : P \to P$ <u>are continuous and isotone</u>,

(iii) $\phi(u) \leq \psi(u)$, $u \in P$,

(iv) <u>there exist</u> $u_0, u_0' \in P$, $u_0 \leq u_0'$, <u>such that</u>

$$\phi(u_0) \leq u_0 , \qquad \psi(u_0') \leq u_0' ,$$

(v) <u>the sequences</u> $\{\phi^n(u_0)\}$, $\{\psi^n(u_0')\}$ <u>converge</u>,

<u>then</u>

$$u^*(\phi, u_0) \leq u^*(\psi, u_0') .$$

The proof of Theorem 4 is very simple. We note also that the same result holds for the minimal fixed point of Φ. □

II. COMPARISON RESULTS FOR FIXED-POINT PROBLEM

5. THE COMPARISON METHOD

In the previous part of this paper, we have discussed inequalities and fixed-point problems in partially ordered spaces. They are naturally related with isotone mappings. Now we ask: What can be said of the fixed-point problem if the mapping is not isotone or if it is defined in a space without any ordering relation? In answering this question, we are going to use the comparison method.

The general idea of the comparison method (see [4], [9], [12]) lies in the following proceeding: The basic space in which a fixed-point equation is discussed, say X, is metrized by elements of some partially ordered groupoid, say G, equipped in some convergence relation of decreasing sequences. Next the basic fixed-point equation is in some way compared with an auxiliary fixed-point equation discussed in G. Now if the last equation is "good," then the fixed-point result for the basic equation is established.

6. ASSUMPTIONS

Let $(G \leq , \searrow , + , 0)$ be the space defined by the following:

ASSUMPTION (A_3). Suppose that

(i) G is partially ordered with minimal element 0.

(ii) In G, convergence (denoted by $\searrow$) having the properties listed in (A_1) is defined.

(iii) There is defined the binary relation : "+" : $G \times G \to G$ having the properties

(a) $u + v = v + u, \quad u + 0 = u,$

(b) $u \leq v \Rightarrow u + w \leq v + w,$

(c) $u + v \leq w \Rightarrow u \leq w,$

(iv) For any sequences $\{u_n\}, \{v_n\} \subset G,$

$$u_n \searrow u, \quad v_n \searrow v \Rightarrow u_n + v_n \searrow u + v .$$

REMARK 7. Note that we do not assume that necessarily all decreasing sequences in G are convergent. This makes the essential distinction of our exposition from those which can be found in [12], [7] and [6].

Let us now introduce the main space $(X, \to, r)$:

ASSUMPTION (A_4). X is an abstract space such that:

(i) For some sequences $\{x_n\}$, $x_n \in X$, $n \in N$, the limit is uniquely determined; we write

$$x = \lim_{n\to\infty} x_n \quad \text{or} \quad x_n \to x, \quad x \in X.$$

(ii) The limit has the properties

(a) $\lim_{k\to\infty} x_{n+k} = \lim_{k\to\infty} x_k$, $n \in N$,

(b) $(x_n = s \in X,\ n \in N) \Rightarrow x_n \to s$.

(iii) The mapping $r : X \times X \to G$ is defined and it has the properties

(a) $r(x,y) = 0 \iff x = y$,

(b) $r(x,y) \le r(x,z) + r(y,z)$, $x,y,z \in X$.

(iv) For any $x^* \in X$, $b \in G$, the ball

$$S(x^*,b) = \{x \mid x \in X,\ r(x,x^*) \le b\}$$

is closed (with respect to the convergence postulated in (i)).

(v) The space X is complete; that is, if for a given $\{x_n\} \subset X$ there exists a sequence $\{c_n\} \subset G$ such that

$$c_n \searrow 0 \quad \text{and} \quad r(x_n, x_{n+p}) \le c_n, \qquad n,p \in N,$$

then the sequence $\{x_n\}$ converges to some $x \in X$.

7. LOCAL COMPARISON FIXED-POINT RESULTS

Now we are in position to formulate a local comparison fixed-point result.

THEOREM 5. Assume:

(i) G and X are defined by assumptions (A_3) and (A_4).

(ii) $f : S(x_0,b) \to S(x_0,b) \subset X$, $x_0 \in X$, $b \in G$.

(iii) There exists a continuous and isotone mapping $a : [0,b] \to [0,b]$, $[0,b] \subset G$, such that

(a) $\{a^n(b)\}$ converges,

(b) $(u \in [0,b],\ u = a(u)) \Rightarrow u = 0$,

(c) for any $x,y \in S(x_0,b)$, $r(x,y) \leq b$,

$$r(f(x),f(y)) \leq a(r(x,y)) .$$

Under these assumptions, there exists in $S(x_0,b)$ a unique fixed point $\bar{x}$ of the mapping f,

$$f^n(x_0) \to \bar{x} , \quad \text{and} \quad r(\bar{x},f^n(x_0)) \leq a^n(b) .$$

Proof. From (ii) it follows that $r(x_0,x_p) \leq b$, $p \in N$. Now by induction we find that

$$r(x_{n+p},x_n) \leq a^n(b) , \quad n,p \in N .$$

By (iii), (a)-(b), we find that $a^n(b) \searrow 0$. This implies that $\{x_n\}$ converges to some $\bar{x}$. It is obviously the fixed point of f. If there exists another fixed point of f, say $\tilde{x}$, then we easily find the evaluation

$$r(\tilde{x},f^n(x_0)) \leq a^n(b) , \quad n \in N ,$$

and this implies $\bar{x} = \tilde{x}$. The error evaluation we infer by the fact that balls are closed in X. □

REMARK 8. If instead of the condition (ii) we have only $f : S(x_0,b) \to X$, then the assertion of Theorem 5 holds if there exists an isotone mapping $A : [0,b] \to G$ and

$$r(f(x_0),f(x)) \leq A(r(x_0,x)) , \qquad x \in S(x_0,b) ,$$

$$q + A(b) \leq b , \qquad q \geq r(x_0,f(x_0))$$

for some $q \in G$.

REMARK 9. It is clear that Theorem 5 is a generalization of the well-known Banach contraction mapping principle.

8. GLOBAL FIXED-POINT RESULTS

In this section, we shall formulate some global fixed-point results. The first of these is based on a lemma concerned with inequalities, and the second one needs the use of the chainability of the space X (see [10]).

LEMMA. Assume:

(i) G is defined by (A_3).

(ii) The continuous and isotone mapping $\varphi : G \to G$ has the property that for any decreasing sequence $\{w_n\} \subset G$ the sequence $\{\varphi(w_n)\}$ converges to some element of G.

(iii) For any $q \in G$, there exists the globally maximal solution $m(\varphi,q)$ of the equation $u = \varphi(u) + q$.

(iv) $p \in G$ and $p \leq \varphi(p) + q$.

Under these assumptions, we have $p \leq m(\varphi,q)$. Moreover, if γ has the property (ii) and $\gamma(u) \leq \varphi(u)$, $u \in G$, then the global maximal solution of the equation $u = \gamma(u) + q$ exists for any $q \in G$, and $m(\gamma,q) \leq m(\varphi,q)$.

Proof. Let u_0 be the global maximal solution of the equation $u = \varphi(u) + (q + p)$. Put

$$u_{n+1} = \varphi(u_n) + q , \qquad n \in N .$$

By induction, we find that

$$u_{n+1} \leq u_n , \quad p \leq u_n , \qquad n \in N .$$

In view of (ii), we see that $\{\varphi(u_n)\}$ converges. This implies that $\{u_n\}$ also converges, say $u_n \searrow \bar{u}$. Obviously, $\bar{u}$ is the solution of the equation $u = \varphi(u) + q$, and $p \leq \bar{u}$. Because $\bar{u} \leq m(\varphi,q)$, the first part of the assertion is proved.

Put

$$v_{n+1} = \gamma(v_n) + q , \qquad v_0 = m(\varphi,q) .$$

Because $v_0 \geq \gamma(v_0) + q$, we see that the sequence $\{v_n\}$ converges to some $\bar{v}$. Obviously $\bar{v}$ is a solution of the equation $v = \gamma(v) + q$, and $\bar{v} \leq m(\varphi,q)$.

For any solution s of the last equation, we have

$$s = \gamma(s) + q \leq \varphi(s) + q .$$

Hence by the first part of the Lemma we get $s \leq m(\varphi,q)$. Now by induction we find that $s \leq v_n$; but this implies $s \leq \bar{v}$. This means that $\bar{v}$ is the globally maximal solution, that is, $\bar{v} = m(\gamma,q)$. □

Now we can formulate:

THEOREM 6. *Suppose*:

(i) G *and* X *are defined by assumptions* (A_3) *and* (A_4).

(ii) $f : X \to X$.

(iii) *There exists a continuous and isotone mapping* $a : G \to G$ *with the property that for any decreasing sequence* $\{w_n\} \subset G$ *the sequence* $\{a(w_n)\}$ *converges to some element of* G.

(iv) *For any* $q \in G$, *there exists the globally maximal solution* $m(a,q)$ *of the equation* $u = a(u) + q$, $m(a,0) = 0$.

(v) *For any* $x,y \in X$,

$$r(f(x),f(y)) \leq a(r(x,y)) .$$

Under these assumptions, there exists in X *a unique fixed point of* f, *say* $\bar{x}$, $f^n(x_0) \to \bar{x}$, *for any fixed* $x_0 \in X$. *Moreover*

$$r(\bar{x},f^n(x_0)) \leq a^n(b) ,$$

where

$$b = m(a,q_0) , \quad q_0 = r(x_0,f(x_0)) .$$

Proof. Let $x_0 \in X$ be given. Suppose that x' is any fixed point of the mapping f. We have

$$r(x',x_0) \leq r(f(x'),f(x_0)) + r(x_0,f(x_0)) \leq a(r(x',x_0)) + q_0 .$$

Now in view of the Lemma, we get

$$r(x',x_0) \leq m(a,q_0) = b .$$

This means that all fixed points of f lie in $S(x_0,b)$. By the same Lemma, it is easy to check that $f(S(x_0,b)) \subset S(x_0,b)$. Now the assertion is implied by Theorem 5. □

REMARK 10. If we assume that for the space G defined by (A_3), (A_2) also holds and the mapping a has the property that for any increasing sequence $\{v_n\} \subset G$ the sequence $\{a(v_n)\}$ converges, then we have the evaluation

$$r(\bar{x},x_0) \leq \nu(a,q_0) ,$$

with

$$\nu(a,q_0) = \lim_{n\to\infty} v_n , \quad \text{where} \quad v_{n+1} = a(v_n) + q_0 , \quad v_0 = 0 .$$

Obviously $\nu(a,q_0)$ is the minimal solution of the equation

$$v = a(v) + q_0 .$$

The assertion is implied by the inequality

$$r(f^n(x_0),x_0) \leq v_n \leq \nu(a,q_0) , \quad n \in N ,$$

which can be obtained by induction.

We have another global result:

THEOREM 7. Assume

(i) G and X are defined by assumptions (A_3) and (A_4).

(ii) $f : X \to X$, $x^* \in X$ are given.

(iii) There exists a continuous and isotone mapping $a : [0,b] \to [0,b]$ such that

- (a) $\{a^n(b)\}$ converges,
- (b) $a(b) + q \leq b$, $q \geq r(x^*,f(x^*))$,
- (c) $(u \in [0,b],\ u = a(u)) \Rightarrow u = 0$,
- (d) for any $x,y \in X$, $r(x,y) \leq b$,

$$r(f(x),f(y)) \leq a(r(x,y)) .$$

(iv) X is b-chainable; that is, for any $x,y \in X$ there exists a finite set of elements of X, say $\{z_1,\ldots,z_m\}$, where m may depend on x,y, such that

$$z_1 = x , \quad z_m = y , \quad \text{and} \quad r(z_i,z_{i+1}) \leq b , \quad i = 1,2,3,\ldots,m-1 .$$

Under these assumptions, there exists in X a unique fixed point of f, say $\bar{x}$,

$$f^n(x_0) \to \bar{x} , \quad \text{for any} \quad x_0 \in X .$$

Moreover,

$$r(\bar{x},f^n(x_0)) \le m\cdot a^n(b) \;, \qquad n \in N \;,$$

where by $m\cdot a^n(b)$ *we mean* $\sum_{i=1}^{m} a^n(b)$, $m(x_0,x^*) \in N$.

Proof. By the assumptions, we see in view of Theorem 5 that in $S(x^*,b)$ there exists a unique fixed point of f. Now we prove the convergence of

$$\{f^n(x_0)\} \quad \text{to} \quad \bar{x} \;.$$

This will imply the uniqueness in the whole space X. By the b-chainability of X, there exists a chain

$$\{y_1,y_2,\dots,y_m\} \;, \qquad m(x_0,x^*) \in N \;,$$

such that $y_1 = x^*$, $y_m = x_0$ and

$$r(y_i,y_{i+1}) \le b \;, \qquad i = 1,2,\dots,m-1 \;.$$

By induction, we find that

$$r(f^n(y_i),f^n(y_{i+1})) \le a^n(b) \;, \qquad i = 1,\dots,m-1, \qquad n \in N \;.$$

Now we have

$$r(\bar{x},f^n(x_0)) \le r(\bar{x},f^n(y_1)) + \sum_{s=1}^{m-1} r(f^n(y_s),f^n(y_{s+1})) \le m\cdot a^n(b) \;.$$

This means that $f^n(x_0) \to \bar{x}$. Thus the proof is completed. □

REFERENCES

1. Z.B. Caliuk, On the convergence of the successive approximations (Russian), *Trud. Semin. Teor. Diff. Urav. s. Otklon. Argumentom*, Univ. Družby Naradov, Moskva 7 (1969), 67-74.

2. J. Eisenfeld, V. Lakshmikantham, Comparison principle and nonlinear contractions in abstract spaces, *J. Math. Anal. Appl.* 49 (1975), 504-511.

3. S. Heikkilä, S. Seikkala, On the estimation of successive approximations in abstract spaces, *J. Math. Anal. Appl.* 58 (1977), 378-383.

4. L. Kantorovich, The method of successive approximations for functional equations, *Acta Mat.* 71 (1939), 63-97.

5. M.A. Krasnosielski, G.M. Vainikko, P.P. Zabreiko, I.B. Rutickii, V.I. Stecenko, On the approximate solutions of operator equations, (Russian), Izdat. "Nauka," Moskva, 1969.

6. N.S. Kurpiel, Projection-iterative methods for solving of operator equations (Russian), Izdat. "Naukova Damka," Kiev, 1968 (see also Transl. Math. Monogr. vol. 46, AMS, Providence, R.I., 1976).

7. M. Kwapisz, On the approximate solution of an abstract equation, Ann. Polon. Math. XIX (1967), 47-60.

8. M. Kwapisz, On the convergence of approximate iterations for an abstract equation, Ann. Polon. Math. XXII (1969), 73-87.

9. J. Schröder, Das Interationsverfahren bei allgemeinerem Abstrandsbegriff, Math. Zeitschr. 66 (1956), 111-116.

10. S. Seikkala, On the method of successive approximations for nonlinear equations in spaces of continuous functions, preprint No. 16, 1978, Dept. Appl. Math. and Statistics, University of Oulu, Finland.

11. A. Tarski, A lattice-theoretical fixed point theorem and its applications, Pacif. J. Math. 5 (1955), 285-309.

12. T. Ważewski, Sur un procéde de prouver la convergance des approximations successive sans utilisation des séries de comparaison, Bull. Acad. Polon. Sci. Sér. Sci. Math. Astr. et Phys. 8 (1960), 54-52.

Geometric and Topological Inequalities

Lorenzenhof, 1946

Left part of the semicircular terrace opening out from the entrance, or reception hall, toward the south. Often used for colloquia

EINE GEOMETRISCHE UNGLEICHUNG UND IHRE ANWENDUNG*

D. Milman
Department of Mathematical Sciences
Tel-Aviv University
Tel-Aviv
ISRAEL

ABSTRACT. The central set of a domain in R_3 is here defined, and the determination of the domain by its central set is discussed.

1. EINFUHRUNG

Sei G ein beschränktes Gebiet in R_3, ∂G -- sein Rand -- eine differenzierbare Fläche mit stetiger äusserer Normale $n(y)$, $|n(y)| = 1$, $y \in \partial G$, und $\overline{G} = G \cup \partial G$. Wir bezeichnen $C(G)$ die Menge der Zentren aller maximalen Kugeln in $\overline{G}$, und nennen $C(G)$ -- die Zentrale Menge des Gebietes $\overline{G}$.

Sei $y \in \partial G$, z -- das Zentrum, und R -- der Radius, einer maximalen Kugel in $\overline{G}$, welche den Rand ∂G in Punkt "y" tangiert. Dann sind "z" und "R" eindeutige Funktionen von $y \in \partial G$: $z = \psi(y)$, $R = R(y)$; im Fall $R(y) = 0$ ist $\psi(y) = y$.

Sei $x \in \overline{G}$ und sei $\rho(x)$, $y(x)$ -- die Entfernung von x zu ∂G bzw. die Punkte in welchem $\rho(x)$ erreicht wird; $y(x)$ ist nicht immer eindeutig bestimmt.

2. RESULTATE

Wir beweisen hier:

SATZ 1. Die Funktion $\rho(x)$ ist differenzierbar in folgendem Sinn:

$$\text{Wenn}\{x_n\}_0^\infty \subset G \ , \quad \lim_{n\to\infty} |x_n - x_0| = 0 \ , \quad x_n \neq x_0 \ , \quad \lim_{n\to\infty} \frac{x_n - x_0}{|x_n - x_0|} = e \ ,$$

und die Werte y_n von $y(x_n)$ so gewählt sind dass

$$\lim_{n\to\infty} |y_n - y_0| = 0 \ ,$$

* Nach Vorbereitung dieses Artikels wurde ich informiert, dass ein Begriff änlich zu "Der zentrale Menge des Gebiets," unter dem Name "Skeleton," ist schon in der "Pattern recognition theory" eingeführt, aber die Resultaten meines Artikels sind nicht bewusst.

<u>dann existiert</u>

$$\lim_{n\to\infty} \frac{\rho(x_n) - \rho(x_0)}{|x_n - x_0|} ;$$

<u>diese Grenze ist</u> $-n(y_0)\cdot e$. <u>Für die Punkte</u> $x_0 \in G\setminus C(G)$ <u>ist die Funktion</u> $y(x)$ <u>eindeutig und stetig,</u>* $\rho'(x_0)$ <u>existiert in gewöhnlichem Sinn, und</u> $\rho'(x_0) = -n(y_0)$.

Wir erhalten diesen Satz auf Grund der folgenden geometrischen Ungleichung:

LEMMA 1. <u>Sei</u>

$$x, x_1 \in G , \quad x_1 \neq x , \quad h = |x_1 - x| , \quad e = \frac{x_1 - x}{h} , \quad y \in y(x) ,$$
$$z = \psi(y) , \quad \cos\alpha = n(y)\cdot e .$$

<u>Falls</u> $h < \rho(x)$, <u>dann</u>

$$\text{(1)} \quad \frac{-h \sin^2\alpha}{|x_1-x| + |x-z| + h\cos\alpha} \leq \frac{\rho(x_1) - \rho(x)}{h} + \cos\alpha \leq \frac{h \sin^2\alpha}{|x_1-y| + |x-y| - h\cos\alpha} .$$

BEMERKUNG. Sei in Lemma 1

$$0 < h < \min[\rho(x), \rho(x_1)] , \quad y_1 \in y(x_1) , \quad e' = \frac{x - x_1}{h} , \quad \cos\alpha' = n(y_1)\cdot e' .$$

Wir vertauschen x und x_1 und benützen die rechte Seite der Ungleichung (1). Dann folgt von Lemma 1

$$\text{(1')} \quad \begin{aligned} -[n(y_1)-n(y)]\cdot\frac{x_1 - x}{h} - \frac{h \sin^2\alpha'}{|x-y_1| + \rho(x_1) - h\cos\alpha} &\leq \frac{\rho(x_1) - \rho(x)}{h} + \cos\alpha \\ &\leq \frac{h \sin^2\alpha}{|x_1-y| + \rho(x) - h\cos\alpha} . \end{aligned}$$

** Im folgendem Sinn: Wenn

$$\lim_{m\to\infty} |x_m - x_0| = 0 \quad \text{und} \quad y_m \in y(x_m) , \quad m = 0,1,\cdots ,$$

dann ist

$$\lim_{m\to\infty} |y_m - y_0| = 0 .$$

(Im Fall

$$\{x_m\}_{m=1}^{\infty} \subset C(G)$$

wissen wir nicht, a priori, folgt von $\lim_{m\to\infty} |x_m - x_0| = 0$, dass $x_0 \in C(G)$, oder nicht.)

Sei ausserdem G ε-offen, dass heisst: G ist eine Vereinigung von Kugeln des Radius ε. Dann, zu jedem Punkt $y \in \partial G$ gibt es eine (einzige) Kugel von Radius "ε", welche zu $\overline{G}$ gehört und den Rand ∂G in Punkt "y" tangiert. Deshalb, gibt es auch eine (einzige) maximale Kugel in $\overline{G}$, welche den Rand ∂G in "y" tangiert. Dabei ist $R(y) = |\psi(y) - y| > 0$ und somit $C(G) \subset G$; wir bemerken dass der Interval $(y,\psi(y))$ enthält keine Punkte von $C(G)$. Es ist klar, dass $\psi(y)$ ∂G auf $C(G)$ abbildet und

$$\psi(y) = y - R(y)n(y) , \qquad y \in \partial G .$$

Jedem Gebiet entspricht eine bestimmte Funktion $\psi(y)$, und wir nennen sie "die zentrale Funktion des Gebietsrandes." Für $z \in C(T)$ wird $\hat{R}(z)$ den Radius der maximaler Kugel in $\overline{G}$ mit Zentrum "z" bezeichnen.

SATZ 2. Hier ist ∂G wie in Satz 1.

(i) Sei $\{z(t)\}_{0\leq t\leq 1} \subset C(G)$ eine stetig differenzierbare Funktion. Dann: für stetige Kurven $\{y(t)\}_{0\leq t\leq 1} \subset \partial G$ mit $\psi[y(t)] \equiv z(t)$, ist der Winkel $\alpha(t)$, wo

$$n[y(t)]\cdot z'(t) = |z'(t)| \cos \alpha(t) , \qquad 0 \leq \alpha(t) \leq \pi ,$$

von der Wahl der Kurve $\{y(t)\}_{0\leq t\leq 1}$ unabhängig,*

(2) $\hat{R}[z(t)] = \hat{R}(z_0) + \int_{t_0}^{t} |z'(t)| \cos\alpha(t)\,dt$, wo $z_0 = z(t_0)$, $0 \leq t \leq 1$,

und die Enveloppe der Familie der Sphären $\{S[z(t),\hat{R}[z(t)]]\}_{0\leq t\leq 1}$, die Linien $\{y(t)\}_{0\leq t\leq 1}$ enthält. Im Fall $C(G) = \{z(t)\}_{0\leq t\leq 1}$ kann man $\overline{G}$ erkennen wenn $C(G)$, $\{\alpha(t)\}_{0\leq t\leq 1}$, und $\hat{R}(z_0)$ gegeben sind, namlich: man bekommt $\hat{R}(z(t))$ von (2), und $\partial\overline{G}$ ist die Enveloppe der Familie der Sphären $\{S[z(t),\hat{R}(z(t))]\}_{0\leq t\leq 1}$.

(ii) Sei $U \subset \partial G$ eine Fläche welche die Funktion $\psi(y)$ homeomorph auf einer glatten Fläche V $(V \subset C(G))$ abbildet. Dann ist $\hat{R}(z)$ im gewöhn-

---

* Im Wesentlichen, das heisst für $z'(t) \neq 0$. Anders: Wenn

$$\psi[y(t)] \equiv z(t) \ \psi[\tilde{y}(t)]$$

und $\pi[y(t)]$, $\pi[\tilde{y}(t)]$ die Tangentenebene in $y(t)$, $\tilde{y}(t)$, bzw., bezeichnet, dann ist $z'(t)$ parallel zu der bissektorialer Ebene zwischen $\pi[y(t)]$ und $\pi[\tilde{y}(t)]$; kurz: $C(G)$ ist bissektorial zu ∂G in den ubereinstimmenden Punkten.

<u>lichen Sinn differenzierbar</u>, $\hat{R}'(z) = -n(y)$, <u>wo</u> $z = \psi(y)$, <u>und die Umkehrungsfunktion</u> $\varphi(z)$ <u>der Restriktion</u> $\psi_u(y)$ <u>von</u> $\psi(y)$ <u>auf</u> "U" <u>ist</u>

$$\varphi(z) = z - \hat{R}(z)\,\hat{R}'(z)\ , \qquad z \in V\ .$$

Weiter unten geben wir die Beweise dieser Resultate.

An anderer Stelle, wird unter der Bedingung dass ∂G stetige Hauptskrümmungen hat, die topologische Struktur der Menge $C(G)$ gegeben ($C(G)$ ist ein Deformationsretrakt von $\overline{G}$; insbesondere ist $C(G)$ immer zusammenhangend), und auch die differenziale Eigenschaften der Funktion $\psi(y)$. Insbesondere, wenn der Ausdruck

$$\left\{\frac{|\psi(y) - \psi(y_0)|}{|y - y_0|}\right\}_{y \neq y_0}$$

beschränkt ist, dann kann man (i) des Satz 2, im Fall $C(G) = \{z(t)\}_{0 \leq t \leq 1}$, so ergänzen

$$k[y(t)] = \frac{1}{\hat{R}[z(t)]}\ , \qquad \lambda[y(t)] = \frac{1 - |z'(t)|\ \sin\alpha(t)}{\hat{R}[z(t)]}\ , \qquad 0 \leq t \leq 1\ ,$$

wo $k(y)$ und $\lambda(y) \leq k(y)$ bezeichnen die Hauptkrümmungen der Fläche ∂G im Punkt $y \in \partial G$.

3. DIE BEWEISE

<u>Beweis der Lemma 1</u>. Aus $h < \rho(x)$ folgt

$$|x_1 - z| \leq |x_1 - x| + |x - z| < \rho(x) + |x - z|\ ,$$

und weil $\rho(x) = |y - x|$, $|y - x| + |x - z| = R(y)$ folgt

$$|x_1 - z| < R(y)\ .$$

Die Kugel mit Zentrum x_1 und Radius $R(y) - |x_1 - z|$ ist enthalten in der Kugel $B(z,R(y))$ mit Zentrum z und Radius $R(y)$, und darum gehört zu $\overline{G}$. Deswegen ist

$$R(y) - |x_1 - z| \leq \rho(x_1) \leq |x_1 - y|\ . \tag{3}$$

Es ist klar $z \neq y$. Sei x_1 nicht auf der Gerade welche "y" und "z" enthält. In der Ebene welche y, z, x_1 enthält, wählen wir die Koordinat

Achsen ξ, η mit "y" als Nullpunkt, so, dass die Achse ξ die Punkte "z" und "y" enthält, von "z" zu "y" gerichtet ist, für $\eta(x_1) > 0$. Dann

$$|\rho(x) + \xi(x_1)| = \sqrt{h^2 - \eta(x_1)^2} ,$$

und damit haben wir zwei Fälle:

$$\rho(x) + \xi(x_1) = -\sqrt{h^2 - \eta(x_1)^2} , \qquad \cos\alpha = -\frac{\sqrt{h^2 - \eta(x)^2}}{h} ,$$

und

$$\rho(x) + \xi(x_1) = \sqrt{h^2 - \eta(x_1)^2} , \qquad \cos\alpha = \frac{\sqrt{h^2 - \eta(x_1)^2}}{h} ,$$

und respektive zu diesen Fällen, nach (3),

$$\frac{R(y) - |x_1 - z| + \xi(x_1) + \sqrt{h^2 - \eta(x_1)^2}}{h} \leq \frac{\rho(x_1) - \rho(x)}{h} \leq \frac{|x_1 - y| - |x - y|}{h} ,$$

und

$$\frac{R(y) - |x_1 - z| + \xi(x_1) - \sqrt{h^2 - \eta(x_1)^2}}{h} \leq \frac{\rho(x_1) - \rho(x)}{h} \leq \frac{|x_1 - y| - |x - y|}{h} .$$

In beiden Fällen bekommen wir

$$(4) \qquad \frac{R(y) - |x_1 - z| + \xi(x_1)}{h} \leq \frac{\rho(x_1) - \rho(x)}{h} + \cos\alpha \leq \frac{|x_1 - y| - |x - y|}{h} + \cos\alpha .$$

Transformiren wir

$$\frac{R(y) - |x_1 - z| + \xi(x_1)}{h} = -\frac{|x_1 - z|^2 - [R(y) - |\xi(x_1)|]^2}{h[|x_1 - z| + R(y) - |\xi(x_1)|]}$$

$$= -\frac{\eta(x_1)^2}{h[|x_1 - z| + R(y) - |\xi(x_1)|]} = \frac{-h\sin^2\alpha}{|x_1 - z| + |x - z| + h\cos\alpha} ,$$

$$\frac{|x_1 - y| - |x - y|}{h} + \cos\alpha = \frac{|x_1 - y| + \xi(x_1)}{h} = \frac{\eta(x_1)^2}{h[|x_1 - y| + |\xi(x_1)|]}$$

$$= \frac{h\sin^2\alpha}{|x_1 - y| + \rho(x) - h\cos\alpha} ,$$

dann erhalten wir von (4) die Formel (1) der Lemma. □

<u>Beweis des Satzes 1</u>. Wir nehmen in (1') x_0 anstatt x, x_k anstatt x_1, und y_k anstatt y_1, $y_k \in y(x_k)$, wo

$$\{x_k\}_{k=0}^{\infty} , \qquad \{y_k\}_{k=0}^{\infty} ,$$

respektive der Forderungen von Satz 1 genommen sind. Dann haben wir anstatt (1'),

$$-[n(y_k) - n(y_0)] \frac{x_k - x_0}{h_k} - \frac{h_k \sin^2\alpha_k'}{|x_0 - y_k| + \rho(x_k) - h_k \cos\alpha_k'} \leq \frac{\rho(x_k) - \rho(x_0)}{h_k} + \cos\alpha_k$$

$$(1^k) \qquad \leq \frac{h_k \sin^2\alpha_k}{|x_k - y_0| + \rho(x_0) - h_k \cos\alpha_k} ,$$

$$\text{wo} \quad h_k = |x_k - x_0| , \quad \cos\alpha_k = n(y_0)\cdot\frac{x_k - x_0}{h_k} , \quad \cos\alpha_k' = n(y_k)\cdot\frac{x_0 - x_k}{h_k} ,$$

$$k = 1,2,\ldots$$

und $0 < h_k < \min[\rho(x_0),\rho(x_k)]$. Aber es ist klar dass $\rho(x)$ ist stetig und somit

$$\lim_{m\to\infty} \rho(x_m) = \rho(x_0) > 0 , \qquad \lim_{k\to\infty} \min[\rho(x_0),\rho(x_k)] = \rho(x_0) > 0 .$$

Deswegen können wir wählen $h_k < \min[\rho(x_0),\rho(x_k)]$ und (1^k) ist erfüllt für grosse "k". Aus

$$\lim_{k\to\infty} \frac{x_k - x_0}{|x_k - x_0|} = e$$

folgt

$$\lim_{k\to\infty} \cos\alpha_k = n(y_0)\cdot e ,$$

und weil die Normale $n(y)$ stetig ist, haben wir

$$\lim_{k\to\infty} [n(y_k) - n(y_0)] \frac{x_k - x_0}{h_k} = 0 .$$

Weil

$$\lim_{k\to\infty} [|x_0 - y_k| + \rho(x_k)] = 2\rho(x_0) > 0 , \qquad \lim_{k\to\infty} [|x_k - y_0|) + \rho(x_0)] = 2\rho(x_0) > 0 ,$$

bekommen wir von (1^k) für $k\to\infty$:

$$\lim_{k\to\infty} \frac{\rho(x_k) - \rho(x_0)}{h_k} = -n(y_0)\cdot e .$$

Es bleibt zu ergänzen unser Resultat im Fall $x_0 \in G\setminus C(G)$.

In diesem Fall ist die Kugel $B(x_0,\rho(x_0))$ in $\overline{G}$ nicht maximal und ihre Grenze $S(x_0,\rho(x_0))$ enthält einen Punkt $y_0 \in \partial G$. Die maximale Kugel in $\overline{G}$ welche $B(x_0,\rho(x_0))$ enthält, enthält auch y_0 an ihrer Grenze. Deswegen enthält $S(x_0,\rho(x_0))$ nur einen Punkt "y_0" des Randes ∂G. So, für

$x_0 \in G \setminus C(G)$ ist $y(x_0)$ eindeutig. Sei

$$x_n \neq x_0 \in G \setminus C(G), \quad \lim_{n\to\infty} |x_n - x_0| = 0, \quad y_n \text{ ein Wert von } y(x_n), \quad \tilde{y} = \lim y_n .$$

Weil

$$\rho(x_n) = |x_n - y_n| , \qquad \lim_{n\to\infty} |x_n - x_0| = 0$$

haben wir

$$|x_0 - \tilde{y}| = \lim_{n\to\infty} |x_n - y_n| = \lim_{n\to\infty} \rho(x_n)$$

und somit

$$|x_0 - \tilde{y}| = \rho(x_0) = |x_0 - y_0| .$$

Weil $y(x_0)$ eindeutig ist, haben wir $\tilde{y} = y_0$. Somit ist bewiesen

$$\lim_{n\to\infty} |y_n - y_0| = 0 ,$$

das heisst $y(x)$ ist stetig in $G \setminus C(G)$. Das ergibt von (1^k)

$$\rho_e'(x_0) = -n(y_0) \cdot e$$

für jedes "e"; somit ist $\rho'(x_0) = -n(y_0)$. Die Interlineare Bemerkung im Satz 1 ist auch begründet. □

<u>Beweis des Satzes 2</u>. (i) Wenn eine Folge $\{t_m\} \subset [0,1]$ existiert so dass

$$\lim_{n\to\infty} t_m = t \quad \text{und} \quad z(t_m) \neq z(t) ,$$

dann kann man annehmen, dass

$$e(t) = \lim_{m\to\infty} \frac{z(t_m) - z(t)}{|z(t_m) - z(t)|}$$

existiert; wenn solch eine Folge $\{t_m\}$ nicht existiert, dann gibt es eine Umgebung von t in welcher $z(t)$ und $\hat{R}[z(t)]$ sind beide konstant und somit ist

$$\hat{R}[z(t)]_t' = 0 = -n[y(t)] \cdot z'(t) .$$

Weil

$$\lim_{m\to\infty} y(t_m) = y(t) ,$$

können wir im ersten Fall dem Satz 1 benützen: $\hat{R}(z)$ ist eine Restriction von $\rho(x)$ auf $C(G)$ und somit haben wir, dass

$$\lim_{m\to\infty} \frac{\hat{R}[z(t_m)] - \hat{R}[z(t)]}{|z(t_m) - z(t)|} = -n[y(t)] \cdot e(t) \; ;$$

von

$$\lim_{m\to\infty} \frac{z(t_m) - z(t)}{t_m - t} = z'(t)$$

folgt

$$\lim_{t_m \downarrow t} \frac{\hat{R}[z(t_m)] - \hat{R}[z(t)]}{t_m - t} = -n[y(t)] \cdot e(t) \; |z'(t)| \; ;$$

im Fall wenn $z'(t) \neq 0$, ist $z'(t) = |z'(t)| \; e(t)$.

Es ist klar dass die letzte Grenzgleichung ist richtig für jede Folge $\{t_m\}_{m=1}^{\infty}$ (obwohl, wenn $z'(t) = 0$, kann $e(t)$ verschiedene Werte für verschiedene Folgen annehmen). Somit haben wir bewiesen, dass

$$R[z(t)]' = -n[y(t)]z'(t) \; , \qquad 0 \leq t \leq 1 \; .$$

Wenn $z'(t) \neq 0$, dann bestimmen wir

$$\cos \alpha(t) = n[y(t)] \cdot e(t) \; ,$$

und wir setzen

$$|z'(t)| \cos \alpha(t) = n[y(t)] \; z'(t) \; , \qquad 0 \leq t \leq 1 \; .$$

Von der Gleichung

$$\hat{R}[z(t)]_t' = |z'(t)| \cos \alpha(t) \; , \qquad 0 \leq t \leq 1 \, , \tag{2'}$$

folgt (2). Wenn wir eine andere stetige Kurve

$$\{\hat{y}(t)\}_{0 \leq t \leq 1} \subset \partial G \qquad \text{mit} \qquad \psi[\hat{y}(t)] \equiv z(t)$$

nehmen, dann bekommen wir dieselbe $\hat{R}[z(t)]_t'$ und für $z'(t) \neq 0$ -- dieselbe $\alpha(t)$.

Weil

$$|y(t) - z(t)| = \hat{R}[z(t)] \qquad \text{für} \qquad z(t) = \psi[y(t)] \; ,$$

sehen wir $y(t) \in \partial G \cap S[z(t),\hat{R}[z(t)]]$. Deswegen liegt $\{y(t)\}_{0 \leq t \leq 1}$ auf der Enveloppe der Familie der Sphären $\{S[z(t), \hat{R}[z(t)]]\}_{0 \leq t \leq 1}$. Die Vereinigung aller maximalen Kugeln in $\overline{G}$ ist $\overline{G}$. Deswegen ist im Fall, wenn $C(G) = \{z(t)\}_{0 \leq t \leq 1}$, die obengenante Enveloppe mit $\partial\overline{G}$ identisch.

(ii) Sei $\pi(z_0)$ die Tangentenebene zu $C(G)$ im Punkt $z_0 \in V$, z_0 -- der Anfangspunkt in $\pi(z_0)$, und $e \in \pi(z_0)$. Dann gibt es auf V eine differenzierbare Kurve $\{z(t)\}_{0\leq t\leq 1}$ mit $z(0) = z_0$ und $z'(0) = e$. Weil $\psi(y)$ bildet U auf V homeomorph ab, gibt es (eindeutig) eine stetige Kurve $\{y(t)\}_{0\leq t\leq 1} \subset U$, so dass $\psi[y(t)] \equiv z(t)$; das gibt uns die Gleichung

$$R[z(t)]'_t = -n[y(t)] \cdot z'(t) \ , \ ^*$$

insbesondere:

$$\hat{R}(z(t))'_{t=0} = -n(y_0)\cdot e \ ,$$

wo $y_0 = y(0)$. Weil "e" ist willkürlich in $\pi(z_0)$, haben wir $\hat{R}'(z_0) = -n(y_0)$, $\psi(y_0) = z_0$.

Damit ist bewiesen, dass $\hat{R}'(z)$ im gewöhnlichen Sinn existiert und

$$\hat{R}'(z) = -n(y) \ , \quad \text{wo} \quad z = \psi(y) \ , \quad z \in V \ , \ y \in U \ .$$

Dabei, von $z = y - \hat{R}(z)n(y)$ folgt

$$y = z - \hat{R}(z)\,\hat{R}'(z) \ , \qquad z \in V \ , \quad y \in U \ . \quad \square$$

4. BEMERKUNGEN

(i) In (i) des Satzes 2, sei $t_0 \in (0,1)$, $z'(t_0) \neq 0$, und $t_1 \to t_0$. Dann ist die Grenzlage von

$$S[z(t_0),\hat{R}[z(t_0)]] \cap S[z(t_1),\hat{R}[z(t_1)]] \ .$$

eine Kreislinie $K(t_0)$ mit Zentrum

$$z(t_0) + R[z(t_0)] \cos \alpha(t_0)\cdot e(t_0)$$

und Radius

$$\hat{R}[z(t_0)] \sin \alpha(t_0) \ ,$$

derer Ebene zu $z'(t_0)$ orthogonal ist. Dabei ist

$$y(t_0) \in K(t_0) \subset S[z(t_0),\hat{R}[z(t_0)]] \subset \overline{G} \ .$$

(ii) In (i) des Satzes 2, sei U eine Umgebung von $z(t_0)$ und $U \cap C(G) \subset \{z(t)\}_{0<t<1}$. Dann ist $K(t_0) \subset C(G)$.

---

* Diese Gleichung bekommen wir ohne der Forderung dass $z'(t)$ stetig ist.

Die Bemerkung (i) ist klar. Für dem Beweis den Bemerkung (ii) nehmen wir $\varepsilon > 0$, so dass

$$0 < t_0 - \varepsilon, \quad t_0 + \varepsilon < 1 \quad \text{und} \quad \{z(t)\}_{t_0-\varepsilon \leq t \leq t_0} \subset U ,$$

und bemerken, dass die Menge

$$\overline{G}_\varepsilon = \bigcup_{t_0-\varepsilon \leq t \leq t_0+\varepsilon} B[z(t),\hat{R}[z(t)]]$$

ein kompaktes Gebiet ist. Ausserdem ist

$$C(\overline{G}_\varepsilon) = \{z(t)\}_{t_0-\varepsilon \leq t \leq t_0+\varepsilon} ,$$

und $K(t_0)$ ist dasselbe wie vorher. Somit ist die Enveloppe der Familie der Sphären $\{S[z(t),\hat{R}[z(t)]]\}_{t_0-\varepsilon \leq t \leq t_0+\varepsilon}$ mit $\partial\overline{G}_\varepsilon$ identisch, und $K(T_0) \subset \partial\overline{G}_\varepsilon \cap \overline{G} \subset \partial G$. □

(iii) Wir haben vorher bemerkt, dass wenn ∂G stetige Hauptkrümmungen hat, dann ist $C(G)$ zusammenhängend. Deswegen folgt aus Bemerkung (ii), dass wenn ∂G Kreislinien nicht enthält, dann muss $C(G)$ in jedem Punkt zweidimensional sein.

(iv) Am Schluss bemerken wir, dass die erbrachte Resultate eine natürliche Verallgemeinerung zulassen, für Gebiete in R_n, wenn $n > 3$.

A STURM-LIOUVILLE INEQUALITY WITH APPLICATIONS TO AN ISOPERIMETRIC INEQUALITY FOR VOLUME IN TERMS OF INJECTIVITY RADIUS, AND TO WIEDERSEHEN MANIFOLDS

Marcel Berger
Laboratoire associé au C.N.R.S. n° 212
Université Paris VII
75005 Paris
FRANCE

Jerry L. Kazdan
Department of Mathematics
University of Pennsylvania
Philadelphia, Pennsylvania 19104
U.S.A.

ABSTRACT. We prove an inequality for Sturm-Liouville systems and apply it to obtain an isoperimetric inequality for the volume of a Riemannian manifold in terms of its injectivity radius. This is used to prove that Blaschke's Wiedersehen manifolds are standard spheres.

1. INTRODUCTION

Around 1920 Blaschke (see [8]) introduced the concept of a Wiedersehenfläche. Intuitively, it is a surface M in $\mathbb{R}^3$ such that if, starting at any point x on M, one moves a distance π along any geodesic, then all of the geodesics meet again at some point x'. The obvious example for M is the standard unit sphere, in which case x' is the antipode of x. A more precise definition of a Wiedersehenfläche is that M is a complete Riemannian manifold such that the "cut locus" of every point x is one point x'. Blaschke conjectured that, in fact, the standard sphere is the only Wiedersehenfläche. This was finally proved by L.W. Green [9] in 1962 (who, in fact, just took M to be any two-dimensional Riemannian manifold, not necessarily embedded in $\mathbb{R}^3$).

One can immediately generalize the problem to higher dimensions, and speak of Wiedersehen manifolds. Our main result (see [3, 10]) is this:

THEOREM A. *The only n-dimensional Wiedersehen manifold is the standard sphere.*

Before going further, we note that there are other generalizations that are still unresolved (see [6, p. 143]). For these, one calls (M,g) a "Blaschke manifold" if for each point x the cut point in any direction occurs at distance π from x; the conjecture is that the only possibilities are the rank-one symmetric spaces with their canonical metrics.

There are two key steps in proving Theorem A. The first step is an isoperimetric inequality. Let (M,g) denote an n-dimensional complete Riemannian manifold with metric g, and let (S^n,can) be S^n with its canonical metric.

THEOREM B. (M. Berger [3] and J.L. Kazdan [10]). *If* (M^n,g) *is a Wiedersehen manifold, then*

$$\mathrm{Vol}(M^n,g) \geq \mathrm{Vol}(S^n,\mathrm{can}) , \tag{1}$$

with equality if and only if (M^n,g) *is* (S^n,can).

The second step uses a topological argument.

THEOREM C. (A. Weinstein [11] (see also [6]) and C.T. Yang [12]). *If* (M^n,g) *is a Wiedersehen manifold, then*

$$\mathrm{Vol}(M^n,g) = \mathrm{Vol}(S^n,\mathrm{can}) .$$

Thus, Wiedersehen manifolds at least have the conjectured volume. Theorem C follows from a more general result concerning the volume of manifolds all of whose geodesics are closed and have length 2π. (Note that Zoll has exhibited many smooth metrics on S^2 with this last property; see [6], Chapter 4.) Weinstein showed that

$$\mathrm{Vol}(M^n,g) = j\ \mathrm{Vol}(S^n,\mathrm{can}) ,$$

where j is an integer. That $j = 1$ was proved for even n by Weinstein and for odd n by Yang.

Theorem A is now obvious, since by Theorem C the equality case of Theorem B is all that can occur.

In this paper we shall sketch the proof of Theorem B. The key new geometric idea is an averaging of solutions of a Sturm-Liouville system, which we carry out in Section 2. In Section 3, we prove an inequality for Sturm-Liouville systems. This is applied in Section 4 to prove both an isoperimetric inequality for volume and, as a special case, Theorem B above. Section 5 contains some applications of these ideas and some open questions.

2. THE AVERAGE VOLUME OF A BALL

If (M,g) is a complete n-dimensional Riemannian manifold, let $B_\pi(x)$ denote the ball centered at x and having radius π. If the manifold is very small in some direction -- as a cylinder of small radius -- then this ball may overlap itself. The technical way one avoids this is to assume the "injectivity radius" at x is at least π. Then the ball $B_\pi(x)$ is a genuine differentiable ball. Since we shall want this for all x in M, we assume the injectivity radius is at least π for all x.

We need a formula for $\mathrm{Vol}(B_\pi(x))$. Introduce polar coordinates (r,u) on the tangent space, TM_x, at x, where r is the distance from x, and where the angular variable u is on the unit sphere in TM_x (we denote this sphere by UM_x). In this tangent space, let the vectors $Y_j(r)$, $j = 2,\dots,n$, denote the solutions of the Sturm-Liouville problem (= the Jacobi equation)

(2) $$Y_j'' + RY_j = 0 \;, \qquad Y_j(0) = 0 \;, \qquad Y_j'(0) = e_j \;,$$

where $e_1,\dots,e_n$ are orthonormal unit vectors in TM_x with $e_1 = u$, and where R is the curvature of (M,g). The desired formula (see [7], p. 256) is

(3) $$\mathrm{Vol}(B_\pi(x)) = \int_{UM_x}\int_0^\pi f(u,r;x)\,dr\,d\sigma_x \;,$$

where $d\sigma_x$ is the element of "area" on UM_x, and where

(4) $$f(u,r;x) = \det(Y_2(r),\dots,Y_n(r)) \;.$$

For example, on $(\mathbb{R}^n, \mathrm{can})$, we have

$$f(u,r) = r^{n-1} \;,$$

while on (S^n,can) we have

$$f(u,r) = \sin^{n-1} r \;,$$

just as expected. Integrating (3) over M, we obtain a formula for the average volume of the ball of radius π,

$$\begin{aligned}\overline{\mathrm{Vol}}(B_\pi) &= V^{-1}\int_M \mathrm{Vol}(B_\pi(x))\,dx \\ &= V^{-1}\int_{UM}\int_0^\pi f(u,r;x)\,dr\,d\mu \;,\end{aligned}$$

where $d\mu$ is the element of volume on the unit tangent sphere bundle UM, and where $V = \mathrm{Vol}(M,g)$.

More mysteriously, we average (5) once again. By Liouville's theorem on invariance of $d\mu$ under geodesic flow $u \mapsto \xi^s(u)$ of the vector u for a distance s along the geodesic, we can rewrite (5) as

$$\overline{\mathrm{Vol}}(B_\pi) = V^{-1} \int_{UM} \int_0^\pi f(\xi^s(u),r;x)\, dr\, d\mu ,$$

so we can average with respect to s for $0 \leq s \leq \pi$ to obtain

$$\overline{\mathrm{Vol}}(B_\pi) = (\pi V)^{-1} \int_{UM} \int_0^\pi \left(\int_0^\pi f(\xi^s(u),r;x)\, dr \right) ds\, d\mu . \tag{6}$$

In view of (2), let the $(n-1) \times (n-1)$ matrix $A(t;s)$ denote the solution of

$$A'' + RA = 0 , \quad A(s;s) = 0 , \quad \text{and} \quad A'(s;s) = I , \tag{7}$$

where $' = d/dt$, and where I is the identity. Then

$$f(\xi^s(u),r;x) = \det A(s+r\,;\,s) . \tag{8}$$

Our goal is to find a sharp lower bound on the right-hand side of (6), since this will give a lower bound on $\mathrm{Vol}(M,g)$.

3. AN INEQUALITY FOR STURM-LIOUVILLE SYSTEMS

At this stage one could, in principle, ignore the geometric origin of the problem; however, the geometry supplies vital hints. We use the notation from (7) above, except that one can allow $R(t)$ to be any self-adjoint matrix. The geometric assumption that the injectivity radius of (M,g) is at least π implies that the matrix solution $A(r;t)$ is invertible, i.e., has no conjugate points for $0 < r < \pi$ and for all t. For convenience, let $N = n - 1$ and $A(r) = A(r;0)$.

MAIN INEQUALITY. <u>Let</u> $R = R^*$, <u>and let</u> A <u>be a solution of</u> (7). <u>If</u> A <u>has no conjugate points for</u> $0 < t,s < \pi$, <u>then for any continuous functions</u> $m(r) \geq 0$, $g(r) \geq 0$ $(\not\equiv 0)$ <u>such that</u>

$$m(\pi - r) = m(r) \quad \underline{\text{and}} \quad g(\pi - r) = g(r) ,$$

<u>we have</u>

$$\int_0^{\pi}\int_r^{\pi} [\det A(t;r)]\, m(t-r)\, dt\, dr$$

(9)

$$\geq \frac{\left[\int_0^{\pi}\int_r^{\pi} \sin(t-r) g^{N-1}(t-r) m(t-r) dt\, dr\right]^N}{\left[\int_0^{\pi}\int_r^{\pi} g^N(t-r) m(t-r) dt\, dr\right]^{N-1}} ,$$

with equality if and only if both

(10) $g(t) = \sin t$ and $R(t) = I$ (i.e., $A(t;r) = \sin(t-r)I$) .

REMARK. For the special choice $g(r) = \sin r$, (9) is a striking inequality for Sturm-Liouville systems:

(11) $$\int_0^{\pi}\int_r^{\pi} [\det A(t;r)] m(t-r) dt\, dr \geq \int_0^{\pi}\int_r^{\pi} \sin^N(t-r) m(t-r) dt\, dr .$$

Since

$$A(t;r) = \sin(t-r)$$

in the general case when $R = I$, this compares the solution of (7) with the special case $R = I$.

We sketch the proof of this inequality in a sequence of steps.

LEMMA 1. We have

(a) $A^*(t)A'(t) = A'^*(t)A(t)$

and

(b) $$A(t;r) = A(t)\int_r^t [A^*(s)A(s)]^{-1}\, ds\, A^*(r) .$$

Proof. (a) Since $R^* = R$, we have $(A^*A' - A'^*A)' = 0$, so

$$A^*A' - A'^*A = \text{const} = 0 .$$

(b) Since $A(t)$ is a solution of (7), we use "reduction of order" to find $A(t;r)$. Thus let

$$A(t;r) = A(t)C(t;r) .$$

Substitute this into (7) to find that $(A^*AC')' = 0$. Integrating twice and solving for C yields the result. □

LEMMA 2. (Jensen's Inequality). If $F(B)$ is a convex real-valued function defined on the convex set of positive-definite matrices, then for any positive measure μ we have

$$F\left[\mu(\Omega)^{-1}\int_\Omega B(s)\, d\mu(s)\right] \le \mu(\Omega)^{-1}\int_\Omega F(B(s))\, d\mu(s) ,$$

with equality if and only if $B(s)$ is a constant matrix.

COROLLARY. Let $\varphi(t) = [\det A(t)]^{1/N}$. Then

$$[\det A(t;r)]^{1/N} \ge \varphi(t)\varphi(r)\int_r^t \varphi^{-2}(s)\, ds ,$$

with equality if and only if $A(t) = \varphi(t)I$.

Proof. By a computation, $F(B) = (\det B)^{-1}$ is convex on positive definite matrices. Let

$$B(s) = [A^*(s)A(s)]^{-1}\,\varphi^2(s) \quad \text{and} \quad d\mu = \varphi^{-2}(s)\, ds .$$

Then by Lemma 2 we have

$$(12)\qquad \det\int_r^t [A^*(s)A(s)]^{-1}\, ds \ge \mu(\Omega)^N = \left[\int_x^y \varphi(s)^{-2}\, ds\right]^N ,$$

which, together with Lemma 1(b), gives the desired inequality. Equality occurs only if B is a constant matrix. But, by using Lemma 1(a), this is equivalent to

$$0 = (B^{-1})' = 2(A^*/\varphi)(A/\varphi)' .$$

Thus, equality occurs if and only if

$$A(s)/\varphi(s) = \text{constant matrix} .$$

Evaluating this at $s = 0$ shows that equality occurs only when $A = \varphi I$. □

In view of this Corollary, it is natural to apply Hölder's inequality to the left-hand side of (9), with measure $d\nu = m(t-r)dt\, dr$, to find that

$$(13)\qquad \int_0^\pi\int_r^\pi \det A(t;r)\, d\nu \ge \frac{\left[\int_0^\pi\int_r^\pi [\det A(t;r)]^{1/N} g^{N-1}(t-r)\, d\nu\right]^N}{\left[\int_0^\pi\int_r^\pi g^N(t-r)\, d\nu\right]^{N-1}} ,$$

where the weight $g \geq 0$ $(\not\equiv 0)$ is arbitrary, and where equality occurs only if

$$g(t-r)^N = \det A(t;r) .$$

Together with the Corollary, this shows that

$$(14) \qquad \int_0^\pi \int_r^\pi [\det A(t;r)] m(t-r)\, dt\, dr \geq \frac{G^N(\varphi)}{\left[\int_0^\pi \left(\int_r^\pi g^N(t-r) m(t-r) dt\right) dr\right]^{N-1}} ,$$

where

$$(15) \qquad G(\varphi) = \int_0^\pi \left[\int_r^\pi \left(\int_r^t \frac{\varphi(r)\varphi(t)}{\varphi^2(s)} \rho(t-r)\, ds\right) dt\right] dr ,$$

and where $\rho = g^{N-1} m$. Equality occurs in (14) only if both

$$g(t-r)^N = \det A(t;r) \quad \text{and} \quad A(t) = \varphi(t) I .$$

To obtain (14), we could have used any nonnegative functions $m(t,r)$ and $g(t,r)$. The special form $m = m(t-r)$ is not used until the next (and last) lemma.

Let $S \subset C[0,\pi]$ be the subset of positive continuous functions having zeros of order at most 1 at $t = 0$ and π, so if $f \in S$ then

$$f(t) = t^\alpha (\pi - t)^\beta h(t)$$

for some continuous $h > 0$ on $[0,\pi]$ with $0 \leq \alpha, \beta \leq 1$ (all we actually use is $-1 < \alpha, \beta < 2$). Notice that if

$$\varphi(t) = [\det A(t)]^{1/N} ,$$

as above, then $\varphi \in S$ since A has no conjugate points for $0 < t < \pi$. Comparing (14) with (9) shows that all we need in order to complete the proof of the Main Inequality is the following lower bound on the functional G.

LEMMA 3. <u>If</u> $\rho \in C[0,\pi]$ <u>is a given nonnegative function</u> $(\not\equiv 0)$ <u>satisfying</u> $\rho(\pi - t) = \rho(t)$, <u>then for any</u> $\psi \in S$ <u>we have</u>

$$(16) \qquad G(\psi) \geq G(\sin) ,$$

<u>with equality if and only if</u> $\psi(t) = c \sin t$, <u>where</u> $c > 0$ <u>is a constant</u>.

Proof. If $\psi \in S$, the quotient appearing in (15) and the expected case of equality lead us to write ψ as

$$\psi(t) = \sin t \, \exp u(t)$$

for some $u \in C(0,\pi)$, which is possibly singular at $t = 0$ or π. Then

$$G(\psi) = J(u) = \int_\Omega \exp[u(r) + u(t) - 2u(s)] \, d\mu ,$$

where $\Omega \subset \mathbb{R}^3$ is the region of integration in (15), and where

$$d\mu = \frac{\sin r \sin t}{\sin^2 s} \rho(t-r) \, ds \, dt \, dr .$$

Inequality (16) then reads $J(u) \geq J(0)$, with equality if and only if u is a constant. But by Jensen's inequality applied to exp, we have

$$J(u) \geq \mu(\Omega) \exp[\mu(\Omega)^{-1} K(u)] = J(0) \exp[\mu(\Omega)^{-1} K(u)] ,$$

where K is the linear functional

$$K(u) = \int_\Omega [u(r) + u(t) - 2u(s)] \, d\mu .$$

The proof is completed by showing that $K(u) = 0$ for all u. In fact, $K(u) = 0$ for all u if and only if

$$\rho(\pi - t) = \rho(t) .$$

To prove this, one manipulates K to rewrite the integral as

$$K(u) = \int_0^\pi u(t) f(t) \sin^{-2} t \, dt ,$$

where $f \in C^2[0,\pi]$ satisfies $f(0) = 0$, $f'(\pi/2) = 0$, and

$$[\sin^{-2} t \, f'(t)]' = \sin^{-2} t [\sin^3 t(\rho(t) - \rho(\pi - t))]' .$$

If $\rho(t) = \rho(\pi - t)$, then clearly $f = 0$ and hence $K = 0$. Conversely, if $f = 0$ then $\rho(t) = \rho(\pi - t) = \text{const}$. Evaluating this at $t = \pi/2$, we find that $K = 0$ implies the symmetry condition on ρ. □

4. AN ISOPERIMETRIC INEQUALITY FOR VOLUME

We begin by substituting (8) into (6) and then splitting the integral into two parts:

(17) $$\overline{\mathrm{Vol}}(B_\pi) = (\pi V)^{-1}\int_{UM}\int_0^\pi\left(\int_0^{\pi-s} + \int_{\pi-s}^{\pi}\right)\det A(s+r;s)\,dr\,ds\,d\mu = I_1 + I_2 .$$

Making the change of variable $t = s + r$ in I_1, we obtain

(18) $$I_1 = (\pi V)^{-1}\int_{UM}\int_0^\pi\left(\int_s^\pi \det A(t;s)\,dt\right)ds\,d\mu .$$

Therefore, by the Main Inequality (11) in the special case $m = 1$, $g(t) = \sin t$, we find (recall $N = n - 1$) that

$$I_1 \geq (\pi V)^{-1}\int_{UM}\int_0^\pi\left(\int_0^\pi \sin^{n-1}(t-s)\,dt\right)ds\,d\mu .$$

But

$$\int_0^\pi\int_s^\pi \sin^{n-1}(t-s)\,dt\,ds = \pi\omega_n/2\omega_{n-1} ,$$

where ω_k is the volume of (S^k,can), and where

$$\int_{UM} d\mu = \omega_{n-1} V .$$

Consequently, we have

$$I_1 \geq \frac{1}{2}\omega_n .$$

Because $I_2 > 0$, we have proved that

(19) $$\overline{\mathrm{Vol}}(B_\pi) \geq \frac{1}{2}\mathrm{Vol}(S^n,\mathrm{can}) + I_2 > \frac{1}{2}\mathrm{Vol}(S^n,\mathrm{can}) .$$

This assumes the injectivity radius is at least π. Scaling the metric, we obtain this result:

ISOPERIMETRIC INEQUALITY. If (M,g) is an n-dimensional complete Riemannian manifold of finite volume with injectivity radius at least ρ, then

(20) $$\mathrm{Vol}(M,g) \geq \overline{\mathrm{Vol}}(B_\rho) > \frac{1}{2}\frac{\rho^n}{\pi^n}\mathrm{Vol}(S^n,\mathrm{can}) .$$

Since $\mathrm{Vol}(M,g) \geq \overline{\mathrm{Vol}}(B_\rho)$ (in fact these are equal on a Wiedersehen manifold), to prove Theorem B from (19), we only need the observation that on a Wiedersehen manifold one can prove that $I_1 = I_2$ in (17). This proves inequality (1). In addition, the Main Inequality states that equality occurs in (1) if and only if the curvature R satisfies $R = I$, which implies that

$$(M,g) = (S^n,\text{can})$$

and completes the proof of Theorem B. □

5. OTHER APPLICATIONS AND QUESTIONS

Two immediate questions spring to mind. First, can one improve the constant 1/2 in our Isoperimetric Inequality? This will require an estimate for the integral I_2. In particular, one suspects that the correct inequality is

$$\text{Vol}(M,g) \geq \overline{\text{Vol}}(B_\rho) \geq \text{Vol}(S^n,\text{can}) ,$$

with equality only for (S^n,can). Berger [1] has proved the special result

$$\text{Vol}(M,g) \geq \text{Vol}(S^2,\text{can})$$

if $\dim M = 2$.

Next, can one obtain an estimate for the volume of any ball, not just the average ball? One wants a constant $c > 0$ such that

$$\text{Vol}(B_\rho) \geq c\, \rho^n\, \text{Vol}(S^n,\text{can}) ,$$

provided the manifold (M,g) has injectivity radius at least ρ. The cases $n \leq 3$ were treated by Berger in [2].

The inequalities and ideas of this paper have been used by Berger [4] to obtain some information on the general Blaschke conjecture mentioned in the Introduction. He proves the analogue of Theorem B under an additional totally geodesic assumption. This work requires the general version (9) of our Main Inequality, rather than the special case of (11) with $m = 1$ which sufficed here.

Berger [5] has also used this method to obtain an upper bound for the first eigenvalue of the Laplacian for the Dirichlet problem of a disc in (M,g) in terms of the injectivity radius. The idea is to use our inequalities to estimate the Rayleigh quotient.

Work on this article by the second author was supported in part by N.S.F. Grant MCS77-02167.

REFERENCES

1. Marcel Berger, Some relations between volume, injectivity radius, and convexity radius in Riemannian manifolds, in Differential Geometry and Relativity, D. Reidel, 1976.

2. Marcel Berger, Volume et rayon d'injectivité dans les variétés riemanniannes de dimension 3, Osaka J. Math. 14 (1977), 191-200.

3. Marcel Berger, Blaschke's conjecture for spheres, Appendix D in the book [6] by A. Besse.

4. Marcel Berger, Sur certaines variétés à géodésiques toutes fermées, Boletin da Sociedade Brasileira de Matematica 9 (1978).

5. Marcel Berger, Une inégalité universelle pour la première valeur propre du laplacien, Bull. Soc. Math. France 107 (1979), 1-7.

6. A. Besse, Manifolds All of Whose Geodesics are Closed, Ergebnisse der Mathematik No. 93, Springer-Verlag, Berlin, 1978.

7. R. Bishop and R. Crittenden, Geometry of Manifolds, Academic Press, New York, 1964.

8. W. Blaschke, Vorlesungen über Differentialgeometrie, 3rd Edition, Springer-Verlag, Berlin, 1930.

9. L.W. Green, Auf Wiedersehenflächen, Annals of Math. 78 (1963), 289-299,

10. J.L. Kazdan, An inequality arising in geometry, Appendix E in the book [6] by A. Besse.

11. A. Weinstein, On the volume of manifolds all of whose geodesics are closed, J. Diff. Geom. 9 (1974), 513-517.

12. C.T. Yang, Odd dimensional Wiedersehen manifolds are spheres, J. Diff. Geom. (to appear).

THE FORMULAS OF WEIERSTRASS AND THE FUNDAMENTAL THEOREM OF ALGEBRA FOR MINIMAL SURFACES

E. F. Beckenbach
Department of Mathematics
University of California
Los Angeles, California 90024
U.S.A.

ABSTRACT. The fundamental theorem of algebra for rational or logarithmico-rational minimal surfaces is the statement that for such a surface S of degree $n \geq 1$ in $\overline{R}^3$ (R^3 closed with a single ideal point at ∞), and for each point a of $\overline{R}^3$, the sum of the orders of the a-points on S, plus the degree of the spherical, or Gaussian, representation of S (on the unit sphere $\mathfrak{S}_a$ with center at a), plus the degree of the counterspherical representation of S on $\mathfrak{S}_a$, is equal to n. If S is a plane surface (for which, it so happens, there can be no logarithmic terms), then the degree of the spherical representation is identically 0; the degree of the counterspherical representation on $\mathfrak{S}_a$ is 0 if a is on S, and is n if a is not on S; and the number of a-points on S is n if a is on S (the classical theorem), and is 0 if a is not on S. Our present purpose is to use the Weierstrass formulas for the coordinate functions of a minimal surface in isothermal representation to gain further insight into the possible relative magnitudes of these three integer components of n in general.

1. SPHERICAL AND COUNTERSPHERICAL REPRESENTATIONS: INTUITIVE CONSIDERATION

As it will appear from the definitions in Section 2, below, the catenoid in $\overline{R}^3$ defined by the coordinate equations

$$(1)\qquad \begin{cases} x_1(u,v) = \Re(\frac{1}{w} + w) = \dfrac{(1 + u^2 + v^2)u}{u^2 + v^2} = (\frac{1}{r} + r) \cos \theta, \\ x_2(u,v) = \Re(\frac{i}{w} - iw) = \dfrac{(1 + u^2 + v^2)v}{u^2 + v^2} = (\frac{1}{r} + r) \sin \theta, \\ x_3(u,v) = \Re(2 \log w) = \log(u^2 + v^2) = 2 \log r, \end{cases}$$

where $w = u + iv = r(\cos \theta + i \sin \theta)$, is a logarithmico-rational minimal surface of degree 2; it has poles or order 1 at $w = 0$ and $w = \infty$.

The spherical, or Gaussian, representation of a point P of a surface S is the terminal point P_0' of the unit vector, with initial point at the origin $O(0,0,0)$, that is equivalent to (has the same magnitude and direction as) the positively directed unit normal to S at P (even at a point $P = \infty$ on a rational or logarithmico-rational minimal surface S, there is a positively directed unit normal). As P ranges over S, P_0' remains on the unit sphere $\mathfrak{S}_0$ with center at the origin and generates the <u>spherical representation of</u> S (on $\mathfrak{S}_0$) [13, p. 141].

For example, the half-plane $x_1 = 0$, $x_2 \geq 0$ intersects the catenoid (1) in a catenary, and it is easy to verify geometrically that the spherical representation of the points on the catenary cover the semicircle

$$x_2^2 + x_3^2 = 1, \qquad x_1 = 0, \qquad x_2 \leq 0$$

exactly once. Rotating the catenary once about the x_3-axis, we generate the catenoid and at the same time see that its spherical representation covers $\mathfrak{S}_0$ exactly once.

One can verify, further, by computing direction cosines, that the positive direction of the normals to the spherical representation of (1) on $\mathfrak{S}_0$ is the <u>inward</u> direction on $\mathfrak{S}_0$. We also choose the orientation of the sphere $\mathfrak{S}_0$ itself so that its normals are directed inward, that is, so that the positive direction of the normals to $\mathfrak{S}_0$ is the inward direction on $\mathfrak{S}_0$.

If a compact oriented surface without boundary, such as the catenoid (1) in $\overline{R}^3$, is mapped on an oriented sphere, then the map must cover the sphere "algebraically" an integral number of times, called the <u>degree</u> of the map [14, p. 124]. Thus, for example, the degree of the spherical representation of the catenoid (1) on $\mathfrak{S}_0$ is + 1.

The counterspherical representation, on the unit sphere $\mathfrak{S}_0$, of a surface S is defined as follows: If P is a point of S, and P'_0 is the spherical representation (on $\mathfrak{S}_0$) of P, then the line P'_0P intersects $\mathfrak{S}_0$ in a second point P''_0, usually distinct from P'_0. The point P''_0 is called the counterspherical representation of the point P of S on $\mathfrak{S}_0$. As P ranges over S, P''_0 remains on $\mathfrak{S}_0$ and generates the <u>counterspherical representation of</u> S <u>on</u> $\mathfrak{S}_0$ [3, p. 290].

For the catenoid (1), and for the catenary we have considered on it, one can readily verify geometrically that the counterspherical representation on $\mathfrak{S}_0$ of the points on the catenary cover the semicircle

$$x_2^2 + x_3^2 = 1, \qquad x_1 = 0, \qquad x_2 \geq 0$$

exactly once. Again rotating the catenary once about the x_3-axis, we generate the catenoid and at the same time see that its counterspherical representation on $\mathfrak{S}_0$ covers $\mathfrak{S}_0$ exactly once. Again one can verify that the covering is positive, and accordingly that the degree of the counterspherical representation of the catenoid on $\mathfrak{S}_0$ is + 1.

For a finite point a other than the origin, to define the counterspherical representation of a surface S on the unit sphere $\mathfrak{S}_a$ with center at a, we start with the spherical representation of S on $\mathfrak{S}_a$. That is, for each point P of S we consider the terminal point P'_a of the unit vector with initial point at a that is equivalent to the unit normal to S at P. Then P'_a is the spherical representation on $\mathfrak{S}_a$ of the point P of S; and as P ranges over S, P'_a remains on $\mathfrak{S}_a$ and generates the spherical representation of S on $\mathfrak{S}_a$. Of course, the spherical representation of S on $\mathfrak{S}_a$ is congruent to the usual spherical representation of S on $\mathfrak{S}_0$.

The line P'_aP intersects $\mathfrak{S}_a$ in a second point P''_a, usually distinct from P'_a. The point P''_a is called the counterspherical representation of the point P of S on $\mathfrak{S}_a$. As P ranges over S, P''_a remains on $\mathfrak{S}_a$ and generates the <u>counterspherical representation of</u> S <u>on</u> $\mathfrak{S}_a$. This last map ordinarily is <u>not</u> congruent to the counterspherical representation of S on $\mathfrak{S}_0$.

Since the spherical representations of a surface S on $\mathfrak{S}_a$ and $\mathfrak{S}_b$ are congruent for all finite a and b, it follows that the degree of the spherical representation of S on $\mathbb{S}_a$ is the same integer for all finite a, including finite points a on S. We take this integer also to be the degree of the spherical representation of S "on $\mathbb{S}_\infty$," although of course the symbol $\mathbb{S}_\infty$ itself is meaningless.

In particular, since the degree of the spherical representation of the catenoid (1) on $\mathbb{S}_0$ is $+1$, the degree is $+1$ also for its spherical representation on $\mathbb{S}_a$ for all $a \in \overline{R}^3$.

Though the counterspherical representations of a surface S on $\mathbb{S}_a$ and $\mathbb{S}_b$ ordinarily are not congruent for distinct finite points a and b, the representation on $\mathbb{S}_a$ varies continuously as the finite point a varies continuously in a component of the complement of S in $\overline{R}^3$. Therefore, since the degree of the representation is always an integer, it must be constant for all finite a in such a complement.

Thus the degree of the counterspherical representation of the catenoid (1) on $\mathbb{S}_a$ is $+1$ for all finite a "inside" the catenoid [in the component of the complement of (1) in $\overline{R}^3$ that contains the origin], since the degree is $+1$ when a is at the origin. Similarly, the degree is also a fixed integer for all finite a in the "outside" component of the complement of the catenoid. We shall return to a discussion of the value of the latter integer in Section 3, and also shall discuss its value in the case that a is a finite point <u>on</u> the catenoid.

We find it convenient to take the degree of the counterspherical representation of a surface S on $\mathbb{S}_\infty$ to be the negative of the degree of the spherical representation on $\mathbb{S}_\infty$, so that the sum of these two degrees is 0.

2. MINIMAL SURFACES: A BRIEF INTRODUCTION

We shall use <u>isothermal parameters</u> in studying minimal surfaces S, that is, parameters u, v for which the representation

$$S : x_j = x_j(u,v), \qquad j = 1,2,3,$$

where the $x_j(u,v)$ are single-valued real functions of (u,v) for (u,v) in a domain D, or simply

$$S : x = x(u,v), \tag{2}$$

where $x(u,v)$ denotes the vector function $(x_1(u,v), x_2(u,v), x_3(u,v))$, is such that

$$(3) \qquad E = G = \lambda(u,v), \qquad F = 0,$$

in which the scalar products

$$E = \frac{\partial x}{\partial u} \cdot \frac{\partial x}{\partial u}, \qquad F = \frac{\partial x}{\partial u} \cdot \frac{\partial x}{\partial v}, \qquad G = \frac{\partial x}{\partial v} \cdot \frac{\partial x}{\partial v}$$

are the coefficients of the first fundamental quadratic form of S. Such an isothermal representation is conformal, or angle-preserving, except at points where $\lambda(u,v) = 0$.

According to a theorem of Weierstrass, a necessary and sufficient condition that a surface S given in isothermal representation be minimal is that its coordinate functions be harmonic. For us, then, a <u>minimal surface</u> is simply a harmonic vector function $x(u,v)$ that satisfies the conformality conditions (3).

If, for some finite (u_0, v_0), the minimal surface S is given in isothermal representation by (2) in the annulus

$$(4) \qquad R_1 < r < R_2,$$

where $u - u_0 = r \cos \theta$, $v - v_0 = r \sin \theta$, then [17, p. 692] the harmonic vector function $x(u,v)$ can be represented there by

$$(5) \qquad x(u,v) = c \log r + \sum_{k=-\infty}^{\infty} r^k (a_k \cos k\theta + b_k \sin k\theta).$$

The real-valued constant vector coefficient b_0 is arbitrary; for simplicity, we take $b_0 = 0$. The other real-valued constant vector coefficients c, a_k, b_k are uniquely determined by $x(u,v)$.

For the present theory, we extend the (u,v)-plane R^2, and also Euclidean 3-space R^3, to $\bar{R}^2$ and $\bar{R}^3$, respectively, by postulating a single ideal <u>point at</u> ∞ for each.

If $R_1 = 0$ in (4), then S has an <u>isolated singularity</u> at the finite point (u_0, v_0).

If S has an isolated singularity at the finite point (u_0, v_0), if there is a lowest value of k for which

(6) $$a_k \cdot a_k + b_k \cdot b_k \neq 0,$$

and if this value τ is negative, then we say that S has a pole of order $|\tau|$ at (u_0,v_0).

The conditions (3) imply that if (6) does not hold for any $k < 0$, then also $c \cdot c = 0$. Thus, a minimal surface given in isothermal representation by (2) cannot have an isolated ∞-point that is merely logarithmic. There can also be no logarithmic terms in any case if S lies on a plane.

If S has an isolated singularity at the finite point (u_0,v_0), if there is a lowest value of k for which (6) holds, and if this value is non-negative, then the singularity is removable, and S is regular at (u_0,v_0). Then either $x(u,v) \equiv a_0$, S reduces to a point, and we say that S is a constant minimal surface; or there is a least positive index τ for which (6) holds, and we say that S has an a_0-point of order τ at (u_0,v_0)

If $R_2 = +\infty$ in (4), we say that S has an isolated singularity at ∞. By means of an inversion, we treat an isolated singularity at ∞ as an isolated singularity at the origin [7, pp. 22-24].

If, except for poles, S is a regular minimal surface given in isothermal representation by (2) for (u,v) in a domain D, then we say that S is a meromorphic minimal surface for (u,v) in D; if D is the entire finite plane R^2, then we simply say that S is a meromorphic minimal surface.

If the minimal surface S, given in isothermal representation by (2), is meromorphic in the closed (u,v) plane $\bar{R}^2$, then, since the poles of S are isolated, S can have at most a finite number of poles in all. The surface is then a logarithmico-rational minimal surface, or a rational minimal surface, according as there is, or is not, a logarithmic term in any of the expansions (5) at the poles of S.

The sum of the orders of the poles of a rational or logarithmico-rational minimal surface S is called the degree of S.

One can verify, for example, that the coordinate functions of the catenoid (1) are harmonic and satisfy the conditions (3) for $0 < u^2 + v^2 < +\infty$, so that the catenoid is indeed a minimal surface. One can verify further that the surface has poles of order 1 at the origin and at ∞. Since there is a logarithmic term in the formula for $x_3(u,v)$ in (1), the catenoid is therefore a logarithmico-rational minimal surface of degree 2.

The Nevanlinna theory of meromorphic functions of a complex variable [15, 1] can be generalized [7, 2] to meromorphic minimal surfaces. Inequalities add zest to the generalization, especially as a result of the fact that two particular functions are subharmonic [8, 9] when evaluated for minimal surfaces: the logarithm of the distance function in the generalized first fundamental theorem [7, 2], and the logarithm of the deformation function in the generalized second fundamental theorem [4].

The reader familiar with the classical Nevanlinna theory will recall that for a nonconstant meromorphic function f of a complex variable, the spherical affinity function $\mathfrak{A}^\circ(r,a;f)$ is the sum of a proximity function, an enumerative function, and a constant function, and that the first fundamental theorem in this theory is the statement that $\mathfrak{A}^\circ(r,a;f)$ is independent of a, $a \in \overline{R}^2$:

$$\mathfrak{A}^\circ(r,a;f) = T^\circ(r;f),$$

where $T^\circ(r;f)$ is the spherical characteristic function of f.

For a nonconstant meromorphic minimal surface S, and for each $a \in \overline{R}^3$, the corresponding hyperspherical affinity function $\mathfrak{A}^\circ(r,a;S)$ is the sum of three functions analogous to those in $\mathfrak{A}^\circ(r,a;f)$, <u>plus</u> a nonnegative "visibility" function consisting of an integral of the (nonnegative) Laplacian of the logarithm of the distance function. Again, $\mathfrak{A}^\circ(r,a;S)$ is independent of a, $a \in \overline{R}^3$:

$$\mathfrak{A}^\circ(r,a;S) = T^\circ(r;S),$$

where $T^\circ(r;S)$ is the hyperspherical characteristic function of S.

In the classical theory, the enumerative function ordinarily dominates, while in the extended theory the visibility function usually takes over. As a working principle, results involving the enumerative function in complex-variable theory, such as value-distribution theorems, can be expected to have analogues involving the sum of the enumerative function and the visibility function in minimal-surface theory.

For example, the fundamental theorem of algebra has been so extended, first [5] analytically for S in $\overline{R}^n$ and then [3] in the following elegant geometric formulation for S in $\overline{R}^3$.

3. THE FUNDAMENTAL THEOREM OF ALGEBRA: MINIMAL-SURFACE VERSION

For any nonconstant rational or logarithmico-rational minimal surface S in $\bar{R}^3$, and for any point a in $\bar{R}^3$, let

$\deg(S)$ = degree of S,

$n(a;S)$ = number of a-points on S, counting multiplicities,

$\deg(\mathcal{S}_a;S)$ = degree of spherical representation of S on $\mathcal{S}_a$,

$\deg(C_a;S)$ = degree of counterspherical representation of S on $\mathcal{S}_a$.

The fundamental theorem of algebra, as extended to minimal surfaces, is then the following:

FUNDAMENTAL THEOREM OF ALGEBRA (FOR MINIMAL SURFACES). *If S is a rational or logarithmico-rational minimal surface of degree ≥ 1 in $\bar{R}^3$, and a is a point of $\bar{R}^3$, then*

$$\deg(S) = n(a;S) + \deg(\mathcal{S}_a;S) + \deg(C_a;S). \tag{7}$$

For example, if S is the catenoid (1), then the values of the various terms in (7) are as shown in Table 1.

Table 1. Values for the One-layered Catenoid

a	$n(a;S)$	$\deg(\mathcal{S}_a;S)$	$\deg(C_a;S)$	sum = $\deg(S)$
Finite, on S	1	1	0	2
Finite, not on S	0	1	1	2
∞	2	1	-1	2

Thus, since the finite part of the catenoid is simply covered, for a finite we have $n(a;S) = 1$ or $n(a;S) = 0$ according as a is, or is not, on S; and $n(\infty;S) = 2$ because of the simple poles at $w = 0$ and $w = \infty$. Further, we have seen that $\deg(\mathcal{S}_a;S) = 1$ for all finite a, and that $\deg(C_a;S) = 1$ for all points a in the interior component of the complement of S in $\bar{R}^3$; and we have agreed to take $\deg(\mathcal{S}_\infty;S) = 1$, $\deg(C_\infty;S) = -1$.

By the theorem, then, we must also have $\deg(C_a;S) = 0$ for a finite and on S, and $\deg(C_a;S) = 1$ for a in the exterior component of the complement of S in $\bar{R}^3$. We shall verify these last two relations not by direct computation for any particular point, but rather by examining what happens in general to $\deg(C_a;S)$ as the point a moves continuously from the complement of S to a finite point of S itself.

For simplicity, consider first the case in which S is a plane map, say the map given by

$$(8) \qquad x_1(u,v) + ix_2(u,v) = (u + iv)^3, \quad x_3(u,v) = 0.$$

Then, for a finite, the spherical representation of the three-sheeted plane surface S on $\mathfrak{S}_a$ is a single point, the "north pole" P of $\mathfrak{S}_a$. Further, if a is not on S, the counterspherical representation of S on $\mathfrak{S}_a$ is the stereographic projection on $\mathfrak{S}_a$, from P, of the three-sheeted plane surface $\mathfrak{P}$ parallel to and one unit "above" S; and one can verify that the three-sheeted covering of $\mathfrak{S}_a$ by the projection is in the positive sense, that is, with normal directed inward, both for a above S and for a below S. For a finite and on S, the counterspherical representation of S on $\mathfrak{S}_a$ is just the point P itself. Thus we have the arrangement of values shown in Table 2 for the three-sheeted plane surface S given by (8).

Table 2. Values for a Three-sheeted Plane Surface

a	n(a;S)	$\deg(\mathfrak{S}_a;S)$	$\deg(C_a;S)$	sum = deg(S)
Finite, on S	3	0	0	3
Finite, not on S	0	0	3	3
∞	3	0	0	3

Though the sum $n(a;S) + \deg(C_a;S)$ is invariant, each addend is discontinuous between S and its complement. Notice, however, that as the variable point x in the complement of the plane surface S in $\bar{R}^3$ approaches the fixed finite point a of S, whether from above S or from below S, less and less of S is mapped, in the counterspherical representation, on more and more of the three-sheeted covering of $\mathfrak{S}_x$ (draw a sketch, with x quite close to a). In the limit, with x = a, the "thinly covered" three-sheeted map is lost as the three-fold a-point is gained.

A similar discussion would hold for any n-sheeted plane map, with 3 replaced throughout by n, in particular in Table 2.

Since in the small every nonconstant minimal surface is essentially a plane surface (perhaps with winding points, self-intersections, and self-overlays), the same sort of discontinuous transfer of values between $\deg(C_x;S)$ and $n(x;S)$ occurs for minimal surfaces S in general as x passes continuously between the complement of S and S itself.

In particular, for the catenoid (1), as the variable point x moves from the interior component of the complement of (1) in $\overline{R}^3$, where $n(x;S) = 0$ and $\deg(C_x;S) = 1$, to a finite point a of S, for which $n(a;S) = 1$, the foregoing heuristic but factual discussion shows that $\deg(C_x;S)$ must decrease discontinuously by 1 to $\deg(C_a;S) = 0$; then as x moves from a into the exterior component of the complement, where again $n(x;S) = 0$, the same argument shows further that $\deg(C_x;S)$ must increase discontinuously by 1, again to $\deg(C_x;S) = 1$. This completes our verification of the entries in Table 1 on page 386.

From a different point of view, since as

$$x \to a, \quad a \in S, \quad x \in \operatorname{comp} S,$$

less and less of S near a is mapped on more and more of $n(a;S)$ sheets of the counterspherical covering of $\mathcal{S}_x$, and these spherical sheets are discontinuously lost in the limiting position $x = a$, we could reasonably alter the definition of counterspherical representation on $\mathcal{S}_a$ by adjoining, to the counterspherical representation on $\mathcal{S}_a$, $n(a;S)$ covering sheets of $\mathcal{S}_a$ on which the single point a is considered as being mapped.

For example, under the altered definition, for the catenoid (1) the counterspherical representation on $\mathcal{S}_x$ would be a single-sheeted covering of $\mathcal{S}_x$ not only for x in the complement of (1) but also for x finite and on (1). Similarly for the three-sheeted plane map S given by (8), the counterspherical representation would be a three-sheeted covering of $\mathcal{S}_x$ both for x in the complement of S and for x finite and on S.

Also, in the altered definition, $\deg(C_\infty;S)$ would be increased by the amount $n(\infty;S)$. With these conventions, not only $\deg(\mathcal{S}_a;S)$ but also $\deg(C_a;S)$ would be invariant over $\overline{R}^3$, the extended fundamental theorem of algebra would be the statement that the sum of these two integer invariants is equal to the degree of the surface, and equation (7) would appear in the attractive and suggestive form

$$\deg(S) = \deg(\mathcal{S}_a;S) + \deg(\mathcal{C}_a;S). \tag{9}$$

4. MINIMAL-SURFACE COORDINATE FUNCTIONS: THE WEIERSTRASS FORMULAS

Recall from Section 2 that for us a minimal surface is a triple of conjugate harmonic functions [6], that is, a set of three harmonic functions $x_j(u,v)$, $j = 1,2,3$, satisfying the conformality conditions (3).

Since the $x_j(u,v)$ are harmonic, they are the real parts of analytic functions of a complex variable:

$$x_j(u,v) = \Re f_j(w + iv) = \Re f_j(w), \quad j = 1,2,3. \tag{10}$$

The conditions (3) can now be written in the equivalent form

$$\sum_{j=1}^{3} f_j'^2 = 0. \tag{11}$$

It should be noted that, because of the possible logarithmic term in the vector equation (5), the "functions" $f_j(w)$ might also contain logarithmic terms $c_j \log(w - w_0)$, with c_j real, and so might not be single valued. As indicated in (10) and (11), however, we shall be concerned only with the functions $\Re f_j(w)$ and $f_j'(w)$, which are single valued, and so we shall retain the notation $f_j(w)$.

Since we shall be working in detail with the Weierstrass formulas for the coordinate functions of a minimal surface, we shall now give their brief derivation.

If the minimal surface S given by (10) is not a plane surface parallel to the (x_1,x_2)-plane, then $f_3' \not\equiv 0$ and equation (11) can be written equivalently as

$$\frac{f_1' + if_2'}{-f_3'} = \frac{f_3'}{f_1' - if_2'} = \varphi(w), \tag{12}$$

where $\varphi(w)$ $[\varphi(w) \not\equiv 0]$ is simply the common value or limiting value of the other two expressions. Solving (12), we obtain

$$(13)\qquad \begin{cases} f_1' = (1 - \varphi^2)\psi, \\ f_2' = i(1 + \varphi^2)\psi, \\ f_3' = 2\varphi\psi, \end{cases}$$

where $\psi(w)$ is defined by

$$(14)\qquad \psi(w) = \frac{f_3'(w)}{2\varphi(w)} .$$

Hence, writing φ for $\varphi(\zeta)$ and ψ for $\psi(\zeta)$, we have

$$(15)\qquad \begin{cases} x_1(u,v) = \Re \int^w (1 - \varphi^2)\psi \, d\zeta, \\ x_2(u,v) = \Re \int^w i(1 + \varphi^2)\psi \, d\zeta, \\ x_3(u,v) = \Re \int^w 2\varphi\psi \, d\zeta. \end{cases}$$

If S is a plane surface parallel to the (x_1,x_2)-plane, then $f_3' \equiv 0$ and either $f_1' + if_2' \equiv 0$ or $f_1' - if_2' \equiv 0$. In the former case, the limiting values from (12) and (14), namely

$$(16)\qquad \varphi(w) = 0, \qquad \psi(w) = f_1'(w),$$

give the correct values of the coordinate functions when substituted in (15). In the latter case, the values (16) give the correct values of the coordinate functions except for the sign of $x_2(u,v)$; but this is sufficient for our purposes since we are investigating value distributions, not actual values. [Properly to treat the case $f_3' \equiv 0$, $f_1' - if_2' \equiv 0$, adjustments would have to be made in the formulas (12)-(16), starting with the ratios in (12). The (improper) limiting values from (12) and (14) in this case are $\varphi = \infty$, $\psi = -f_1'/\infty^2$.]

Thus, for our purposes, any minimal surface S given by (10) can be adequately represented by equations of the form (15).

Conversely, for given analytic functions φ and ψ, the <u>Weierstrass formulas</u> in the right-hand members of (15) give the coordinate functions [not necessarily single-valued functions of (u,v), though, unless additional restrictions are added] of a minimal surface S in isothermal representation.

Computations now give, for the area-deformation ratio $\lambda(u,v)$ [see equation (3)] of the surface (15),

$$\lambda(u,v) = \tfrac{1}{2}(E + G) = \tfrac{1}{2} \sum_{j=1}^{3} |f_j'|^2 = |\psi|^2(1 + |\varphi|^2)^2. \tag{17}$$

The function

$$\lambda^{1/2} = |\psi|(1 + |\varphi|^2) \tag{18}$$

corresponds to $|f'|$ in complex-variable theory. Thus $\lambda^{1/2}$ is the linear-deformation ratio for S; and if $\lambda^{1/2}$ has a zero of order h at (u_0,v_0), then the corresponding point a on S is a branch, or winding, point (see [17] for references) of order h: angles are multiplied by h + 1 at a, and a curve on S about a must wind h + 1 times about a before it closes. Such a winding contributes h + 1 to the multiplicity of a as a point on S. [We say that a is a <u>simple</u> point on S if $n(a;S) = 1$, a <u>double</u> point on S if $n(a;S) = 2$, and a <u>multiple</u> point on S if $n(a;S) \geq 2$. The point a might be a multiple point on S because it is a winding point of S, or a point of self-intersection of S with itself, or a point of S where two or more sheets, or layers, of S coincide, or a combination of these.]

For the direction cosines of the positively directed normal to the surface S given by (15), that is, for the coordinates of the spherical representation of S on $\mathfrak{S}_0$, computations give

$$\begin{cases} X_1 = \dfrac{\varphi + \bar{\varphi}}{1 + |\varphi|^2} = \dfrac{2\Re(\varphi)}{1 + |\varphi|^2}, \\[2ex] X_2 = \dfrac{i(\bar{\varphi} - \varphi)}{1 + |\varphi|^2} = \dfrac{2\Im(\varphi)}{1 + |\varphi|^2}, \\[2ex] X_3 = \dfrac{|\varphi|^2 - 1}{1 + |\varphi|^2}. \end{cases} \tag{19}$$

Notice that the coordinate functions (19) of the spherical representation of the surface S given by (15) on $\mathfrak{S}_0$ are independent of ψ. Notice further (see, e.g., [12, p. 120]) that <u>the functions (19) have a familiar appearance: They are the coordinate functions of the stereographic projection on</u> $\mathfrak{S}_0$, <u>from the pole</u> (0,0,1), <u>of the map on the equatorial plane of</u> $\mathfrak{S}_0$

given by the function $\varphi(w)$.

The minimal surface S given in isothermal representation by (2) is rational or logarithmico-rational if and only if the representation can be written equivalently [5, p. 362] in the form

$$(20) \qquad x_j(u,v) = \Re f_j(w) = \Re \frac{p_j(w)}{q(w)} + \log \prod_{k=1}^{\ell} |w - w_k|^{c_{jk}}, \qquad j = 1,2,3,$$

where the c_{jk} are real constants and p_1, p_2, p_3, q $[q(w) \not\equiv 0]$ are relatively prime polynomials:

$$(21) \qquad (p_1, p_2, p_3, q) = 1.$$

Then

$$(22) \qquad \deg(S) = \max[\deg(p_1), \deg(p_2), \deg(p_3), \deg(q)].$$

If S is a rational or logarithmico-rational minimal surface in isothermal representation, then equations (20) for the coordinate functions of S imply that each $f_j'(w)$ is rational; and that, at each pole $w = w_k$ of S, the residue of each $f_j'(w)$ [that is, the coefficient c_{jk} of $(w - w_k)^{-1}$ in the partial-fraction expansion of each $f_j'(w)$] is a real value. Therefore, by the defining equations (12), (14), and (16) for φ and ψ, the functions φ and ψ for such a surface S are rational and are such that each of the three derivative expressions in the right-hand members of equations (13) has a real-valued residue.

Since the converse also clearly is true, it follows that necessary and sufficient conditions that the minimal surface S be rational or logarithmico-rational is that the functions φ and ψ in the equations (15) for S be rational, and that the three derivative expressions in the right-hand members of equations (13) have real-valued residues.

Since, as we have seen, the spherical representation of S on $\mathcal{S}_0$ coincides with the stereographic projection, on $\mathcal{S}_0$ from the point $(0,0,1)$, of the φ-map on the equatorial plane of $\mathcal{S}_0$, and since the degree of the spherical representation of S on $\mathcal{S}_a$ is invariant, it follows that for all $a \in \overline{R}^3$,

$$(23) \qquad \deg(\mathcal{S}_a; S) = \deg(\varphi).$$

Therefore, since $\deg(\varphi) \geq 0$, we have

$$\deg(\mathfrak{S}_a;S) \geq 0 \tag{24}$$

for all rational or logarithmico-rational minimal surfaces. This result (24) follows also from the fact that for nonconstant minimal surfaces the positively directed normal to the spherical representation on $\mathfrak{S}_0$ always points inward. The sign of equality holds in (24) if and only if S is a plane surface.

The situation is rather different for the counterspherical representation, which actually can fold back on itself with the positively directed normal pointed outward. Thus the covering of the sphere must be considered algebraically in the counterspherical representation.

Of course, the third integer term on the right-hand side of (7) is always nonnegative,

$$n(a;S) \geq 0, \tag{25}$$

with the sign of equality holding if and only if a is not on S.

The sum of $\deg(\mathfrak{S}_a;S)$ and $\deg(C_a;S)$ is known [3, p. 297] to be nonnegative,

$$\deg(\mathfrak{S}_a;S) + \deg(C_a;S) \geq 0, \tag{26}$$

the sign of equality holding if and only if either $a = \infty$ or S is a plane surface and a is on S.

Several additional inequalities can be read off from (7), (24), (25), and (26), including

$$n(a;S) \leq \deg(S), \tag{27}$$

the sign of equality holding if and only if either $a = \infty$ or S is a plane surface and a is on S.

In the remainder of this paper, we shall use the Weierstrass formulas (15) further to explore the possible values of the integers in the right-hand member of (7), and the possible relationships amongst these integers. In general, our purpose will be, for a given class $\mathfrak{K}$ of surfaces S, and with a given nonnegative integer specified as $\deg(\mathfrak{S}_0;S)$, to seek to determine the range of possible values of $\deg(S)$ for $S \in \mathfrak{K}$; and then, for a given

$\deg(\mathcal{S}_0;S)$ and compatible $\deg(S) > 0$, to seek a surface $S \in \mathcal{K}$ and a point $a \in R^3$ that maximize $n(a;S)$ for $S \in \mathcal{K}$, $a \in R^3$ [or, equivalently, that minimize $\deg(C_a;S)$ for $S \in \mathcal{K}$, $a \in R^3$].

5. ENTIRE RATIONAL MINIMAL SURFACES: POLYNOMIAL MINIMAL SURFACES

Let S be a rational or logarithmico-rational minimal surface given in isothermal representation by (15). If all the poles of S are at ∞, then S is a polynomial, or entire rational, minimal surface. [There are no logarithmico-polynomial minimal surfaces, or surfaces having coordinate functions of the form (20), with $q(w) \equiv 1$ and some $c_{jk} \neq 0$.]

A sufficient condition for (15) to be an entire rational minimal surface is that φ and ψ be polynomials.

For example, if

$$\varphi(\zeta) = \zeta, \qquad \psi(\zeta) = 3,$$

then (15) yields the minimal surface of Enneper:

$$(28)\qquad \begin{cases} x_1(u,v) = 3u + 3uv^2 - u^3, \\ x_2(u,v) = -3v - 3u^2v + v^3, \\ x_3(u,v) = 3u^2 - 3v^2. \end{cases}$$

This surface has no winding points, since for it, by (17), we have

$$\lambda(u,v) = 9(1 + |w|^2)^2 \neq 0.$$

Nevertheless, the surface does have double points, for it intersects itself; for instance, both

$$(u,v) = (0,\sqrt{3}) \qquad \text{and} \qquad (u,v) = (0,-\sqrt{3})$$

are mapped on $(x_1,x_2,x_3) = (0,0,-9)$. For this surface, in part by (23), we have the values shown in Table 3.

Table 3. Values for the Minimal Surface of Enneper

a	$n(a;S)$	$\deg(\mathcal{S}_a;S)$	$\deg(C_a;S)$	sum = $\deg(S)$
Finite, simple on S	1	1	1	3
Finite, double on S	2	1	0	3
Finite, not on S	0	1	2	3
∞	3	1	-1	3

It is not necessary, however, for both φ and ψ to be polynomials in order that (15) be an entire rational minimal surface. For example, if

$$\varphi(\zeta) = \frac{1}{\zeta}, \qquad \psi(\zeta) = 3\zeta^2,$$

then (15) again yields the same minimal surface of Enneper [except for the sign of the first coordinate function $x_1(u,v)$].

To determine necessary and sufficient conditions on the rational functions φ, ψ for (15) to be a nonconstant entire rational minimal surface, write

$$\varphi = \frac{p}{q}, \qquad \psi = \frac{r}{s}, \qquad\qquad q \neq 0,\ s \neq 0,$$

as quotients of polynomials in lowest terms. Then (15) becomes

$$(29) \qquad \begin{cases} x_1(u,v) = \Re \displaystyle\int^w \left(\frac{q^2 - p^2}{q^2}\right)\frac{r}{s}\, d\zeta, \\ x_2(u,v) = \Re \displaystyle\int^w i\left(\frac{q^2 + p^2}{q^2}\right)\frac{r}{s}\, d\zeta, \\ x_3(u,v) = \Re \displaystyle\int^w 2\frac{pr}{qs}\, d\zeta. \end{cases}$$

Here the integrals must be polynomials, and therefore the integrands must also be polynomials. Since p and q are relatively prime, so are $q^2 - p^2$ and $q^2 + p^2$, and therefore the polynomial s must be a nonzero constant, which we can take to be 1. Furthermore, to balance the q^2 in the first two denominators in (29), r must be of the form $r = q^2t$, where t is also a polynomial, $t \neq 0$. Thus we must have $\psi = q^2t \neq 0$, and this choice yields a polynomial expression not only for $x_1(u,v)$ and for $x_2(u,v)$, but also for $x_3(u,v)$.

Hence, (15) _is an entire rational minimal surface if and only if_ φ _is a rational function_, $\varphi = p/q\ [q \not\equiv 0]$ _with_ $(p,q) = 1$, _and_ ψ _is an entire rational function of the form_ $\psi = q^2 t$.

Since the degree of the integral of a nonzero polynomial is greater by 1 than the degree of the integrand, it is easy to verify that if

$$\varphi = \frac{p}{q}, \quad \psi = q^2 t, \qquad (p,q) = 1, \quad q \not\equiv 0, \ t \not\equiv 0, \tag{30}$$

then (15) is an entire rational minimal surface with degree given by

$$\begin{aligned} \deg(S) &= 2\deg(\varphi) + \deg(t) + 1 \\ &= 2\deg(\mathfrak{S}_a;S) + \deg(t) + 1. \end{aligned} \tag{31}$$

Since $\deg(t) \geq 0$, it follows that _for any nonconstant entire rational minimal surface_ S,

$$\deg(S) \geq 2\deg(\mathfrak{S}_a;S) + 1. \tag{32}$$

The sign of equality holds in (32) _if and only if_ t _is a constant; the excess of the left-hand member over the right-hand member can be any given nonnegative integer_.

For a nonconstant entire rational minimal surface S determined by the functions (30), by (18) we have

$$\lambda^{1/2} = |q^2 t|\left(1 + \frac{|p|^2}{|q|^2}\right) = |t|(|q|^2 + |p|^2). \tag{33}$$

Since p and q are relatively prime, we have $|q|^2 + |p|^2 \not\equiv 0$, and therefore the zeros of $\lambda^{1/2}$ are the zeros of t.

Consider now the entire rational minimal surface S with coordinate functions determined by

$$\varphi = \zeta^{\alpha}, \qquad \psi = \zeta^{\beta}, \tag{34}$$

where α and β are nonnegative integers. Substituting from (34) into (15), we obtain

$$(35)\quad \begin{cases} x_1(u,v) = \dfrac{r^{\beta+1}}{\beta+1}\cos(\beta+1)\theta - \dfrac{r^{2\alpha+\beta+1}}{2\alpha+\beta+1}\cos(2\alpha+\beta+1)\theta, \\[2ex] x_2(u,v) = -\dfrac{r^{\beta+1}}{\beta+1}\sin(\beta+1)\theta - \dfrac{r^{2\alpha+\beta+1}}{2\alpha+\beta+1}\sin(2\alpha+\beta+1)\theta, \\[2ex] x_3(u,v) = 2\dfrac{r^{\alpha+\beta+1}}{\alpha+\beta+1}\cos(\alpha+\beta+1)\theta. \end{cases}$$

For this surface S, which is of degree $2\alpha+\beta+1$, we have

$$\lambda^{1/2} = |w|^{\beta}(1+|w|^{2\alpha}),$$

so that there is a winding point of order β [a (0,0,0)-point of order $\beta+1$] at $w = 0$, but no other finite winding points on S.

The surface (35) does not otherwise pass through the origin (0,0,0), since we have

$$x_3(u,v) = 0 \quad \text{for} \quad u^2+v^2 = r^2 > 0$$

if and only if θ is a value θ_0 such that

$$\cos(\alpha+\beta+1)\theta_0 = 0.$$

But then, by symmetry properties of the cosine and sine functions about points where $\cos\theta = 0$, for such a point we have

$$\cos(2\alpha+\beta+1)\theta_0 = -\cos(\beta+1)\theta_0, \quad \sin(2\alpha+\beta+1)\theta_0 = \sin(\beta+1)\theta_0.$$

Substituting these values in the expressions for $x_1(u,v)$ and $x_2(u,v)$ in (35), squaring, and adding, we see that

$$x_1^2+x_2^2 > 0 \quad \text{at all points} \quad (u,v) \quad \text{where} \quad x_3 = 0,\ w^2+v^2 = r^2 > 0;$$

that is, we have

$$x_1^2+x_2^2+x_3^2 > 0 \quad \text{for all} \quad (u,v) \quad \text{satisfying} \quad u^2+v^2 = r^2 > 0.$$

For the entire rational minimal surface S with coordinate functions given by (35), we have the values shown in Table 4.

Table 4. Values for the Entire Rational Minimal Surface (35)

a	$n(a;S)$	$\deg(\mathcal{S}_a;S)$	$\deg(C_a;S)$	sum = $\deg(S)$
(0,0,0)	$\beta + 1$	α	α	$2\alpha + \beta + 1$
Finite, simple on S	1	α	$\alpha + \beta$	$2\alpha + \beta + 1$
Finite, not on S	0	α	$\alpha + \beta + 1$	$2\alpha + \beta + 1$
∞	$2\alpha + \beta + 1$	α	$-\alpha$	$2\alpha + \beta + 1$

The foregoing example shows that <u>in the class</u> $\mathcal{E}_{\alpha\beta}$ <u>of nonconstant entire rational minimal surfaces</u> S <u>with a given nonnegative integer</u> α $(\alpha \geq 0)$ <u>as</u> $\deg(\mathcal{S}_0;S)$ <u>and a given compatible integer</u> $2\alpha + \beta + 1$ $(\beta \geq 0)$ <u>as</u> $\deg(S)$, <u>we have</u>

(36) $$\max_{\substack{S\in\mathcal{E}_{\alpha\beta}\\ a\in R^3}} n(a;S) \geq \deg(S) - 2\deg(\mathcal{S}_0;S),$$

<u>or equivalently</u>,

(37) $$\min_{\substack{S\in\mathcal{E}_{\alpha\beta}\\ a\in R^3}} \deg(C_a;S) \leq \deg(\mathcal{S}_0;S).$$

Thus, for the surface (35), for which

$$\deg(\mathcal{S}_0;S) = \alpha \geq 0 \quad \text{and} \quad \deg(S) = 2\alpha + \beta + 1 \ (\beta \geq 0),$$

and for the point $a = (0,0,0)$, we have

$$\begin{aligned} n(a;S) = \beta + 1 &= (2\alpha + \beta + 1) - 2\alpha \\ &= \deg(S) - 2\deg(\mathcal{S}_0;S) \end{aligned}$$

and

$$\deg(C_a;s) = \alpha = \deg(\mathcal{S}_0;S),$$

whence (36) and (37) follow for this surface.

In the plane case, namely, in the case

$$\deg(\mathcal{S}_0;S) = \alpha = 0, \quad \beta \geq 0 \text{ arbitrary}, \quad \deg(S) = 2\alpha + \beta + 1 = \beta + 1 > 0,$$

the sign of equality holds in (36),

$$n(a;S) = \beta + 1 = (2\alpha + \beta + 1) - 2\alpha = \deg(S) - 2\deg(\mathcal{S}_0;S),$$

and in (37),

$$\deg(C_a;S) = 0 = \alpha = \deg(\mathcal{S}_0;S),$$

for <u>each</u> point $a \in S$.

At least in the simplest nonplane case, namely in the case

$$\deg(\mathcal{S}_0;S) = \alpha = 1, \quad \beta = 0, \quad \deg(S) = 2\alpha + \beta + 1 = 3,$$

the minimal surface of Enneper, discussed earlier in this section, shows that the values in the right-hand members of (36) and (37) can be improved <u>as a consequence of the intersection of the surface with itself</u>. Thus, if a is a double point of this surface, then (see Table 3 on page 395) we have

$$n(a;S) = 2 = 3 - 2 + 1 = \deg(S) - 2\deg(\mathcal{S}_0;S) + 1 > \deg(S) - 2\deg(\mathcal{S}_0;S)$$

and

$$\deg(C_a;S) = 0 = 1 - 1 = \deg(\mathcal{S}_0;S) - 1 < \deg(\mathcal{S}_0;S).$$

6. RATIONAL AND LOGARITHMICO-RATIONAL MINIMAL SURFACES: PARTIAL FRACTIONS AND PARTIAL RESULTS

With a given nonnegative integer α specified as $\deg(\mathcal{S}_0,S)$,

$$\deg(\mathcal{S}_0;S) = \deg(\varphi) = \alpha, \tag{38}$$

determination of the range of values of $\deg(S)$ in the class of rational and logarithmico-rational minimal surfaces is less immediate than it is in the special case of the class of entire rational minimal surfaces. Complicating factors in the general case are (a) the present lack of a practicable characterization of the set of pairs φ, ψ of rational functions for which the three integrands in (15) all have real-valued residues, and (b) the fact that the expression for $\deg(S)$ is less simple for members of the general class than it is for members of the special class of entire rational minimal surfaces. We shall not here attempt a complete analysis of the general class.

Heuristic considerations of (a) and (b), however, seem to indicate that perhaps the entire range of $\deg(S)$ for a given value of α in (38) is covered by simple functions of the form (c) $\varphi = 1/q$, $\psi = r/1$, and (d) $\varphi = p/1$, $\psi = 1/s$, and that, if this is so, then a single simple family extending the family (35) of surfaces contains the answers to many of our questions.

(a) The determination of practicable necessary and sufficient conditions on rational functions φ and ψ for all three of the integrands in (15) to be real valued might be difficult, since the evaluation of each separate residue can require a lengthy computation.

Sometimes, as for the functions

$$\varphi = -\zeta, \qquad \psi = -\frac{1}{\zeta^2}, \tag{39}$$

one can quickly verify from (13) that each of the three residues is real valued:

$$f_1' = -\frac{1}{\zeta^2} + 1, \quad f_2' = i\left(\frac{1}{\zeta^2} + 1\right), \quad f_3' = \frac{2}{\zeta} .$$

In fact, in this case S is the catenoid (1).

For the functions

$$\varphi = \frac{-i(\zeta + i)}{\zeta - 1}, \qquad \psi = \frac{(\zeta - i)^2}{2\zeta^2},$$

by contrast, rather more of a computation is required before one establishes again that the three integrands have real-valued residues - and discovers, perhaps unexpectedly, that these functions also determine the catenoid (1), except that this time the coordinate functions $x_2(u,v)$ and $x_3(u,v)$ are interchanged!

(b) A consideration of partial fractions shows that the degree of the rational part R (there might also be a logarithmic part L) of the integral of a rational function p/q, where p and q are relatively prime polynomials, $q \neq 0$, is given by

$$\deg(R) = \max[\deg(p) + 1, \deg(q)] - k(q), \tag{40}$$

where $k(q)$ is the number of distinct linear factors of q.

With a given value of α in (38), say $\alpha = 2$, in order to take full advantage of the term $k(q)$ in (40) when choosing the rational functions φ and ψ to minimize $\deg(S)$ for the surface (15), we might begin by trying

$$\varphi = \frac{p}{q} = \frac{\zeta - w_3}{(\zeta - w_1)(\zeta - w_2)}, \quad \psi = \frac{r}{s} = 1, \tag{41}$$

where the linear factors in φ are distinct and the degree of p is less than that of q. But then the residues of the first two integrands in (15) do not vanish; and accordingly, by their form, they cannot both be real valued.

Help in making the residues be real valued for the choice of the denominator q in (41), and in other similar cases, must come not at all from the numerator p of φ but only, at the cost of a corresponding increase in the value of $\deg(S)$, from the numerator r of ψ.

(c) Consider now the surface S determined by the functions

$$\varphi = \frac{1}{(\zeta - 1)(\zeta + 1)}, \quad \psi = 4\zeta. \tag{42}$$

Substituting these expressions in (15), we obtain the coordinate functions

$$\begin{cases} x_1(u,v) = \Re\left(2w^2 + \dfrac{1}{w-1} - \dfrac{1}{w+1}\right), \\ x_2(u,v) = \Re i\left(2w^2 - \dfrac{1}{w-1} + \dfrac{1}{w+1}\right), \\ x_3(u,v) = \Re[4 \log(w-1) + 4 \log(w+1)] \end{cases} \tag{43}$$

of a logarithmico-rational minimal surface S of degree 4; it has poles of order 1 at $w = 1$ and $w = -1$, and a pole of order 2 at $w = \infty$.

Notice that for the surface (43) determined by the functions (42), which are of the form $\varphi = 1/q$, $\psi = r/1$, we have

$$\deg(\mathcal{S}_0;S) = \deg(\varphi) = 2, \quad \deg(S) = 4. \tag{44}$$

(d) Notice also that for the catenoid (1) determined by the functions (39), which are of the form $\varphi = p/1$, $\psi = 1/s$, we have

(45) $$\deg(\mathfrak{S}_0;S) = \deg(\varphi) = 1, \qquad \deg(S) = 2.$$

The values in (44), and those in (45), do not satisfy the inequality (32) for $\deg(S)$ relative to $\deg(\mathfrak{S}_0;S)$ for entire rational minimal surfaces S. They do suggest, however, that perhaps in general for rational and logarithmico-rational minimal surfaces S we have

(46) $$\deg(S) \geq 2 \deg(\mathfrak{S}_0;S).$$

Convinced that (46) is valid, one might possibly be able to establish it without a great deal of effort. In any case, the inequality (46) holds for each member of the following extension of the family (35) of surfaces, with the sign of equality holding throughout one portion of the extension.

Consider now the functions $\varphi = \zeta^\alpha$ and $\psi = \zeta^\beta$ of (34) with the integer α remaining nonnegative, but, corresponding to each α, β taking on all negative values except

(47) $$\beta = -1 \text{ and } \beta = -2\alpha - 1.$$

The values (47) are special. If $\alpha = 0$, then these values are equal and the corresponding surface S determined by (15) is the logarithmic map

$$x_1(u,v) + ix_2(u,v) = \log(u - iv) = \log \overline{w}, \quad x_3(u,v) = 0,$$

which covers the (x_1,x_2)-plane with an infinite number of sheets. If $\alpha > 0$, then the surfaces corresponding to the values β in (47) again have logarithmic singularities: They are logarithmic right helicoids, minimal surfaces but not rational or logarithmico-rational ones.

For

(48) $$\beta < -2\alpha - 1, \qquad \alpha \geq 0,$$

the roles of $w = 0$ and $w = \infty$ in (35) are interchanged from those for $\beta \geq 0$, $\alpha \geq 0$: There is now a pole at $w = 0$ and a $(0,0,0)$-point at $w = \infty$. Mutatis mutandis (with β replaced by the nonnegative integer $\delta = -\beta - 2\alpha - 2$), the values for S are again those shown in Table 4.

There remain, sandwiched between the values (47), the values β satisfying

$$(49) \qquad -2\alpha - 1 < \beta < -1, \quad \text{or} \quad 0 < -\beta - 1 < 2\alpha \quad (\alpha > 0).$$

For each of these values, the corresponding surface S has exactly <u>two</u> poles, one at $w = \infty$ and the other at $w = 0$; with each successively lower value of β, a pole is transferred from $w = \infty$ to $w = 0$ in exchange for a $(0,0,0)$-point. We shall conclude this section with a consideration of these surfaces.

For notational convenience, we write

$$(50) \qquad \gamma = -\beta - 1, \quad \text{so that} \quad 0 < \gamma < 2\alpha,$$

and also for convenience we change the signs of φ and ψ.

Substituting

$$\varphi = -\zeta^{\alpha}, \quad \psi = \frac{-1}{\zeta^{\gamma+1}}, \quad \alpha > 0, \quad 0 < \gamma < 2\alpha,$$

in (15), for $\gamma \neq \alpha$ we obtain the coordinate functions

$$(51) \qquad \begin{cases} x_1(u,v) = \dfrac{1}{\gamma r^{\gamma}} \cos \gamma\theta + \dfrac{r^{2\alpha-\gamma}}{2\alpha - \gamma} \cos(2\alpha - \gamma)\theta, \\[2ex] x_2(u,v) = \dfrac{1}{\gamma r^{\gamma}} \sin \gamma\theta + \dfrac{r^{2\alpha-\gamma}}{2\alpha - \gamma} \sin(2\alpha - \gamma)\theta, \\[2ex] x_3(u,v) = 2\,\dfrac{r^{\alpha-\gamma}}{\alpha - \gamma} \cos(\alpha - \gamma)\theta, \end{cases}$$

while for $\gamma = \alpha$ we get

$$(52) \qquad \begin{cases} x_1(u,v) = \left(\dfrac{1}{r^{\alpha}} + r^{\alpha}\right)\dfrac{\cos \alpha\theta}{\alpha}, \\[2ex] x_2(u,v) = \left(\dfrac{1}{r^{\alpha}} + r^{\alpha}\right)\dfrac{\sin \alpha\theta}{\alpha}, \\[2ex] x_3(u,v) = 2 \log r. \end{cases}$$

For the surface S given by (51), there is a pole of order $2\alpha - \gamma$ at $w = \infty$, and a pole of order γ at $w = 0$. There are no $(0,0,0)$-points on this surface [see the discussion on pages 397-398 of the surface with coordinate functions given by (35)]. We shall not here consider the multiplicity of other points on this surface. The surface is of degree 2α, independent of γ. Some of its values are shown in Table 5.

Table 5. Values for the Rational Minimal Surface (51)

a	n(a;S)	$\deg(\mathfrak{S}_a;S)$	$\deg(C_a;S)$	sum = deg(S)
(0,0,0)	0	α	α	2α
∞	2α	α	$-\alpha$	2α

The surface S given by (52) is an α-layered catenoid, with fundamental region $0 \leq \theta < 2\pi/\alpha$. The map of a curve around $w = 0$ goes α times around the catenoid before it closes. For $\alpha > 1$, there are branch points, of order $\alpha - 1$, at $w = 0$ and $w = \infty$, but they are both at ∞ on S!

All the values for this surface are shown in Table 6, which contains the values shown in Table 1 on page 386 as a special case.

Table 6. Values for the α-layered Catenoid

a	n(a;S)	$\deg(\mathfrak{S}_a;S)$	$\deg(C_a;S)$	sum = deg(S)
Finite, on S	α	α	0	2α
Finite, not on S	0	α	α	2α
∞	2α	α	$-\alpha$	2α

7. REMARKS AND PROBLEMS: CONJECTURES

For the extension of the fundamental theorem of algebra to minimal surfaces (page 386), the proof proceeded in two stages: First it was shown [5] by analytical methods that

$$\deg(S) = n(a;S) + h(a;S), \tag{53}$$

where h(a;S) is a certain integral expression, a "visibility" function; and then it was shown [3] by methods of differential geometry that, for $a \in R^3$,

$$h(a;S) = \deg(\mathfrak{S}_a;S) + \deg(C_a;S),$$

whence (7) follows.

Of the terms in the right-hand members of (7) and (53), $n(a;S)$ clearly is nonnegative, and $h(a;S)$ is nonnegative since its integrand is nonnegative. Again, $\deg(\mathcal{S}_a;S)$ is nonnegative because it also is the integral of a nonnegative expression. The integrand in the expression for $\deg(C_a;S)$, on the other hand, is positive on part of its domain of integration, and negative on part, and $\deg(C_a;S)$ is discontinuously variable as a function of a, so the foregoing derivation appears not at all to indicate whether or not $\deg(C_a;S)$ also is nonnegative for $a \in R^3$.

In the present paper, for given compatible values of $\deg(\mathcal{S}_a;S)$ and $\deg(S)$, we have sought to maximize $n(a;S)$, or equivalently to minimize $\deg(C_a;S)$, for $a \in R^3$. We have found examples where $\deg(C_a;S) = 0$, and in fact where $\deg(C_a;S)$ plummets from an arbitrarily large value discontinuously to 0, but never where $\deg(C_a;S) < 0$. This suggests that $\deg(C_a;S) \geq 0$ for all rational or logarithmico-rational minimal surfaces. The suggestion is supported by heuristic examination of the topological structure of the counterspherical representation of S. Reserving a detailed and rigorous treatment of this representation for another occasion, we shall here merely state the following conjecture.

CONJECTURE C-1. At least for all rational and logarithmico-rational minimal surfaces S, and for all $a \in R^3$, $\deg(C_a;S)$ satisfies the inequality

$$\deg(C_a;S) \geq 0.$$

Confirmation of this conjecture would complete the extended fundamental theorem of algebra to minimal surfaces in a most satisfying way.

The extended fundamental theorem of algebra does not hold exclusively for minimal surfaces. Thus the rational or logarithmico-rational minimal surface S can be distorted in a smooth and one-to-one way without altering $\deg(\mathcal{S}_a;S)$ or $\deg(C_a;S)$ for a point a not on S, and therefore without invalidating the conclusion of the theorem.

For a concrete and suggestive example of a different sort, consider the map [cf. (19)] given by

$$x_1(u,v) = \frac{2u}{1 + u^2 + v^2}, \qquad x_2(u,v) = \frac{2v}{1 + u^2 + v^2}, \qquad x_3(u,v) = \frac{u^2 + v^2 - 1}{1 + u^2 + v^2}.$$

For this spherical map S, it is easy to verify for the point $O(0,0,0)$ that

$$\deg(\mathcal{S}_0;S) = -1, \qquad \deg(C_0;S) = +1.$$

Further, since S does not extend to ∞, the "degree" of S is 0; and since the sphere does not pass through the origin, for this point we have $n(0;S) = 0$. Thus the conclusion of the theorem is valid for this point,

$$0 = \deg(S) = 0 - 1 + 1 = n(0;S) + \deg(\mathcal{S}_0;S) + \deg(C_0;S),$$

and accordingly, by the discussion given in Section 3, it is valid in general.

The foregoing considerations suggest the following conjecture.

CONJECTURE C-2. The fundamental theorem of algebra for minimal surfaces is a special case of a general result concerning maps of $\overline{R}^2$ into $\overline{R}^3$ that, except for winding points, are one-to-one and continuous in the small, and that have unique unit normal vectors at all their points, including any points at ∞ in $\overline{R}^3$.

The proof of (53) is valid for rational and logarithmico-rational minimal surfaces in $\overline{R}^n$. Further, S. S. Chern [10] has extended the notion of spherical representation to minimal surfaces in R^n. This suggests the following conjecture.

CONJECTURE C-3. The fundamental theorem of algebra can be extended to maps from $\overline{R}^2$ into $\overline{R}^n$ in terms of $n(a;S)$ and representations on spheres, and for minimal surfaces all the corresponding degrees are nonnegative.

The investigation in this paper of the relative magnitudes of the terms in equation (7) has been useful but inevitably incomplete, since except for a minor observation concerning the minimal surface of Enneper we have not at all investigated self-intersection of minimal surfaces.

Improved estimates could yield valuable information. For example, if the maximum value in (36) were shown to be less than or equal to

$\deg(S) - \deg(\mathcal{S}_0;S)$, then Conjecture C-1 would be verified for the class of surfaces involved. Or if it were shown for a single rational or logarithmico-rational minimal surface to be greater than this difference, then we would have a counterexample disproving the conjecture; this would be so, for instance, if there were shown - contrary to fact - to be a finite triple point on the minimal surface of Enneper.

We list here some problems suggested by the developments in this paper.

PROBLEM P-1. Determine the value of the maximum expressed in (36), and also the maximum for other significant classes $\mathcal{K}$ of rational or logarithmico-rational minimal surfaces.

PROBLEM P-2. Determine whether or not inequality (46) is valid; and if it is not, determine what is the best lower bound of $\deg(S)$ for rational and logarithmico-rational minimal surfaces with a given value for $\deg(\mathcal{S}_0;S)$.

PROBLEM P-3. Determine whether or not multiple-sheeted plane maps and multiple-layered catenoids (we use "layered" rather than "sheeted" here to avoid confusion with the meaning of "sheeted" in "hyperboloid of two sheets") are the only rational or logarithmico-rational minimal surfaces S for which the two-dimensional (outer Lebesgue) measure of the set of points a with $n(a;S) > 1$ is positive.

While we have sought to maximize $n(a;S)$, problems in the opposite direction also are attractive (cf. [18]). For example:

PROBLEM P-4. For significant classes $\mathcal{K}$ of rational and logarithmico-rational minimal surfaces, determine $\min_{S \in \mathcal{K}} \max_{a \in R^3} n(a;S)$.

Unlike plane maps, nonplane minimal surfaces must intersect themselves in specific curves as they wind about branch points. Soap-film experiments [11, pp. 385-397] would not reveal the nature of these curves, for the physical forces do not properly reflect the mathematics involved [19]. By <u>computer graphics</u> or other methods, one might determine the location of these curves in simple cases (cf. [16, p. 235]). For example, the functions

$$\varphi = k\zeta, \quad \psi = 3\zeta^2$$

determine a polynomial minimal surface of degree 5 when substituted in the Weierstrass formulas. As $k \to 0$, the surface converges to the map

$$x_1(u,v) + ix_2(u,v) = \bar{w}^3, \qquad x_3(u,v) = 0,$$

and thus, perhaps, Determines the "natural" (in this context) location of the branch cuts for the map $z = w^3$.

PROBLEM P-5. Apply computer graphics or other methods to the location of self-intersections of specific rational or logarithmico-rational minimal surfaces in the neighborhood of branch points.

REFERENCES

1. L. V. Ahlfors, Beiträge zur Theorie der meromorphen Funktionen, Den syvende skandinaviske matematikerkongress i Oslo, 19-22 August, 1929, pp. 84-91, A. W. Brøggers Boktrykkeri A/S, Oslo, 1930.

2. E. F. Beckenbach, An introduction to the theory of meromorphic minimal surfaces, Proceedings of symposia in pure mathematics, vol. 11, Entire Functions and Related Parts of Analysis, American Mathematical Society, Providence, R.I., 1968.

3. E. F. Beckenbach, The counterspherical representation of a minimal surface, pp. 277-299 in E.F. Beckenbach (ed.) General Inequalities 1, (Proceedings of the First International Conference on General Inequalities, Oberwolfach, 1976), ISNM 41, Birkhäuser Verlag, Basel, Stuttgart, 1978.

4. E. F. Beckenbach and T. A. Cootz, The second fundamental theorem for meromorphic minimal surfaces, Bull. Amer. Math. Soc., 76 (1970), 711-716.

5. E. F. Beckenbach, F. H. Eng, and R. E. Tafel, Global properties of rational and logarithmico-rational minimal surfaces, Pacific J. Math., 50 (1974), 355-381.

6. E. F. Beckenbach and J. W. Hahn, Triples of conjugate harmonic functions and minimal surfaces, Duke Math. J., 2 (1936), 698-704.

7. E. F. Beckenbach and G. A. Hutchison, Meromorphic minimal surfaces, Bull. Amer. Math. Soc., 68 (1962), 519-522; Pacific J. Math., 28 (1969), 17-47.

8. E. F. Beckenbach and T. Radó, Subharmonic functions and minimal surfaces, Trans. Amer. Math. Soc., 35 (1933), 648-661.

9. E. F. Beckenbach and T. Radó, Subharmonic functions and surfaces of negative curvature, Trans. Amer. Math. Soc., 35 (1933), 662-674.

10. Shiing-Shen Chern, Minimal surfaces in Euclidean space of N dimensions, Differential and combinatorial topology, A Symposium in Honor of Marston Morse, Princeton University Press, Princeton, N.J., 1965.

11. Richard Courant and Herbert Robbins, What is Mathematics?, Oxford University Press, London, New York, Toronto, 1941.

12. L. R. Ford, Automorphic Functions, McGraw-Hill, New York, 1929.

13. W. C. Graustein, Differential Geometry, Macmillan Company, New York, 1935.

14. S. Lefschetz, Introduction to Topology, Princeton University Press, Princeton, N.J., 1949.

15. R. Nevanlinna, Zur Theorie der meromorphen Funktionen, Acta Math., 46 (1925), 1-99.

16. Johannes C. C. Nitsche, On new results in the theory of minimal surfaces, Bull. Amer. Math. Soc., 71 (1965), 195-270.

17. W. F. Osgood, Lehrbuch der Funktionentheorie, vol. 1, G. G. Teubner, Leipzig, 1928.

18. R. Osserman, Global properties of classical minimal surfaces, Duke Math. J., 32 (1965), 565-573.

19. R. Osserman, A proof of the regularity everywhere of the classical solution to Plateau's problem, Ann. of Math. (2) 91 (1970), 550-569.

SOME INEQUALITIES FOR UNIVALENT FUNCTIONS WITH QUASICONFORMAL EXTENSIONS

Jochen Becker
Technische Universität Berlin
Fachbereich Mathematik
D-1000 Berlin 12
WEST GERMANY

ABSTRACT. Some inequalities for univalent functions with quasiconformal extensions are discussed. The emphasis lies on inequalities being sufficient for a univalent function to have a quasiconformal extension.

1. INTRODUCTION

Let S denote the class of normalized univalent functions $f(z) = z + a_2 z^2 + \cdots$ in the unit disk $D = \{|z| < 1\}$, and let $S_{k,R}$ $(0 \leq k < 1, 1 < R \leq \infty)$ be the class of functions $f \in S$ having a quasiconformal extension F onto $\{|z| < R\}$ with $F(z) \neq \infty$ and

$$|F_{\bar{z}}| \underset{\text{a.e.}}{\leq} k|F_z| .$$

Many of the known estimates for the functions of class S have been improved (compare, e.g., [7]) for the subclasses $S_{k,R}$. The following two inequalities are necessary conditions for $S_{k,\infty}$ and are of particular interest here:

$$\text{(1)} \qquad \left|\frac{f''(z)}{f'(z)}\right| \leq \frac{6k}{1 - |z|^2} , \qquad (|z| < 1)$$

$$\text{(2)} \qquad |S_f(z)| \leq \frac{6k}{(1 - |z|^2)^2} ,$$

where

$$S_f = \left(\frac{f''}{f'}\right)' - \frac{1}{2}\left(\frac{f''}{f'}\right)^2$$

denotes the Schwarzian derivative [4], [5], [6]. For $k = 1$, these are well-known estimates for $f \in S$.

Corresponding sufficient conditions for an analytic function $f(z) = z + \cdots$ to belong to the class $S_{k,\infty}$ are also known [1], [2]:

$$\text{(1')} \qquad \sup_{|z|<1} |(1 - |z|^2)\, z \frac{f''}{f'}(z) + c|z|^2| \leq k ,$$

(2') $$\sup_{|z|<1} \left|(1-|z|^2)^2 \frac{z}{\bar{z}} S_f(z) + 2c(1+c)|z|^2\right| \le 2k|1+c| ,$$

where c is a given constant with $|c| < 1$. For $k = 1$, these are univalence criteria.

Since the existence of a quasiconformal extension depends only on the boundary curve of the image domain, the question arises as to whether or not there are also sufficient limsup conditions corresponding to (1'), (2'). Indeed, we have the following result:

THEOREM 1. Let $f \in S$ be a univalent function such that the image domain $f(D)$ is a Jordan domain. Then each of the following two conditions implies that f belongs to a class $S_{k,R}$, where k,R can be chosen suitably:

(1") $$\limsup_{|z|\to 1} \left|(1-|z|^2)\, z \frac{f''}{f'}(z) + c\right| < 1 ,$$

(2") $$\limsup_{|z|\to 1} \left|(1-|z|^2)^2 \frac{z}{\bar{z}} S_f(z) + 2c(1+c)\right| < 2|1+c| \quad \text{and}$$
$$\limsup_{|z|\to 1} (1-|z|^2) \left|\frac{f''}{f'}(z)\right| < 2|1+c| .$$

Condition (1") for $c = 0$ was proved already in [3].

2. PROOF OF THEOREM 1

In order to show that (1") and (2") imply the existence of a quasiconformal extension over the unit circle, we need a result on the Löwner differential equation,

(3) $$\frac{\partial}{\partial t} f(z,t) = z p(z,t) \frac{\partial}{\partial z} f(z,t) .$$

Here

$$p(z,t) = c_0(t) + c_1(t)z + \cdots \qquad (|z| < 1,\ 0 \le t \le \alpha)$$

denotes a function which is analytic for every $t \in [0,\alpha]$ and measurable as a function of t, with the property

(4) $$\left|\frac{p(z,t) - 1}{p(z,t) + 1}\right| \le k < 1 \qquad (|z| < 1,\ 0 \le t \le \alpha) .$$

We consider general solutions

$$f(z,t) = a_1(t)z + z_2(t)z^2 + \cdots ,$$

being analytic for every $t \in [0,\alpha]$ and absolutely continuous with respect to t (for each fixed z), satisfying (3) for almost every $t \in [0,\alpha]$.

THEOREM 2. Let $f(z,t) = a_1(t)z + \cdots$ $(|z|<1,\ 0\leq t\leq\alpha)$ be a solution of (3) such that (4) is satisfied. Let $f(z,0)$ be univalent and let the image domain $f(D,0)$ be a Jordan domain. Let $f(z,\alpha)$ be locally univalent in D. Then there is a $\tau \in (0,\alpha)$ such that $f(z,t)$ is univalent for every $t \in [0,\tau]$, and the image domains $f(D,t)$ are also Jordan domains. Furthermore,

$$F(re^{i\varphi}) := f(e^{i\varphi}, \log r), \qquad 1 \leq r \leq e^{\tau} ,$$

is a k-quasiconformal extension of $f(z,0)$ onto $\{|z| < e^{\tau}\}$ with

$$\frac{F_{\bar z}(re^{i\varphi})}{F_z(re^{i\varphi})} \underset{\text{a.e.}}{=} e^{2i\varphi} \frac{p(e^{i\varphi},\log r) - 1}{p(e^{i\varphi},\log r) + 1} ,$$

where $p(e^{i\varphi},t)$ denotes the radial limit.

A proof of Theorem 2 for the normalized case

$$c_0(t) \equiv 1 , \quad a_1(t) = e^t$$

can be found in [3]. The general case can be reduced to this case (compare [2]). □

Now it is not difficult to prove that each of the conditions (1"), (2") implies quasiconformal extension.

In the first case, we consider

$$f(z,t) = f(e^{-t}z) + \frac{e^t - e^{-t}}{1 + c} zf'(e^{-t}z) = \frac{e^t + ce^{-t}}{1 + c} z + \cdots .$$

This is a solution of (3) (which is even continuously differentiable with regard to t), with $p(z,t)$ given by

$$\frac{p(z,t) - 1}{p(z,t) + 1} = -(1 - e^{-2t})\, e^{-t}z\, \frac{f''(e^{-t}z)}{f'(e^{-t}z)} - ce^{-2t} .$$

By (1") it follows that there is a $k < 1$ and an $\alpha > 1$ such that $p(z,t)$ satisfies (4). Since

$$f'(z,t) = \frac{e^t f'(e^{-t}z)}{1+c}\left(1 - \frac{p(z,t)-1}{p(z,t)+1}\right) \neq 0 ,$$

and since by assumption $f(D,0) = f(D)$ is a Jordan domain, Theorem 2 shows that

$$F(re^{i\varphi}) = f\left(\frac{1}{r}\, e^{i\varphi}\right) + \frac{r - \frac{1}{r}}{1+c}\, e^{i\varphi}\, f'\left(\frac{1}{r}\, e^{i\varphi}\right)$$

is a k-quasiconformal extension of $f(z) = f(z,0)$ onto a disk which is a little larger than the unit disk. The complex dilatation is

$$\frac{F_{\bar z}(re^{i\varphi})}{F_z(re^{i\varphi})} = -e^{2i\varphi}\left[\frac{c}{r^2} + \left(1 - \frac{1}{r^2}\right)\frac{1}{r}\, e^{i\varphi}\, \frac{f''\left(\frac{1}{r}\, e^{i\varphi}\right)}{f'\left(\frac{1}{r}\, e^{i\varphi}\right)}\right] .$$

In the second case, we consider

$$f(z,t) = f(e^{-t}z) + \frac{(e^t - e^{-t})\, z\, f'(e^{-t}z)}{(1+c) - \frac{1}{2}(e^t - e^{-t})\, z\, \frac{f''}{f'}(e^{-t}z)} .$$

The second inequality of condition (2") implies that the denominator is $\neq 0$ for sufficiently small t, and hence $f(z,t)$ is analytic satisfying (3) with $p(z,t)$ defined by

$$\frac{p(z,t)-1}{p(z,t)+1} = -ce^{-2t} - \frac{(1-e^{-2t})^2}{2(1+c)}\, z^2\, S_f(e^{-t}z) .$$

By the first inequality of (2"), it follows that $p(z,t)$ satisfies (4) with suitable k,α. Again we have $f'(z,t) \neq 0$ for small t. Hence, by Theorem 2,

$$F(re^{i\varphi}) = f\left(\frac{1}{r}\, e^{i\varphi}\right) + \frac{\left(r - \frac{1}{r}\right) e^{i\varphi}\, f'\left(\frac{1}{r}\, e^{i\varphi}\right)}{(1+c) - \frac{1}{2}\left(r - \frac{1}{r}\right) e^{i\varphi}\, \frac{f''}{f'}\left(\frac{1}{r}\, e^{i\varphi}\right)}$$

is a quasiconformal extension of $f(z) = f(z,0)$ over the unit circle. □

3. REMARK

In the case $c = 0$, condition (2") has the form

$$\begin{cases} \limsup\limits_{|z|\to 1}\, (1-|z|^2)^2\, |S_f(z)| < 2 \quad \text{and} \\ \limsup\limits_{|z|\to 1}\, (1-|z|^2)\left|\frac{f''(z)}{f'(z)}\right| < 2 . \end{cases}$$

I do not know whether one or even each of these two inequalities alone is already sufficient for quasiconformal extension (under the assumption that f(D) is a Jordan domain). The constant 2 would be best possible in both cases. This is shown for the second inequality by $f(z) = z + \frac{1}{2} z^2$ satisfying

$$\limsup (1 - |z|^2) \left|\frac{f''(z)}{f'(z)}\right| = 2 .$$

The boundary curve of the image domain has a zero angle; hence f cannot have a quasiconformal extension.

In the first case, a suitable transformation of

$$f(z) = \log \frac{1 + z}{1 - z} ,$$

for instance, shows that the constant 2 would be best possible. The transformation uses Möbius transformations and the square root such that the image domain is mapped onto a Jordan domain, while

$$\limsup (1 - |z|^2)^2 \, |S_f(z)| = 2$$

remains unchanged.

REFERENCES

1. L.V. Ahlfors, Sufficient conditions for quasiconformal extension, in Discontinuous Groups and Riemann Surfaces (Proc. Conference, Univ. of Maryland, 1973), pp. 23-29. Ann. of Math. Studies, No. 79, Princeton University Press, Princeton, N.J., 1974.

2. J. Becker, Über die Lösungsstruktur einer Differentialgleichung in der konformen Abbildung, J. Reine Angew. Math. 285 (1976), 66-74.

3. J. Becker u. Chr. Pommerenke, Über die quasikonforme Fortsetzung schlichter Funktionen, Math. Z. 161 (1978), 69-80.

4. Z. Göktürk, Estimates for univalent functions with quasiconformal extensions, Ann. Acad. Sci. Fenn., Ser. AI (1974), 589.

5. R. Kühnau, Verzerrungssätze und Koeffizientenbedingungen von Grunskyschen Typ für quasikonforme Abbildungen, Math. Nachr. 48 (1971), 77-105.

6. O. Lehto, Schlicht functions with a quasiconformal extension, Ann. Acad. Sci. Fenn. Ser. AI (1971), 500.

7. G. Schober, Univalent functions - selected topics, Springer, Berlin-Heidelberg-New York, 1975.

Inequalities of Probability and Information Theory

ON A FAMILY OF FUNCTIONAL INEQUALITIES

Claudi Alsina
Dept. Matemàtiques i Estadística (ETSAB)
Univ. Politècnica de Barcelona
Diagonal 649, Barcelona 28
SPAIN

ABSTRACT. We study some inequalities relating the behavior of certain binary operations of the unit interval on some numerical series.

1. INTRODUCTION

In a previous paper [1], we established an inequality dealing with the study of countable products of probabilistic metric spaces. Our aim now is to study the same inequality under weaker hypotheses and to solve some questions related to it.

In the sequel 'I' will denote the unit interval $[0,1]$, and the set of two-place functions from $I \times I$ into I will be considered partially ordered with respect to the usual pointwise ordering of functions.

2. ON THE FUNCTIONAL INEQUALITY (Σ)

Let T be a two-place function from $I \times I$ into I, and let (Σ) be the following functional inequality:

$$(\Sigma) \qquad T\left(\sum_{i=1}^{\infty} \frac{a_i}{2^i}, \sum_{i=1}^{\infty} \frac{b_i}{2^i}\right) \leq \sum_{i=1}^{\infty} \frac{1}{2^i} T(a_i, b_i),$$

for all sequences (a_i), (b_i) in I.

Our chief concern in this section is to find, under very weak restrictions on T, the strongest solution of (Σ).

First, consider a family of solutions for (Σ).

EXAMPLE 2.1. For any $a \in \mathbb{R}$, $a \geq 1$, consider T_a to be the two-place function from $I \times I$ into I defined by

$$T_a(x,y) = \mathrm{Max}(\mathrm{Min}(x,y) + a\,\mathrm{Max}(x,y) - a, 0).$$

A straightforward computation shows that T_a satisfies (Σ) and that the unique associative T_a is $T_1(x,y) = \mathrm{Max}(x + y - 1, 0)$. This operation T_1

is usually denoted by T_m.

THEOREM 2.1. <u>Let</u> T <u>be a two-place function</u> $I \times I$ <u>into</u> I <u>such that</u> $T(0,0) = T(0,1) = T(1,0) = 0$. <u>If</u> T <u>satisfies the functional inequality</u> (Σ), <u>then</u> $T(x,y) \le T_m(x,y)\, T(1,1)$, <u>for all</u> $(x,y) \in I \times I$.

<u>Proof</u>. Let $x \in I$ and let

$$x = \sum_{i=1}^{\infty} \left(\frac{x_i}{2^i}\right)$$

be any binary expansion of x, where, for each i, $x_i \in \{0,1\}$. Using (Σ) and the conditions $T(0,0) = T(1,0) = 0$, we have

$$T(x,0) = T\left(\sum_{i=1}^{\infty} \frac{1}{2^i} x_i \,,\, \sum_{i=1}^{\infty} \frac{0}{2^i}\right) \le \sum_{i=1}^{\infty} \frac{1}{2^i} T(x_i,0) = 0 \ ,$$

and similarly $T(0,x) = 0$. Moreover,

$$T(x,1) = T\left(\sum_{i=1}^{\infty} \frac{1}{2^i} x_i \,,\, \sum_{i=1}^{\infty} \frac{1}{2^i}\right) \le \sum_{i=1}^{\infty} \frac{1}{2^i} T(x_i,1) = x\,T(1,1) \ ,$$

and $T(1,x) \le xT(1,1)$, that is, $T(x,y) \le T_m(x,y)\, T(1,1)$ on the boundary of $I \times I$. We must show that

$$T(x,y) \le T_m(x,y)\; T(1,1)$$

for all $(x,y) \in \mathring{I} \times \mathring{I}$, where $\mathring{I} = (0,1)$. To this end, let $B_0 = 0$ and, for any $n \ge 1$, let $B_n = 1/2 + \cdots + 1/2^n$. Consider the partition

$$\mathring{I} \times \mathring{I} = \bigcup_{n=1}^{\infty} (R_n \cup S_n) \ ,$$

where

$$R_n = \{(x,y) \in \mathring{I} \times \mathring{I} \mid 1 + B_{n-1} < x + y \le 1 + B_n\}$$

and

$$S_n = \{(x,y) \in \mathring{I} \times \mathring{I} \mid 1/2^n < x + y \le 1/2^{n-1}\} \ .$$

Fix $n \ge 1$ and let $(x,y) \in R_n$, that is, $x + y = 1 + B_{n-1} + b$, where $0 < b \le 1/2^n$, so that at least one of x,y must be greater than B_n. Suppose $x > B_n$ and consequently

$$x = B_n + \sum_{i=n+1}^{\infty} \left(\frac{x_i}{2^i}\right) ,$$

where $x_i \in \{0,1\}$ for each $i \geq n+1$. Since $1 - B_n = 1/2^n$, we have

$$y = 1 + B_{n-1} + b - x = B_{n-1} + \frac{2^n b}{2^n} + \sum_{i=n+1}^{\infty} \left(\frac{1-x_i}{2^i}\right) ,$$

and

$$x = B_{n-1} + \frac{1}{2^n} + \sum_{i=n+1}^{\infty} \left(\frac{x_i}{2^i}\right),$$

so, applying (Σ), we obtain

$$\begin{aligned} T(x,y) &\leq B_{n-1}\, T(1,1) + \frac{1}{2^n} T(1,2^n b) + \sum_{i=n+1}^{\infty} \frac{1}{2^i} T(x_i, 1-x_i) \\ &\leq B_{n-1}\, T(1,1) + bT(1,1) = T_m(x,y)\, T(1,1) . \end{aligned}$$

If $x \leq B_n$, then reversing the roles of x and y yields the same conclusion.

Next, fix $n \geq 1$ and let $(x,y) \in S_n$, that is,

$$x + y = \frac{1}{2^n} + a , \quad \text{with } 0 < a \leq \frac{1}{2^n} .$$

At least one of x,y is greater than $1/2^{n+1}$, and, as above, without loss of generality, we consider the case $x > 1/2^{n+1}$. If $(1/2^{n+1}) < x \leq (1/2^n)$, then

$$x = \frac{1}{2^{n+1}} + \sum_{i=n+2}^{\infty} \left(\frac{x_i}{2^i}\right),$$

where $x_i \in \{0,1\}$ for each $i \geq n+2$. In that case,

$$y = \frac{1}{2^n} + a - x = \frac{2^n a}{2^n} + \sum_{i=n+2}^{\infty} \left(\frac{1-x_i}{2^i}\right),$$

and (Σ) yields

$$\begin{aligned} T(x,y) &\leq \frac{1}{2^n} T(0,2^n a) + \frac{1}{2^{n+1}} T(1,0) + \sum_{i=n+2}^{\infty} \frac{1}{2^i} T(x_i, 1-x_i) \\ &= 0 = T_m(x,y)\, T(1,1) . \end{aligned}$$

Finally, if $(1/2^n) < x < (1/2^n) + a$, then

$$x = \frac{1}{2^n} + \sum_{i=n+1}^{\infty} \left(\frac{tx_i}{2^i}\right)$$

(with $x_i \in \{0,1\}$ for $i \geq n+1$ and $t \in (0,1)$) and

$$y = \sum_{i=n+1}^{\infty} \frac{(1-t)x_i}{2^i} .$$

If

$$t = \sum_{i=1}^{\infty} \left(\frac{t_i}{2^i}\right)$$

is any binary expansion of t (with $t_i \in \{0,1\}$ for each i), then

$$T(t,1-t) \leq \sum_{i=1}^{\infty} \frac{1}{2^i} T(t_i, 1-t_i) = 0 ,$$

and consequently

$$T(x,y) \leq \frac{1}{2^n} T(1,0) + \sum_{i=n+1}^{\infty} \frac{1}{2^i} T(tx_i, (1-t)x_i) = 0 . \quad \square$$

COROLLARY 2.1. <u>If</u> T <u>satisfies the hypothesis of Theorem</u> 2.1 <u>and</u> $T(1,1) = 1$, <u>then</u> $T \leq T_m$, <u>that is</u>, T_m <u>is the strongest solution of</u> (Σ).

If we associate to T the two-place function T^* from $I \times I$ into I defined by

$$T^*(x,y) = \inf\left\{\sum_{i=1}^{\infty} \frac{1}{2^i} T(x_i,y_i) \mid \sum_{i=1}^{\infty} \frac{x_i}{2^i} = x, \ \sum_{i=1}^{\infty} \frac{y_i}{2^i} = y, \ (x_i),(y_i) \subset I\right\} ,$$

then T satisfies (Σ) if and only if $T \leq T^*$. If $T \leq T^*$, then T^* is also a solution of (Σ), so by Corollary 2.1, $T_m^* = T_m$.

The next theorem is an application of Theorem 2.1 to the solution of a functional inequality in the set $\mathcal{D}^+$ of positive probability-distribution functions. Let C be a copula, that is, a two-place function from $I \times I$ into I such that

(i) $C(0,x) = C(x,0) = 0$, $C(1,x) = C(x,1) = x$, for all $x \in I$,

(ii) $C(x_1,y_1) - C(x_1,y_2) - C(x_2,y_1) + C(x_2,y_2) \geq 0$, whenever $x_1 \leq x_2$ and $y_1 \leq y_2$.

It follows that any copula C is stronger than T_m $(C \geq T_m)$ and induces a binary operation ρ_C in $\mathcal{D}^+$ defined by

$$\rho_C(F,G)(x) = \begin{cases} 0 , & \text{if } x \leq 0 , \\ \inf\{F(a) + G(v) - C(F(a),G(v)) \mid a + v = x\}, & \text{if } x > 0 . \end{cases}$$

These operations have been studied recently in [2].

THEOREM 2.2. *Let* C *be a copula. Then*

$$(*)\qquad \rho_C\left(\sum_{i=1}^{\infty}\frac{1}{2^i}F_i\,,\ \sum_{i=1}^{\infty}\frac{1}{2^i}G_i\right)\geq\sum_{i=1}^{\infty}\frac{1}{2^i}\rho_C(F_i,G_i)\,,$$

for all sequences (F_i), (G_i) *in* $\mathcal{D}^+$ *if and only if* $C = T_m$.

Proof. Sufficiency follows from the fact that T_m satisfies (Σ). To prove necessity, suppose that $(*)$ holds. Let (a_i), (b_i) be arbitrary sequences in I. For each $i\in N$, consider the functions $F_i, G_i \in \mathcal{D}^+$ given by

$$F_i(x)=\begin{cases}0\,, & \text{if } x\leq 0\,,\\ a_i\,, & \text{if } 0<x\leq 1,\\ a_i+b_i-C(a_i,b_i), & \text{if } 1<x\leq 2,\\ 1\,, & \text{if } x>2\,,\end{cases}\qquad G_i(x)=\begin{cases}0\,, & \text{if } x\leq 0,\\ b_i\,, & \text{if } 0<x\leq 1,\\ a_i+b_i-C(a_i,b_i), & \text{if } 1<x\leq 2,\\ 1\,, & \text{if } x>2\,.\end{cases}$$

Then we have

$$\begin{aligned}\sum_{i=1}^{\infty}\frac{1}{2^i}(a_i+b_i)-C\left(\sum_{i=1}^{\infty}\frac{a_i}{2^i}\,,\ \sum_{i=1}^{\infty}\frac{b_i}{2^i}\right)&\\ =\sum_{i=1}^{\infty}\frac{1}{2^i}(F_i(1)+G_i(1))&+C\left(\sum_{i=1}^{\infty}\frac{1}{2^i}F_i(1)\,,\ \sum_{i=1}^{\infty}\frac{1}{2^i}G_i(1)\right)\\ \geq\rho_C\left(\sum_{i=1}^{\infty}\frac{1}{2^i}F_i\,,\ \sum_{i=1}^{\infty}\frac{1}{2^i}G_i\right)(2)&\geq\sum_{i=1}^{\infty}\frac{1}{2^i}\rho_C(F_i,G_i)(2)\\ =\sum_{i=1}^{\infty}\frac{1}{2^i}(a_i+b_i)&-\sum_{i=1}^{\infty}\frac{1}{2^i}C(a_i,b_i)\,,\end{aligned}$$

that is,

$$C\left(\sum_{i=1}^{\infty}\frac{a_i}{2^i}\,,\ \sum_{i=1}^{\infty}\frac{b_i}{2^i}\right)\leq\sum_{i=1}^{\infty}\frac{1}{2^i}C(a_i,b_i)\,,$$

so by Theorem 2.1, $C\leq T_m$; and being a copula, C satisfies $C\geq T_m$, so that $C = T_m$. □

3. ON THE FUNCTIONAL INEQUALITIES (Σ,n)

Given a two-place function T from $I\times I$ into I, and given a fixed $n\in N$, we can consider the following functional inequality:

$$(\Sigma,n)\qquad T\left(\sum_{i=1}^{n}\frac{a_i}{2^i}\,,\ \sum_{i=1}^{n}\frac{b_i}{2^i}\right)\leq\sum_{i=1}^{n}\frac{1}{2^i}T(a_i,b_i)\,,$$

for all n-sequences $(a_1,\ldots,a_n)$, $(b_1,\ldots,b_n)\in I^n$.

Obviously, if T satisfies (Σ), then T is a solution of (Σ, n) for all $n \in N$; and if T is continuous, then the reciprocal statement holds. By the next theorem, it will be possible to show that, without continuity assumptions on T, the conclusion of Theorem 2.1 holds whenever T satisfies (Σ, n), for all $n \in N$.

THEOREM 3.1. <u>Let</u> T <u>be a two-place function from</u> $I \times I$ <u>into</u> I <u>such that</u> $T(x,0) = T(0,x) = 0$ <u>and</u> $T(x,1) = T(1,x) = x$, <u>for all</u> $x \in I$. <u>If, for a fixed</u> $n \geq 2$, T <u>satisfies the functional inequality</u> (Σ,n), <u>then</u>

$$T(x,y) \leq \operatorname{Max}\left(x + y - 1 + \frac{1}{2^n}, 0\right),$$

<u>for any</u> $(x,y) \in K_n$, <u>where</u>

$$K_n = \left[0, 1 - \frac{1}{2^n}\right]^2 - \bigcup_{i=1}^{2^n-1} \left[\frac{i-1}{2^n}, \frac{i}{2^n}\right] \times \left[1 - \frac{1+i}{2^n}, 1 - \frac{i}{2^n}\right].$$

<u>Proof</u>. For $i \in \{1,2,\ldots,2^n-1\}$, let

$$\frac{i}{2^n} = \sum_{k=1}^{n} \frac{1}{2^k} t_k^i$$

be a binary expansion, where $t_k^i \in \{0,1\}$ for $k = 1,2,\ldots,n$. In order to prove that

$$T(x,y) \leq \operatorname{Max}\left(x + y - 1 + \frac{1}{2^n}, 0\right)$$

on K_n, we distinguish two cases.

<u>Case 1</u>. $(x,y) \in K_n$ and $x + y \leq 1 - 1/2^n$. Then there exists $i \in \{1,2,\ldots,2^n-2\}$ such that

$$(x,y) \in \left[\frac{i-1}{2^n}, \frac{i}{2^n}\right] \times \left[0, 1 - \frac{i+1}{2^n}\right],$$

and consequently there are $\theta, \lambda \in I$, such that

$$(*) \qquad \begin{aligned} x &= \frac{i-1}{2^n} + \frac{\theta}{2^n} = \sum_{k=1}^{n} \frac{1}{2^k} t_k^i + \frac{\theta}{2^n} - \frac{1}{2^n}, \\ y &= \lambda\left(1 - \frac{i+1}{2^n}\right) = \sum_{k=1}^{n} \frac{1}{2^k} \lambda(1 - t_k^i). \end{aligned}$$

If $t_n^i = 1$, applying (Σ,n) to the expansions $(*)$ we obtain

$$T(x,y) \le \sum_{k=1}^{n-1} \frac{1}{2^k} T(t_k^i, \lambda(1 - t_k^i)) + \frac{1}{2^n} T(\theta,0) = 0 ,$$

because $T(t,\lambda(1 - t)) = 0$ whenever $t \in \{0,1\}$. If $t_n^i = 0$, consider

$$k_0 = \mathrm{Max}\{k \mid t_k^i = 1,\ k = 1,2,\dots,n-1\}$$

and rewrite $(*)$ as follows:

$$x = \sum_{k=1}^{k_0-1} \frac{1}{2^k} t_k^i + \frac{1}{2^{k_0}} \left(1 - \frac{1 - \theta}{2^{n-k_0}}\right),$$

$$y = \sum_{k=1}^{k_0-1} \frac{1}{2^k} \lambda(1 - t_k^i) + \frac{0}{2^{k_0}} + \sum_{k=k_0+1}^{n} \frac{\lambda}{2^k} ,$$

so that, using (Σ,n), we have as above $T(x,y) = 0$. This completes case 1.

<u>Case 2</u>. $(x,y) \in K_n$ and $x + y \ge 1 - 1/2^n$. Then there exists $i \in \{2,3,\dots,2^n-1\}$ such that

$$(x,y) \in \left[\frac{i - 1}{2^n} , \frac{i}{2^n}\right] \times \left[1 - \frac{i}{2^n} , 1 - \frac{1}{2^n}\right] ;$$

that is, there are two parameters $\theta,\lambda \in I$ such that

$$(**) \quad \begin{aligned} x &= \frac{i - 1}{2^n} + \frac{\theta}{2^n} = \sum_{k=1}^{n} \frac{t_k^i}{2^k} + \frac{\theta}{2^n} - \frac{1}{2^n} \\ y &= 1 - \frac{i}{2^n} + \lambda \frac{i - 1}{2^n} = \sum_{k=1}^{n} \frac{1}{2^k} (1 - t_k^i(1 - \lambda)) + \frac{1 - \lambda}{2^n} . \end{aligned}$$

If $t_n^i = 1$, applying (Σ,n) to the expansion $(**)$ we have

$$\begin{aligned} T(x,y) &\le \sum_{k=1}^{n-1} \frac{1}{2^k} T(t_k^i, 1 - t_k^i(1 - \lambda)) + \frac{1}{2^n} T(\theta,1) \\ &= \sum_{k=1}^{n-1} \frac{\lambda}{2^k} t_k^i + \frac{\theta}{2^n} = \lambda \frac{i - 1}{2^n} + \frac{\theta}{2^n} = x + y - 1 + \frac{1}{2^n} , \end{aligned}$$

where we have used the fact that $T(t, 1 - t(1 - \lambda)) = \lambda t$ for $t \in \{0,1\}$. If $t_n^i = 0$, we define

$$k_0 = \mathrm{Max}\ \{k \mid t_k^i = 1,\ k = 1,2,\dots,n-1\} ,$$

and $(**)$ can be rewritten as follows:

$$x = \sum_{k=1}^{k_0-1} \frac{1}{2^k} t_k^i + \frac{1}{2^{k_0}} \frac{\theta}{2^{n-k_0}} + \sum_{k=k_0+1}^{n} \frac{1}{2^k},$$

$$y = \sum_{k=1}^{k_0-1} \frac{1}{2^k} (1 - t_k^i(1-\lambda)) + \frac{1}{2^{k_0}} \cdot \frac{1}{2^{n-k_0}} + \sum_{k=k_0+1}^{n} \frac{\lambda}{2^k}.$$

Applying (Σ,n) to these expansions, we obtain, as above,

$$T(x,y) \le \sum_{k=1}^{k_0-1} \frac{\lambda}{2^k} t_k^i + \frac{\theta}{2^n} + \sum_{k=k_0+1}^{n} \frac{\lambda}{2^k} = x + y - 1 + \frac{1}{2^n}. \quad \square$$

COROLLARY 3.1. <u>If</u> T <u>satisfies</u> (Σ,n) <u>for all</u> $n \in N$, <u>then</u> $T \le T_m$.

In the following theorem, some conditions on T are given in order to satisfy (Σ,n).

THEOREM 3.2. <u>Let</u> T <u>be a two-place function from</u> $I \times I$ <u>into</u> I. <u>If either of the following statements holds</u>:

(i) $\mathrm{Max}\left(x + y - \frac{2^n}{2^n - 1}, 0\right) \le T(x,y) \le T_m(x,y)$, <u>for all</u> $(x,y) \in I \times I$;

(ii) $\mathrm{Sup}\{|T(x,y) - T_m(x,y)| \; ; x,y \in I\} \le \frac{1}{2^{n+1} - 1}$ <u>and</u> $T(x,y) = 0$ <u>whenever</u> $x + y \le 1$;

<u>then</u> T <u>satisfies the functional inequality</u> (Σ,n).

To end, consider the following suggestive example.

EXAMPLE 3.1. Given the partition

$$[0,1] = \left[0, 1 - \frac{1}{2^n}\right] \cup \left(1 - \frac{1}{2^n}, 1\right],$$

consider the associated ordinal sum of T_m and Min; that is, let S be the two-place function from $I \times I$ into I defined by

$$S(x,y) = \begin{cases} \mathrm{Max}\left(x + y - 1 + \frac{1}{2^n}, 0\right), & \text{if } (x,y) \in \left[0, 1 - \frac{1}{2^n}\right]^2, \\ \mathrm{Min}(x,y), & \text{if } (x,y) \in I^2 - \left[0, 1 - \frac{1}{2^n}\right]^2. \end{cases}$$

It is easy to show that S satisfies functional inequalities (Σ,k) for $k = 1,\dots,n$, but S does not satisfy (Σ,k) for $k \ge n + 1$.

ACKNOWLEDGMENT. The author gratefully acknowledges Professor B. Schweizer (University of Massachusetts, Amherst) for his helpful suggestions.

REFERENCES

1. C. Alsina, On countable products and algebraic convexifications of probabilistic metric spaces, Pacific J. Math., to appear.

2. R. Moynihan, B. Schweizer, and A. Sklar, Inequalities among operations on probability distribution functions, pp. 133-149, in E.F. Beckenbach (ed.) General Inequalities 1 (Proceedings of the First International Conference on General Inequalities, Oberwolfach, May 10-14, 1976), ISNM 41, Birkhäuser Verlag, Basel and Stuttgart, 1978.

HOW TO DERIVE ALL L_p-METRICS FROM A SINGLE PROBABILISTIC METRIC

B. Schweizer
Department of Math. and Stat.
University of Massachusetts
Amherst, MA 01003
U.S.A.

A. Sklar
Department of Mathematics
Illinois Institute of Technology
Chicago, IL 60616
U.S.A.

ABSTRACT. It is shown that all the L_p-metrics on a given vector space of functions can be derived from a single and very natural probabilistic metric on that space. In addition, it is indicated how the close connection between these concepts can be exploited to generate a large variety of inequalities, e.g., for special functions, by a uniform method.

1. INTRODUCTION

The L_p-metrics play a central role in modern analysis. Probabilistic metrics, on the other hand, are not as well known. Nevertheless, the two concepts are closely related. In this note we shall demonstrate this fact by showing that all the L_p-metrics on a given vector space S of functions can be recovered from one probabilistic metric. This single probabilistic metric thus yields as much information about S as all these ordinary metrics combined, and more information than any individual L_p-metric or finite collection of such metrics. (For a concise survey of the theory of probabilistic metric spaces, see [3]; cf. also [4], [5], [6], [8], and [10].)

2. THE SPACE $(S,\mathfrak{F})$

For a given positive integer m, let X be a (Lebesgue-)measurable subset of Euclidean m-space E^m and let μ be a measure, absolutely continuous with respect to m-dimensional Lebesgue measure, such that $\mu(X) = 1$. Let n be a positive integer and let S be a vector space of μ-measurable functions mapping X into E^n; as usual, functions in S that are equal almost everywhere are identified. Let d denote a metric on E^n topologically equivalent to the usual n-dimensional Euclidean metric. For any p, $0 < p < \infty$, let L_p denote the usual L_p-metric on S; and let L_∞ denote the essential supremum metric on S.

For any a,b in S and $x > 0$, the set $\{t \in X \mid d(a(t),b(t)) < x\}$ is measurable. Thus we can define a function F_{ab} on the reals via

$$F_{ab}(x) = \begin{cases} 0, & x \leq 0, \\ \mu\{t \in X \mid d(a(t),b(t)) < x\}, & x > 0 . \end{cases}$$

Clearly, F_{ab} is nondecreasing and left-continuous, with $\inf F_{ab} = 0$ and $\sup F_{ab} = \mu(X) = 1$. Hence F_{ab} is a probability distribution function -- the distribution function of the random variable $d(a,b)$. It is also evident that $F_{ab} = F_{ba}$ and that $F_{ab} = \varepsilon_0$ if and only if $a = b$ a.e., where ε_0 is given by

$$\varepsilon_0(x) = \begin{cases} 0, & x \leq 0, \\ 1, & x > 0 . \end{cases}$$

Next, for any a, b, c in S and $x,y > 0$, let

$$A = \{t \mid d(b(t),c(t)) < x\} ,$$

$$B = \{t \mid d(a(t),c(t)) < y\} ,$$

$$C = \{t \mid d(a(t),b(t)) < x + y\} .$$

Then $A \cap B \subseteq C$, and we have (cf. [10], p. 260)

$$\mu C \geq \mu(A \cap B) = \mu A + \mu B - \mu(A \cup B) \geq \mu A + \mu B - 1 .$$

Consequently, since $\mu C \geq 0$, for any x,y we have

$$F_{ab}(x + y) \geq T_m(F_{bc}(x),F_{ca}(y)) ,$$

where T_m is the function defined on the unit square $[0,1] \times [0,1]$ by

$$T_m(u,v) = \mathrm{Max}(u + v - 1,0) .$$

It follows that

$$F_{ab} \geq \tau_{T_m}(F_{bc},F_{ca}) ,$$

where τ_{T_m} is defined for any two distribution functions F and G and any $t > 0$ via

$$\tau_{T_m}(F,G)(t) = \sup_{x+y=t} T_m(F(x),G(y)) .$$

Now let $\mathfrak{F}$ be the function on $S \times S$ defined by $\mathfrak{F}(a,b) = F_{ab}$. Then we have proved:

THEOREM 1. <u>The pair</u> $(S,\mathfrak{F})$ <u>is a probabilistic metric space</u> (<u>cf</u>. [3]); <u>i.e., for all</u> a, b, c <u>in</u> S <u>we have</u>

(I) $\mathfrak{F}(a,b) = \varepsilon_0$ <u>if and only if</u> $a = b$ <u>a.e.</u>,

(II) $\mathfrak{F}(a,b) = \mathfrak{F}(b,a)$,

(III) $\mathfrak{F}(a,b) \geq \tau_{T_m}(\mathfrak{F}(a,c),\mathfrak{F}(c,b))$.

3. The L_p-METRICS

Let S_∞ denote the set of essentially bounded elements of S. Then S_∞ is a metric space under the essential supremum metric L_∞. An appeal to the definition of F_{ab} immediately yields:

THEOREM 2. <u>For any</u> a, b <u>in</u> S_∞, $L_\infty(a,b) = \sup\{x \mid F_{ab}(x) < 1\}$.

Thus the essential supremum metric L_∞ can be extracted from the probabilistic metric $\mathfrak{F}$.

To obtain the L_p-metrics for $0 < p < \infty$, we use the fact that for any a, b in S the function Q_{ab} defined on the unit interval $[0,1]$ by

$$Q_{ab}(t) = \sup\{x \mid F_{ab}(x) < t\}$$

is equimeasurable with $d(a,b)$ (cf. [1]). Thus for all $x > 0$ we have

$$\lambda\{u \mid Q_{ab}(u) < x\} = \mu\{t \mid d(a(t),b(t)) < x\} ,$$

where λ is linear Lebesgue measure. The function Q_{ab} is therefore a random variable on $[0,1]$ whose distribution function is also F_{ab}. Hence if for some $p > 0$ the p-th moment $m^{(p)}(F_{ab})$ exists, then it is given by

$$m^{(p)}(F_{ab}) = E(Q_{ab}^p) = \int_0^1 Q_{ab}^p \, d\lambda = \int_X (d(a,b))^p \, d\mu .$$

We therefore have:

THEOREM 3. <u>For any</u> $p > 0$, <u>let</u> S_p <u>denote the set</u>

$\{a \in S \mid \int |a|^p \, d\mu < \infty\}$ (whence $S_p = S$ for $0 < p \le 1$). Then for any a,b in S_p,

$$L_p(a,b) = \begin{cases} m^{(p)}(F_{ab}), & 0 < p \le 1, \\ [m^{(p)}(F_{ab})]^{1/p}, & 1 \le p < \infty . \end{cases}$$

Thus for each finite p, the L_p-metric can also be extracted from the probabilistic metric $\mathfrak{F}$.

In the other direction we encounter the moment problem. Using some well-known results concerning its solvability (cf. [9], Theorem 1.11) we obtain the following partial converse to Theorems 2 and 3:

THEOREM 4. Let a, b be functions in S_∞. Then the distribution function F_{ab} (or equivalently the function Q_{ab}) is uniquely determined by the sequence of numbers $\int_X (d(a,b))^n \, d\mu$, $n = 1,2,\ldots$.

4. REMARKS

We conclude with several observations:

(i) The functions F_{ab} and Q_{ab} are quasi-inverses of each other; i.e., if we add appropriate vertical segments to the graphs of F_{ab} and Q_{ab} at places where these functions have jump discontinuities, then the resulting connected graphs are mirror images of each other in the graph of the identity function.

(ii) For $0 < r < 1$, the r-th percentile of F_{ab} is most simply defined as the number $Q_{ab}(r)$; in particular, the median of F_{ab} is $Q_{ab}(1/2)$. In general, there is no way of deriving even one of the r-th percentiles $Q_{ab}(r)$ from any finite combination of the means $m^{(p)}(F_{ab})$ or the closely related distances $L_p(a,b)$. Here, then, is a situation where the probabilistic metric yields information about a and b which is unobtainable from any finite number of the ordinary L_p-metrics.

(iii) The function T_m, originally introduced in [5], is one of a large class of functions called t-norms (t for "triangular"). Given a t-norm T, there is a corresponding operation τ_T which plays the same role in the triangle inequality for a class of probabilistic metric spaces as the operation of addition does in the triangle inequality for ordinary metric spaces. Distinct T's in general yield distinct τ_T's and inequivalent triangle inequalities. For details, see [3] and [4].

(iv) For any t in X, the function d_t defined by $d_t(a,b) = d(a(t),b(t))$ in a pseudo-metric on S. Moreover, the probabilistic metric space $(S,\mathfrak{F})$ is pseudo-metrically generated by the collection $\{d_t \mid t \in X\}$ in the sense that

$$F_{ab}(x) = \mu^*\{d_t \mid d_t(a,b) < x\} ,$$

where μ^* is the measure induced on $\{d_t\}$ by the measure μ on X (cf. [8]). However, the space $(S,\mathfrak{F})$ cannot be pseudo-metrically generated by means of any measure on the collection of metrics $\{L_p\}$. For if this were the case then, since the L_p-metrics are proper, it would follow from a basic result of R. Stevens ([10], Theorem 2) that for any distinct a, b in S, the distribution function F_{ab} would be continuous at 0. But this need not be the case, e.g., if $a = b$ on a set of positive measure.

(v) The spaces $(S,\mathfrak{F})$ of Section 2 are all E-spaces (cf. [8]) over the real line with its usual metric.

(vi) Note that the arguments for Theorems 1 - 4 do not really depend on the facts that X is a subset of a Euclidean space, that S is a vector space, etc. All that is needed to ensure the validity of Theorems 1 - 4 is the following:

a) X is a set on which a probability measure μ is defined;

b) S is a set of functions mapping X into a metric space with metric d;

c) for each pair a, b of functions in S, the real-valued function $d(a,b)$ is μ-measurable.

Now the fact that the p-th order means $m^{(p)}(F_{ab})$ of the distance distribution functions F_{ab} still give rise to metrics on S follows from an observation of Fréchet [2] to the effect that the standard proofs of the Minkowski inequalities remain valid in this more general setting; and all such Fréchet-Minkowski metrics on S are obtainable from a single probabilistic metric.

(vii) In the class of probabilistic metric spaces studied in [6], the Fréchet-Minkowski metrics of the preceding remark yield inequalities for confluent hypergeometric functions (cf. [7]). Similar inequalities for other special functions can be generated from other classes of probabilistic metric spaces.

REFERENCES

1. K.M. Chong and N.M. Rice, Equimeasurable rearrangements of functions, Queen's Papers in Pure and Applied Mathematics, No. 28; Kingston, Ontario, 1971.

2. M. Fréchet, Les éléments aléatoires de nature quelconque dans un espace distancié, Ann. Inst. Henri Poincaré 10 (1948), 215-310.

3. B. Schweizer, Probabilistic metric spaces -- the first 25 years, The New York Statistician 19 (1967), 3-6.

4. B. Schweizer, Multiplications on the space of probability distribution functions, Aequat. Math. 12 (1975), 156-183.

5. B. Schweizer and A. Sklar, Statistical metric spaces, Pacific J. Math. 10 (1960), 313-334.

6. B. Schweizer and A. Sklar, Statistical metric spaces arising from sets of random variables in Euclidean n-space, Teorija Verojat. Primen. 7 (1962), 456-465.

7. B. Schweizer and A. Sklar, Inequalities for the confluent hypergeometric function, J. Math. and Physics 42 (1963), 329-330.

8. H. Sherwood, On E-spaces and their relation to other classes of probabilistic metric spaces, J. London Math. Soc. 44 (1969), 441-448.

9. J.A. Shohat and J.D. Tamarkin, The Problem of Moments, AMS Surveys, No. 1; Providence, R. I., 1943.

10. R. Stevens, Metrically generated probabilistic metric spaces, Fundamenta Math. 61 (1968), 259-269.

ON A FUNCTIONAL INEQUALITY

Peter Kardos
Scarborough College
University of Toronto
West Hill, Ontario
CANADA M1C 1A4

ABSTRACT. In this paper, we give all solutions f, that do not change sign, of the inequality

$$p\,\frac{f(p)}{f(q)} + (1-p)\,\frac{f(1-p)}{f(1-q)} \le 1\,, \qquad 0<p<1, \quad 0<q<1\,.$$

1. INTRODUCTION

A basic concept of information is that of the Rényi information gain of order $c+1$, defined by

$$I_{c+1}(P//Q) = \frac{1}{c}\log_2 \sum_{i=1} p_i\left(\frac{p_i}{q_i}\right)^c \qquad (c>-1, \quad c\neq 0)$$

for all $P,Q \in A_n$, where

$$A_n = \left\{P\in R^n : P=(p_1,p_2,\ldots,p_n)\,, \quad \sum_{i=1}^n p_i = 1\,, \quad p_i>0 \ \text{ for } \ i=1,2,\ldots,n\right\}$$

and for some integer $n\geq 2$. The limit

$$\lim_{c\to 0} I_{c+1} = \sum_{i=1}^n p_i \log_2 \frac{p_i}{q_i}$$

is the Shannon information gain. We expect the gain of information to be nonnegative, and this is the case if $c>-1$ since

$$(1) \qquad \sum_{i=1}^n p_i\left(\frac{p_i}{q_i}\right)^c \le 1 \qquad \text{if} \qquad -1\le c\le 0$$

and

$$(2) \qquad \sum_{i=1}^n p_i\left(\frac{p_i}{q_i}\right)^c \ge 1 \qquad \text{if} \qquad c\ge 0\,.$$

Inequality (1) suggests the functional inequality

$$(3) \qquad \sum_{i=1}^n p_i\,\frac{f(p_i)}{f(q_i)} \le 1\,,$$

valid for all $P,Q\in A_n$, for fixed integer $n\geq 2$, and $f:(0,1)\to R-\{0\}$.

The similar functional inequality arising from (2) was studied in [3]. P. Fischer [2] and A. Rényi [4] showed that the general positive solution of (3) for fixed $n \geq 3$ has the form

$$f(p) = Bp^c , \quad B > 0 , \quad -1 \leq c \leq 0 .$$

For $n = 2$, Fischer [2] proved that the general positive solution of (3) is monotonic nonincreasing and continuous. We want to give the general solution in this case when f does not change sign.

THEOREM 1. <u>All solutions that do not change sign on</u> $(0,1)$, <u>of the inequality</u>

$$p \frac{f(p)}{f(q)} + (1-p) \frac{f(1-p)}{f(1-q)} \leq 1 , \quad 0 < p < 1, \quad 0 < q < 1 , \tag{4}$$

<u>are of the form</u>

$$f(p) = A \exp\left(\int_b^p \frac{G(t)}{t}\, dt\right) , \quad p \in (0,1) , \tag{5}$$

<u>where</u> $A \neq 0$, $b \in (0,1)$, <u>with</u> G <u>arbitrary measurable on</u> $(0,1)$ <u>and satisfying, for almost all</u> $p \in (0,1)$,

$$G(1-p) = G(p) \tag{6}$$

<u>and</u>

$$-1 \leq G(p) \leq 0 . \tag{7}$$

<u>Proof</u>. Since f does not change sign, we may suppose that $f(p) > 0$, $0 < p < 1$, and that $A = 1$ in (5). By interchanging p and q in (4), we obtain

$$q \frac{f(q)}{f(p)} + (1-q) \frac{f(1-q)}{f(1-p)} \leq 1 , \quad 0 < p < 1, \quad 0 < q < 1 . \tag{8}$$

We can write (4) and (8) in the forms

$$\frac{f(1-p)}{f(1-q)} \leq \frac{1 - [pf(p)/f(q)]}{1-p} \quad \text{and} \quad \frac{f(1-q)}{f(1-p)} \leq \frac{1 - [qf(q)/f(p)]}{1-q} .$$

When we multiply these inequalities and rearrange, we get

$$[f(p) - f(q)][pf(p) - qf(q)] \leq 0 . \tag{9}$$

It follows that

(10) $\qquad f$ is nonincreasing on $(0,1)$

and

(11) $\qquad p \to pf(p)$ is nondecreasing on $(0,1)$.

Indeed, let $p < q$. If $f(p) < f(q)$, then the left-hand side of (9) would be positive. The contradiction implies (10). Moreover, if $p < q$ then $f(p) \geq f(q)$ and hence, by (9), we have

$$pf(p) \leq qf(q) .$$

We now prove that f is locally absolutely continuous on $(0,1)$. Let a, b, ε be fixed, $0 < \varepsilon < a < b < 1$, and let s, t be any two numbers satisfying $a \leq s < t \leq b$. By applying (10) and (11), we obtain

$$\begin{aligned} 0 \leq tf(t) - sf(s) &= (t-s)f(t) + s[f(t) - f(s)] \\ &\leq (t-s)f(t) \\ &\leq (t-s)f(\varepsilon) . \end{aligned}$$

Hence

(12) $\qquad |tf(t) - sf(s)| \leq |t-s|f(\varepsilon) \qquad$ for all $\qquad 0 \leq s < t \leq b$,

and (12) also holds with $K = f(\varepsilon)$ for all $t < s$. Thus $p \to pf(p)$ is Lipschitz on $[a,b]$ and therefore*

(13) $\qquad f$ is locally absolutely continuous on $(0,1)$.

Next, we may write (4) and (8) as

$$(1-p)\,\frac{f(1-p) - f(1-q)}{f(1-q)} \leq p\,\frac{f(q) - f(p)}{f(q)}$$

and

$$(1-q)\,\frac{f(1-q) - f(1-p)}{f(1-p)} \leq q\,\frac{f(p) - f(q)}{f(p)} ,$$

respectively. We deduce from these inequalities, if $1 > q > p$, that

(14) $$\frac{f(1-p)}{f(p)} \cdot \frac{q}{1-q} \cdot \frac{f(q) - f(p)}{q-p} \leq \frac{f(1-q) - f(1-p)}{(1-q) - (1-p)} \leq \frac{f(1-q)}{f(q)} \cdot \frac{p}{1-p} \cdot \frac{f(q) - f(p)}{q-p} ,$$

while in the case $q < p$ both inequalities are reversed. In view of (13),

---

*The simple proof of (13) is due to Professor W. Walter.

f is differentiable almost everywhere on $(0,1)$. As q tends to p in (14), we see that if f is differentiable at p, then f is differentiable at $1-p$; and further, we have

$$p\,\frac{f'(p)}{f(p)} = (1-p)\,\frac{f'(1-p)}{f(1-p)}$$

for almost all p on $(0,1)$, say on A. Denoting

$$G(p) = p\,\frac{f'(p)}{f(p)}\ , \qquad p \in A\ ,$$

we have (6). Moreover, from (11),

$$f(p) + pf'(p) \geq 0 \qquad \text{for} \qquad p \in A\ .$$

Thus

$$1 + G(p) \geq 0\ , \qquad p \in A\ ,$$

and, since $f'(p) \leq 0$, (7) is valid. By (13), G is measurable and

$$\frac{G(p)}{p} = \frac{f'(p)}{f(p)} \tag{15}$$

is locally integrable on $(0,1)$. We derive (5) by integrating (15).

Conversely, any f given by (5) satisfies (4). Indeed, let measurable G satisfying (6) and (7) be given. We can show that

$$p \to pf(p) \quad \text{is nondecreasing}\ . \tag{16}$$

Indeed,

$$pf(p) = p\exp\left(\int_b^p \frac{G(t)}{t}\,dt\right) = b\exp\left(\int_b^p \frac{G(t)}{t} + \int_b^p \frac{1}{t}\,dt\right), \qquad b \in (0,1)\ ,$$

$$= b\exp\left(\int_b^p \frac{G(t)+1}{t}\,dt\right),$$

and (7) yields

$$p_2f(p_2) - p_1f(p_1) = \int_{p_1}^{p_2} \frac{G(t)+1}{t}\,dt \geq 0 \qquad \text{for} \quad p_1 < p_2\ .$$

Next, if p and q are fixed, $1 > p > q > 0$, then, since

$$G(u) \leq 0\ , \quad G(1-u) = G(u)\ ,$$

by (16) we have

$$\text{(17)} \qquad \frac{G(1-u)(1-p)f(1-p)}{(1-u)f(1-u)} \geq \frac{G(u)pf(p)}{uf(u)}$$

for almost all $u \in [q,p]$. From (5), we see that

$$G(u) = \frac{uf'(u)}{f(u)}$$

almost everywhere on $(0,1)$, and it follows from (17) that

$$\frac{(1-p)f(1-p)f'(1-u)}{f(1-u)^2} \geq \frac{pf(p)f'(u)}{f(u)^2} \qquad \text{a.e. on} \quad [q,p] ,$$

$$(1-p)f(1-p)\int_q^p \frac{f'(1-u)}{f(1-u)^2}\,du \geq pf(p)\int_q^p \frac{f'(u)}{f(u)^2}\,du ,$$

$$(1-p)f(1-p)\left[-\frac{1}{f(u)}\right]_{1-p}^{1-q} \geq pf(p)\left[-\frac{1}{f(u)}\right]_q^p ,$$

and

$$1 \geq p\,\frac{f(p)}{f(q)} + (1-p)\,\frac{f(1-p)}{f(1-q)} .$$

If $p < q$, we arrive at the same inequality, and the theorem is proved. □

By a similar reasoning, we can prove the following result.

THEOREM 2. <u>All solutions</u> f_i, $i = 1,2$, <u>that do not change signs on</u> $(0,1)$, <u>of the inequality</u>

$$p\,\frac{f_1(p)}{f_1(q)} + (1-p)\,\frac{f_2(1-p)}{f_2(1-q)} \leq 1 , \qquad 0 < p < 1, \quad 0 < q < 1 ,$$

<u>are of the form</u>

$$f_1(p) = a \exp\left(\int_c^p \frac{(1-t)g'(1-t)}{tg(1-t)}\,dt\right) , \qquad f_2(p) = bg(p) , \qquad p \in (0,1) ,$$

<u>where</u> a, b, <u>and</u> c <u>are arbitrary</u>, $ab \neq 0$, $c \in (0,1)$, <u>with</u> g <u>arbitrary continuous, positive, nonincreasing, and</u> $p \to pg(p)$ <u>nondecreasing on</u> $(0,1)$.

REFERENCES

1. J. Aczél and Z. Daróczy, <u>On Measures of Information and their Characterizations</u>, Academic Press, New York, 1975.

2. P. Fischer, On the inequality $\sum_{i=1}^n p_i(f(p_i)/f(q_i)) \leq 1$, <u>Canadian Math. Bull.</u> 17 (1974), 193-199.

3. P. Fischer, On the inequality $\sum_{i=1}^{n} p_i(f(p_i)/f(q_i)) \geq 1$, Pacific J. Math. 60 (1975), 65-74.

4. A. Rényi, On the foundations of information theory, Rev. Inst. Internat. Stat. 33 (1965), 1-14.

GENERAL SOLUTION OF AN INEQUALITY CONTAINING SEVERAL UNKNOWN FUNCTIONS, WITH APPLICATIONS TO THE GENERALIZED PROBLEM OF "HOW TO KEEP THE EXPERT HONEST"

Dedicated to the memory of P. Szász on his 80th birthday

J. Aczél
Fac. of Math.
Univ. of Waterloo
Waterloo, Ontario
CANADA N2L 3G1

P. Fischer
Dep. of Math. & Stat.
Univ. of Guelph
Guelph, Ontario
CANADA N1G 2W1

P. Kardos
Scarborough College
Univ. of Toronto
Toronto, Ontario
CANADA M5S 1A4

The following is a generalization of the problem rhetorically called "how to keep the expert (or forecaster) honest" (see, e.g., McCarthy 1956, Marschak 1959, Good 1952, 1954, Aczél-Pfanzagl 1966, Fischer 1972, Aczél-Ostrowski 1973, Aczél 1973, 1974, Aczél-Daróczy 1975, Walter 1976). Let the events $x_1,\dots,x_n$ be results of an experiment (market situation, weather, etc.). We are interested in their probabilities, so we ask an expert. He may know the true probabilities (or, at least, have subjective probabilities) $p_1,p_2,\dots,p_n$, but tells us $q_1,q_2,\dots,q_n$ instead. Till now everything is very realistic. Now we make the somewhat idealistic assumption that the expert agrees to be paid the amount $f_k(q_k)$ <u>after</u> one (and only one) of the events, x_k, happened. So his expected gain is

$$\sum_{k=1}^{n} p_k f_k(q_k) \quad .$$

We want to keep him honest by a method usually applied for the opposite purpose, namely money: we determine the payoff functions f_k so that his expected gain is maximal if he told the truth, i.e.,

$$\sum_{k=1}^{n} p_k f_k(q_k) \le \sum_{k=1}^{n} p_k f_k(p_k) \quad \text{for all } p_k, q_k \ (k=1,2,\dots,n) \tag{1}$$

satisfying

$$\sum_{k=1}^{n} p_k = \sum_{k=1}^{n} q_k = 1, \ p_k > 0, \ q_k > 0 \quad (k=1,2,\dots,n) \quad . \tag{2}$$

We will solve the above problem <u>without any regularity assumption</u> on f_k.

Also, while the problem allows all $n \geq 2$ in (1), we will suppose (1) only for one fixed $n > 2$ (the theorem is not true if (1) is supposed only for $n = 2$; see Aczél-Pfanzagl 1966, Fischer 1972). The result will turn out to be related to the Shannon entropy.

Most of the attention has been focused (see the works quoted in the previous paragraph) on the case where all payoff functions are the same, $f_1 = f_2 = \dots = f_n = f$ (cf., however, Good 1954). We prove here a theorem for the general case.

THEOREM. The inequality (1) holds for one $n > 2$ and for all p_k, q_k $(k=1,2,\dots,n)$ satisfying (2) if, and only if, there exist constants $\alpha \geq 0$, $\gamma_1,\dots,\gamma_n$ such that

$$f_k(p) = \alpha \log p + \gamma_k \qquad (p \in]0,1[; \quad k=1,2,\dots,n) \quad . \tag{3}$$

Proof. Choose $p_1 = p$, $q_1 = q$, and $p_i = q_i$ for all $i > 2$. Then [cf. (2)] $p + p_2 = q + q_2 = r$, and (1) reduces to

$$pf_1(q) + (r-p)f_2(r-q) \leq pf_1(p) + (r-p)f_2(r-p) ,$$

or

$$p[f_1(p) - f_1(q)] \geq (r-p)[f_2(r-q) - f_2(r-p)] \tag{4}$$

$$\text{for all } p,q \in]0,r[, \quad r \in]0,1[\quad .$$

The domain on which (4) holds is symmetric in p and q, so also

$$q[f_1(q) - f_1(p)] \geq (r-q)[f_2(r-p) - f_2(r-q)] \tag{5}$$

has to hold on the same domain. Multiplying (4) by $(r-q)$ and (5) by $(r-p)$ and adding the two inequalities thus obtained, we get

$$r(p-q)[f_1(p) - f_1(q)] \geq 0 ,$$

or $p \geq q$ implies $f_1(p) \geq f_1(q)$; that is, f_1 is monotonic nondecreasing, and similarly, the same holds for f_2.

Also from (4) and (5)

$$\frac{f_1(p)-f_1(q)}{p-q} \quad \text{lies between}$$

$$\frac{r-p}{p}\,\frac{f_2(r-q)-f_2(r-p)}{(r-q)-(r-p)} \quad \text{and} \quad \frac{r-q}{q}\,\frac{f_2(r-q)-f_2(r-p)}{(r-q)-(r-p)} \quad .$$

Thus, _if_ f_2 is _differentiable at_ $r-p$, _then_ f_1 _is differentiable at_ p and

(6) $$pf_1'(p) = (r-p)f_2'(r-p) \quad .$$

In other words, _if_ f_1 _is not differentiable at_ p, _then_ f_2 _is not differentiable at any_ $r-p \in]0,1-p[$. But this is impossible, since f_2 is monotonic and thus almost everywhere differentiable. Therefore f_1 (and similarly f_2) _is everywhere differentiable and (6) holds for all_ $p \in]0,1[$. So $(s = r-p)$ $pf_1'(p) = sf_2'(s) = \alpha$ (constant), ($\alpha \geq 0$, since f is non-decreasing), i.e.,

$$f_1(p) = \alpha \log p + \gamma_1, \quad f_2(p) = \alpha \log p + \gamma_2 \ ,$$

and similarly

$$f_k(p) = \alpha \log p + \gamma_k \quad (p \in]0,1[;\ \alpha \geq 0,\ \gamma_1,\dots,\gamma_n \text{ constants}) \quad ,$$

which concludes the proof of the "only if" part of Theorem 1. As to the "if" part, it follows immediately from Shannon's inequality (see, e.g., Aczél 1973, Aczél-Daróczy 1975)

(7) $$-\sum_{k=1}^{n} p_k \log q_k \geq -\sum_{k=1}^{n} p_k \log p_k \quad . \quad \square$$

The expression on the right of (7) is _Shannon's entropy_.

In another note (Aczél 1979) an application of the above theorem will be given to the so-called mixed theory of information, where the payoff functions f_k may depend also upon the events x_k themselves, not only on their probabilities.

This research has been supported in part by the Natural Sciences and Engineering Research Council of Canada and in part by the California Institute of Technology.

REFERENCES

J. Aczél 1973 On Shannon's Inequality, Optimal Coding, and Characterizations of Shannon's and Rényi's Entropies, (Convegno Informatica Teoretica, Ist. Naz. Alta Mat., Roma 1973), Symposia Math. 15 (1975), 153-179.

J. Aczél 1974 "Keeping the Expert Honest" Revisited - or: A Method to Prove the Differentiability of Solutions of Functional Inequalities, Selecta Statistica Canadiana vol. 2, pp. 1-14.

J. Aczél 1979 A Mixed Theory of Information - V: How to Keep the (Inset) Expert Honest, J. Math. Anal. Appl.

J. Aczél-Z. Daróczy 1975 On Measures of Information and Their Characterizations, Academic Press, New York-San Francisco-London.

J. Aczél-A.M. Ostrowski 1973 On the Characterization of Shannon's Entropy by Shannon's Inequality, J. Austral. Math. Soc. 16, 368-374.

J. Aczél-J. Pfanzagl 1966 Remarks on the Measurement of Subjective Probability and Information, Metrika 11, 91-105.

P. Fischer 1972 On the Inequality $\sum p_i f(p_i) \geq \sum p_i f(q_i)$, Metrika 18, 199-208.

B. Forte 1977 Subadditive Entropies for a Random Variable, Boll. Un. Mat. Ital. (5) 14B, 118-133.

I.J. Good 1952 Rational Decisions, J. Roy. Statist. Soc. Ser. B 14, 107-114.

I.J. Good 1954 Uncertainty and Business Decisions. Liverpool Univ. Press, Liverpool, 2nd ed. 1957.

J. Marschak 1959 Remarks on the Economy of Information, (Contrib. Sci. Res. Management, Univ. of Calif., Los Angeles, 1959), Univ. of Calif. Press, Berkeley 1960, pp. 79-98.

J. McCarthy 1956 Measures of the Value of Information. Proc. Nat. Acad. Sci. USA 42, 654-655.

C.T. Ng 1977 Universal Parallel Composition Laws and Their Representations. Math. Scand. 40, 25-45.

W. Walter 1976 Remark on a Paper by Aczél and Ostrowski. J. Austral. Math. Soc. 22A, 165-166.

Remarks and Problems

WHY STUDY INEQUALITIES?

Richard Bellman
Departments of Mathematics, Electrical Engineering, and Medicine
University of Southern California
Los Angeles, California 90007
U.S.A.

There are three reasons for the study of inequalities: practical, theoretical, and aesthetic.

In many practical investigations, it is necessary to bound one quantity by another. The classical inequalities are very useful for this purpose.

From the theoretical point of view, very simple questions give rise to entire theories. For example, we may ask when the nonnegativity of one quantity implies that of another. This simple question leads to the theory of positive operators and the theory of differential inequalities. The theory of quasilinearization is a blend of the theory of dynamic programming and that of positive operators. This is typical of mathematics. Each new theory uses parts of existing theories.

Another question which gives rise to much interesting research is that of finding equalities associated with inequalities. We use the principle that every inequality should come from an equality which makes the inequality obvious.

Along these lines, we may also look for representations which make inequalities obvious. Often, these representations are maxima or minima of certain quantities.

Again, we know that many inequalities are associated with geometric properties. Hence, we can go in either direction. We can find the geometric equivalent of an analytic result, or the analytic consequence of a geometric fact such as convexity or duality.

Finally, let us turn to the aesthetic aspects. As has been pointed out, beauty is in the eyes of the beholder. However, it is generally agreed that certain pieces of music, art, or mathematics are beautiful. There is an elegance to inequalities that makes them very attractive.

THE n-TH PARTIAL SUMS OF JACOBI ELLIPTIC FUNCTIONS

Dieter K. Ross
Department of Mathematics
La Trobe University
Victoria 3083
AUSTRALIA

It is well known that the trigonometric sine function satisfies the inequality

$$(-1)^{n+1}\left[\sin x - \sum_{\nu=0}^{n} \frac{(-1)^{\nu}\, x^{2\nu+1}}{(2\nu+1)!}\right] \geq 0, \quad \text{for all } x \geq 0, \quad n = 0,1,2,3,\ldots .$$

Can a similar result be proved for the Jacobi functions

$$S_n(x,k) \quad \text{and} \quad C_n(x,k), \qquad \text{for } x \geq 0 \quad \text{and} \quad -1 \leq k \leq 1 \text{ ?}$$

In the paper by Ross and Mahajan which appears in this volume [1], many results of this kind are proved or indicated for functions which satisfy a linear differential equation. The present problem depends on certain nonlinear differential equations and seems to be much more difficult. Perhaps the theory of monotone functions can be used in some way.

REFERENCE

1. Dieter K. Ross and Arvind Mahajan, On enveloping series for some of the special functions and on integral inequalities involving them, pp. 161-175, in E. F. Beckenbach (ed.), General Inequalities 2 (Proc. Oberwolfach Conference, July 30-August 5, 1978), ISNM 47, Birkhäuser Verlag, Basel and Stuttgart, 1980.

PROBLEMS IN THE THEORY OF INFINITE MATRICES

P. D. Johnson, Jr.
Department of Mathematics
American University of Beirut
Beirut
LEBANON

R. N. Mohapatra
Department of Mathematics
American University of Beirut
Beirut
LEBANON

We give below a few problems related to our paper [1], entitled "Inequalities involving infinite matrices with nonnegative entries," published in this volume. We shall present the problems after some notations and definitions are stated.

The space of all sequences of real numbers will be denoted by ω. Sequence space ℓ_p $(p > 0)$ will be as usual. Let $A = (a_{mn})$ be an infinite matrix with nonnegative entries. If $x \in \omega$, $\lambda \subseteq \omega$, then $x\lambda = \{xy \mid y \in \lambda\}$. If $x \in \omega$ is such that $x = \{x_1, x_2, \dots\}$, then $P_n : \omega \to R$ is the functional $P_n x = x_n$, $n = 1,2,\dots$. We say that $(\lambda, \|\cdot\|)$ is AK (Abschnitt-konvergent) if

$$\|P_n x - x\| \to 0 \quad \text{as} \quad n \to \infty .$$

For $\lambda, \mu \subseteq \omega$, let us write

$$D(\mu,\lambda) = \{x \in \omega \mid x\mu \subseteq \lambda\} .$$

Let us also write

$$\text{nor-}A^{-1}(\lambda) = \{x \in \lambda \mid A|x| \in \lambda\} \qquad (|x| = \{|x_1|, |x_2|, \dots\}) .$$

PROBLEM 1. <u>Is</u> $D(\ell_q, \text{nor-}A^{-1}(\ell_p))$ <u>AK for</u> $0 < p < q < \infty$, $p < 1$?

PROBLEM 2. <u>Suppose</u> $0 < p < q < \infty$, $0 < p < 1$. <u>Then do the following hold</u>?

(a) $D(\ell_q, \text{nor-}A^{-1}(\ell_p)) = b\ell_\infty$ <u>for some</u> $b \in \omega$.

(b) <u>Only finitely many columns of</u> A <u>are in</u> ℓ_p.

(c) $D(\ell_q, \text{nor-}A^{-1}(\ell_p))$ <u>is finite dimensional</u>.

Let us define the space

$$\text{ces}_p^{(r)} = \left\{x \in \omega \;\middle|\; \left\{n^{-r} \sum_{k=1}^{n} |x_k|\right\}_n \in \ell_p\right\}$$

for $p > 0$ and r real.

The following result can be proved without much difficulty:

PROPOSITION. _Suppose_ $1 < p,q \leq \infty$, $rp > 1$, $q^{-1} + q'^{-1} = 1$. _Then_

(1) $$\{n^{r-p^{-1}}\}\ell_{q'} \subseteq D(\ell_q, ces_p^{(r)}) \subset \bigcap_{k>r-p^{-1}} \{n^k\}\ell_{q'} .$$

The inclusion on the right is strict.

We do not know the answer to the following:

PROBLEM 3. _Suppose_ $1 < p < \infty$ _and_ $rp > 1$. _For what_ q, $1 < q < \infty$, _is the left-hand inclusion in_ (1) _strict_?

PROBLEM 4. _For what_ q, $1 < q < p$, is $D(\ell_q, ces_p^{(r)})$ _AK_?

REMARK. An answer to Problem 4 would have bearing on Problem 3 because, for $1 < q < \infty$, $\{n^{r-p^{-1}}\}\ell_{q'}$, being a diagonal copy of $\ell_{q'}$, has a natural FK topology inherited from $\ell_{q'}$ with which it is AK, since $1 \leq q' \leq \infty$.

REFERENCE

1. P. D. Johnson, Jr. and R. N. Mohapatra, Inequalities involving infinite matrices with nonnegative entries, pp. 55 - 80, in E. F. Beckenbach (ed.), _General Inequalities 2_ (Proc. Oberwolfach Conference, July 30-August 5, 1978), ISNM 47, Birkhäuser Verlag, Basel and Stuttgart, 1980.

THE MOTION OF A SIMPLE PENDULUM WITH UNIFORMLY SHORTENING STRING LENGTH

Dieter K. Ross
Department of Mathematics
La Trobe University
Victoria 3083
AUSTRALIA

The motion of a simple undamped pendulum that is confined to a single vertical plane is modified by shortening the string at a constant speed U_0 through a fixed point.

Suppose that the motion begins in the downward vertical position when the string length is ℓ_0, and that its angular speed there is w_0, $w_0 > 0$. If the position of the pendulum bob at time t is specified by its plane polar coordinates (r,θ), then the following apply:

(i) $dr/dt = -U_0$, with $U_0 > 0$;

(ii) the tension T in the string due to the weight mg must remain positive and be given by

$$\frac{T}{mg} = \cos\theta + \frac{rU_0^2}{g}\left(\frac{d\theta}{dr}\right)^2 ;$$

(iii) the equation of motion is

$$r\frac{d^2\theta}{dr^2} + 2\frac{d\theta}{dr} + \frac{g\sin\theta}{U_0^2} = 0 , \qquad (1)$$

with initial conditions

$$\theta = 0 , \quad d\theta/dr = -w_0/U_0 \quad \text{at} \quad r = \ell_0 .$$

Now it is easily shown that, for a long enough string, the tension is a monotonic increasing function of the angle θ during one complete revolution if there exists a function $f(w_0,U_0) \geq C$, where C is a constant. One solution to this problem is

$$f(w_0,U_0) \equiv w_0U_0/g \geq 1/2 . \qquad (2)$$

Is a lesser value for C possible, or is it possible to find a better function $f(w_0,U_0)$?

It is worth mentioning the following points:

(a) The linearized form of equation (1) has Bessel functions of order 1 as its solutions.

(b) If the length r is replaced by ℓ_0/x, then the equation of motion becomes

$$\frac{d^2\theta}{dx^2} = -\frac{g\,\ell_0 \sin\theta}{U_0^2\, x^3} .$$

In case the index 3 is replaced by 2, a solution exists in terms of elliptic functions. On the other hand, we can deduce a differential inequality of the form

$$\frac{-g\,\ell_0}{U_0^2\, x^3} \le \frac{d^2\theta}{dx^2} \le \frac{g\,\ell_0}{U_0^2\, x^3} \qquad \text{in } 1 \le x \le \infty .$$

This can be integrated and adjusted in various ways to give bounds on the tension as well as bounds on the angular velocity $d\theta/dt$. It is from this approach that the inequality (2) was obtained; see Ross [1].

REFERENCE

1. Dieter K. Ross, The behaviour of a simple pendulum with uniformly shortening string length, Internat. J. Non-Linear Mech., to appear.

REMARKS CONCERNING EXTENSIONS OF THE GAMMA FUNCTION

H.-H. Kairies
Mathematisches Institut der Technischen Universität
3392 Clausthal-Zellerfeld
WEST GERMANY

Let $\Gamma_\alpha : \mathbb{R}_+ \to \mathbb{R}_+$ be a family of functions, α a positive real parameter. We want to embed Euler's Γ-function in this family, such that

(E) $$\forall x \in \mathbb{R}_+ : \lim_{\alpha \to 1} \Gamma_\alpha(x) = \Gamma(x)$$

holds. We assume the following normalization condition:

(N) $$\forall \alpha \in \mathbb{R}_+ : \Gamma_\alpha(1) = 1 .$$

The ratio

$$H_\alpha(x) := \frac{\Gamma_\alpha(x + 1)}{\Gamma_\alpha(x)}$$

exists for all $\alpha \in \mathbb{R}_+$ and $x \in \mathbb{R}_+$ and defines a family of functions $H_\alpha : \mathbb{R}_+ \to \mathbb{R}_+$. Hence we have

(F) $$\forall \alpha \in \mathbb{R}_+ \, \forall x \in \mathbb{R}_+ : \Gamma_\alpha(x + 1) = H_\alpha(x)\Gamma_\alpha(x) .$$

The solution set of the functional equation (F) is large: If Γ^*_α is any special solution, then the general solution is given by

$$\Gamma_\alpha(x) = \Gamma^*_\alpha(x) \cdot p_\alpha(x),$$

with $p_\alpha : \mathbb{R}_+ \to \mathbb{R}_+$ of period 1, otherwise arbitrary.

Now we ask for simple properties of Γ_α and H_α which guarantee that (F) has a unique "principal" solution Γ_α with the embedding peoperty (E). Any such family Γ_α may be considered as a "natural" extension of Γ. It turns out that there exist many possibilities of such extensions. Classical examples have been given by Jackson [3] and by Bendersky [2] (here the parameter range has to be extended and shifted to correspond with the above notations). We have

$$H_\alpha(x) = \frac{\alpha^x - 1}{\alpha - 1} , \quad H_1(x) = x \quad \text{and} \quad H_\alpha(x) = x^{x^{\alpha-1}}$$

for the Jackson resp. Bendersky functions.

First a simple consequence of (E): If Γ_α is a "natural" extension of Γ, then necessarily

(1) $$\forall x \in \mathbb{R}_+ : \lim_{\alpha \to 1} H_\alpha(x) = x .$$

Now we show that continuity conditions for H_α and Γ_α are not suitable to characterize solutions of (F). Fix $\alpha > 0$ and assume H_α and the $[1,2)$-restriction of Γ_α to be continuous. Then iteration of (F) shows: Γ_α is continuous on $\mathbb{R}_+$ if and only if

(2) $$\lim_{x \to 2-} \Gamma_\alpha(x) = H_\alpha(1) .$$

Thus any continuous function $G_\alpha : [1,2) \to \mathbb{R}_+$ can be extended by means of (F) to a continuous solution $G_\alpha : \mathbb{R}_+ \to \mathbb{R}_+$, provided (2) is satisfied. A similar reasoning applies to differentiable functions.

Now we sketch how to get the desired characterization of Γ_α as a special solution of (F). Define

$$g_\alpha := \log \circ \Gamma_\alpha \quad \text{and} \quad h_\alpha := \log \circ H_\alpha .$$

Then (F) is equivalent to the difference equation

(D) $$\forall \alpha \in \mathbb{R}_+ \ \forall x \in \mathbb{R}_+ : g_\alpha(x+1) - g_\alpha(x) = h_\alpha(x) .$$

Assume first that Nörlund's principal solution g_α^* of (D) exists. This requires some regularity and growth conditions on h_α (see [8]). Then g_α^* is unique up to a constant, which may be determined by (N). There is another possibility to characterize special solutions of (D): John [4] and Krull [5] proved existence and uniqueness theorems for monotonic resp. convex solutions of (D). Their results and more general statements can be found in Kuczma's book [6]. These theorems may as well be applied to the n-th derivatives:

$$g_\alpha^{(n)}(x+1) - g_\alpha^{(n)}(x) = h_\alpha^{(n)}(x) ,$$

and they may give characterizations in cases where Nörlund's theory is not applicable. Hence for a large class of functions h_α we can obtain "principal" solutions g_α of (D) which give distinguished solutions Γ_α of (F).

The well-known Bohr-Mollerup characterization of the Γ-function is a very special case of the procedure described above. Recently Askey [1] and Moak [7] proved characterization and embedding theorems for the Jackson functions, which may serve as illustrations for our procedure.

REFERENCES

1. R. Askey, The q-gamma and q-beta functions, Applicable Analysis, to appear.

2. L. Bendersky, Sur la fonction gamma généralisée, Acta Math. 61 (1933), 263-322.

3. F.H. Jackson, On q-definite integrals, Quart. J. Pure Appl. Math. 41 (1910), 193-203.

4. F. John, Special solutions of certain difference equations, Acta Math. 71 (1939), 175-189.

5. W. Krull, Bemerkungen zur Differenzengleichung $g(x + 1) - g(x) = \varphi(x)$, I, II. Math. Nachr. 1 (1948), 365-376; Math. Nachr. 2 (1949), 251-262.

6. M. Kuczma, Functional Equations in a Single Variable, Polish Scientific Publishers, Warszawa, 1968.

7. D. Moak, The q-gamma function for $q > 1$, Aequationes Math., to appear.

8. N.E. Nörlund, Vorlesungen über Differenzenrechnung, Springer, Berlin, 1924.

A PROBLEM ON NORMED KÖTHE SPACES

F. Fehér
Lehrstuhl A für Mathematik
Rheinisch-Westfälische Technische Hochschule
Aachen
WEST GERMANY

Let L^ρ denote a complete normed Köthe space, K a nonnegative, Lebesgue-measurable function on $(0,\infty) \times (0,\infty)$ which is homogeneous of degree γ $(\gamma \in \mathbb{R})$, and

$$(1) \qquad (Kf)(t) := \int_0^\infty K(t,s)f(s)\,ds \qquad (f \in L^\rho, \quad t > 0) .$$

A generalized version of the Schur-Hardy inequality states that for $(\cdot)^{1+\gamma} f \in L^\rho$,

$$\|Kf\|_\rho \le A_\rho \|(\cdot)^{1+\gamma} f\|_\rho$$

if

$$A_\rho := \int_0^1 K(1,s)h(s,L^\rho)\,ds < \infty ,$$

where $h(s,L^\rho)$ denotes the indicator function of L^ρ (see [1]). In particular, if $K = P_\theta$, $\theta \in \mathbb{R}$, the averaging operator, then $A_\rho < \infty$ if and only if the index condition

$$(2) \qquad \alpha := \inf_{0<t<1} - \frac{\log h(s,L^\rho)}{\log s} < \theta$$

holds.

QUESTION. What about the general situation (1)? Does there also exist an index condition involving the kernel $K(t,s)$ which is equivalent to the condition $A_\rho < \infty$? Note that with

$$K(t,s) = t^{-\theta} s^{\theta-1} \chi_{(0,t)}(s) ,$$

(2) can be rewritten as

$$\alpha < 1 + \inf_{0<s<1} \frac{\log K(1,s)}{\log s} .$$

REFERENCE

1. F. Fehér, A generalized Schur-Hardy inequality on normed Köthe spaces, pp. 277-286, in E.F. Beckenbach (ed.), General Inequalities 2 (Proc. Oberwolfach Conference, July 30-August 5, 1978), ISNM 47, Birkhäuser Verlag, Basel and Stuttgart, 1980.

REMARKS ON A GENERALIZATION OF THE SCHUR-HARDY INEQUALITY

R. N. Mohapatra
Department of Mathematics
American University of Beirut
Beirut
LEBANON

Let the function space L_p and the norm $\|\cdot\|_p$ $(1 \leq p < \infty)$ be as usual. Let $K(t,s)$ denote a nonnegative, measurable function of $t,s > 0$, and let K be the operator defined by

$$(Kf)(t) = \int_0^\infty K(t,x)f(x)\,dx \qquad (t > 0, \quad f \in L_p) . \tag{1}$$

The well-known Schur-Hardy inequality is given by the following:

THEOREM A. *Let* $K(t,s)$ *be homogeneous of degree* -1, *such that*

$$A(p) \equiv \int_0^\infty K(t,x)\, x^{-1/p}\, dx < \infty ,$$

and let $f \in L_p$ $(1 \leq p < \infty)$. *Then* $Kf \in L_p$ *and*

$$\|Kf\|_p \leq A(p)\|f\|_p . \tag{2}$$

Fehér in her talk [1] at the Second International Conference on General Inequalities, held in 1978 at Oberwolfach, proved amongst other things the following generalization of Theorem A:

THEOREM B. *Let* $K(t,x)$ *be homogeneous of degree* r, $r \geq -1$, *such that*

$$A \equiv \int_0^\infty K(1,x)\, x^{-(1+r)}\, h(x)\, dx < \infty ,$$

and let $(\cdot)^{1+r} f \in L_p$ $(1 \leq p < \infty)$. *Then* $Kf \in L_p$ *and*

$$\|Kf\|_p \leq A\|(\cdot)^{1+r} f\|_p . \tag{3}$$

Let an operator on the vector space of all measurable, Lebesgue integrable functions on $(0,\infty)$ be defined by

$$T_r(f)(t) \equiv t^{-r} \int_0^t f(x)\, dx .$$

The kernel of this operator is homogeneous of degree $-r$. If $r \leq 1$, then we obtain the following from Theorem B:

THEOREM 1. *Let* $1 \leq p < \infty$, $1/p < r \leq 1$, *and let* $(\cdot)^{1-r} f \in L_p$. *Then*

$$\|T_r f\|_p \leq \frac{p}{pr - 1} \|(\cdot)^{1-r} f\|_p . \tag{4}$$

This leads to the following problem:

PROBLEM 1. *Does there exist an analogue of* (4) *for* $r > 1$?

REMARK. An answer to Problem 1 is related closely to an extension of Theorem B for $r < -1$, if that is possible.

Also by using another result of Fehér [2; Theorem 1^*], one can obtain:

THEOREM 2. *Let* $1/p \leq r \leq 1$, *and let* $f \in L_p$ $(1 \leq p < \infty)$. *Then*

$$\|T_r f\|_p \leq (1 + p(1 - r))^{-1/p} \left(\frac{p}{pr - 1}\right)^2 \|f\|_{p/(1 + p(1 - r))} .$$

These remarks are based on my discussion on the paper of Dr. Fehér referred to above and a communication from her.

REFERENCES

1. F. Fehér, A generalized Schur-Hardy inequality on normed Köthe spaces, pp. 277-286, in E. F. Beckenbach (ed.), *General Inequalities 2* (Proc. Oberwolfach Conference, July 30-August 5, 1978), ISNM 47, Birkhäuser Verlag, Basel and Stuttgart, 1980.

2. F. Fehér, A note on a paper of E. R. Love, *Bull. Austral. Math. Soc.*, to appear.

A NOTE ON THE FOREGOING REMARKS OF R. N. MOHAPATRA

F. Fehér
Lehrstuhl A für Mathematik
Rheinisch-Westfälische Technische Hochschule Aachen
5100 Aachen
WEST GERMANY

In the meantime, I have been able to prove Theorem B of the foregoing remarks [2] by Professor Mohapatra without the restriction $r \geq -1$ (compare Theorem 1.1 of my paper [1] applied to the Lebesgue norm); hence the answer to Problem 1 of Mohapatra is "Yes." The analogous problem for his Theorem 2 is still open.

REFERENCES

1. F. Fehér, A generalized Schur-Hardy inequality on normed Köthe spaces, pp. 277-286, in E. F. Beckenbach (ed.), General Inequalities 2 (Proc. Oberwolfach Conference, July 30-August 5, 1978), ISNM 47, Birkhäuser Verlag, Basel and Stuttgart, 1980.

2. R. N. Mohapatra, Remarks on a generalization of the Schur-Hardy inequality, pp. 459-460, in E. F. Beckenbach (ed.), General Inequalities 2 (Proc. Oberwolfach Conference, July 30-August 5, 1978), ISNM 47, Birkhäuser Verlag, Basel and Stuttgart, 1980.

A PROBLEM IN UNIVALENT-FUNCTION THEORY

Jochen Becker
Fachbereich Mathematik
Technische Universität Berlin
D-1000 Berlin 12
WEST GERMANY

Let g, g_n $(n = 1,2,\ldots)$ be univalent functions in $\{|z| > 1\}$, all with the customary normalization

$$g(z) = z + b_0 + \frac{b_1}{z} + \cdots .$$

Let

$$S_g = \left(\frac{g''}{g'}\right)' - \frac{1}{2}\left(\frac{g''}{g'}\right)^2$$

denote the Schwarzian derivative.

PROBLEM. Does

$$\sup_{|z|>1} (|z|^2 - 1)^2 \, |S_{g_n}(z) - S_g(z)| \to 0 , \quad n \to \infty ,$$

imply

$$\sup_{|z|>1} (|z|^2 - 1) \left|\frac{g''_n(z)}{g'_n(z)} - \frac{g''(z)}{g'(z)}\right| \to 0 , \quad n \to \infty \ ?$$

This is known to be true if g_n, g are in the subclass of univalent functions with quasiconformal extensions onto the plane. It is easy to show that the converse is generally true.

ON A MAJORIZATION OF DISTANCES BETWEEN THE VALUES OF A FAMILY OF FUNCTIONS AND A FIXED POINT

Karol Baron
Department of Mathematics
Silesian University
40-007 Katowice
POLAND

Suppose that X is a subset of a set endowed with a metric ρ, and let a function $f : S \times X \to X$ be given, where S is a nonvoid set, together with a $\xi \in \mathrm{Cl}\, X$ and a neighbourhood U of ξ. The following condition (1) appears in a natural way when considering the problem of extending solutions of functional equations (cf. [1]) as well as of uniqueness of solutions of functional equations and inequalities (cf. [2] and [4]):

$$(1) \qquad \wedge (x \in X) \vee (n \in N) \wedge (s_1,\dots,s_n \in S)(f(s_1,\cdot) \circ \dots \circ f(s_n,\cdot)(x) \in U) .$$

It is very easy to see that (1) is fulfilled whenever there exists an increasing and right-continuous real function γ defined on an interval I containing the origin such that

$$(2) \qquad \wedge (t \in I \setminus \{0\})(\gamma(t) < t)$$

and

$$(3) \qquad \wedge (s \in S) \wedge (x \in X)(\rho(f(s,x),\xi) \leq \gamma(\rho(x,\xi))) .$$

Hence, the following question arises: Under what condition does such a function γ exist? An answer is contained in the following theorem, proved in [3].

THEOREM. <u>If the set</u> $\{\xi\} \cup \{x \in X : \rho(x,\xi) \leq \rho(\bar{x},\xi)\}$ <u>is compact for every</u> $\bar{x} \in X$, <u>the family</u> $\{f(s,\cdot) : s \in S\}$ <u>is locally equicontinuous, and</u>

$$\sup\{\rho(f(s,x),\xi) : s \in S\} < \rho(x,\xi)$$

<u>whenever</u> $x \in X \setminus \{\xi\}$, <u>then</u> (3) <u>holds with an increasing, continuous real function</u> γ <u>defined on an interval</u> I <u>containing the origin and fulfilling condition</u> (2).

REFERENCES

1. K. Baron, On extending solutions of a functional equation, Aequationes Math. 13 (1975), 285-288.

2. K. Baron, On the uniqueness of continuous solutions of a functional inequality of n-th order, Report of Meeting, Fourteenth international symposium on functional equations, May 21-28, 1976, Aequationes Math. 15 (1977), 278-279.

3. K. Baron, Functional equations of infinite order, Prace Naukowe Uniwersytetu Sląskiego w Katowicach, 265 (1978).

4. K. Baron and M. Sablik, On the uniqueness of continuous solutions of a functional equation of n-th order, Aequationes Math. 17 (1978), 295-304.

AREA OF A TRIANGLE AND THE PRODUCT OF ITS SIDE LENGTHS

O. Shisha
Department of Mathematics
University of Rhode Island
Kingston, Rhode Island 02881
U.S.A.

The recent English translation of Pólya and Szegö [4] contains the following problem (17.1 on p. 161, Vol. II). Let ABC be a triangle with side lengths

$$\overline{BC} = a , \quad \overline{CA} = b , \quad \overline{AB} = c$$

and area S. Then

$$S \leq (\sqrt{3}/4)(abc)^{2/3} , \tag{1}$$

with equality if and only if ABC is equilateral. The solution offered treats the problem as one of maximizing a suitable function of two variables, equating partial derivatives to zero.

The reviewer [2, p. 61] of [4] expresses his preference for another method of proof, for which he suggests use of Lagrange multipliers.

The purpose of this note is to point out that (1) is much more elementary than use of the above methods seems to imply. For let R be the radius of the circle in which ABC is inscribed. Then since $abc = 4RS$, (1) states that

$$S \leq (3\sqrt{3}/4)R^2 ,$$

with equality if and only if ABC is equilateral. This, in turn, is just the elementary, well-known theorem that of all triangles ABC inscribed in a circle of radius R, the equilateral triangle alone has maximal area.

Observe how elementary this theorem is, following from these two facts:

(a) If $\overline{BC} \neq \overline{AC}$, then the isosceles triangle ABC' has a greater area than ABC, where C' is the point of the circle, on the same side of AB as C, lying on the perpendicular bisector of AB.

(b) If $\overline{BC} = \overline{AC}$, if α denotes the angle CAB, and if $u = \sin^2\alpha$, then

$$S^2 = (2R^2 \sin^2\alpha \sin 2\alpha)^2 = 432R^4\left(\frac{u}{3}\right)^3(1-u) \leq 432R^4\left[\frac{\frac{u}{3}+\frac{u}{3}+\frac{u}{3}+(1-u)}{4}\right]^4 = \frac{27R^4}{16},$$

by

(2) the inequality between the arithmetic and geometric means ,

with equality if and only if $u = 3/4$, i.e., if and only if $\alpha = \pi/3$.

Incidentally, both the formula $abc = 4RS$ and (2) are used in [4] in the solution of the next two problems!

Observe also that of (2) we have used only the particularly simple case of means of four numbers. The extreme simplicity of this case is seen from Cauchy's classical proof of (2) [1, p. 4; 3, p. 17; 4, Vol. I, p. 64].

REFERENCES

1. E.F. Beckenbach and R. Bellman, Inequalities, Springer-Verlag, Berlin, 1961.

2. H. Flanders, review of [4], Bull. Amer. Math. Soc. 84, 53-62 (1978).

3. G.H. Hardy, J.E. Littlewood, and G. Pólya, Inequalities, Cambridge University Press, 2nd Edition, 1952.

4. G. Pólya and G. Szegö, Problems and Theorems in Analysis, Springer-Verlag, New York; Vol. I, 1972; Vol. II, 1976.

A MINIMUM PROPERTY OF THE SQUARE

J. Aczél
Faculty of Mathematics
University of Waterloo
Waterloo, Ontario
CANADA N2L 3G1

Inscribe a polygon into a circle and, by drawing at the vertices tangents to the circle, get the corresponding circumscribed polygon. By use of simple calculus (differential conditions for minima of functions of a single variable) and after lengthy calculations, it has been proved 30 years ago [1] that the sum of the areas of these two polygons takes its minimum (among all such polygons belonging to the same circle, whatever the number of vertices) for the pair of squares.

It would be nice to find a truly elementary (though not necessarily purely geometric) proof without using calculus.

The following historical remark may give an amusing background to the above result. One of the "solvers" of the "quadratura circuli problem" has, in his publication, given thanks to the Lord for letting him find the following solution. He draws exactly the above extremal situation of a pair of squares. Since, in the unit circle, the area of the inscribed square is 2, while that of the circumscribed square is 4, "evidently" the area of the circle "has to be 3." The above result shows that, taking the arithmetic means of the areas of inscribed and of corresponding circumscribed polygons, he could not get a worse approximation from below than what he got, that for two squares. (Approximations from above can be as bad as one wants; see also the paper [1] quoted above.)

REFERENCE

1. J. Aczél and L. Fuchs, A minimum-problem on areas of inscribed and circumscribed polygons of a circle, Compositio Math. 8 (1950), 61-67.

Indexes

NAME INDEX

(including citations by reference number)

SUBJECT INDEX